Apache Tomcat Bible

Apache Tomcat Bible

Jon Eaves, Rupert Jones, and Warner Godfrey

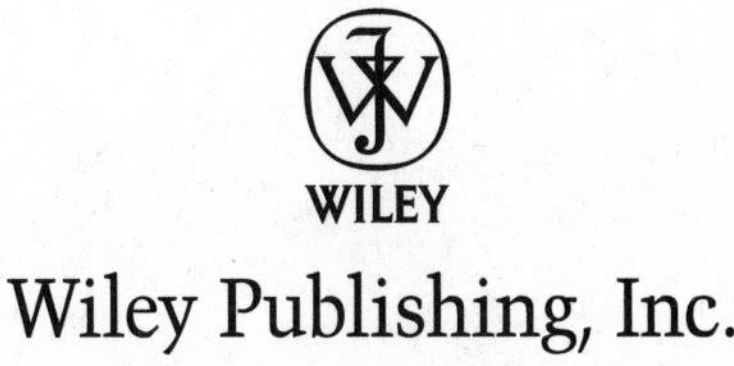

Wiley Publishing, Inc.

Apache Tomcat Bible

Published by
Wiley Publishing, Inc.
10475 Crosspoint Boulevard
Indianapolis, IN 46256
www.wiley.com

Published simultaneously in Canada

Library of Congress Control Number: 2003101873

ISBN: 0-7645-2606-5

Manufactured in the United States of America

10 9 8 7 6 5 4 3 2 1

1B/RU/QV/QT/IN

About the Authors

Jon Eaves is the Chief Technology Officer of ThoughtWorks Australia and has over 15 years of software development experience in a wide variety of application domains and languages. Jon spends his working hours developing large-scale enterprise systems using J2EE, and when he can find spare time developing J2ME/MIDP applications and working on the BouncyCastle Java Cryptographic APIs (`http://www.bouncycastle.org`). He can be reached at `jon@eaves.org`.

Warner Godfrey is a dedicated software engineer, who with 4 years' experience is constantly looking for new technical challenges. Past experience has seen Warner involved in many large-scale Web-based projects. Warner has recently taken a position as Chief Technology Officer at LiveEvents Wireless, a wireless content aggregator developing J2ME applications for mobile devices. An avid surfer, Warner will most likely be found down the coast after writing this book, making up for lost time catching a few waves. Surf conditions not permitting, he may be found kicking up some dust on a mountain bike trail in the nearby hills. Warner may be reached via email at `warner@godfrey.name`.

Rupert Jones has been a Technical Lead for large-scale Internet projects for the past 4 years. He has a wealth of experience in Internet-related application development (J2EE and other) and has been involved in a number of open source projects in his spare time. Outside of work and writing this book Rupert enjoys traveling, reading and dining on fine food and wine. Rupert can be reached at `rup@rupertjones.com`.

Credits

Acquisitions Editor
Jim Minatel

Project Editor
Sharon Nash

Technical Editor
David Wall

Copy Editor
Howard Jones

Editorial Manager
Mary Beth Wakefield

Vice President & Executive Group Publisher
Richard Swadley

Vice President and Executive Publisher
Bob Ipsen

Vice President and Publisher
Joseph B. Wikert

Executive Editorial Director
Mary Bednarek

Project Coordinator
Ryan Steffen

Graphics and Production Specialists
Beth Brooks
Amanda Carter
Jennifer Click
Sean Decker
Carrie Foster
Jackie Nicholas

Quality Control Technicians
Laura Albert
John Tyler Connoley
Andy Hollandbeck
Carl Pierce

Proofreading and Indexing
TECHBOOKS Production Services

Jon Eaves: This book is dedicated to my grandfather, Keith George. Thanks Pop for never tiring of answering my questions.

Warner Godfrey: I would like to dedicate this book to my parents, Dolland and Elizabeth Godfrey, who helped me embrace technology at a young age and without knowing paved a successful and fulfilling career.

Rupert Jones: This book is dedicated to my parents. Julia and Michael. whose unconditional love has always seen me through.

Preface

Welcome to the *Apache Tomcat Bible*, a book designed to help you understand how to make the most effective use out of the Apache Tomcat Servlet Container. This book is aimed at Java developers and administrators using Tomcat for development and deployment. It is written for developers who have a familiarity with the Java language, but not necessarily with the Java 2 Platform, Enterprise Edition (J2EE). Because the book provides detailed information about the installation and configuration of software packages an understanding of how to install software on your chosen platform is helpful, but not required.

Why Do You Need This Book?

One of the great strengths of the Apache Group is the high quality of the software it produces. One of the weaknesses of the Apache Group is the often limited or incomplete documentation for their products. The documentation that does exist is generally aimed at more experienced or advanced developers and has limited assistance for developers new to Tomcat. This is particularly noticeable in the areas of installation, configuration, and real-world examples of use for their products. This book provides a detailed guide of the use of Tomcat from installation through configuration and use of advanced development topics such as using frameworks and configuration of database connections.

Tomcat has grown into a highly complex product, and is often a starting point for developers entering the world of Java server-side development. Tomcat is a great choice for server-side development, but the learning curve now required is significant and many developers with a background in other server-side development tools like PHP, ASP, and Perl expect Tomcat to work exactly the same as the Web environments that they are used to. This is not the case: Tomcat provides a richer environment for development that while different, is equally simple to use once the appropriate skills have been learned.

How This Book Is Organized

The book is divided into four major parts that lead the reader from the simplest to the most complex aspects of developing and deploying with Tomcat. This book covers the fundamentals of using Tomcat, including administration and deployment as well as software development practices for development.

Part I: Getting Started with Tomcat and Web Applications

The book begins by explaining what Tomcat is and how the Apache Group is involved in its development. The book continues by explaining installation of Tomcat and the associated software required for the examples developed in the book. This part concludes with an overview of Web applications, the recommended deployment model for Tomcat.

Part II: Packaging, Compiling, and Deploying Applications for Tomcat

This section builds on the earlier fundamentals to provide details about the compiling, packaging, and deployment of the Web components to Tomcat utilizing an IDE and standard development tools. This part closes with a step-by-step development and deployment example to bring together all the information from the prior chapters.

Part III: Tomcat Configuration and Applications

This section contains the major software development activities for the book. It starts with a detailed examination of the configuration of Tomcat, both from the structure of the configuration files and use of the Administration application. The part contains a fully worked application using an MVC Model 2 framework, a tutorial for debugging Web applications using an IDE, and instructions about how to implement appropriate security in a Web application.

Part IV: Advanced Tomcat Techniques

Frameworks provide enhanced developer productivity and are key middleware components utilized extensively in Tomcat development. This portion of the book covers some of the leading frameworks that can be integrated with Tomcat including Struts and Velocity for user interface development and the Apache SOAP framework for developing Web services. This part includes advanced topics such as high availability and clustering as well as examples of how to customize Tomcat by extending some of the Tomcat functionality.

What You'll Need

To obtain the maximum benefit from this book, you need to install some software on a computer and work through the examples provided in the book. The book provides all the information needed to install the software, but for completeness you need the following products:

- Tomcat 4.1.12 (`http://jakarta.apache.org/tomcat`)
- Sun's J2SE 1.3.1 SDK (`http://java.sun.com/j2se`)
- Struts 1.1b2 (`http://jakarta.apache.org/struts`)

Optional items include:

- An SQL database of some form is required to complete the exercises in the book. The examples use MySQL (`www.mysql.org`)
- The Java-based build tool, Ant 1.5 (`http://jakarta.apache.org/ant`)
- A Java development IDE such as Sun ONE Studio Community Edition (`www.sun.com/software/sundev/jde/buy/index.html`) or Eclipse (`www.eclipse.org`).

The optional items and the specific version numbers are not required for the development of the examples in the book, however these are the software that the authors used to create the examples in the book as well as to test that they compiled and executed correctly.

Conventions Used in This Book

All the programming code and URLs in this book appear in this `fixed-width font`.

Sections of code shown in bold are used to highlight sections that are relevant to accompanying text, or sections that have changed and require modification from a current version of that code.

Throughout this book, you will find icons in the margins that highlight special or important information. Keep an eye out for the following icons:

A Caution icon indicates a procedure that could cause difficulty or even data loss; pay careful attention to Caution icons to avoid common and not-so-common programming pitfalls.

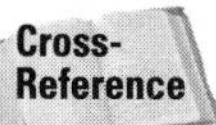

Cross-Reference icons point to additional information about a topic, which you can find in other sections of the book.

A Note icon highlights interesting or supplementary information and often contains extra bits of technical information about a subject.

Tip icons draw attention to handy suggestions, helpful hints, and useful pieces of advice.

Web Site

The book Web site is located at `http://www.wiley.com/compbooks/eaves`. On this site you will find the latest information regarding updates to this book, along with downloadable source code for each chapter.

Tell Us What You Think

We are very interested in finding out what you think of this book. Please feel free to register this book at the Wiley Publishing Web site (`www.wiley.com`) and give us your feedback. If you are interested in contacting us directly, send e-mail to one or all of the authors. We will do our best to respond promptly.

Acknowledgments

We would like to thank Jim Minatel, our Acquisitions Editor, and Sharon Nash, our Project Editor, for keeping three new authors on track with liberal doses of helpful advice and humor.

This book would not be readable without the phenomenal efforts of its Copy Editor, Howard Jones. His meticulous work to transform our jumbled words into the well structured, clearly phrased and consistently spelled prose you are now reading should be considered nothing short of miraculous.

Thanks go to the community surrounding the tomcat-user mailing list; we have not seen a more accommodating and friendly group of people. Many of the questions posed on the list provided structure for the book and focused us on the task of creating a book that would answer some of the commonly raised issues. Special thanks must go to the Tomcat developers and evangelists who spend many hours answering questions and helping users of all levels of ability.

There are many who donate their time to answer questions on the Tomcat mailing lists, all who deserve accolades, but we feel the need to mention two important contributors. Craig McClanahan, you have the patience of a saint, your answers are always clear and concise and are targeted perfectly to the level of ability of the questioner. John Turner, without your help and your FAQ there would be far fewer working installations of Tomcat with the Apache Web Server. Filip Hanik for his fantastic work on the tomcat-javagroups project, which has made in memory session replication possible in Tomcat 4. We all look forward to the inclusion of tomcat-javagroups clustering in Tomcat 5.

I'd like to thank my co-authors who are consummate professionals and fantastic friends. Without your hard work, this book could not have been completed. Thanks also go to another great friend, Peter Grant; your insightful reviews dramatically increased the quality of this book.

The long hours of writing and research were made more bearable by my cats, Boo and Maddy, who were delighted to find a warm lap on many late nights.

Finally, none of this would have been possible without the incredible support I was given by my beautiful wife, Sue. You are a remarkable woman, and your patience for my latest 'whimsy' can never be adequately repaid. I love you to the moon and back, the long way.

– Jon Eaves

I would also like to thank my co-authors who helped make this book possible. I simply would not have taken on a project of such scale without having complete trust in the capabilities of my fiends and colleagues. Against better advice I still underestimated the amount of work involved in such and undertaking, but the professionalism of both Jon, Rupert and all those involved at Wiley made this book a reality.

Just prior to this book my lovely girlfriend Stacey-Lee completed a nine-month-long thesis as part of her Honors degree, during this time I learned the virtue of patience and how to cherish even short amounts of time we spend together. I thank you Stacey-Lee for showing me the same patience and understanding. The last twelve months, however difficult, has still been a wonderful journey and I am looking forward sharing many more bottles of fine wine over the months and years to come.

– Warner Godfrey

It seems Jon has stolen my thunder as far as thanking the Wiley team goes, so I won't bore the reader by reiterating it, but my sincere thanks to these fine people still stands.

I would also like to acknowledge two people I am proud to call close friends, my co-authors Jon and Warner. Their awesome technical knowledge constantly amazes me and sets new standards for me to achieve in my own development. I would undertake work in any field with these two people and I would be assured of two things, I would learn extensively in doing so and we would all enjoy a laugh about it afterwards.

I should also extend a big thank you to Peter Grant for reviewing work. Pete's breadth of technical experience constantly bewilders me.

I would also like to thank my brother Nick and sister Caroline who, although had nothing to do with this book directly, have always counseled me on technical and personal issues and in doing so have influenced some of the most important decisions of my life.

To my beautiful girlfriend Valentina, who has had to put up with my many foibles (a big one being this book), your relentless support and kind words have seen me through many a late night and bleary-eyed morning. My love and appreciation for you cannot be quantified by my feeble words, thank you for being there, and still being there.

– Rupert Jones

Contents at a Glance

Contents

PART I

Getting Started with Tomcat and Web Applications

✦ ✦ ✦ ✦

In This Part

✦ ✦ ✦ ✦

What Is Tomcat?

In This Chapter

About the Apache Group

About the Java Community Process

The Servlet and JSP specifications

Understanding different Tomcat deployment strategies

The Tomcat development environment used in the book

This chapter provides a background to the history of Tomcat, the Apache Software Foundation, and the process by which new versions of Tomcat are developed. It also shows where Tomcat fits within the range of technologies used in server-side development and the Java 2 Enterprise Edition platform and specifications. The chapter concludes with a brief introduction to the tools and frameworks used in the examples in later chapters.

The Apache Software Foundation

The Apache Software Foundation (`www.apache.org`) is a non-profit organization that has grown out of The Apache Group. The Apache Group consists of the individuals who were originally responsible for the development of the Apache HTTP Server (often known as just Apache), which is now a project within the Apache Software Foundation.

The Apache Software Foundation is a coordinating body that is responsible for the management and direction of software projects, and is not completely responsible for providing the development resources to complete the projects. The Apache Software Foundation, through the Board of Directors, manages the organizational aspects of the projects, providing legal protection and financial support for the open source projects and their participants. The Apache Software Foundation provides support for projects, but it is the volunteer developers who provide the majority of the code for projects.

Apache projects are developed under the Apache Software License, which enables people to download and use the software for personal or commercial use completely free of charge. More information on the License can be found on the Apache Web site at (`www.apache.org/foundation/licence-FAQ.html`).

Apache Projects

The Apache Software Foundation oversees a number of different projects, each with potential sub-projects. The main projects include the following:

- HTTP Server (`http://httpd.apache.org/`). This HTTP server is the most widely used Web server on the Internet in August 2002. To be fair, the Apache HTTP server has been the most widely used Web server on the Internet since early 1996!

The Apache HTTP Server has more than 60 percent of the market for Web servers, with Microsoft IIS coming a very distant second with about 25 percent.

✦ PHP (`www.php.net`). This software is a general purpose scripting language that is targeted at server-side Web development. PHP is the most popular Apache module and installed on over 35 percent of all Apache HTTP servers.

✦ mod_perl (`http://perl.apache.org/`). This software is a module for Apache to enable Perl (www.perl.com) to be efficiently utilized as a server-side Web development scripting language. `mod_perl` is the second most popular Apache module, also installed on over 35 percent of all Apache HTTP servers.

✦ XML Project (`http://xml.apache.org/`). This project was founded to provide standards-based XML solutions in a variety of languages (for example Java, C, Perl). This project is responsible for the development of Xerces and Xalan, two of the most widely used XML/XSLT processing libraries for Java. Xerces is used by Tomcat for the XML processing of the configuration files.

✦ Jakarta Project (`http://jakarta.apache.org/`). This project is responsible for the development of open source Java server-side solutions. The Jakarta project is responsible for maintaining and enhancing some of the most widely used and important freely available Java software. This includes:

- **Ant**, the Java build tool
- **Cactus**, a server-side automated testing framework
- **Log4J**, an extensible Java logging framework
- **Struts**, a Web application development framework
- **Velocity**, a Java-based template engine
- **Tomcat**, the Servlet container reference implementation and topic of discussion for this book.

Without a doubt, the Apache Software Foundation, and the multitudes of developers who donate time and code to the projects, are currently providing some of the most important and fundamental software projects. The fact that these software projects are all freely available for general use is extraordinary.

The Apache projects have developed taxonomy for the contributors involved in the projects. It is valuable to examine this taxonomy because it describes clearly the roles and authority of the contributors within the projects.

Apache projects have the following structure for contributors:

✦ **Users** are people who use the software. Users provide feedback to developers in the form of bug reports and are involved in the project mailing lists.

✦ **Developers** are people who contribute code or documentation to a project. The contributions are sent to the project mailing lists.

✦ **Committers** are developers who have been granted write access to the CVS repository for the project. These contributors are the people who decide what new code will be introduced and what defects will be fixed.

✦ **Project Management Committee (PMC)** is a group of the committers who are responsible for the long term direction of their project.

As can be seen, the Apache Software Foundation considers the projects and the organizational infrastructure very important, and as a result, the level of quality of the software in the Apache projects tends to be very high.

Apache Tomcat Project

Apache Tomcat is a sub-project of the Jakarta project, and is the Reference Implementation for the Java Servlet Specification and the Java Server Pages Specification. However, it was not always Tomcat that fulfilled that role. The original project was JSWDK, which was also developed by Sun Microsystems. Apache had another project, JServ, a Servlet container that supported the Java Servlet API's version 2.0 and was designed to work with the Apache HTTP Server using the `mod_jserv` plug-in. JServ has now been retired and replaced by Tomcat. While it is still accessible at `http://java.apache.org`, only maintenance releases are available.

History of Tomcat

Tomcat started in late 1999 when Sun Microsystems contributed the JSWDK source code to the Apache Software Foundation. The Tomcat project became the reference implementation of the Java Servlet Specification and the Java Server Pages Specification. As a result, the major releases of Tomcat coincide with new versions of the specifications. The specifications are developed using the Java Community Process, and periodic updates as a result of requests result in new versions of the specifications.

There are currently 3 production-ready versions of Tomcat. Tomcat 3.3.1 still uses much of the original Sun supplied code base and supports the Servlet Specification 2.2. Tomcat 4.0.5 supports the Servlet Specification 2.3. The 4.0.x release stream is a complete rewrite of the original code base and includes a completely new architecture for the Servlet container. Tomcat 4.1.12 also supports the Servlet Specification 2.3, and is similar to the 4.0.5 production release. The Tomcat 4.1.x release stream is a refactoring of the 4.0.x stream including many performance enhancements and additional features for management and administration that previously were not well supported.

At the time of writing the book the Servlet 2.4 and JSP 2.0 specifications had achieved final Ddraft status and were approaching final release. Because Tomcat is the Reference Implementation for the Servlet and JSP specifications there is a new version of Tomcat, version 5.0, which will implement the new specifications.

Java Community Process

The Java Community Process is an open mechanism that guides the development of the Java platform. Sun has provided a process to allow community input, guidance, and in many cases, leadership, to direct the future product features of the Java platform. Membership is open to all, and companies or individuals may join as appropriate. The JCP includes all of the major companies involved in Java products like IBM, BEA, Oracle, and Sun itself.

The process of making changes to the Java platform involves the submission of a Java Specification Request (JSR) and this may be new features, or enhancements of existing features, that exist within the Java platform. It should be noted that the JCP covers the entire Java platform, from J2ME through to J2EE, and submission of a JSR is open to all. After submission the next step is the gathering of experts to form the expert group. This process involves specific requests from the submitter, to open invitations on the JCP Web site and relevant mailing lists. During this time, the JSR is open for review, and there is an initial ballot of the Executive Committee to see if the JSR should proceed. This step is in place to ensure that the JSR meets a widely accepted need within the Java platform, and that it fits within the currently existing framework for Java. If the ballot succeeds, the JSR enters active status. It is then the responsibility of the JSR Expert Group to create what is known as the *Community Draft*. This is an initial document reviewed by members and the responsible Executive Committee. The review of the Community Draft ensures that the JSR is proceeding as planned, and provides the opportunity to review and revise the document before proceeding to Public Draft. When a JSR achieves this milestone, the documents are available for anybody to read, review, and provide feedback. During this feedback process the Expert Group is working on developing a reference implementation.

One of the highlights of the JCP is that each JSR must have a reference implementation as part of the process. This is a fantastic decision by the creators of the JCP and means that the specifications produced are already tested in the real world, and capable of being implemented. This leads to standards and specifications that reflect the reality of development activities, completely unlike many of the specifications that tend to plague the computer industry.

At the end of the Public Review period, the documents are updated to reflect the input from the public and a Final Draft is created. At the same time the reference implementation is being completed to reflect the changes made from the Public Draft to the Final Draft. The final step in the process is the Final Approval Ballot, where the Executive Committee votes to accept or reject the JSR. After successfully passing the Final Approval Ballot, the JSR is accepted and the documents and reference implementation is then considered to be the Final Release. The Expert Group, after many months of tireless (and often thankless) work is disbanded.

This process is used to develop new versions of the Servlet and Java Server Pages specifications. For more information on the JCP, visit the Web site at `http://www.jcp.org`.

JSR-53, JSR-152, JSR-154

These rather innocuous numbers are the specifications for the Servlet and JSP specifications, and have driven the features and development of Tomcat to the present day.

Table 1-1 presents the resulting specifications and the version(s) of Tomcat that support those specifications.

Table 1-1: JSR, Specifications, and Tomcat Versions

JSR Number	*JSR Name*	*Start Date*	*Release Date*	*Tomcat Version*
JSR-53	Java Servlet 2.3 and Server Pages 1.2 Specifications	7th Feb 2000	25th Sep 2001	Tomcat 4.0.x, Java Tomcat 4.1.x
JSR-152	Java Server Pages 2.0 Specification	22nd Oct 2001	16th Aug 2002 (*)	Tomcat 5.0.x
JSR-154	Java Servlet 2.4 Specification	22nd Oct 2001	8th Aug 2002 (*)	Tomcat 5.0.x

As can be seen from Table 1-1, the JSR process and the resulting software take considerable time to develop and mature to stable, production-ready products.

What is a Reference Implementation?

Tomcat is the reference implementation for the Java Servlet and JSP specifications, and more correctly, the reference implementation for JSR-53. It is soon to be the reference implementation for JSR-152 and JSR-154.

A reference implementation is a prototype, or proof of concept of the defined specification.

The logical question is of course, "How do I know the reference implementation meets the specification?"

That question has a complicated answer, but fortunately the JCP has foreseen that eventuality and part of the JCP process which wasn't mentioned previously is the development of the *Technology Compatibility Kit (TCK)*. The TCK is a set of tools, tests, and documentation that defines the specification in such a way that a developer can test that their implementation meets the requirements of the specification. The developers of other Servlet containers like IBM (for WebSphere) and BEA (for WebLogic) utilize the TCK to ensure their software meets the standards defined in the specification. Tomcat (and any reference implementation) is the initial product developed to demonstrate the specification can be implemented, and to assist in the process of clarification of the wording in the specification.

Current Specifications

The current specifications and the specifications that are supported by Tomcat 4.x are Java Servlet Specification 2.3 and Java Server Pages Specification 1.2. The details of these specifications can be found on the JCP site, or from Sun's `java.sun.com` site at `http://java.sun.com/products/servlet` and `http://java.sun.com/products/jsp`.

These specifications are very important to Tomcat because they define exactly what Tomcat must be. The servlet and JSP specifications are relatively long documents, and as a result are a little daunting to read. However, to fully understand the capabilities of Tomcat it is important to have a reasonable understanding of what the specifications require to be supported.

The following sections provide a brief introduction to the specifications. This is meant as a guide to further study as when problems arise during development it is often highly instructive to review the specifications to understand the behavior of Tomcat.

Java Servlet Specification

The Java Servlet Specification defines a mechanism for extending a Web server to provide functionality for developing dynamic content generation similar to that provided by a CGI approach.

The Java Servlet Specification covers a wide spectrum of topics, all with the goal of defining the runtime environment and the development of APIs for servlets. This goal has been well achieved. Across the wide variety of servlet containers, the inconsistencies are minor, and in many cases inconsistencies are a direct result of not following the specification adequately.

The following sections provide summaries of chapters of the specification, and their relevance.

Servlet Interface

The Servlet Interface, where `interface` is the Java language construct and not just the architectural construct, is the fundamental component of the Servlet API. The Servlet Interface is most commonly implemented and used as the `HttpServlet` in Web applications. The examples in this book use `HttpServlet` exclusively, and do not examine the other classes of Servlet (like `GenericServlet`).

The specification for the Servlet Interface defines the semantics of the request handling methods, and this is defined by the `service()` method which is the single point of entry into a class implementing Servlet. In the case of the `HttpServlet` there are additional methods defined for the purposes of handling the HTTP protocol. The most commonly used methods are `doGet()` and `doPost()`, but there is also `doPut()`, `doDelete()`, `doHead()`, `doOptions()` and `doTrace()`.

The next important consideration for the Servlet Interface is the definition of how a servlet container may create servlets to service the external requests. The normal case is for each servlet to be instantiated only once and hence require multi-threading consideration when writing the servlet. However, a servlet can implement the `SingleThreadModel` and the container may create a pool of multiple servlets, each for the processing of individual requests, or force the requests to be processed serially. This may have negative consequences on performance because the flow of control through the servlet limits the number of requests that can be handled.

Finally, the Servlet Interface defines the life cycle of a servlet. This defines not only the mechanism the servlet container must use to execute the servlet, but also what methods are invoked in the servlet so the application developer can use the methods to his advantage. The life cycle of a servlet is defined by the invocation of the `init()`, `service()`, and `destroy()` methods.

An important consideration of the life cycle is that a servlet isn't in a valid, useable state until the `init()` method has been called, so the servlet constructor and any static initialization should not attempt to perform external actions, such as connection to databases, until `init()` is called.

Servlet Context

The `ServletContext` interface provides a servlet the ability to obtain access to the information about the Web application in which the servlet is running. The `ServletContext` is provided by the Container developer (in this case Tomcat) and provides access to resources such as:

- Logging
- Parameters defined in the context configuration
- External resources such as properties, files, or images

The `ServletContext` also provides the capabilities to set and get attributes (an object bound to a name) that can be retrieved by other servlets within the same context.

A single instance of a `ServletContext` is associated with each Web application that is deployed in a servlet container. This ensures that servlets with the Web application have the same view of the Web application, and can use the same `ServletContext`.

An important consideration in the use of a ServletContext is that context attributes are only valid in the VM where they were created. Developers using an implementation of a container that makes use of a distributed environment must be aware that the context attributes are not available to a remote VM.

The Request

The Request Object (ServletRequest) contains all the information from the client request to the servlet container. For the HTTP protocol, this includes elements such as HTTP headers and message body. The servlet container takes the raw information and bundles it into a subclass of ServletRequest called HttpServletRequest.

The HttpServletRequest object is created by the container and passed to the service() method of the servlet. The HttpServletRequest provides access to information such as:

- ✦ Authentication type, such as BASIC or SSL
- ✦ The cookies sent by the client
- ✦ The headers sent by the client
- ✦ The session associated with this request

The ServletRequest also provides access to attributes associated with the request. Attributes are objects that have been set by the container (as with the ServletContext) to be associated with the request and are used to communicate information between servlets. This mechanism makes use of the RequestDispatcher and is utilized heavily by the Model 2 architecture to facilitate communication between a controlling servlet and the JSP responsible for display.

For more information on the Model 2 architecture, see the following section titled "Java Server Pages Specification."

The specification also defines the lifetime of the request object. That is, the request object is only valid within the scope of the service() method invoked by the container (and in the case of an HttpServlet the internally called doPost() or doGet() methods). A developer making a reference to the ServletRequest that is then used outside that scope may find the data is invalidated because a container potentially re-uses the objects in a pool rather than having the overhead of creation and destruction of the objects. Clearly this is not a practice that leads to correctly working Web applications.

The Response

The Response Object (ServletResponse) provides the encapsulation of the data that is transmitted from the server to the client. For the HTTP protocol, this includes elements such as HTTP headers and message body, and is a subclass of ServletResponse called HttpServletResponse.

The ServletResponse object does not provide as much abstraction from the response to the client compared to the ServletRequest. A servlet developer must still use low level constructs to produce the output to the client. The ServletRequest provides convenient mechanisms for dealing with cookies and headers, but the message body is still produced via directly writing (via a PrintWriter) the response.

To assist, the ServletResponse provides capabilities for accessing the buffering, and being able to increase or decrease the size of the buffer depending on the application's requirements.

The specification also defines convenience methods for reporting the more common error conditions to the client. These conditions redirect the client to an alternative URL, and produce an error.

As with the Request Object, the Response Object is only valid within the scope of the `service()` method and maintaining a reference to the Response Object carries the same risks as with the Request Object.

Filtering

Filtering is newly introduced to the servlet specification and is somewhat like a servlet in that it is invoked within the context of the servlet container; however filtering allows transformation of body and header information in both the request and response. A filter is not normally responsible for creating a response, but tends to act on client or servlet produced information by modifying a request, or a response.

Some potential examples of filters follow:

- ✦ Implementing a cache
- ✦ Data conversion, such as removal of particular tags from HTML, or transforming XML using XSLT to create the HTML response
- ✦ Encryption of a response
- ✦ Logging of user requests

Filters are configured in a similar manner to a servlet by requiring entries in the deployment descriptor of the Web application.

The specification defines a lifecycle for a filter, and an API for implementing a filter. Like a servlet, a filter has an `init()` and a `destroy()` but in contrast to the `service()` method, the filter only has a `doFilter()` method for implementing the required filtering action.

The specification defines the ability for filters to exist in a chain, so that multiple filters can operate on the same request and response. The ordering of filters is defined to be their order of declaration in the deployment descriptor.

Finally, the specification defines a mechanism for wrapping request and response objects to override methods and behavior to make the objects more useful to downstream filter or Web resources.

Sessions

An important point that was not lost on the implementers of the servlet specification is that HTTP is a stateless protocol. Web applications need to have a concept of a session to map series of client requests together to define a logical flow of events. There are many ways that this can be achieved with HTTP, so to abstract the concept of a session the specification defines the `HttpSession` interface. This then allows a servlet container to use any of the session tracking mechanisms defined in the specification without requiring the Java developer to make a specific choice.

The specification defines the session tracking approaches that are covered by the interface. These are cookies, SSL sessions, and URL rewriting.

To work with sessions effectively, the specification defines how and when a session is created, the scope of the session, and how a session can be completed. The scope of a session is defined to only operate on the Web application (or context) level, and therefore limits the access to session variables to a single Web application.

Sessions provide a mechanism for binding attributes (objects stored with a name) to the session. Any servlet sharing the same servlet context (part of the same Web application) can access the objects stored in the session.

Because HTTP is a stateless protocol there is no explicit means of determining that a client has stopped visiting the Web application. To facilitate the cleanup of inactive sessions, the specification defines a mechanism for removing the sessions once an inactivity timeout has been reached. This timeout value is defined by the servlet container and is generally configurable via the servlet container configuration files.

Finally, the specification defines how sessions should behave under specific circumstances relating to threading, distributed environments, and multiple window client simultaneous access.

Dispatching Requests

A Web application may gain benefit from taking the results of processing and forwarding those results to another servlet for further processing or display. This facility can be performed using the new Filter capabilities, or using a `RequestDispatcher`. A request dispatcher works similarly to a client side redirect, but without the round trip to the client, making the processing far more efficient.

The servlet specification defines how to obtain a request dispatcher and the specific semantics surrounding the dispatcher. A request dispatcher can be obtained from either the `ServletContext` or from the `ServletRequest`, but the manner in which they can be used differs slightly.

A request dispatcher can be used in one of two methods. The first is to invoke the `include()` method. This allows the target of the include to write data to the output stream of the response object. Using the include method does not allow for modification of header information in the response, but the include method can be invoked at any time during the output processing.

The second method is to invoke the `forward()` method. This method may only be called if no output has been sent to the client. This method of invocation is used in the Model 2 architecture for dispatching processed results to a JSP page for output.

Web Applications

The servlet specification provides broad instruction for the processing of Web applications by the Web application container. A Web application is defined by the specification as a:

"Collection of servlets, html pages, classes, and other resources that make up a complete application on a Web server" (Java Servlet Specification Version 2.3, Chapter SRV.9).

This is an important portion of the specification as it crosses from defining how servlets should be processed by the Web application container into defining how a group of assets should be treated during processing by the Web application container. This chapter details what the elements of a Web application are, the deployment hierarchy, and even the directory structure of the Web application.

The benefit of this level of specification is that it guarantees consistency of deployment of packaged Web applications over Web application containers implemented by different vendors. This is a tremendous benefit to the Web application developer because it gives a very strong write-once run-anywhere capability to their products.

Included in a Web application is a Web application deployment descriptor that is used to define various aspects of the Web application. This is discussed in more detail in the section titled "Deployment Descriptor" later in this chapter.

The specification has identified that Web applications may rely on external libraries which are installed into the servlet container separately from the Web application. The specification recommends that application developers list the dependencies as part of their Web application to enable the container to reject the Web application with an appropriate error message.

The specification defines the behavior of the Web application class loader and what classes should and should not be available to the Web application as well as the order of preference for loading the classes.

The final part of this chapter of the specification defines a naming environment for the Web application. Some elements in the naming environment are not appropriate or relevant for a Web application only application server, but provide a defined interface when dealing with an integrated application server such as a fully compliant J2EE server. The naming entries that are important to a standalone Web application container (such as Tomcat) are the environment (`env-entry`) and resources (`resource-ref`) that define resources such as database pools.

Application Lifecycle Events

The application lifecycle events are new functionality defined in this version of the specification. This functionality provides for registration of a servlet event listener that can receive events when state changes occur in a `ServletContext` or `HttpSession` object.

The specification defines four types of events. These are:

- ✦ Servlet context lifecycle events. These events are sent when a servlet context is created or is just about to be destroyed.
- ✦ Servlet context attribute events. These events are sent when attributes of a servlet context are added, removed, or replaced.
- ✦ HTTP session lifecycle events. These events are sent when an `HttpSession` is created, explicitly invalidated, or is just about to time out.
- ✦ HTTP session attribute events. These events are sent when attributes of an HTTP session are added, removed, or replaced.

As with the servlets and filters, the listener classes require configuration and are part of the deployment descriptor for the Web application.

The specification has defined the behavior of listeners in distributed containers to be the same as the behavior for `HttpSession` and `ServletContext` objects. The listeners only receive events relating to the local VM, and distributed containers are explicitly not required to forward these events to remote VMs.

Mapping Requests to Servlets

To make effective use of Web applications and the context they are defined in, the specification defines how a client request URL is mapped to particular servlets. This covers explicit mappings defined in deployment descriptors or Web container configuration as well as implicit mappings. Implicit mappings include how to process requests for particular files such as *.jsp, or *.shtml.

The specification enables the container to include any implicit mapping desired, provided that explicit mapping can override the implicit mapping.

This chapter of the specification is very important for application developers but also important for determining how the deployment of the Web application occurs on a server. The mapping allows for all requests to be directed to a particular servlet, or for just a very specific match by specifying the full URL of the request.

Security

There are two types of security defined in the servlet specification. The first is , which is controlled by the Web container and is external to the Web application, providing security for Web applications that have no explicit code implemented for security within the application.

Declarative security can be changed during deployment time by modifying an external file or data source, such as an LDAP or SQL database containing user and access data. An important point is that declarative security is not enforced during an internal dispatch via a `RequestDispatcher` or a servlet using forward or include. This particular feature means that declarative security must be carefully applied as it only is applied to direct requests from the client and not any internal redirection by the server.

The second type of security defined is *programmatic security*. Programmatic security is explicitly implemented within the Web application and uses methods within the `Http ServletRequest` interface to obtain information about the user making the request. This information can then be programmatically compared to determine the desired behavior.

The specification defines the authentication styles that can be used by the Web client. These mechanisms are:

- ✦ Basic auth, a standard HTTP 1.0 authentication mechanism. The Web client is responsible for obtaining a username and password from the user by any means necessary and transmits this information to the server.
- ✦ Digest auth, a standard HTTP authentication mechanism. Unlike basic auth the password is not transmitted to the server in clear text. The client applies simple base64 encoding to obfuscate the information during transit.
- ✦ HTTPS client authentication is an optional authentication mechanism for servlet containers that are not part of a J2EE compliant server. This authentication uses the strong identification mechanisms of client public key certificates.
- ✦ Form based authentication, which provides for a means to customize a login screen according to the needs of the Web application rather than having the Web client provide a standard dialog box for user data entry. The form-based authentication provides a standard HTML page with specific names for form fields for the username and password of the user. The form-based authentication uses the container and configuration in the deployment descriptor to display the login form when access to a restricted resource is requested.

The specification recognizes the authentication information may be handled externally to the Web application and as a result requires the container, and not the Web application, to be responsible for tracking the authentication information. This requirement has the effect of having container-wide, or cross-context, authentication and applications may take advantage of this behavior by allowing access to any resources managed by the container.

Finally, the specification defines how security constraints should be configured and applied to resources within a Web application. This information is defined in the deployment descriptor and the configuration is applied to the request using the same algorithm as the mapping of requests to servlets.

Deployment Descriptor

This chapter of the specification describes the requirements for a conforming Web application server to process a deployment descriptor. The specification defines the rules for processing the syntax of the deployment descriptor, and the DTD for the XML grammar that is used to define the elements of the deployment descriptor.

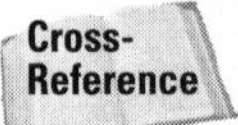

The deployment descriptor is fully described in Chapter 3.

javax.servlet and javax.servlet.http API

The specification is completed with automatically generated content from the `javadoc` comments contained in the Java classes and interfaces for `javax.servlet` and `javax.servlet.http`.

Java Server Pages Specification

The Java Server Pages Specification was developed to provide a consistent and simple means for creating HTML output as opposed to explicit coding of HTML fragments in a servlet.

The JSP specification provides more application developer information in the form of defining syntax and semantics for the use of JSP scripting and tags. This is due to the lifecycle of JSP pages, as they are parsed and compiled into servlets as part of their processing. This is good news, because all the information in the previous section is also relevant to JSP.

The following sections provide summaries of chapters of the specification, and their relevance.

Core Syntax and Semantics

The JSP specification has an introductory section that defines the concepts involved in the JSP technologies and how those concepts relate to each other and other technologies, such as servlets.

The items covered in this chapter include definitions for:

- A JSP page
- A Web or JSP container
- Web components
- Events in JSP pages (init and destroy)
- Compiling of JSP pages and their packaging in Web applications
- The handling of errors during translation time and request time

The specification also covers the syntax of the pages including definitions for:

- Syntactic elements of a JSP page. These are either elements or template data. Elements are those parts of the JSP page that the JSP translator can process. Template data is everything else.
- The element syntax, start, and end tags; empty elements; attribute values; valid names for actions and attributes; white space.
- Comments (HTML comments, JSP comments).
- Quoting and escape conventions applying to JSP pages.

A JSP page is a server-side Java component, and it can access normal Java objects and objects provided as part of the Web container environment. The specification defines the manner in which objects can be accessed, the scope, and what objects are implicit to a JSP page. The implicit objects available include request (`ServletRequest`) and response (`ServletResponse`) objects, session (`HttpSession`) and application (`ServletContext`) objects, and the `JspWriter` for output.

A JSP-specific object, the pageContext (`javax.servlet.jsp.PageContext`) is available for storage of page specific references to objects, similar in capabilities to the `ServletContext` object.

Finally, this chapter of the specification defines the allowable directives and their behavior, the scripting elements, and actions. All these elements are part of what is commonly used in the creation of a JSP page.

A directive has a syntax of `<%@ directive {attr="value"}* %>` and the purpose is to provide information to the JSP container. The directives deal with behavior such as:

- Importing namespaces, `<%@ page import="java.sql.*" %>`
- Choosing the scripting language, `<%@ page language="java" %>`
- Buffering control, `<%@ page buffer="none" %>`
- Using a tag library, `<%@ taglib uri="http://www.bar.com/tags prefix="foo" %>`
- Including a script or HTML fragment, `<%@ include file="header.html" %>`

Scripting elements are the declarations, fragments of code called *scriptlets*, and expressions. Expressions are a single statement that the return value is converted into a String object for display.

Actions are commands that use a tag syntax for invoking and the specification includes a definition of standard actions and a mechanism for defining and introducing new actions for use in JSP pages.

Localization Issues

The JSP specification defines the requirements associated with localization support for conforming containers. These specifications cover the configuration of the JSP page character encoding and the ability to statically or dynamically modify the content type of the response.

Standard Actions

The specification defines a set of standard actions that are to be provided by a JSP container for use within JSP pages. The syntax for using a standard action is similar to using an action defined in a tag library.

The standard actions are:

- `<jsp:useBean>`. This action provides mapping between a Java object and a scripting variable. This action provides an attribute to define the scope of the object, which determines where the object is available for use. Objects of scope `request` are located in the current page's `ServletRequest`, `session` scoped objects are located in the page's `HttpSession`, and objects of `application` scope are located in the `ServletContext` for the current page.
- `<jsp:setProperty>` and `<jsp:getProperty>`. These actions set and get properties associated with a JavaBean.
- `<jsp:include>` and `<jsp:forward>`. These actions provide similar functionality to the `include` and `forward` methods in `RequestDispatcher` with similar constraints and behavior.
- `<jsp:param>`. This action is used to provide key/value pairs as part of the `<jsp:include>`, `<jsp:forward>`, and `<jsp:params>` actions.
- `<jsp:plugin>`. This action is a convenient mechanism for providing a way of generating the appropriate browser-specific HTML for downloading the Java Plugin software.

JSP Documents

The JSP specification defines XML syntax for JSP pages. This XML syntax is provided in addition to the JSP syntax and has additional benefits over the JSP syntax, including validation of the JSP page syntax prior to processing, use of standard XML manipulation tools on the JSP pages, and enhanced white space processing.

The XML syntax replaces the directives, declaration, scriptlets, and expression JSP syntax with XML tags. For example, the `<%@ page { attr="value"}* %>` syntax is replaced with `<jsp:directive.page { attr="value" }* />`.

The JSP syntax and XML syntax can be used interchangeably within a Web application, but each JSP page must use only one syntax style.

Scripting

The entire purpose of having JSP pages is to embed some form of scripting within the template data. The specification defines the syntax and structure of the JSP scripting elements when the page language directive is Java. The only page language directive required to be supported by a 1.2 conforming JSP container is the Java language, so this specification provides a complete definition of the current scripting language requirements. This is not always the case, however, because any language may be supported by the JSP container in the future.

The specification defines the overall structure of the scripting elements, including what defines a JSP Page, the reserved names, declarations, elements, initialization of the implicit objects, and the transformation from the JSP page into the code to be executed by the container.

The transformation of the main section defines the approach required for template, scriptlet, expression, and action elements on a JSP page.

Tag Extensions

To provide additional support for removing the Java scriptlets from the JSP pages the specification defines facility for introducing new actions into a JSP page. This facility is known as a tag library, or *taglib*.

This section of the specification covers how to create and package tag libraries, including definitions of the structure of the libraries and the library descriptor file.

JSP Container

This chapter of the specification defines what is required to be implemented by the JSP container. It is of particular importance to the JSP container developers and provides interesting information for JSP page authors.

The JSP container chapter covers the protocols between the JSP pages and the JSP container, the contracts and interfaces required to be supported, and the JSP page lifecycle. An item of particular interest is the transformation of JSP pages to implementation classes. The specification defines that the implementation classes must implement the `Servlet` interface, however it explicitly states that the created object will be placed in an implementation dependent package, and of an implementation dependent class. The class may be specified by the use of the `page extends` directive, however this is strongly cautioned against as it may prevent the JSP container from performing optimization on the class.

Using Java Server Pages

Shortly after the release of the JSP Specification, developers found that there was a tendency to mix business logic and presentation in the JSP pages, even though the JSP pages were using beans for significant amounts of the processing. The other difficulty was that as the JSP page was responsible for the request (1) and the response (3) the entire flow was through an individual page. This worked very well for small applications where workflow and processing was simple, but quickly became very cumbersome when workflow was not linear. This rapidly led to using fragments of JSP code as include files and significant amounts of Java code embedded in the JSP page.

This was known as the *Model 1 architecture* and is shown in Figure 1-1.

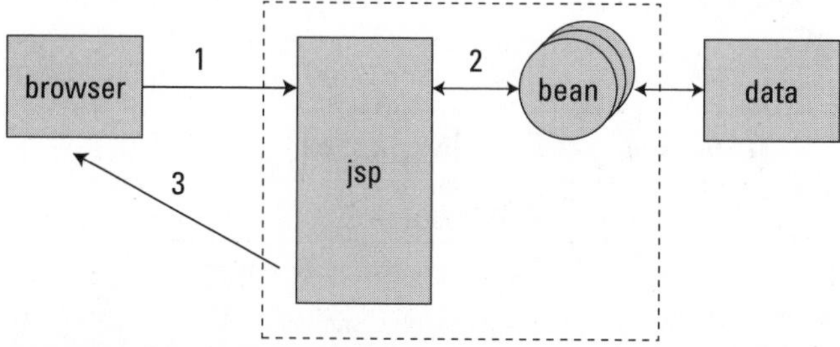

Figure 1-1: Model 1 architecture

After a short period of time, developers identified an architecture utilizing servlets and JSP that would lead to good scalability and robustness, both in application development and in system engineering. This way of developing Web applications is known as *Model 2 architecture*, shown in Figure 1-2.This architecture uses a servlet as a controller for the application taking requests from the browser (1), creating the beans required for processing (2), and then invoking the appropriate JSP page for the display of the results (3 and 5). The JSP page makes use of the beans created by the Servlet for the display (4). This has great benefits in reducing the Java code in the JSP pages, leading to increased maintainability and in many cases speed improvements as the JSP page compilations were simplified.

It is an implementation of the Model-View-Controller (MVC) software development pattern. MVC is an important development pattern because it separates the user interface (view) from the business logic (model) and is coordinated by a controller which is normally a servlet.

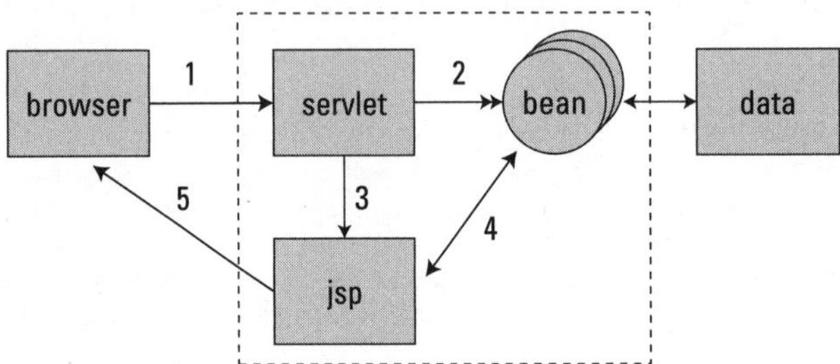

Figure 1-2: Model 2 architecture

The implementation of the Model 2 architecture allows for good separation between the components of the application, providing the capability for scheduling of development by appropriate skill sets (JSP development by HTML and design specialists, and the architecture and other infrastructure by server-side software developers).

What about J2EE?

J2EE, or *Java 2 Platform Enterprise Edition* to use its full name, is a standard environment for developing and deploying enterprise applications using the Java language. J2EE consists of a set of coordinated specifications, standards, and practices relating to the development, deployment, and management of server-side applications. Table 1-2 shows the technologies involved in the J2EE platform.

Table 1-2: J2EE Technologies

Name	*Purpose*
Java Server Pages (JSP)	User Interface Development
Java Servlets	Application control and flow
Enterprise JavaBeans (EJB)	Distributed Component Architecture
Java DataBase Connectivity (JDBC)	Connecting to databases

Name	*Purpose*
Java Naming and Directory Interface (JNDI)	Unified interface to naming and directory services
Java Transaction API (JTA)	Transaction management system
CORBA	RMI over IIOP, Java IDL, EJB to CORBA mapping
XML Support (JAXP)	Parsing and transforming XML documents
JavaMail API	Libraries for sending a receiving mail
Java Message Service (JMS)	Asynchronous messaging
Java Connector Architecture (JCA)	Architecture for integrating heterogeneous IESs

As can be seen from the Table 1-2, the J2EE specification covers a very wide technology base, and despite the most common uses of J2EE today it is not only for Web and Internet developments. The infrastructure supported by J2EE is also very well suited to thick client development (for example, Swing-based Java clients).

If we are to represent J2EE in a diagram it could potentially look like Figure 1-3:

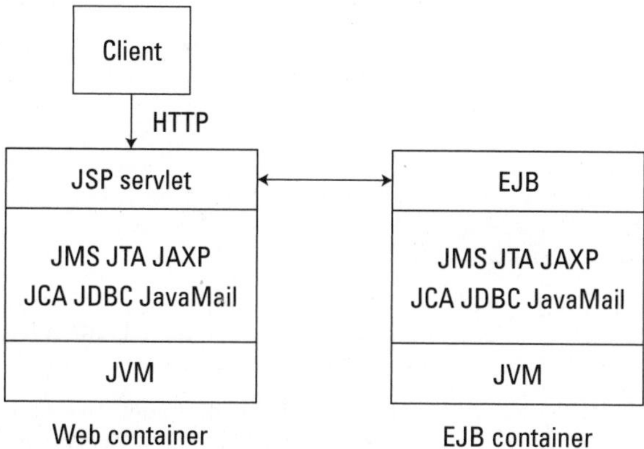

Figure 1-3: J2EE architecture

From Table 1-2 and Figure 1-3 we can see that Tomcat provides J2EE technology services for the Java Server Pages and Java Servlets components of the platform.

As we also can see, J2EE is a much wider scoped platform than Tomcat attempts to provide. There is good reason for this. A major contributor to the creation of the J2EE platform specifications was the existence of the JSP and Servlet specifications and the server-side development opportunities provided by those specifications.

There is often a great deal of confusion surrounding the J2EE platform and the use of the platform. By utilizing Tomcat as a Web application server (or servlet container) we are using technologies defined by the J2EE platform, because the JSP and Servlet specifications fall under the jurisdiction of the JCP Executive Committee responsible for the J2EE platform.

An implementation of the entire J2EE technology specification suite is called a J2EE Application Server and Table 1-3 shows some examples of the vendors and the availability of the servers.

Table 1-3: J2EE Application Servers

Server	*Vendor*	*Availability*	*URL*	*Comments*
WebLogic	BEA	Commercial Terms	www.bea.com	No comment
WebSphere	IBM	Commercial Terms	www.ibm.com	No comment
JRun	MacroMedia	Commercial Terms	www.macromedia.com	No comment
SunONE	Sun	Free/Commercial Terms	www.sun.com	No comment
JoNAS	ObjectWeb	Free	www.objectweb.org/jonas	No comment
JBoss	JBoss Group	Free	www.jboss.org	Uses Jetty or Tomcat as the Servlet container
J2EE-RI	Sun	Free	java.sun.com/j2ee	Useful for proof of concept development

Why Tomcat and Not a J2EE Server?

The short answer to this question is, "It depends on the problem you are trying to solve." The full answer to this question is outside the scope of this book, but in a nutshell, the full power and capabilities of a J2EE server is very often overkill for many problems.

Tomcat provides a Servlet container for running servlets and JSP, JDBC connections for communication with databases. For many Web applications this is sufficient to provide the functionality to solve the problem elegantly and rapidly. The introduction of J2EE technologies such as Enterprise JavaBeans may have some additional benefits, but should be weighed carefully against the additional development complexity.

The real benefit of choosing Tomcat is that if the solution requires greater complexity at a later stage, or could benefit from some of the additional J2EE features, the migration to a J2EE server can be easily performed. The ease of migration often depends on the application development architecture. Those applications that are more closely aligned with a Model 2 MVC architecture have a greater benefit during migration than an application with an architecture that is not as well defined.

Of course, this is assuming that the migration to a J2EE application server is to take advantage of the additional features provided by J2EE, such as Enterprise JavaBeans. A J2EE application server must provide the capabilities matching the Servlet and JSP specifications, so an application executing on Tomcat should be able to be moved unchanged to a J2EE application server.

Some advantages of using Tomcat over a full J2EE application server are:

- ✦ Smaller footprint. Tomcat requires fewer resources to operate than a J2EE application server that must provide all of the J2EE technology infrastructure even if the solution does not take advantage of those additional capabilities.
- ✦ Less complexity. Because Tomcat does not provide all the additional capabilities of a J2EE application server, the configuration and administration of the server is significantly simpler.

Using Tomcat

It would be very convenient at this stage to launch straight into using Tomcat. However, there are still more choices to be made, and a few more items to be explored.

What Tomcat Version?

At the time the book was written there are three versions of Tomcat that can be chosen for use. The version that you decide to use in your environment will depend on what factors are most important.

- ✦ Tomcat 3.3.1. This version of Tomcat is the most stable, and has been used in production environments for an extended period of time. This version would be a good choice if stability and reliability is of paramount importance. Unfortunately, this version is based on the Java Servlet Specification 2.2 and Java Server Pages Specification 1.0, which are both nearly 2 versions old, so some of the more advanced functionality is not available.
- ✦ Tomcat 4.0.5. This version of Tomcat replaced the 3.x versions and is based on the Java Servlet Specification 2.3 and Java Server Pages Specification 1.1. The 4.0.x code base has significant advances over the 3.x code base in modularity and function, and includes all the new functionality prescribed in the newer specifications. This version is used extensively in production and is considered to be the most stable version available. Unfortunately, this version does not include some of the newer administration and deployment features available in the latest releases.
- ✦ Tomcat 4.1.12. This version of Tomcat is a re-factoring of the 4.0.x code base and contains many major advances in functionality including a comprehensive Web-based administration and management system. This version also includes very good integration with the Ant development tool to ease some of the issues associated with the Web application development. Other major improvements include a re-written JSP compiler which is significantly faster and requires considerably fewer resources than the 4.0.x counterpart.

As will become a little clearer soon, the Tomcat release philosophy makes it a little difficult to select a version of Tomcat to use in this book. Tomcat 4.1.12 has been used for examples because this version has become significantly more stable than previous releases and there are many users deploying this version in production environments.

Astute readers will have noticed that the 5.0.x code base is also available, but in the authors' opinion this server is not robust enough at this stage even for development or educational activities. As time passes, the 5.0.x versions will surpass the other versions in functionality, stability, and ease of use.

Apache Tomcat Release Philosophy

The Apache Tomcat project has an interesting release philosophy that can cause confusion and frustration if the user of the project isn't aware of the methodology. Tomcat has a continual development cycle, with releases being created "when they are ready" and release numbers assigned. This tends to generate a large number of releases of products, with relatively rapid iteration through minor version numbers.

The confusing aspect of this development is that while the project teams consider the version numbered release to be ready for use, it doesn't mean that it's defect free, or suitable for large scale use. A project will generate a "release build" and assign a version number. However, that version will only become a stable version if it lasts for some period of time without defects being found, and the level of quality is appropriate.

This sounds a little bit confusing and haphazard. The reality is that if you download only what are identified as the production quality releases from the Web site, you are guaranteed to have the most stable, well-tested version of Tomcat available to you at that time. If you want to help out the testing and development efforts or live on the leading edge of features, then downloading the stable releases and reporting defects is your best option.

Future versions of the 4.1.X development stream should also work with the examples used in this book, but there may be minor incompatibilities introduced, so ensure that the release notes are read thoroughly when downloading new releases.

Development and Deployment

One of the advantages of the servlet specification is that it defines a format for deploying the applications. This means that the developer needs to have a structured development environment and that it must support the deployment format. This is advantageous because when deployment to production is required, it is a relatively simple matter of taking the deployment bundle (called a *Web archive,* or *WAR*) generated and tested in the development cycle and deploying it in the project. The exact details of these development environments and the deployment archive are expanded in later chapters.

This separation between development and deployment also allows the development activities on a developer's workstation to be a completely different environment from the production or system testing environments. In fact, there is no need for the development and production machines to even run the same operating system. This is where the power and flexibility of the multi-platform capabilities of Java become evident. The multi-platform capabilities of Java gives flexibility in machine configuration, especially as the resource requirements for Tomcat are relatively low, depending on the size and scope of the application under development.

This difference in production and development environments is manifested in instances where Tomcat is linked with the Apache HTTP Server in production. During development the developer uses Tomcat for serving static content as well as the dynamic execution of the servlets and JSP pages. In production the Apache HTTP Server serves the static content and passes requests through the Servlet to Tomcat to fulfill.

An appropriately architected application is capable of moving between the two environments with no change in the application code, only requiring changes to the deployment environment and configuration files.

Should Tomcat Serve Static Pages?

There are two schools of thought about using Tomcat in a production environment.

- Use an HTTP server (Apache, IIS) to serve static pages and images
- Use Tomcat to serve static pages and images

Both of these approaches have merit, and like many things depend on the application that is being developed and the scale of the deployment.

Two of the most common reasons cited for using an HTTP Server as a "front" for Tomcat is that the HTTP Server serves static content much faster than Tomcat, and that by using the HTTP Server to server static content then the load can be taken from Tomcat and Tomcat can utilize its resources solely for serving dynamic content.

Tomcat 3.x was not as fast as the 4.x versions and for many the convenience of setting up just one server and avoiding the complexity of connecting the two far outweighs any speed benefits that are found by using an HTTP Server. For many applications, "fast enough" is more than adequate as opposed to being "the fastest possible."

There may be good reasons for deploying Tomcat with an HTTP server. Here are some of the reasons why that configuration should be considered more closely:

- The HTTP server may have extra features provided by the server that Tomcat cannot provide. A good example is integration with an existing PHP or ASP solution. Using an HTTP server obviates the need to redevelop the entire application.
- A Web browser connects to a Web server using port 80. In some environments (Unix) this requires the use of accounts that have elevated access privileges. HTTP servers like the Apache HTTP server are capable of working with that in a more appropriate manner than Tomcat.
- The system administration team may already be using an HTTP server, and is experienced in deployment and configuration of the server. This reduces the learning curve when connecting the HTTP server with Tomcat, and assists greatly in identifying issues if they occur.
- Tomcat is written in Java and uses a JVM for its runtime so thereare times when the JVM garbage collection (removing objects that are no longer needed from memory) can stall the JVM and cause increased latency on responses to users. If response times could be considered critical then the introduction of an HTTP server may reduce the load on Tomcat and the garbage collection will occur less frequently.
- Finally, a topic is examined in Chapter 16 is the use of an HTTP server to act as a load balancer for Tomcat. For example, the Apache HTTP server can act as a load balancer with session affinity (or sticky sessions) in front of a number of Tomcat instances.

Essentially the greatest benefit of using Tomcat to server static content is the ease of configuration, installation, and deployment of Web applications. This benefit should be carefully considered because considerable time and skilled resources are required to configure the HTTP Server and Tomcat together.

The decision of how to deploy Tomcat should only be made on a case-by-case basis and an appropriate time for consideration is during the analysis phase of a project. For the majority of the examples in the book Tomcat is used to serve the static content and not to configure an HTTP Server.

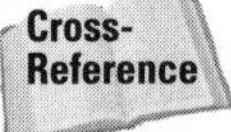

Chapter 15 will provide examples that show how to integrate Web Servers with Tomcat. Chapter 16 has detailed information about configuration of Tomcat with a Web Server for load balancing and clustering.

Tomcat Environment

Tomcat is a servlet/JSP container that is capable of serving static content. The servlet and JSP specifications allow for the development of complex dynamic applications that can perform many tasks. To use Tomcat there must be a means of writing Java code, deploying that code to the Tomcat server, and completing a database for the applications to read and write data for the enterprise picture.

For the purposes of completing the examples in the book the authors have chosen to use the tools in Table 1-4. It is highly recommended that these tools are obtained and used when completing the examples, because the authors have tested the applications and environments using these tools. However, these are not the only tools that can be used, and the application development environment of any particular organization may dictate different tools.

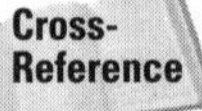

Chapter 2 provides details on the installation and configuration of all of these tools.

Table 1-4: Tomcat Development Tools

Tool	*Version*	*Download URL*	*Comment*
Tomcat	4.1.12	`jakarta.apache.org/tomcat`	The Tomcat servlet container
Ant	1.5	`jakarta.apache.org/ant`	A Java based software build tool
Java SDK	1.3.1	`java.sun.com/j2se`	The Java compiler and runtime environment
Struts	1.1b2	`jakarta.apache.org/struts`	A Java based Web application framework
MySQL	3.23.51	`www.mysql.org`	An open source relational database with JDBC driver

These tools have been chosen because they are all freely available for download at no cost, and have no restriction on their use. The other benefits from choosing these tools are that they are all being used by commercial developers, for commercial applications. These are not academic or research and development tools, but real world tools; in many cases they are very widely deployed and tested.

Summary

This chapter has covered a lot of introductory material that provides background to Tomcat and the specifications that Tomcat implements. The specifications are only part of the picture, and the environment that is required to develop and deploy Tomcat is as important as choosing to use Tomcat in the first place.

Topics such as development and deployment covered in this chapter will be covered in much greater detail in later chapters.

✦ ✦ ✦

Installing Tomcat

✦ ✦ ✦ ✦

In This Chapter

Prerequisites for installing

Installing Tomcat

Connecting to a database

Installing Struts

Advanced setup

✦ ✦ ✦ ✦

This chapter guides you through the creation of an environment for the use of Tomcat. Over the course of the chapter you will see the prerequisites that must exist before installation, and learn how to install Tomcat, connect Tomcat to a database, install the struts UI framework, and see the post-install configuration.

To keep the instructions as simple as possible, and to prevent confusion from repeating very similar information, the installation is only described for one operating system platform.

All of the installation instructions describe the installation of the various software products in a Microsoft Windows 2000 environment.

Users of other operating systems should have no difficulty translating these instructions to their native environments. Because these products are all multi-platform, the processes are very similar in all cases. To ensure compatibility the installations use directory structures that are easily replicated on various platform.

The installation of the software in this chapter requires the setting of environment variables to successfully complete the installations. It is important to be able to perform this operation, and to understand how to make the changes permanent.

The installations specifically avoid using directories with spaces in the filenames because in many instances this creates unusual and incorrect behavior.

The installation for each of the software components follows the same format. There is a download section that describes where to obtain the software, and an installation section that describes the steps required to install the software. There is a testing section that provides some simple tests to validate that the installation is proceeding successfully and to give confidence that the building blocks are placed on solid foundations. In some of the installations there is a configuration section that describes some additional steps that should be performed to create users or an environment that is required.

Prerequisites

There are two important goals to achieve in this chapter. The first is to understand how to install the Tomcat server so that it can be used to develop the examples in the book. The second goal is to provide some assistance in installing the software commonly used with

Tomcat. This includes the user interface frameworks, development code, and databases. The only software that is really required to be installed to have a working version of the Tomcat server is a JDK.

Java SDK

The first software to be installed is a Java Software Development Kit. It is required for a development environment to compile to Java classes. The SDK is normally required for a deployment-only environment to compile the JSP pages during the transformation process; however the JSP pages can be precompiled as part of the development process. These processes are covered in Chapter 5.

Download

The download URL for the Java SDK used for this environment is `http://java.sun.com/j2se/1.3/download.html`.

1. Select the SDK version and not the JRE version.
2. Download the j2sdk-1_3_1_05-windows-i586.exe and save it to the computer.

Installation

The executable that has been downloaded is the installer for the SDK. To begin the installation, run this program.

After a few moments the screen displays a message: "Unpacking Java 2 SDK." A few moments later a splash screen is displayed.

1. Read the instructions on the Welcome Screen and press Next.
2. This displays the license screen. Read the license agreement and press Yes.
3. The next screen displayed should look like Figure 2-1.
4. Choose destination location as `c:\jdk1.3.1` and press Next.
5. The next step is a screen for selecting the installation components; leave the values on the default selection and press Next.

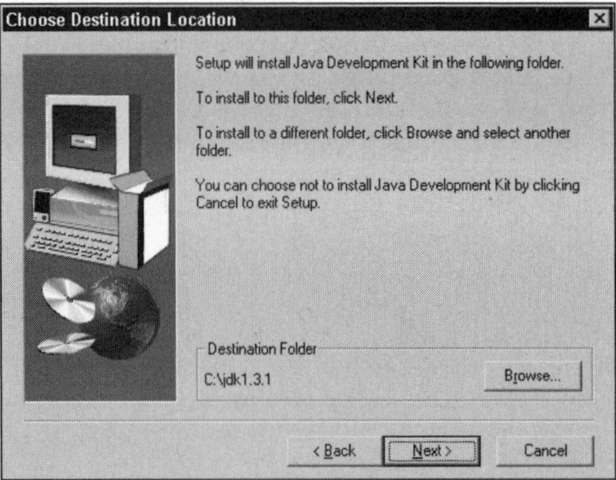

Figure 2-1: The Choose Destination Location screen

6. A dialog box shows the installer copying Java source files, setting up Java 2 Runtime Environment, and then there is a final pause before a screen showing the setup was successful.

7. On the setup complete screen, click Finish to end the installation process.

The Java SDK and Runtime Environment is now installed, to complete the installation so Java can be used easily set the following environment variables:

```
set JAVA_HOME=c:\jdk1.3.1
set PATH=%PATH%;%JAVA_HOME%\bin
```

Testing

To test that the installation has proceeded successfully, open a command window and enter the command `java -version`. The results should look like Figure 2-2.

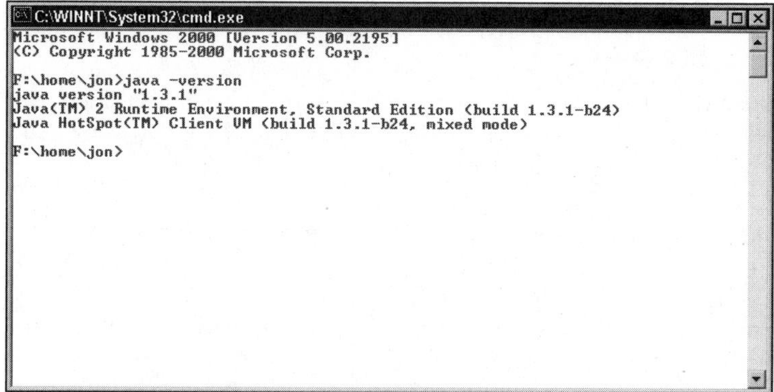

Figure 2-2: Results of `java -version`

Finally, check the correct setting of the PATH to the Java compilation command open a command window and enter the command `javac`. Unfortunately `javac` doesn't have a version option, so look for the usage information similar to Figure 2-3.

```
C:\WINNT\System32\cmd.exe
Microsoft Windows 2000 [Version 5.00.2195]
(C) Copyright 1985-2000 Microsoft Corp.

F:\home\jon>javac
Usage: javac <options> <source files>
where possible options include:
  -g                        Generate all debugging info
  -g:none                   Generate no debugging info
  -g:{lines,vars,source}    Generate only some debugging info
  -O                        Optimize; may hinder debugging or enlarge class file

  -nowarn                   Generate no warnings
  -verbose                  Output messages about what the compiler is doing
  -deprecation              Output source locations where deprecated APIs are us
ed
  -classpath <path>         Specify where to find user class files
  -sourcepath <path>        Specify where to find input source files
  -bootclasspath <path>     Override location of bootstrap class files
  -extdirs <dirs>           Override location of installed extensions
  -d <directory>            Specify where to place generated class files
  -encoding <encoding>      Specify character encoding used by source files
  -target <release>         Generate class files for specific VM version

F:\home\jon>
```

Figure 2-3: Results of `javac`

If everything is working fine at this point, congratulations; move on to install the ant development tool. If the installation didn't proceed as planned, or the testing didn't end up with the same results, double-check the location of the JDK installation directory and the setting of the `JAVA_HOME` and `PATH` environment variables.

Ant

Ant is a Java-based build tool used extensively by Java developers. Ant is supported and developed by the Apache Software Foundation and is a supported build tool for the Tomcat environment.

Ant is not required if you are using an IDE, however if you want to use some of the advanced features of the Tomcat management applications and automatic deployment options, then it is worth installing.

Download

To download Ant, the latest versions and archive versions are available from the Ant Web site at `http://jakarta.apache.org/ant`.

1. To find the download area select Download/Binaries from the left navigation bar. Then scroll down to Release Builds and select the latest version of Ant. The version that is recommended for installing is Ant 1.5.1 and the direct URL for that is `http://jakarta.apache.org/builds/jakarta-ant/release/v1.5.1/bin/`.
2. Select: `jakarta-ant-1.5.1-bin.zip` and when prompted save the file to disk.

Installation

The installation of Ant is very simple as all it involves is unpacking a zip file and setting some environment variables.

1. Extract the zip file to `c:\`. This creates a directory `c:\jakarta-ant-1.5.1` and subdirectories.
2. Rename the directory `c:\jakarta-ant-1.5.1` to `c:\ant` to make later configuration and use easier.
3. Create the environment variables:

```
set ANT_HOME=c:\ant
set PATH=%PATH%:%ANT_HOME%\bin
```

To integrate the Tomcat manager application with Ant there is a Tomcat specific JAR file (`catalina-ant.jar`) that will need to be copied from the Tomcat installation distribution into the Ant `lib` directory. Tomcat is installed a bit later in this chapter and the copy will be done in the configuration section so pay careful attention at that point.

Testing

To test the Ant installation, create a file called `build.xml` in a directory (for example c:\devel) containing the following:

```
<project name="test-ant" default="init" basedir=".">
     <property environment="env" />
     <target name="init">
            <echo message="Checking environment" />
            <echo message="JAVA_HOME  = ${env.JAVA_HOME}" />
            <echo message="ANT_HOME   = ${env.ANT_HOME}" />
     </target>
</project>
```

Open a command window and change directory to where the build.xml file was saved.

At the prompt type ant and you should have results similar to Figure 2-4.

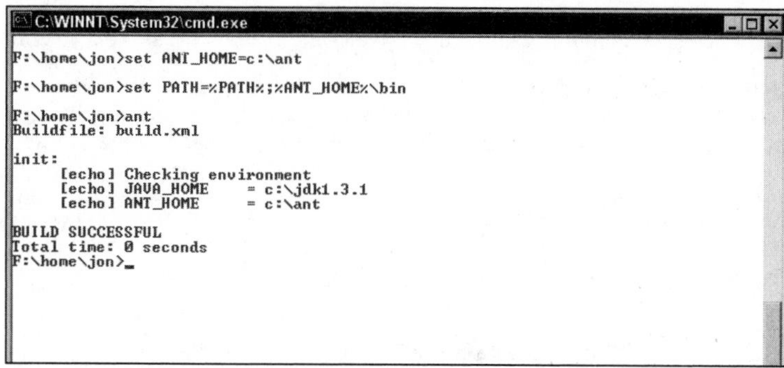

Figure 2-4: Results of ant testing

If the results aren't similar to those above, double-check the settings for the ANT_HOME and PATH environment variables. Try setting the variables as shown in Figure 2-4, and if the ant command works at that stage then the problem is related to not saving the variables permanently in the environment.

After Ant is working, proceed to the installation of MySQL.

MySQL

The installation and configuration of MySQL is the most complicated procedure that needs to be performed in this chapter. Particular care must be taken during this installation because the steps can be quite fiddly and missing a step can cause problems later in the installation, testing, and development.

The installation guide provided in this section should not be considered a comprehensive guide to all the options in installing MySQL. The detail required to provide that is well beyond the scope of the book. The guide does, however, provide all the information required to get MySQL installed, tested, and working in a manner suitable for developing the example applications in this book.

Download

To download MySQL go to: `http://www.mysql.com/`

1. Select MySQL 3.23.52 from Versions/Production on the right side of the browser.
2. Scroll down to Windows downloads and choose the download link on the Windows 95/98/NT/2000/XP build.
3. Select a mirror closest to you and save the `mysql-3.23.52-win.zip` file to disk.

Installation

To start the installation process, unzip the files to a temporary directory and run the `setup.exe` program.

1. After a short pause the installer will display a Welcome screen. Press Next to continue.
2. The next screen provides an information screen about changing the default directory. This screen displays the steps to be performed if the default directory is changed. As luck has it, the default directory is exactly what you want, so to continue to the next step press Next.
3. The next step is to choose a destination location. As described in the previous step the location that is used is the default destination. The destination folder should be c:\mysql, as shown in Figure 2-5. Press Next to proceed.

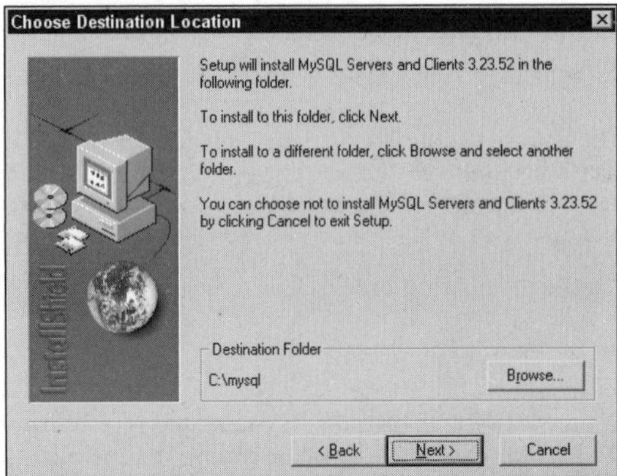

Figure 2-5: MySQL Destination Folder configuration

4. The next screen describes the setup type for the installation. Select Typical and press Next.
5. The installation process now installs the MySQL components. When the installation has completed the installer displays a dialog box similar to Figure 2-6.
6. Press Finish to exit the installer.

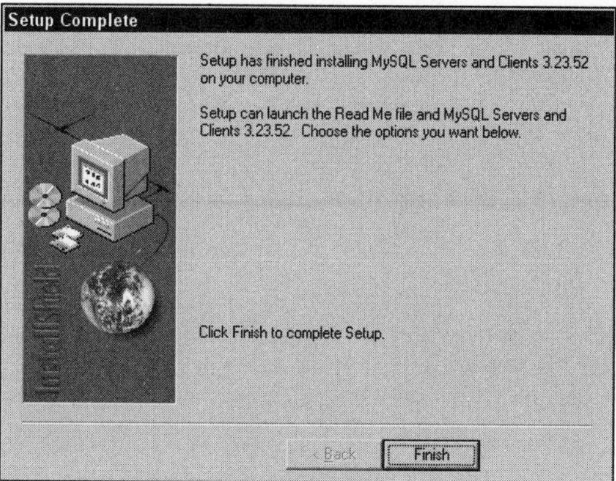

Figure 2-6: MySQL Installation complete!

Update the PATH environment variable to include the MySQL `bin` directory.

```
set PATH=%PATH%;c:\mysql\bin
```

This makes it easier to run some of the commands during testing.

The next step that needs to be completed is to perform post installation setup. The setup is quite different under different operating systems, so the safest path is to examine the MySQL documentation. The installation process has copied the MySQL documentation into the `c:\mysql\Docs` directory.

Using a Web browser, open the file `c:\mysql\Docs\manual_toc.html`. This is the table of contents for the MySQL reference manual.

Select the link for the section titled "2.4 post installation setup and testing." This section describes in detail the steps that need to be taken for various operating systems. The MySQL documentation also provides comprehensive information to resolve any issues during installation.

The post installation says to run `c:\mysql\bin\mysql_install_db`, but if you look at the directory, this executable doesn't exist. The purpose of running this program is to create the initial user environment for MySQL. This program would create the initial user authentication databases and a test database if it existed. However, if you examine the directory `c:\mysql\data`, the `mysql` and test directories are already created. So, at least for Windows 2000 using the MySQL installer, that step is performed by the installer, and not required as an additional step.

The next step in the installation process is to install MySQL as a service. This makes it very easy to start and stop the database from a command prompt, and by completing this step MySQL can be configured to start and stop when the workstation is started and stopped.

To install MySQL as a service under Windows NT or Windows 2000 type the following at a command prompt.

```
c:\mysql\bin\mysqld-nt --install
```

Caution The full path must be specified for the command or the installation (as a service) will be corrupted and will not work. If you accidentally do not provide the full path use the `--remove` option to remove the service and then re-install using the full path to the command.

To start and stop the database from a command prompt, it is as simple as using the following commands:

- `net start mysql` to start the mysql service, and
- `net stop mysql` to stop the service.

If the command fails, then check that the service was installed correctly, or the MySQL database is not already running. If the commands still do not work then read the MySQL reference documentation because it provides further information on resolving installation issues.

Testing

To test that the installation of MySQL was successful, first ensure the database is running. To find out if the database is running enter `net start` at a command prompt. This shows a list of all the started services. Look through the list for a line displaying the text `MySql`. If this is missing, then start the service with `net start mysql`.

Open a command prompt and type the following commands:

```
mysqlshow
mysqlshow -u root mysql
mysqladmin version status proc
```

The results should look like Figure 2-7.

Configuration

Finally, the MySQL default configuration is rather insecure, with no password for the root user, and remote access to the database enabled by default. Because we will be using this database exclusively locally to be accessed by Tomcat, you should remove the default user and any users with remote access.

To do this, open a command window and run the `mysql` command line client (called `mysql`) using the database mysql with the rather confusing command `mysql mysql`.

This should result in a response similar to the screen shown in Figure 2-8.

At the `mysql>` prompt type in the commands

```
delete from user where host='localhost' and user='';
delete from user where host='%';
quit
```

This exits the `mysql` command line client.

At the command prompt type `mysqladmin reload`. This reloads the `GRANT` permissions tables after the deletions made previously.

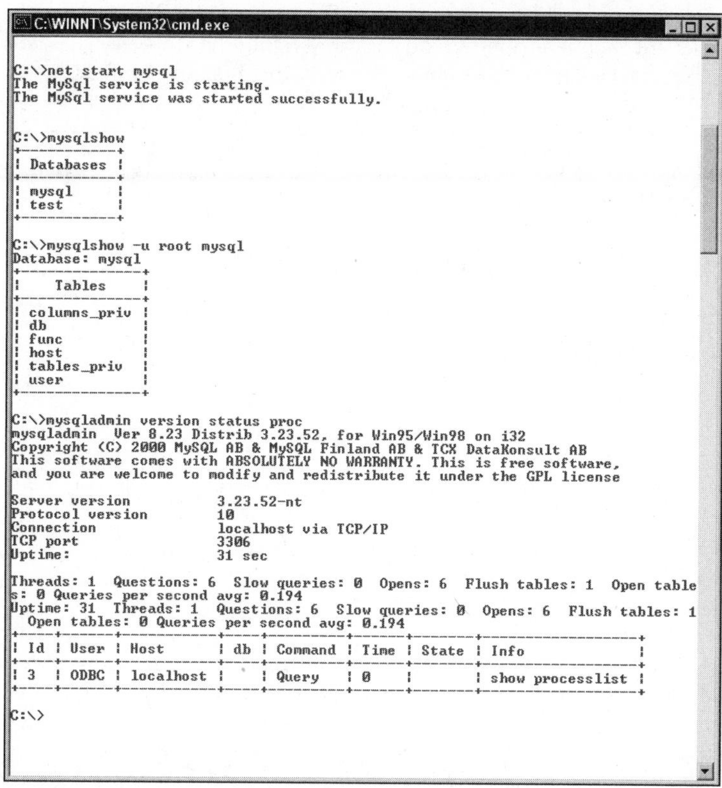

Figure 2-7: Results of running MySQL testing commands

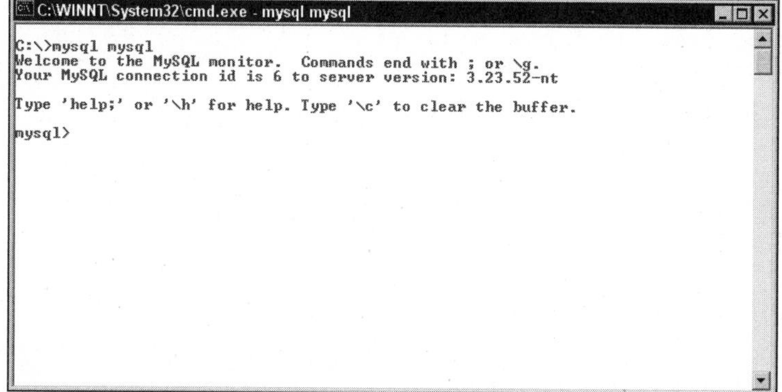

Figure 2-8: Starting MySQL on the `mysql` database

To change the root password from the current blank to something less guessable, type in the following command and choose an appropriate password rather than the very guessable `root_password`. For the remainder of the book where required to enter the MySQL root user password it will be shown as `root_password` but remember to use the password you chose here instead.

At a command prompt type `mysqladmin -u root password root_password` and the results should be similar to Figure 2-9.

```
C:\WINNT\System32\cmd.exe

C:\>mysql mysql
Welcome to the MySQL monitor.  Commands end with ; or \g.
Your MySQL connection id is 6 to server version: 3.23.52-nt

Type 'help;' or '\h' for help. Type '\c' to clear the buffer.

mysql> delete from user where Host='localhost' and User='';
Query OK, 1 row affected (0.00 sec)

mysql> quit
Bye

C:\>mysqladmin reload

C:\>mysqladmin -u root password root_password

C:\>
```

Figure 2-9: Setting the MySQL root user password

To test that this worked correctly, try to access the database as was done before with `mysql mysql`. You should receive the error message displayed in Figure 2-10.

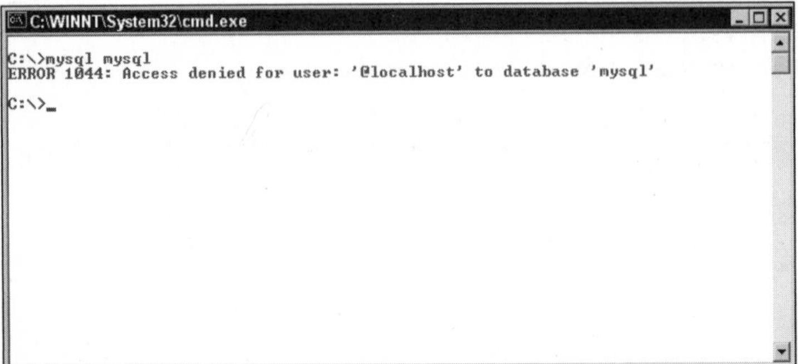

Figure 2-10: Accessing MySQL without a username and password

To continue the testing, when provided with the password using

```
mysql -u root -p mysql
```

The `-p` option asks for the password to be entered interactively, or more conveniently it can be provided using either:

```
mysql -u root -proot_password mysql
```

or

```
mysql -u root --password=root_password mysql
```

This should display results similar to those shown in Figure 2-11.

At this stage, we can claim victory over MySQL because the install has been completed and shown to work successfully. It is important to remember to start and stop the MySQL database as required. If this is not remembered it will be a source of continual frustration during further installation and testing in this chapter, and during development of the applications in later chapters.

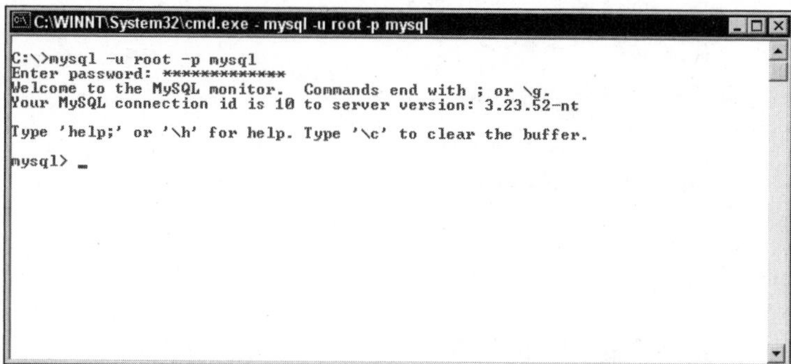

Figure 2-11: Accessing MySQL using a username and password

Installing Tomcat

The Tomcat installation is straightforward and provided the previous installations have completed successfully, getting Tomcat installed correctly should present no difficulties.

Download

To download Tomcat, the latest versions and archive versions are available from the Tomcat Web site at `http://jakarta.apache.org/tomcat`.

1. To find the download area select Download/Binaries from the left navigation bar. Scroll down to Release Builds and select the latest version of Tomcat. The version that is recommended for installing is Tomcat 4.1.12.
2. From the download page, select the directory labeled `bin`.
3. Select: `jakarta-tomcat-4.1.12.exe` and when prompted save the file to disk.

Installation

To start the installation, execute the installer that was downloaded.

After a brief pause the installer detects the Java SDK that was installed earlier. This should result in a screen identical to that shown in Figure 2-12.

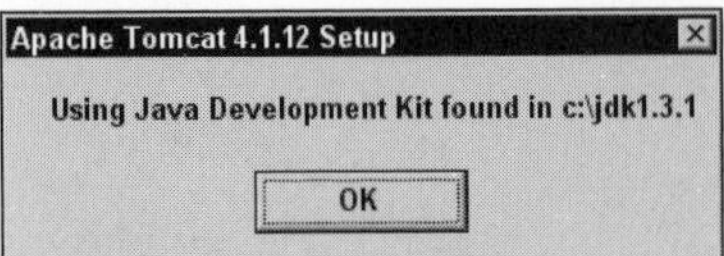

Figure 2-12: Tomcat Setup screen

Click OK to proceed.

The next screen displayed is the License Agreement for Tomcat. Read the License Agreement and select "I agree" to proceed.

The next step defines the type of installation. Select Normal as shown in Figure 2-13 and then press Next.

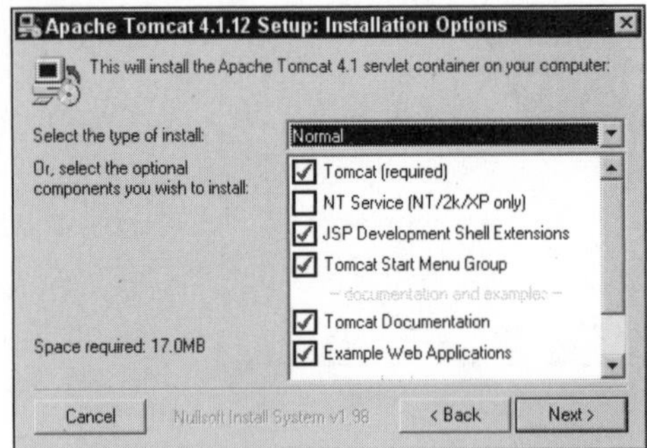

Figure 2-13: Tomcat Installation Options screen

The next step is to configure the installation directory. Change the installation directory to `c:\tomcat` as shown in Figure 2-14 and press Install. This is an important change because the default directory has spaces in the path, and simplifying the path reduces the likelihood of unusual behavior.

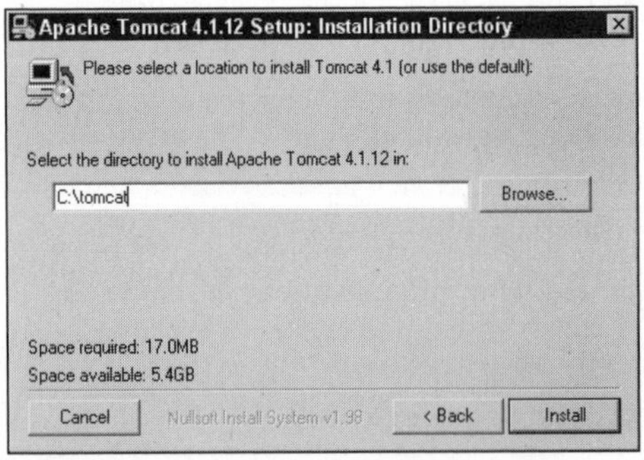

Figure 2-14: Tomcat Installation Directory screen

The installer proceeds to copy all the required files to `c:\tomcat` and subdirectories, as shown in Figure 2-15.

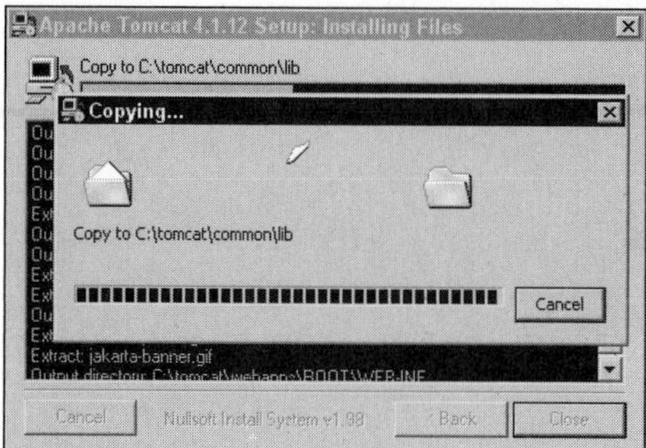

Figure 2-15: Installing Tomcat

At this stage the Tomcat software is now installed. The installer proceeds through a few more steps to collect information to configure the administration application.

The next screen shown is for the initial Tomcat configuration and looks like Figure 2-16. The title for the dialog box is very confusing, so you should just ignore it.

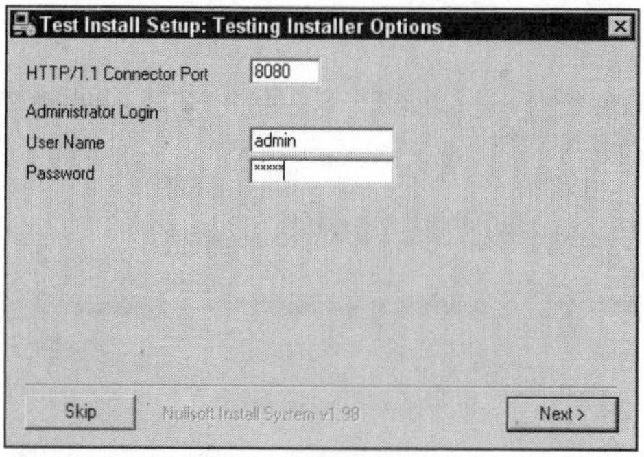

Figure 2-16: Tomcat configuration

This dialog box configures the port that tomcat is running on, and the username and password for the administrative user. Do not change the port# and username from the defaults, and type a secure password for the admin user. For simplicity the password used in the book will be "admin."

This user is known as the administrator user and is separate from the manager user that will be configured manually after the automated installation has completed.

After entering the Tomcat administrator password, press Next.

The installer copies the remaining configuration files to the Tomcat directories and the installation completes, as shown in Figure 2-17.

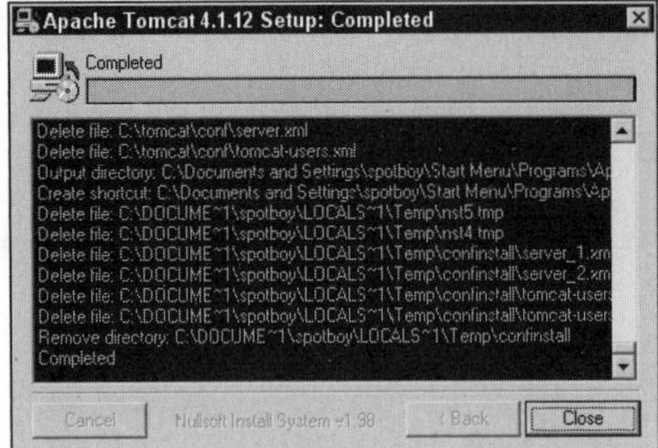

Figure 2-17: Tomcat setup completed

Press close to exit the installer.

The dialog box closes, and the installer exits. A window opens containing a series of shortcuts to manipulate the tomcat server, access documentation, and access the tomcat directory.

Copy the "Start Tomcat" shortcut and put it on your Windows desktop, Quickstart bar or somewhere else convenient. This will make it easier to start and stop Tomcat during development.

Testing

Now, using the "Start Tomcat" shortcut, start Tomcat. This should display the Tomcat console in a command window, as shown in Figure 2-18.

Start Tomcat

```
[INFO] Registry - -Loading registry information
[INFO] Registry - -Creating new Registry instance
[INFO] Registry - -Creating MBeanServer
[INFO] Http11Protocol - -Initializing Coyote HTTP/1.1 on port 8080
Starting service Tomcat-Standalone
Apache Tomcat/4.1.12
[INFO] Http11Protocol - -Starting Coyote HTTP/1.1 on port 8080
[INFO] ChannelSocket - -JK2: ajp13 listening on tcp port 8009
[INFO] JkMain - -Jk running ID=0 time=0/80  config=C:\tomcat\conf\jk2.properties
```

Figure 2-18: Tomcat console

To ensure that the server is correctly working, open a browser and type in the URL, `http://localhost:8080/`. A screen resembling Figure 2-19 should be displayed.

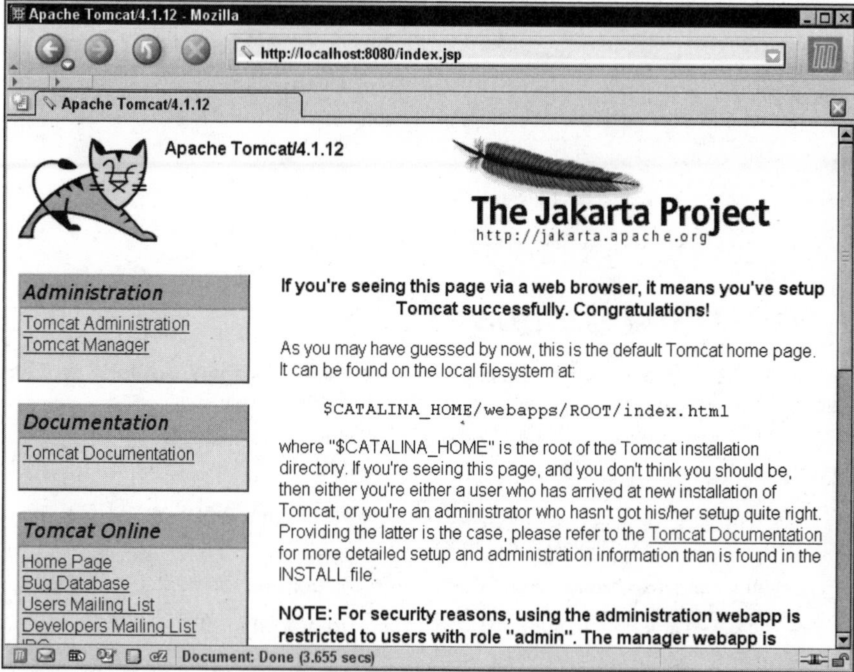

Figure 2-19: Tomcat Default Home Page

Configuration

Another other option to using the Start Tomcat shortcut is to start Tomcat from a command prompt. To enable that set the following environment variables.

```
set CATALINA_HOME=c:\tomcat
set PATH=%PATH%;%CATALINA_HOME%\bin
```

Then type `startup` at the command prompt.

Starting Tomcat using the shortcut or the command prompt provide the same basic functionality, however the command prompt gives access to some further options, such as being able to start Tomcat in a debugger and see error messages if things go awry.

To stop Tomcat either use the Stop Tomcat shortcut, or simply close the Tomcat console window.

The final step in configuration of Tomcat is to integrate the Ant build tool with the Tomcat manager application for use during development.

The Ant build tool was installed earlier in this chapter, but required a JAR file from the Tomcat installation to complete the installation. This step will link Ant and the Tomcat manager application.

To integrate Ant with Tomcat copy the file `catalina-ant.jar` from the `server\lib` directory into the Ant `lib` directory. This file contains the classes that implement additional functionality for Ant.

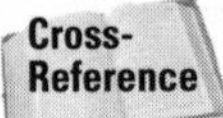

The Ant build tool is described in detail in Chapter 5.

The command to copy the JAR file would be:

```
copy c:\tomcat\server\lib\catalina-ant.jar c:\ant\lib
```

Connecting to a Database

Connecting to the MySQL database using Java requires the installation of JDBC compliant drivers. Fortunately MySQL provides a suitable set of drivers to use.

Download

The MySQL drivers that are recommended are now part of the MySQL site and can be downloaded from `http://www.mysql.com/`.

1. Select Connector/J 2.0.14 from "Versions/Production" on the right side of the browser.
2. Scroll down and download the MySQL Connector/J 2.0.14 (ZIP).
3. Select the closest mirror and when prompted save the `mysql-connector-j-2014.zip` file to disk.

Installation

The downloaded zip file contains the source, class files, and a packaged JAR file. To perform the installation only the JAR file is required.

1. Unpack the archive to a temporary directory.
2. Copy the file `mysql-connector-j-2.0.14-bin.jar` into `c:\tomcat\common\lib\`.
3. That's it. The installation is complete.

Test

The easiest method to test the connection with the MySQL database is to create a very simple JSP file in the following directory: `c:\tomcat\Webapps\ROOT\mysql.jsp`.

mysql.jsp

```
<%@ page import="java.sql.*" %>
<html>
<%
```

```
    Connection con = null;
    try
    {
        Class.forName("com.mysql.jdbc.Driver").newInstance();
        con = DriverManager.getConnection
("jdbc:mysql://localhost/mysql?user=root&password=root_password");
        Statement s = con.createStatement();
        ResultSet rs =
            s.executeQuery("SELECT Host, User, Password FROM user");
%>
<table border=1 width=60% >
<tr><th>Host</th><th>User</th><th>Password</th></tr>
<%
    while(rs.next())
    {
%>
    <tr>
        <td><%= rs.getString("Host") %></td>
        <td><%= rs.getString("User") %></td>
        <td><%= rs.getString("Password") %></td>
    </tr>
<%
    }
    s.close();
%>
</table>
<%
    } // close of try
    catch (Exception e)
    {
%>
        <h1>Error Occurred</h1>
        <b>Exception:</b> <%= e.getMessage() %>
<%
    }
    finally
    {
        if ( con != null )
        {
            con.close();
        }
    }
%>
```

Using a browser, enter the URL: `http://localhost:8080/mysql.jsp`

This should display similar results to those shown in Figure 2-20.

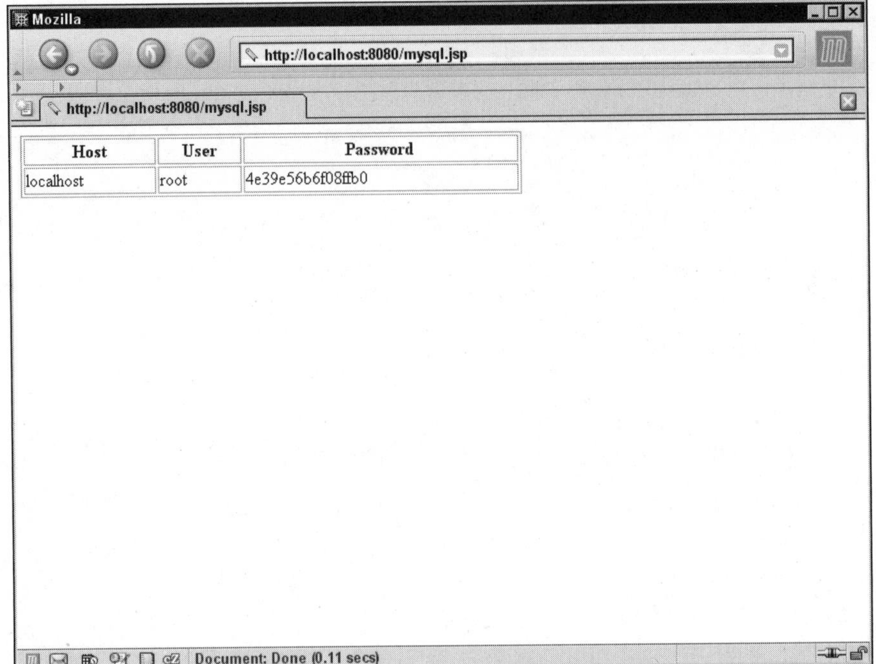

Figure 2-20: Successful results from Tomcat and MySQL integration

Installing Struts

Struts is an implementation of an MVC Model 2 UI framework written in Java for building Web applications. Struts is being used successfully in the commercial world as a Web application productivity tool. Struts provides a very configurable and structured framework for rapid building and deploying of Web applications.

Download

To download Struts, the latest versions and archive versions are available from the Struts Web site at `http://jakarta.apache.org/struts`.

1. To find the download area select Download/Binaries from the left navigation bar. Then scroll down to Milestone Builds and select Struts version 1.1beta2. This is important because only the latest beta versions of Struts have the functionality required to develop some of the examples.
2. Select: `jakarta-struts-1.1.b2.zip` and when prompted save the file to disk.

Installation

The downloaded zip file contains the Struts classes, jar files, and documentation. Struts is used in the example applications and is packaged as part of the individual Web applications.

1. To start the install process, unzip the downloaded file to `c:\`.
2. This creates a `c:\jakarta-struts-1.1-b2` directory and subdirectories.
3. Copy the `c:\jakarta-struts-1.1-b2\struts\Webapps\struts-example.war` into `c:\tomcat\ \Webapps`.
4. Start Tomcat. If Tomcat is already running, stop, then start Tomcat.
5. Using a Web browser open the URL: `http://localhost:8080/struts-example`.

This should display the same results shown in Figure 2-21.

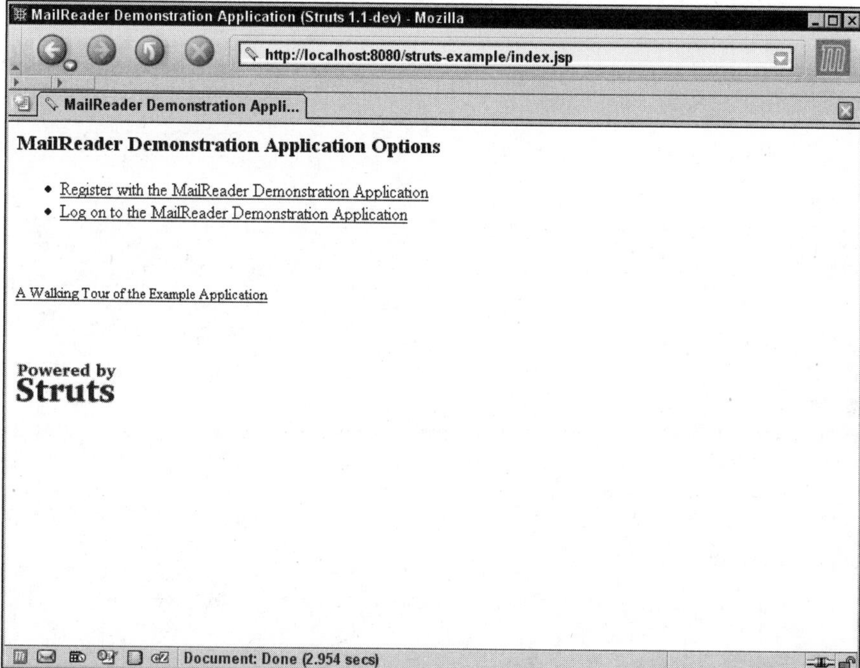

Figure 2-21: Struts Demonstration Application

Congratulations; that's all the required software installed. The following section contains information about additional configuration required in later chapters.

Advanced Setup

Manager User

To use the administrator application and manager application provided by Tomcat we need to add and set the password on some users. During installation of Tomcat the administrator user was created. A manager user needs to be created as part of the installation to use the manager application.

There are a few methods that can be used to add the manager user, but the simplest and least error prone is to use the administration tool. Start Tomcat using either the shortcut or the startup script and enter the following URL into a browser.

```
http://localhost:8080/admin
```

This accesses the administration tool and display a screen identical to that shown in Figure 2-22.

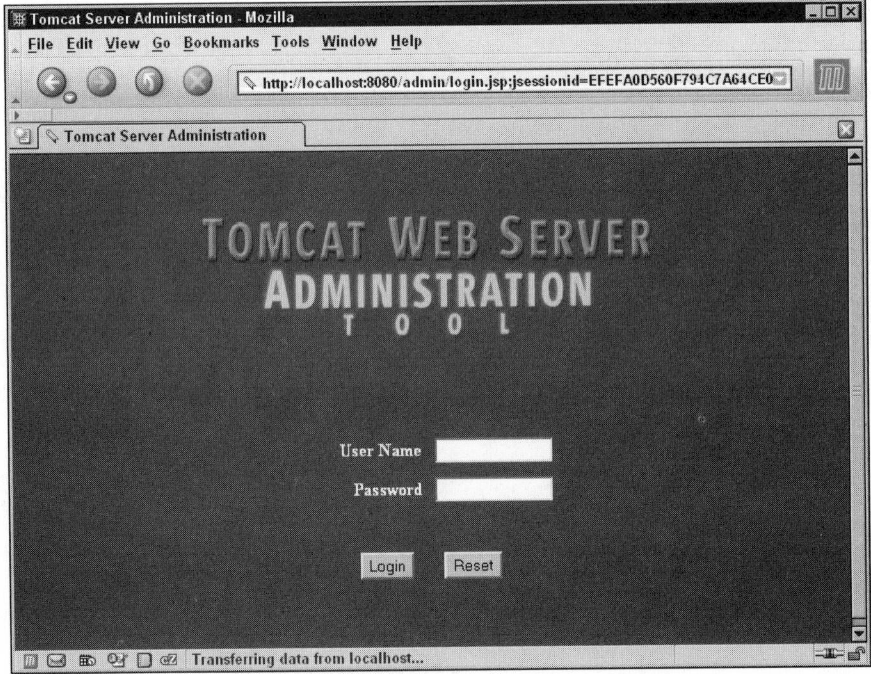

Figure 2-22: Tomcat Administration Tool Login screen

Enter the user and password that was configured during the Tomcat installation process. These should be username of `admin` and password of `admin` from the installation instructions. Then press Login. This displays the main control screen of the administration tool, as shown in Figure 2-23.

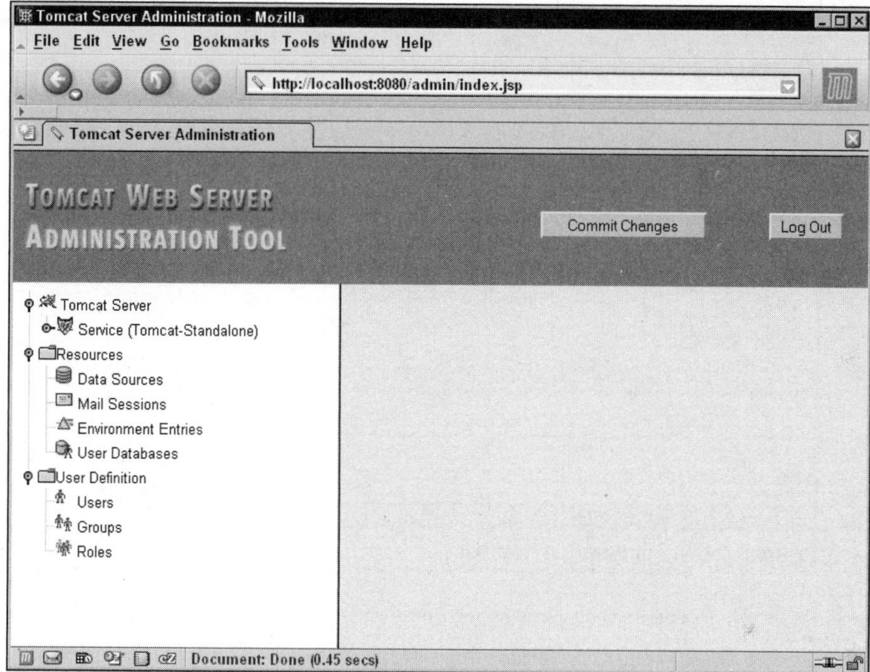

Figure 2-23: Tomcat Administration Tool Main screen

Chapter 9 fully describes how to use the administration tool, so this section describes only how to add the manager user with the correct role.

1. Click the navigation item Users, under the menu item User Definition. This opens a frame on the RHS. The resulting screen should look like Figure 2-24.
2. Under the drop-down list “Available Actions” select “Create New User.” This displays a data entry screen similar to that shown in Figure 2-25.

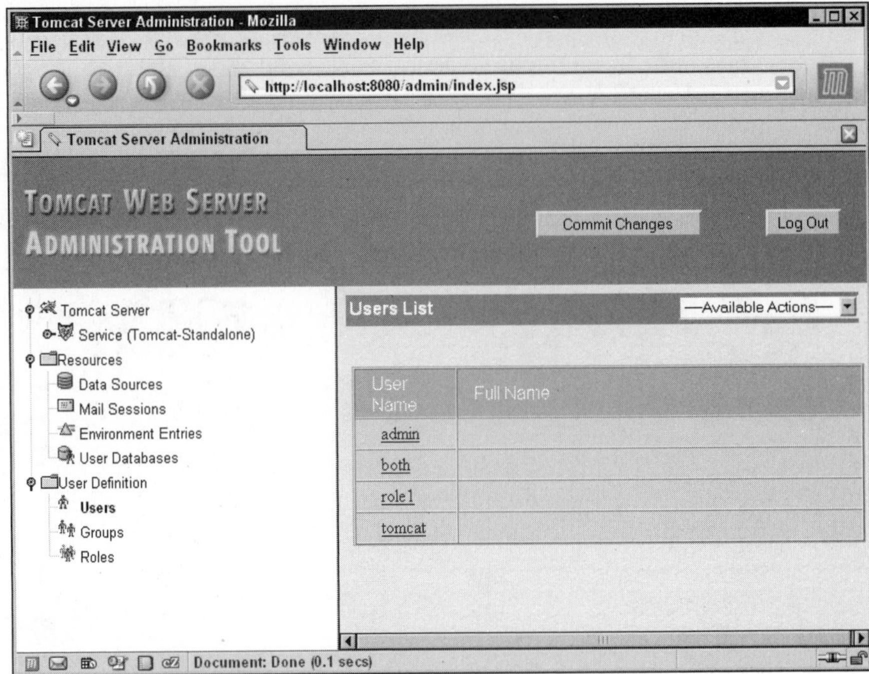

Figure 2-24: Administration Tool User list

3. Enter into the fields the following information:
   - **User Name:** ant-install
   - **Password:** ant-install
   - **Full Name:** Tomcat Bible Ant Installer
4. From the Role Name table, select the manager role and then press Save. This adds the new user into memory; however to make this user permanent, press the "Commit Changes" button, which adds the user to the Tomcat configuration files.
5. Press Log Out and close the browser window.

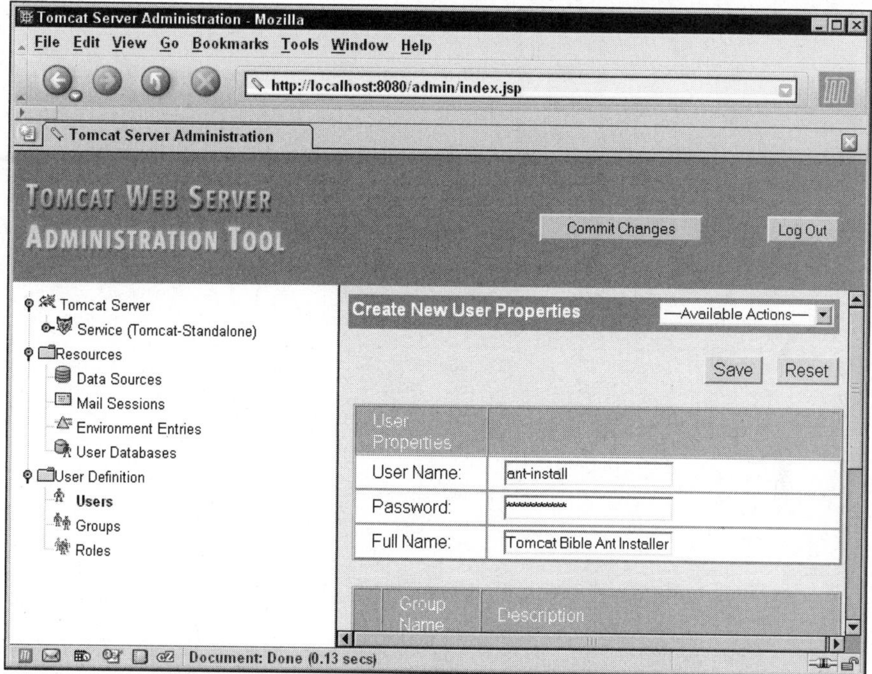

Figure 2-25: Administration Tool adding a user

Summary

This chapter we have downloaded, installed and tested all the software necessary for an installation of Tomcat. This environment will provide the base for the remainder of the book and with minimal additions is all that is required to develop sophisticated Web applications.

To start developing right away, skip forward and read Chapter 7 on building a simple Web application, or for more background on Web applications and development process continue to the next chapter.

✦ ✦ ✦

Overview of Web Applications

✦ ✦ ✦ ✦

In This Chapter

What is a Web application?

Structure and components of a Web application

The Web application deployment descriptor

✦ ✦ ✦ ✦

This chapter examines the structure, components, and configuration options for Web applications.

The structure of Web applications is defined in the servlet specification and influences the development and deployment options available to developers. This structure gives Web application developers a platform for development that is consistent across all servlet containers. This of course is only specific to the actual Web application, and the deployment descriptor options. The configuration and operation of the server is specific to each different server. Tomcat options are examined in later chapters.

What Is a Web Application?

A Web application is a collection of components that comprise a complete application on a server. The components may include HTML pages, CSS files, images, servlets, JSP pages, Java classes for business logic, third-party libraries, and other resources such as XML files.

A Web application deployed in a server has a number of attributes. These are:

- A Web application has a one-to-one mapping with a `ServletContext`. This `ServletContext` is common for all assets within the application, and as such any servlet or JSP page can obtain access to the same `ServletContext`.
- A Web application has a defined path for the root of the application within the server. This path may be `www.foo.com/bar`, or even `www.bar.com/~username/`. All requests sent to the server that match the path are handled by the `ServletContext` responsible for the Web application.
- A Web application has a classloader that is specific to that Web application. This has some benefits in that the Web application can not gain access to resources outside of the defined loading scope. The negatives include quite a degree of confusion about packaging and deploying Web applications that make use of third-party libraries (like Struts, or a cryptographic library).

Chapter 4 provides details about how the classloader works in Tomcat.

✦ A Web application has a directory structure. The root of the directory structure is also the root of the Web application. This results in a request for the file `foo.jsp` in the Web application with a context path of `/bar` formed from the URL `www.bletch.com/bar/foo.jsp`. Any subdirectories are a further part of the structure, so `/www.bletch.com/bar/images/pixel.gif` is found in the `images` subdirectory of the Web application.

A Web application deployed to Tomcat as a WAR file does not need to be unpacked to be used. The servlet specification makes no promises as to what happens when the servlet container uses the Web application. Due to this, access to resources within the Web application (such as a properties file) should not be performed using file based paths (`WEB-INF/my.properties`) but instead use `getResourceAsStream("/my.properties")` to obtain the resource.

Structure and Components of a Web Application

The Web application must conform to a standard directory structure. This structure is not particularly complicated and can be displayed as shown in Figure 3-1.

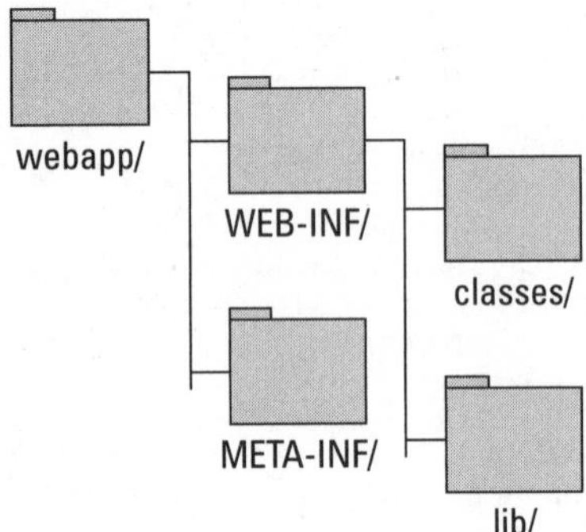

Figure 3-1: Web application structure

The Web application structure shown in Figure 3-1 describes the layout, but doesn't provide a really clear idea of what the various directories contain, and how they are presented to the user.

The root directory of the Web application contains a directory hierarchy of pages that are presentation based. These directories contain the JSP, HTML, images, and other presentation elements of the Web application. A common directory hierarchy and contents are shown in Figure 3-2.

There is no limit on the complexity of the directories in the hierarchy, and in very large Web applications there are many components and directories to reflect the partitioning of the resources.

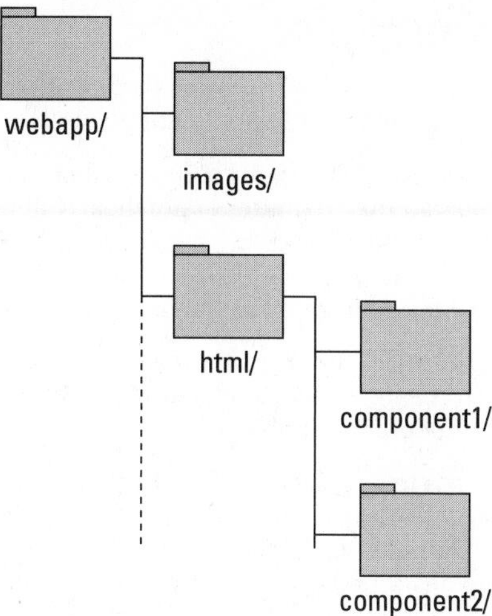

Figure 3-2: Web Application root directory

The next component of the Web application structure is the `WEB-INF` directory hierarchy. This contains a number of directories with specific purposes.

- The `WEB-INF` directory contains the `web.xml` deployment descriptor for the application. This directory also can be used to contain other descriptors and Web application configuration files such as the Struts configuration files `struts-config.xml` and tag library descriptor files such as `struts-html.tld`.
- The `WEB-INF/lib` directory contains JAR files that are used by the application. These JAR files may contain servlets, JavaBeans, third-party libraries, and other utility classes.
- The `WEB-INF/classes` directory contains Java class files that are used by the application. As with the `WEB-INF/lib` directory these may be used for servlets, utility classes, or JavaBeans.

The classloader for the Web application loads classes from the `WEB-INF/classes` directory first, and then classes from the JAR files in the `WEB-INF/lib` directory.

The final component of the Web application structure is the `META-INF` directory. This is an optional component, and only occurs when the Web application is packaged as a JAR. The `META-INF` directory contains a `MANIFEST.MF` and potentially other files called `*.SF`.

- The `MANIFEST.MF` file is used to provide information to Java archive tools relating to the contents of the JAR. The `MANIFEST.MF` may list the files present in the archive, but is not required to do so, and as a result may be empty. If there are any files in the archive that are signed, they must be in `MANIFEST.MF`.
- The `*.SF` files are signature files are used to validate the files signed in the JAR, and specified in the `MANIFEST.MF`. These files do not exist if there are no signed files in the JAR.

Web Application Deployment Descriptor

The Web application deployment descriptor, or `web.xml` file, is used by the application developer to define the attributes required for the operation of the Web application.

The deployment descriptor is an XML file with a defined DTD. The DTD is described in detail in the servlet specification, however the use of many of the attributes is not clearly defined or placed in a context that a developer can use as a template for creating a deployment descriptor. The remainder of this chapter examines the elements of the deployment descriptor, places them in context for their use, and identifies potential traps for the unwary.

One of the first traps for the unwary is that there is a strict order for the `web.xml` file. Developers often add elements to the descriptor in the incorrect order, leading to a broken `web.xml`. As a result the Web application will fail to deploy to the server.

The first area to be examined is the order of elements in `web.xml`, and after that the use and syntax for the elements. Not all elements have a detailed explanation; some are only elements that exist within a particular parent element. For example the `<small-icon>` element only exists within the `<icon>` element and as a result is described within that context.

Order of Elements in `web.xml`

The `web.xml` file is used to define a single Web application, and the outermost element that encloses all other elements is the `<web-app>` element. Within the `<web-app>` the following elements must occur in the order shown in Table 3-1. Where noted there may be more than one element of that type, and if those elements occur, they must be grouped together.

Table 3-1: Order of elements in <web-app>

Element Name	*Number*
`<icon>`	1
`<display-name>`	1
`<description>`	1
`<distributable>`	1
`<context-param>`	many
`<filter>`	many
`<filter-mapping>`	many
`<listener>`	many
`<servlet>`	many
`<servlet-mapping>`	many
`<session-config>`	many
`<mime-mapping>`	many
`<welcome-file-list>`	many
`<error-page>`	many
`<taglib>`	many

Element Name	Number
<resource-env-ref>	many
<resource-ref>	many
<security-constraint>	many
<login-config>	1
<security-role>	many
<env-entry>	many
<ejb-ref>	many
<ejb-local-ref>	many

<icon>

The `<icon>` element is used to specify a filename containing GIF or JPEG images representing the parent element to be displayed by a GUI tool.

The icon element has two elements:

✦ <small-icon>

✦ <large-icon>

Both of the elements are optional.

The icon element can be located in the following parent elements:

✦ <filter>

✦ <servlet>

✦ <web-app>

An example of the use of the <icon> element follows:

```
<web-app>
    <icon>
        <small-icon>helloicon-sml.gif</small-icon>
        <large-icon>helloicon-lrg.gif</large-icon>
    </icon>
    . . . .

    <servlet>
        <icon>
            <small-icon>important-sml.gif</small-icon>
            <large-icon>important-lrg.gif</large-icon>
        </icon>
        <servlet-name>important</servlet-name>
        . . . .
    </servlet>
    . . . .
</web-app>
```

<display-name>

The <display-name> element is a short name that is displayed by tools. The contents of the display-name element can be any text.

The display-name element can be located in the following parent elements:

- <filter>
- <servlet>
- <security-constraint>
- <web-app>

An example of the use of the <display-name> element is as follows:

```
<web-app>
    <icon>
        <small-icon>helloicon-sml.gif</small-icon>
        <large-icon>helloicon-lrg.gif</large-icon>
    </icon>
    <display-name>HelloWorld Application</display-name>
    . . . .

    <servlet>
        <servlet-name>important</servlet-name>
        <display-name>An important servlet</display-name>
        . . . .
    </servlet>
    . . . .
</web-app>
```

<description>

The <description> element is used to contain information relevant to the parent element to be displayed to a user of the Web application. The <description> element is contained in many of the elements of a Web application. These generally relate to elements that a deployer of the Web application may find informative.

The description element can be found in the following parent elements:

- <auth-constraint>
- <context-param>
- <ejb-local-ref>
- <ejb-ref>
- <env-entry>
- <filter>
- <init-param>
- <resource-env-ref>
- <resource-ref>

- <run-as>
- <security-role>
- <security-role-ref>
- <servlet>
- <user-data-constraint>
- <web-app>
- <web-resource-collection>

An example of the use of the <description> element follows:

```
<web-app>
    . . . .
    <context-param>
          <param-name>developer</param-name>
          <param-value>developer@foo.com</param-value>
          <description>
              The email of the developer of this
              application. Send all complaints to this
              address.
          </description>
    </context-param>
    . . . .
</web-app>
```

<distributable>

The <distributable> element indicates to the server that the Web application has been developed in a manner that allows it to be deployed into a distributed servlet container.

There are certain constraints that the developer of a Web application must follow if the Web application is to be marked as distributable. An example of the constraint is that the developer must not rely on a single ServletContext for the Web application. The ServletContext may have different instances on each JVM that the servlet container is distributed over, and as a result storing an application state in the context may result in the Web application not working as expected.

The <display-name> element is only contained within the <web-app> parent, and is used simply as follows:

```
<web-app>
    . . . .
    <distributable/>
    <context-param>
          <param-name>developer</param-name>
          <param-value>developer@foo.com</param-value>
    </context-param>
    . . . .
</web-app>
```

<context-param>

The <context-param> element is used to define Web applications ServletContext initialization parameters. There may be more than one <context-param> element, each defining a separate initialization parameter. The values are obtained by using the getInitParameterNames() and getInitParameter() methods of ServletContext.

The <context-param> contains the following elements:

- <param-name> (required)
- <param-value> (required)
- <description> (optional)

The <param-name> contains the value of a parameter, and the <param-value> contains the value of the parameter.

The <context-param> is only contained in the <web-app> element and is used as follows:

```
<web-app>
    . . . .
    <context-param>
          <param-name>minUsers</param-name>
          <param-value>0</param-value>
    </context-param>
    <context-param>
          <param-name>maxUsers</param-name>
          <param-value>150</param-value>
    </context-param>
    <context-param>
          <param-name>defaultTeam</param-name>
          <param-value>Kangaroos</param-value>
    </context-param>
    . . . .
</web-app>
```

<filter>

The <filter> element is used to declare a filter in the Web application. Filters are new to version 2.3 of the servlet specification and are declared and used in a similar manner to the <servlet> element. There may be more than one filter element, each defining a different filter.

The filter element contains the following elements:

- <icon> (optional),
- <filter-name> (required),
- <display-name> (optional),
- <description> (optional),
- <filter-class> (required), and
- <init-param> (optional, more than one may be defined)

The <filter-name> is a unique name given to the <filter> element and is used to map the name of the filter to a URL pattern or servlet in a filter-mapping element. The <filter-class> is the fully qualified classname of the filter class. The <filter-class> must extend the interface javax.servlet.Filter.

The <init-param> elements are similar to <context-param> elements in that they provide a mechanism for specifying initialization values to the filter. The values are obtained by using the getInitParameterNames() and getInitParameter() methods of FilterConfig.

The <filter> element is only contained in the Web-app element. An example of its use follows:

```
<web-app>
. . . .
    <filter>
        <filter-name>CryptoFilter</filter-name>
        <filter-class>bouncycastle.AESFilter</filter-class>
        <init-param>
            <param-name>KeySize</param-name>
            <param-value>256</param-value>
        </init-param>
        <init-param>
           <param-name>BlockSize</param-name>
            <param-value>128</param-value>
        </init-param>
    </filter>
    . . . .
    <filter-mapping>
        <filter-name>CryptoFilter</filter-name>
        <url-pattern>/secret/*</url-pattern>
    </filter-mapping>
. . . .
</web-app>
```

<filter-mapping>

The <filter-mapping> element defines the mapping of the <filter-name> to a URL pattern, or <servlet-name>. There may be more than one filter-mapping element and the order of the <filter-mapping> elements determines the order in which the filters are invoked. The <filter-mapping> element uses the same rules for request URI matching as the <servlet-mapping> element to determine if a filter is invoked.

The <filter-mapping> element contains the following elements:

- <filter-name> (required)
- one of <url-pattern> or <servlet-name> (required)

The <filter-name> element must match a <filter-name> element from a <filter> element defined in the deployment descriptor. The rules for matching the <url-pattern> are defined in the servlet specification.

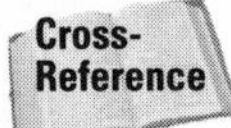

See the <servlet-mapping> element for a description of how the <url-pattern> is matched against a request URI.

The filter-mapping is only contained in the <web-app> element, and an example of use follows:

```
<web-app>
. . . .
    <filter>
        <filter-name>CryptoFilter</filter-name>
        <filter-class>org.bouncycastle.AESFilt</filter-class>
    </filter>
    . . . .
    <filter-mapping>
        <filter-name>CryptoFilter</filter-name>
        <url-pattern>/secret/*</url-pattern>
    </filter-mapping>
    <filter-mapping>
        <filter-name>CryptoFilter</filter-name>
        <servlet-name>AdminServlet</servlet-name>
    </filter-mapping>
    . . . .
    <servlet>
        <servlet-name>AdminServlet</servlet-name>
        <servlet-class>com.foo.adm.AdminCtrl</servlet-class>
    </servlet>

. . . .
</web-app>
```

<listener>

The <listener> element is used to define an application state change listener. The <listener> element is new in version 2.3 of the servlet specification. More than one <listener> element may be defined.

The <listener> element only contains one element, the <listener-class> element. The <listener-class> element defines a fully-qualified class that must implement one of the application state change listener interfaces. These interfaces are:

- javax.servlet.ServletContextListener
- javax.servlet.ServletContextAttributesListener
- javax.servlet.http.HttpSessionListener
- javax.servlet.http.HttpSessionAttributesListener

The listener element is only contained in the <web-app element>, and an example of use follows:

```
<web-app>
. . . .

    <listener>
        <listener-class>
            bible.tomcat.ActiveSessionCounter
```

```
        </listener-class>
    </listener>
    <listener>
        <listener-class>
            bible.tomcat.UserLoginWatcher
        </listener-class>
    </listener>
. . . .
</web-app>
```

<servlet>

The <servlet> element is used to define a <servlet> in the Web application. The <servlet> element is used with the <servlet-mapping> element to map the appropriate request URI to the servlet.

A <servlet> contains the following elements:

- <icon> (optional)
- <servlet-name> (required)
- <display-name> (optional)
- <description> (optional)
- one of <servlet-class> or <jsp-file> (required)
- <init-param> (optional, more than one may be defined)
- <load-on-startup> (optional)
- <run-as> (optional)
- <security-role-ref> (optional, more than one may be defined)

The <servlet-name> is a unique name given to the <servlet> element and is used to map the name of the servlet to a URL pattern or servlet in a <servlet-mapping> element. The <servlet-class> is the fully qualified classname of the <servlet> class and the <jsp-file> is a path to the JSP file from the root of the Web application and beginning with a '/'.

The <init-param> elements are similar to <context-param> elements in that they provide a mechanism for specifying initialization values to the servlet. The values are obtained by using the getInitParameterNames() and getInitParameter() methods of ServletConfig.

The <load-on-startup> element is used to inform the servlet container that this Web application should be loaded on startup. Loading on startup instantiates and invokes the init() method on the servlet. The value for the <load-on-startup> defines a priority for the loading of the servlets. Lower values are loaded first, however, for a negative value the servlet container may load the servlet at any time. If two or more servlets have the same priority, the servlet container may choose any order for loading of those particular servlets.

The <run-as> element is used to specify the identity to be used for the execution of the Web application. The <run-as> element contains an optional description element, and the <role-name>. The <role-name> element contains the name of a <security-role> that is the identity of the execution of the Web application.

The <security-role-ref> defines a security role reference in the Web applications code. The <security-role-ref> element contains an optional description, a role-name, and an optional role link. The <role-name> contains the name of a security role, and the <role-link> references a defined security role from the security-role elements. There may be more than one <security-role-ref> defined.

The <security-role-ref> element allows a Web application that has a defined set of roles used internally by the application code to be mapped to roles defined externally by the application deployer.

The <servlet> element is only contained in the <web-app> element. An example of use follows:

```
<web-app>
. . . .
    <servlet>
        <servlet-name>AdminServlet</servlet-name>
        <servlet-class>
            bible.tomcat.MyAdminServlet
        </servlet-class>
        <load-on-startup>1</load-on-startup>
    </servlet>
    <servlet>
        <servlet-name>UserServlet</servlet-name>
        <servlet-class>/TheUserJSP.jsp</servlet-class>
    </servlet>
    . . . .
    <servlet-mapping>
        <servlet-name>AdminServlet</servlet-name>
        <url-pattern>/secret/*</url-pattern>
    </servlet-mapping>
. . . .
</web-app>
```

<servlet-mapping>

The <servlet-mapping> element defines the mapping of the <servlet-name> to a URL pattern. There may be more than one <servlet-mapping> element defined.

The <servlet-mapping> element contains the following elements:

✦ <servlet-name> (required)

✦ <url-pattern> (required)

The <servlet-name> element must match a <servlet-name> element from a servlet element defined in the deployment descriptor. The <servlet-mapping> element only exists within the <web-app> element.

The <url-pattern> is defined according to the following:

- A pattern starting with a '/' and terminating with a '/*' is used for path mapping. For example:

  ```
  <url-pattern>/secret/*</url-pattern>
  ```

- A pattern starting with a '*.' is used as an extension mapping. For example:

  ```
  <url-pattern>*.shtml</url-pattern>
  ```

- A pattern that consists of only a '/' matches the default servlet of the application.
- All other patterns are used for exact matches.

A request URI is mapped to a servlet according to the following rules, and in the specified order. The first successful match that occurs terminates the checking and no further matches are tried.

1. **Exact Match.** The servlet container attempts to find an exact match from the defined servlet-mapping elements. If an exact match occurs, that servlet is selected and the matching process terminates.
2. **Longest path-prefix.** The servlet container attempts to match the path against the defined servlet-mapping elements. If there are no matches, the parent directory is used for the path. The servlet-mapping element that has the longest match (in terms of number of directories) is the servlet that is selected.
3. **Extension match.** If the URL contains an extension such as `*.html` the servlet container attempts to match the servlet that handles requests for that extension.
4. **Default.** Finally, if nothing has matched the request URL, the servlet container attempts to serve content appropriate to the request. For example, if a request URL has a valid path such as `www.foo.com/webapp/` then the servlet container may return a directory listing. If the Web application has a default servlet defined, then that servlet is used.

Consider the following example definitions:

```
<servlet-mapping>
    <servlet-name>AdminServlet</servlet-name>
    <url-pattern>/admin/secret/*</url-pattern>
</servlet-mapping>
<servlet-mapping>
    <servlet-name>LoginServlet</servlet-name>
    <url-pattern>/login</url-pattern>
</servlet-mapping>
<servlet-mapping>
    <servlet-name>XMLHandlerServlet</servlet-name>
    <url-pattern>*.xml</url-pattern>
</servlet-mapping>
```

Table 3-2 describes the servlets that would handle the requests, given the specified request.

Table 3-2: Incoming requests to example servlet mapping

Request	*Servlet*
/admin/secret/payroll.html	AdminServlet
/admin/secret/payroll.xml	AdminServlet
/login/index.html	default servlet
/login	LoginServlet
/user/data/accounts.xml	XMLHandlerServlet

<session-config>

The `<session-config>` element is used to define session parameters for the Web application. There is only one element contained in the session-config, the `<session-timeout>` element, and it is optional.

The `<session-timeout>` element defines the session timeout value (in minutes) for sessions created in this Web application. If the session timeout value is zero (0) or negative then the servlet container never expires sessions automatically.

The `<session-config>` element only exists in the `<web-app>` element. An example of its use follows:

```
<web-app>
. . . .
    <servlet-mapping>
        <servlet-name>AdminServlet</servlet-name>
        <url-pattern>/secret/*</url-pattern>
    </servlet-mapping>
    <session-config>
        <session-timeout>10</session-timeout>
    </session-config>
. . . .
</web-app>
```

<mime-mapping>

The `<mime-mapping>` element is used to map between an extension and a mime type. The `<mime-mapping>` element consists of the following elements:

- ✦ `<extension>` (required)
- ✦ `<mime-type>` (required)

The `<extension>` element is a string containing a file extension, and the `<mime-type>` element is a string containing a defined mime type.

The `<mime-mapping>` element only exists in the `<web-app>` element. An example of its use follows:

```
<web-app>
. . . .
    <servlet-mapping>
        <servlet-name>AdminServlet</servlet-name>
```

```
        <url-pattern>/secret/*</url-pattern>
    </servlet-mapping>
    <mime-mapping>
        <extension>bin</extension>
        <mime-type>application/octet-stream</mime-type>
    </mime-mapping>
. . . .
</web-app>
```

<welcome-file-list>

The <welcome-file-list> element defines the files that are to be treated as welcome files (like index.html) for the Web application. This definition allows for the mapping of additional elements to a request URL to determine validity of the request.

The <welcome-file-list> element consists of only one type of element; the <welcome-file> element. There may be more than one <welcome-file> element and if there is, the order of the <welcome-file> list determines the match priority for directories that may contain more than one match. The first match in the <welcome-file> list is the file that is served.

Tip A servlet cannot be defined as a welcome file. To configure a servlet as the welcome file for a Web application without defining an '/*' match in the url-pattern, create a JSP file called welcome.jsp that contains a single line as <jsp:forward name="servlet-name">. Now define welcome.jsp as a <welcome-file> element in the <welcome-file-list>. Browsing to that directory invokes the servlet.

The <welcome-file-list> element only exists in the <web-app> element. An example of use follows:

```
<web-app>
. . . .
    <servlet-mapping>
        <servlet-name>AdminServlet</servlet-name>
        <url-pattern>/secret/*</url-pattern>
    </servlet-mapping>
    <welcome-file-list>
        <welcome-file>index.shtml</welcome-file>
        <welcome-file>index.jsp</welcome-file>
        <welcome-file>welcome.jsp</welcome-file>
    </welcome-file-list>
. . . .
</web-app>
```

<error-page>

The <error-page> element defines a mapping between an error and a resource in the Web application that will be invoked when that condition occurs. The <error-page> is capable of mapping both HTTP errors (like 404 Not Found) and Web application exceptions (like bible.tomcat.LoginRefusedException). More than one <error-page> element may be defined with different <error-code> elements.

An <error-page> has the following elements:

✦ one of <error-code> or <exception-type> (required)

✦ <location> (required)

The <error-code> element contains a numeric HTTP error code and the <exception-type> contains a fully qualified Java class name of an exception. The <location> element is the path to a resource in the Web application and must start with a '/'.

The <error-page> only exists in the <web-app> element. An example of use follows:

```
<web-app>
. . . .
    <welcome-file-list>
        <welcome-file>index.jsp</welcome-file>
    </welcome-file-list>
    <error-page>
        <error-code>404</error-code>
        <location>/notfound.html</location>
    </error-page>
    <error-page>
        <exception-type>
            bible.tomcat.LoginRefusedException
        </exception-type>
        <location>/login.jsp</location>
    </error-page>
    <error-page>
        <exception-type>
            bible.tomcat.PasswordExpiredException
        </exception-type>
        <location>/user/admin</location>
    </error-page>

. . . .
</web-app>
```

<taglib>

The <taglib> element is used to define a JSP tag library that is utilized by the Web application. There may be more than one <taglib> element defined.

A <taglib> contains the following two elements:

- ✦ <taglib-uri> (required) and
- ✦ <taglib-location> (required)

The <taglib-uri> describes how the <taglib> is to be referenced by resources in the Web application, and the <taglib-location> contains a path relative to the root of the Web application to the <taglib> library descriptor file (*.tld).

The error-page only exists in the <web-app> element and an example of use follows:

```
<web-app>
. . . .
    <error-page>
        <error-code>404</error-code>
        <location>/notfound.html</location>
    </error-page>
```

```
        <taglib>
            <taglib-uri>/citytag</taglib-uri>
            <taglib-location>
                /WEB-INF/lib/citytaglib.tld
            </taglib-location>
        </taglib>

    . . . .
    </web-app>
```

Using the <taglib> in a JSP file would consist of code similar to the following:

```
<%@ taglib uri="/citytag" prefix="city" %>
<jsp:useBean id="theName" class="java.lang.String" scope="request" />
<html>
<head>
<title>Taglib Demo</title>
</head>
<body>
<h1><city:greeting /><%= theName %> </h1>
</body>
</html>
```

<resource-env-ref>

The <resource-env-ref> element is used to define for the Web application a reference to an object associated with a resource in the Web application's environment. The <resource-env-ref> is a element that is new in version 2.3 of the servlet specification and was introduced to simplify configuration of resources that do not require authentication. Resources requiring authentication should use the <resource-ref> element. There may be more than one <resource-env-ref> element defined for the Web application.

The <resource-env-ref> contains the following elements:

- <description> (optional),
- <resource-env-ref>-name (required), and
- <resource-env-ref-type> (required)

The <resource-env-ref-name> element is a unique JNDI name relative to the java:comp/env context and contains the name of the resource. The <resource-env-ref-type> element is a fully qualified Java class name of the resource.

The <resource-env-ref> only exists in the <web-app> element and an example of use follows:

```
    <web-app>
    . . . .
        <error-page>
            <error-code>404</error-code>
            <location>/notfound.html</location>
        </error-page>
        <resource-env-ref>
            <resource-env-ref-name>
```

```
            jms/ErrorQueue
        </resource-env-ref-name>
        <resource-env-ref-type>
            javax.jms.Queue
        </resource-env-ref-type>
    </resource-env-ref>
. . . .
</web-app>
```

<resource-ref>

The <resource- ref> element is used to define for the Web application a reference to an object associated with a resource in the Web application's environment. There may be more than one <resource-ref> element defined for the Web application. The <resource-ref> element is often used to define database connection pool information for use by the Web application.

The <resource-ref> contains the following elements:

- <description> (optional),
- <res-ref-name> (required),
- <res-type> (required),
- <res-auth> (required), and
- <res-sharing-scope> (optional)

The <res-ref-name> element is a unique JNDI name relative to the java:comp/env context and contains the name of the resource manager factory. The <res-ref-type> element is a fully qualified Java class or interface of the type of the data source.

The <res-auth> specifies whether the Web application or the servlet container is responsible for authentication with the resource manager. There are two allowable values for <res-auth>:

- Application
- Container

If the container is responsible, the container relies on the Web application deployer to provide the authentication details to access the resource.

The <res-sharing-scope> defines if the connections obtained from the resource manager can be shared. There are two allowable values for <res-sharing-scope>:

- Shareable,
- <unshareable>Unshareable

The <resource-ref> only exists in the <web-app> element. An example of use follows:

```
<web-app>
. . . .
    <error-page>
        <error-code>404</error-code>
        <location>/notfound.html</location>
    </error-page>
```

```
    <resource-ref>
        <description>Corporate Asset Database</description>
        <res-ref-name>jdbc/Assets</res-ref-name>
        <res-type>javax.sql.DataSource</res-type>
        <res-auth>Container</res-auth>
  </resource-ref>
. . . .
</web-app>
```

<security-constraint>

The <security-constraint> element defines the security constraints that are applied to a list of <web-resource-collection> elements. The <web-resource-collection> elements define a subset of the Web application resources and potentially the HTTP methods that apply to those resources. This allows more fine-grained declarative security mechanisms on the Web application resources. There may be more than one security-constraint for a Web application.

The security-constraint consists of the following elements:

✦ <display-name> (optional)

✦ <web-resource-collection> (one or more required)

✦ <auth-constraint> (optional)

✦ <user-data-constraint> (optional)

The <web-resource-collection> element is used to define a subset of resources and methods and consists of the following elements:

✦ <web-resource-name> (required)

✦ <description> (optional)

✦ <url-pattern> (optional, more than one may be defined)

✦ <http-method> (optional, more than one may be defined)

The <web-resource-name> contains the name of the collection. The <url-pattern> follows the same rules for request URI matching for the <filter> and <servlet> elements. The <http-method> defines an HTTP method such as GET or POST. Any valid HTTP method is allowed for the http-method, but if none are defined then the security constraint applies to all HTTP methods.

The <auth-constraint> element is used to define the user roles that are able to access the resource collection. The <auth-constraint> element consists of the following:

✦ <description> (optional)

✦ <role-name> (optional, more than one may be defined)

The <auth-constraint> must contain the <role-name> of a <security-role> element or use '*' to indicate all roles in the Web application. If a '*' and< role-names> are used then all roles have permission to access the resource. If no roles are defined, then no user has access to the defined resources.

The <user-data-constraint> defines the method of transport between the user and container. The <user-data-constraint> consists of the following:

✦ <description> (optional)

✦ <transport-guarantee> (required)

The <transport-guarantee> element is one of the following:

✦ NONE. There are no transport guarantees.

✦ INTEGRAL. The data between the client and server is protected against modification.

✦ CONFIDENTIAL. The data between the client and server is protected against observation.

The <security-constraint> only exists in the <web-app> element. An example of use follows:

```
<web-app>
. . . .
    <error-page>
        <error-code>404</error-code>
        <location>/notfound.html</location>
    </error-page>
    <security-constraint>
        <display-name>Protect Administration</display-name>
        <web-resource-collection>
            <web-resource-name>
                Administration
            </web-resource-name>
            <url-pattern>/admin/*</url-pattern>
            <http-method>GET</http-method>
            <http-method>POST</http-method>
       </web-resource-collection>
       <auth-constraint>
           <role-name>boss</role-name>
           <role-name>adminstaff</role-name>
       </auth-constraint>
       <user-data-constraint>
           <transport-guarantee>
               CONFIDENTIAL
           </transport-guarantee>
       </user-data-constraint>
  </security-constraint>
. . . .
</web-app>
```

<login-config>

The <login-config> element defines the authentication scheme to be used, the realm name for the Web application, and, if required, the configuration for use by the form login.

The <login-config> consists of the following elements:

✦ <auth-method> (optional),

✦ <realm-name> (optional) and

✦ <form-login-config> (optional)

The <auth-method> defines the mechanism for the authentication scheme to be used by the Web application. To gain access to any resources protected by a security constraint, a user must first authenticate using the method defined by the <auth-method> element. There are four legal values for <auth-method>:

- BASIC. The authentication is handled by HTTP Basic Authentication.
- DIGEST. The authentication is handled by HTTP Digest Authentication.
- FORM. The authentication is handled using custom forms. The configuration of the form login mechanism is defined in the <form-login-config> element.
- CLIENT-CERT. The authentication is handled by HTTPS Client Authentication. This mechanism involves client-side certificates.

The <realm-name> element defines the realm name used for HTTP Basic and HTTP Digest Authentication.

The <form-login-element> consists of two elements:

- <form-login-page> (required)
- <form-error-page> (required)

The <form-login-page> and <form-error-page> are locations of resources in the Web application where the login page and error page can be found. The error page is displayed when a login attempt is unsuccessful.

The <login-config> only exists in the <web-app> element. A simple example of use follows:

```
<web-app>
. . . .
    <error-page>
        <error-code>404</error-code>
        <location>/notfound.html</location>
    </error-page>
    <login-config>
        <auth-method>DIGEST</auth-method>
        <realm-name>Administration Application</realm-name>
    </login-config>
<web-app>
```

Using the <form-login> mechanism is more complex. An example of use follows:

```
<web-app>
. . . .
    <error-page>
        <error-code>404</error-code>
        <location>/notfound.html</location>
    </error-page>
    <login-config>
        <auth-method>FORM</auth-method>
        <form-login-config>
            <form-login-page>/login.jsp</form-login-page>
            <form-error-page>/fail.jsp</form-error-page>
        </form-login-config>
    </login-config>
<web-app>
```

The <form-login-page> must contain fields for entering a username and password, and what is more, the fields must be named j_username and j_password. The form should post with the action of j_security_check. An example of the HTML required to achieve this follows:

```
<form method="POST" action="j_security_check">
    <input type="text" name="j_username">
    <input type="password" name="j_password">
</form>
```

<security-role>

The <security-role> element defines a security role for the Web application. There may be more than one security-role defined for a Web application.

The <security-role> contains the following elements:

- ✦ <description> (optional)
- ✦ <role-name> (required)

The <role-name> contains the name of a <security-role> for the Web application.

The <security-role> only exists in the <web-app> element. An example of its use follows:

```
<web-app>
. . . .
    <login-config>
        <auth-method>DIGEST</auth-method>
        <realm-name>Administration Application</realm-name>
    </login-config>
    <security-role>
        <description>The Big Boss</description>
        <role-name>boss</role-name>
    </security-role>
    <security-role>
        <description>Administration Staff</description>
        <role-name>adminstaff</role-name>
    </security-role>
    <security-role>
        <description>General Staff</description>
        <role-name>staff</role-name>
    </security-role>
<web-app>
```

<env-entry>

The <env-entry> element describes an environment entry for a Web application. There may be (and often is) more than one <env-entry> defined for a Web application.

The <env-entry> contains the following elements:

- ✦ <description> (optional)
- ✦ <env-entry-name> (required)
- ✦ <env-entry-value> (optional)
- ✦ <env-entry-type> (required)

The <env-entry-name> is a unique JNDI name relative to the java:comp/env context that contains the name of the environment entry. The contents of <env-entry-name> are used to obtain the value during runtime.

The <env-entry-value> contains the value of the environment entry and the <env-entry-type> contains a fully qualified Java class name for the type of the entry. The <env-entry-type> must be one of the following values:

- java.lang.Boolean
- java.lang.Byte
- java.lang.Character
- java.lang.String
- java.lang.Short
- java.lang.Integer
- java.lang.Long
- java.long.Float
- java.long.Double

The <env-entry-value> is a string that must be valid for the object constructor of <env-entry-type> that takes a string as the parameter.

The <env-entry> only exists in the <web-app> element and an example of use follows:

```
<web-app>
. . . .
    <env-entry>
        <description>Debugging On ?</description>
        <env-entry-name>debug</env-entry-name>
        <env-entry-value>true</env-entry-value>
        <env-entry-type>java.lang.Boolean</env-entry-type>
    </env-entry>
    <env-entry>
        <description>Debugging Level</description>
        <env-entry-name>debugLevel</env-entry-name>
        <env-entry-value>10</env-entry-value>
        <env-entry-type>java.lang.Integer</env-entry-type>
    </env-entry>
<web-app>
```

<ejb-ref>

This element defines the access to EJB resources through an EJBs Home interface.

The <ejb-ref> contains the following elements:

- <description> (optional)
- <ejb-ref-name> (required)
- <ejb-ref-type> (required)

- ✦ <home> (required)
- ✦ <remote> (required)
- ✦ <ejb-link> (optional)

The <ejb-ref-name> is the name of the reference to the Enterprise Bean used by the web application. The standard convention for the name recommends starting with ejb.

The <ejb-ref-type> is the expected type of the EJB. There are only two allowable values for <ejb-ref-type>:

- ✦ Entity
- ✦ Session

The <home> contains the fully qualified name of the home interface for the EJB.

The <remote> contains the fully qualified name of the remote interface for the EJB.

The <ejb-link> contains a path to uniquely identify the EJB to be used by the EJB reference. This element is used when there are more than one EJB that has the same name, and packaged in multiple JAR files. The path is relative to the WAR file containing the web application.

The <ejb-ref> only exists in the <web-app> element and an example of use follows:

```
<web-app>
. . . .
    <ejb-ref>
        <description>Authentication EJB</description>
        <ejb-ref-name>ejb/Auth</ejb-ref-name>
        <ejb-ref-type>Session</ejb-ref-type>
        <home>bible.AuthHome</home>
        <remote>bible.Auth</remote>
        <ejb-link>../ejb/auth.jar#Auth</ejb-link>
    </ejb-ref>
<web-app>
```

<ejb-local-ref>

This element defines the access to EJB resources through an EJBs Local interface. The use of the <ejb-local-ref> element is the same as the <ejb-ref> except the access to the EJB is via the Local interface rather than the Remote interface.

The <ejb-local-ref> contains the following elements:

- ✦ <description> (optional)
- ✦ <ejb-ref-name> (required)
- ✦ <ejb-ref-type> (required)
- ✦ <local-home> (required)
- ✦ <local> (required)
- ✦ <ejb-link> (optional)

The <ejb-ref-name>, <ejb-ref-type> and <ejb-link> elements in <ejb-local-ref> have the same meaning as the elements in <ejb-ref>, however they refer to the EJBs local interface, rather then the remote interface.

The <local-home> contains the fully qualified name of the local home interface of the EJB.

The <local> contains the fully qualified name of the local interface of the EJB.

The <ejb-local-ref> only exists in the <web-app> element and an example of use follows:

```
<web-app>
. . . .
    <ejb-local-ref>
        <description>Local Auth EJB</description>
        <ejb-ref-name>ejb/LocalAuth</ejb-ref-name>
        <ejb-ref-type>Session</ejb-ref-type>
        <home>bible.LocalAuthHome</home>
        <remote>bible.LocalAuth</remote>
    </ejb-ref>
<web-app>
```

Summary

This chapter has covered the structure and content of a Web application and then provided a detailed view of the Web application deployment descriptor complete with examples. This chapter should provide all the groundwork for the application developer to confidently proceed to building and configuring Web applications.

If it's time to start some coding, then jump directly to Chapter 7, where some of this theory is put into practice. If a little more theory is desired, or a computer isn't within easy reach, continue on to Chapter 4, where designing and building web applications for Tomcat are discussed.

✦ ✦ ✦

P A R T

Packaging, Compiling, and Deploying Applications for Tomcat

✦ ✦ ✦ ✦

In This Part

✦ ✦ ✦ ✦

Creating Web Applications for Tomcat

✦ ✦ ✦ ✦

In This Chapter

Designing a Web application

The Tomcat environment

Packaging a Web application

✦ ✦ ✦ ✦

This chapter examines the processes behind designing, building, and packaging Web applications for Tomcat.

This chapter explores the common areas that need to be examined when starting a Web application project and identifies a number of important questions to be answered prior to writing any code.

The section devoted to building Web applications relies on the environment that Tomcat or any compliant servlet container provides. It is a guide to the design and operation of the environment as it is implemented by Tomcat, and supplies useful insight into how to structure applications and avoid potential causes for application error

The chapter concludes with information about the packaging of a Web application from the development and deployment perspectives as well as some important configuration options that are specific to Tomcat.

Why Design?

A Web application is more than just the collection of resources provided in the package. The resources developed by the application developer are the controlling resources and are the implementation of the solution desired by the developer. However, there are other factors to consider. There is interaction with third party libraries, databases, and potentially services provided by the application server, in this case Tomcat.

The interaction with these other components leaves the application developer with decisions to make. The application developer must consider how to identify the components and how to best to make use of these components if and where they exist.

The design of a Web application should consider:

- **What components?** Identify the components of the Web application. Components include the graphical assets, the JSP and servlets, the Java classes that comprise the business logic, and external data sources.
- **What libraries?** Identify the libraries used by the application. The versions, their locations, and how they should be included by the application. The libraries to be used also require integration into the development environment so this can be an important step in the process.
- **What structure?** This includes the components and how they will interact. The use of an MVC pattern and access to data sources all influence the structure of the Web application. Security and authentication methods also heavily influence the final structure of the Web application.
- **What packaging?** This is to identify the deployment packaging of components, and deployment descriptor. This, combined with the structure, determines the user access to the Web application.

Making these decisions requires knowledge of the environment the Web application is operating within. Tomcat, like all Web application servers, provide facilities for the Web application in the form of processing the user requests, invoking the appropriate Web application, loading and compiling the JSP pages, and loading the classes for the servlets and business classes.

Exactly how Tomcat performs these operations can give the application developer a better insight into the way the Web application will execute, as well as guidance for identifying likely problems during application execution.

Tomcat Execution Environment

Tomcat is an implementation of the Servlet Specifications and therefore is constrained in the manner in which it operates in many areas. However, reading the Servlet Specification doesn't always provide a clear understanding of what to expect when a Web application is deployed. This section provides an understanding of how Tomcat operates when:

- Loading a Web application
- Processing JSP files
- the servlet lifecycle,
- Loading classes,
- Responding to user requests

However, before those items are examined, first we shall take a look at what is the directory structure for Tomcat. This shows where various files are located and what purpose the Java class files serve within directories.

This section contains an examination of the base environment of Tomcat and how the environment can be correctly extended to serve the needs of the Web applications deployed on that instance of Tomcat.

Tomcat Directory Structure

The standard installation of Tomcat has a directory structure as shown in Figure 4-1.

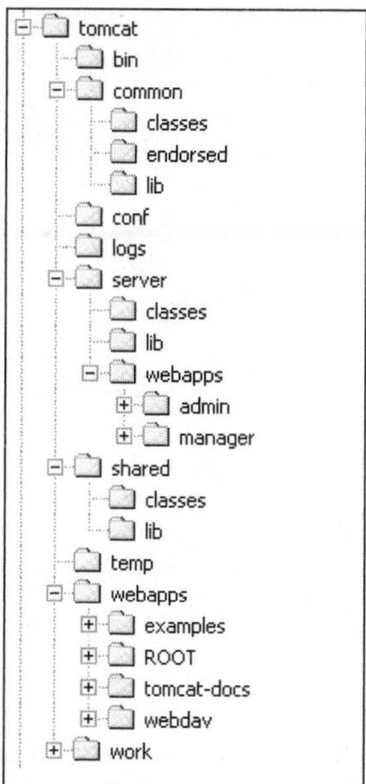

Figure 4-1: Tomcat directory structure

The directories in Figure 4-1 are used for the following purposes in the default configuration of Tomcat. Tomcat provides an absolute plethora of configuration options for modifying just about every aspect of runtime behavior and the following descriptions relate to the situation prior to any configuration changes..

Some directories, such as `bin` and `common`, are relative to the installation of Tomcat and therefore are relative to the `CATALINA_HOME` environment variable. The other following directories, such as `conf` and `shared`, are relative to the `CATALINA_BASE` environment variable.

The use of `CATALINA_HOME` and `CATALINA_BASE` are further explored in Chapter 8, where multiple instances of Tomcat are configured using these environment variables.

Setting the environment variable `CATALINA_HOME` is part of the installation process and is described in Chapter 2.

bin

The `bin` directory contains the scripts for starting and stopping Tomcat as well as utility scripts for the execution of the jspc compiler Jasper. The `bin` directory also contains the bootstrap classes for starting up Tomcat, which includes the standard class loader for loading the Web applications.

common

The `common` directory contains 3 subdirectories:

✦ `classes`

✦ `endorsed`

✦ `lib`

These directories contain the common runtime classes (in the lib directory) that are required for general use including the servlet.jar that contains all the javax.servlet.* classes to implement the APIs required by the Servlet and JSP specifications.

The classes in the common directory are available for use by Web applications as part of the runtime environment of Tomcat.

Despite the name of the directory, the common directory is not the recommended directory to use for Web application classes that are utilized by multiple Web applications; these should be placed in the shared directory, or incorporated into the WEB-INF/lib directory for each Web application.

conf

The conf directory contains the configuration files for the Tomcat server. This includes the server.xml which is described in more detail in Chapter 8. Other configuration also includes the tomcat-users.xml for configuration of users and roles in the default security realm as well as web.xml, containing the default configuration for all Web applications.

logs

Not surprisingly the logs directory contains the runtime logging output files for Tomcat. This is the place to look for logging from the Web applications and from the Tomcat runtime as well.

server

The server directory contains the implementation of the Tomcat specific classes responsible for the server. This includes many classes that relate to the configuration and setup of Tomcat that are not directly specified in the Servlet or JSP specification, but are required to implement a useful Web application server.

The directory contains 3 subdirectories:

✦ classes

✦ lib

✦ webapps

The classes and lib directories contain classes that are used by Tomcat. The webapps directory contains the Administration and Manager Web applications provided in Tomcat 4.1.

The classes in the server directory are not available for use by Web applications as part of the runtime environment of Tomcat. These classes are only for use by the Tomcat application.

shared

The shared directory is used to place classes that are shared over multiple Web applications. There are two sub-directories in shared:

✦ classes

✦ lib

classes is for unpacked classes and resources, and JAR files can be located in the lib directory.

temp

The temp directory is used by the JVM for temporary file storage on behalf of Tomcat. For security reasons this directory is used by Tomcat rather than the default value for java.io.tmpdir.

Interestingly enough, the temp directory contains a README file by default that explains the use of the directory.

webapps

The webapps directory is the default location for 3 types of files.

- WAR files
- unpacked WAR files
- XML files

The WAR files are the Web application archives described in Chapter 3 and serve as the source for a Web application. Unpacked WAR files are a directory structure where the root directory is the name of the WAR. So mywebapp.war unpacks into the directory webapps/mywebapp/.

Finally, the XML files are fragments of configuration and contain a single <Context> element that specifies the configuration for a Web application. Normally the <Context> element us used to deploy an application that is not in the webapps directory structure, or has configuration requirements that are different from the default configuration of a <Context> in server.xml.

To deploy applications in this form has a great advantage during development, and also during deployment as there is no need to modify the server.xml file because individual Web applications can have configuration of parameters applied in the <Context> element of the XML file.

work

The work directory is used to contain scratch files used by Tomcat. These may be where Web applications are deployed using the Ant administration tasks, or where JSP files are translated into Java code for servlets prior to compilation.

The structure of the work directory in Tomcat is a hierarchy formed by the <Engine>, <Host>, and <Context> nodes of the server.xml file. Any additional <Context> nodes added either automatically, or via a <Context> XML file in the webapps directory are also included in the directory hierarchy.

A subdirectory of the work directory, specific to a particular Web application, is made available as the temporary directory for the Web application as required by the Servlet Specification.

Web Applications and Class Loading

One of the most confusing aspects of working with Web applications is that they don't follow the standard Java mechanisms of utilizing the CLASSPATH for finding classes. This causes no end of problems for developers who charge into Web application development without spending some time understanding this particular difference.

Tip

Ignore the CLASSPATH. Setting JAVA_HOME and CATALINA_HOME is enough to get Tomcat working successfully.

There are many options for including third-party classes into the class loading structures of Tomcat. Tomcat has been designed to work this way and placing the additional classes into the common, shared, or WEB-INF directory structures assists in the smooth development and deployment of the Web applications.

It is important to understand that with Tomcat there are two sorts of class loaders. The first are for the system classes that implement Tomcat. These classes are only available to Tomcat, and under no circumstances do the class loaders share those classes with a Web application. The second is for the classes that are available to the Web application. Some of the latter classes also are available to Tomcat.

Tomcat arranges the class loaders in a hierarchical arrangement according to Figure 4-2.

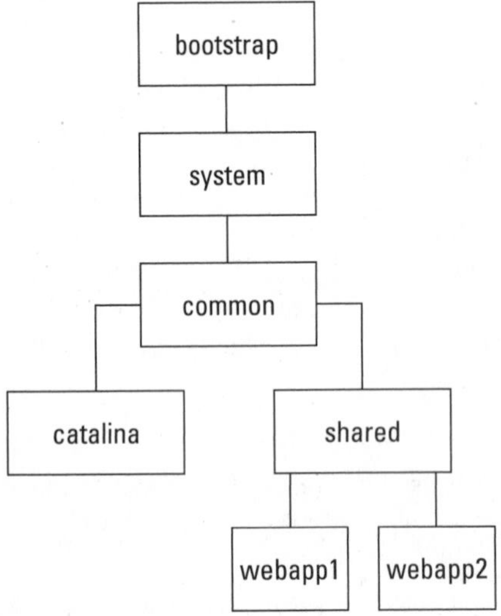

Figure 4-2: Tomcat class loader hierarchy

It is important to recognize that the class loaders named in Figure 4-2 do not relate to specific directories, but groups of directories and/or JAR files. The source of classes and the visibility of the classes are described in the following sections.

bootstrap

The bootstrap class loader contains the minimal runtime classes for the Java Virtual Machine and any JAR files in $JAVA_HOME/jre/lib/ext. Classes loaded by the bootstrap class loader are only visible to Tomcat, and in some circumstances may not be visible at all.

system

The `system` class loader normally includes the classes that are found in the `CLASSPATH` environment variable. However, in the standard Tomcat startup scripts the `CLASSPATH` is explicitly ignored and instead a custom class path is build consisting of the following:

- `$CATALINA_HOME/bin/bootstrap.jar`
- `$JAVA_HOME/lib/tools.jar`

The classes loaded by system are visible to Tomcat and to Web applications.

common

The `common` class loader includes additional classes available to Tomcat and to Web applications. The common classes are located in:

- `$CATALINA_HOME/common/classes,`
- `$CATALINA_HOME/common/endorsed`
- `$CATALINA_HOME/common/lib`

By default, these classes include support for JNDI, the servlet ,and JSP, API, and XML processing.

catalina

The `catalina` class loader is used to load the classes that are used to implement Tomcat. These classes are loaded from:

- `$CATALINA_HOME/server/classes` and
- `$CATALINA_HOME/server/lib`

These classes include the Tomcat servlet implementation, implementation of the Coyote, HTTP/1.1, JK and JK2 connectors, and utility classes for implementing the connectors.

These classes are not visible to Web applications.

shared

The `shared` class loader is the first class loader that can be configured for use by the Web applications. To add classes or resources that are utilized across more than one Web application, place them in a directory loaded by the `shared` class loader. These classes are loaded from:

- `$CATALINA_HOME/shared/classes`
- `$CATALINA_HOME/shared/lib`

Obviously, these classes are visible to all Web applications.

webapp<n>

The final class loader used by Tomcat is the Web application specific class loader. Each Web application has a class loader for the specific classes and resources located in the `WEB-INF/classes` and `WEB-INF/lib` directories for the Web application.

The Web application class loader is significantly different from the other class loaders in Tomcat and is different from the default Java 2 model for class loaders.

The default Java 2 class loader behavior is to delegate a request for a class to parent class loader first, and then if the class is not located, the child searches the local resources.

The Web application class loader examines the local resources first, then delegate to the parent if not found.

These classes and resources are only visible to a specific Web application.

With the class loaders defined above and with all the directories involved, the resulting search path for classes, in order of evaluation, is:

- /WEB-INF/classes
- /WEB-INF/lib/*.jar
- bootstrap classes of the local JVM
- system class loader classes
- $CATALINA_HOME/common/classes
- $CATALINA_HOME/common/endorsed/*.jar
- $CATALINA_HOME/common/lib/*.jar
- $CATALINA_HOME/shared/classes
- $CATALINA_HOME/shared/lib/*.jar

Common Class Loading Problems

Due to the relatively complex class loading structure that Tomcat uses sometimes what seems to be the correct course of action unfortunately isn't.

The basic problem with class loading in Tomcat can be summed up quite simply as a problem of visibility. This generally manifests as a class higher in the class loading tree attempting to load a class lower in the tree. A good example of this is classes in `WEB-INF/classes` do not have visibility to classes in `shared/lib`.

So what? Well, the Tomcat environment is well suited to using frameworks to simplify the development activities. Struts is a good example of one of these frameworks. Struts uses dynamic class loading based on configuration files to load the Web application classes implementing the business logic for the application.

The Struts JAR file (`struts.jar`) weighs in at a hefty 450k. It would seem to make sense if there are many Web applications using the Struts framework to place the `struts.jar` into `shared/lib`. However, doing what seems to be sensible causes the Web application to not work because the class loader responsible for loading files from `common/lib` does not have visibility to the classes in `WEB-INF/classes`.

So, the `struts.jar` file must be placed into the `WEB-INF/lib` directory for each and every Web application.

The other side of the coin is problems caused by too much visibility. This circumstance is easier to identify, and easier to rectify. Generally this is a result of packaging versions of JAR or class files in a Web application that conflict with versions existing in the Tomcat common or shared directory structures.

The simplest way to resolve class loading problems in Tomcat is to include the classes at their lowest level of required visibility. This basically means not to try and throw all the classes and JAR files into the shared directory hierarchy unless absolutely necessary. There are other good software engineering reasons for wanting to keep Web application dependencies within a Web application as much as possible. The most important of these is modularity and resistance to outside changes. If a Web application is modular and self-contained, then the normal chaos caused by an administrator removing an "unneeded" JAR file from the shared library directory, or upgrading it "because it seemed like a good idea" will be reduced to a minimum.

JSP Compiling

The JSP files deployed as part of a Web application undergo a two-stage transformation process. The first stage converts the JSP files into Java source code, and the second stage compiles the Java source code into class files. These two stages together are called *translation* by the JSP specification.

Errors can occur in either of these stages, and as a result it is often desirable to pre-compile the JSP files prior to deployment. One of the drawbacks in pre-compiling JSP files is that there is no standard mechanism for the JSP compilation and any Web application that has pre-compiled the JSP files into servlets may only be deployed to a specific JSP/Servlet container.

Cross-Reference Pre-compiling JSP files for Tomcat is covered in Chapter 5.

An advantage in using a JSP compiler during development and deployment is that it is often much easier and faster to find and correct errors rather than deploying to a Web server and running the application to find syntax errors.

Another advantage is the removal of the delay that occurs when a JSP page is first used. This delay is caused by the translation, mostly due to the Java compilation from the servlet to the class files.

Caution There is a defect in the Sun javac which contains a memory leak. It causes the Tomcat process to grow when compiling the JSP files; it may become very large over a period of time if JSP files are changed frequently.

Servlet Lifecycle

Servlets in a Web application are loaded by the Tomcat servlet container according to the lifecycle defined in the Servlet Specifications. Appropriately using the lifecycle methods provides opportunities for Web application developers during creation and destruction of the servlet.

The servlet container performs the following actions on a servlet:

- Loading and instantiation
- Initialization
- Request handling
- End of service

During loading and instantiation the servlet container loads the servlet class file and instantiates it. This calls the constructor for the servlet. At this point the servlet is not connected with the container so any calls to access the Web context return null until after initialization.

After initialization the servlet is available to service requests. The initialization of the servlet is managed via the `init()` method, which provides the Web application developer a hook into the initialization process to perform "once-off" activities for the servlet.

Servlets can be loaded and unloaded, created and destroyed, at any time according to the whims of the servlet container. Any external resources obtained during the `init()` method should be released in the `destroy()` method.

During request handling the Tomcat servlet container hands requests matching the context and servlet mapping to the `service()` method of the servlet. This is where the normal operation of the servlet occurs and either the `service()` method is overridden or more commonly the `doPost()` or `doGet()` methods.

Finally, the servlet container can dispose of a servlet at any time; this may be after a period of inactivity, to recover resources such as memory, or when the servlet container is shutting down. The servlet container invokes the `destroy()` method of the servlet, which provides the opportunity to release any resources acquired during the running of the servlet.

Classes involved in the running of the servlet and JSP files once loaded by the Web application class loader are not released until the class loader is removed. This only occurs when Tomcat is restarted, or the individual Web application is restarted.

Request Handling

Tomcat has a pipeline of elements that are involved in handling a user request for resources. These elements are internal to Tomcat and only after the pipeline has completed is the request handed to the Web application.

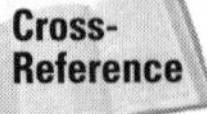

The configuration of the following elements can be found in Chapter 8.

- **Connector.** Receives an HTTP connection from a client and dispatches the request to the associated Engine.
- **Engine.** Executes all Valves explicitly specified and contained in the Engine, including an implicitly defined Valve that dispatches the request to the appropriate Host based on the requested host name.
- **Host.** Executes all Valves explicitly specified and contained in the Host, including an implicitly defined Valve that dispatches the request to the appropriate Context, based on the requested context path.
- **Context.** Executes all Valves explicitly specified and contained in the Context, including an implicitly defined Valve that dispatches the request to the appropriate servlet Wrapper, based on the servlet mappings defined in the Web application deployment descriptor.
- **Wrapper.** If the servlet is not currently loaded then loads the servlet and calls the `init()` method. Executes all the filters mapped to this request URI via the filter mapping elements in the Web application deployment descriptor. Provided the filter chain completes successfully it is followed by a call to the `service()` method of the servlet.

An important consideration of this pipeline is that the some of the elements can be dynamically created during Web application loading. Authentication within Tomcat is handled by the dynamic creation of an Authenticator Valve in the processing pipeline. This valve is created if Tomcat processes the Web application deployment descriptor and identifies a `login-method` element.

The impact of this on the Web application is that authentication by Tomcat is handled before the execution of filters or the servlet. This affects the user experience of Web applications under many circumstances and should be taken into consideration during design.

Implementing security in a Web application is covered in more detail in Chapter 12.

Tomcat Default Behavior

Tomcat is a highly configurable servlet container and there are often many ways to achieve a particular result. For example, there are at least two different options for providing the `Context` configuration for a Web application and there are at least four different options for installing a Web application.

However, it is possible for configuration changes to limit and in some cases extend the available functionality.

This section covers the default behavior of Tomcat for many of the elements that can affect how a Web application may be designed or implemented and what potential configuration changes are required to fulfill some of the requirements.

Details on configuring Tomcat and the `server.xml` can be found in Chapter 8.

Web Application Installation

The default configuration of Tomcat Installa Web applications as follows:

- ✦ A directory structure that is an unpacked WAR file in the `webapps` directory is assigned a context path that matches the subdirectory name.
- ✦ A Web application archive file (`WAR`) in the `webapps` directory is expanded into a directory structure matching the `WAR` file name without the `.war` extension. The Web application is then installed as above. If a matching directory name exists the WAR file is not unpacked.
- ✦ An XML file in the `webapps` directory that contains a Context fragment that refers to a packed or unpacked WAR file is assigned a context path that matches the definition in the Context fragment
- ✦ A Context entry in the `conf/server.xml` that refers to a packed or unpacked WAR file is assigned a context path that matches the definition in the Context

The Web applications that are installed that do not provide a `Context` entry use the `DefaultContext` element to determine the behavior.

Default web.xml

The installation of Tomcat provides a default `web.xml` file that is found in `conf/web.xml`. This Web application deployment descriptor file is processed prior to the processing of the Web application specific `WEB-INF/web.xml`. This provides a default set of configuration elements that are used, or can be overridden, by elements in the application specific `web.xml`.

The following sections describe various elements within the default `web.xml`.

The servlet and servlet-mapping elements are shown together in the following sections. This is not the order the elements are configured in the `web.xml`, but have been shown this way for easier comprehension.

Default Servlet

```
<servlet>
    <servlet-name>default</servlet-name>
    <servlet-class>
      org.apache.catalina.servlets.DefaultServlet
    </servlet-class>
    <init-param>
        <param-name>debug</param-name>
        <param-value>0</param-value>
    </init-param>
    <init-param>
        <param-name>listings</param-name>
        <param-value>true</param-value>
    </init-param>
    <load-on-startup>1</load-on-startup>
</servlet>

<!-- The mapping for the default servlet -->
<servlet-mapping>
    <servlet-name>default</servlet-name>
    <url-pattern>/</url-pattern>
</servlet-mapping>
```

The default servlet is the servlet that processes all requests for resources that are not explicitly handled by servlet mappings in the Web application. This servlet is generally invoked to handle requests for static resources such as the images and HTML files. The main configuration change that is performed on the default servlet is to change the `listings` parameter to `false` so that directory listings are not performed when a request is made for a directory that does not have a file that matches a welcome file.

The name of the servlet is not the important consideration when defining a default servlet, but the servlet mapping to `'/'` means that this servlet will receive all unhandled requests to this Web application.

The default servlet can be configured via the following `init-param` elements:

- ✦ `debug`.Set the debugging level, default of zero (0).
- ✦ `input`. Set the input buffer size in bytes for reading of resources to be served to the client, default of 2048.
- ✦ `listings`. Used to determine if directory listings are generated if there are no matching welcome file in the directory, default of true.

- `output`. Set the output buffer size in bytes for writing the resources to be served to the client, default of 2048.
- `readonly`. Used to determine if the Web application context is read-only. This automatically rejects `HTTP PUT` and `DELETE` commands if set to true. The default value is true.

Invoker Servlet

```
<servlet>
    <servlet-name>invoker</servlet-name>
    <servlet-class>
      org.apache.catalina.servlets.InvokerServlet
    </servlet-class>
    <init-param>
        <param-name>debug</param-name>
        <param-value>0</param-value>
    </init-param>
    <load-on-startup>2</load-on-startup>
</servlet>

<!-- The mapping for the invoker servlet -->
<servlet-mapping>
    <servlet-name>invoker</servlet-name>
    <url-pattern>/servlet/*</url-pattern>
</servlet-mapping>
```

The invoker servlet provides an implementation to allow anonymous servlets to be accessed via their class names without providing servlet or servlet-mapping elements in `web.xml`.

The servlets are accessed via a URL of the following form:

```
http://host/context/servlet/{class}
```

where `{class}` is of the form:

```
/com.mycompany.mypackage.MyServlet
```

The invoker servlet is disabled by default for all versions of Tomcat after (and including) version 4.1.12. This has caused a number of migration issues for developers moving Web applications from the 3.X and 4.0.X versions of Tomcat that used this functionality.

The invoker servlet was disabled because it exposed a security risk to the Web applications. However, while the use of the invoker servlet to access servlet classes directly is convenient it does have some drawbacks from a software engineering point of view.

- Using the invoker servlet exposes the class name being used. This makes it much harder to refactor your Web application.
- Using the invoker servlet does not require explicit definition of servlets. This makes maintenance harder because using the `web.xml` file provides a list of the servlets that are utilized, and the description element provides additional documentation when used.
- Not having an explicit list of the servlets used in a Web application introduces additional complications when reviewing the Web application to remove redundant, unneeded, or antique code.
- Using the invoker servlet does not allow for providing initialization parameters to the servlets. This increases the likelihood of hard-coded or environment specific information when developing the application.

When migrating an application there are two options for providing the same visible functionality. This can be important when a URL has been used as part of a redirect, or coded into other systems.

The first option is to enable the invoker servlet. This is as simple as removing the comments from around the servlet-mapping element. This is not a generally recommended approach because it exposes the security risk that was closed by removing the invoker servlet in the first place. This may be suitable in a very small number of trusted and well defined situations.

The second option is to define the servlet mappings that would act as if the invoker servlet existed. This is a simple case of defining the servlets with a unique name and then a servlet mapping to map the name to the URL that the invoker servlet would have used.

This is best illustrated by a simple example. In the example there are 2 servlets that have the following classes.

```
bible.tomcat.hello.HelloWorld
bible.tomcat.hello.HelloCity
```

These could be accessed via the invoker servlet using the following URLs.

```
http://localhost/hello/servlet/bible.tomcat.hello.HelloWorld
http://localhost/hello/servlet/bible.tomcat.hello.HelloCity
```

With the invoker servlet disabled, create the entries shown in Listing 4-1 in the `web.xml` of the Web application to provide the same results for requests directed at the URLs.

Listing 4-1: **Disabled Invoker Servlet Mappings**

```
<servlet>
  <servlet-name>HelloWorld</servlet-name>
  <servlet-class>
      bible.tomcat.hello.HelloWorld
  </servlet-class>
</servlet>

<servlet>
  <servlet-name>HelloCity</servlet-name>
  <servlet-class>
      bible.tomcat.hello.HelloCity
  </servlet-class>
</servlet>

<servlet-mapping>
  <servlet-name>HelloWorld</servlet-name>
  <url-pattern>
    /servlet/bible.tomcat.hello.HelloWorld/*
  </url-pattern>
</servlet-mapping>

<servlet-mapping>
  <servlet-name>HelloCity</servlet-name>
  <url-pattern>
```

```
      /servlet/bible.tomcat.hello.HelloCity/*
    </url-pattern>
  </servlet-mapping>
```

The invoker servlet can be configured via the following `init-param` elements:

✦ last:debug; set the debugging level, default of zero (0).

JSP Servlet

```
<servlet>
    <servlet-name>jsp</servlet-name>
    <servlet-class>org.apache.jasper.servlet.JspServlet</servlet-class>
    <init-param>
        <param-name>logVerbosityLevel</param-name>
        <param-value>WARNING</param-value>
    </init-param>
    <load-on-startup>3</load-on-startup>
</servlet>

<!-- The mapping for the JSP servlet -->
<servlet-mapping>
    <servlet-name>jsp</servlet-name>
    <url-pattern>*.jsp</url-pattern>
</servlet-mapping>
```

The JSP servlet is responsible for handling the support for Java Server Pages within the Tomcat server. By convention the mapping of the servlet is generally to `*.jsp`, however for Web application or deployment-specific reasons this may be modified.

The Tomcat 4.1.X releases use a newly developed JSP compiler called Jasper that does the translation of the JSP files and uses the Ant build tool for the compilation of the generated Java files to classes.

The JSP servlet can be configured via the following `init-param` elements:

✦ `checkInterval`. Set the number of seconds between checks to see if a JSP page needs to be recompiled, default of 300. The `checkInterval` parameter is modified by the development parameter and the reloading parameter.

✦ `classpath`. Set the `classpath` to be used when compiling the servlets created by the JSP translation process. The default is automatically generated based on the current Web application.

✦ `compiler`. Set which compiler Ant will use to compile JSP pages, default is `javac`.

✦ `classdebuginfo`. Determines if the classes will be compiled with debugging, default is true.

✦ `development`. Determines if the Jasper compiler will be used in development mode and check JSP files for modifications on every access, default is true. This parameter should be set to false in a deployment environment due to the additional overhead that is incurred by the checking.

✦ `enablePooling`. Determines if the Tag handler poling is enabled, default is true.

✦ ieClassId. Set the class-id value to be sent to IE when the jsp:plugin tag is used in a JSP. This is implemented as a parameter so that should Microsoft change the identifier, updating any Web application is a trivial exercise.

✦ javaEncoding. Set the encoding to be used when generating the Java source code for the JSP servlets, default is UTF8.

✦ keepgenerated. Determines if the generated Java source code is to be saved, or deleted when the class files have been created, default is true.

✦ largefile. Determines if the HTML from the JSP files should be stored as a separate file from the generated Java code, default is false. Setting largefile to true reduces the size of generated servlets.

✦ logVerbosityLevel. Set the detail of messages to be produced by the JSP servlet when processing requests, default is WARNING. Valid values are FATAL, ERROR, WARNING, INFORMATION, and DEBUG.

✦ mappedfile. Determines if the Java code for the servlet should be generated so that each HTML line in the JSP file is a separate print statement, default is false. Setting mappedfile to true can be used to aid in debugging of JSP files.

✦ reloading. Determines if the JSP servlet should check for modifications to the JSP files for recompilations, default is true. Setting reloading to false may be appropriate in a deployment environment to reduce processing overheads.

✦ scratchdir. Set the working directory to be used when translating and compiling the JSP pages, default is the work directory for the current Web application.

SSI Servlet

```
<servlet>
    <servlet-name>ssi</servlet-name>
    <servlet-class>
      org.apache.catalina.ssi.SSIServlet
    </servlet-class>
    <init-param>
      <param-name>buffered</param-name>
      <param-value>1</param-value>
    </init-param>
    <init-param>
      <param-name>debug</param-name>
      <param-value>0</param-value>
    </init-param>
    <init-param>
      <param-name>expires</param-name>
      <param-value>666</param-value>
    </init-param>
    <init-param>
      <param-name>isVirtualWebappRelative</param-name>
      <param-value>0</param-value>
    </init-param>
    <load-on-startup>4</load-on-startup>
</servlet>
```

```
<!-- The mapping for the SSI servlet -->
<servlet-mapping>
    <servlet-name>ssi</servlet-name>
    <url-pattern>*.shtml</url-pattern>
</servlet-mapping>
```

The SSI servlet provides Server Side Include functionality similar to the Apache HTTP Server processing of directives in HTML pages. This servlet is disabled by default and if required to be enabled, the JAR file in `server/lib` that provides the functionality must be renamed from `servlets-ssi.renametojar` to `servlets-ssi.jar`.

The functionality provided by the SSI servlet may be a convenient alternative to installing the Apache HTTP Server to provide this support for existing applications or during a migration from an existing SSI/CGI environment to a Java Web application.

Caution When processing the parameters the SSI servlet uses `'0'` for false and `'1'` for true as the parameter values rather than `'false'` or `'true'`.

The SSI servlet can be configured via the following `init-param` elements:

✦ `buffered`. Determines if the output from the servlet should be buffered, default is 0 (false).

✦ `debug`. Sets the debugging level, default of zero (0).

✦ `expires`. Sets the number of seconds before a page generated from the SSI directives through the SSI servlet will expire. There is no default value.

✦ `isVirtualWebappRelative`. Determines if virtual paths in the pages are interpreted as relative to the Web application context root or the Tomcat server root. The default is 0 (false).

CGI Servlet

```
<servlet>
    <servlet-name>cgi</servlet-name>
    <servlet-class>
      org.apache.catalina.servlets.CGIServlet
    </servlet-class>
    <init-param>
      <param-name>clientInputTimeout</param-name>
      <param-value>100</param-value>
    </init-param>
    <init-param>
      <param-name>debug</param-name>
      <param-value>6</param-value>
    </init-param>
    <init-param>
      <param-name>cgiPathPrefix</param-name>
      <param-value>WEB-INF/cgi</param-value>
    </init-param>
     <load-on-startup>5</load-on-startup>
</servlet>
```

```
<!-- The mapping for the CGI Gateway servlet -->
<servlet-mapping>
    <servlet-name>cgi</servlet-name>
    <url-pattern>/cgi-bin/*</url-pattern>
</servlet-mapping>
```

The CGI servlet supports execution of applications that conform to the Common Gateway Interface (CGI) specification.

This servlet is disabled by default and if required to be enabled, the JAR file in `server/lib` that provides the functionality must be renamed from `servlets-cgi.renametojar` to `servlets-cgi.jar`.

The functionality provided by the CGI servlet may be a convenient alternative to installing the Apache HTTP server to provide this support for existing applications or during a migration from an existing SSI/CGI environment to a Java Web application.

The CGI servlet can be configured via the following `init-param` elements:

- ✦ `cgiPathPrefix`. Set the search path for the CGI executable, default is `WEB-INF/cgi`. Setting `cgiPathPrefix` results in a search path of

  ```
  {web app root dir} + File.separator + cgiPathPrefix
  ```

- ✦ `clientInputTimeout`. Set the timeout in milliseconds to wait for input from a client, default is 100.

- ✦ `debug`. Set the debugging level, default of zero (0).

Default session-timeout

```
<session-config>
    <session-timeout>30</session-timeout>
</session-config>
```

The default `sessiontimeout` sets the idle timeout in minutes for any sessions in the Web application. Setting the `session-timeout` to 0 or less means that sessions do not expire due to timeout.

This value may be modified in an individual session by the use of the `Session.setMax InactiveInterval(int seconds)` method.

Mimetype Mappings

```
<mime-mapping>
    <extension>au</extension>
    <mime-type>audio/basic</mime-type>
</mime-mapping>
<mime-mapping>
    <extension>bin</extension>
    <mime-type>application/octet-stream</mime-type>
</mime-mapping>
<mime-mapping>
    <extension>bmp</extension>
    <mime-type>image/bmp</mime-type>
</mime-mapping>
    <extension>htm</extension>
    <mime-type>text/html</mime-type>
</mime-mapping>
```

```
<mime-mapping>
    <extension>html</extension>
    <mime-type>text/html</mime-type>
</mime-mapping>
<mime-mapping>
    <extension>xml</extension>
    <mime-type>text/xml</mime-type>
</mime-mapping>
```

The MIME mapping elements are used to generate Content-Type headers based on the resource extension from the request.

The preceding list is a very small subset of the over 120 mappings provided in the default `web.xml`. Additional MIME types can be added either in the default `web.xml` or in an individual Web application as required.

Default welcome Welcome Files

```
<welcome-file-list>
    <welcome-file>index.html</welcome-file>
    <welcome-file>index.htm</welcome-file>
    <welcome-file>index.jsp</welcome-file>
</welcome-file-list>
```

The common default welcome files are provided in the `web.xml` and are generally sufficient for most Web applications. The welcome file list is used when a request URL refers to a directory. The default servlet searches through the welcome file list to find a matching file in the directory to be served.

If the default servlet cannot find a matching welcome file, then a directory listing or a 404 status error is returned to the client depending on the configuration of the default servlet with regards to directory listings.

Caution If a Web application defines a `welcome-file-list` in the Web application deployment descriptor, this replaces the default `welcome-file-list`. Any of the default values above that are to be used by such a Web application need to exist in the deployment descriptor for the Web application.

Packaging the Web Application

As part of the development and deployment cycles of a Web application the mechanism for creating and installing the Web application has many options.

Shown previously, the Web application can be installed as a WAR file, an unpacked WAR file in a directory structure, using a context fragment, or even editing the server configuration file. These files and directories can exist under the directory structure of Tomcat, or can be located separately if that is more convenient.

In Chapter 7 and Chapter 10 many of these options are shown, and the focus is on the options that provide the most convenient development environment to maximize the productivity of the development of the Web applications. This is an important consideration because the development cycle occurs many times in rapid succession; however the deployment cycle is generally a single event.

Chapter 8 provides information about how to configure Tomcat using `server.xml`.

During development, the packaging of the WAR should be done in such a way as to minimize the effort on behalf of the developer for each cycle and change that occurs. This normally results in the following installation and configuration changes.

- ✦ Install using a context fragment with the Web application root as part of the development environment directory structure.
- ✦ The context fragment will be used for the majority of changes to the Tomcat configuration to modularize the changes to configuration of the Tomcat server in circumstances where many developers may be using the same server.
- ✦ Compilation of class files will be directly into the development directory structure minimizing manual copying.
- ✦ Tomcat and Web application configuration include the setting of options to immediately recognize modified class files and JSP files.

During deployment the packaging of the WAR should be done in such a way as to modularize the deployment package to minimize the likelihood of unforeseen changes or reliance on external behavior. This normally results in the following installation and configuration changes.

- ✦ Install using a specific entry in the Tomcat configuration file `server.xml`.
- ✦ Install the Web application as a packaged WAR file.
- ✦ Tomcat and Web application configuration include the setting of options to not recognize changes to the Web application unless the context is reloaded.
- ✦ JSP files are precompiled and deployed as servlets with appropriate servlet mapping in the deployment descriptor to avoid potential delays with JSP compilation and the reliance on a build environment on the server.

Summary

This chapter has provided an insight into the decision making process required for developing Web applications with Tomcat. The chapter has covered the general installation environment of Tomcat and how those directories and resources are used by Tomcat during execution.

An important area covered has been how Tomcat loads classes for a Web application. This topic is one of the most confusing areas for beginners when developing a Web application and a thorough understanding of how to package classes and libraries can make the development and deployment of Web applications a very simple task.

The chapter also has covered the default configuration of Tomcat for a Web application. The features in the way of default servlet mappings for the default and invoker servlets are commonly misunderstood functionality and the configuration of these servlets can provide benefits to a Web application developer.

Finally, some brief coverage was provided of the differences between development and deployment of a Web application. This topic is discussed in much greater depth in Chapter 7, where a simple Web application is developed.

✦ ✦ ✦

Compiling and Deploying Using Ant

In This Chapter

What is Ant?

A development environment for Ant and Tomcat

Using Ant with Tomcat

Ant is a comprehensive, flexible, and extensible Java-based build tool. Ant is a tool that covers the same area of development process as the Unix `make` tool, however the philosophy of the implementation is somewhat different. Because Ant is Java based it is cross platform and ideal for use in Java software development, which also can be cross platform.

To perform the operations the execution of Ant is controlled by a build file. The build file is an XML formatted file consisting of elements that represent properties, tasks, and targets that can be used to configure, compile, or even copy resources.

The purpose of this chapter is to provide familiarity with the Ant build tool so that it can be used with Tomcat and to give a solid foundation that can be built on if desired. To fully describe the multitude of features and options that are available in Ant would take an entire book!

The build environment required for Tomcat and the default build files provided in the Tomcat installation are simple enough to be explained without having to cover detailed explanations of advanced Ant functionality.

We hope that this introduction will provide motivation to explore Ant further and utilize some of these features in your development environments.

This chapter covers the history of Ant introduces the concepts and features that make up the language.

It also covers the setup of a development environment for using Ant, how to create a new project for a Web application, the use of the Tomcat-specific build commands, and how to extend the Ant tasks to perform new functionality.

Finally, the chapter examines some uses of Ant for packaging Web applications including pre-compilation of JSP pages.

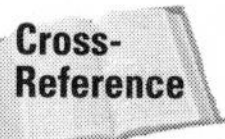

The examples in this chapter require the installation of Ant and Tomcat before proceeding. The details on the installation of Ant and Tomcat are in Chapter 2.

This chapter focuses on the use of Ant with Tomcat as a Java developer and provides the information required to modify the standard Tomcat build files, create simple build files, and understand how to fix any failures that may occur.

The History of Ant

Ant and Tomcat have a very close relationship, because Ant was originally developed to build Tomcat. That was its only purpose. The author of Ant, James Duncan Davidson, is also the original author of Tomcat and when Tomcat was donated to the Apache Software Foundation, so was Ant.

Many of the Jakarta projects recognized the value of a Java-based build tool for integration into the development environments because it solved problems associated with using the Unix `make` in that environment.

Ant was incorporated into a number of Jakarta projects and soon the reputation of the tool spread. As a result of its fame, Ant was moved out of the Tomcat source code repository and into one of its own. At that point in time the product was named Apache Ant, gaining independent status within the Jakarta projects.

With the release of Tomcat 3.1 in April 2000 a version of Ant was released for the first time to a wide audience in July 2000, closely following the first official release of Ant, version 1.1.

Functionality in Ant is implemented as elements known as tasks. Ant has been steadily increasing in functionality and with the addition of more and more third-party tasks Ant is a comprehensive framework for building Java projects from J2ME all the way through to J2EE.

Ant provides a solid basis for the controlled extension of functionality to suit individual environments. Tomcat is one such environment that not only has tasks for compilation of Java classes, but for creating WAR files and then finally deployment of the Web applications to Tomcat using an interface into the manager application.

Ant version 1.4 and above supports the Tomcat tasks that interface with the manager application described in this chapter.

Ant Philosophy

Many of the original development build tools originated in the Unix environment, and hence have a relatively Unix-centric view of development activities. Not only that, but the tools were constructed for compilers of the Fortran and C languages that do not support many of the Java compiler features such as automatic loading of referenced classes and packages.

This behavior led to much frustration using `make`-like tools for Java development because `javac` is ideally suited to compiling all the classes for an application in one invocation, as opposed to compiling each of the Java files to class files as a separate process.

Another important feature of Ant is that extensions to the base functionality of Ant are done via Java classes, and not via an external scripting interface to the operating system. This decision gives Ant cross-platform capabilities; however there are facilities within Ant to identify the underlying operating system, make decisions based on that operating system, and even run native operating system-specific commands.

To create an extension for Ant, it is simply a matter of creating a Java task that extends the `org.apache.tools.ant.Task` class. Ant provides an extensive array of tasks for performing common activities and the need to create new tasks is drastically lessening.

To operate successfully, Ant requires the Java source files to be arranged in their package hierarchy, and to have the classes compiled into a similar hierarchy. These may overlap, but it is not a recommended practice, and certainly all the default Tomcat build files provide a separate directory (`build`) that the class files are compiled into. Ant then checks the timestamps on the source Java file against the destination class file, and if the Java file is newer, it recompiles the class file; otherwise that source file is skipped.

Not following the recommended hierarchy causes Ant to recompile the source file each time as the source and destination files do match correctly. This is generally nothing more than a nuisance, but can cause development time to increase dramatically if classes are being recompiled when not required.

Finally, Ant is built on three fundamental core elements:

- ✦ Property
- ✦ Target
- ✦ Task

The `property` element is the Ant equivalent of variables. Properties have a name and a value and some examples are as follows:

```
<property name="src" location="src"/>
<property name="app.name" value="helloworld">
<property name="app.jar" value="${app.name}.jar"/>
<property environment="env" />
```

The `target` element is a flow control mechanism and the manner in which different activities can be grouped and then executed. A target generally contains tasks to be executed. Targets may also depend on other targets, in which case a chain of targets may be invoked by specifying an individual target. Some examples of targets are as follows:

```
<target name="jar" depends="compile" >
<target name="dist" depends="compile,javadoc" >
```

The final core element is the task. Tasks are the units of functionality that are provided by Ant and by third-parties. They can even be implemented as part of a local installation if required. The significant difference between properties and targets and the task is that the task element uses the name of the task being performed rather than using a name attribute. Some examples of tasks follow:

```
<javac srcdir="${src}" destdir="${build}/WEB-INF/classes" />
<copy file="${app.jar}" todir="${webapps}"/>
```

The properties, tasks, and targets used in the Tomcat build file are described in more detail later in the chapter.

Using Ant

Ant is a very simple tool to run, provided the installation and configuration was successful. Ant is installed with convenience scripts for both Windows and Unix to easily invoke the Java classes.

Note: To use Ant it must have been installed as described in Chapter 2. If Ant is not installed and will be used for development then follow the instructions in Chapter 2 before continuing this chapter.

One of the main reasons that Ant may not work correctly is due to the `ANT_HOME` environment variable being set correctly. This should be one of the first configuration items to check if Ant fails.

Running Ant is performed by entering the following command:

```
ant
```

Pretty simple!

Ant starts, looks in the current directory for a build file named `build.xml`, and run the default target. Of course, Ant is capable of dealing with various options including debugging and choosing the targets to be executed.

Note: The Ant installation comes with extensive documentation about all aspects of using and extending Ant. This documentation can be found in the `docs` directory of the Ant installation.

The Ant Command Line Options

The Ant `build` command is described as follows:

```
ant [options] [target [target2 [target3] . . . .]]
```

Ant has many command line options. The most commonly used are:

✦ `-help`

✦ `-projecthelp`

✦ `-D<property>=<value>`

✦ `-verbose (also -v)`

✦ `-debug`

✦ `-logfile<file> (also -l)`

The `help` option lists all the command line options. This is useful when exploring new options for Ant, or when a new version of Ant is released to see what additional functionality has been included.

The `projecthelp` option provides a list of the targets defined in the build file, and displays the description information associated with each target. This is useful to determine what target should be executed to perform a particular action. The results of using `ant -projecthelp` on the HelloWorld Tomcat `build.xml` used in Chapter 7 is as follows:

```
Buildfile: build.xml
Main targets:

 all       Clean build and dist directories, then compile
 clean     Delete old build and dist directories
 compile   Compile Java sources
 context   Install to container using context.xml
```

```
    deploy    Deploy web application
    dist      Create binary distribution
    install   Install application to servlet container
    javadoc   Create Javadoc API documentation
    list      List installed applications on servlet container
    reload    Reload application on servlet container
    remove    Remove application on servlet container
    undeploy  Undeploy web application

Default target: compile
```

The D option defines a property to be used in the build execution. This property can be used in the same manner as a property defined directly in the build file. An example of using this option is:

```
ant -Dapp.release=V1.0 dist
```

This is the equivalent as having the following in the build.xml.

```
<property name="app.release" value="V1.0" />
```

The verbose and debug options provide additional output on the execution of the build. The debug option produces a very large amount of output, even for a very simple application.

Note Using debug with the HelloWorld build file produces over 300 lines of output to execute the compile target, so be prepared to look through a lot of information if you need to use the debug option.

Finally, the logfile option provides a mechanism for directing the output from the execution of the build to a file. This option is very useful when combined with the verbose or debug options to save the debugging information to a file to be examined or searched in a more convenient manner.

The targets (target, target2, target3, and so on) are an optional list of targets to be executed. If more than one target is defined on the command line, the targets are executed sequentially within a single instance of Ant. A common example of this follows.

```
ant compile jar dist
```

This command is the same as performing three separate ant commands:

```
ant compile
ant jar
ant dist
```

The advantage of using the first approach is that it avoids the overhead of starting the JVM and evaluating the property elements for each run and as a result is significantly faster.

Ant Build Scripts

The Ant build scripts by default are stored in a file named build.xml. This file must contain a project element and at least one target. Listing 5-1 contains the simple Ant build file created in Chapter 2.

Listing 5-1: Simple build.xml

```
<project name="test-ant" default="init" basedir=".">
    <property environment="env" />
    <target name="init">
        <echo message="Checking environment" />
        <echo message="JAVA_HOME  = ${env.JAVA_HOME}" />
        <echo message="ANT_HOME   = ${env.ANT_HOME}" />
    </target>
</project>
```

As shown in Listing 5-1 the project element is the root element and contains all the other elements of the build file. Property elements exist within the project element and are resolved at run time to determine their values. There is only one property in Figure 5-1 and that is a special type of property that loads the environment into many individual properties prefixed with the name of the environment attribute.

These properties can be then used in other properties, or in this case as part of a task. The second echo task is evaluating the `env.JAVA_HOME` property, which contains the value of the `JAVA_HOME` environment variable.

Target elements contain the addressable items within the build file, and contain tasks. In Figure 5-1 there is only target named `init`. This target contains three echo tasks. The echo task prints the value of the message attribute to the standard output stream.

The result of executing the command `ant` is as follows:

```
Buildfile: build.xml

init:
     [echo] Checking environment
     [echo] JAVA_HOME  = c:\jdk1.3.1
     [echo] ANT_HOME   = c:\ant

BUILD SUCCESSFUL
Total time: 2 seconds
```

With only one target this build file isn't very useful, but it does provide a useful way of showing what happens when Ant is called with a target that doesn't exist.

The command:

```
ant hello
```

produces the following output:

```
Buildfile: build.xml

BUILD FAILED
Target `hello' does not exist in this project.

Total time: 2 seconds
```

Tip

When this error message is displayed, use the projecthelp option to list all the available targets in the build file. This error is normally caused by a spelling mistake in the target in build.xml or on the command line.

Project

The project element is the root element of the build file and contains all the other elements.

A project has three attributes:

- name (optional)
- default (required)
- basedir (optional)

The name attribute is the name of the project.

The default attribute defines the target to be used when no target is supplied to the ant command.

The basedir attribute defines the base directory for all relative path calculations.

A project contains one or more targets. One of the targets has a name attribute with the value that matches the value of the default attribute.

The project may also contain a description element. This element contains information that is displayed when the projecthelp option is used.

An example of the project element follows:

```
<project name="test-ant" default="init" basedir=".">
    <description>
        This is the ant install test build file
    </description>
    <target name="init">
        <echo message="JAVA_HOME  = ${env.JAVA_HOME}" />
    </target>
</project>
```

Property

A property defines a single variable, or a group of variables to be used in the build execution. The property can be set in the build file using the property element, or set on the command line using the -D option.

A property element exists in two forms. The first has two attributes:

- name (required)
- value or location (required)

The name attribute represents the name of the property. This attribute is used when referencing the value of the property.

The value or location attribute contains the value of the property set.

Tip

Use the location specification for properties that contain path names, like to a JAR file or a directory. Ant is smart enough to be able to convert the file separators (like a slash "/") to the right type for the operating system.

The second only has one attribute:

- `environment` (required)
- `file` (required)

The `environment` and `file` versions of the property task create a number of properties. Using the `environment` variant all the environment variables are converted into properties and prepended with the argument to the attribute as shown in the preceding example build file.

Using the `file` variant, the value of the `file` attribute is expected to identify a file that can be loaded using `java.util.Properties.load()`. The property element using the `file` attribute is very useful for defining system specific configuration (such as root directories for build or installation) and these files can be created so that a single build file can operate unchanged in multiple environments.

There are a number of predefined properties that can be used in the build files. These properties come from two sources, the first being the `System` properties set by the JVM:

- `file.separator`
- `java.class.path`
- `java.class.version`
- `java.ext.dirs`
- `java.home`
- `java.specification.name`
- `java.specification.vendor`
- `java.specification.version`
- `java.vm.specification.name`
- `java.vm.specification.vendor`
- `java.vm.specification.version`
- `java.vm.name`
- `java.vm.vendor`
- `java.vm.version`
- `line.separator`
- `os.arch`
- `os.name`
- `os.version`
- `path.separator`
- `user.dir`

- `user.home`
- `user.name`

The second source for the predefined properties is Ant, and these properties are:

- `ant.file`
- `ant.java.version`
- `ant.project.name`
- `ant.version`
- `basedir`

This is a lot of properties, and in general use many are rarely used, however the `user.home` and `basedir` attributes are frequently utilized in build scripts and the `os.name` property can be very useful when working with tasks that can perform operating system specific activities (such as the `exec` task).

Using a property is done by generating a reference to the property. A property is referenced by enclosing the value of the name attribute in `"${" and "}"`. An example of using a property is:

```
<echo message="The user home directory is: ${user.home}" />
```

Examples of the property element are:

```
<project name="test-ant" default="init" basedir=".">
    <property file="${user.home}/my_properties" />
    <property environment="env" />

    <property name="dist" location="${install.root}/dist" />
    <property name="src" location="${basedir}/src" />

    <property name="app.version" value="1.0" />
    <property name="app.name" value="myapp" />
    <property name="app.jar" value="${myapp}.jar" />

    <target name="init">
        <echo message="JAVA_HOME  = ${env.JAVA_HOME}" />
    </target>
</project>
```

The file `my_properties` may have the following format and contents:

```
install.root=c:\root
manager.username=ant-install
manager.password=ant-install
manager.url=http://localhost:8080/manager
```

Paths and Files

In addition to the `property` element Ant provides elements for describing a collection of paths and files. These elements are used for the generating the Java `classpath`, identifying the set of directories that are compiled using Javac or the set of files for use in copying.

These structures are superior to explicitly defining a property that would contain the same information because they provide means of re-using sub-elements and pattern matching. The pattern matching provides a compelling alternative to long-winded static definitions, which are frequently error-prone and resistant to changes in a single environment and require constant modification when transporting to multiple environments.

It is important to remember that the `CLASSPATH` for compiling classes used in a Web application must reference many of the Tomcat provided JAR files as well as class file directories. Any means of automating the generation of the `classpath` results in a far more robust development environment.

There are many types of path elements, however one of the best examples is the compilation classpath `path` element from the default Tomcat `build.xml`. This element is shown in Listing 5-2:

Listing 5-2: Example <path> element

```
<path id="compile.classpath">
    <pathelement location="${myjar.jar}"/>
    <pathelement location="${catalina.home}/common/classes"/>
    <fileset dir="${catalina.home}/common/endorsed">
        <include name="*.jar"/>
    </fileset>
    <fileset dir="${catalina.home}/common/lib">
        <include name="*.jar"/>
    </fileset>
    <pathelement location="${catalina.home}/shared/classes"/>
    <fileset dir="${catalina.home}/shared/lib">
        <include name="*.jar"/>
    </fileset>
</path>
```

The `id` attribute defines a name for the `path` element. This allows the path to be used in the javac task as follows:

```
<javac srcdir="${src.home}"
    destdir="${build.home}/WEB-INF/classes"
    debug="${compile.debug}"
    deprecation="${compile.deprecation}"
    optimize="${compile.optimize}">
    <classpath refid="compile.classpath"/>
</javac>
```

The `pathelement` elements define a single file or directory that is to be included in the path.

The `fileset` element is used to create a group of files. The `dir` attribute defines the root directory and the `include` elements define the files to be added to the `fileset`. As shown in Figure 5-2 these can be specified as regular expressions.

Note

There is also an `exclude` element that can be used to prevent the addition of the named files to the `fileset`.

If there are no `include` elements in the `fileset` then all files under the root directory are added.

Target

The target element is used as an addressable element that contains tasks to be executed. Targets may depend on other targets, and what this means is that prior to a target activating the targets listed in the depends attribute are evaluated for activation. As the depends attribute may contain a list of other targets, this process can get quite complicated.

Tip To see the Ant target dependency checking and evaluating in action, use the `ant -verbose dist` command in the HelloWorld example in Chapter 7. Near the top of the output is a line that starts with "Complete build sequence." Notice how many targets are evaluated, just from the single target specified on the command line.

A target has the following attributes:

- `depends` (optional)
- `description` (optional)
- `if` (optional)
- `name` (required)
- `unless` (optional)

The `depends` attribute is a comma separated list of targets that are evaluated for activation. The order of the list is significant because the activation occurs from left to right. Targets may depend on some targets which in turn depend on others. This may cause the situation where a target is listed multiple times.

Note A target is only evaluated once regardless of how many times it is listed in a `depends` attribute.

Targets dependencies may never create a loop. This causes a Circular Dependency error when running the build script, and the build script will need to be corrected before any further work can be done.

Tip While this sounds very ominous the standard Tomcat build file works correctly, and the minor changes that are needed to customize it for the projects in the book are all very simple and straightforward.

An example of using the depends attribute is that the "jar" target will depend on the "compile" target. So, if the command `ant jar` is issued from the command line, then the "compile" target is evaluated and possibly activated before the "jar" target.

Note A target may be evaluated and not activated (or executed) due to the presence of the `if` and `unless` attributes in the target element.

The `description` attribute is used by the `projecthelp` option.

The `if` attribute controls the execution of the target depending on the value of the attribute. The value of the `if` attribute is the name of a property, and if this named property is set then the target executes.

Caution The value of the `if` attribute is the name of a property and not a reference to the property. That is, the property name is not enclosed in `"${" and "}"`.

The `name` attribute defines the addressable name of the target. This value is used on the command line to execute the target, in the `default` attribute in the property task and in the `depends` attribute of targets. The name may be any string that is valid in the encoding of the XML file, however it is recommended not to use a blank string as the name or a space or commas in the name because these are likely to be removed as valid in later versions of Ant.

Tip If the name of the target starts with a hyphen '-', then the target cannot be called from the command line because the Ant option processor will reject it as an unknown option or process the option rather than the target. This provides a useful mechanism to create private targets in the build file that are not exposed externally.

The `unless` attribute is the logical opposite of the `if` attribute. The `unless` attribute prevents a target from executing if the property named in the attribute is set.

Examples of the target element are:

```
<project name="test-ant" default="init" basedir=".">
    <property name="test.execute" value="anything" />

    <target name="init">
        <echo message="JAVA_HOME  = ${env.JAVA_HOME}" />
    </target>

    <target name="compile" depends="init">
    . . . .
    </target>

    <target name="test" if="test.execute" >
    . . . .
    </target>
</project>
```

Task

The `task` element is the core to the flexibility and power of Ant. A task describes an activity that is to be performed. This could be a Java compilation, creating a JAR file, copying files, or even performing substitution on tokens in a file.

Each task has its own attributes and these vary widely depending on the task. The general structure for a task is as follows:

```
<name attr1="value1" attr2="value2" . . . . />
```

Basic Tasks

The tasks that are used for any particular development vary widely depending on the project and the nature of the development environment.

In general, the most likely tasks that are used during development are:

- `copy`
- `delete`
- `echo`
- `jar`
- `java`
- `javac`
- `javadoc`
- `mkdir`

This very small list is insignificant when compared to the extensive list of tasks that are available in the Ant Core Tasks, the Ant Optional Tasks, and the many third-party extensions, however most Java projects could be built and managed by only using this small subset.

Some of the examples used in this section are taken directly from the default Tomcat `build.xml`.

copy

The `copy` task is used to copy files and directories. The source files can be specified using a `fileset` element and are normally copied only if they are newer than the destination files, or the destination files do not exist.

Some examples of the copy task are as follows:

Copy a file to a directory

```
<copy file="${app.jar}" todir="${catalina.base}/webapps"/>
```

Copy a set of files to a directory

```
<copy  todir="${build.home}/WEB-INF/classes">
    <fileset dir="${src.home}" excludes="**/*.java"/>
</copy>
```

Note: The `excludes` attribute provides the same functionality as a single `exclude` element.

delete

The `delete` task is used to delete files and directories. When deleting directories subdirectories are also deleted. The delete task can also use a `fileset` to specify particular files to be deleted or retained.

An example of a use of the `delete` task follows:

```
<target name="clean"
    description="Delete old build and dist directories">
    <delete dir="${build.home}"/>
    <delete dir="${dist.home}"/>
</target>
```

jar

The jar task is used to create JAR files. The jar task can also create WAR files provided the basedir attribute is referencing a directory structure that is consistent with the layout of an unpacked WAR file.

There is a war task that can be used to create WAR files if the directory structure is not appropriate. The default Tomcat build files create an appropriate directory structure and then simply use the jar task as follows.

```
<jar jarfile="${dist.home}/${app.name}.war"
     basedir="${build.home}"/>
```

java

The java task is used to execute a Java class either within the current Ant JVM or to start a separate JVM depending on the values of the fork attribute.

The java task is often used to execute arbitrary test classes as part of a build script, however, the optional jUnit task provides a more sophisticated and comprehensive alternative to writing custom test classes.

The java task can contain other elements, and the most common are the classpath element for the execution libraries and the arg element for options that are passed to the Java class.

The java task can be used as follows:

```
<target name="test.run" >
    <java classname="test.Main" fork="yes">
        <classpath>
            <pathelement path="${emulator.classpath}" />
        </classpath>
        <arg line="${app.count} -file ${app.config}" />
    </java>
</target>
```

javac

The javac task is used to compile Java source files into class files. Using this task is why most developers look at Ant in the first place. The javac task only compiles source files that are newer than their respective class files, or if the class files do not exist.

> **Caution**
>
> The heuristic that Ant uses to determine if a source file requires compilation is to check the timestamps of only the source and class file. The javac task does not scan for dependencies and so any classes that might rely on the modified class (for public static values for example) are not recompiled.
>
> There are two commons methods to resolve this. In circumstances where classes that are used by other classes are modified the simplest option is to delete all the class files and recompile. This guarantees that the dependencies are resolved correctly.
>
> The second option is to use the depend task. This task scans for dependencies in modified classes and removes those class files that are now out of date due to a dependency changing.
>
> The choice of method is entirely dependent on the complexity of the class hierarchy and the general project structure. In many cases it may be faster to clean out the compiled class files when circumstances warrant rather than have the depend task execute each time.

Like the `java` task the `javac` task may contain other elements to construct the `classpath` for compilation, the file or directory sets for the source files to compile, and attributes that can even control the version of the compiler to use.

Some examples of the `javac` task are as follows:

```
<javac srcdir="${src.home}"
    destdir="${build.home}/WEB-INF/classes"
    debug="${compile.debug}"
    deprecation="${compile.deprecation}"
    optimize="${compile.optimize}">
    <classpath refid="compile.classpath"/>
</javac>
```

and

```
<javac destdir="${master.classes}"
    bootclasspath="${midp.classes}"
    includeJavaRuntime="no"
    debug="off"
    optimize="off">
    <src path="${client.src}" />
    <src path="${server.src}" />
    <patternset refid="client.files" />
    <classpath refid = "compile.cp" />
 </javac>
```

The `java`, `javac`, and `javadoc` tasks provide convenient but fairly transparent facades to access the underlying Java SDK tools of the same name. The documentation on the Java SDK tools can be directly used because the attributes closely match the options passed to the SDK tools.

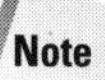

For those unfamiliar with command line environments, the Java SDK has a number of tools that are used for development and other activities. These tools cover the compilation of Java classes (`javac`), the execution of those classes (`java`), documentation generation for the classes (`javadoc`), a viewer for applets (`appletviewer`), a java archive creator (`jar`), a java debugger (`jdb`), and many others.

For more information about the tools provided, read the documentation provided at `http://java.sun.com/j2se/1.3/docs/tooldocs/tools.html`. This documentation is also available for download with the SDK.

javadoc

The `javadoc` task is used to generate documentation from the Java source files. The `javadoc` task requires that the Java source files have been commented according to the Sun Java Javadoc Doc Comments (`http://java.sun.com/j2se/javadoc/index.html`) as the `javadoc` task provides a collation of the files involved on the process and then passes these files and the options to the JDK javadoc tool.

Documentation on the use of the javadoc tool can be found at `http://java.sun.com/j2se/1.3/docs/tooldocs/javadoc/index.html`

The `javadoc` task is used as follows:

```
<target name="javadoc" depends="compile">
    <mkdir          dir="${dist.home}/docs/api"/>
    <javadoc sourcepath="${src.home}"
                destdir="${dist.home}/docs/api"
           packagenames="*">
        <classpath refid="compile.classpath"/>
    </javadoc>
  </target>
```

mkdir

The last of our basic tasks for Ant, `mkdir` is used to create directories. The `mkdir` task creates the specified directory as well as any parent directories that are required.

The `mkdir` task is used as follows:

```
<target name="compile" depends="prepare" >
    <mkdir    dir="${build.home}/WEB-INF/classes"/>
    <javac srcdir="${src.home}"
          destdir="${build.home}/WEB-INF/classes"
            debug="${compile.debug}"
      deprecation="${compile.deprecation}"
         optimize="${compile.optimize}">
        <classpath refid="compile.classpath"/>
    </javac>
    . . . .
</target>
```

With the introduction to Ant completed, the next section describes how to use Ant with Tomcat, including setting up a development environment and how to modify the build file for use with your application.

Ant and Tomcat

It is no surprise that Ant and Tomcat integrate very well given the origins of both products. To make the best use of Ant with Tomcat the development environment configuration follows the practices recommended by the Tomcat developers.

There are no issues if the standard practices do not fit into the development environment of your organization. Ant is very flexible and the environment recommended can be modified with very little effort.

This book follows the standard environment because it is the simplest path for most developers and provides a solid basis for enhancement to fit within alternative development environments.

Development Environment

The development environment is the compile, build, and test environment for a software product. It encompasses the tools, the physical hardware, and network infrastructure required to perform the development activities. This section describes how to set up the Ant build tool so that it can effectively be utilized in any environment.

For the purposes of simplicity it is required that the compiling and testing activities are performed on the same computer as the Tomcat installed in Chapter 2. Of course your environment may differ from this, but for consistency the following examples and setup require that the tools are installed as described in Chapter 2.

Don't panic if your environment is not the same, Ant is flexible enough to use environment variables and property configuration (such as the `JAVA_HOME` environment variable and `catalina.home Ant configuration property`) to allow for these minor variations. Just be aware that some of the instructions may have to be changed slightly to suit your particular environment.

Web Application Project

Using Ant with Tomcat requires the creation of some new files and the modification of the default Tomcat build files. This process only needs to occur once for all the Tomcat projects that you do, so when the changes are made, save them in a directory so they can be used later.

Creating Directories

The first step is to create the directory structure for the Web application development. The Tomcat recommended practice is to have the following directories in the project.

- `src`
- `docs`
- `web`

The `src` directory contains the Java source files for the application, the docs directory contains static documentation (if any), and the Web directory contains the static HTML, JSP, and other Web resources, including the `WEB-INF` directory and the associated `web.xml`.

So, create this structure using the following commands:

```
mkdir <project>
cd <project>
mkdir src
mkdir docs
mkdir web\WEB-INF
```

The `mkdir` command should create the required parent directories if they do not exist. For Unix users, `mkdir -p web/WEB-INF` should be the command to use.

Creating web.xml and build.xml

The next step in preparing a development environment for a Web application project is to create a `web.xml` file in the `web/WEB-INF` directory.

Without knowing more about the project, such as the servlets or any of the other Web components, the best that can be achieved is to create a template version. Listing 5-3 shows the initial version of the `web.xml`. The bold text represents information that needs to be changed when creating the file, or before the Web application is first used.

Listing 5-3: web.xml

```
<?xml version="1.0" encoding="ISO-8859-1" ?>

<!DOCTYPE web-app
  PUBLIC "-//Sun Microsystems, Inc.//DTD Web Application 2.3//EN"
  "http://java.sun.com/dtd/web-app_2_3.dtd" >

<web-app>
    <display-name>This is the display name</display-name>
    <description>
        This is a description of the application.
    </description>

    <servlet>
        <servlet-name>myservlet</servlet-name>
        <description>
            My Servlet
        </description>
        <servlet-class>
            com.mycompany.package.MyServlet
        </servlet-class>
    </servlet>

    <servlet-mapping>
        <servlet-name>myservlet</servlet-name>
        <url-pattern>/myservlet</url-pattern>
    </servlet-mapping>

</web-app>
```

To use Ant in the development process, copy the sample build file from the Tomcat installation.

```
copy c:\tomcat\webapps\tomcat-docs\appdev\build.xml.txt build.xml
```

Before looking at the configuration of `build.xml` for a particular Web application there are some minor modifications to integrate all of the Tomcat specific tasks and to add some tasks that will streamline development.

Adding Tomcat Tasks

The standard build file has the following tasks defined:

```
<taskdef name="install" classname="org.apache.catalina.ant.InstallTask"/>
<taskdef name="list"    classname="org.apache.catalina.ant.ListTask"/>
<taskdef name="reload"  classname="org.apache.catalina.ant.ReloadTask"/>
<taskdef name="remove"  classname="org.apache.catalina.ant.RemoveTask"/>
```

After the `remove` task definition add the lines shown in Listing 5-4:

Listing 5-4: deploy and undeploy targets

```
<taskdef name="deploy" classname="org.apache.catalina.ant.DeployTask"/>
<taskdef name="undeploy" classname="org.apache.catalina.ant.UndeployTask"/>

<target name="deploy" description="Deploy Web application">
    <deploy
        url="${manager.url}"
        username="${manager.username}"
        password="${manager.password}"
        path="${app.path}"
        war="file:///${dist.home}/${app.name}-${app.version}.war"/>
</target>

<target name="undeploy" description="Undeploy Web application">
    <undeploy
        url="${manager.url}"
        username="${manager.username}"
        password="${manager.password}"
        path="${app.path}"/>
</target>
```

Listing 5-4 defines the deployment related tasks `deploy` and `undeploy`.

The next step is to add a custom target that is related to the install target that will install a Web application and use a `context.xml` fragment for configuration.

Locate the install target (the target is near the middle of the build file) and add the following contents just after the target.

```
<target name="context" depends="compile"
    description="Install to container using context.xml">

    <install url="${manager.url}"
        username="${manager.username}"
        password="${manager.password}"
        path="${app.path}"
        config="file:///${build.home}/WEB-INF/context.xml"/>
</target>
```

This creates a new target called `context` that will be used extensively during development. To make use of this new target the file specified in the `config` attribute needs to contain an XML file.

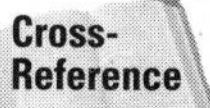

The details of the `context.xml` file is described in Chapter 8.

Create a file called `template.context.xml` using Listing 5-5 as the information in the root directory of the Web application. In this example it would be the `<project>` directory.

Listing 5-5: template.context.xml

```
<Context path="@context.path@" docBase="@context.docbase@"
    reloadable="true" debug="99" >
    <Loader checkInterval="1" />
    <Logger
        className="org.apache.catalina.logger.FileLogger"
        debug="99"
        prefix="@context.appname@_dbglog." suffix=".txt" />
</Context>
```

This context fragment template is designed for use with the build file to substitute in the values `context.path`, `context.docbase` and `context.appname` so this template can be used unchanged in many places if desired. The default configuration of the template context fragment is to have the Web application automatically reload classes and check for changes every second.

There also is a logger defined for use during development, however, it can be easily removed.

The next step in configuring the `build.xml` is to add support for the `template.context.xml`. The template needs to be copied into the `WEB-INF` directory where the class files are created and because this file should not change very much during development, the most appropriate place to add this functionality is in the `"prepare"` target.

Locate the `"prepare"` target in the `build.xml`. This target is near the end of the build file. Insert the XML as shown in Listing 5-6. The new lines are displayed in bold.

Listing 5-6: Modifying the Prepare Target

```
<target name="prepare">
    . . . .
    <!-- Copy static content of this Web application -->
    <copy todir="${build.home}">
        <fileset dir="${web.home}"/>
    </copy>

    <!-- Create a context file if needed -->
    <filter token="context.docbase" value="${build.home}" />
    <filter token="context.path" value="${app.path}" />
    <filter token="context.appname" value="${app.name}" />
    <copy todir="${build.home}/WEB-INF" filtering="true" >
        <fileset dir="${basedir}">
            <present present="srconly" targetdir="${basedir}">
                <mapper type="glob" from="template.*" to="*" />
            </present>
        </fileset>
        <mapper type="glob" from="template.*" to="*" />
    </copy>
```

```
    <!-- Copy external dependencies as required -->
    . . . .
</target>
```

At this stage the files that have been created and the modifications made to `build.xml` are ready for the Web application and environment-specific changes.

Caution

There is a defect in the standard Tomcat build.xml where the `dist` target has an error in a `mkdir` task. This is obvious the first time the `dist` target is executed during development.

To check to see if this defect still exists in the Tomcat build.xml that you are using look for a `mkdir` task with the `todir` attribute. This needs to be changed from:

```
<mkdir todir="${dist.home}/docs"/>
```

to:

```
<mkdir dir="${dist.home}/docs" />
```

The default state of the Tomcat `build.xml` needs to have a few additional properties defined to enable the configuration of the Tomcat installation and the Manager application. There are two ways to configure this; the first is to modify the `build.xml` file directly. This has the benefit of keeping the entire configuration in one file, but if the project will be developed in one environment, then tested in another, or there are multiple developers working on the project then each time a new environment is set up, the file must be changed to suit that particular environment.

This can be especially irritating when using a source code management system like CVS because the installation specific changed invariably find their way back into the source code repository and the next time a developer checks out the changed files, their development environment stops working!

So, the recommended approach is to remove the configuration that is specific to an instance of the development environment and put those configuration elements in a properties file.

The standard build file looks for properties in a file called `build.properties` in the current directory and in the users home directory.

Caution

The users home directory is very easy to find under Unix because it is the value of the `HOME` environment variable, however Windows seems to not be as consistent with the value of the `user.home` directory. The simplest way to find out where the `user.home` directory is located is to add a target that echoes the value of `user.home`. Place the `build.properties` file in that directory.

In Windows 2000 the value of `user.home` is `"c:\Documents and Settings\<username>"`.

The `build.xml` has some property definitions that need to be removed to keep all the environment configuration in the `build.properties` file. Edit `build.xml` to remove the properties lines shown in bold in Listing 5-7.

Listing 5-7: Property Definitions in build.xml

```
<property name="app.name"      value="myapp"/>
<property name="app.path"      value="/${app.name}"/>
<property name="app.version"   value="0.1-dev"/>
<property name="build.home"    value="${basedir}/build"/>
<property name="catalina.home" value="../../../.."/>
<property name="dist.home"     value="${basedir}/dist"/>
<property name="docs.home"     value="${basedir}/docs"/>
<property name="manager.url"   value="http://localhost:8080/manager"/>
<property name="src.home"      value="${basedir}/src"/>
<property name="web.home"      value="${basedir}/web"/>
```

This removes the `catalina.home` and `manager.url` properties. This group of property elements is located near the start of `build.xml`.

Now, create the file `build.properties` in the `user.home` directory with the following contents:

```
# the same as CATALINA_HOME
catalina.home=c:/tomcat

# the configuration for using the manager application
# with the Ant tasks
manager.url=http://localhost:8080/manager
manager.username=ant-install
manager.password=ant-install
```

The values here are specific to the installation and are the appropriate values for the environment configured in Chapter 2.

The Tomcat and environment-specific changes are now completed. These changes are a little time consuming, but only need to be done once so it's not going to make much of a difference to project schedule! The next section examines the changes required for each individual Web application.

The `build.xml` and `template.context.xml` files can be saved away for use in many Web applications. The modifications made in these sections are suitable for all Web applications, and not for a specific Web application. The Web application specific configuration is detailed in the next section.

Configuration for a Web Application Project

The setup of the files and the modifications in the previous section put the developer in a strong position to make minimal changes for each Web application that needs to be built.

To configure the development environment for a specific Web application there are only two activities to be considered. The first is to modify the `template.context.xml` for the Web application. This might be the addition of extra elements such as resources for using a database or additional logging or tracing facilities.

The second is to modify the configuration for the Web application, and this is a simple matter of changing the following elements:

1. Modify the project element attribute `name` to reflect the name of the application. This can be descriptive and the initial value of the element is set as:

```
<project name="My Project" default="compile" basedir=".">
```

2. Modify the `app.name` property to reflect the name of the application used in the Web application path and the `jar` file and the name of the log file in the `template.context.xml`. This should be short and the initial value of the element is set as:

```
<property name="app.name"      value="myapp"/>
```

Tip

The default Tomcat configuration uses a property `app.version` when constructing a WAR file so that each version of the WAR file reflects the version of the application.

If this behavior is not required, it is a simple matter of modifying the `"dist"` and `"deploy"` targets to remove the reference to `app.version` in the relevant attributes of the tasks.

Congratulations, that's all that is required to configure a development environment to use Ant and Tomcat together. It should be noted that this configuration is more sophisticated than the standard Tomcat build file, however we feel that the additional flexibility that is gained easily outweighs the minor increase in complexity.

Development

The changes to the build file have resulted in the availability of some additional targets. To identify what targets exist in the build file use the command:

```
ant -projecthelp
```

This should result in the following output:

```
Buildfile: build.xml
Main targets:

 all       Clean build and dist directories, then compile
 clean     Delete old build and dist directories
 compile   Compile Java sources
 context   Install to container using context.xml
 deploy    Deploy web application
 dist      Create binary distribution
 install   Install application to servlet container
 javadoc   Create Javadoc API documentation
 list      List installed applications on servlet container
 reload    Reload application on servlet container
 remove    Remove application on servlet container
 undeploy  Undeploy web application

Default target: compile
```

These targets are explained in more detail in this section, however, the development process is quite simple. Use the `compile` task to compile the Java sources and use the `context`, `deploy`, or `install` tasks to register the Web application with Tomcat. The deployment process is similarly easy; the `deploy` task automatically deploys the Web application and the `dist` target creates a WAR file to be used for an alternative deployment option.

Tomcat Targets

This section briefly describes the "public" targets available in the Web application build file. These targets create and delete directories in the project directory, so don't be too confused if these directories appear and disappear as various targets are executed.

The `build` directory is the target for the compiled Java classes. This directory also has the contents of the `web` directory copied into it (including the `WEB-INF` directory hierarchy). This creates an unpacked WAR structure with the `build` directory as the root.

The `dist` directory is created by the `dist` or `javadoc` targets and contains Java API documentation in a `docs` subdirectory and a Web application WAR file.

Caution The Tomcat targets and the Tomcat tasks are often called the same name, such as the `"install"` target and the `"install"` task. Pay careful attention in this next section because the description often uses both terms to describe the activities that are occurring.

all

The `all` target deletes the `build` and `dist` directories and then recompiles all the classes.

clean

The `clean` target deletes the `build` and `dist` directories.

compile

The `compile` target creates the `build` directory hierarchy, if it doesn't exist, in the same structure as an unpacked WAR file and then compile all the Java sources in the `src` directory into the `build/WEB-INF/classes` directory.

The compile target also copies any resources in the `src` directory into the `build/WEB-INF/classes` directory. Resources in this instance are any files that are not Java source files.

The `compile` target depends on the `prepare` target. The `prepare` target is not normally executed directly (and doesn't appear on the `projecthelp` list) and is responsible for copying the files in the `web` directory into the `build` directory as well as creating the `context.xml` file from the `template.context.xml`.

context

The `context` target is not part of the standard Tomcat build file, and was added in the previous section to aid in the development process.

The `context` target uses the Tomcat `install` task to install the `build` directory as a Web application using the `context.xml` stored in `build/WEB-INF/` for configuration of the Web application context.

The `install` task does not install Web applications that will survive restarts of Tomcat. If Tomcat is stopped for any reason, then all Web applications that have been installed using the `context` or `install` targets need to be installed again to be available.

If a Web application is already installed using `context`, `deploy` or `install`, then attempting to re-register the Web application results in an error. Also, if the Web application is configured in `server.xml`, then using the `context`, `deploy`, or `install` also results in an error.

Tomcat must be running to use this target because it uses the Tomcat manager application to perform the server configuration.

When in doubt as to the status of the Tomcat server, or the Web applications installed, then use the `list` target. If the `list` target fails, then the server is either not running or the manager application configuration in `build.properties` is incorrect.

If the `list` target succeeds, then the information returned provides an indication about the reason for the error.

deploy

The `deploy` target deploys a Web application to the Tomcat server. This task provides the only Tomcat management functionality that cannot be executed from the HTML interface.

The `deploy` task uses an HTTP PUT to deploy the Web application and actually copies the WAR file to the server. As a result,this target also can be used on remote Tomcat servers, unlike the `context` and `install` targets, which must always use a local server.

Note To deploy to a remote Tomcat server and still use the `install` task on a local server requires additional modifications to the `build.xml` to configure the URL of the remote server and the username and password of the remote manager user. The deploy target needs to be modified to successfully use these additional parameters.

Web applications that are installed using the deploy task are persistent and will survive the shutdown and restart of Tomcat.

Caution The deploy task rewrites the `server.xml` file when the Web application is installed to create a `Context` entry. This rewriting of the file causes any elements that are commented out to be lost, and the formatting of the server.xml is significantly modified as the default values of attributes are explicitly written to the `Context` elements.

If you modify the `server.xml` file using an editor and not the Tomcat Administration GUI, then using the `deploy` target is not recommended because it will make the manual editing of the file extremely difficult.

Tomcat must be running to use this target because it uses the Tomcat manager application to perform the server configuration.

dist

The `dist` target is used to create a distribution of the Web application. This target invokes the `javadoc` target to create the documentation, copies any static documentation in the `docs` directory, invokes the `compile` target, and creates a WAR file from the `build` directory structure.

The `install` target depends on the `compile` and `javadoc` targets.

install

The `install` target registers a Web application using the `build` directory as an unpacked WAR file. The install target depends on the compile target as the Web application needs to be built prior to registration with the Tomcat server.

Because the `install` target uses the `install` task the same restrictions apply as specified in the `context` target description.

Tomcat must be running to use this target because it uses the Tomcat manager application to perform the server configuration.

javadoc

The `javadoc` target creates the Java API documentation for the Web application. This target is normally invoked as part of the execution of the `dist` target, however it may be executed manually if required.

list

The `list` target displays the currently installed Web applications on the Tomcat server. These applications may be installed in `server.xml`, as WAR files or unpacked Web applications in the `webapps` directory, or Web applications installed using the `context` or `install` targets.

Tomcat must be running to use this target because it uses the Tomcat manager application to obtain the server configuration.

reload

The `reload` target causes the Web application to gracefully shutdown and restart. This target is useful for restarting Web applications after changes to class files or resources and the `Context` for the Web application does not have the `reloadable` attribute set to `"true"`.

The most common error when using `reload` is that the Web application is not installed with Tomcat. To see which Web applications are currently available use the `list` target.

Tomcat must be running to use this target because it uses the Tomcat manager application to perform the server manipulation.

remove

The `remove` target is the opposite of the `install` target and causes the Web application to shut down gracefully and remove the registration from the Tomcat server.

The `remove` target uses the Tomcat `remove` task, so the `remove` target also removes Web applications installed using the `context` target.

Tomcat must be running to use this target because it uses the Tomcat manager application to perform the server configuration.

undeploy

The `undeploy` target is the opposite of the `deploy` target. This target removes the Web application from the Tomcat server as well as deleting the Web application files and resources that were installed.

jspc

The `jspc` task is an optional Ant task that is used to run the Tomcat JSP compiler to convert JSP pages into Java source code.

The main benefits of using the `jspc` task are:

- ✦ JSP files do not need to have the initial delay when first accessed and the JSP file is converted to Java source and then compiled into class files.
- ✦ The server environment does not needs to have the full Java SDK installed, and a JRE is all that is required.
- ✦ The JSP files can be checked for syntax errors without having to start Tomcat and view them in a browser.

To use the jspc task in the development environment add the XML shown in Listing 5-8 to the build.xml.

Listing 5-8: jspc Target

```
<taskdef classname="org.apache.jasper.JspC" name="jasper" >
    <classpath refid="compile.classpath" />
</taskdef>

<target name="jspc" depends="compile"
    description="Invoke Jasper JSP compiler" >
    <mkdir dir="${basedir}/gensrc" />

   <jasper verbose="0"
           uriroot="${web.home}"
           webXmlFragment="${basedir}/web.inc"
           outputDir="${basedir}/gensrc" />

    <javac
        srcdir="${basedir}/gensrc"
        destdir="${build.home}/WEB-INF/classes" >
        <classpath refid="compile.classpath" />
    </javac>

    <!-- remove any *.jsp files in the build directory -->
    <delete>
        <fileset dir="${build.home}" includes="**/*.jsp" />
    </delete>

</target>
```

Using the jspc target is a little more complicated than the standard Ant targets. This target will generate a file called web.inc that includes the <servlet> and <servlet-mapping> elements required for inclusion in the web.xml.

This fragment containing the elements will need to be included every time additional JSPs are added to the Web application. This can prove to be somewhat error prone, so it is a task best left until the deployment and release cycles of a project.

To ensure the JSP files are no contained as part of the deployment, they are deleted from the build directory.

Summary

This chapter contains an introduction to the Ant build tool, and the common elements that can be found in a build script. The topics covered in this chapter have been focused to provide sufficient knowledge to create, modify and debug Ant build scripts with Tomcat.

✦ ✦ ✦

Compiling and Deploying with an IDE

✦ ✦ ✦ ✦

In This Chapter

What is an IDE?

Advantages of using an IDE

Popular IDEs

SunONE Studio CE

The Eclipse Platform

✦ ✦ ✦ ✦

An Integrated Development Environment (IDE) is a very personal thing. Developers are particular about the tools they use, and IDE preferences, or even the preference not to use one, can spark heated debates within the developer community. For a developer to be truly productive they must have the appropriate tools for the job, and feel comfortable with those tools.

In this chapter two freely available IDEs suitable for use in Web-based projects are discussed; the Eclipse Project and the SunONE Studio CE. These IDEs allow the streamlined integration of all aspects of a Web-based development process, including project creation, building, deploying, and testing.

The fundamentals of an Integrated Development Environment are discussed first, followed by a discussion of how an IDE can benefit your project. After this comes a detailed section on how to use each IDE, including details about how to integrate Tomcat into the development environment.

The aim of this chapter is to familiarize the reader with inner workings of each IDE before applying that knowledge to a Web-based project, using Tomcat. At the conclusion of this chapter, the reader will be able to make an informed decision regarding the suitability of each IDE for the development of Web-based projects, and have a feeling of their personal preference of developing in each environment.

What Is an IDE?

An Integrated Development Environment is just that, an environment with all aspects of the development process integrated into a single tool. IDEs are typically GUI applications allowing the developer to complete all day-to-day development activities using the one tool.

In practice, however, this may not be the case. There are many useful standalone tools, especially in the Unix environment, which developers have begun to know and love. These tools were designed to do one thing and do it well. IDEs go against this philosophy, and attempt to encompass everything in one. In the past, this has lead to many compromises, especially with the capabilities of the integrated editor.

The current set of available IDEs have gone a long way toward improving the quality of the tools available, and also allow a high degree of customization so the user can feel at home in the environment. Some IDEs also offer the ability to customize the editor key bindings, or even to apply the key bindings of your favorite editor, for example EMACS. However, the authors are unaware of any IDE that supports key bindings for the de-facto Unix editor 'Vi'.

In essence an IDE is made up of the following components.

- An integrated build environment, forming the core of the IDE
- Project frameworks allowing the management of source code and associated resources in a defined project structure
- A rich text editor; including syntax highlighting and tight integration with the compiler to highlight compile-time errors
- Object browsers to navigate the hierarchy of objects, and object properties
- The ability to run and deploy applications
- Debugger and tracing tools to track down run-time errors
- Productivity tools; including wizards, code-generators, defect tracking and source code control, to increase the efficiency of the developer

All these components together make up an all-in-one toolset that is designed to assist developers with the task of programming. In addition to these components an IDE may offer a visual environment, allowing the developer to rapidly develop GUI applications. Visual programming is used extensively in 4th Generation Languages (4GL) to offer Rapid Application Development (RAD).

Beware however, not all IDEs are created equal. Some tools over a complete feature set, while others only focus on a narrow area of development (for instance, EJB). It is important to select a tool that suits the developer's domain and the scope of the application being developed. Hence, many larger vendors are releasing specialized editions of their IDE targeted towards GUI, enterprise and mobile device application development.

Advantages of Using an IDE

As mentioned previously, an IDE provides an integrated toolset that enables a developer to use a single tool to perform all development activities, therefore streamlining the development process and increasing efficiency.

The end result is an environment that applies a best practice application/project framework avoiding the need of a roll-your-own development environment. This allows the developer(s) to focus on delivering required functionality, instead of peripheral tasks.

This section outlines the best practices that an IDE may provide you, and also some of the caveats of using an IDE over a custom development environment.

Not all IDEs offer all of the following features. Please consult the data sheet for the IDE for more details.

Best Practices

IDEs are becoming increasingly useful in agile software development methodologies with an increased importance placed on testing, continuous integration, and constant refactoring. For more information on agile methodologies, including extreme programming (XP) refer to `http://agilemanifesto.org/`.

Using a traditional methodology, you still benefit from the best practices evangelized by the agile community. They will just not be taken to the extreme. An IDE may also provide an overall project framework conforming to best practices at the time.

Project Framework

Project frameworks enforce a structure on the project. A project structure dictates the location of source code, compiled classes, and additional resources with regard to the packaging requirements of the project. This structure is a reflection of the best practices for the type of project being created.

The accepted best practice may differ depending on the context of the application, requiring the ability to support various project structures. For example, a J2EE project has specific packaging requirements, including Web Application archive (WAR) and Enterprise Application aRchive (EAR) files; therefore the project structure differs greatly from a Swing-based application.

IDEs assist developers creating new projects by suggesting accepted best practice project frameworks via the use of project creation wizards. Developers can therefore focus on the business logic of the application, not the project structure.

Automatic Code-Generation

In addition to streamlining development, an IDE also can offer various productivity tools to automate, often, tedious development tasks. Automatic code generation is an example of such a tool.

For example, EJB developers are well aware of the large amount of replication and duplication between entity and session beans, and their home, remote and local interfaces, an IDE can assist with the construction of these interfaces using wizards and code-generation tools.

Build Environment

An integrated build environment is the core of any good IDE. It provides integral ability to build the entire application. The build process performs dependency checking, compilation, packaging, and possibly even deployment.

Unfortunately, vendors seem to have their own proprietary build environments, locking the project into a particular IDE. It is, however, encouraging to see that many newer IDEs are beginning to support freely available build tools such as Jakarta Ant, allowing projects to be shared by a team of developers over a heterogeneous development environment.

Debugging

Most IDEs offer a facility to debug applications while they are running. This allows the developer to identify run-time errors in the code that are not apparent during the build phase. A debugger allows the developer or tester to step through each line of code in the application and inspect the variables contained in the stack at runtime. Breakpoints may be set, allowing inspection of crucial parts of the code, avoiding the need to step through the entire application.

Testing

In addition to debugging, the IDE may also provide a unit-testing framework, enabling black box testing of the individual components of the application. Testing is a crucial part of continuous integration.

Refactoring

Code refactoring is the process of applying a design change to an entire code base. Refactoring may be as simple as changing the class or package name, or can be as complex as reworking the entire object model.

Regardless of the change, refactoring results in the change propagating through large amounts of referencing code (for example, when changing the name of a class, all type declarations for that class must be changed). With the aid of tools, the process of refactoring may be automated, reducing the manual effort required to change all reference to the modified element.

Due to the reduced likelihood of human error, a refactoring tool reduces the number of errors resulting from design changes. Coupled with a continuous integration and testing strategy, it will become immediately apparent if the design change has introduced any defects.

Refactoring is essential for agile methodologies to keep up with changing requirements. Developers are less inhibited to make design changes if they know their actions will not result in defects being introduced into the code. Refactoring is also beneficial for traditional methodologies because up-front designs are very rarely 100 percent correct, and even perfect designs are not immune to changing customer requirements.

When an IDE Is Not Advantageous

Of course, it is not absolutely necessary for a developer to use an integrated toolset provided by an IDE. Many developers dislike the reliance on a mouse-driven interface, and persist on using command line tools in conjunction with their favorite text editor. Experienced developers also use scripting languages to automate common tasks, a feature not available in many GUI-based IDEs. In this case, a suite of separate tools can offer a comparable set of features to an integrated environment.

It is important to choose a toolset that suits your development requirements, and not to get tied up with the bells and whistles offered by tool vendors. Remember, the purpose of a development environment is to transparently support your development process, and to make developers as productive as possible. Some IDEs may do this, and may even improve your process, by enforcing development best practices. However, IDE is not a substitute for good software engineering practices and a well thought out development environment. Hence, if you constantly find yourself working against the IDE or tinkering with the tool to customize it to your needs, you may need to reevaluate your IDE, your development process, or both.

Popular IDEs

The sheer volume and the constantly changing landscape of Java IDEs makes it impossible to exhaustively list every available IDE. Table 6-1 lists some of the most popular IDEs available today. For an up-to-date rundown of the latest IDE trends try the Development Tools section of the JavaWorld site `www.javaworld.com/channel_content/jw-tools-index.shtml`.

Table 6-1: Popular Integrated Development Environments

Name	*Vendor*	*URL*
BEA WebLogic Workshop	BEA Systems	`www.bea.com/`
CodeWarrior	Metrowerks	`www.metrowerks.com/`
IDEA	IntelliJ	`www.intellij.com/`
JBuilder	Borland	`www.borland.com/`
NetBeans IDE	NetBeans.org	`www.netbeans.org/`
Oracle 9i JDeveloper	Oracle Corporation	`http://otn.oracle.com/`
SunOne Studio	Sun Microsystems	`wwws.sun.com/`
The Eclipse Project	eclipse.org	`www.eclipse.org/`
Together ControlCenter	TogetherSoft	`www.togethersoft.com/`
WebSphere Studio Application Developer	IBM Corporation	`www.ibm.com/`

The remainder of this chapter discusses in detail two of the aforementioned IDEs; the Eclipse Platform and the Sun ONE Studio IDE. The following sections explain the installation, configuration, and Tomcat integration for each IDE.

SunONE Studio Community Edition

SunONE Studio Community Edition (CE) Release 4 update 1 is a free Java IDE released by Sun Microsystems. The original code base for this product was acquired by Sun in their purchase of NetBeans in 1999[1]. Originally this product was called Forte for Java but it has since developed into SunONE Studio. There are three editions of SunONE Studio now available from Sun; all have evolved from the same code base acquired from NetBeans.

- ✦ Community Edition Release 4, Update 1: This version of SunONE Studio is discussed in this chapter. The community edition is released by Sun for free.
- ✦ Mobile Edition Release 4 Update 1: This is a customized version for the development of J2ME applications. This edition is also released free by Sun.
- ✦ Enterprise Edition Release 4 Update 1: A non-free product from Sun. The enterprise edition provides extra functionality over and beyond the free versions.

In this chapter the Community Edition is used.

In 2000 Sun released as open source a code base that would become the NetBeans IDE we know today. NetBeans IDE would continue to be developed under an open source basis, with members of the community contributing to its extension and continued development.

---

[1] History of Netbeans: http://www.netbeans.org/

SunONE Studio forms one part of the SunONE fleet of products. This line includes a range of products that can be integrated for enterprise level applications. The SunONE Application Server is one of these (formerly iPlanet).

SunONE Studio offers a vast array of features and tools to use in the development of an application. This is enhanced furthermore by the Update Center available, where both NetBeans and SunONE modules can be chosen and installed into the IDE. Unsupported modules also are available as add-ons through the update center. This makes the possibilities of this product almost limitless.

For instance, a Tomcat integration plug-in and a version of Tomcat comes installed with SunONE Studio. The Tomcat instance that comes with the IDE is configured to work with the plug-in. Useful Tools such as Ant (see Chapter 5) and CVS (Concurrent Versioning System) can be fully integrated into SunONE Studio. These and the range of available tools make this a very powerful product that is ever expanding through its alliance with the open source NetBeans.

Where to Get It

SunONE Studio Release 4 Update 1 is available from Sun's Developer section (`www.sun.com/developer/`). Registration is required to complete the download.

When selecting the version to download be careful not to select the Enterprise Edition by accident; its license will expire if you don't purchase it. Choose the Community Edition Release 4 update 1 for your platform, with or without the Java 2 Platform Standard Edition (J2SE) Co bundle, depending on your environment.

Installation

Depending on which platform version you downloaded, the executable install file should be called `ffj_ce_win32.exe`. Double click this file and the installation process will begin.

In the first few steps you are only asked to locate the installation directory and agree to the terms and conditions of using the software. The installation then asks which version of the Java SDK to use with the IDE. Figure 6-1 displays this step:

Choose the appropriate JDK installation and press Next.

Once the remaining installation steps have been completed, you can start SunONE Studio by clicking the icon on your desktop or in the Programs section of the start menu.

Update Center

When you start SunONE for the first time the main Window displays the welcome screen and some options to get started. First, though, close the start-up screen and head to the menu. Select `Tools > Update Center`. This area allows patches and new modules to be installed directly into the IDE.

Upon starting the Update Center you are asked to specify which Center(s) you wish to browse the modules of for installation. To be safe just select the SunONE Studio Update Center. If you don't mind using open source unsupported components on your system, the other centers also can be selected. This step appears as in Figure 6-2:

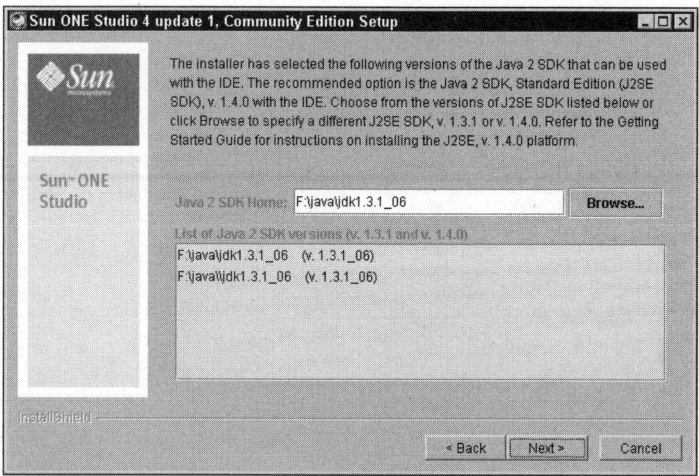

Figure 6-1: SDK specification step of the SunONE Studio CE installation

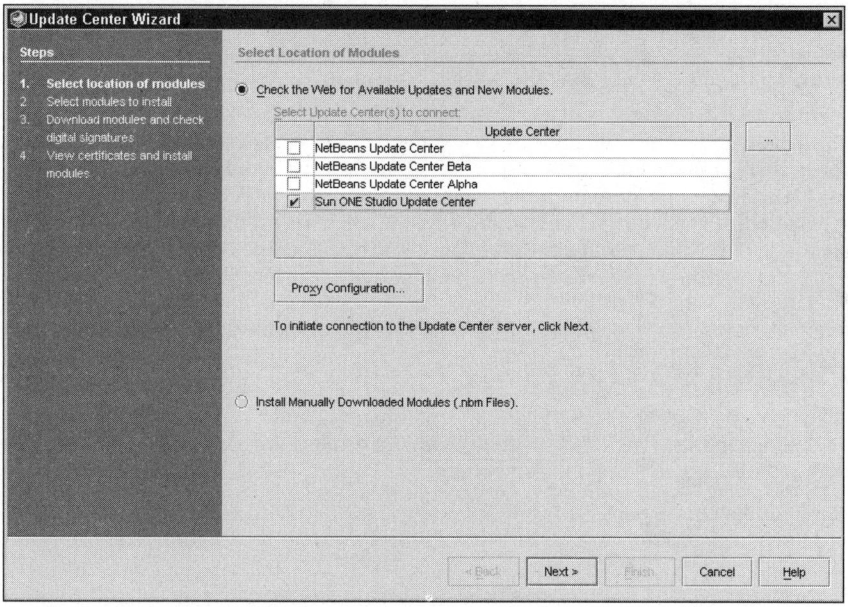

Figure 6-2: SunONE Studio CE Update Center

Press next and you are prompted to enter your username and password to access the SunONE Update Center. Enter the same username and password you used to download SunONE Studio. Pressing Next from this step begins communications from your IDE to the remote server from where patches and modules are downloaded. If the username and password was entered correctly, the next screen displays the available downloads, as shown in Figure 6-3.

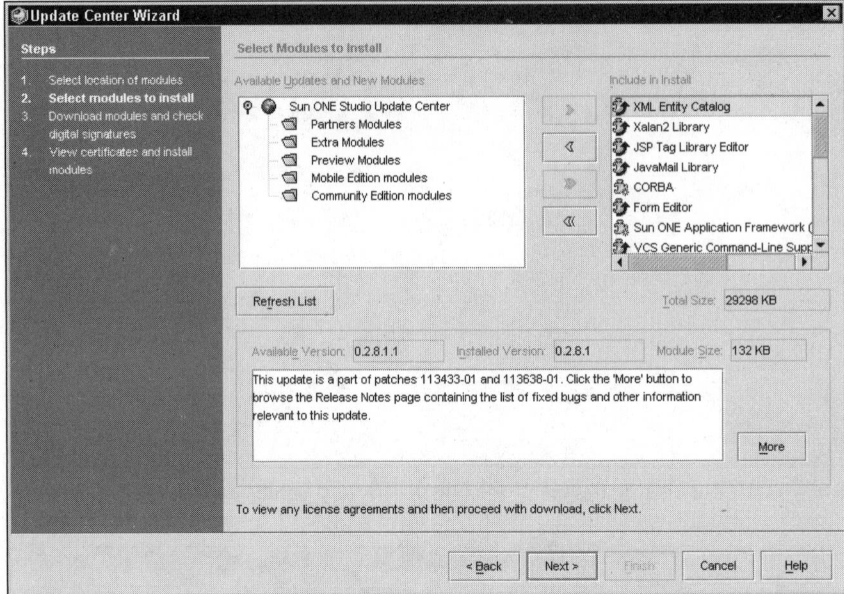

Figure 6-3: Update Center listing the patches and modules available

At the top of the Wizard's window are two panels. The left lists the available modules and patches. Select the desired patch and press the arrow keys in the center to add or remove items from the update. More information about each item can be gained by highlighting the items, then pressing More. When you are finished, click Next. The screen that follows presents the modules and patches selected for download. The rest of the process walks your through downloading the modules selected and then choosing which of these to install in the IDE.

Ant Configuration

We can now configure the SunONE Studio environment to allow us to use some of the projects outlined in this book. This section deals with configuring SunONE Studio to use Ant 1.5.1 as well as utilize custom tasks in Ant scripts.

SunONE Studio comes packaged with Ant 1.4.1. The integration of Ant into this IDE is excellent, allowing you to execute specific Ant tasks from within the GUI interface.

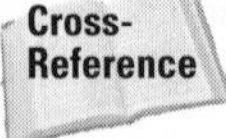

Refer to Chapter 5 for more information on how to use and configure Ant. This chapter only covers integrating and using Ant in the context of the IDE.

We are now going to walk through two configuration steps with regards to Ant and the IDE.

- ✦ Upgrading the IDE to Ant 1.5.1. Unfortunately there is no module for SunONE Studio that will do this for us. It is therefore required to perform the upgrade manually.
- ✦ Configuring SunONE Studio to use custom Ant tasks

Upgrade to Ant 1.5.1[2]

From within the SunONE Studio main interface the version of the current Ant integration can be found by selecting `Tools > Options`. Click the Building node and select Ant Settings. The right hand panel displays the current `Ant Version` as well as some other settings that can be changed. The version should indicate that 1.4.1 is being used.

In short, we are going to replace the Ant files being referenced by SunONE to be the newer 1.5.1 files, however their file names must remain the same. To get 1.5.1 working follow these steps:

1. Close SunONE Studio.
2. Copy `ant.jar` and `ant-optional.jar` from your `ANT_HOME/lib` directory and place them in a temporary folder on your desktop. Where `ANT_HOME` is where you installed Jakarta Ant 1.5.1.
3. Rename these files to `ant-1.4.1.jar` and `ant-optional-1.4.1.jar` respectively.
4. Use Windows Explorer browser to the modules/ext directory where you installed SunONE Studio. Move the files `ant-1.4.1.jar` and `ant-optional-1.4.1.jar` to a safe location as backup.
5. Copy the two files you renamed from your desktop into the modules/ext directory from before. It is very important that you do not overwrite a file in this directory called `ant.jar`.
6. Restart SunONE Studio.

If you now go to Ant Settings as before, the version number reported is 1.5.1 and the upgrade has been completed. This process may seem a little half baked until an Ant 1.5.1 module update is available for SunONE Studio. Figure 6-4 shows the Ant Setting information with Ant 1.5.1 as the version:

Configuration to use custom Ant tasks[3]

The examples in this book use a series of custom Ant tasks to communicate with Tomcat. By default SunONE Studio does not know about these tasks, we therefore need to add them to its classpath. There are various methods for achieving what we are doing here. It basically boils down to a classpath problem. But seeing as changing the classpath being used in the Ant scripts is not really within the scope of this chapter, we must use another method. For more information about achieving this in other ways refer to the SunONE Studio Documentation.

---

[2] NetBeans Ant Web site: http://ant.netbeans.org.

[3] SunONE Studio Documentation

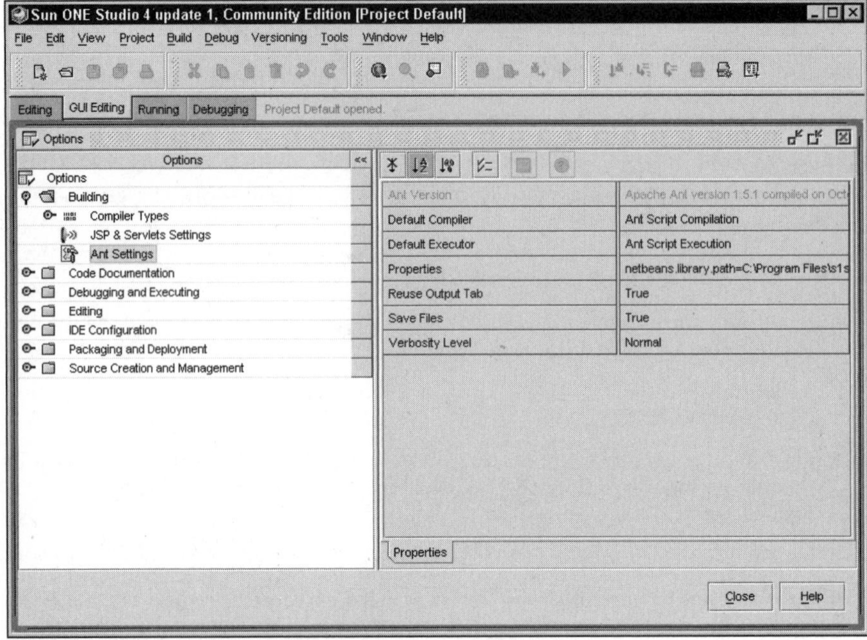

Figure 6-4: SunONE Studio with upgraded Ant version 1.5.1

Follow these steps to get the Catalina custom Ant tasks available to Ant in SunONE Studio:

1. Close down SunONE Studio.
2. Copy the file `catalina-ant.jar` from your `ANT_HOME/lib` directory (remember this file originally came with Tomcat, not Ant) into the `\modules\patches\org-apache-tools-ant-module` directory of your SunONE Studio installation directory.
3. Start up SunONE Studio.
4. Select `Tools > Options` and from the list of options click Building and then Ant Settings. Figure 6-4 should again be displayed. Select the properties item in the right panel and click the (...) at the end of the value column. An edit window should appear showing various classpath entries. Delete the line `build.sysclasspath=ignore`. Press OK and close the Options window[4].

Once this is completed, Ant in SunONE Studio should be able to use Custom Ant tasks.

How to Use SunONE Studio

Like many such tools, the use of SunONE Studio can be as easy or complicated as you like, depending on the extent to which the tool has become your development environment and how much reliance you place on it to get stuff done. The guide in this chapter is by no means a definitive list of features and functionality, but it should give the new user some idea as to whether the tool will suit their needs.

---

[4] Removing this item affects the CLASSPATH value used by the Ant script when run inside the IDE. Consult the SunONE Studio Documentation for further information.

The SunONE Studio environment is a logical and mature one. This product (in its NetBeans form, and onto Forte) has been through a number of versions. So by now you can rest assured that the interface will not introduce any major new concepts.

Workspaces[5]

The SunONE Studio interface provides us with a number of views of the environment without cluttering the screen. Upon starting SunONE Studio, you are met with a left panel with tabs across the top and bottom,and a display frame between them. The tabs across the top represent your workspaces, as shown in Figure 6-5.

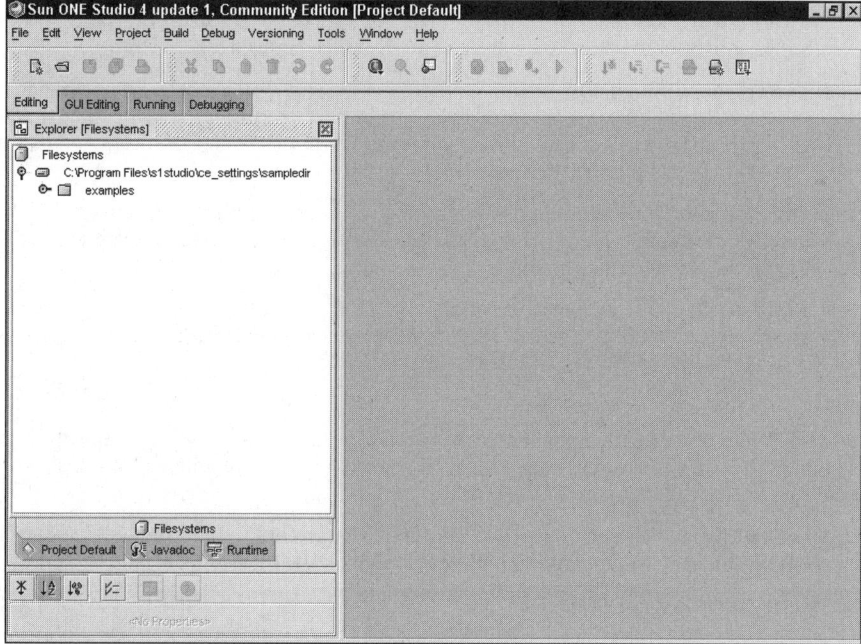

Figure 6-5: SunONE Studio showing Workspaces

The workspaces are:

✦ **Editing:** This workspace is used to display the Explorer in the display frame as well as provide editor capability.

✦ **GUI editing:** Used for the development of Graphical User Interfaces (GUI). This section includes access to the Editor and Form Designer as well as the Explorer.

✦ **Running:** When a project is executed for testing, or a process is started, the view is changed to the Running workspace to display any initialization errors. An Output window will display any output.

✦ **Debugging:** This workspace provides access to a debugger window and an output window. May also display the source editor if there are errors in any code. In this workspace Watches and breakpoints can be set and monitored.

[5] SunONE Studio Documentation

Think of workspaces as being modeled on the way a developer will work. There is an area where the developer will edit and manage files within a project, an area where processes that are running such as servers can be debugged or monitored, and an area where debugging is worked on.

Workspaces can be created, changed, removed, or renamed by right clicking a workspace tab and selecting Customize Workspaces.

At the base of the Explorer workspace pane are some tabs that allow you to see what are basically different views of the file system, or the environment.

- ✦ **File-systems tab:** Listing and navigation of any file systems you may have made the IDE aware of (by mounting). A File system can include directories on your hard disk or network, source-controlled areas or even archive files such as JAR or Zip.
- ✦ **Project tab:** Contains the resources that have been added to the current project. For instance if a directory is mounted from within the File-systems tab, it can be added to the current project. Individual files and other resources such as servers and databases can also be added to the Project view.
- ✦ **Javadoc tab:** This tab contains listings of javadoc resources registered with the IDE. Javadoc resources can point to a URL, local Javadoc directories, or even archive files containing Javadoc information.
- ✦ **Runtime tab:** For the management of processes running within the IDE. For instance, this tab contains a listing of all servers registered with the IDE, as well as databases and the database drivers that are available.

Editor

SunONE Studio comes with a sophisticated text editor that is tightly integrated with other aspects of the IDE such as debugging tools, and the compiler. The editor also does all the usual syntax highlighting you would expect.

Multiple files that are open can be easily accessed via tabs at the base of the browser. These tabs also can be used to perform various operations on the files such as closing and saving.

The editor can be seen in Figure 6-6.

The editor also has tools to search across the file system using regular expressions and replace ability in documents. Searching can also be executed across a file system by object name, content or version control status.

Project Creation

No IDE description in a book would be complete without a project creation walkthrough. A project in SunONE Studio is created simply by selecting Project from the menu and clicking Project Manager. A list of the current projects within the IDE will appear. Click New... and the IDE asks for the new project's name. Enter the name of the project, press OK, and the IDE creates a namespace for Projects settings.

Details of each project are saved to where you specified your individual user settings would be kept under the `system/projects` folder of the IDE installation directory.

Once you have created a new project the IDE will be quite blank and empty. To be useful, some access to the file system is required. This can be achieved by mounting a part of the file system to include in the project.

For instance, let's create a project called Hello and use it to house the Hello servlet example described in Chapter 7. Start by creating a project called Hello in the way described previously.

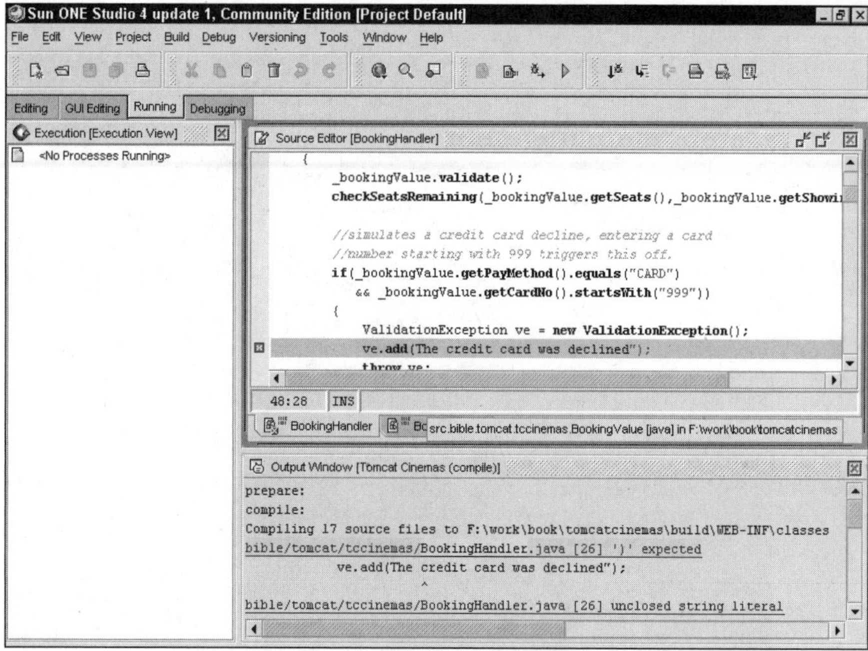

Figure 6-6: SunONE Studio Editor integrated with compiler

Once the project has been created, select the File system tab of the Explorer pane. In the pane should be a single node, File systems, with no leaf nodes. We are about to register a part of the file system that relates to the Hello example. In short we are going to **mount** a part of the file system.

Right click the File systems node and select `Mount > Local Directory`. This should appear as in Figure 6-7.

A dialog box appears, prompting you to select where on your computer the Hello example is located. Select the top-most directory of the example and press Finish. The Explorer pane, File-system tab now shows the directory structure from where you selected downwards.

Note You also should notice that the Explorer has recognized you have an Ant build script located in this directory. Thisis covered in more detail in the next section.

Now we have the top-most directory of the example mounted in the IDE. If you expand this node you will see the familiar subdirectories listed. For the IDE to correctly recognize the package structure in the `src` directory, these must be visible in the same way as the container directory.

It is therefore required to mount the `src/` and `web/` directories in the same way we have mounted the Hello example container directory. When you mount the `web/` directory, SunONE Studio recognizes the structure as being J2EE compliant. It tells you that it has created an alternative view for this directory in the Project view. Press OK when SunONE tells you about this; you will see the effect soon.

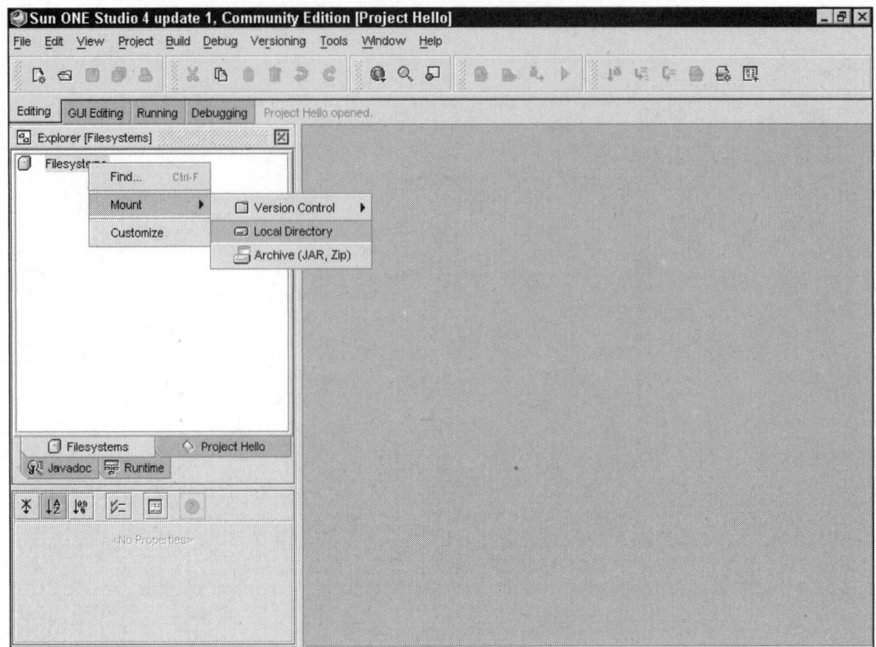

Figure 6-7: Mounting a local directory in Sun ONEStudio

Once this is completed you should have three items in the file-systems view:

```
/hello
/hello/src
/hello/web
```

Once these directories have been mounted we can add the `src/` directory and `build.xml` file to the Project View. Right click the `src/` directory mounting and select `Tools > Add to Project`. This is illustrated in Figure 6-8.

Once this is done for the `src/` directory, expand the container file system mounting (probably the top one) until you can see the build file (`build.xml`) recognized as an Ant script. Right click this file and select `Tools > Add To Project.`

If you now click the Project tab in the explorer, you will see the `src/` directory is visible as well as the `web/` directory that SunONE allocated to the Project view for us. You can expand these directories and have a look at the contents. The `src/` directory expands into the package structure, while the `web/` directory (actually a Web module in SunONE Studio) expands representing the contents of our `web/` directory:

✦ Document base: Contains JSP files used in the application

✦ Classes: (short-hand view to `WEB-INF/classes`) Where class files are kept in a Web application

✦ Lib directory: Representing the directory at `WEB-INF/lib`

✦ Web: Representing the `web.xml` file in `WEB-INF/` directory

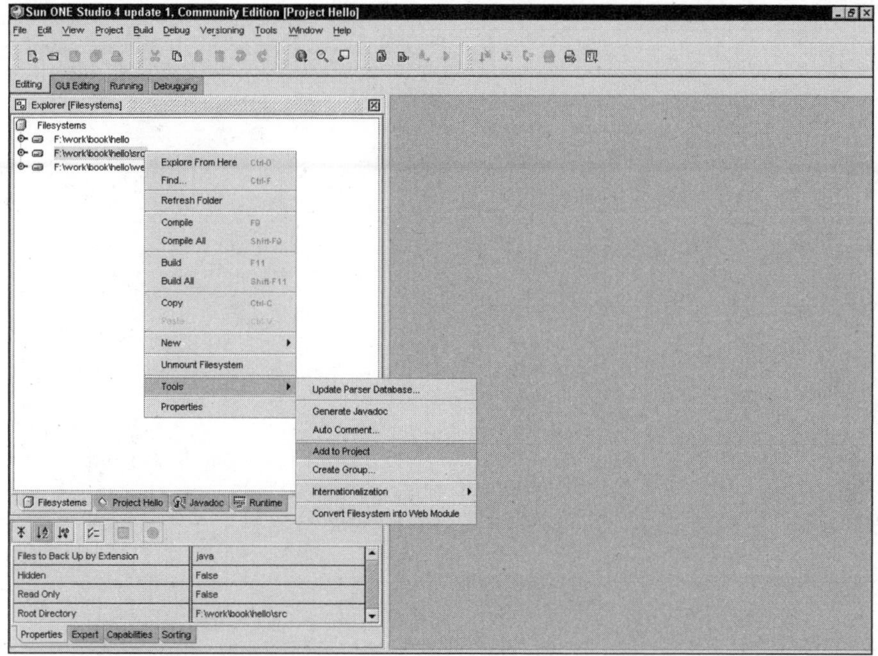

Figure 6-8: Adding a mounted directory to the project view

The project setup is now complete. All files can be accessed via the project view. We now need to look at registering an external Tomcat Server so that the Hello project can be compiled and viewed through the IDE using Ant.

External Tomcat Server

SunONE Studio comes packaged with an internal 4.0.1 server. However, in this example we register the 4.1.12 server we have been using so far in this book. This will lead on to an illustration of how developers can use SunONE Studio as a tool to develop applications without being tied to the internal server the IDE comes with.

We start by having a look at the Runtime tab of the Explorer pane. Listed in this pane are various runtime resources we may need to administer. If you select the Server Registry node and then Installed Servers you will see Tomcat 4.0 listed with a further sub node called Internal. This is SunONE Studios internal Tomcat Server. You cannot delete it. However, it can be started, stopped, and manipulated via the IDE. We are going to create another node alongside the Internal Server, representing another server, or the server we have been using in this book.

Note SunONE Studio only supports adding Tomcat 4.x servers in this way. 3.x and below will not work.

Right-click the Tomcat 4.0 node in the list just described and select Add Tomcat 4.0 Installation. A dialog appears as shown in Figure 6-9:

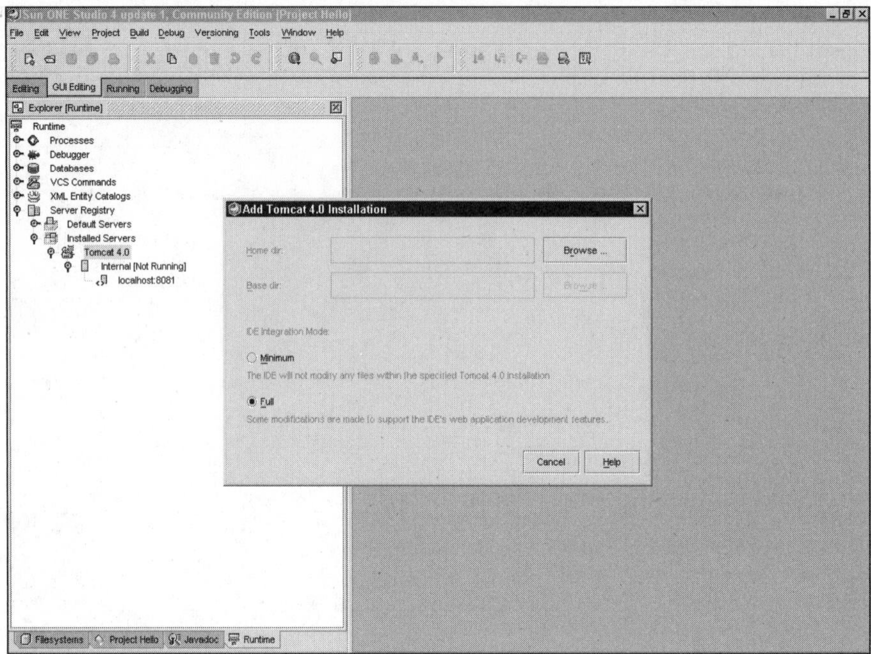

Figure 6-9: Adding a Tomcat 4.0 Installation to SunONE Studio

Place the equivalent of `CATALINA_HOME` in the Home fields. You only need to specify the Base dir if your external Tomcat installation is used in a multi-server environment. For IDE Integration mode select Minimum.

Selecting minimum for IDE integration means that SunONE will not change our external server instance at all. However, this also means that some of the debugging and tool integration facilities will not be available.

Caution

Allocating a Tomcat 4.1.x server in Full IDE Integration mode will not work. There were differences made to the Jasper engine between 4.0 and 4.1 that are incompatible with the Tomcat plug-in for SunONE Studio. Minimum mode can be used, however, at the sacrifice of some of SunONEs Web application development features. If these are important, and the use of Tomcat 4.0 is not a problem, you can just use the internal Tomcat server for your development, which runs at full integration mode. For more information consult the NetBeans Users mailing list.

Press OK and the server is added to the list. You can check that the registered server is still working by trying to start it from within the IDE. Right-click the new server and select Start Server. The workspace changes to Running and a progress bar indicating the server that is starting is displayed, as shown in Figure 6-10.

Once the server has started the progress meter disappears and the output console shows the output messages that Tomcat displays when it starts. A browser also appears, going to the default page of the server with Tomcat's welcome message and menus to access documentation and the Manager application. The execution view within the Running workspace now shows the Tomcat server process running.

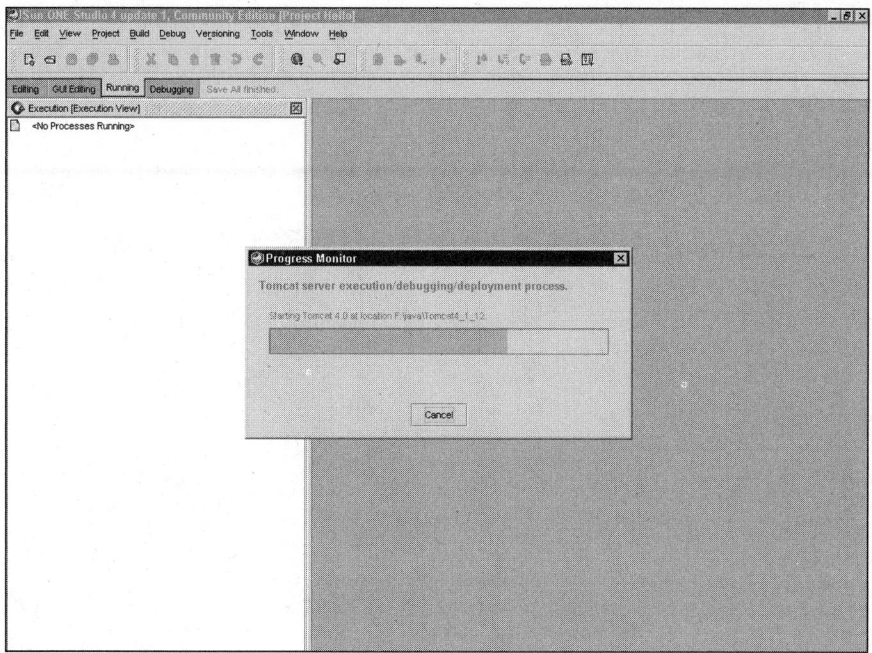

Figure 6-10: External Tomcat Server starting under SunONE Studio

Other J2EE servers, such as the SunONE Application server, also can be integrated into SunONE Studio in this fashion. The Jserver Plug in Integration module provides this. An API for this module allows vendors of J2EE servers to create server plug-ins for this IDE. The Tomcat plug-in is an example of this[6].

From the Runtime tab of the Explorer pane various administrative commands can run against the server from within the IDE. For Tomcat these include:

- ✦ Configure server.xml
- ✦ Add a new Host
- ✦ Viewing log files
- ✦ Adding a context
- ✦ Removing a context
- ✦ Removing a Host

Basically these tools allow for another way to edit the `server.xml` of the server.

---

[6] SunONE Studio Documentation

Using Ant

As mentioned before, Ant 1.4.1 comes as one of the build tools available under SunONE Studio. The SunONE studio interface makes executing and manipulating Ant scripts and targets very simple. SunONE Studios Explorer view of files recognizes the XML structure of an Ant build file and displays this structure appropriately.

Figure 6-11 shows the `build.xml` file from the Hello Project started earlier:

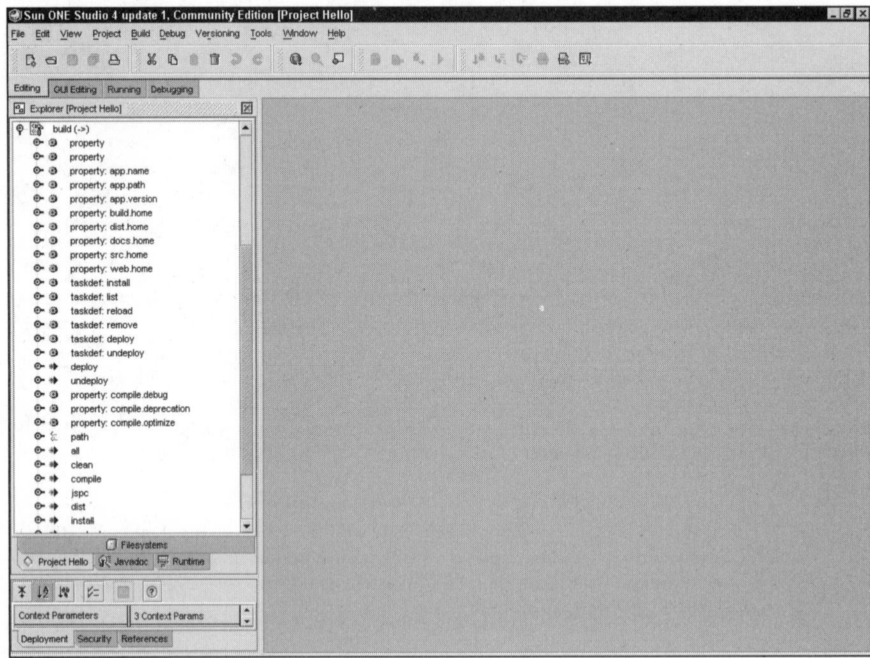

Figure 6-11: Ant properties and targets displayed in the Explorer view

The IDE matches each type of node within the `build.xml` with a different symbol for ease of recognition. You can execute one of these targets simply by double-clicking it. By right-clicking a target, task def or property more options become available. The context menu that results allows you to change the order of the targets, delete targets, or add new targets. An individual target or property also can be added to a project in the same way we added Mounted directories.

Let's use this view of the Ant build script to compile the Hello application.

Remember to upgrade the IDE's Ant version to 1.5.1 and configure the IDE to use Custom Ant tasks for Tomcat before trying to run the example applications in this book from the IDE. The instructions for doing this are presented earlier in this chapter.

Firstly ensure that the IDE has started your external copy of Tomcat successfully. Now right-click the clean target node within the Ant `build.xml`. The workspace changes to the Running view where an output window displays the messages Ant prints when this task is run. It should say something like:

```
clean:
Deleting directory F:\work\book\hello\build
BUILD SUCCESSFUL
Total time: 0 seconds
```

With the directory location being wherever you have the application on disk. Now run the 'context' target in the same way. The task runs the 'prepare', 'compile', and 'context' targets, installing the application into the Tomcat instance. If you now start up a browser and browse to the hello context on the server:

```
http://localhost:8080/hello
```

You should be presented with the Hello application as discussed in Chapter 7.

If you make subsequent compiles you only need to run the 'compile' task and then the 'reload' task to see your changes reflected in the server.

You also can make changes to the SunONE Studios settings so that the Ant script is executed when using the IDE's `compile` or `build` commands.

Compiling and Building with the IDE

If Ant is not available to build your application the IDE offers integrated methods for performing similar tasks. As part of this SunONE Studio allows the developer to compile using a range of compilers[7]:

- ✦ Internal Compiler: The internal compiler is a variant of the `javac` compiler.
- ✦ External Compiler: The compiler that comes with the JDK installed on the computer in which the IDE is running.
- ✦ Fastjavac: A compiler that allows Java code to be compiled for specific environments such as Windows, Linux or Solaris.
- ✦ Jikes compiler: An open source java compiler.

The choice can be set per class or as a general default.

Compiling in SunONE Studio means compiling new files or files that have changed in the folder selected, and Compile All means compiling new files or files that have changed in all directories below the currently selected one. Files that require compiling have a small red badge next to them.

A Build in the context of SunONE Studio means removing any class files and recompiling all files in the folder selected. Build All would mean all folders below as well.

JSP files also can be compiled in SunONE Studio, which can help with the debugging process. The developer doesn't have to view the JSP output in the browser to discover errors; rather the JSP files can be compiled and checked for errors before hand. To compile a JSP file simply right-click its node within the Explorer Workspace and select Compile. Any errors will be output within the IDE's Output Window.

Note Notice in the IDE that there are definable settings for compilation or execution, such as which is the default executor, and which is the default compiler. The executor is the method the IDE uses to run your application. For instance, when we create a Web module within the IDE later on, the executor is the J2EE Server, Tomcat. Whereas we may use a choice of compilers to actually compile the classes.

[7] SunONE Studio Documentation

Some common configurations you may want to change:

✦ The default compiler can be set by selecting `Tools > Options > Editing >Java Sources` and changing the `Default Compiler` property.

✦ The destination for the output directory of a compile can be set by selecting `Tools > Options > Building > Select the Compiler you wish to change`. Change the target property to a mounted file-system directory. For packages, nominate the directory above the first item in the package name, in other words, `classes` directory. If `<not set>` is chosen, the class files are placed alongside the source file after compilation.

✦ The IDE parses source files every two seconds, but this value can be changed or set to zero in which case the parse is done only on save.

Classpath in SunONE Studio

By default the IDE uses a classpath built up around the file systems you have mounted as well as packages within the system and user directories. The system classpath is ignored.

Note When we configured Ant in SunONE Studio to use custom tasks we told it to not ignore the system classpath.

The internal Tomcat Servers classpath is configurable via its properties. Select the Runtime tab of the Explorer workspace then select `Server Register > Installed Servers > Tomcat 4.0 > Internal`. Right-click the Internal (this is the internal Tomcat Server) node and select properties. The External Execution Process property contains the classpath configuration for this server.

MySQL Database Integration

As mentioned before, the Runtime tab of the Explorer workspace contains runtime processes such as servers. Included in here is the ability to reference data sources that might be available. Once we have registered a database, its contents can be browsed and queried, or its structure can be exported into XML.

Seeing as we are using MySQL in this book, the following steps walk you through installing the Connector/J JDBC Driver for MySQL and then registering a database on the local MySQL server.

First click the runtime tab of the Explorer menu and expand the Databases node. This reveals a node labeled Drivers that lists all the database drivers that have been registered with the IDE (you can see that SunONE Studio has quite a few by default). One of these is the MM.MySQL driver. The version of this driver that we use in this book is slightly later than the version SunONE Studio comes with, so this gives us the opportunity to register a new one.

Note For details about obtaining the MySQL `Connector/J` driver, see Chapter 2.

First the MySQL Connector/J driver (a JAR file) is placed in the `lib/ext` directory of your SunONE Studio installation. Right-click the Drivers node under Databases in the Runtime tab of the Explorer menu, and select Add Driver. A dialog box is displayed as shown in Figure 6-12:

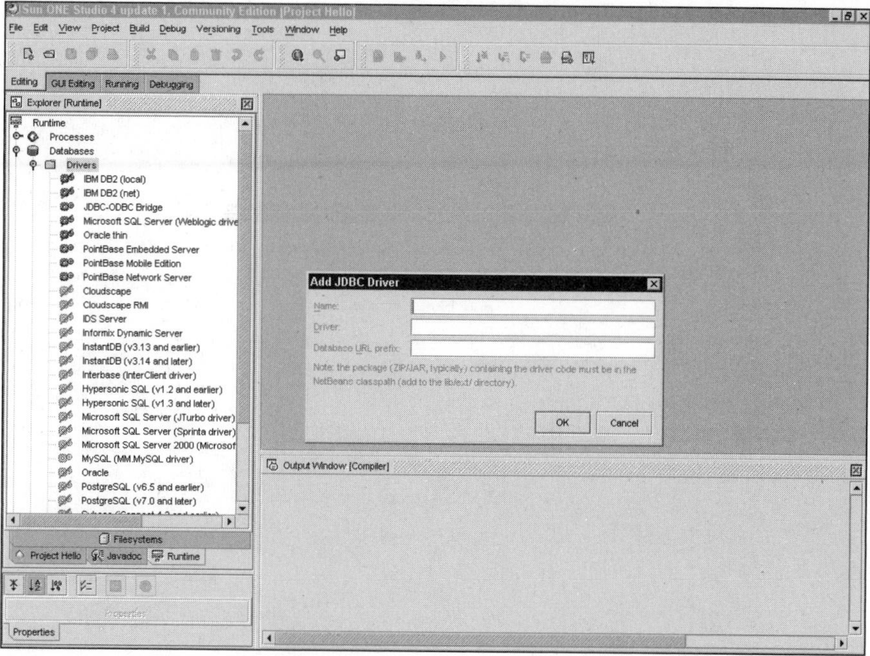

Figure 6-12: Adding a new JDBC Driver

Populate the three fields with the following:

- ✦ Name: `MySQL Connector/J`. This is just a name to apply to this driver.
- ✦ Driver: `com.mysql.jdbc.Driver`. This is the package and class for the Driver class of the driver.
- ✦ URL Prefix: `jdbc:mysql://localhost:3306/`. This is merely a prompt for how the JDBC URL should be formed when a connection is made using this driver.

Once these details have been entered press OK and the new Driver is added to the list.

From here we can simply test a connection to a database using the Driver or push ahead and create a connection to a MySQL database you might have running. The latter is more interesting.

Right-click the Databases node (above Driver) in the Runtime tab and select Add Connection... . A dialog box asks for configuration input for this database. For the purposes of this demonstration we are going to create a connection to a database called `tomcatcinemas` that is used in Chapter 10. The dialog box is displayed in Figure 6-13.

In the name field, select the Driver we just added from the drop-down list provided. The Driver class name is populated correctly. In Database URL we only need to append 'tomcatcinemas' onto the prefix we specified when the driver was added, so the full URL becomes:

```
jdbc:mysql://localhost:3306/tomcatcinemas
```

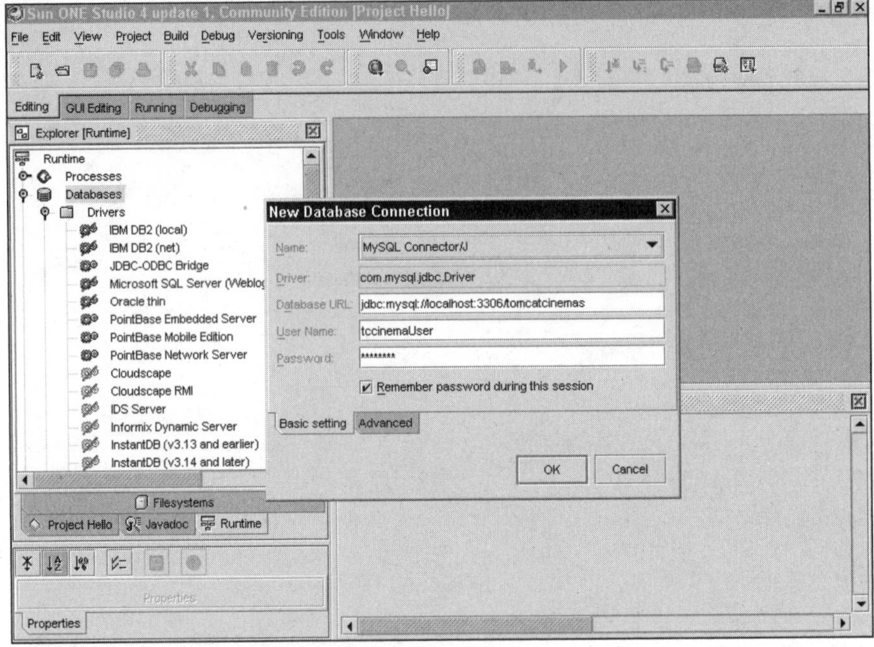

Figure 6-13: New Database Connection

In username and password we enter the details for the user who has been granted appropriate rights. Click Remember Password during this session and press OK. If all the details entered were correct, the database should be listed under the Databases node in the list.

Now that the database is registered we can run queries against it, browse its schema, and even change the schema by adding columns or tables. Figure 6-14 shows some of these features in action:

Integration of SunONE Studio and Tomcat

SunONE Studio comes packaged with an Internal Tomcat Server. The internal server cannot be deleted and is excellent for debugging and testing Web applications within the convenient services of the IDE.

To explain the use of the Tomcat Internal Server we are going to create a small Web Application (or Web Module in SunONE Studio) and display some of its integration capabilities.

We start by creating a new project in SunONE Studio called `MyWebApp`. We then add a simple JSP page and servlet to the application.

Note This process describes the use of a single Web Module within the IDE. The process is different when there are multiple Web modules that needed to be executed against the Internal Server.

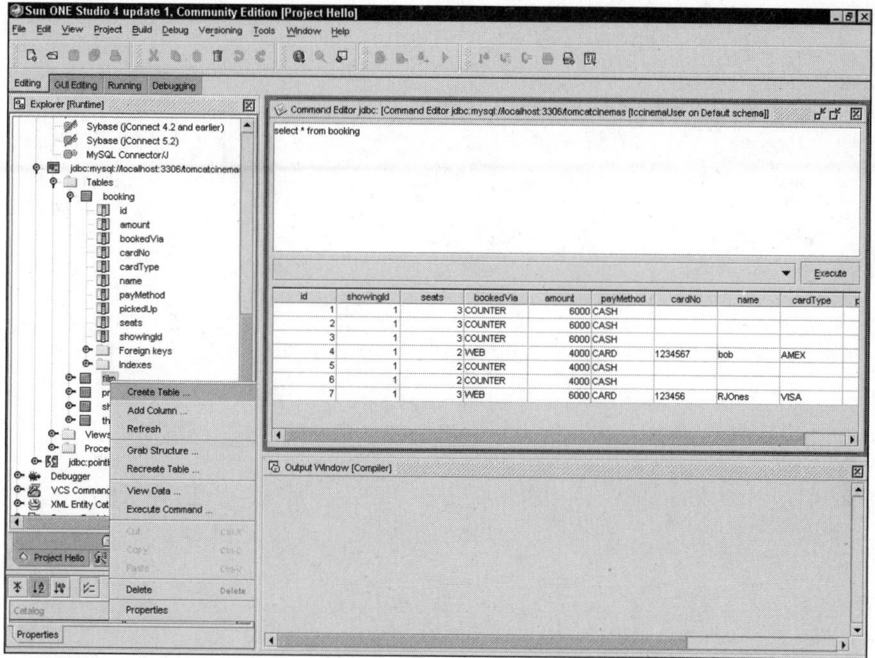

id	showingId	seats	bookedVia	amount	payMethod	cardNo	name	cardType
1	1	3	COUNTER	6000	CASH			
2	1	3	COUNTER	6000	CASH			
3	1	3	COUNTER	6000	CASH			
4	1	2	WEB	4000	CARD	1234567	bob	AMEX
5	1	2	COUNTER	4000	CASH			
6	1	2	COUNTER	4000	CASH			
7	1	3	WEB	6000	CARD	123456	RJOnes	VISA

Figure 6-14: Database administration functionality within SunONE Studio

Firstly let's create a Web module called `MyWebApp`:

1. Mount an appropriate directory on your computer such as `C:\MyWebApp`.
2. Right-click the new mounted directory and select `New > JSP & Servlet > Web Module`.
3. Choose OK when the IDE asks you to convert the file system to a J2EE Web module.
4. Choose OK again, when the IDE informs you that an alternate view of the Web module has been created in the Project view.
5. Select the MyWebApp project view and examine the structure it has created.

The resulting Web module should appear as shown in Figure 6-15.

As explained previously, the document base node contains the JSP files we create, and the servlet is placed within the `Classes` node. The `web.xml` file for this Web application is the Web node in the tree.

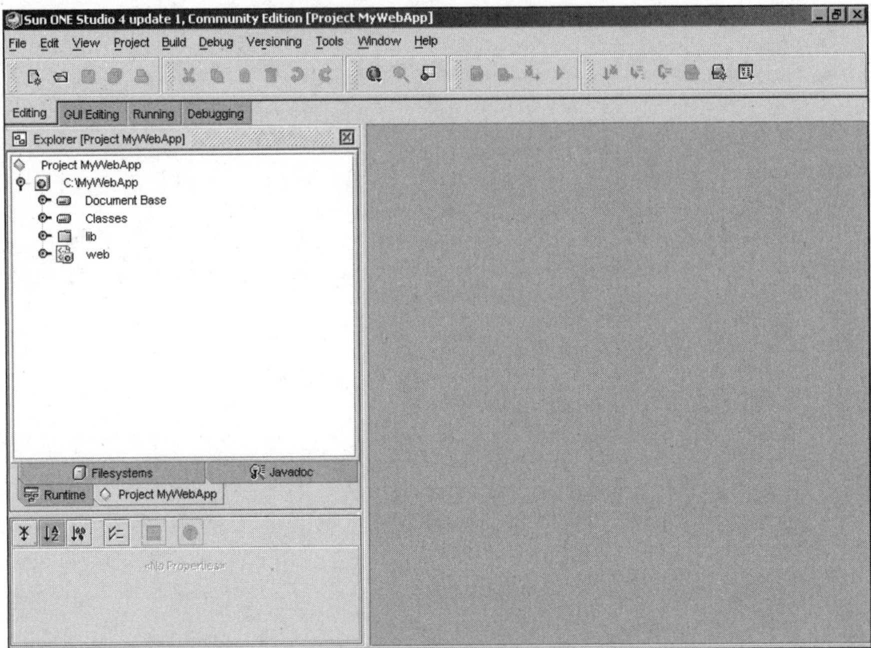

Figure 6-15: Web Module created in SunONE Studio

To create the JSP file right-click the Document Base node and select `New > JSP & Servlet > JSP`. A dialog box asks for a name; type '`MyJSP`' and press Finish. The document editor now displays some default content for the JSP file. In the demonstration JSP file I have added some simple looping code to print out a `String` in descending font size:

```
<%
String foo = "this is my test JSP file";

for(int i=1; i < 7; i++)
{
%>
    <H<%=i%>><%=foo%></H<%=i%>><br>
<%
}
%>
```

Once you have added this code, save the file. We can now tell this Web Module which server we want to test it on. Right-click the `WEB-INF` node under Document Base and select Properties. Properties for `WEB-INF` directories have various tabs across the bottom of the properties display dialog box., Select Execution. Change the `Target Server` property by using the drop-down list provided. Ensure you select `Tomcat 4.0 Internal`. The default server for executing this Web application has now been set.

We can now execute the JSP file to see the output it returns. Simply right-click the JSP file in the Explorer menu and select Execute.

The server starts, as does the browser that navigates to the URL of the internal server. The JSP page executed is shown. You should see something like Figure 6-16:

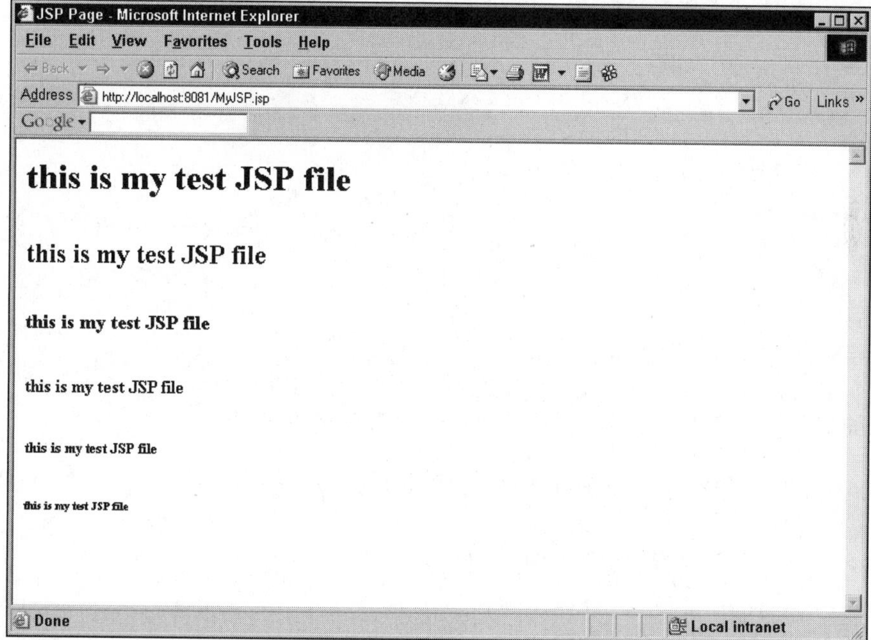

Figure 6-16: Test JSP file executed in SunONE Studios internal Tomcat server

If you look back in SunONE Studio you should notice that the Workspace has changed to Running and the output window includes tabs for the server output and an access log for the server.

If we make a minor change then go through the same process again, you will see the changed content appear in the browser, as shown in Figure 6-17.

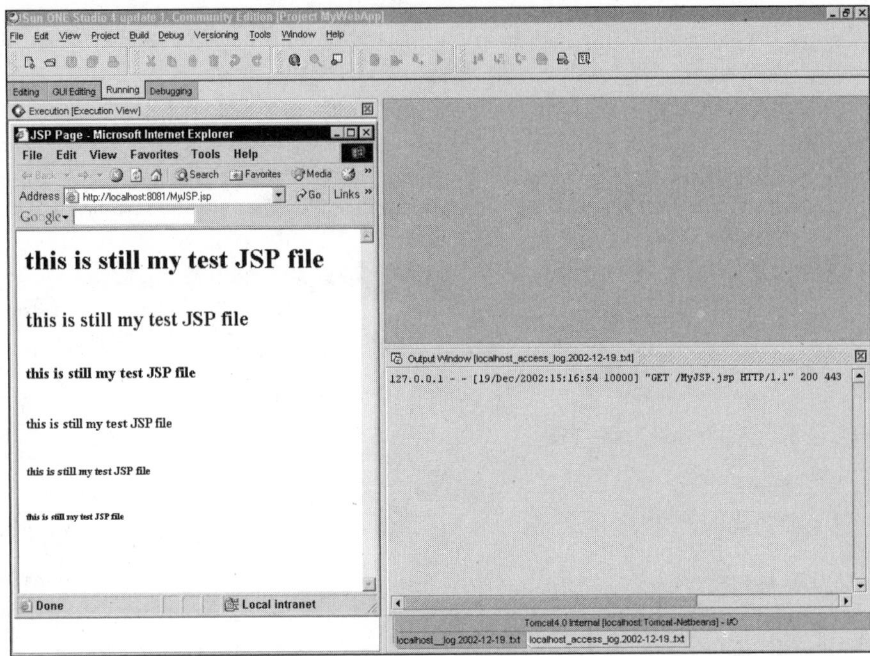

Figure 6-17: Changed JSP page in browser and output window in SunONE Studio

Let's now create a simple servlet to include in the Web Module. The servlet has to sit within a package structure, say `bible.tomcat.sunonetest`.

1. From the Project view in the Explorer workspace, right-click the `Classes` node under the Web Module. Select `New > Java Package`. A dialog box askes for the package details; simply type **`bible.tomcat.sunonetest`** and press Finish. The package structure is created automatically.

2. Expand the package until the `sunonetest` node appears. Right-click this directory and select `New > JSP & Servlet > Servlet`. Another dialog box appears, asking for the name of the servlet. Type **`MyServlet`** (don't add .java, it will do this automatically) then press Next.

3. The next dialog asks for the servlet deployment configuration information. Much of the information provided here goes to populating the `web.xml` file within this Web Module. In the Display Name Field type `myservlet` and then enter a short description. Now go down to the URL pattern and change this to just `/test`. Press Finish.

The servlet has now been created and the appropriate descriptor elements have been added to the `web.xml` file for this Web module. If you open the `Web` node (this denotes the `web.xml` file) you will see the servlet has been properly added.

Amongst the other standard servlet methods, SunONE Studio has placed a `processRequest` method in the servlet. This is where you can now type some content for the servlet to display. For comparison, type the same code as in the JSP file (without the `<% %>` delimiters of course) and press Save. The `processRequest` method should now appear as shown in Listing 6-1.

Listing 6-1: processRequest in MyServlet

```
protected void processRequest(HttpServletRequest request,
                              HttpServletResponse response)
     throws ServletException, java.io.IOException
{
     response.setContentType("text/html");
     java.io.PrintWriter out = response.getWriter();

     String foo = "this is my test servlet";

     for(int i=1; i < 7; i++)
     {
         out.println("<H" + i + ">" + foo + "</H" + i + "><br>");
     }
     out.close();
 }
```

Find the servlet file in the package nodes and right-click it. Then select Execute. The Server again goes through its startup; open a browser and show the output of the servlet. It should look something like Figure 6-18:

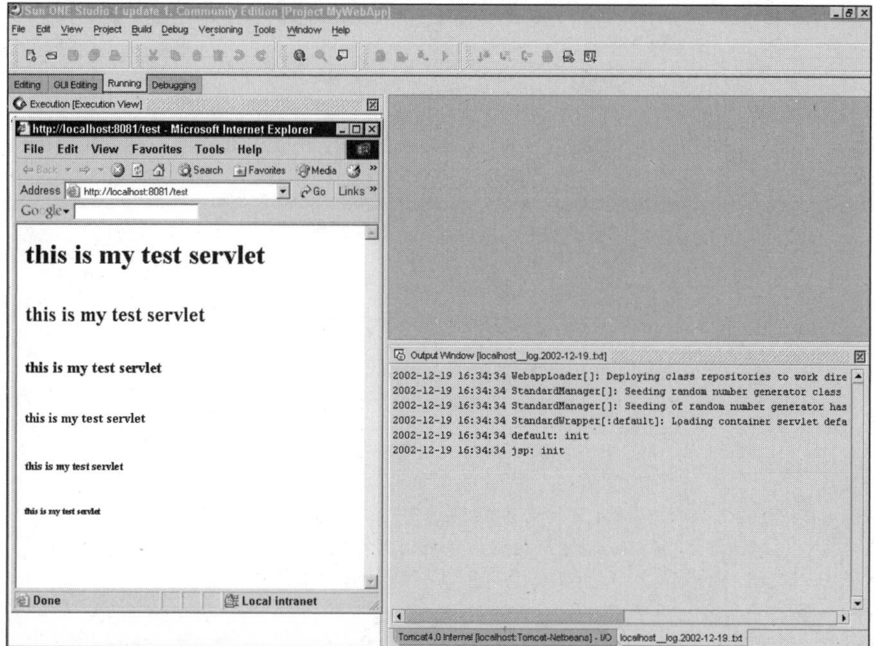

Figure 6-18: Servlet loaded in browser

Running the `Execute` command actually compiles the classes in the Classes node for you, if required, and then runs the application.

SunONE Studio offers extensive debugging facilities for applications, including the ability to debug JSP files. Debugging is discussed in detail in Chapter 11.

From the simple examples displayed here you can see how SunONE Studio can be used closely with its Internal Tomcat Server in the development of Web Applications.

Tips and Tricks

The following are some odds and ends available in the IDE that we consider extremely useful and important in any IDE discussion.

Code Completion

SunONE Studio offers powerful code completion, allowing the developer quickly program without having to manually lookup classes, methods, or member variables. By typing part of an expression the IDE is able to provide a list of the next possible values for the developer to choose.

For instance, by typing `Calendar.` the IDE can infer that we are obviously trying to access methods or member variables of the `Calendar` class and provide a scrollable list of the possible entries to continue the line of code. Figure 6-19 illustrates this example.

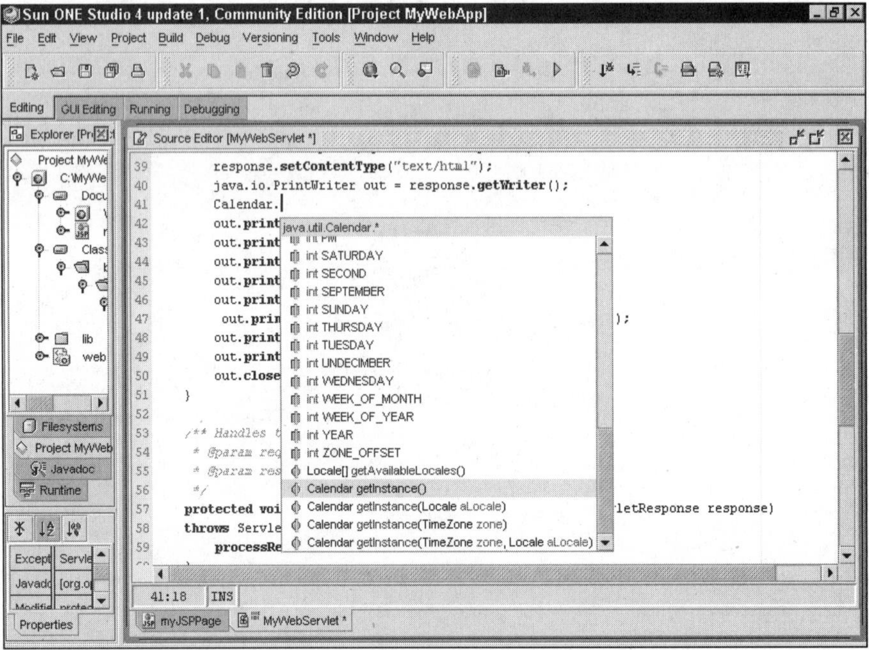

Figure 6-19: Code completion

As you can see, the IDE is able to recognize the Class we are accessing and provide an appropriate list of the next possible part of the code. As typing continues the list is reduced to include only the next possible values based on what has just been typed. Therefore if `Calendar.getI` was being typed, the list would shrink to only include the `getInstance` methods of the `Calendar` class.

Parser Database

There may be occasions where the relevant API is not available for the object you are referencing. Code Completion uses the Parser Database to store the APIs it needs. The Parser Database can be updated with new APIs by following these steps:

Assume the database driver JAR that was added to SunONE Studio earlier needed to be included in the Parser Database, as an example. (It doesn't have to be a JAR file.)

Mount the JAR file in the File-system view of the Explorer workspace.

Right-click the file in the File-system view and select `Tools > Update Parser Database...`

The IDE displays a dialog box asking what it should call the database it is about to create and what information from the JAR file it should store. The parser database can store different combinations of public, protected, and private classes, fields, and methods.

Once the parser database is updated code completion is available for the contents of the JAR file.

Auto Comment and Javadoc Tool

If you're like most developers, you find comments a chore, "Hey, the code *is* documentation!" SunONE Studio includes a tidy little tool that enables you to enter Javadoc comments into your java files from the IDE interface, Auto comment. Once the comments are placed in the code, there is another tool to automatically generate the Javadoc html files for you without executing Javadoc from the command line.

To explain, let's assume you have a small bean class to which we want to add Javadoc comments. Start the Auto comment tool by right-clicking the Java file within the Project or File-system tab of the Explorer Workspace, and select Tools then Auto comment. Figure 6-20 shows the Auto comment tool at work.

As you can see from Figure 6-21 we have added some comments to the first item in the list that is the class definition itself. The remaining items in the list relate to properties and methods that are not commented. A green tick appears next to the item that has comments; a red cross marks those that don't. There is also the facility to add Taglets to the comments, for instance, `@version 0-1`, that Javadoc recognizes when the documentation is created.

Once the code is full of meaningful comments SunONE Studio can run the Javadoc tool by right-clicking any node in the tree that contains classes and selecting `Tools > Generate Javadoc`. The IDE then asks if the Javadoc should be displayed in the default browser; selecting yes displays the completed Javadoc HTML.

Version Control

SunONE Studio allows for the integration of CVS (Concurrent Versions System) or any Version Control System that has a command-based interface.

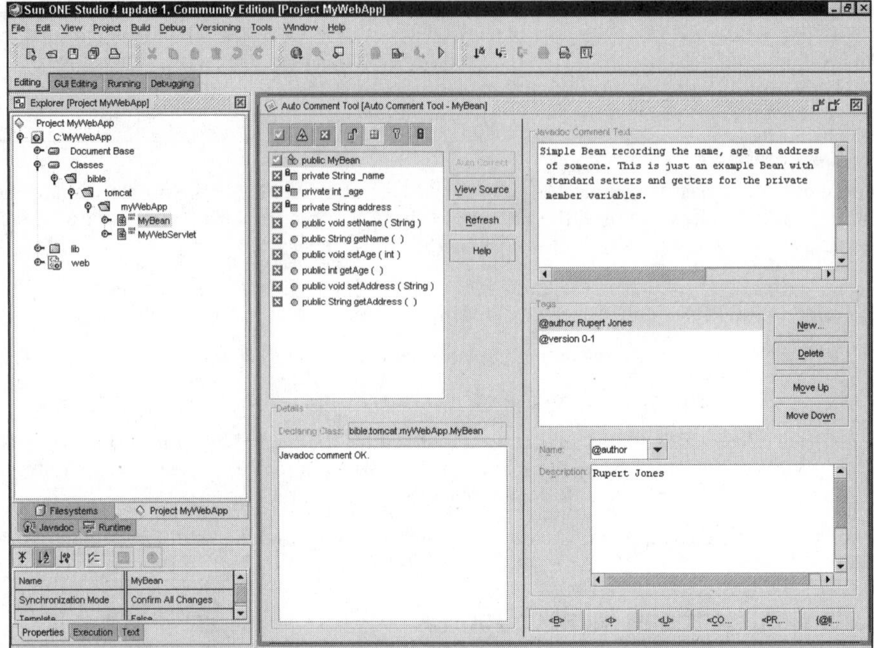

Figure 6-20: Auto comment tool

CVS is an excellent tool for managing your source. It can be run from both Windows- and Unix-based platforms. You can find more information about it at http://www.cvshome.org.

CVS can be fully integrated with the IDE, so much so that most commands available under CVS can be executed on a file or directory basis within the source tree.

Summary

This concludes a very brief introduction into SunONE Studio CE. By no means is this a definitive description of its features and functionality, but what *is* described should give you some knowledge of its ins and outs. We recommend doing further reading in the SunONE Studio documentation and other resources such as mailing lists.

The Eclipse Platform

The Eclipse Platform was formed as part of the Eclipse Project, the purpose of which was to create a universal platform for tools integration. The platform forms the foundation for the IBM WebSphere Application Studio in much the same way that NetBeans is the foundation for the SunOne Developer Studio. Eclipse is an open source and freely available platform written in Java[8].

---

[8] The Standard Windowing Toolkit (SWT) does, however, require native libraries to interface with the native windowing environment.

The Eclipse Platform is primarily a tool integration platform, not a Java IDE. It is a generic platform containing frameworks and services that can be used for general purpose applications.

The Eclipse Platform uses a custom windowing toolkit called Standard Widget Toolkit (SWT), developed by the Eclipse Project. This toolkit is a replacement for AWT and Swing, which utilizes native widgets wherever possible, giving the platform an unparalleled native look and feel. SWT is used in conjunction with the platform independent JFace toolkit, to provide a set of reusable UI components simplifying graphical programming tasks. Unlike AWT, SWT is not limited to the lowest common denominator of widgets available on all platforms; custom widgets are provided to give a set of distinguishing features that still adhere to the native user interface design guidelines. This, in comparison to Swing; which entirely replicates the entire set of widgets and attempts to give them a native look and feel.

The extensible nature of Eclipse is limitless. Using the Plug-in Development Environment (PDE), anyone can write extensions to the platform, customizing all aspects of the GUI, and introducing new features to the platform. Installation and updates of the plug-ins is as simple as extracting a zip file into the `plugins` directory and customizing the display options to make the plug-in visible.

Eclipse comes packaged with Java Development Tools (JDT), enabling the platform to be used as a Java development environment. JDT is a plug-in that supports Java development with the addition of a Java builder and a customized perspective to the UI. Various other tools and wizards are added to the platform as part of the plug-in.

Eclipse is a multi-language IDE, and although Java is supported by default this does not prevent the use of numerous plug-ins adding support for other languages. See the Useful Add-ons section later in this chapter for more details.

Where to Get It

The latest builds for the Eclipse Platform are available from `www.eclipse.org`. There are two build types that should be of interest; the latest release and the current stable release. Milestone 3 (M3) is the current stable release in the 2.1 branch; it has more features but may contain more bugs. The latest release, 2.0.2, has fewer bugs, but as it is still part of the 2.0 branch it has fewer features.

For the purposes of this chapter the latest release, 2.0.2, will be used. To download the latest release go to `www.eclipse.org` and select the “download” link to the left of the page.

Select the link for the latest release with build name `2.0.2` from the Latest Downloads section.

The Version 2.0.2 download page enables you to select from a variety of packages, including the Eclipse Platform bundled with various tools. The Eclipse SDK comes with the Eclipse Platform, the Java development tools, and user documentation, making it the most appropriate package.

Select the Windows 98/ME/2000/XP version: `eclipse-SDK-2.0.2-win32.zip`, and when prompted, save the file to disk.

Installation

The file that has been downloaded is a zip file containing the Eclipse platform. Installation is as simple as extracting the zip file to your hard drive.

Extract the `eclipse-SDK-2.0.2-win32.zip` file to the `C:\`. This creates a directory titled `C:\eclipse` and subdirectories.

Note

The Eclipse SDK does not come with a JDK or JRE; one must be installed before you proceed.

JDK 1.4.x is recommended for debugging with Eclipse because it supports the hot code replacement feature. However, throughout this chapter JDK 1.3.1 is used to retain consistency with the rest of the book. Without a 1.4.x JDK the Eclipse Platform cannot hot swap code from the development environment straight into the in-process Tomcat, requiring Tomcat to be restarted.

You can now create a shortcut on the start menu or desktop for `C:\eclipse\eclipse.exe`.

Start eclipse by double-clicking the Eclipse icon.

The first time Eclipse is run a splash screen shown in notifying the user to Please Wait ... Completing the Install.

Upon completion of the installation the Eclipse workbench is displayed with a welcome screen, as shown in Figure 6-21. The welcome page contains many useful links, including to the Workbench User Guide.

If you want to get back to the Welcome screen at a later stage, select `Help>Welcome...` from the menu. In the Welcome dialog box select the Eclipse Platform.

Configuration

It is necessary to set eclipse to use a JDK instead of the JRE; this is important to allow compilation of JSP using the Tomcat plug-ins described later in this section.

If necessary, start Eclipse.

Select `Window>Preferences` from the menu. This displays a Preferences dialog box, allowing the user to customize the behavior of Eclipse.

Navigate to `Java>Installed JRE`. The Preferences dialog box will change, allowing the user to reconfigure Eclipse to use a new JRE or JDK.

Click Add... to add a JRE definition used to build and run Java programs.

A dialog box is displayed; fill in the details, as shown in Figure 6-22, to define a JDK for Eclipse to use. Name the new JRE definition JDK 1.3.1, and click OK.

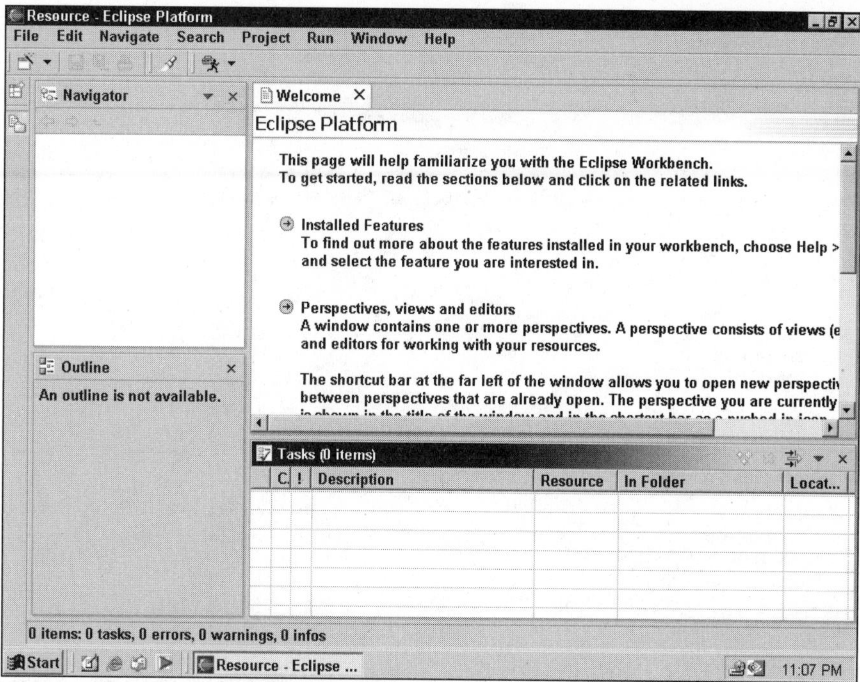

Figure 6-21: Eclipse workbench with welcome screen

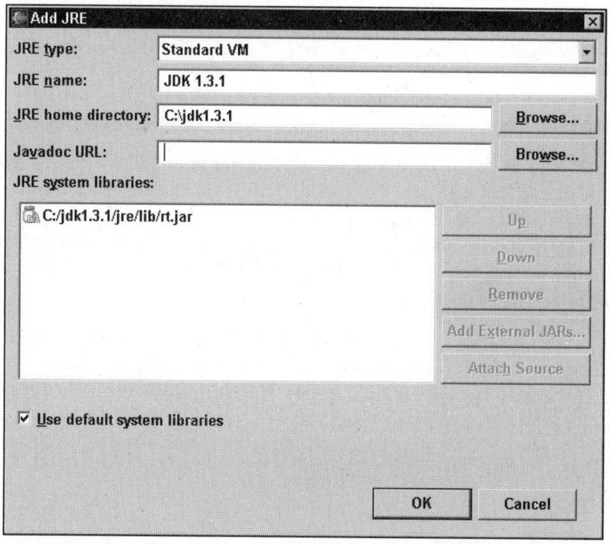

Add JRE
JRE type: Standard VM
JRE name: JDK 1.3.1
JRE home directory: C:\jdk1.3.1 Browse...
Javadoc URL: Browse...
JRE system libraries:
C:/jdk1.3.1/jre/lib/rt.jar
Up
Down
Remove
Add External JARs...
Attach Source
Use default system libraries
OK Cancel

Figure 6-22: Adding a new JRE definition so Eclipse uses the JDK to build and run Java programs

So the JDK is used by default, click the check box to the left of the JDK 1.3.1 definition as shown in Figure 6-23.

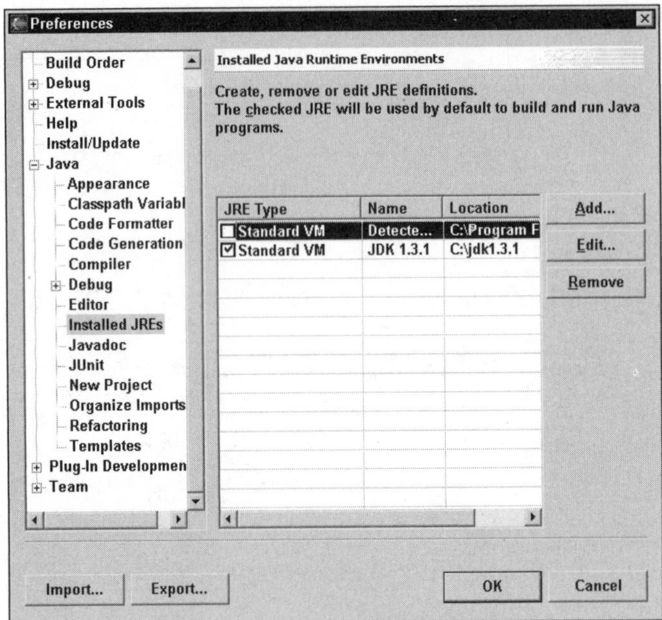

Figure 6-23: Making JDK 1.3.1 Eclipse's default JRE

Click OK to complete the configuration. You are now returned to the Eclipse workbench.

How to Use Eclipse

The Eclipse Platform is a large and in-depth application of which it is impossible to cover all the features in only one section. Fortunately the Eclipse distribution comes bundled with very good quality user documentation. Documentation is available through the Help view by selecting `Help>Help Contents` from the menu. If, for some reason, the Eclipse package did not come bundled with documentation, an online version is also available from `http://dev.eclipse.org:8080/help/help.jsp`.

This section provides a very brief introduction to the Eclipse Platform environment, just enough to get familiar with Eclipse and set up a Web-based Java project using Tomcat. For a more detailed tour of the features and benefits of Eclipse, it is recommended to read both the Workbench User Guide and the Java Development User Guide accessible through the Help view.

The concepts explained during the familiarization section are referenced throughout the remainder of this chapter.

Getting Familiar with the Environment

The concepts explained in this section familiarize you with the Eclipse environment, and define the terminology essential to the understanding of the integration of Eclipse with Tomcat.

Workbench

The most fundamental piece of the Eclipse User Interface (UI) is the workbench. The workbench metaphor is used to describe a set of specialized tools, and a space on which to work. All the tools and features to complete a task are available in the one location, the workbench.

When you first open Eclipse you are confronted with a multi-windowed environment complete with menus, toolbars, and components, this is the workbench.

Perspectives

The perspective controls what is displayed on a workbench. There are various perspectives available in the standard Eclipse Platform, and new perspectives can be added with the use of plug-ins.

Standard perspectives available after the installation of Eclipse include:

- **Resource Perspective:** shows a directory-like view workspace and the resources located within.
- **Java Perspective:** a view of the java resources contained in a project workspace.
- **Java Browsing Perspective:** alternate view of java resources, more suited to browsing through packages, classes, methods, and properties.
- **Debug Perspective:** shows all the tools required to debug the application.

Many other perspectives are available.

To make new perspectives visible select the perspective name from the menu `Window>Open Perspective>...`.

Figure 6-24 outlines the various components contained in the Resource Perspective.

Menu

Each perspective can have a custom menu. The features available from the menu will be context sensitive. Standard `File`, `Edit`, `Window`, and `Help` entries are accessible from menus across all perspectives.

Toolbars

There are two toolbars visible in each perspective; a standard toolbar and the perspective toolbar. The standard toolbar behaves like any other toolbar found in a GUI application, making features available through the menu quickly accessible with the click of a button.

The perspective toolbar allows quick navigation between perspectives without having to use the `Window` menu.

Editors

The editor pane normally takes up a large portion of the perspective. This real estate is essential for editing any sort of document. Editors are also typically visible across multiple perspectives, allowing edit to file based resources in a variety of contexts.

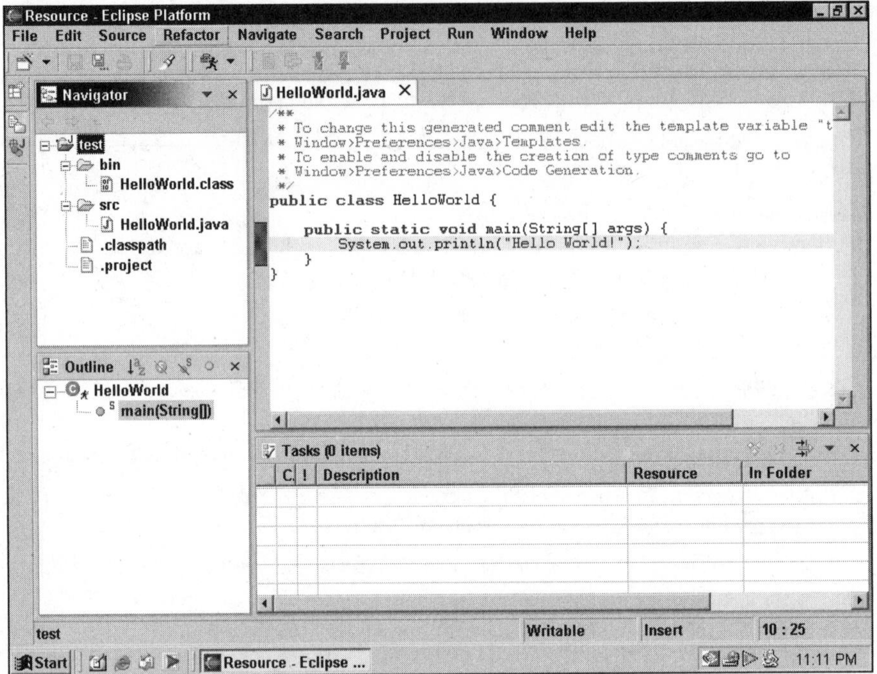

Figure 6-24: Eclipse workbench, showing the Resource Perspective

The editor pane is also tabbed, allowing switching between multiple open documents. You may notice that double-clicking an editor tab expands the editor to take up nearly the entire perspective.

Eclipse comes with a feature-rich text editor by default, and supports the embedding of other OLE compliant editors such as Microsoft Word, further exemplifying the workbench metaphor. Eclipse also supports the use of external system editors for registered file types. External editors can be launched from the Navigator View, and open as a separate window on top of the workbench.

Users are therefore able to utilize their favorite text editor via an external program. Alternatively, the Eclipse text editor can support custom key bindings, or there may be a plug-in available that includes an embedded version of your favorite editor.

Tasks and markers appear as icons in the left margin of the Eclipse text editor. The left margin is referred to as the *vertical ruler. Task icons* highlight an area of the document that requires the user's attention; for example, a compiler error notifying the user of a syntactical error in the code, or an Eclipse quick hint offering the user a suggestion.

Markers identify a point in the document that may be referenced at a later time. Examples of markers include bookmarks and debug breakpoints.

Views

Views are the most diverse workspace component. There are many different views available across all perspectives; generally they display information regarding a resource or project, or provide navigation through resources in the project.

Examples of standard views include:

- **Navigator View:** Allows a user to navigate through resources across projects, similar to the Windows Explorer interface.
- **Package Explorer View:** A Windows Explorer-like interface enabling the user to navigate through the source tree, including packages, classes, methods, and properties.
- **Type Hierarchy View:** Displays both the class hierarchy and the outline of a particular object.
- **Outline View:** A narrowed-down view of all the methods and properties contained in a class.
- **Bookmark View:** Displays all bookmarked files in the project. Users may navigate directly to the bookmarked file by double clicking the bookmark.
- **Task View:** A to-do list of outstanding tasks to be completed. Eclipse will also display system and compilation errors/warnings/information in the Task View.

Many other views are available.

New views may be opened and added to the perspective by selecting the desired view from the `Window>Show View>...` menu.

Workspace

Each project has its own *workspace*. A workspace is simply a directory or folder containing all the project resources and configuration files. By default Eclipse stores workspaces in `C:\eclipse\workspace`. Workspaces may however, live anywhere on the disk.

To create a new a new project workspace select `File>New>Project...` from the menu. A dialog box is displayed, allowing the user to select from the available project *natures*. Each project nature defines the structure and behavior of the project, including directory structure, location of source and output directories, a build path, and any customized build tasks to perform on the project.

It is very important when creating a new project that the project name does not contain any spaces or special characters.

Many plug-ins offer new project natures when installed. These natures are available from the New Project dialog box. During the integration with Tomcat section we install two new project types, enabling the creation of J2EE Web-based projects.

The project structure can be viewed and modified using the Navigator or Package Explorer. These views behave like Windows Explorer folders, enabling the creation of files and folders, and rename/copy/move/delete functionality all resources. Drag-and-drop functionality from other Windows applications is also supported.

Table 6-2 outlines the various types of folders that may be contained in a project workspace. It is important to understand the purpose of each folder type as their use is very important to the project structure, and in particular the build process.

Table 6-2: Workspace Structure

Folder Type	*Purpose*
Project Root	All project files, including source code, resources, and binary output are to be located under the project root.
Web Application Root	All JSP files and static Web content are to be placed in the Web application root.
Source Folder	All source files are to be located within one or more source directories. A project may have many source directories containing source code or other resources that are to be built with the project. Source code can be organized using packages. The Eclipse Java Builder only compiles source code contained in source directories.
Packages	A directory hierarchy corresponding to the package name. Each delimited identifier within the package name will correspond to a directory within the hierarchy.
Output Folder	The source code contained in source directories is compiled by the Java Builder and object files are placed in the output directory. If the source directory contains other resources, they are simply copied to the output directory. The output directory is also referred to as the *Build* output folder.
Sub Folder	Normal subdirectories may be created within the project root to logically organize other project resources such as specification documentation etc. Subdirectories have no special behavior or properties unless specified by the project nature.

Build Path

The most important part of the Eclipse workspace is the build path; this controls how the source code is built into binary objects. As mentioned previously in Table 6-2, all source code must be located in a source folder to be compiled by a custom JCK-compliant Java compiler called the Java Builder.

Caution Eclipse does support other builders apart from the default Java Builder. Theoretically a build tool like Ant could be used instead. The setup and configuration of Ant, however, is not trivial. It is recommended to consult the Java Developer's User Guide for more information.

Compiled objects are then placed into the output folder. New source folders and the output folder can be specified using the Java Build path properties.

To open the Java Build path properties, select `File>Properties` from the menu and navigate to Java Build Path in the left pane. Figure 6-25 shows the initial Source tab for the Java Build Path properties.

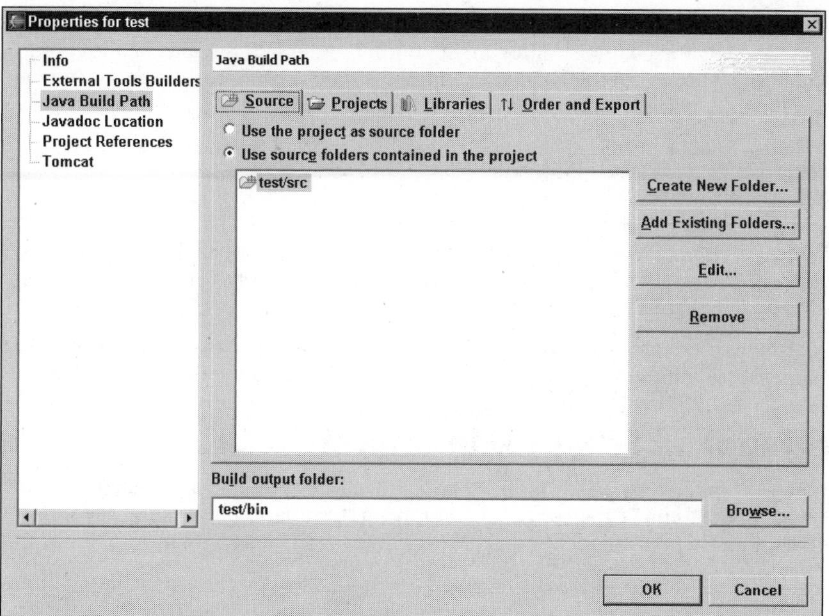

Figure 6-25: Java Build Path properties

It also is possible to include third party Java libraries that are required by the project. In the Java Build Path properties, select the Libraries tab and insert references to classpaths and JAR files containing classes required by the project source. Java libraries and class files contained in the build path are accessed by the Code Assist feature of Eclipse, suggesting a list of possible method and property names while typing code in the editor.

There also is the ability to control what resources are built and included in the output folder. The Order | Export tab allows the build order to be specified, along with the inclusion or exclusion of source directories and libraries to be exported into the output folder.

Incremental Build

Incremental compilation is an integral part of the project builder framework. This allows developers to be immediately notified of compilation errors, and avoids a lengthy full build process that can take minutes, even hours to complete.

The automatic build process is triggered upon the saving of a source file. Then files that have changed since the last build are compiled into the output folder. Any compile-time syntactical errors are entered into the Task View.

Tip The behavior of build process to can be changed from custom to manual if need be by clearing the `Window>Preferences>Perform build automatically on resource modification` check box.

Full Build

A full build cleans the contents of the project output folder and rebuilds all the resources contained in the project. A full build is recommended before a release to ensure no unnoticed changes have slipped past the incremental build process.

To start a full build, select `Project>Rebuild Project` from the menu.

Running the Project

Project source code may be run from within Eclipse as Java applications or JUnit tests. To run the application, select `Run>Run As>...` from the menu, and choose the appropriate type of application. The output of the application appear in either a Console View, or a custom view provided by the plug-in.

The next section explains the setup and configuration of a Web-based project using Tomcat. Web-based applications may be run and debugged from within the Eclipse workbench.

Integration of Eclipse with Tomcat

Although the commercial WebSphere Studio Application Developer comes bundled with built-in Tomcat support, the Eclipse project must rely on third-party plug-ins to provide integration with the Tomcat Server.

There are several Tomcat plug-ins available for Eclipse, two of which are covered in this section. An introduction is given to each plug-in describing how to install the software, and how to create a Tomcat project in both environments. To demonstrate, a simple Web project containing a JSP and servlet is created using each of the plug-in environments.

Sysdeo Eclipse Tomcat Launcher

The Sysdeo Eclipse Tomcat Launcher is a simple plug-in enabling the creation of Web-based projects using JSP and servlet technology. Development is targeted to the Tomcat server allowing the developer to deploy directly to a local Tomcat instance.

Download

The Sysdeo Eclipse Tomcat Launcher can be downloaded from `http://www.sysdeo.com/eclipse/tomcatPlugin.html`.

Select the plug-in corresponding to the version of Eclipse you are using: `tomcatPluginV201.zip`, and when prompted save the file to disk.

Installation

As mentioned previously, Eclipse plug-in installation is as simple as extracting the zip file into the `C:\eclipse\plugins` directory. Once this is complete, the features of plug-in are made available by customizing the perspective.

Extract the `tomcatPluginV201.zip` file to the `C:\eclipse`. This creates a directory `C:\eclipse\plugins\ com.sysdeo.eclipse.tomcat` and subdirectories.

Caution Tomcat 4.1.12 must be installed before using this plug-in.

Stop Eclipse if necessary the plug-in is registered when Eclipse next starts.

Configuration

To configure the Sysdeo Tomcat Launcher plug-in, the Eclipse Platform must first be started. The following steps outline the process of configuring the Tomcat plug-in to operate with `Tomcat 4.1.12` installed on the local machine.

To activate the plug-in select `Window>Customize Perspective...` from the menu. A Customize Perspective dialog box appears.

Navigate to `File>New`, and then check the box next to Tomcat Project. This adds the facility to create a new Tomcat project from the menu and the New Project wizard.

Next, navigate to Other, and check the box next to Tomcat. This adds Restart, Start, and Stop Tomcat buttons to the workbench toolbar. Press OK to commit the changes.

Next we need to customize the Tomcat preferences. Select `Windows>Preferences` from the menu. The Preferences dialog box is displayed.

Navigate to Tomcat in the left pane, and in the Tomcat Preferences change the Tomcat version to `4.1.x`, and change the Tomcat home directive to `C:\tomcat`. The configuration file should be automatically updated and the screen should look like Figure 6-26.

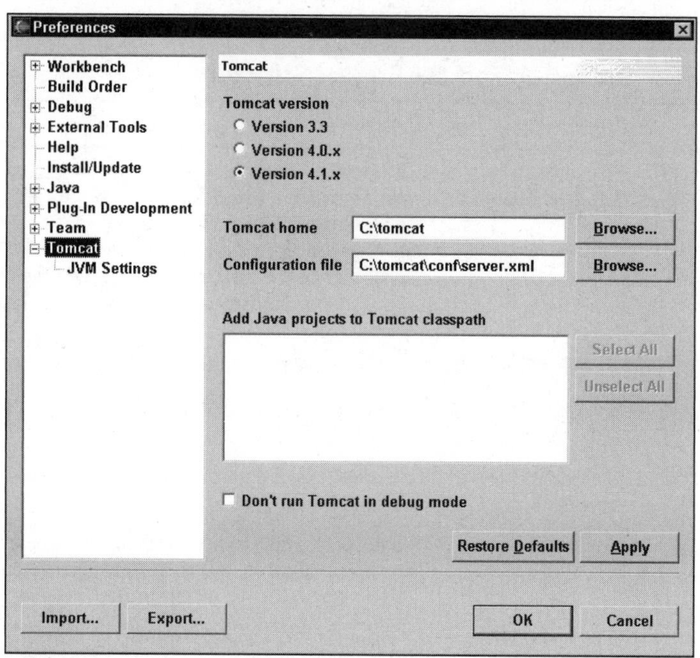

Figure 6-26: Tomcat Launcher preferences

Navigate to `Tomcat>JVM Settings` in the left pane, and in the JVM Settings dialog box change the JRE to `JDK1.3.1`.

If JDK 1.3.1 does not appear in the list of available JREs repeat the steps outlined previously in the Eclipse Configuration section.

The selected JRE specified must be a JDK for Tomcat JSP compilation to work successfully.

Press OK to close the preferences dialog and apply the changes. The Sysdeo Tomcat Launcher is now configured and we are ready to create a Tomcat project in Eclipse.

Creating a New Tomcat Project

The Tomcat Launcher plug-in has added a new project type to the Eclipse Platform. Every eclipse project has a nature. This project nature determines a project's structure and behavior. The project nature also defines a default compilation build path appropriate for Tomcat projects.

When a new Tomcat project is created by the wizard the directory structure is created as outlined in Table 6-3.

Table 6-3: Tomcat Project Structure

Directory	*Directory Type*	*Description*
`/project`	Project root, Web Application Root	The project root serves as the document root of the Web application. This also doubles as the Web application root. All JSP files and static Web content are to be placed in this directory. The Web application root of the project may alternatively be specified as a subdirectory under the project root.
`/project/WEB-INF`	Subdirectory	Configuration directory containing deployment descriptors and other configuration files.
`/project/WEB-INF/classes`	Output directory	Destination for compiled servlet object files.
`/project/WEB-INF/src`	Source directory	Location of servlet source and other resources such a properties files.
`/project/WEB-INF/lib`	Subdirectory	Contains Java Archive (JAR) files or libraries used by the Web application, along with any other resources required at runtime.
`/project/work`	Source directory	Working directory containing pre-compiled JSP files generated by the Jasper compiler.
`/project/work/org/apache/jsp`	Package	Working directory with a pre-defined package hierarchy used by Tomcat.

Any new Tomcat projects created with the new project wizard have a familiar directory structure to that used inside Web Application aRchive (WAR) files. The directory layout makes deployment easy, the project root is simply zipped up and packaged as a WAR file ready for deployment.

The Tomcat project directory may also be used directly as a Tomcat context root. This is useful for development purposes where it is desirable to have changes made to the source code immediately available on the Tomcat server without the need to package and deploy the project.

Structuring the developer's workspace like a WAR file simplifies packaging and allows a Tomcat context to point directly at the project root, however the Tomcat Application Developer's Guidelines recommends against this practice. Unfortunately the nature of the project cannot be changed to conform to these guidelines, but don't worry Tomcat projects will still function as normal. See the Tomcat Application Developer's Guidelines section for more information.

The following procedure describes the steps involved in creating a new Tomcat project using the Wizard.

Select `File>New>Project...` from the Eclipse workbench menu. A New Project dialog box is displayed as shown in Figure 6-27. Select Tomcat Project and click Next.

Tomcat Application Developer's Guidelines

Many of the Tomcat plug-in project directory structures are not consistent with the Application Developer's Guidelines suggested by the Jakarta Tomcat project `http://jakarta.apache.org/tomcat/tomcat-4.1-doc/appdev/processes.html`.

The guidelines suggest a build area is created, separate from the developer's workspace. A build area structure should be laid out like a Web application; static content and JSP files should be placed at the root of the build area, configuration files and deployment descriptors are placed in the `/WEB-INF` directory, third party libraries are placed in the `/WEB-INF/lib` directory, and compiled object class files are placed in the `/WEB-INF/classes` directory. At this stage the build area may be zipped up and packaged as a WAR file, or a new Tomcat context can be registered to point directly at the build area. The Tomcat project structures do not generate a separate build area, instead the developer's workspace is made to resemble the structure of a WAR file. Source is compiled and object file placed in the `/WEB-INF/classes` directly under the developer's workspace. Deploying the Web application selectively packages the contents of the workspace as a WAR file, or registers a new context to point directly to the developer's workspace where both source code and object code are kept.

It is preferable to have the source code and the built Web-application separate, but unfortunately it is difficult to modify the Sysdeo or Lomboz Tomcat project natures to comply with the Tomcat guidelines.

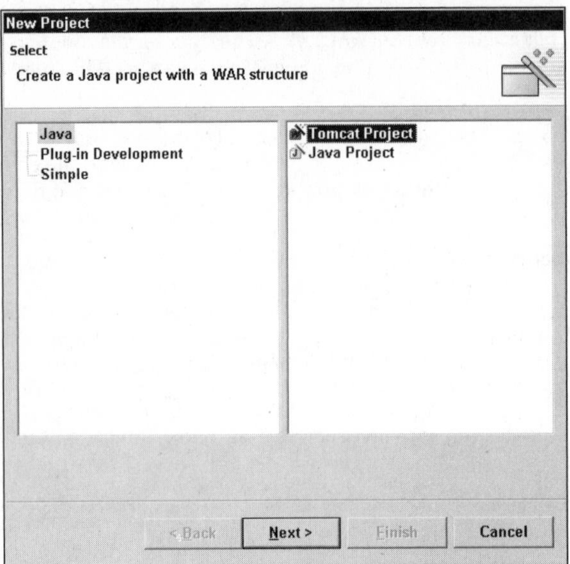

Figure 6-27: New Project dialog box, including a Tomcat Project

For the purposes of this example we create a simple project called `hello` in the New Tomcat Project dialog box and type the Project Name **hello** in the text field. You can have the project created in the default workspace directory by ensuring the Project Contents: Use default check box is checked. Click Next to proceed.

In the New Tomcat Project Settings dialog box as seen in Figure 6-28, ensure the Context name corresponds to the name given to your project in the previous step; this name must have a leading slash to correctly register the Tomcat project in a context. If the Can update server.xml file option is checked, this enables the project to add, update, or create contexts in the Tomcat configuration. Check the box if you are developing on the same machine as Tomcat and would like a Tomcat context to point directly at the project workspace.

The Subdirectory to set as Web application root (optional) field can be left as is unless you require the Web application document root to be separate from the project root.

Click Finish to commence the construction of the new Tomcat project, which may take a little while as the project structure is created. At the conclusion of this process a new Tomcat project is displayed in a Java perspective on the workbench, as seen in Figure 6-29.

Implementing a Tomcat Project

We are now ready to add resources to our project to test the integration between Tomcat and Eclipse. This section sets up a working Web application containing a simple JSP and servlet.

All source code and deployment descriptor locations are relative to the Tomcat project document root `C:\eclipse\workspace\hello`.

Create a new JSP file `HelloWorldJSP.jsp` in the under the Web application root directory `/hello` with the source in Listing 6-2.

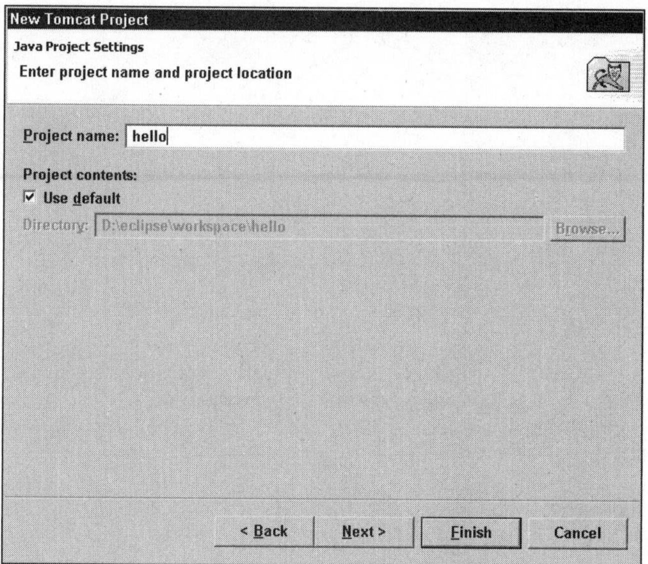

Figure 6-28: New Tomcat Project Settings dialog box

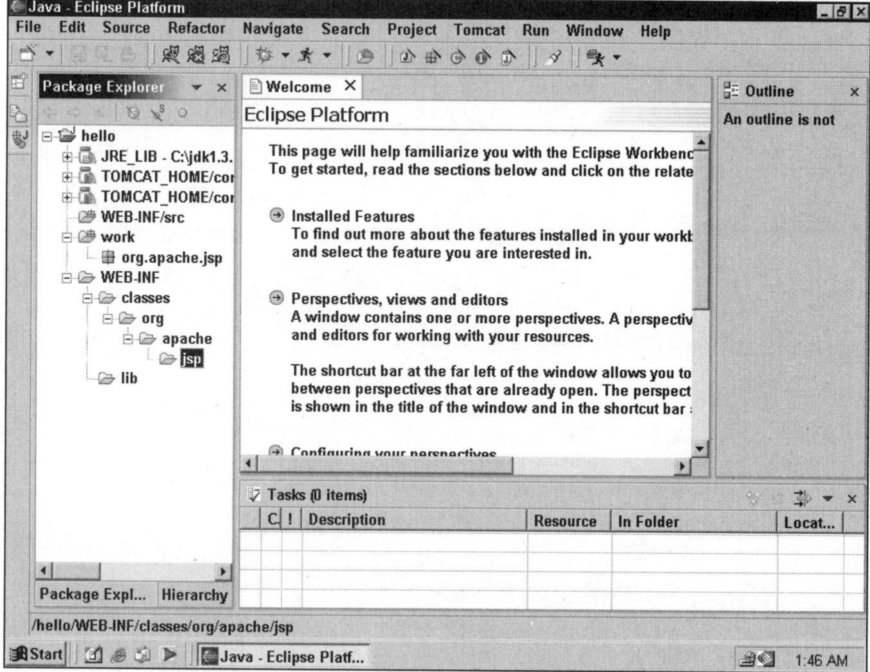

Figure 6-29: Finished new Tomcat project

Listing 6-2: **HelloWorldJSP.jsp**

```
<%
    String helloMessage = "Hello World!";
%>
<html>
<body>
<h1><%=helloMessage %></h1>
</body>
</html>
```

Create a new servlet `HelloWorldServlet.java`, shown in Listing 6-3, under the source directory `/hello/WEB-INF/src`. It is necessary to create the appropriate `bible.tomcat.hello` package under the source directory before creating the file.

Listing 6-3: **HelloWorldServlet.java**

```
package bible.tomcat.hello;

import java.io.*;

import javax.servlet.http.*;
import javax.servlet.*;

public class HelloWorldServlet extends HttpServlet
{
    public void doGet(HttpServletRequest request,
            HttpServletResponse response)
    throws ServletException, IOException
    {
        // pass on the request to doPost
        doPost(request,response);
    }

    public void doPost(HttpServletRequest request,
            HttpServletResponse response)
    throws ServletException, IOException
    {
        PrintWriter out = response.getWriter();
        String helloMessage = "Hello World!";

        // set the response type
        response.setContentType("text/html");

        // now write it out
        out.println("<html>");
        out.println("<body>");
```

```
        out.println("<h1>"+helloMessage+"</h1>");
        out.println("</body>");
        out.println("</html>");
    }
}
```

Finally, create the Web application deployment descriptor defined in Listing 6-4 in the `/hello/WEB-INF` folder.

Listing 6-4: WEB-INF\web.xml

```
<?xml version="1.0" encoding="ISO-8859-1" ?>

<!DOCTYPE web-app
  PUBLIC "-//Sun Microsystems, Inc.//DTD Web Application 2.3//EN"
  "http://java.sun.com/dtd/web-app_2_3.dtd" >

<web-app>
    <icon>
    </icon>
    <display-name>Hello World Application</display-name>
    <description>
        This is the simple Hello World! application
    </description>

    <servlet>
        <servlet-name>world</servlet-name>
        <description>
            The Hello World! Servlet
        </description>
        <servlet-class>
            bible.tomcat.hello.HelloWorldServlet
        </servlet-class>
    </servlet>

    <servlet-mapping>
        <servlet-name>world</servlet-name>
        <url-pattern>/world</url-pattern>
    </servlet-mapping>
</web-app>
```

After the files have been created and added to the project, the workbench should look like the one in Figure 6-30.

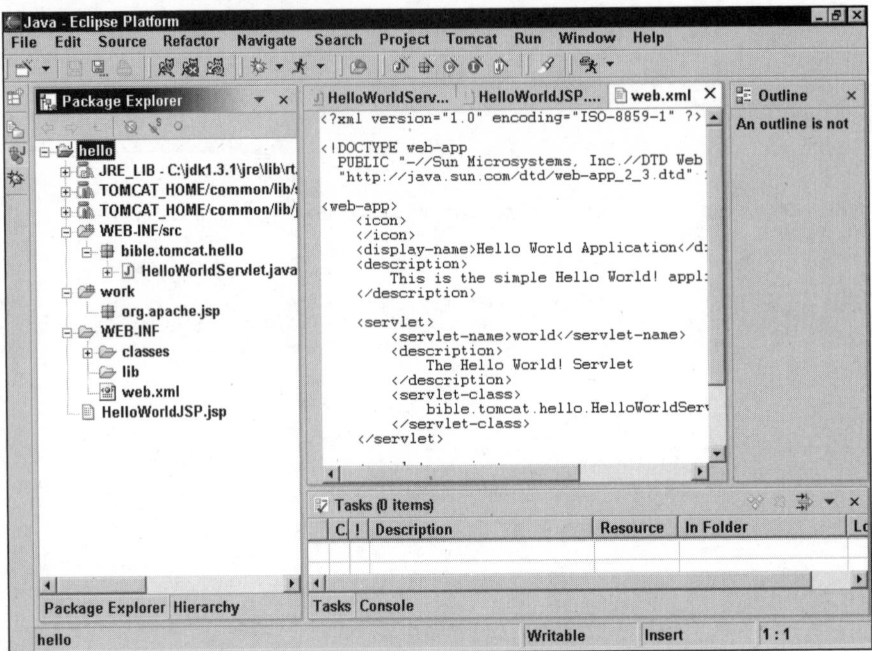

Figure 6-30: Java Perspective in workbench containing new files

To test the application it must first be deployed on the Tomcat server.

Deployment

The Tomcat Launcher plug-in can deploy Web applications using a distributable WAR file by simply setting a single project property. Once created, the WAR file may be placed in the `webapps` directory of the Tomcat server or be deployed using the Tomcat Manager application.

Unfortunately the Sysdeo plug-in does utilize the hot deployment features of the Tomcat Manager application. Instead the WAR file must be deployed manually to the Tomcat server.

The Sysdeo plug-in creates a WAR file based on the contents of the document root. Because the project structure is designed to reflect the layout of a WAR file, packaging the Web application is simple. The plug-in handles the packaging of the document root upon each incremental compilation. All compiled objects, deployment files, and resources are included in the WAR file. By default source code is excluded from the WAR, unless explicitly specified.

To configure the Tomcat project to deploy the Web application as a WAR file, open the Tomcat project properties by selecting the project name in the Package View, right-clicking, and selecting Properties, or select `File>Properties` from the menu.

A Properties dialog box similar to Figure 6-31 is displayed. Enter the desired location of WAR file for export and click OK.

If you are developing on the same machine as the Tomcat server, the location of the exported WAR file can point directly at Tomcat's `webapps` directory, avoiding the need to manually deploy the WAR file.

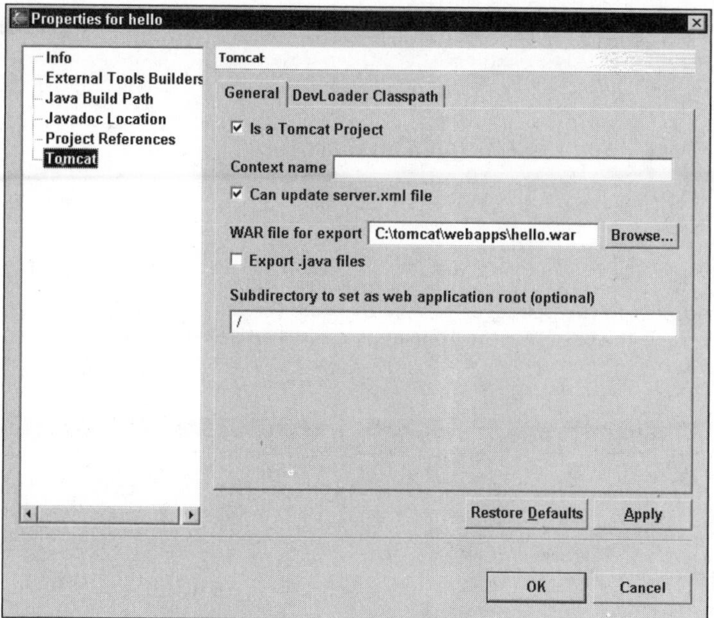

Figure 6-31: Tomcat properties for the hello project

Upon the next incremental build a distributable WAR file is created in the specified location. This file may then be deployed on the Tomcat server.

Testing

Update the context in the Tomcat config, by right clicking on the hello project and selecting `Tomcat project>Update context in server.xml` from the pop-up menu. This deploys the application to the local Tomcat server for testing.

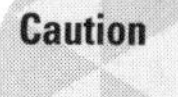

As mentioned in the Deployment section, this practice is only suggested for development. For details regarding the creation of a distributable version of your Web application that can be deployed on a remote production server, please package the project as a WAR file.

An alert box should be displayed notifying you that the Operation was successful. Click OK to proceed.

If you look at the `C:\tomcat\conf\server.xml` file you will see that the Tomcat Launcher plug-in has created a new context for our Tomcat project. See the XML branch outlined in Listing 6-5 showing the context created by the Sysdeo plug-in.

The `docBase` argument defines the document root of Web application. The document root defined in the context points straight at the project workspace allowing the developer to make changes in the development environment, and the continuous compile feature ensures that the changes are immediately reflected on the server.

Note

Unless you have a target VM that does support hot code replace, Eclipse is not able to update servlets without restarting the Tomcat server. The user will be prompted with a warning to the effect during each continuous compile of the servlet source code. Updates to JSP, are, however, immediate, regardless of the JVM used.

Listing 6-5: server.xml (fragment)

```
...
<Context path="/hello" docBase="C:\eclipse\workspace\hello"
    workDir="C:\eclipse\workspace\hello\work\org\apache\jsp" />
...
```

Start the Tomcat server by clicking the Start Tomcat button on the workbench toolbar.

The workbench switches to the Debugger perspective, and the Console view at the bottom of the workbench displays the output of the Tomcat process. The Debugger perspective is shown in Figure 6-32.

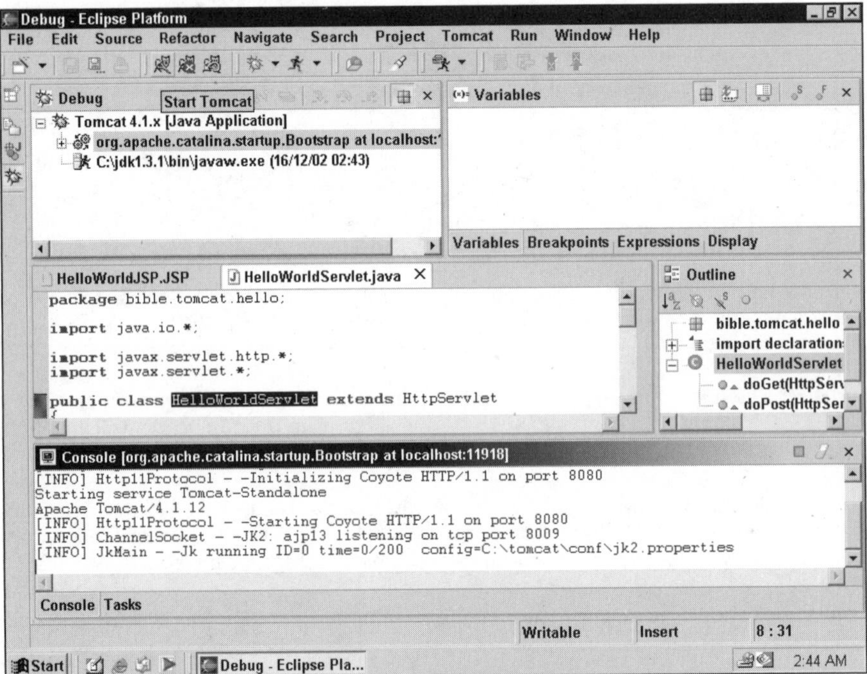

Figure 6-32: The debugger perspective incorporating the Tomcat log

After Tomcat has completed its startup routine, it is necessary to test the Tomcat project. Firstly, to test the simple JSP, navigate to `http://localhost:8080/hello/HelloWorldJSP.jsp` using a browser; the result should reflect the output shown in Figure 6-33.

Figure 6-33: Expected result after testing simple JSP

The previous test established that the Tomcat project context has been registered successfully with the Tomcat. It is now necessary to test the execution of a simple servlet by using a browser to navigate to `http://localhost:8080/hello/world`. A result very similar to the JSP example in Figure 6-33 should be displayed.

Congratulations, you now have successfully created a working Tomcat Web application using Eclipse.

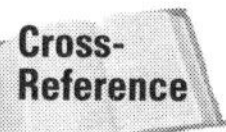

Debugging is discussed extensively in Chapter 11.

Lomboz J2EE Plug-in

OpenLearn `http://www.objectlearn.com/` provide an excellent Eclipse plug-in that brings the full capabilities of a J2EE project to the Eclipse Platform. Lomboz J2EE projects support JSP, servlet, and EJB technologies over a wide variety of J2EE platforms.

This book focuses on the JSP and servlet support for the Tomcat server.

Download

To download the Lomboz plug-in, go to the OpenLearn site `http://www.objectlearn.com/` and navigate to the Lomboz section. Click the Download link in the left hand toolbar.

Before the download can proceed, you are required to enter some registration information. Enter all the required fields and click Download to proceed.

It is necessary to download all three files and save them to disk:

✦ `lomboz.096.zip`

✦ `install.pdf`

✦ tutorial.pdf

Installation

Again, installation of plug-ins is a trivial task. Simply extract the contents of `lomboz.096.zip` into `C:\eclipse\`. The directory `plugins\com.objectlearn.jdt.j2ee` is created under the Eclipse home.

Caution Tomcat 4.1.12 must be installed before using this plug-in.

After restarting Eclipse the Lomboz plug-in is installed and is ready to configure.

Configuration

Select `Window>Customize Perspective`, expand `File>New`, and ensure all the Lomboz items are selected as shown in Figure 6-34.

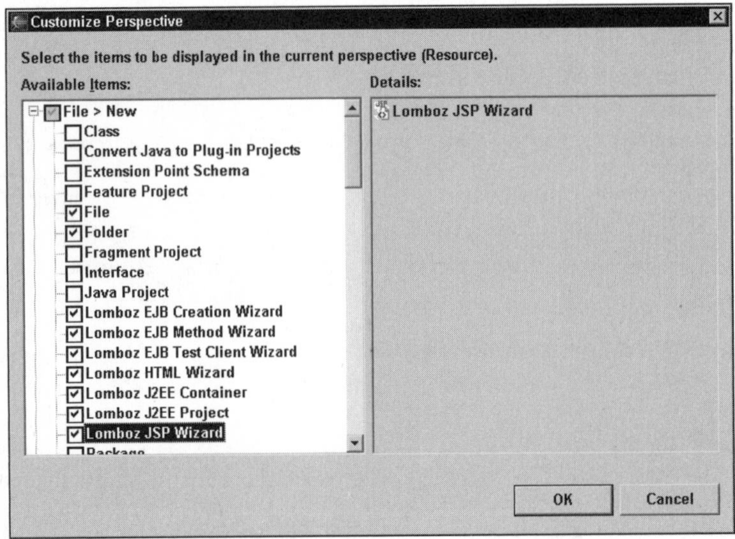

Figure 6-34: Activate Lomboz J2EE plug-in.

Under Available items, expand the `Window>Show View` tree and check Lomboz J2EE View.

Finally expand the Other tree and check the Lomboz Actions item.

Click OK to complete the plug-in activation.

It is now necessary to modify the workbench preferences. Select Window>Preferences from the menu.

Check the source and output location for the creation of new projects. In the left pane navigate to Java>New Project. Make sure the Folders radio button is checked, the Source Folder Name is set to src, and the Output Folder Name is set to bin. This sets the source and output locations in all new projects created; if these are not set to src and bin respectively, the Lomboz plug-in will not operate properly.

Like the Sysdeo plug-in, Lomboz must point to a JDK, not a JRE to enable JSP compilation. In the Lomboz entry under the Preferences dialog box, enter the location of JDK Tools.jar as C:\jdk1.3.1\lib\tools.jar. See Figure 6-35 for details.

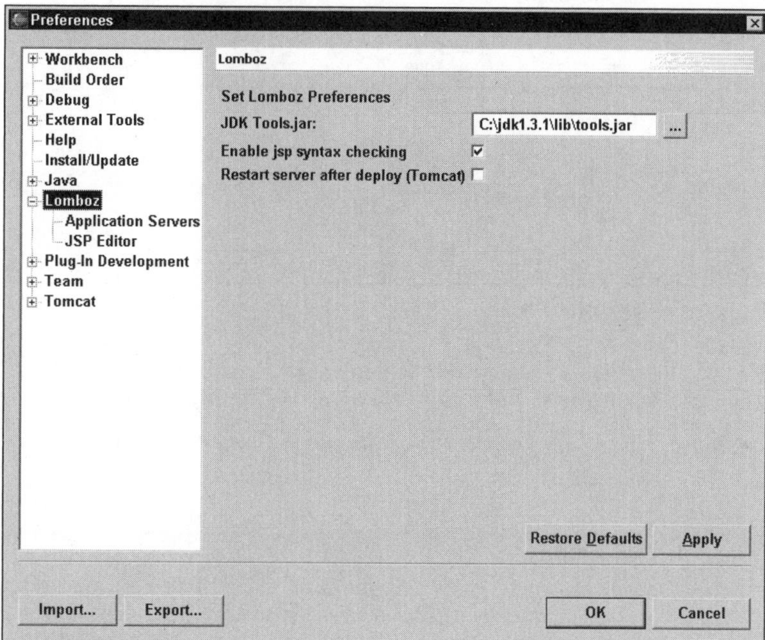

Figure 6-35: Lomboz JDK preferences

Navigate one level down to the Application Servers branch, and click the Tomcat tab in the dialog box. Set the location of the Tomcat home directory as C:\tomcat. The version must be set to 4.1.x.

Finally the configuration of classpath variables must be verified. Classpath variables avoid the use of hard-coded pathnames in the project Library preferences.

Navigate to Java>Classpath Variables, and verify that the Defined classpath variables at least contain a TOMCAT4 and TOMCAT_HOME entries, reflecting the location of your Tomcat installation. See the example configuration in Figure 6-36.

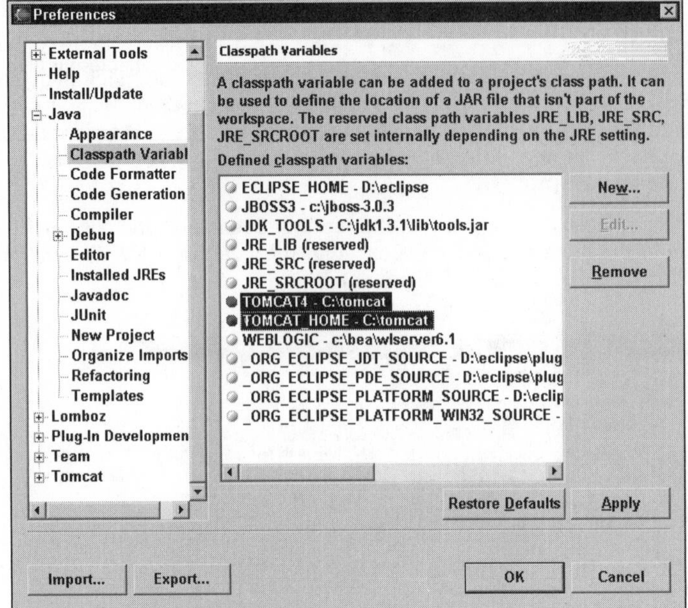

Figure 6-36: Verify Classpath variables.

If the classpath variables do not exist create two new variables named `TOMCAT4` and `TOMCAT_HOME` by clicking the New... button and following the prompts.

After the classpath variables have been verified, press OK to close the preferences dialog box.

Creating a New J2EE Project

We are now ready to add resources to our J2EE project. Like the Sysdeo Tomcat project example we shall setup a Web application containing a simple JSP and servlet.

Table 6-4 describes the typical structure of a J2EE project. Unlike the Sysdeo Tomcat project, the Lomboz J2EE project can support many J2EE servers. Therefore, each container subdirectory structure will reflect the deployment requirements of the target server. In our case Tomcat is the target server so the container directory will reflect the structure of a WAR file.

Table 6-4: J2EE Project Structure

Directory	*Directory Type*	*Description*
`/project`	Project root	All project files, including source code, resources, and binary output, are to be located under the project root.
`/project/container`	Web Application root	The document root of the Web application. All JSP files and static Web content are to be placed in this directory. The name of the Web application root depends on the name given to the container when the project is created.

Directory	Directory Type	Description
/project/src	Source directory	Location of servlet source and other resources such a properties files.
/project/container/WEB-INF	Subdirectory	Configuration directory containing deployment descriptors and other configuration files.
/project/container/WEB-INF/lib	Subdirectory	Contains Java Archive (JAR) files or libraries used by the Web application, along with any other resources required at run-time.
/project/j2src	Source directory	Working directory containing pre-compiled JSP files generated by the Jasper compiler.
/project/j2src/org/apache/jsp	Package	Working directory with a pre-defined package hierarchy used by Tomcat.
/project/bin	Output directory	Destination for compiled servlet object files.

To create a new J2EE project select `File>New Project` from the menu. as shown in Figure 6-37 navigate to Java>Lomboz J2EE Wizards and select Lomboz J2EE Project. Click Next to proceed.

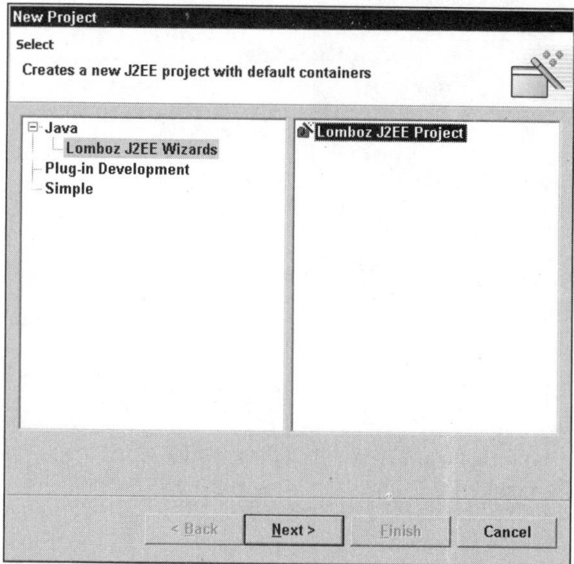

Figure 6-37: Creating a new J2EE project

Create a new J2EE project, enter **hello** into the project name field, and press Next to continue.

Caution

After creating a Tomcat project in the Sysdeo Eclipse Tomcat Launcher section there may already exist a project named hello. Either remove the existing project named hello, or uniquely name the new J2EE project.

A Java Settings dialog box is displayed with the Source tab displayed, like the one in Figure 6-38. Verify that the Use source folders contained in the project radio button are checked, and that the source folder is displayed as `hello/src`, and the output folder is specified as `hello/bin`.

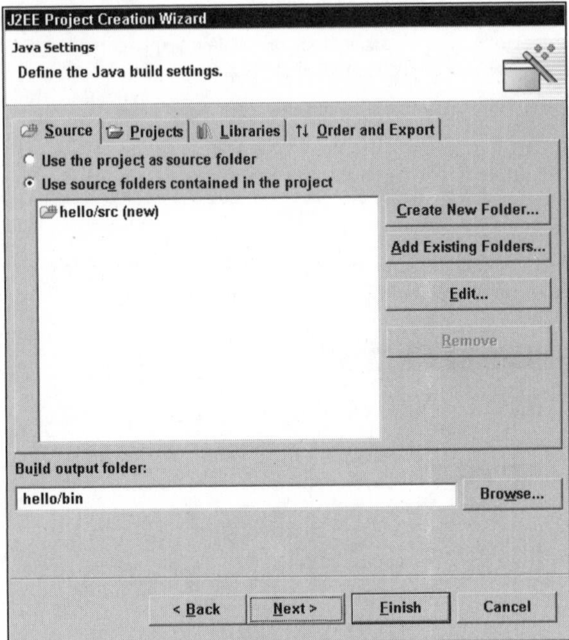

Figure 6-38: New J2EE project Java settings

To successfully debug the project it is necessary to place the jasper runtime libraries in the project's build path.

Click the Libraries tab. To include internal and external JAR files and classpaths into the build path, click the Add Variable button. The Add Variable feature enables you to reference file and folder locations using pre-defined variables instead of hard coded paths.

A list of pre-defined variables is displayed. Click on TOMCAT4, then press the Extend button. A Variable extension like that in Figure 6-39 appears. In the variable extension select `common/lib/jasper-runtime.jar` from the menu.

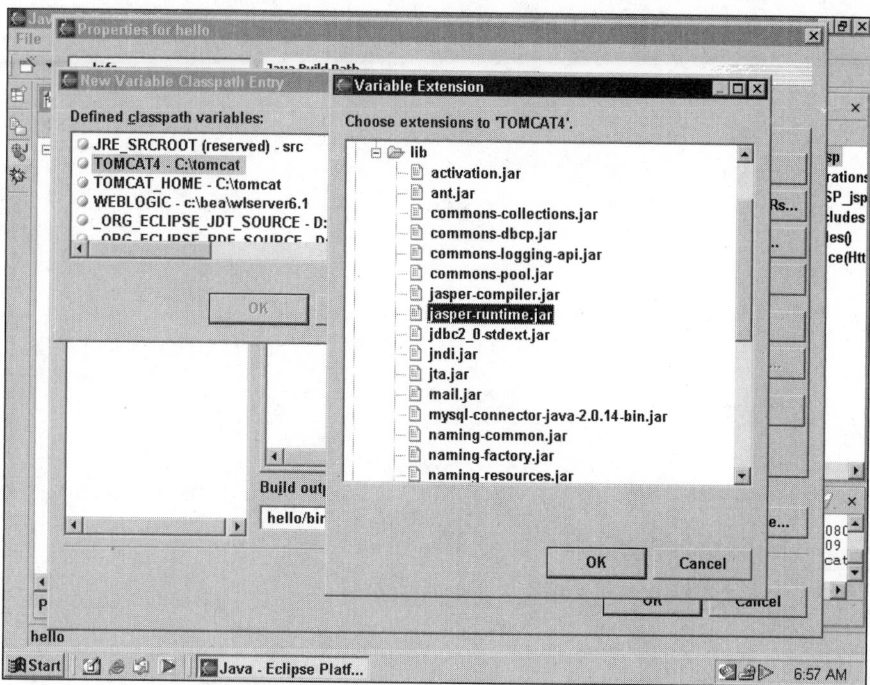

Figure 6-39: Adding the jasper runtime library to the project build path

Click OK; you are then taken back to the Java Setting dialog box.

Click Next. You are prompted to set up the container on which the application runs. A project may have many containers, each container referrers to a Web or J2EE deployment and is tied to a server, in our case the Tomcat server. Enter the container name **hello** in the text box as shown in Figure 6-40, and press OK when complete.

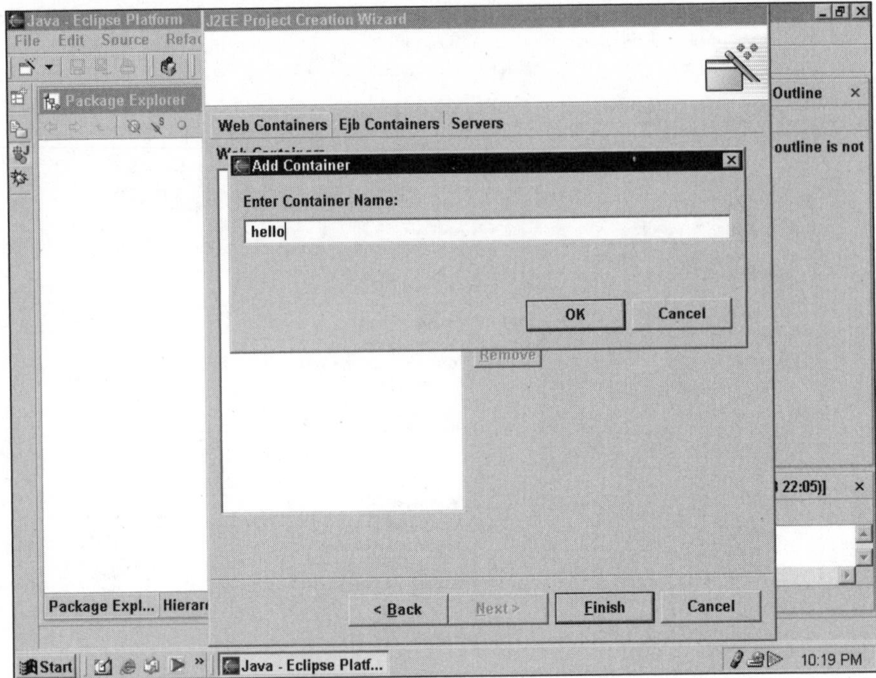

Figure 6-40: Creating a new Web container

The type of container must now be selected. Go to the Servers tab and in the Type drop-down box select Tomcat. The correct Tomcat configuration details should appear as shown in Figure 6-41. If not, please correct the Tomcat home directory and version before proceeding.

Click Finish. The new J2EE project is constructed and a new workbench is displayed with a Java Perspective, as shown in Figure 6-42.

Implementing a J2EE Project

We are now ready to add resources to our project to test the integration between Tomcat and Eclipse. This section sets up a working Web application containing a simple JSP and servlet.

All source code and deployment descriptor locations are relative to the Tomcat project document root `C:\eclipse\workspace\hello`.

Create a new JSP file `HelloWorldJSP.jsp` in the under the context root directory `/hello/helo` with the source contained in Listing 6-6.

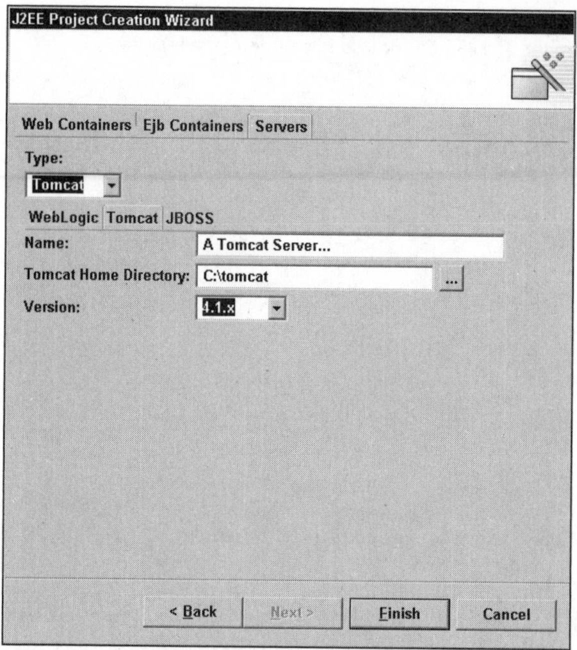

Figure 6-41: Selecting a Tomcat container type

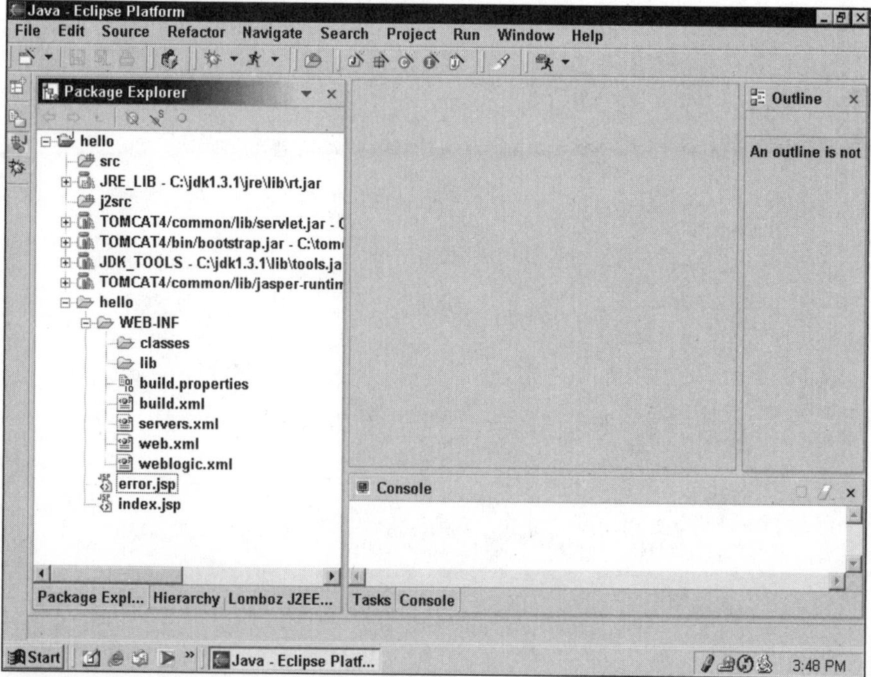

Figure 6-42: Successful creation of new J2EE project

The JSP Editor that comes with the Lomboz plug-in enables compilation tasks and markers just like the standard Java Editor. The JSP Editor also has Code Assist features.

Listing 6-6: HelloWorldJSP.jsp

```
<%
    String helloMessage = "Hello World!";
%>
<html>
<body>
<h1><%=helloMessage %></h1>
</body>
</html>
```

Create a new servlet `HelloWorldServlet.java` under the source directory `/hello/hello/src` with the source listes in Listing 6-7. It is necessary to create the appropriate `bible.tomcat.hello` package under the source directory before creating the file.

Listing 6-7: HelloWorldServlet.java

```
package bible.tomcat.hello;

import java.io.*;

import javax.servlet.http.*;
import javax.servlet.*;

public class HelloWorldServlet extends HttpServlet
{
    public void doGet(HttpServletRequest request,
            HttpServletResponse response)
    throws ServletException, IOException
    {
        // pass on the request to doPost
        doPost(request,response);
    }

    public void doPost(HttpServletRequest request,
            HttpServletResponse response)
    throws ServletException, IOException
    {
        PrintWriter out = response.getWriter();
        String helloMessage = "Hello World!";

        // set the response type
        response.setContentType("text/html");
```

```
            // now write it out
            out.println("<html>");
            out.println("<body>");
            out.println("<h1>"+helloMessage+"</h1>");
            out.println("</body>");
            out.println("</html>");
        }
}
```

Finally, update the application deployment descriptor located in /hello/hello/WEB-INF/web.xml. The result should look like that shown in Listing 6-8.

Tip To open the XML file in a normal text editor, select the file and from the pop-up menu select Open With>Text Editor.

Listing 6-8: **web.xml**

```
<?xml version="1.0" ?>
<!DOCTYPE web-app PUBLIC
    "-//Sun Microsystems, Inc.//DTD Web Application 2.2//EN"
    "http://java.sun.com/j2ee/dtds/web-app_2_2.dtd">

<web-app>

    <icon>
    </icon>

    <display-name>Hello World Application</display-name>

    <description>
        This is the simple Hello World! application
    </description>

    <servlet>
        <servlet-name>world</servlet-name>
        <description>
            The Hello World! Servlet
        </description>
        <servlet-class>
            bible.tomcat.hello.HelloWorldServlet
        </servlet-class>
    </servlet>

    <servlet-mapping>
        <servlet-name>world</servlet-name>
        <url-pattern>/world</url-pattern>
    </servlet-mapping>
```

```
    <welcome-file-list>
        <welcome-file>index.jsp</welcome-file>
    </welcome-file-list>

    <error-page>
        <error-code>404</error-code>
        <location>error.jsp</location>
    </error-page>

</web-app>
```

After the files have been created and added to the project, the workbench should look like the one shown in Figure 6-43.

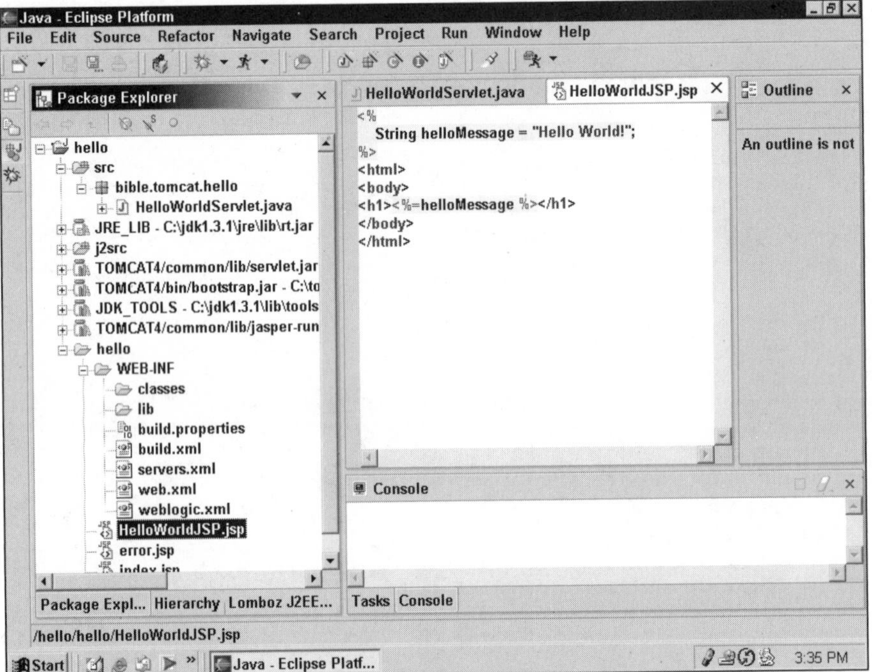

Figure 6-43: Completion of the J2EE project

We have now completed the application. Save the files and resolve any compilation errors that may have occurred.

To test the application it must firstly be deployed on the Tomcat container.

Deployment

Open the Lomboz J2EE view using the new icon on the toolbar, or by selecting `Window>Show View>Lomboz J2EE View` from the menu. The result should look like Figure 6-44.

Tip When the new view is added, it may be nested in the lower area of the screen where it is not very visible. The view is better viewed if it is dragged on top of the Package Explorer View.

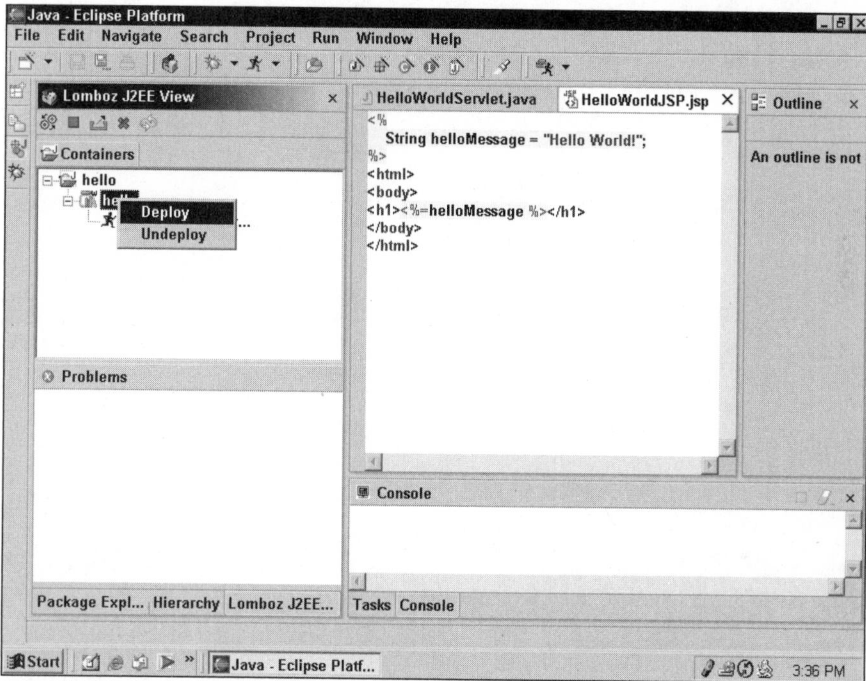

Figure 6-44: Lomboz J2EE view

The Tomcat server must be stopped before deploying a J2EE project. Right click on the A Tomcat Server... entry and select Stop Server.

To deploy the Web application to the container right-click the container named hello and select Deploy. This will copy the generated WAR file `hello.war` to the `C:\tomcat\webapps directory`.

Restart the Tomcat server after the application has been deployed by right-clicking the A Tomcat Server... entry and selecting Run Server.

Unfortunately the Lomboz plug-in does utilize the hot deployment features of the Tomcat Manager application. The WAR file must be deployed to the Tomcat server using the method described previously.

Testing

After tomcat has completed its startup routine, it is necessary to test the Tomcat project. Firstly, to test the simple JSP navigate to `http://localhost:8080/hello/HelloWorldJSP.jsp` using a browser; the result should reflect the output shown in Figure 6-45.

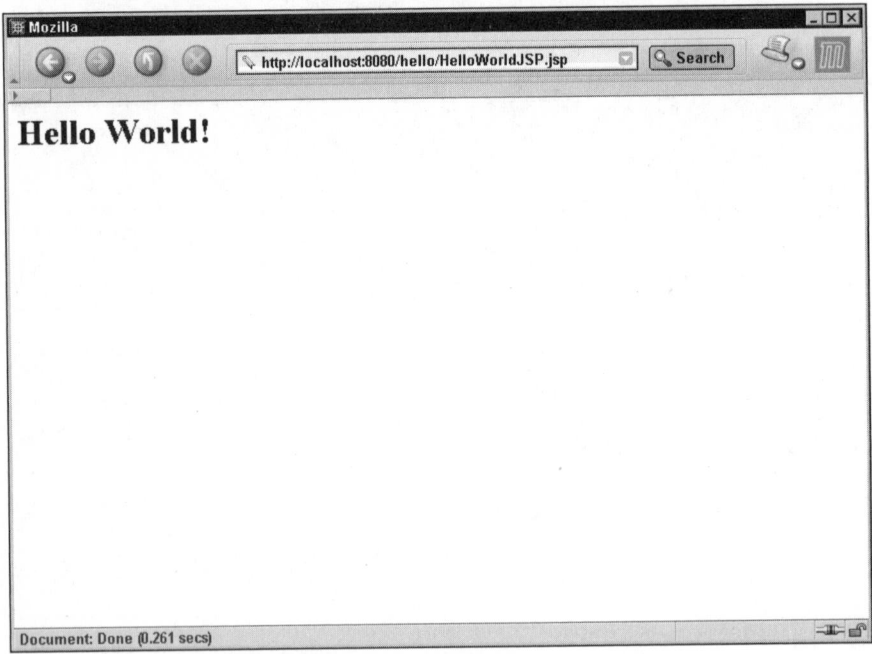

Figure 6-45: Expected result after testing simple JSP

The previous test established that the Tomcat project context has been registered successfully with the Tomcat. It is now necessary to test the execution of a simple servlet by using a browser to navigate to `http://localhost:8080/hello/world`. Congratulations, you now have successfully created a working Tomcat Web application using Eclipse.

Debugging is discussed extensively in Chapter 11.

Tips and Tricks

The use of an IDE can bring with it huge productivity gains. It does, however, require the user to be fluent with all the ins and outs of the environment. Just to get you started, here are a few tips and tricks to make the use of Eclipse a little more productive.

Code Assist

Whilst coding, the code assist feature can suggest method and field names that are available for the given class. For example, in the text editor, type:

```
System.out.
```

Then type **CTRL+Space** to activate code assist. A list of available fields and methods for the system output stream will be displayed. Select the appropriate field or method from the list by using the arrow keys, and then press Enter. The correct field name, or method declaration is displayed for you.

To change the behavior of Code Assist select `Window>Preferences` from the menu, then `Java>Editor>Code Assist` in the properties dialog box. Code Assist has many additional features that are explained in the Java Development User Guide.

Templates

The output for the Code Assist feature can be customized using Templates. To add/modify/delete templates, go to the Eclipse properties by selecting `Window>Properties` from the menu, then navigating to `Java>Templates` in the left pane.

Templates operating on Java code or Javadoc comments may be specified. Please refer to the Java Development User Guide for more information.

Quick Fix

If the Java editor is configured to automatically identify problems, notice while writing code, or after incremental compilation, that light bulb icons appear in the left margin, or vertical ruler, of the editor. These are identity suggested quick fixes to problems in the code. Click the light bulb icon to select the appropriate fix, if any.

Problem indication may be turned on or off using the properties window accessible from the menu by selecting `Window>Preferences` then `Java>Editor>Problem Indication` inside the properties dialog box.

Quick fixes are sometimes available for compile errors. To apply a suggested fix, place the cursor inside the code containing a compiler error and type `CTRL-1` or select `Edit>Quick Fix` from the menu. Select the appropriate solution, if any, and press Enter to continue.

Local History

Eclipse offers local users a simple version control system called the Local History. Developers can get the local history of an individual method or field by selecting the element in the Outline or Type Hierarchy view and then choose `Replace With>Element From Local History` from the pop-up menu.

This shows you the history of this particular method or field in a new window. Each version of the code is time stamped in the local history; if a previous version is selected, differences between the current version and the one from the local history are displayed in the Java Source Compare view. The user can then choose whether or not to replace the code with a version from the local history.

If version control over a team of developers is required a tool like CVS should be used. Information about CVS can be found at `http://www.cvs.org/`.

Refactoring

Eclipse has many useful refactoring features; these include the renaming of member variables, arguments, methods, classes, packages, and so on. The changes are made not only to the local source file, but also to all references of the renamed element throughout the entire code base. The build path limits the scope of the referred changes.

To refactor code, select the relevant element in an open editor, or alternatively in the Package Explorer, Outline, or Type Hierarchy view, and select the relevant feature from the `Refactor` menu. You also may get access to the refactor menu via the right-click pop-up menu.

There are many other neat refactoring features such as the encapsulation of methods and fields and the promotion of methods and fields to the parent class. Please refer to the Java Development User Guide for more information.

Task View

The Task View is very useful for keeping track of to-do items. Developer using agile methodologies will like this facility because the action items for future releases can be noted easily, without taking the focus away from developing the current iteration.

The task view is very tightly integrated with the Java Builder and the Java Editor. Eclipse displays system and compilation errors/warnings/information in the Task View. By double-clicking the task entry an editor is opened with the relevant line of code highlighted.

Resetting Perspectives

The layout of each perspective may be customized to the user's personal preferences. A very helpful feature to remember before customizing perspectives is that it is possible to reset the perspective, undoing any changes you have made. This is useful if a user inadvertently moves or deletes a view and cannot get the perspective back to normal.

To reset the current visible perspective, select `Window>Reset Perspective` from the menu, and click `OK` when prompted to reset the perspective back to the default layout.

Useful Add-ons

The extensibility of the Eclipse Platform is a major draw card, allowing developers to customize and enhance nearly any aspect of the workbench. Developers may create their own plug-ins using the Plug-in Development Environment (PDE) available as part of the Eclipse SDK.

Alternatively there are a plethora of useful plug-ins available from `http://eclipse-plugins.2y.net/eclipse/`. Plug-ins may customize the workbench, providing new views, editors, and customized perspectives, and also may provide integration with third-party products. The following is a list of just some of the types of plug-ins available for the Eclipse Platform:

- ✦ Application server integration, including support for major J2EE environments
- ✦ Custom editors, offering enhanced features and custom key bindings
- ✦ Database design and administration tools
- ✦ Profiling tools
- ✦ Testing frameworks
- ✦ UML Modeling tools for software design

Additionally, plug-ins are available for the following languages:

- AspectJ
- C#
- C/C++
- Cobol
- Eiffel
- Pascal
- PHP
- Python

Java support is enabled by default using Java Development Tooling (JDT) packaged with the Eclipse Platform.

There are a host of other plug-ins that, although are not strictly productivity tools, may make the development environment a little more pleasant. These include MP3 players, IRC clients, the Google search facility, and news feeds like Slashdot.

Summary

This completes a brief walkthrough of the Eclipse IDE. We have touched on a number of topics, including the Eclipse environment in general and its integration with Tomcat and developing using Projects. It is not within the scope of this book to provide an exhaustive account of every feature available, but the description here at least gets you going within the context of some of the examples contained in this book. For further reading we recommend you consult the Eclipse documentation and other resources such as mailing lists.

✦ ✦ ✦

Building a Simple WAR: HelloWorld WAR

In This Chapter

Understanding WAR components

Development and deployment

Setting up a development environment

Developing using Tomcat

Deploying using Tomcat

Now that you have read about what is involved in creating a Web application, and how to deploy it within the Tomcat environment, this chapter takes that theory and puts it into practice.

For the impatient readers, this chapter is a good starting point to dive straight into developing Web applications. However it is very important to have completed the installation steps in Chapter 2 prior to development. This ensures that applications are developed on a sound foundation and that any errors can be easily identified and fixed.

The first part of the chapter looks at the different use and configuration of Tomcat for development and deployment and identify a few mechanisms for performing the deployment.

It describes how to set up a development environment compatible with the Tomcat-supplied Ant scripts.

Cross-Reference Chapter 5 provides a comprehensive coverage of compiling and building Web applications using the Ant build tool.

The chapter provides all the code required to build a version of the standard Hello World! example as a Web application and step through the development process using command line tools and the Tomcat-provided administration interfaces.

The chapter then provides examples of how to deploy the packaged Web application to Tomcat using the Ant scripts and the Tomcat-provided administration interfaces.

This chapter uses the command-line or Ant for the examples of creating directories and building the Web application. If you are using an IDE such as Eclipse, or SunONE, then many of these steps will be managed by the IDE. However, it is important to understand the basic principles behind the management of Tomcat. This is best illustrated by the more manual process of using the command-line or Ant.

Cross-Reference Users of an IDE should examine Chapter 7 for more detailed information about using an IDE in development and deployment.

Development and Deployment

To make the most out of Tomcat, it is worth defining and separating the development and deployment cycles. This is generally advantageous in software development, but even more with Tomcat, because the nature of Web applications and distribution and deployment using WAR files leads to a more formal release procedure.

For the examples in the book, and to clearly identify the separation of the two concepts, let's define development and deployment as follows:

- **Development:** The process involved in creating the Web application. This includes writing code, debugging, unit testing, and configuration of the environment to support those activities. The development stage ends with a fully working Web application.
- **Deployment:** The process involved in installing a completed Web application. This includes identifying the WAR file to be installed and configuration of Tomcat to support the application.

One of the more commonly raised issues about Tomcat is the lack of support for the developer during the development compile/test/debug cycle.

This concern has been addressed somewhat with the 4.1.x release of Tomcat, because there are now many ways of managing the configuration both during development and for deployment.

These are:

- The Manager Application
- The Administration Tool
- Ant/Tomcat task definitions
- Manual editing of `server.xml`
- Using a `context.xml`

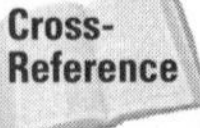

See Chapter 9 for more detailed information about the use of the Manager and Administration applications.

Manager Application

The manager application has been available as part of the Tomcat distribution since version 4.0x, however, the application was not easy to use, and the feedback provided was not very clear, leading to it not being very useful. In Tomcat 4.1.x this has been enhanced with the use of an HTML interface, providing a great run-time mechanism for checking the status of the server and management of the Web applications.

The application is accessed by a user that has been configured with the role of manager. For the book, we use the manager user that was configured during Chapter 2.

Remember in Chapter 2 there were two users configured. The first user, the administrator user, was admin with the password of admin and the second user, the manager user, was called ant-install with the password of ant-install.

The manager application HTML interface can be accessed by entering the following URL into a browser.

```
http://localhost:8080/manager/html
```

This should result in a browser display similar to that shown in Figure 7-1.

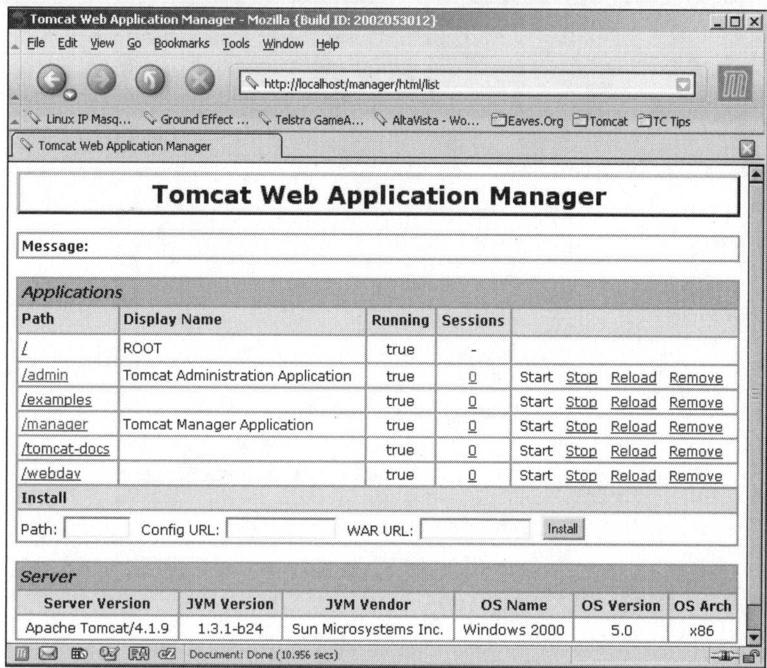

Figure 7-1: The Tomcat Web Application Manager

As Figure 7-1 shows, the Web application manager is used to install, start, stop, reload, remove, and list Web applications. There are more configuration options available to the administrator, and they can be configured graphically using the Administration Tool user interface.

Administration Tool

The Tomcat Administration Tool is new with 4.1.x and provides a completely graphical interface to configure the `server.xml`, and Tomcat `-users.xml` files. The tool is accessed by the user that was configured during installation. For this book, we use the administrator user that was configured during Chapter 2.

This application provides all the necessary configuration options for developing and deploying applications to Tomcat and is started by entering the following URL into a browser.

```
http://localhost:8080/admin
```

This displays a screen similar to that shown in Figure 7-2.

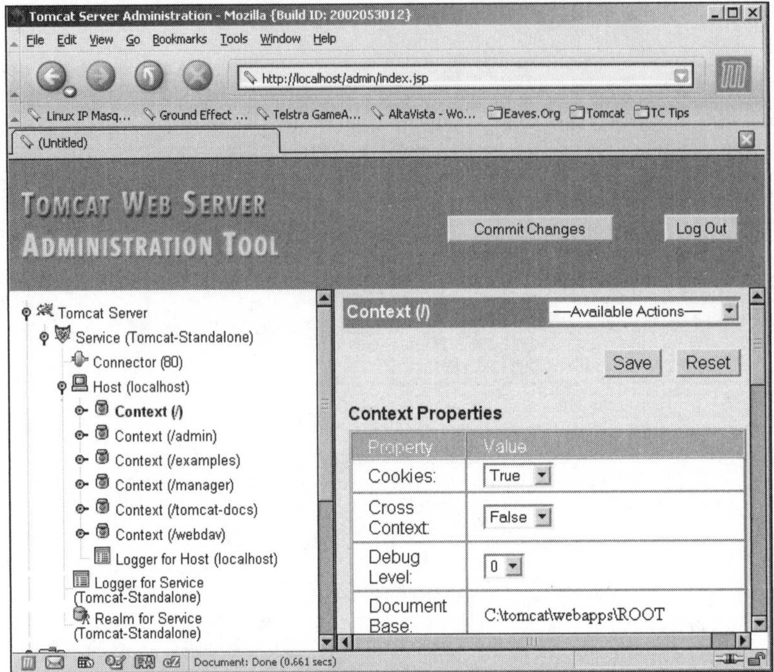

Figure 7-2: The Tomcat Web Server Administration Tool

Ant/Tomcat Task Definitions

With the release of 4.1.x, the Tomcat release includes a number of Ant tasks to simplify development and deployment using Tomcat. The tasks provide the same functionality as the Manager Application, but are packaged so they can be used with the Ant build scripts. The Ant build tasks provide the most benefit when used during development, but do provide some useful deployment capabilities.

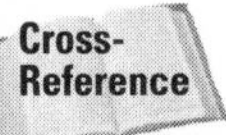

The use of these tasks is covered in detail in Chapter 5.

Manual Editing of the server.xml file

A further option to the developer and deployment administrator is the manual editing of the `server.xml` file. This has a number of advantages, the greatest being the fine-grained control over specific aspects of the Web application and the Tomcat server.

The node of most relevance, while adding new Web applications to the Tomcat configuration, is the `<Context>` node. This controls the options for development and deployment of the Web application.

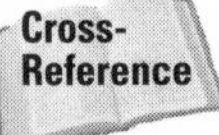

The contents of the `server.xml` file and the instructions on configuring Tomcat are covered in detail in Chapter 9.

Using a context.xml

Finally, the development option used in this chapter is the creation of a `context.xml` file and the use of the Ant build file to install and deploy the application. This is a fantastic option for users of Tomcat because it provides a mechanism for developing and deploying Web applications without having to make changes to the `server.xml`.

Differences

There is one fundamental and important difference between development and deployment. During development, there are a large number of changes in the contents of the Web application (from changing Java and JSP files). These changes occur frequently, and the compile/test/debug cycle can be accelerated by limiting other steps in the process.

During deployment it is important to have a well structured, well managed release of the application, and because the deployment releases are relatively infrequent additional steps in the process cause less impact.

This difference means that it is important to have a development and deployment environment that can support the rapid iterations required during development and the controlled releases during deployment. During this chapter, an environment that can support this is created to illustrate these processes.

Setting Up a Development Directory Structure

To facilitate the transition from development to deployment, and to minimize the number of activities in the compile/test/debug cycle, it is recommended practice to set up the development directory structure similar to the structure of the WAR file. As the example progresses, the configuration is modified to reflect the updated requirements, so pay careful attention to this example because the end result is quite different from the start.

First we identify the package to develop the Hello World! application. For the sake of convenience, all example code in the book uses the `bible.tomcat` as a base and used packages under that. Not surprisingly for this example the package will be `bible.tomcat.hello`.

As with the installation procedures, the example uses Windows directory structure and command lines.

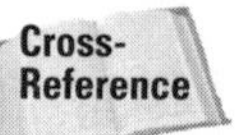

A full description of setting up a development directory structure using Ant is described in Chapter 5.

Now create the development directory.

```
mkdir c:\devel
cd c:\devel
mkdir hello
cd hello
```

Copy the Ant build file from the Tomcat installation.

```
copy c:\tomcat\webapps\tomcat-docs\appdev\build.xml.txt build.xml
```

Create the source and document directories, and the source sub-directories.

```
mkdir src
mkdir docs
cd src

mkdir bible\tomcat\hello
mkdir web\WEB-INF
```

This gives the base directory structure required for this example application. The next task is to modify the `build.xml` file to suit this application.

First, copy the `build.xml` created in Chapter 5 to the base directory and perform the following tasks:

1. **Modify the project and `app.name` of `build.xml`.** Near the top of the file is the project directive, and the property for `app.name`. Modify the two lines as follows:

   ```
   <project name="hello" default="compile" basedir=".">
   <property name="app.name"      value="hello"/>
   ```

2. **Copy the `template.context.xml` created in Chapter 5 to the base directory.** This may seem like a lot of effort, but it is a once-only configuration and the benefits that are gained during development and deployment are quite significant. Steps 2 and 3 add the configuration required to use the Ant manager tasks. Steps 4-6 add in an additional option for development that allows changes that are made during development to be immediately used by the running Web application without having to perform a server or Web application restart. This significantly decreases development time.

Creating the Web Application

The Web application that will be built in this chapter is very simple. The only requirement is to display the text Hello World! to the user when the Web application is accessed.

Using Java and Web applications there are many ways to achieve this result, and some methods are superior to others. This example describes a few of the methods and the advantages and disadvantages of each, starting from the simplest and moving to a more complicated version. (If you could call any Hello World application complicated, that is!)

As the more complicated versions are introduced, be aware that an application so simple does not need the complexity described, but as we examine more complex requirements in Chapter 10, and examine the frameworks utilized in Chapter 13 the reasons for the additional complexity will become clear.

Servlet Version

The first version of Hello World! uses a simple servlet to process all of the input and create the output for the user. Listing 7-1 shows the code for the servlet. This should be created in the `src/bible/tomcat/hello`.

The code begins by declaring the package the servlet will exist in, and importing the `javax.servlet` packages. This provides access to the `HttpServlet` class that `HelloWorldServlet` is extending.

The first method defined is `doGet()`. This method is invoked by the servlet container to handle `GET` requests from the browser, and as can be seen, all it does is pass off the request to the `doPost()` method.

The second (and last) method defined is `doPost()`. This method is used to handle the `POST` requests from the browser. It obtains access to a `PrintWriter` to produce the output, and then proceeds to set the response content type to HTML via `response.setContentType ("text/html")` and then, using the `PrintWriter`, writes out the HTML for the response page.

Note

Pay attention to how much effort is required to generate even simple HTML output in the servlet using the `PrintWriter`. Imagine how much of a mess it would be trying to get complex HTML formatting like tables, input forms, and fields generated this way. Luckily there is an easier way; using JSP to output the HTML.

Listing 7-1: **HelloWorldServlet.java**

```
package bible.tomcat.hello;

import java.io.*;

import javax.servlet.http.*;
import javax.servlet.*;

public class HelloWorldServlet extends HttpServlet
{

    public void doGet(HttpServletRequest request,
            HttpServletResponse response)
    throws ServletException, IOException
    {
        // pass on the request to doPost
        doPost(request,response);
    }

    public void doPost(HttpServletRequest request,
            HttpServletResponse response)
    throws ServletException, IOException
    {
        PrintWriter out = response.getWriter();
        String helloMessage = "Hello World!";

        // set the response type
        response.setContentType("text/html");
        // now write it out
        out.println("<html>");
        out.println("<body>");
```

Continued

Listing 7-1 *(continued)*

```
            out.println("<h1>"+helloMessage+"</h1>");
            out.println("</body>");
            out.println("</html>");
        }
    }
```

The web.xml file describes the Web application deployment properties. Listing 7-2 provides the source for the initial version. This should be created in the web\WEB-INF directory.

Cross-Reference The details of the web.xml file are covered in Chapter 3.

The important nodes in this XML file are servlet and servlet-mapping, which define the servlet and the class that implements that servlet, as well as the mapping of the URL pattern to the servlet.

Listing 7-2: **web.xml**

```
<?xml version="1.0" encoding="ISO-8859-1" ?>

<!DOCTYPE web-app
  PUBLIC "-//Sun Microsystems, Inc.//DTD Web Application 2.3//EN"
  "http://java.sun.com/dtd/web-app_2_3.dtd" >

<web-app>
    <display-name>Hello World Application</display-name>
    <description>
        This is the simple Hello World! application
    </description>

    <servlet>
        <servlet-name>world</servlet-name>
        <description>
            The Hello World! Servlet
        </description>
        <servlet-class>
            bible.tomcat.hello.HelloWorldServlet
        </servlet-class>
    </servlet>

    <servlet-mapping>
        <servlet-name>world</servlet-name>
        <url-pattern>/world</url-pattern>
    </servlet-mapping>
</web-app>
```

At this point, the application is ready to go, and the environment is correctly configured. Compile the Web application with:

```
ant compile
```

This should produce output similar to:

```
Buildfile: build.xml
prepare:
    [mkdir] Created dir: C:\devel\hello\build
    [mkdir] Created dir: C:\devel\hello\build\WEB-INF
    [mkdir] Created dir: C:\devel\hello\build\WEB-INF\classes
     [copy] Copying 2 files to C:\devel\hello\build
     [copy] Copied 1 empty directory to C:\devel\hello\build
     [copy] Copying 1 file to C:\devel\hello\build\WEB-INF
compile:
    [javac] Compiling 1 source file to C:\devel\hello\build\WEB-INF\classes
BUILD SUCCESSFUL
Total time: 9 seconds
```

If there are any compilation errors, fix those before proceeding. Providing the environment is the same as the setup from Chapter 2 there shouldn't be any issues other than errors in the files that have just been created.

Executing the Ant command has created the build directory that will be installed as a Tomcat Web application using the Ant tasks and the context file `context.xml`.

Finally, start Tomcat and issue the following command at a console:

```
ant context
```

This should display a result similar to:

```
Buildfile: build.xml
prepare:
compile:
context:
  [install] OK - Installed application from context file file:///C:\devel\
\hello/build/WEB-INF/context.xml

BUILD SUCCESSFUL
Total time: 2 seconds
```

Any errors that occur at this stage are generally due to either Tomcat not starting properly, or the username and password for the manager user has not been correctly specified in the `build.xml` file. Check the configuration of the username and password for the manager user in Chapter 2, and check that they match the values in the build files.

Now, after all this, the result of all the hard work is a fairly simple display of text that can be seen by entering the URL `http://localhost:8080/hello/world` into a browser. This should give a result similar to that shown in Figure 7-3.

Figure 7-3: Output from HelloWorldServlet.java

JSP Version

To compare against the servlet version, the next step is to create a JSP version that produces the same output.

Listing 7-3 shows the code for the JPS page. Create the file `HelloWorldJSP`.jsp in the `web` directory.

The very simple JSP file contains a scriptlet with a declaration of a variable that is initialized to the string that is going to be displayed to the user. Following that are standard HTML tags with an expression for displaying the variable. The file finishes with some more standard HTML tags.

Listing 7-3: **HelloWorldJSP.jsp**

```
<%
   String helloMessage = "Hello World!";
%>
<html>
<body>
<h1><%=helloMessage %></h1>
</body>
</html>
```

After that very simple piece of code test the JSP page. First, deploy the JSP file to the build environment. Remember that the changes to the JSP page are only in the source directory (`web`) and need to be deployed into the build directory (`build`) where Tomcat has currently installed the application. To deploy the page issue the following command in a console window:

```
ant compile
```

This command recompiles any class files and then deploys the `servlet` and `bean` classes to the build directory and copy the JSP files to the build directory. For now, the only change will be the new JSP file that has been added.

This produces output similar to the following:

```
Buildfile: build.xml

prepare:
     [copy] Copying 1 file to C:\devel\hello\build

compile:

BUILD SUCCESSFUL
Total time: 2 seconds
```

Now, test the JSP page by entering the URL `http://localhost:8080/hello/HelloWorldJSP.jsp` in a browser. This should give the result seen in Figure 7-4.

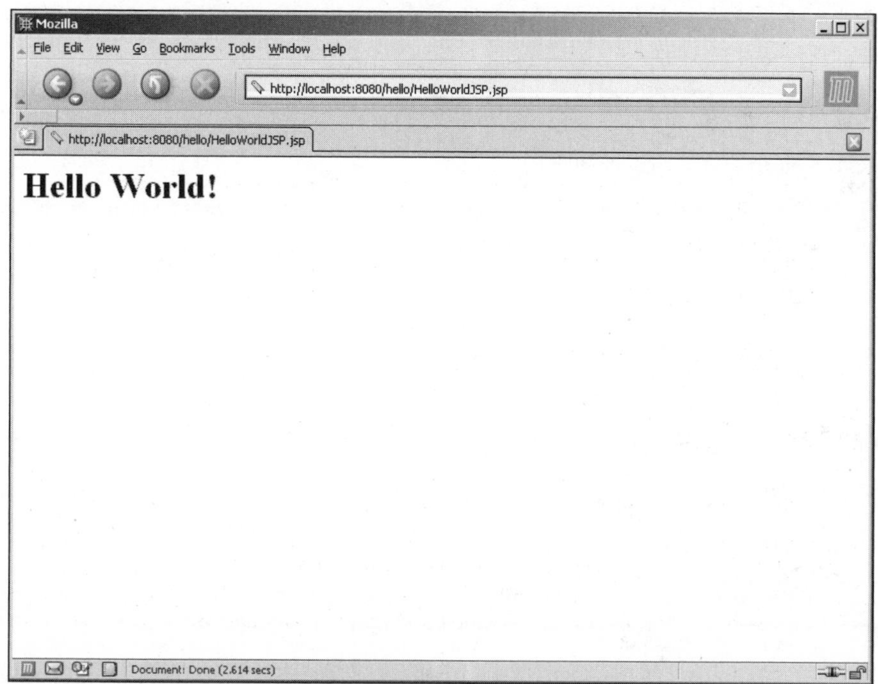

Figure 7-4: Output from HelloWorldJSP.jsp

With these two versions of Hello World! created, it has just about exhausted the possibilities for examples in these simple versions. The next step is to introduce a little complexity and take input from a user.

Hello City!

Chapter 1 contains a brief discussion of the introduction of JSP, the resulting Model 1 architecture, and the transition to the MVC Model 2 architecture. The following example puts that architecture into practice by providing a controller servlet that takes some user input, performs some processing, and displays the results using a JSP page.

This section will present a number of examples refining the original concept and introducing new techniques at each stage. The learning curve should not be too onerous, but pay close attention to each example as future versions build on knowledge and code from previous versions.

This example presents a user with a form to enter their name and allow them to choose a city. The Web application performs some validation on the data entered and represents the form if any errors exist, or displays a greeting in the language of the city that was chosen.

These interactions can be illustrated as shown in Figure 7-5.

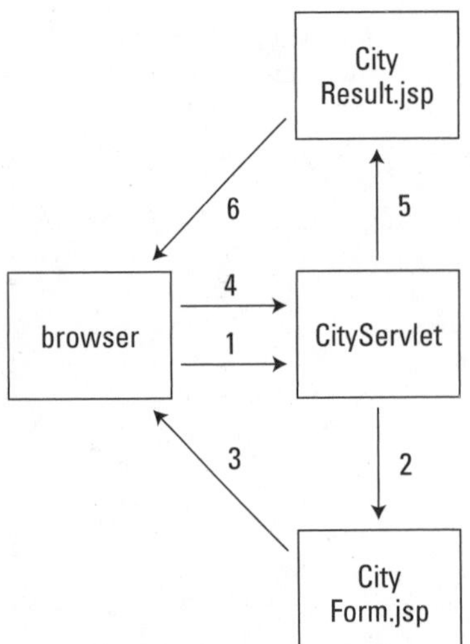

Figure 7-5: Hello City! Web application

The simplest path of the flow of control for the Web application can be described as follows:

1. Browse to `http://localhost:8080/hello/city` where the servlet container calls `doGet()` on `CityServlet`. The servlet invokes `doPost()` internally where logic determines that the name and city information has not been sent to the controlling servlet. `CityServlet` performs a server-side forward from a request dispatcher to the `CityForm.jsp` page.

2. The servlet container forwards the request to the JSP page.
3. The JSP page is executed and the resulting output is sent to the browser. This output is a form for the user to complete.
4. The user enters the form details and submits the results. The servlet container calls `doPost()` on `CityServlet`. The servlet examines the user-supplied information and if there are any errors performs a server-side forward to the `CityForm.jsp` page. Otherwise, the business logic of the servlet determines the correct output and then performs a server-side forward to the `CityResult.jsp` page.
5. The servlet container forwards the request to the JSP page.
6. The JSP page is executed and the resulting output is sent to the browser.

So, start at the core of the matter and create the controlling servlet contained in Listing 7-4.

Listing 7-4: CityServlet.java

```
package bible.tomcat.hello;

import java.io.*;
import java.lang.*;
import java.util.*;

import javax.servlet.http.*;
import javax.servlet.*;

/*
 * This is the main controlling servlet for the Hello City
 * application.
 *
 * This HttpServlet controls the simple interactions between
 * a form (created by CityForm.jsp) and the results page
 * (created by CityResult.jsp)

 */
public class CityServlet
extends HttpServlet
{
    public final String FORM_PAGE   = "/CityForm.jsp";
    public final String RESULT_PAGE = "/CityResult.jsp";

    /*
     * These are identifiers used by the FORM_PAGE for the
     * form processing.
     */
    public final String NAME_FIELD      = "NAME";
    public final String CITY_FIELD      = "CITY";
```

Continued

Listing 7-4 *(continued)*

```
/*
 * Invoke doPost() from doGet(), if ever called.
 */
public void doGet(HttpServletRequest req, HttpServletResponse res)
throws ServletException, IOException
{
    doPost(req, res);
}

/*
 * doPost() provides the body of the servlet controller,
 * and invokes the business logic
 *
 * doPost() is also responsible for determining what page
 * should be displayed.  If the servlet is invoked with no
 * parameters, it is assumed that the request is for the
 * display of the form page.
 */
public void doPost(HttpServletRequest req,
        HttpServletResponse res)
throws ServletException, IOException
{
    String incPath = FORM_PAGE;
    String error = "";

    /*
     * Has the servlet been invoked from the FORM_PAGE ?
     */
    String action = req.getParameter("action");
    if (action != null)  // yes !
    {
        boolean gotError = false;
        incPath = RESULT_PAGE;

        /*
         * Grab the fields (name and city) from the HTTP request
         */
        String name = req.getParameter(NAME_FIELD);
        String city = req.getParameter(CITY_FIELD);

        /*
         * Now calculate the results
         */
        if ((name == null) || (name.length() < 1))
        {
            error = "Please enter a name!";
            gotError = true;
            name = null;
        }
```

```
        if ((city == null) || (city.length() < 1))
        {
            if (gotError)
            {
                error += " and ";
            }
            error += "Please choose a city";
            gotError = true;
        }

        if (gotError)
        {
            incPath = FORM_PAGE;
            req.setAttribute("errorMessage", error);
            performRedirect(incPath, req, res);
            return;
        }

        // we've got real values, so we'll use them in the JSP
        req.setAttribute("theCity", city);
        req.setAttribute("theName", name);
        String greeting = null;

        if (city.equals("MEL"))
        {
            greeting = "G'day";
        }
        else if (city.equals("PAR"))
        {
            greeting = "Bonjour";
        }
        else if (city.equals("MIL"))
        {
            greeting = "Ciao";
        }

        req.setAttribute("theGreeting", greeting);
    }

    /*
     * Now we've done our calculations, got some results, or
     * some sort of error, so let the user know what's been
     * going on!
     */
    performRedirect(incPath, req, res);
}

private void performRedirect(String incPath,
        HttpServletRequest req,
        HttpServletResponse res)
throws ServletException, IOException
```

Continued

Listing 7-4 (continued)

```
    {
        String servletName;
        if (incPath != null)
        {
            servletName = req.getServletPath();
            req.setAttribute("servletPath",
                    req.getContextPath()+servletName);
            req.setAttribute("nameField", NAME_FIELD);
            req.setAttribute("cityField", CITY_FIELD);

            /*
             * Now, forward the results to the appropriate JSP page
             */
            RequestDispatcher rd = req.getRequestDispatcher(incPath);
            rd.forward(req, res);
        }
    }
}
```

When you examine the code for this servlet it should be obvious that while it is somewhat more complicated than the initial version provided by `HelloWorldServlet.java`, the structure is similar. To understand the differences, let's look at the components of the `CityServlet` and their purposes.

`CityServlet` starts with the declaration of some useful constants. These are used by the servlet to forward to the correct JSP page for output processing.

```
public final String FORM_PAGE   = "/CityForm.jsp";
public final String RESULT_PAGE = "/CityResult.jsp";
```

The next declarations are used to select the input form fields from the request.

```
public final String NAME_FIELD      = "NAME";
public final String CITY_FIELD      = "CITY";
```

Tip It is very convenient to define the fields used for the forms on the JSP pages in the controller servlet. These fields can then be used by the JSP page to construct the form and help keep the input form and the form processing synchronized.

The next interesting component of `CityServlet` is the `doPost()` method. This is where all the logic processing is performed, so this is examined in some detail.

First, `incPath` is used to hold the name of the JSP page that generates the output to the browser. This is set to the form page (`CityForm.jsp`) by default. `error` is used to hold the value of any error messages that are generated during the processing of the request. `error` is set to the an empty string by default. This isn't the most elegant Java code, but in keeping the examples as short as possible some sacrifices have been made.

```
String incPath = FORM_PAGE;
String error = "";
```

Next we check to see if a hidden parameter as part of the input form has been set.

```
String action = req.getParameter("action");
```

Tip This is a simple mechanism that can be extended to include examination of the value of the action parameter if the controlling servlet is processing the input from many input forms or submission types.

If the action parameter is not null, then we proceed to processing the input fields from the form. This code fragment shows the setting of the `name` and `city` variables with the values from the input form stored in the request object.

```
String name = req.getParameter(NAME_FIELD);
String city = req.getParameter(CITY_FIELD);
```

Next, perform some error checking on the fields to make sure they are sensible.

```
if ((name == null) || (name.length() < 1))
{
    error = "Please enter a name!";
    gotError = true;
    name = null;
}
```

If any errors were found, then store the value into the `HttpServletRequest` object and forward the processing back to the form page so the user can fix the errors.

```
if (gotError)
{
    incPath = FORM_PAGE;
    req.setAttribute("errorMessage", error);
    performRedirect(incPath, req, res);
    return;
}
```

If there are no errors, store the values of variables used by `CityResult.jsp` and forward the processing to that JSP page.

```
req.setAttribute("theCity", city);
req.setAttribute("theName", name);
String greeting = null;

if (city.equals("MEL"))
{
    greeting = "G'day";
}
. . . .
req.setAttribute("theGreeting", greeting);
performRedirect(incPath, req, res);
```

The final section of code is the processing of the forward to the appropriate JSP page. To enable the input forms to direct their responses to the correct servlets the code creates a `servletPath` object that is used by the JSP pages.

Tip

Obtaining the context path and pre-pending to the servlet name in the same way as the example allows the Web application to be deployed using a different context and still continue to work. This adds greater flexibility in development and deployment of Web applications.

```
servletName = req.getServletPath();
req.setAttribute("servletPath",
                 req.getContextPath()+servletName);
req.setAttribute("nameField", NAME_FIELD);
req.setAttribute("cityField", CITY_FIELD);

RequestDispatcher rd = req.getRequestDispatcher(incPath);
rd.forward(req, res);
```

To enable the controller servlet and to complete the input side of the picture Listing 7-5 provides the code for the input form JSP page. Create this, and all other JSP files, in the `web` directory.

Listing 7-5: CityForm.jsp

```
<jsp:useBean id="errorMessage" class="java.lang.String" scope="request" />
<jsp:useBean id="servletPath" class="java.lang.String" scope="request" />
<jsp:useBean id="nameField" class="java.lang.String" scope="request" />
<jsp:useBean id="cityField" class="java.lang.String" scope="request" />
<%
    // work out if an error has occurred
    boolean anError = true;
    if ((errorMessage == null) || (errorMessage.length() < 1))
    {
        anError = false;
    }
    String screenName = "Hello City! - Input Form";
%>
<html>
<head>
    <title><%=screenName%></title>
</head>
<body bgcolor="#ffffff">
<form action="<%=servletPath%>" method="POST" name="frmInput">
<input type="hidden" name="action" value="input">
<table border="0" width="80%">
<tr>
    <td colspan=2>
        <h1><%=screenName%></h1>
    </td>
```

```
</tr>
<tr><td colspan=2> </td></tr>
<%
    if (anError)
    {
        %>
        <tr>
        <td colspan=2>
            <font color="red"><b><%=errorMessage%></b></font>
        </td>
        </tr>
        <%
    }
%>

<tr>
    <td width=30%>
        <b>Enter Your Name: </b>
    </td>
    <td>
        <input type="text" name="<%=nameField%>" size="32" >
    </td>
</tr>
<tr>
    <td>
        <b>Choose Your Home City: </b>
    </td>
    <td>
    <select name="<%=cityField%>">
        <option value="" >Select City
        <option value="" >-----------
        <option value="MEL">Melbourne
        <option value="PAR">Paris
        <option value="MIL">Milan
    </select>
    </td>
</tr>
<tr><td colspan=2> </td></tr>
<tr>
    <td>   </td>
    <td>
        <input type="submit" value="Say Hello!">
        <input type="reset" >
    </td>
</tr>
</table>
</form>
</html>
```

CityForm.jsp is considerably more complicated than HelloWorldJSP.jsp, so the following section describes some of the additional code.

The first part of the JSP page is the useBean actions that obtain the attributes stored in the HttpRequest object by CityServlet.

```
<jsp:useBean id="errorMessage" class="java.lang.String" scope="request" />
<jsp:useBean id="servletPath" class="java.lang.String" scope="request" />
<jsp:useBean id="nameField" class="java.lang.String" scope="request" />
<jsp:useBean id="cityField" class="java.lang.String" scope="request" />
```

The next code fragment is using errorMessage to determine if any errors need to be displayed and initializing a variable to be used in displaying the page title and as a heading.

```
boolean anError = true;
if ((errorMessage == null) || (errorMessage.length() < 1))
{
    anError = false;
}
String screenName = "Hello City! - Input Form";
```

The remainder of the file is fairly simple HTML code, with the occasional JSP expression to make use of the objects stored by CityServlet.

Finally, to finish off the Web application, Listing 7-6 contains the code for CityResult.jsp.

Listing 7-6: **CityResult.jsp**

```
<jsp:useBean id="errorMessage" class="java.lang.String" scope="request" />
<jsp:useBean id="servletPath" class="java.lang.String" scope="request" />
<jsp:useBean id="theName" class="java.lang.String" scope="request" />
<jsp:useBean id="theGreeting" class="java.lang.String" scope="request" />
<%
    // work out if an error has occurred
    boolean anError = true;
    if ((errorMessage == null) || (errorMessage.length() < 1))
    {
        anError = false;
    }

    String screenName = "Hello City! - Results Page";
%>
<html>
<head>
    <title><%=screenName%></title>
</head>
<body bgcolor="#ffffff" >
<table border="0" width="80%">
<tr>
    <td colspan=2>
        <h1><%=screenName%></h1>
    </td>
```

```
</tr>
<tr><td colspan=2> </td><tr>
<tr>
<%
    if (anError)
    {
        %>
        <td width="40%" >
        An error occurred while running the Hello City!
        Web application.
        </td>
        <td >
            <%=errorMessage%>
        </td>
        <%
    }
    else
    {
        %>
        <td width="30%">
        <b>Your greeting is: </b>
        </td>
        <td>
            <%=theGreeting%> <%=theName%> !
        </td>
        <%
    }
%>
</tr>
<tr>
    <td> </td>
    <td>
        <a href="<%=servletPath%>">Try again</a>
    </td>
</tr>
</table>
</html>
```

With all the code created, all that is left is to update the `web.xml` file to include the new servlet. Add the lines shown in bold in Listing 7-7 to deploy the servlet.

Listing 7-7: **web.xml**

```
<?xml version="1.0" encoding="ISO-8859-1" ?>
<!DOCTYPE web-app
  PUBLIC "-//Sun Microsystems, Inc.//DTD Web Application 2.3//EN"
  "http://java.sun.com/dtd/web-app_2_3.dtd" >
```

Continued

Listing 7-7 *(continued)*

```
    <web-app>
    <display-name>Hello World Application</display-name>
    <description>
        This is the simple Hello World! application
    </description>

    <servlet>
        <servlet-name>world</servlet-name>
        <description>The Hello World! Servlet</description>
        <servlet-class>
            bible.tomcat.hello.HelloWorldServlet
        </servlet-class>
    </servlet>

    <servlet>
        <servlet-name>city</servlet-name>
        <description>The Hello City! Servlet</description>
        <servlet-class>
            bible.tomcat.hello.CityServlet
        </servlet-class>
    </servlet>

    <servlet-mapping>
        <servlet-name>world</servlet-name>
        <url-pattern>/world</url-pattern>
    </servlet-mapping>

    <servlet-mapping>
        <servlet-name>city</servlet-name>
        <url-pattern>/city</url-pattern>
    </servlet-mapping>
</web-app>
```

Testing Hello City!

Now it is time to compile and test the Web application. Normally this is more of an iterative process where the Java, JSP, and descriptors are changed during development as more of the application is built, so there may be a few mistakes to be fixed before the results can be properly appreciated.

Make sure that Tomcat is running and issue the following command at a console:

```
ant context
```

Chapter 5 describes compiling and deploying using Ant in detail, but it is important to remember that each time Tomcat is started, the application needs to be installed using the `context` target. After the `context` target has been used, subsequent development activities only need to use the `compile` target. If there is any doubt that the Web application has not been installed, use the `list` target to display all the installed Web applications.

When all of the errors have been fixed and the Web application is ready to be tested this should result in output similar to the following:

```
prepare:
    [mkdir] Created dir: C:\devel\hello\build
    [mkdir] Created dir: C:\devel\hello\build\WEB-INF
    [mkdir] Created dir: C:\devel\hello\build\WEB-INF\classes
     [copy] Copying 4 files to C:\devel\hello\build
     [copy] Copied 1 empty directory to C:\devel\hello\build

compile:
    [javac] Compiling 2 source files to C:\devel\hello\build\WEB-INF\classes
     [copy] Copying 1 file to C:\devel\hello\build\WEB-INF

context:
  [install] OK - Installed application from context file
file:///C:\devel\hello/build/WEB-INF/context.xml
```

To see the results of the development of the Web application browse to the newly added URL, `http://localhost:8080/hello/city` and the output should be similar to that shown in Figure 7-6.

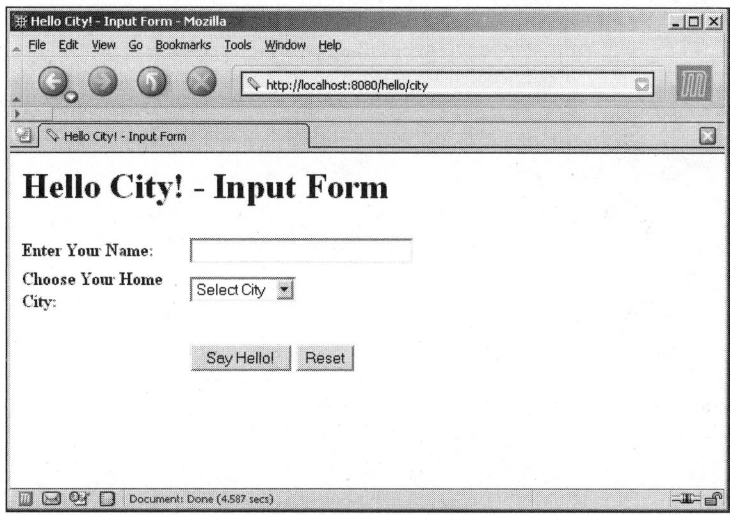

Figure 7-6: Hello City! Web application input form

First check error handling. Without entering any data into the form, press the Say Hello! button, which should result in output similar to that shown in Figure 7-7.

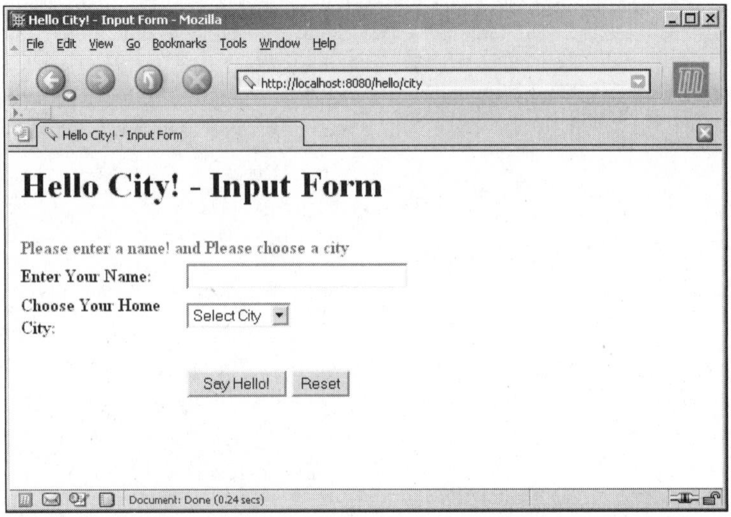

Hello City! - Input Form - Mozilla
File Edit View Go Bookmarks Tools Window Help
http://localhost:8080/hello/city
Hello City! - Input Form

Hello City! - Input Form

Please enter a name! and Please choose a city
Enter Your Name:
Choose Your Home City:
Select City
Say Hello! Reset
Document: Done (0.24 secs)

Figure 7-7: Displaying validation errors

Finally, enter your name and choose a city from the drop-down menu to display output similar to that shown in Figure 7-8.

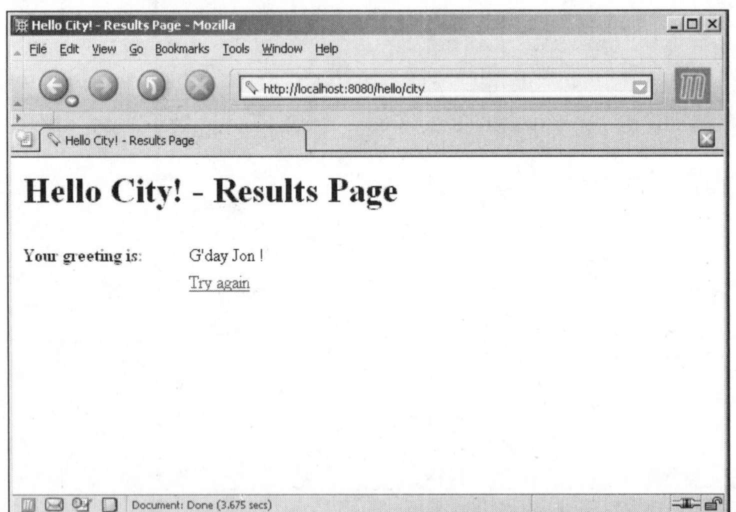

Figure 7-8: Displaying the successful results of the Hello City! Web application

The results from Hello City! are the first steps toward building a more complex Web application, however, there are a few more refinements that can be included before it is completed.

There is an area of concern in the Web application. Both `CityForm.jsp` and `CityServlet.java` have sections of code that have "hard coded" values for the cities. While this is a simple application, imagine how hard it will be to keep the two lists synchronized as the application grows in complexity. The next version of Hello City! shows a convenient way to use the one list for both parts of the application.

Using the ServletContext

Chapter 1 described the `ServletContext` and how all the components of a Web application have access to the `ServletContext`. This becomes a convenient object to use as a repository for static, application wide data. It allows the code in `CityForm.jsp` and the code in `CityServlet.java` to share the same city information.

So, to upgrade the Web application, first make changes to `CityServlet.java` as shown in Listing 7-8 and Listing 7-9. The changes are shown in bold.

The final completed code for the Web application (servlets, JSP pages, and `web.xml`) is included at the end of the development section of this chapter and also is available for download from the Web site.

Listing 7-8: Adding an Object to the ServletContext in CityServlet.java

```
public final String NAME_FIELD      = "NAME";
public final String CITY_FIELD      = "CITY";

/*
 * An array list containing the greetings
 */
private ArrayList greetings;

public void init()
throws ServletException
{
    /*
     * On initialisation, load the static lookup information
     * into the ServletContext for use by the Web application
     */
    greetings = new ArrayList();
    greetings.add(new CityBean("MEL", "Melbourne", "G'day"));
    greetings.add(new CityBean("MIL", "Milan", "Ciao"));
    greetings.add(new CityBean("PAR", "Paris", "Bonjour"));

    ServletContext ctx = getServletContext();
    ctx.setAttribute("greetings", greetings);
}
```

Continued

Listing 7-8 *(continued)*

```
public void doGet(HttpServletRequest req, HttpServletResponse res)
throws ServletException, IOException
{
    doPost(req, res);
}
```

Listing 7-8 shows the creation of an `ArrayList` used to store the objects that encapsulate the (very limited) business logic of the Web application. This `ArrayList` is then stored in the `ServletContext` via the use of the `setAttribute()` method using the name of greetings.

Listing 7-9: Finding the Correct Greeting in doPost() of CityServlet.java

```
public void doPost(HttpServletRequest req, HttpServletResponse res)
throws ServletException, IOException
{
    String incPath = FORM_PAGE;
    String error = "";

    String action = req.getParameter("action");
    if (action != null)
    {
. . . . . . . . . .
. . . . . . . . . .

        // we've got real values, so we'll use them in the JSP
        req.setAttribute("theCity", city);
        req.setAttribute("theName", name);

        for (int i=0;i<greetings.size();i++)
        {
            CityBean cb = (CityBean)greetings.get(i);
            if (city.equals(cb.getCityAbbrev()))
            {
                req.setAttribute("theGreeting",
                                 cb.getCityGreeting());
            }
        }
    }
    else
    {
. . . . . . . . . .
. . . . . . . . . .
```

Listing 7-9 shows the processing of the input fields from the user. The code fragment shows the searching through the array comparing the abbreviation stored in the `CityBean` with the value from the drop-down list.

To complete the application, enter the code for the `CityBean` shown in Listing 7-10.

Listing 7-10: CityBean.java

```
package bible.tomcat.hello;

public class CityBean
{
    private String  cityName;
    private String  cityAbbrev;
    private String  cityGreeting;

    public CityBean()
    {
        cityName = null;
        cityAbbrev = null;
        cityGreeting = null;
    }

    public CityBean(String ca, String cn, String cg)
    {
        setCityAbbrev(ca);
        setCityName(cn);
        setCityGreeting(cg);
    }

    public void setCityName(String cn)
    {
        cityName = cn;
    }

    public void setCityAbbrev(String ca)
    {
        cityAbbrev = ca;
    }

    public void setCityGreeting(String cg)
    {
        cityGreeting = cg;
    }

    public String getCityName()
    {
        return cityName;
    }
```

Continued

Listing 7-10 *(continued)*

```
    public String getCityAbbrev()
    {
        return cityAbbrev;
    }

    public String getCityGreeting()
    {
        return cityGreeting;
    }
}
```

The changes that have been implemented allow for the storage of the objects, and using them to check for the response. In doing this, there has been no change to the results page; it still shows the same simple greeting that was displayed previously. However, the drop-down list needs to be updated on `CityForm.jsp` to read the information stored in the `ServletContext`. These changes are shown in Listing 7-11. The updates are shown in bold.

Listing 7-11: Updating CityForm.jsp

```
<%@page import="bible.tomcat.hello.*" %>
<jsp:useBean id="errorMessage" class="java.lang.String" scope="request" />
<jsp:useBean id="servletPath" class="java.lang.String" scope="request" />
<jsp:useBean id="nameField" class="java.lang.String" scope="request" />
<jsp:useBean id="cityField" class="java.lang.String" scope="request" />
<jsp:useBean id="greetings" class="java.util.ArrayList" scope="application" />
. . . . . . . . .
. . . . . . . . .
<tr>
    <td>
        <b>Choose Your Home City: </b>
    </td>
    <td>
    <select name="<%=cityField%>">
        <option value="" >Select City
        <option value="" >-----------
        <%
        for (int i=0;i<greetings.size();i++)
        {
            CityBean cb = (CityBean)greetings.get(i); %>
            <option value="<%=cb.getCityAbbrev()%>"><%=cb.getCityName()%><%
        }
        %>
    </select>
    </td>
</tr>
```

The first line of the file is a page directive. This import statement provides the JSP page with the ability to access the classes in the `bible.tomcat.hello` package, which of course is where the `CityBean` class is packaged.

The next change of importance is the following line:

```
<jsp:useBean id="greetings" class="java.util.ArrayList" scope="application" />
```

This is the `ArrayList` that is stored in the `ServletContext`.

Notice how the scope of the objects in the `ServletContext` is `application`, where the scope of the objects in the `HttpServletRequest` is `request`. The use of the `scope` attribute is how the JSP page identifies where to find the objects named in the `useBean` directive. `request` is for the `HttpServletRequest` object, `session` is for the `HttpSession` object, and `application` is for the `ServletContext` object.

The final change is the `for()` loop that iterates through the `ArrayList` displaying the information stored in the `CityBean` objects.

With this stage of the application completed it is time to test. So, ensure Tomcat is started and issue the following command:

```
ant compile
```

If Tomcat has been restarted, the Web application must be re-installed using `ant context`. Use the `ant list` command to check if the `city` application has been installed.

This should produce the following results:

```
prepare:
     [copy] Copying 1 file to C:\devel\hello\build

compile:
    [javac] Compiling 2 source files to C:\devel\hello\build\WEB-INF\classes

BUILD SUCCESSFUL
Total time: 3 seconds
```

Check the results by browsing to the URL `http://localhost:8080/hello/city`. This should display results similar to those shown in Figure 7-9.

As can be seen from comparing Figure 7-9 to Figure 7-6, they are identical. This should be expected because the changes occur to replace code that will be hard to maintain, rather than change how the application works. It may seem considerably effort to use a technique like this for such a simple application. This is true, but imagine dealing with many lists like this over an application that has many servlets and JSP pages and trying to keep them synchronized manually.

Currently the application is working well, but there is always the customer wanting to change things after development has finished. Wouldn't it be nice if the application could be modified to read the information from a data source rather than having the information stored in the Java code? The next (and final) change to the application is to read the greetings from the `web.xml` file. This shows a technique for reading properties from the deployment file for the Web application.

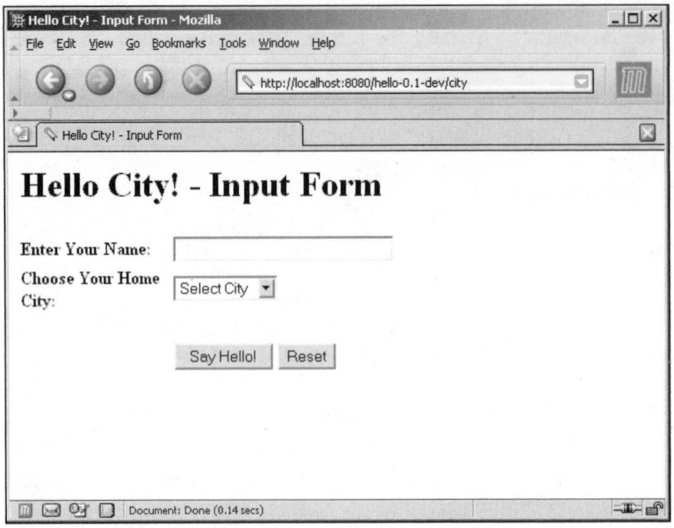

Figure 7-9: Updated Hello City! application

Reading the <context-param> in web.xml

The `<context-param>` nodes in the `web.xml` deployment descriptor file are processed by the servlet container and made available to the Web application via the `ServletContext`. To obtain the `<context-param>` data, there are two methods used to obtain the information. The first is `getInitParameterNames()`. This method returns an `Enumeration` of `String` objects that contain the `<param-name>` node of the `<context-param>`. The second is `getInitParameter()`. This method returns a `String` object that contains the `<param-value>` node of the `<context-param>`.

These two methods and a simple naming convention provide a simple means for providing initialization data to a Web application. The final version of the Web application deployment descriptor is shown in Listing 7-12. The changes are displayed in bold.

Listing 7-12: web.xml

```
<?xml version="1.0" encoding="ISO-8859-1" ?>

<!DOCTYPE web-app
  PUBLIC "-//Sun Microsystems, Inc.//DTD Web Application 2.3//EN"
  "http://java.sun.com/dtd/web-app_2_3.dtd" >

<web-app>
    <display-name>Hello World Application</display-name>
    <description>
        This is the simple Hello World! application
    </description>
```

```
    <context-param>
        <param-name>city.param.1</param-name>
        <param-value>MEL:Melbourne:G'day</param-value>
        <description>The Melbourne Greeting</description>
    </context-param>
    <context-param>
        <param-name>city.param.2</param-name>
        <param-value>MIL:Milan:Ciao</param-value>
        <description>The Milan Greeting</description>
    </context-param>
    <context-param>
        <param-name>city.param.3</param-name>
        <param-value>PAR:Paris:Bonjour</param-value>
        <description>The Paris Greeting</description>
    </context-param>

    <servlet>
        <servlet-name>world</servlet-name>
        <description>
            The Hello World! Servlet
        </description>
        <servlet-class>
            bible.tomcat.hello.HelloWorldServlet
        </servlet-class>
    </servlet>

    <servlet>
        <servlet-name>city</servlet-name>
        <description>
            The Hello City! Servlet
        </description>
        <servlet-class>
            bible.tomcat.hello.CityServlet
        </servlet-class>
    </servlet>

    <servlet-mapping>
        <servlet-name>world</servlet-name>
        <url-pattern>/world</url-pattern>
    </servlet-mapping>

    <servlet-mapping>
        <servlet-name>city</servlet-name>
        <url-pattern>/city</url-pattern>
    </servlet-mapping>

</web-app>
```

The only changes are the addition of the three `<context-param>` structures. The `<param-value>` nodes are simple colon (:) delimited fields with the city abbreviation, the city name, and the city greeting stored as one value. The `<param-name>` nodes all have the same prefix. This prefix (`city.param.`) is used by the `CityServlet` to identify the `<context-param>` nodes that are used for the drop-down list. With a more complicated application there may be many `<context-param>` nodes that are used for many purposes, so this provides a mechanism for determining the correct parameters.

The only other change to the Web application is the modification to the `CityServlet` to process the initialization parameters. Listing 7-13 contains the `CityServlet` with the final changes shown in bold.

Listing 7-13: **CityServlet.java**

```
package bible.tomcat.hello;

import java.io.*;
import java.lang.*;
import java.util.*;

import javax.servlet.http.*;
import javax.servlet.*;

/*
 * This is the main controlling servlet for the Hello City
 * application.
 *
 * This HttpServlet controls the simple interactions between
 * a form (created by CityForm.jsp) and the results page
 * (created by CityResult.jsp)

 */
public class CityServlet
extends HttpServlet
{
    public final String FORM_PAGE   = "/CityBeanForm.jsp";
    public final String RESULT_PAGE = "/CityResult.jsp";

    /*
     * These are identifiers used by the FORM_PAGE for the
     * form processing.
     */
    public final String NAME_FIELD      = "NAME";
    public final String CITY_FIELD      = "CITY";

    /*
     * An array list containing the greetings
     */
    private ArrayList greetings;
```

```
public void init()
throws ServletException
{
    /*
     * On initialization, load the static lookup information
     * into the ServletContext for use by the Web application
     * from the Web application files.
     */

    ServletContext ctx = getServletContext();
    Enumeration en = ctx.getInitParameterNames();

    greetings = new ArrayList();

    while (en.hasMoreElements())
    {
        String p = (String)en.nextElement();

        if (p.startsWith("city.param"))
        {
            String v = ctx.getInitParameter(p);
            greetings.add(createCityBean(v));
        }
    }
    ctx.setAttribute("greetings", greetings);
}

private CityBean createCityBean(String composite)
{
    CityBean rv = new CityBean();
    StringTokenizer st = new StringTokenizer(composite, ":");
    rv.setCityAbbrev(st.nextToken());
    rv.setCityName(st.nextToken());
    rv.setCityGreeting(st.nextToken());

    return rv;
}

/*
 * Invoke doPost() from doGet(), if ever called.
 */
public void doGet(HttpServletRequest req, HttpServletResponse res)
throws ServletException, IOException
{
    doPost(req, res);
}

/*
 * doPost() provides the body of the servlet controller,
 * and invokes the business logic
```

Continued

Listing 7-13 *(continued)*

```
 *
 * doPost() is also responsible for determining what page
 * should be displayed. If the servlet is invoked with no
 * parameters, it is assumed that the request is for the
 * display of the form page.
 */
public void doPost(HttpServletRequest req,
        HttpServletResponse res)
throws ServletException, IOException
{
    String incPath = FORM_PAGE;
    String error = "";

    /*
     * Has the servlet been invoked from the FORM_PAGE ?
     */
    String action = req.getParameter("action");
    if (action != null)  // yes !
    {
        boolean gotError = false;
        incPath = RESULT_PAGE;

        /*
         * Grab the fields (name and city) from the HTTP request
         */
        String name = req.getParameter(NAME_FIELD);
        String city = req.getParameter(CITY_FIELD);

        /*
         * Now calculate the results
         */
        if ((name == null) || (name.length() < 1))
        {
            error = "Please enter a name!";
            gotError = true;
            name = null;
        }

        if ((city == null) || (city.length() < 1))
        {
            if (gotError)
            {
                error += " and ";
            }
            error += "Please choose a city";
            gotError = true;
        }
```

```
        if (gotError)
        {
            incPath = FORM_PAGE;
            req.setAttribute("errorMessage", error);
            performRedirect(incPath, req, res);
            return;
        }

        // we've got real values, so we'll use them in the JSP
        req.setAttribute("theCity", city);
        req.setAttribute("theName", name);

        for (int i=0;i<greetings.size();i++)
        {
            CityBean cb = (CityBean)greetings.get(i);
            if (city.equals(cb.getCityAbbrev()))
            {
                req.setAttribute("theGreeting", cb.getCityGreeting());
            }
        }
    }
    else
    {
    }

    /*
     * Now we've done our calculations, got some results, or
     * some sort of error, so let the user know what's been
     * going on!
     */
    performRedirect(incPath, req, res);
}

private void performRedirect(String incPath,
        HttpServletRequest req,
        HttpServletResponse res)
throws ServletException, IOException
{
    String servletName;
    if (incPath != null)
    {
        servletName = req.getServletPath();
        req.setAttribute("servletPath",
                req.getContextPath()+servletName);
        req.setAttribute("nameField", NAME_FIELD);
        req.setAttribute("cityField", CITY_FIELD);

        /*
         * Now, forward the results to the appropriate JSP page
         */
```

Continued

Listing 7-13 *(continued)*

```
                RequestDispatcher rd = req.getRequestDispatcher(incPath);
                rd.forward(req, res);
            }
        }
}
```

For completeness, Listing 7-14 contains the final version of `CityForm.jsp`.

Listing 7-14: **CityForm.jsp**

```
<%@page import="bible.tomcat.hello.*" %>
<%-- Simple form for obtaining the name and home fields --%>
<jsp:useBean id="errorMessage" class="java.lang.String" scope="request" />
<jsp:useBean id="servletPath" class="java.lang.String" scope="request" />
<jsp:useBean id="nameField" class="java.lang.String" scope="request" />
<jsp:useBean id="cityField" class="java.lang.String" scope="request" />
<jsp:useBean id="greetings" class="java.util.ArrayList" scope="application" />

<%
    // work out if an error has occurred
    boolean anError = true;
    if ((errorMessage == null) || (errorMessage.length() < 1))
    {
        anError = true;
    }

    String screenName = "Hello City! - Input Form";
%>

<html>
<head>
    <title><%=screenName%></title>
</head>

<body bgcolor="#ffffff">

<form action="<%=servletPath%>" method="POST" name="frmInput">
<input type="hidden" name="action" value="input">

<table border="0" cellpadding="0" cellspacing="0" width="80%">
<tr>
    <td colspan=2>
        <h1><%=screenName%></h1>
    </td>
</tr>
<tr><td colspan=2> </td></tr>
```

```
<%
    if (anError)
    {
        %>
        <tr>
        <td colspan=2>
            <font color="red"><b><%=errorMessage%></b></font>
        </td>
        </tr>
        <%
    }
%>

<tr>
    <td width=30%>
        <b>Enter Your Name: </b>
    </td>
    <td>
        <input type="text" name="<%=nameField%>" size="32" >
    </td>
</tr>
<tr>
    <td>
        <b>Choose Your Home City: </b>
    </td>
    <td>
    <select name="<%=cityField%>">
        <option value="" >Select City
        <option value="" >-----------
        <%
        for (int i=0;i<greetings.size();i++)
        {
            CityBean cb = (CityBean)greetings.get(i); %>
            <option value="<%=cb.getCityAbbrev()%>"><%=cb.getCityName()%><%
        }
        %>
    </select>
    </td>
</tr>
<tr><td colspan=2> </td></tr>
<tr>
    <td>   </td>
    <td>
        <input type="submit" value="Say Hello!">
        <input type="reset" >
    </td>
</tr>
</table>
</form>

</html>
```

The final versions of the files in the Web application should be exactly the same as the following list:

✦ `web.xml`, Listing 7-12

✦ `CityServlet.java`, Listing 7-13

✦ `CityForm.jsp`, Listing 7-14

✦ `CityResult.jsp`, Listing 7-6

Again, compile and test the Web application. There should be no changes to the display.

The order of the items in the drop-down list of `CityForm.jsp` depends upon the order in which the `<context-param>` entries are defined. This may result in changes to the order of the list, but that will not affect how the application operates.

The final step is to create the Web archive that will be used for deployment. At a console, type the following command.

```
ant dist
```

This creates a new directory, `c:\devel\hello\dist`, which contains the documentation for the project, created Javadocs, and a WAR file called `hello-0.1-dev.war`. The WAR file is the deployment package used in the next section of this chapter.

With the Web application completed, the developers can go home and sleep well. However, the customer still needs to have application deployed on their server. The next section of the chapter shows how to deploy the Hello City! Web application using some of the tools that are provided by Tomcat.

Deploying the Web Application

During the development of the application, deployment to Tomcat was done using the `context` task. This installs the Web application temporarily using the current build environment as the Web application root. This can be demonstrated effectively by performing the following operations.

1. Start up Tomcat.
2. Install the Web application with `ant context`.
3. List the installed applications with `ant list`.

This should produce output that is similar to:

```
context:
  [install] OK - Installed application from context file file:///C:\devel
\hello/build/WEB-INF/context.xml
```

and

```
list:
     [list] OK - Listed applications for virtual host localhost

     [list] /hello:running:1:C:\devel\hello/build
```

```
    [list] /examples:running:0:examples

    [list] /webdav:running:0:C:\tomcat\webapps\webdav

    [list] /tomcat-docs:running:0:C:\tomcat\webapps\tomcat-docs

    [list] /manager:running:0:../server/webapps/manager

    [list] /admin:running:0:../server/webapps/admin

    [list] /:running:0:C:\tomcat\webapps\ROOT
```

The `list` shows that the `/hello` Web application is installed using an application root of `c:\devel\hello\build`.

Now, if Tomcat is stopped and restarted, performing an `ant list` produces the following results.

```
list:
    [list] OK - Listed applications for virtual host localhost

    [list] /examples:running:0:examples

    [list] /webdav:running:0:C:\tomcat\webapps\webdav

    [list] /tomcat-docs:running:0:C:\tomcat\webapps\tomcat-docs

    [list] /manager:running:0:../server/webapps/manager

    [list] /admin:running:0:../server/webapps/admin

    [list] /:running:0:C:\tomcat\webapps\ROOT
```

The `hello` Web application is now missing! The `install` target (and the modified version `context`) does not install applications permanently.

Tip Using the development `build` directory for a permanent deployment option is a potentially very unsafe option because when the development environment changes, or the class files are deleted, the Web application stops working.

The question now is, "How can we deploy our application permanently?" The covered methods are:

- ✦ Manual deployment
- ✦ Deploying using the Tomcat Ant Task

Manual Deployment

This option is the simplest and the most common deployment technique. Simply copy the deployment WAR to the `webapps` directory for the install of Tomcat.

```
copy c:\devel\hello\dist\hello-0.1-dev.war c:\tomcat\webapps
```

This deployment uses the default options in the `server.xml` to change the options for this Web application edit `server.xml` or use a `context.xml`. Chapter 9 contains details about the modification of `server.xml`. Chapter 4 contains details about using a `context.xml` file.

Restart Tomcat and enter `ant list` at a console. This should result in output similar to:

```
list:
     [list] OK - Listed applications for virtual host localhost

     [list] /examples:running:0:examples

     [list] /webdav:running:0:C:\tomcat\webapps\webdav

     [list] /hello-0.1-dev:running:0:C:/tomcat/webapps/hello-0.1-dev

     [list] /tomcat-docs:running:0:C:\tomcat\webapps\tomcat-docs

     [list] /manager:running:0:../server/webapps/manager

     [list] /admin:running:0:../server/webapps/admin

     [list] /:running:0:C:\tomcat\webapps\ROOT
```

Now browse to the URL `http://localhost:8080/hello-01.-dev/city`.You should see results similar to those shown in Figure 7-10.

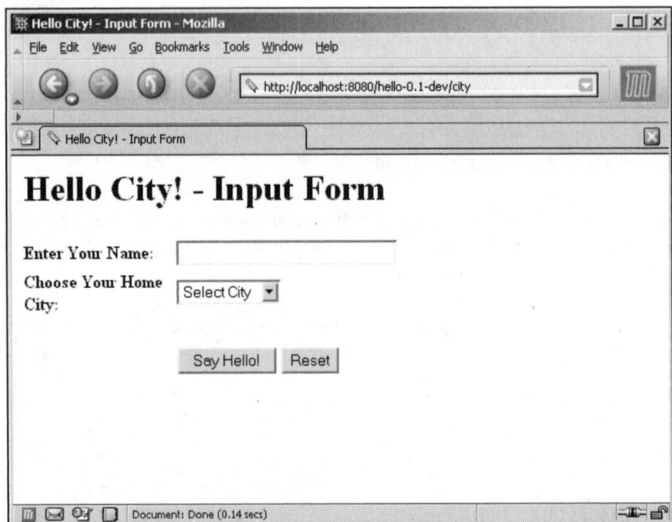

Figure 7-10: Manual deployment of Hello City!

Certainly a Web site that looks like this won't impress anyone. It doesn't look very friendly. There are ways to address this. The simplest is to change the name of the WAR file prior to restarting Tomcat, or as part of the copy process. Changing the name can be achieved by using the following command:

```
copy c:\devel\hello\dist\hello-0.1-dev.war c:\tomcat\webapps\hello.war
```

Now when Tomcat is restarted the application can be accessed using the URL `http://localhost:8080/hello/city`.

Placing WAR files in the `webapps` directory results in Tomcat unpacking the WAR files to subdirectories and accessing the Web application from the unpacked directory. Changes to the WAR file will not be reflected in the Web application because Tomcat does not overwrite the unpacked directory with the new WAR file contents. To re-deploy the WAR, the subdirectory (hello-0.1-dev or hello) needs to be deleted before Tomcat is restarted. Chapter 5 contains more details about options for Web application deployment in Tomcat.

To remove the Web application, perform the following tasks:

1. Stop Tomcat (or remove the Web application using the Manager Application)
2. Delete `c:\tomcat\webapps\hello-0.1-dev.war`
3. Delete the directory tree `c:\tomcat\webapps\hello-0.1-dev\`

The next area of concern is that to install a Web application Tomcat has been started and stopped. This might not be an issue if this is the only Web application Tomcat is running, but in a service or hosting environment, or at a customer site where downtime for other applications might not be acceptable, there needs to be other ways of achieving the same objectives. This can be performed using the Tomcat Ant Task.

Deploying Using the Tomcat Ant Task

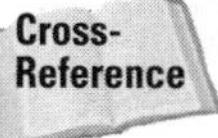

To deploy using the Tomcat Ant tasks, the project `build.xml` file needs to be modified to include the deploy task and a deploy target. Details about these modifications are found in Chapter 5.

Using the Tomcat Ant Task for deployment provides the advantage of performing remote deployment (and removal).

To deploy the application, perform the following tasks:

1. Start Tomcat
2. Create the WAR file with `ant dist`
3. Deploy the WAR file with `ant deploy`

This should result in output similar to:

```
Buildfile: build.xml

deploy:
   [deploy] OK - Installed application at context path /hello
```

If the an application is already installed, or deployed using the context path `/hello` then an error occurs, producing output similar to the following:

```
deploy:
   [deploy] FAIL - Application already exists at path /hello


BUILD FAILED
file:c:/devel/hello/build.xml:529: FAIL - Application already exists at
path /hello
```

At this point either use `ant undeploy` or `ant remove` to free up the context.

Tip An application that has been deployed with `deploy` can only be removed with `undeploy`. An application that has been installed with `install` or `context` can only be removed with `remove` or by restarting Tomcat. Attempting to `undeploy` an application that has been installed with `install` will result in an error.

To examine the results of the deployment use the `ant list` command, which should produce the following:

```
list:
     [list] OK - Listed applications for virtual host localhost

     [list]
/hello:running:1:C:\tomcat\work\Standalone\localhost\manager\hello.war

     [list] /examples:running:0:examples

     [list] /webdav:running:0:C:\tomcat\webapps\webdav

     [list] /tomcat-docs:running:0:C:\tomcat\webapps\tomcat-docs

     [list] /manager:running:0:../server/webapps/manager

     [list] /admin:running:1:../server/webapps/admin

     [list] /:running:0:C:\tomcat\webapps\ROOT
```

Notice that the deployment of the WAR is not within the Tomcat `webapps` directory.

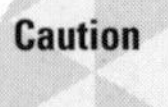

Caution If an application has been configured with an `explicit <Context>` directive either manually or via the `deploy` task, then a WAR file in the `webapps` directory with the same name is silently ignored. For example, the `<Context>` path is `/hello` and the WAR file is `hello.war`. There are no errors generated in the log entries or to the Tomcat console.

The development and deployment of the Hello City! Web application in this chapter were chosen as a simple example of the activities that need to be performed to develop and deploy Web applications with Tomcat. The scope of the example is deliberately limited to focus on the essential elements.

To gain a full understanding of particularly the development and deployment options available, examine Chapters 3 and 4 for more detail on the `web.xml` deployment descriptor, Chapter 9 for the configuration of Tomcat using the `server.xml`, and Chapters 10 and 16 for configuration relating to external data sources.

Summary

This chapter has provided a starting point for development and deployment of web applications. Using very simple possible examples the chapter provided some of the most commonly used techniques for web application development.

These included a simplified Model-View-Controller architecture which is covered in further detail in Chapter 10 as well as techniques for reading the configuration parameters from the `web.xml` file and working with HTML forms.

✦ ✦ ✦

PART

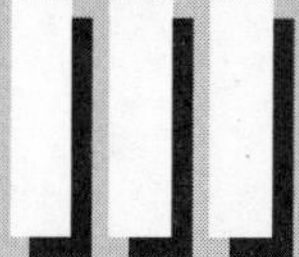

Tomcat Configuration and Applications

✦ ✦ ✦ ✦

In This Part

✦ ✦ ✦ ✦

CHAPTER 8

Configuring the Tomcat Server

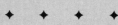

✦ ✦ ✦ ✦

In This Chapter

Tomcat Configuration Elements

Using the Administration Application

Common Configuration Scenarios

✦ ✦ ✦ ✦

This chapter examines the configuration of Tomcat in detail, enabling a developer or a system administrator to modify the configuration of a default Tomcat installation to appropriately reflect their requirements. This examination also includes configuration that will be useful during development, such as debugging and logging support for identifying errors.

The examination begins with the structure of the Tomcat configuration file, the elements in the file and how the elements may be nested together.

It then turns to options available for the elements and the values that can be used for a default Tomcat installation. This includes details of external data sources and other configuration files that are part of the Tomcat distribution.

The chapter concludes with a series of HOWTO guides for configuring common scenarios including:

- Logging
- Debugging
- SSL
- Multiple hosts
- Multiple instances of Tomcat

Configuration Overview

`server.xml` is the Tomcat configuration file and is an XML file consisting of the elements that describe the structure of the installation, including Hosts and Contexts for the Web applications.

The elements of `server.xml` can be broken into five broad categories:

- Top Level Elements
- Connectors
- Containers
- Nested components
- Special components

Top level elements are the `Server` and `Service` elements, which define the highest level the runtime parameters like shutdown port number and connection capabilities.

`Connector` elements are contained within a `Service` and work with a single `Engine` element for processing of incoming requests. `Connector` elements handle the various protocols such as HTTP, HTTPS, and the custom connectors for communicating with Web servers.

`Containers` are elements that hold other elements, including other containers and nested elements. Nested components are elements that exist within a container. Some nested components may exist in any container, while some nested components only exist in specific containers.

`Hosts` and `Context` elements are good examples of containers and `Valve` and `Logger` elements are good examples of nested components.

Special components either exist within a single container, or have different semantics depending on the container they are located.

The `server.xml` contains the elements shown in Table 8-1.

Table 8-1: server.xml Elements

Element Name	*Type*
`Server`	Top Level Element
`Service`	Top Level Element
`Coyote HTTP/1.1`	Connector
`Coyote JK2`	Connector
`Engine`	Container
`Host`	Container
`Context`	Container
`Default Context`	Nested
`GlobalNamingResources`	Nested
`Loader`	Nested
`Logger`	Nested
`Manager`	Nested
`Realm`	Nested
`Resources`	Nested
`Valve`	Nested
`Alias`	Special
`Environment`	Special
`Listener`	Special
`Parameter`	Special

Element Name	Type
Resource	Special
ResourceLink	Special
ResourceParams	Special

The arrangement of the elements can be shown in Figure 8-1.

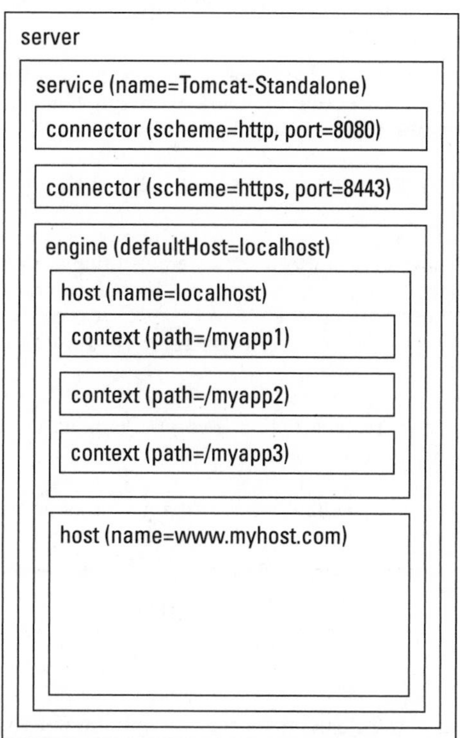

Figure 8-1: Tomcat configuration elements

Figure 8-1 shows the nature of the containers and the collection of the elements within containers. The next section describes the elements and their configuration parameters.

Configuration Directories

With the configuration options available to Tomcat, there is also the option to run multiple instances of Tomcat, all based on a single installation. This provides the advantage that there is only one version of Tomcat installed on the machine, and yet, many different configurations can be supported.

To create this configuration, first create a directory structure containing the following directories:

- `conf`
- `logs`
- `temp`
- `webapps`
- `work`

Now, with `CATALINA_HOME` pointing to the Tomcat installation root directory, set `CATALINA_BASE` to the root of this directory structure.

For example, the installation instructions in Chapter 2 have Tomcat installed in the directory `c:\tomcat`. The value of `CATALINA_HOME` is set to `c:\tomcat`. The separate instance of Tomcat is to be installed at `c:\myinstance`, and this is the value for `CATALINA_BASE`.

Note If `CATALINA_BASE` is not set then it will default to the value of `CATALINA_HOME`.

Obviously there is more configuration that should be performed, such as editing `conf/server.xml` and installing Web applications into `webapps`, but to start Tomcat for the new instance set `CATALINA_HOME` to `c:\tomcat` and `CATALINA_BASE` to `c:\myinstance`. Further details about configuring multiple Tomcat instances are described later in the How To Configure Tomcat" section of this chapter.

Cross-Reference Setting the startup options and starting and stopping Tomcat is covered in more detail in Chapter 2.

Some of the configuration elements described in this chapter have attributes that are relative to specific directories. Normally the paths are relative to `CATALINA_HOME`, however the `Engine`, `Host`, and `Context` elements have attributes that are relative to `CATALINA_BASE` for enabling the configuration of separate Tomcat instances.

Configuration Elements

This section contains a detailed description of the elements for the configuration of Tomcat. The elements are grouped according to the first four of the five broad categories described in the previous section.

Many of the configuration elements have a class name as one of their attributes. The attribute is included as the Tomcat designers have had the foresight to recognize the need to extend the capabilities of Tomcat to suit the needs of the users.

To keep the implementations and extensions consistent, the Tomcat designers have provided Java interfaces to represent the element, and then provided a standard implementation as a concrete class.

For example, the standard context element implements the interface `org.apache.catalina.Context` and is defined in the `org.apache.catalina.core.StandardContext` class.

Caution The final result of the configuration of the Web applications and resources surrounding the Web applications depend on interactions between the configuration options in the server.xml file, and in many cases the individual Web application configuration in WEB-INF/web.xml. This results in a situation where it is very difficult to provide explicit guidance on the exact behavior of a configuration setting.

A good example of this is the debug attribute in a container (such as a Host) and the interaction with a Logger. The debug attribute determines the level of messages that are generated by the Host, but with no specified Logger no messages will be logged. Likewise, if a Logger is configured but the parent container does not have the debug attribute set to a non-zero value no messages will be logged.

There are many interactions like this in the configuration, and where they occur we have tried to highlight it in the appropriate sections.

Top Level Elements

The top level elements provide the highest level containers for the configuration for the Tomcat instance.

Note The use of the word container for the top level elements is a general term for describing the relationship of the Server and Service elements with other elements. Within the Tomcat class libraries and documentation there is a specific use for the word container that pertains specifically to the Context, Engine, and Host elements. In this section where the word has a special meaning it will be shown as Container, with an initial capital letter.

Server

The Server element is the root element for the configuration and must exist as the outermost container. There is little need to change any of the attributes in the Server element, except when multiple instances of the Tomcat server are configured on the same device.

All implementations of the Server element have the following attributes:

- className (optional, default is the standard implementation)
- port (required)
- shutdown (required)

The standard implementation of the Server element also includes the optional attribute debug.

The className is the Java class implementing the server to be utilized. This class must implement the org.apache.catalina.Server Java interface. The standard implementation is the Java class org.apache.catalina.core.StandardServer and is suitable for most purposes.

The port is the TCP/IP port the server will listen on to await the shutdown command.

shutdown is a string that represents the command sent to the server to shut down this instance of Tomcat. To shut down Tomcat, the shutdown string must be sent from the local machine (the same machine Tomcat is running on) to the port number specified in the port attribute.

The debug attribute is the debug level that will be logged by the server element to a Logger.

> **Note** The standard server element does not have any logging code implemented, so no logging will be performed, nor is the specified file created. However, this attribute is presumably provided to allow for future enhancements.

The Server element contains the following components:

✦ Service (required, more than one may be defined)

✦ GlobalNamingResources (optional)

An example of a server element is follows:

```
<Server port="8005" shutdown="SHUTDOWN" debug="0" >
    <Service name="Tomcat" debug="0" >
    . . . . .
    </Service>
</Server>
```

Service

The Service element is used as a container to group Connectors and an Engine together to process requests.

All implementations of the Service element have the following attributes:

✦ className (optional, default is the standard implementation)

✦ name (required)

The standard implementation of the Service element also includes the optional attribute debug.

The className is the Java class implementing the service to be used. This class must implement the org.apache.catalina.Service Java interface. The standard implementation is the Java class org.apache.catalina.core.StandardService and is suitable for most purposes.

The name attribute is a string used for logging as part of the service, and is used by the Server element to uniquely identify the services it manages.

> **Note** The standard Service element does not have any logging code implemented, so no logging is performed, nor is the specified file created. However, this attribute is presumably provided to allow for future enhancements.

The Service element contains the following components:

✦ Connector (required, more than one may be defined)

✦ Engine (required, exactly one must be defined)

An example of the Service element follows:

```
<Server port="8005" shutdown="SHUTDOWN" debug="0" >
    <Service name="Standalone" debug="0" >
        <Connector
```

```
            className="org.apache.coyote.tomcat4.CoyoteConnector"
            port="8080"  />
        <Engine name="Standalone" defaultHost="localhost" debug="99">
        . . . .
        </Engine>
    </Service>
</Server>
```

Connectors

Connectors are the functionality within Tomcat to allow requests from other sources to be delivered to Tomcat and processed by the `Engine` that is configured in the same `Service`.

Tomcat has two types of connectors. The first type allows browsers to connect directly to Tomcat, and the second type allows a Web server (such as Apache) to connect to Tomcat.

There is one main connector for direct connection, which is the Coyote HTTP/1.1 connector. The use of connectors that are in past versions of Tomcat such as the HTTP/1.1 connector is now deprecated and should be avoided. Fortunately, the Coyote HTTP/1.1 connector supports all the HTTP protocols so there is no need to rely on older connectors.

There are two main connectors for Web server integration.

- Coyote JK2
- JK

JK is in the process of being deprecated and Coyote JK2, while quite new, has surpassed the capabilities of JK and has the advantage of being written to support many of the new features in Apache 2.0. Many people still use the JK connector and probably will continue to do so for quite a while, however because the differences between the two is relatively small, we shall focus on the newer of the two.

All implementations of a Connector support the following attributes:

- `className` (required)
- `enableLookups` (optional)
- `redirectPort` (optional)
- `scheme` (optional)
- `secure` (optional)

The `className` attribute is a class which implements `org.apache.catalina.Connector`, and in the case of the following connectors is required to be set to `org.apache.coyote.tomcat4.CoyoteConnector`.

If the `enableLookups` attribute is set to true then the `Connector` performs DNS lookups to return the host name of the client connecting to Tomcat. If `enableLookups` is set to false no lookup is performed and the IP address of the client is returned as a string. The default value is true; setting to false improves performance.

The `redirectPort` attribute is used if the `Connector` is not supporting SSL requests and the request is for a resource protected by a `<security-constraint>` requiring SSL transport. This configures Tomcat to redirect the request to the specified port.

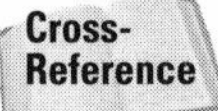

The detail of the <security-constraint> configuration option is described in Chapter 3.

The `scheme` attribute is the protocol handled by the `Connector` and the value to be returned by a call to `request.getScheme()`. The default value is http. To configure the scheme for SSL the value is https.

The `secure` attribute controls the value returned by a call to `request.isSecure()` that is handled by this `Connector`. The default value is false. To configure the secure attribute for SSL the value is true.

Coyote HTTP/1.1

The Coyote HTTP/1.1 connector is used to enable Tomcat to act as a standalone Web server capable of servicing requests of the following types:

- HTTP/1.0
- HTTP/1.1
- HTTPS

In addition to the attributes available to a general Connector the Coyote HTTP/1.1 connector also includes the following:

- `acceptCount` (optional)
- `address` (optional)
- `bufferSize` (optional)
- `connectionTimeout` (optional)
- `debug` (optional)
- `maxProcessors` (optional)
- `minProcessors` (optional)
- `port` (required)
- `proxyName` (optional)
- `proxyPort` (optional)
- `tcpNoDelay` (optional)

The `acceptCount` attribute is the length of the queue for unprocessed incoming requests. When this value is exceeded the Coyote HTTP/1.1 connector refuses incoming requests. The default value of this attribute is 10.

The `address` attribute is used when a server has more than one IP address and the value specifies the IP address to be used when listening on the specified port. The default value is to listen on all addresses.

The `bufferSize` attribute is used to configure the number of bytes in the buffer for the input streams used by the connector. The default value is 2048 bytes.

The `connectionTimeout` attribute is used to configure the number of milliseconds the Coyote HTTP/1.1 will wait between accepting an incoming connection and the URI being written to the connector. If this value is exceeded, the connection is closed. The default value is 60000 milliseconds, or 60 seconds.

The `debug` attribute is the level of detail of messages that will be generated by the connector. The higher the number, the greater the level of detail of messages generated. The default value for `debug` is 0.

The `maxProcessors` and `minProcessors` attributes control the number of request processing threads to be created by the connector. The value of the `maxProcessors` attribute sets the limit on the maximum number of simultaneous requests that can be handled, and the value of the `minProcessors` attribute is the number of threads that will be created when the connector is first started. The default values for `maxProcessors` and `minProcessors` is 20 and 5 respectively.

The `port` attribute is the TCP port number the connector will listen to for incoming requests. This port number must be unique and different for all applications running on the server, not only Tomcat, but any other process. This includes Web servers like Apache and IIS. The Coyote HTTP/1.1 connectors configured in the default `server.xml` has the port number attribute set to 8080 and 8443 for HTTP and HTTPS respectively.

Caution

Changing the port numbers from the default configuration to 80 and 443 is only possible if there are no other applications using those port numbers. On Unix systems this configuration is only possible if the user starting Tomcat has root privileges, because the port numbers below 1024 are reserved for system use only.

The `proxyName` and `proxyPort` attributes are used when Tomcat is operating behind a proxy server, such as Apache using `mod_proxy`. These settings enable calls to `request.getServerName()` and `request.getServerPort()` to return the values specified in the attributes rather than the server and port values from the proxy. This is important for Web applications that construct URLs using the preceding methods because the client browser must be redirected to the URLs based on the proxy, not on the Tomcat server, which may not be directly accessible.

The `tcpNoDelay` attribute controls the setting of `TCP_NO_DELAY` on the socket connections. The default value is true.

The Coyote HTTP/1.1 connector can contain an optional element, the `Factory` element. The `Factory` element is used to define additional parameters when this connector is configured to accept SSL connections.

Cross-Reference

Details about configuring Tomcat to support SSL connections are described later in the How To . . . section of this chapter. Additional software that is freely available from the `java.sun.com` Web site is required to be installed prior to the configuration and use of a connector supporting SSL.

The `Factory` element contains the following attributes:

✦ `algorithm` (optional)

✦ `className` (required)

✦ `clientAuth` (optional)

✦ `keystoreFile` (optional)

- ✦ `keystorePass` (optional)
- ✦ `keystoreType` (optional)
- ✦ `protocol` (optional)

The algorithm attribute defines the certificate encoding algorithm for the keys. The default value is SunX509.

The `className` attribute is the fully qualified class name of the SSL server socket factory and must be set to `org.apache.coyote.tomcat4.CoyoteServerSocketFactory`.

The `clientAuth` attribute determines if the SSL protocol will require a valid certificate chain from the client prior to accepting the connection. The default value is false and is only overridden by a resource that is protected by a `<security-constraint>` requiring `CLIENT-CERT` authentication.

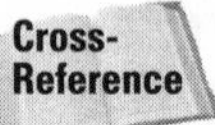

The details of the `<security-constraint>` configuration options are described in Chapter 3.

The `keystoreFile` and `keystoreType` attributes define the keystore that contains the server certificate. The `keystorePass` attribute is the password that was used to secure the keystore. The default value for `keystoreFile` is the file `.keystore` in the home directory of the user starting Tomcat. The default value for the `keystoreType` is JKS, and the default value for `keystorePass` is `changeit`.

The protocol attribute is the version of SSL to use. The default value of this attribute is TLS.

An example of the Coyote HTTP/1.1 element follows:

```
<Server port="8005" shutdown="SHUTDOWN">
    <Service name="Standalone" >
        <!-- Define a non-SSL HTTP/1.1 Connector on port 8080 -->
        <Connector
            className="org.apache.coyote.tomcat4.CoyoteConnector"
            port="8080"  />
        <!-- Define an SSL Connector on port 8443 -->
        <Connector
            className="org.apache.coyote.tomcat4.CoyoteConnector"
            port="8443" scheme="https" secure="true">
            <Factory
                className="org.apache.catalina.net.SSLServerSocketFactory"
                clientAuth="false" protocol="TLS"
                keystoreFile="c:/keystore/mykeystore"
                keystorePass="verysecret"
            />
        </Connector>

        <Engine name="Standalone" defaultHost="localhost" debug="99">
        . . . .
        </Engine>
    </Service>
</Server>
```

If the port number is changed for an SSL connector from 8443 then it is important to remember to change the `redirectPort` attribute in the non-SSL connector to match the new value.

Coyote/JK2

The Coyote/JK2 connector is an implementation of a connector that communicates between Tomcat and a Web server using the AJP protocol. AJP stands for the *Apache JServ Protocol*. The Web server connectors consist of two components, the Web server plug-in and the servlet container connector. The Web server plug-in is written in C and the servlet container connector is written in Java and they exist together as a pair.

Using the Coyote/JK2 connector with Apache requires the `mod_jk2` plug-in available from the Apache Web site.

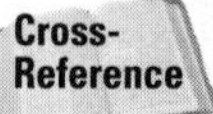

Details of downloading, installing, and configuring the Apache `mod_jk2` plug-in is covered in detail in the "How to . . ." section of this chapter.

`mod_jserv` was the first Apache plug-in to communicate with a servlet container, at that stage Apache JServ. This provided the name of the protocol which has been extended and is now specified including a version number, so AJP12 is version 1.2 of the protocol.

The Coyote/JK2 connector supports load balancing with appropriate configuration of the `Engine` element.

Cross-Reference

The details of how to configure Tomcat and Apache to perform load balancing are described in Chapter 15.

The Coyote JK2 includes the following attributes in addition to those in a general Connector:

- `acceptCount` (optional)
- `debug` (optional)
- `maxProcessors` (optional)
- `minProcessors` (optional)
- `port` (required)
- `protocolHandlerClassName` (required)

The attributes that are common to both the HTTP/1.1 and JK2 connectors have the same semantics. The only additional attribute is the `protocolHandlerClassName` attribute and that must be set to `org.apache.jk.server.JkCoyoteHandler` to use the JK 2 handler.

```
<Server port="8005" shutdown="SHUTDOWN" >
    <Service name="Standalone" >
        <!-- Define a Coyote/JK2 connector on 8009-->
        <Connector
            className="org.apache.coyote.tomcat4.CoyoteConnector"
            port="8009"
            enableLookups="false"
            protocolHandlerClassName="org.apache.jk.server.JkCoyoteHandler"/>
```

```
        <Engine name="Standalone" defaultHost="localhost" debug="99">
        . . . .
        </Engine>
    </Service>
</Server>
```

Containers

The containers section of the configuration file is the area that is most likely to be modified for a particular installation of Tomcat. The Host and Context containers provide the most significant customization opportunities, with the ability to add multiple hosts and the creation of Web applications all controlled by a specific container.

Engine

The Engine container represents the request-processing component of a Service. There may be only one Engine for any particular Service, and it must follow all of the configured connectors for that Service.

The Engine is responsible for handling the configuration of the load balancing scenarios for a Service, and the standard Engine implementation supports session affinity, ensuring requests for the same session are forwarded by the front-end load balancer to the appropriate Engine.

The Engine processes all the requests received by the connectors for a Service, and once the processing is complete the response is sent to the connector for communication with the client.

All implementations of the Engine element have the following attributes:

- className (optional, default is the standard implementation)
- defaultHost (required)
- jvmRoute (optional)
- name (required)

The standard implemention of the Engine element also includes the following attribute:

- debug (optional)

The className is the Java class implementing the engine to be utilized. This class must implement the org.apache.catalina.Engine Java interface. The standard implementation is the Java class org.apache.catalina.core.StandardEngine.

The defaultHost is a string identifying the Host element that will process requests from clients accessing host names on this server that are not explicitly configured. The defaultHost must match a name attribute of a Host element contained in the engine. It is common for Tomcat to only have a single Host element, so the defaultHost will be configured to match that element.

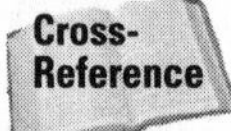

For detailed instructions on setting up Tomcat with virtual hosts, see the "How to . . ." section of this chapter.

The jvmRoute attribute is an identifier used in a load balancing environment. The value of the attribute must exactly match an identifier used in the load balancing configuration. The value of this attribute must be unique across all Tomcat servers used in the load balancing configuration.

Cross-Reference

For detailed instructions on setting up Tomcat with load balancing, see the "How to . . ." section of this chapter.

The name attribute is used to identify the Engine element. This attribute is used in logging and error messages.

The debug attribute is the debug level of messages that will be logged by the Engine element to the nested Logger.

Note

In this element, the debug level and logging actually work!

The Engine element contains the following components:

- ✦ DefaultContext (optional)
- ✦ Host (required, more than one may be defined)
- ✦ Listener (optional)
- ✦ Logger (optional)
- ✦ Realm (optional)
- ✦ Valve (optional, more than one may be defined)

An example of the Engine element follows:

```
<Server port="8005" shutdown="SHUTDOWN" >
    <Service name="Standalone" >
        <Connector
            className="org.apache.coyote.tomcat4.CoyoteConnector"
            port="8080"  />
        <Engine name="Standalone" defaultHost="localhost" debug="99">
            <Logger className="org.apache.catalina.logger.FileLogger"
                prefix="catalina_log." suffix=".txt" timestamp="true" />
            <Realm className="org.apache.catalina.realm.MemoryRealm" />
            <Host name="localhost" appBase="webapps" debug="0">
            . . . .
            </Host>
        </Engine>
    </Service>
</Server>
```

Host

The Host element represents an addressable network host name configured to an IP address for the server that Tomcat is executing. These are names like www.wiley.com and www.eaves.org. The most common host used in Tomcat, especially during development, is `localhost`, because this represents the IP address for the local machine and is represented in a local hosts file as the IP address 127.0.0.1.

Unlike the `Server` and `Service` elements, the `Host` element needs to be configured specifically for each Tomcat instance, and potentially is quite different for development and deployment. As can be seen from the list of attributes below, the `Host` element defines the operational aspects of the runtime for this implementation of Tomcat.

All implementations of the `Host` element have the following attributes:

- ✦ `appBase` (required)
- ✦ `autoDeploy` (optional)
- ✦ `className` (optional, default is the standard implementation)
- ✦ `name` (required)

The standard implementation also includes the following attributes:

- ✦ `debug` (optional)
- ✦ `deployXML` (optional)
- ✦ `errorReportValveClass` (optional)
- ✦ `liveDeploy` (optional)
- ✦ `unpackWARs` (optional)
- ✦ `workDir` (optional)

The `appBase` attribute is the root directory for the Web applications. It is either a directory relative to `CATALINA_BASE` or an absolute path to a directory. The `server.xml` that is included in the default configuration of Tomcat uses `webapps` as the value for the `appBase` attribute.

The `autoDeploy` attribute controls whether Web applications placed in the `appBase` are automatically deployed as part of this host. Automatic deployment considers directories, WAR files, and XML context fragments as Web applications to be deployed on host initialization. The default value for this attribute is true.

The `className` is the Java class implementing the `Host` to be utilized. This class must implement the `org.apache.catalina.Host` Java interface. The standard implementation is the Java class `org.apache.catalina.core.StandardHost`.

The `name` attribute represents the name of the virtual host. One of the `Host` elements configured for an `Engine` must have a name attribute matching the `defaultHost` attribute for the `Engine`.

The `debug` attribute is the debug level of messages that will be logged by the `Engine` element to the nested `Logger`.

The `deployXML` attribute controls the deployment of applications using XML Context fragments in the `webapps` directory. If the `deployXML` attribute is true, then Tomcat attempts to load XML files as `Context` fragments. If the attribute is false, then no loading occurs. The default value of the `deployXML` attribute is true.

The errorReportValveClass attribute controls the Java class used to generate the error pages by Tomcat. This class must implement the org.apache.catalina.Valve Java interface. If no errorReportValveClass is specified then the standard implementation org.apache.catalina.valves.ErrorReportValve is used.

The liveDeploy attribute controls the behavior of Tomcat when new Web applications are placed into the appBase directory while Tomcat is running. If liveDeploy is set to true, new applications are automatically deployed. The liveDeploy attribute defaults to true.

The unpackWARs attribute controls the behavior of Tomcat when WAR files are placed in the appBase directory. If unpackWARs is set to true, then WAR files are unpacked into a directory structure of the same name. For example, helloworld.war unpacks into the root of webapps as the directory helloworld. If unpackWARs is false, then the Web application is run directly from the WAR.

Caution A WAR file never expands if a directory of the same name exists. This prevents new WAR files of the same name deploying over an existing directory. To update the Web application the expanded directory structure must be deleted. Then, when there is no directory, the new WAR file expands to create a directory structure.

The workDir attribute represents a directory that is used by Tomcat as a temporary directory, often for compiled results of JSP files and other implementation-specific files. Each Web application has a temporary directory that is either configured specifically in the Context element or assigned a subdirectory under the workDir attribute from the Host element.

A temporary directory is required by the Servlet Specification to be made available to the servlet defined by the servlet context attribute javax.servlet.context.tempdir.

The Host element contains the following components:

- Alias (optional, more than one may be defined)
- Context (required, more than one may be defined)
- DefaultContext (optional)
- Listener (optional)
- Logger (optional)
- Realm (optional)
- Valve (optional, more than one may be defined)

An example of a Host element follows:

```
<Server port="8005" shutdown="SHUTDOWN" >
    <Service name="Standalone" >
        <Connector
            className="org.apache.coyote.tomcat4.CoyoteConnector"
            port="8080"  />
        <Engine name="Standalone" defaultHost="localhost" debug="99">
            <Host name="localhost" appBase="webapps" debug="0">
                <Context docBase="ROOT" path="" >
                . . . .
                </Context>
```

```
                <Context docBase="hello.war" path="/hello" >
                . . . .
                </Context>
            </Host>
        </Engine>
    </Service>
</Server>
```

Context

The Context elements represent the Web applications that are being serviced by the Tomcat instance. The Context element is the part of the server.xml file that is most likely to be modified as Web applications are added, removed, and modified. There may be any number of Context elements defined within a Host, however each Context must have a unique context path. The other requirement is that there must be a Context element mapped to the default Web application for the Host. This Context element is identified by a path attribute with an empty string.

Contexts are serviced by requests received on a connector that is associated with an Engine. The Engine then dispatches the requests to the appropriate Host, where a specific Context is chosen.

The Context is selected by identifying the longest possible prefix of the request URI against the context path of each defined Context. Once a Context is chosen, the servlet mappings in WEB-INF/web.xml determine the servlet or filter to process the request.

The Context element is used to define specific contexts and to define particular attributes of a context. If the Context attributes are required to be the same by the deployment then using a DefaultContext element can prevent the requirement to define a Context for each Web application.

All implementations of the Context element contain the following attributes:

- className (optional, default is the standard implementation)
- cookies (optional)
- crossContext (optional)
- docBase (required)
- override (optional)
- privileged (optional)
- path (required)
- reloadable (optional)
- wrapperClass (optional)

The standard implementation of the Context element also includes the following attributes:

- debug (optional)
- swallowOutput (optional)
- useNaming (optional)
- workDir (optional)

The `className` is the Java class implementing the `Context` to be utilized. This class must implement the `org.apache.catalina.Context` Java interface. The standard implementation is the Java class `org.apache.catalina.core.StandardContext`.

The cookies attribute controls how the session identifiers are communicated between the Web applications and the clients (normally a browser). If the cookies attribute is set to true, then cookies may be used for the session identifiers. If the cookies attribute is set to false, then cookies may not be used, and the Web application must rely on URL rewriting to maintain the session information.

Note

Setting the cookies attribute to true does not guarantee that cookies will be used in by a Web application for the session identifier communication. The browser may reject cookies and a fully interoperable Web application should also support URL rewriting under these circumstances.

The `crossContext` attribute may be set to true to allow a Web application to obtain a request dispatcher using `ServletContext.getContext(uri)`. This enables the Web application to gain access to various contexts within Tomcat. The default value for the `crossContext` attribute is false, which will force `ServletContext.getContext(uri)` to return null, rather than a `ServletContext`.

The `docBase` attribute contains the path of the Web application. This is either a fully qualified path name, or relative to the `appBase` of the `Host` element the `Context` element is defined within. The `docBase` may be the root directory containing a `WEB-INF` subdirectory, or a WAR file.

The `override` attribute controls how the `Context` attributes interact with the `DefaultContext` attributes for this `Host`. If the `override` attribute is set to true, then the explicit values of `Context` attributes will take precedence over values of the `DefaultContext`. The default value for the `override` attribute is false.

Caution

The use of the `DefaultContext` and the interaction with `Context` elements is not immediately obvious. The values in a defined `DefaultContext` will take priority over values in a `Context`, unless the `override` attribute is set in the `Context`. Creating a `DefaultContext` may have unintended consequences, because `Context` elements do not automatically override the `DefaultContext`.

The `privileged` attribute determines if the `Context` will allow servlets to have access to the container classloader rather than the standard class loader. Setting the `privileged` attribute to true enables the use of the container classloader and access to classes to which Web applications do not normally have access. The `privileged` attribute needs to be set to true for the contexts that define the manager and administration applications. The default value for the `privileged` attribute is false.

The `path` attribute defines the context path for the Web application. This value is used to match against the request URI to determine the Web application that is to process the request. If the value for the path attribute is the empty string `""` then that `Context` element defines the default Web application for that `Host`.

Note

The default Web application for Tomcat after installation is stored in the Web application directory named `ROOT`.

The default Web application is used as the Web application invoked when no context path is specified, such as `www.mywebsite.com/`. This is often known as the *root* of the Web server, hence the name chosen for the default Web application in the Tomcat installation.

There must be a default Web application defined for the `Host`, so there needs to be a `Context` with a `path` attribute matching the empty string as part of the configuration. If this is not provided, and `autoDeploy` is set to true, Tomcat will search for a Web application named `ROOT` (or `ROOT.war`) in the `webapps` and will provide a `Context` mapping that binds `ROOT` to the default Web application. If Tomcat cannot find the `ROOT` named Web application, then it will fail to start. However, if `autoDeploy` is set to false, then Tomcat will start, but return a status 500 error message when attempting to access the default Web application.

Tip

As this is all quite confusing, the simplest and safest option is to ensure that there is always a `Context` defined for the `Host` that has a path attribute of the empty string " ", and therefore always a default Web application.

The `reloadable` attribute determines if Tomcat monitors the Web application classes for changes. If the `reloadable` attribute is set to true, then Tomcat will monitor the `WEB-INF/lib and WEB-INF/classes` and if any changes are detected, will automatically reload the Web application. The default value of the `realoadable` attribute is false.

Note

Setting the `reloadable` attribute to true increases the load on Tomcat and therefore is generally not used in a production environment. However, in a development environment it is an invaluable configuration option to enable changes to be made to the Web application without needing to restart Tomcat to have the changes reflected.

The default configuration of Tomcat defines a Loader with a `checkInterval` of 15 seconds. This means that it takes up to 15 seconds for Tomcat to notice changes in the classes and libraries of the Web application. During development it is very worthwhile to set `checkInterval` to a much smaller value such as 1 or 2 seconds.

The `wrapperClass` attribute defines the Java class used to invoke the servlets defined in this `Context` element. The `wrapperClass` is responsible for the management of an individual servlet within a Web application and controls the startup, shutdown, and other lifecycle events of the servlet. This class must implement the `org.apache.catalina.Wrapper` interface. The default value is to use the standard implementation, `org.apache.catalina.core.StandardWrapper`.

The `debug` attribute is the debug level of messages that will be logged by the `Context` element to the nested `Logger`.

When the `swallowOutput` attribute is set to true, all output via `System.out` and `System.err` will be sent to the Web application logger. The default value for `swallowOutput` is false.

Note

During development the `swallowOutput` attribute should be set to true to enable debugging messages using `System.out.println()` and `System.err.println()` to appear in the nested `Logger`.

The `useNaming` attribute determines if Tomcat will create a JNDI `InitialContext` for the Web application. The default value for `useNaming` is true and indicates that an `InitialContext` will be created.

The `workDir` attribute represents a directory that is used by Tomcat as a temporary directory, often for compiled results of JSP files and other implementation specific files. Each Web application will have a temporary directory that is either configured specifically in the Context element, or assigned a subdirectory under the `workDir` attribute from the `Host` element.

A temporary directory is required by the Servlet Specification to be made available to the servlet defined by the servlet context attribute `javax.servlet.context.tempdir`.

The `Context` element contains the following elements:

- `Environment` (optional)
- `Listener` (optional)
- `Loader` (optional)
- `Logger` (optional)
- `Manager` (optional)
- `Parameter` (optional)
- `Realm` (optional)
- `Resource` (optional)
- `ResourceLink` (optional)
- `ResourceParams` (optional)
- `Resources` (optional)
- `Valve` (optional, more than one may be defined)

An example of a `Context` element follows:

```
<Server port="8005" shutdown="SHUTDOWN" >
    <Service name="Standalone" >
        <Connector
            className="org.apache.coyote.tomcat4.CoyoteConnector"
            port="8080"  />
        <Engine name="Standalone" defaultHost="localhost" debug="99">
            <Host name="localhost" appBase="webapps" debug="0">
                <Context docBase="ROOT" path="" reloadable="true"
                    debug="99" swallowOutput="true">
                    <Loader checkInterval="1" />
                    <Valve
                      className="org.apache.catalina.valves.AccessLogValve"
                      prefix="ROOT_access." suffix=".txt"
                      pattern="common" />
                    <Logger
                      className="org.apache.catalina.logger.FileLogger"
                      directory="logs"  prefix="ROOT_log." suffix=".txt"
                      timestamp="true"/>
                </Context>
            </Host>
```

```
        </Engine>
    </Service>
</Server>
```

Nested Elements

The nested elements are components that exist within the hierarchy of containers in the `server.xml` file. Some of the dested elements, such as the `Alias`, only exist within a single type of container, the `Host`, whereas other nested element, such as the `Logger` or `Listener`, may exist in many.

Some of the nested elements, such as the `Valve`, cover a wide range of capabilities, and the various configurations are only valid in particular containers. The attributes of the nested elements are described in this section as well as their use, and where they can be defined within the `server.xml`.

Default Context

The `DefaultContext` element defines some of the `Context` configuration attributes and is used to provide configuration for Web applications that are automatically deployed to a particular `Host`.

Note Automatic application deployment is controlled via the Host attributes `autoDeploy`, `deployXML`, and `liveDeploy`. Further details about automatic application deployment are covered in the configuration How To . . . section in this chapter.

The attributes defined in the `DefaultContext` element also act as the value for `Context` elements explicitly defined in the particular `Host`, provided that the `override` attribute has not been set to true.

Caution Attributes defined in the `DefaultContext` take priority over attributes defined in `Context` elements in the same `Host`. Setting the `override` attribute in a `Context` element to true enables the `Context` element attributes to be used, rather than the attribute values from the `DefaultContext`.

If an attribute is not defined in the `Context` and `override` is set to true, then the default value of that attribute is used and not the value specified in `DefaultContext`.

The `DefaultContext` only provides a subset of the `Context` element attributes. All implementations of the `DefaultContext` element contain the following attributes:

- `cookies` (optional)
- `crossContext` (optional)
- `reloadable` (optional)
- `wrapperClass` (optional)

The standard implementation of the `DefaultContext` element also contains the following attributes:

- `swallowOutput` (optional)
- `useNaming` (optional)

All the attributes have the same values and descriptions as the matching attributes in the Context element.

The DefaultContext element is contained in the Host element.

The DefaultContext element contains the following elements:

- ✦ Environment (optional)
- ✦ Listener (optional)
- ✦ Parameter (optional)
- ✦ Resource (optional)
- ✦ ResourceLink (optional)
- ✦ ResourceParams (optional)

Caution A parameter defined in the DefaultContext is accessible to any Context in the Host using ServletContext.getInitParameter(). However, if the override attribute is set to true, then the parameter in the DefaultContext is no longer available.

To access the parameter, it must be defined in the Context element.

An example of a DefaultContext element follows:

```
<Server port="8005" shutdown="SHUTDOWN" >
    <Service name="Standalone" >
        <Connector
            className="org.apache.coyote.tomcat4.CoyoteConnector"
            port="8080"  />
        <Engine name="Standalone" defaultHost="localhost" debug="99">
            <Host name="localhost" appBase="webapps" debug="0">
                <DefaultContext reloadable="true"
                    swallowOutput="true">
                    <Parameter name="isDefault" value="YES" />
                </DefaultContext>
            </Host>
        </Engine>
    </Service>
</Server>
```

GlobalNamingResources

The GlobalNamingResources element defines the global JNDI resources available to the server.

The GlobalNamingResources element has no attributes.

The GlobalNamingResources element is contained in the Server element.

The GlobalNamingResources element contains the following elements:

- ✦ Environment (optional)
- ✦ Resource (optional)
- ✦ ResourceParams (optional)

An example of a GlobalNamingResources element follows:

```
<Server port="8005" shutdown="SHUTDOWN" >
    <GlobalNamingResources>
        <Environment name="simpleValue"
            type="java.lang.Integer" value="30"/>
        <Resource name="UserDatabase"
            scope="Shareable"
            type="org.apache.catalina.UserDatabase"
            auth="Container"
            description="User database that can be updated and saved"/>
        <ResourceParams name="UserDatabase">
            <parameter>
                <name>factory</name>

<value>org.apache.catalina.users.MemoryUserDatabaseFactory</value>
            </parameter>
            <parameter>
                <name>pathname</name>
                <value>conf/tomcat-users.xml</value>
            </parameter>
        </ResourceParams>
    </GlobalNamingResources>

    <Service name="Standalone" >
    . . . .
    </Service>
</Server>
```

Loader

The Loader element defines the class loader for the Web application. The class loader is used to load the classes for the Web application, plus any static resources in the Web application.

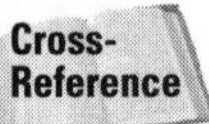

Details of the Tomcat standard class loading mechanisms can be found in Chapter 4.

All implementations of the Loader element have the following attributes:

- ✦ className (optional, default is the standard implementation)
- ✦ delegate (optional)
- ✦ reloadable (optional)

The standard implementation also provides the following attributes:

- ✦ checkInterval (optional)
- ✦ debug (optional)
- ✦ loaderClass (optional)
- ✦ workDir (optional)

The className is the Java class implementing the Loader to be utilized. This class must implement the org.apache.catalina.Loader Java interface. The standard implementation is the Java class org.apache.catalina.loader.WebappLoader.

The delegate attribute controls the mechanism of class loading by the class loader. If the delegate attribute is set to true, then the class loader follows the Java 2 model for class loading and queries the parent class loader before examining the Web application. If the delegate attribute is false, the class loader examines the Web application for resources prior to querying the parent class loader. The default for the delegate attribute is false.

The reloadable attribute is inherited from the parent Context element. Any value set in the Loader is ignored.

The checkInterval attribute defines the number of seconds the Loader waits before looking for modified classes and resources. The Loader only utilizes the checkInterval if the reloadable attribute is set to true. The default value of checkInterval is 15 seconds.

Tip A checkInterval of 15 seconds is quite long for development. Set checkInterval to a much lower value, such as 1 or 2 seconds for use during development.

The debug attribute is the same as the debug attribute in any of the previously defined elements.

The loaderClass attribute is the name of the Java class that extends the java.lang.ClassLoader abstract class. If the loaderClass attribute is not defined, the default value is org.apache.catalina.loader.WebappClassLoader.

The workDir attribute is the same as the workDir attribute in the Context element.

The Loader element is contained in the Context element.

The Loader element contains no elements.

An example of a Loader element follows:

```
<Server port="8005" shutdown="SHUTDOWN" >
    <Service name="Standalone" >
        <Connector
            className="org.apache.coyote.tomcat4.CoyoteConnector"
            port="8080"  />
        <Engine name="Standalone" defaultHost="localhost" debug="99">
            <Host name="localhost" appBase="webapps" debug="0">
                <Context docBase="ROOT" path="" reloadable="true" >
                    <Loader checkInterval="1" />
                </Context>
            </Host>
        </Engine>
    </Service>
</Server>
```

Logger

The Logger element is a multi-purpose element that can be contained in any of the containers. The Logger serves as the target for messages emitted from the containers according to the level of the debug attribute configured on the container.

The Logger elements exist in a hierarchy that matches the hierarchy of the containers. For example, the Host and Context elements inherit the Logger from the Engine if no Loggers are defined for the Host or Context. However, defining a Logger in a Host or Context element overrides the behavior of the parent container.

All implementations of the Logger element have the following attributes:

✦ className (required)

✦ verbosity (optional)

The className attribute defines the type of Logger that is to be used. All Logger elements must implement the org.apache.catalina.Logger interface. Tomcat provides three standard implementations for a Logger. These are:

✦ org.apache.catalina.logger.FileLogger,

✦ org.apache.catalina.logger.SystemErrLogger

✦ org.apache.catalina.logger.SystemOutLogger

The verbosity attribute determines the level of messages that the Logger will process. Tomcat elements emit messages of specific levels, and these will be compared against the verbosity value. Any messages emitted that have no specific level are always logged.

The FileLogger contains the following additional attributes:

✦ directory (optional)

✦ prefix (optional)

✦ suffix (optional)

✦ timestamp (optional)

The directory attribute is a relative or absolute path to a directory in which the log file will be created. If the directory is relative, it will be relative to the CATALINA_BASE environment variable. The default value for the directory attribute is logs.

The prefix attribute is the root file name of the log file. The default value for the prefix attribute is catalina.

The suffix attribute is the extension for the log file. The default value for the suffix attribute is .log.

The prefix and suffix attributes are combined with a date to create the log file name and the resulting file is <prefix>YYYY-MM-DD<suffix>.

The timestamp attribute controls how messages are logged into the log file. If the timestamp attribute is set to true, then each message is prefixed with a date and time stamp. If the value is false, no prefix is applied. The default value for the timestamp attribute is false.

The SystemErrLogger and SystemOutLogger duplicate all logged messages and send them to the respective standard error or standard output stream. There are no additional attributes for these Logger implementations.

The Logger element may be contained in the following:

✦ `Engine`

✦ `Host`

✦ `Context`

The `Logger` element contains no elements.

Tip If no `Logger` is defined all messages fall through to the standard output and error streams and appear in the console. This may, or may not be what is desired at any time. During development it is sometimes useful to only deal with a single source of information.

An example of the use of the `Logger` element follows:

```
<Server port="8005" shutdown="SHUTDOWN" >
    <Service name="Standalone" >
        <Connector
            className="org.apache.coyote.tomcat4.CoyoteConnector"
            port="8080"  />
        <Engine name="Standalone" defaultHost="localhost" debug="99">
            <Logger
              className="org.apache.catalina.logger.FileLogger"
              prefix="ENGINE_log." suffix=".txt"
              timestamp="true" />
            <Host name="localhost" appBase="webapps" debug="0">
                <Logger
                  className="org.apache.catalina.logger.FileLogger"
                  directory="logs"  prefix="HOST_log." suffix=".txt"
                  timestamp="true" />
                <Context docBase="ROOT" path="" reloadable="true" >
                    <Logger
                      className="org.apache.catalina.logger.FileLogger"
                      directory="logs"  prefix="ROOT_log." suffix=".txt"
                      timestamp="true" />
                </Context>
            </Host>
        </Engine>
    </Service>
</Server>
```

Manager

The `Manager` element defines the session manager used by the Web application for the creation and maintenance of HTTP sessions.

All implementations of the `Manager` element contain the following attributes:

✦ `className` (optional, default is the standard implementation)

✦ `distributable` (optional)

The `className` attribute defines the type of `Manager` that is to be used. All `Logger` elements must implement the `org.apache.catalina.Manager` interface.

The `distributable` attribute provides the same functionality and constraints as the use of the `<distributable>` element in the Web application `web.xml`.

As with the `Logger`, Tomcat provides multiple implementations of the `Manager` element as part of the standard distribution. The two implementations are:

- `org.apache.catalina.session.StandardManager`
- `org.apache.catalina.session.PersistentManager`.

The standard implementation that is utilized if no `className` attribute is explicitly specified is the `StandardManager`.

The `StandardManager` provides the default session management mechanisms for Tomcat, which include the capabilities of persisting session information over graceful restarts of the Web application. Because this persistence is done via Java serialization, for the session to be successfully saved and restored, all session attributes must implement the `java.io.Serializable` interface.

The `StandardManager` contains the following attributes:

- `algorithm` (optional)
- `checkInterval` (optional)
- `debug` (optional)
- `entropy` (optional)
- `maxActiveSessions` (optional)
- `pathname` (optional)
- `randomClass` (optional)

The `PersistenceManager` provides a more robust session persistence that supports non-graceful failure modes and the swapping out of idle (but still active) sessions to a store. The `PersistenceManager` is currently highly experimental and likely to change. Therefore further information on the `PersistenceManager` is best sought from the Apache Tomcat configuration documentation in the version of Tomcat downloaded.

The `algorithm`, `entropy`, and `randomClass` attributes are used to define the mechanism by which session identifiers are created. The algorithm defines an implementation of a `java.security.MessageDigest`, of which MD5 is used by default.

The `checkInterval` attribute is used to determine how frequently the Manager checks for expired sessions. The default value for `checkInterval` is 60 seconds.

The `debug` attribute is the same as any of the `debug` attributes in the `server.xml` configuration file.

The `entropy` attribute is a string used as the initial seed for the random number generator used in calculating the session identifiers. The default value is calculated internally by the `Manager` if none is provided. It is recommended to use a long string for the value of an `Manager` used in sensitive environments.

The `maxActiveSessions` attribute defines the limit of active sessions created by the `Manager`. If the value is (-1) then there is no limit to the number of sessions created. The default value for this attribute is (-1).

The pathname attribute is an absolute or relative pathname of a file where the serialized session information is to be stored on shutdown of the Web application. If the pathname is relative, it is calculated as relative from the workDir directory for the Web application. The default value is SESSIONS.ser.

The randomClass attribute is a Java class that implements the java.util.Random interface. The default value for this attribute is an instance of java.security.SecureRandom.

The Manager element may be contained in the Context element.

The StandardManager implementation of the Manager element contains no elements.

Realm

The Realm element represents the user authentication model defined in the Servlet Specification. The Realm provides support for users with passwords and allocated to specific roles. The Realm element provides the capability for the container-managed security and as such abstracts the location or style of storage of the authentication information within the implementation of the Realm.

All implementations of the Realm element contain the following attributes:

- className (required)

The className attribute defines the type of Realm that is to be used. All Realm elements must implement the org.apache.catalina.Realm interface.

As with the Logger, Tomcat provides multiple implementations of the Manager element as part of the standard distribution. The four implementations are:

- org.apache.catalina.realm.MemoryRealm
- org.apache.catalina.realm.UserDatabaseRealm
- org.apache.catalina.realm.JDBCRealm
- org.apache.catalina.realm.JNDIRealm

The MemoryRealm is the simplest Realm implemented in the default installation of Tomcat. The MemoryRealm provides the capabilities for loading an XML file into memory with no capabilities for modification.

The only attribute contained in the MemoryRealm element is the pathname. This is an absolute or relative path to a file containing XML configuration of the users and roles. If the path is relative, it is relative to CATALINA_BASE. If the pathname is not specified then the default value is conf/tomcat-users.xml.

An example of the file follows:

```
<?xml version='1.0' encoding='utf-8'?>
<tomcat-users>
    <role rolename="admin"/>
    <role rolename="manager"/>
    <user username="admin" password="admin" roles="admin,manager"/>
    <user username="ant-install" password="ant-install"
        fullName="Tomcat Bible Ant Installer" roles="manager"/>
</tomcat-users>
```

The `JDBCRealm` and `JNDIRealm` implementations provide mechanisms for integrating Tomcat with enterprise authentication systems.

The `JDBCRealm` defines a `Realm` that provides an interface with a relational database. Access to the `JDBCRealm` is via a JDBC driver.

The `JDBCRealm` contains the following attributes:

- `connectionName` (required)
- `connectionPassword` (required)
- `connectionURL` (required)
- `digest` (optional)
- `driverName` (required)
- `roleNameCol` (required)
- `userCredCol` (required)
- `userNameCol` (required)
- `userRoleTable` (required)
- `userTable` (required)

The `connectionName` and `connectionPassword` attributes are the username and password for a particular user that is needed to access the database.

The `connectionURL` attribute is the JDBC- and database-specific URL passed to the JDBC driver to define the connection to the database.

The `digest` attribute specifies the name of the `MessageDigest` algorithm that is used to hash the user passwords in the database. If the `digest` attribute is not provided, then the passwords are stored in plain text in the database.

The `driverName` attribute is the fully qualified Java class name of the JDBC driver used to access the database.

The `roleNameCol` attribute is the name of the column in the `userRoleTable` that matches a role name assigned to a user.

The `userCredCol` attribute is the name of the column in the `userTable` that contains the password of the user.

The `userNameCol` attribute is the name of the column in the `userTable` and the `userRoleTable` that contains the username of the user.

The `userRoleTable` attribute is the name of the database table in the database that contains columns matching the `userNameCol` and the `roleNameCol`. This table is used to map the user to roles.

The `userTable` attribute is the name of the database table in the database that contains columns matching the `userNameCol` and the `userCredCol`. This table is used to identify users with their passwords.

An example of using the `JDBCRealm` follows:

```
<Server port="8005" shutdown="SHUTDOWN" >
    <Service name="Standalone" >
        <Connector
            className="org.apache.coyote.tomcat4.CoyoteConnector"
            port="8080"  />
        <Engine name="Standalone" defaultHost="localhost" debug="99">
            <Host name="localhost" appBase="webapps" debug="0">
                <Context docBase="ROOT" path="" reloadable="true" >
                    <Realm className="org.apache.catalina.realm.JDBCRealm"
                        driverName="com.mysql.jdbc.Driver"
                        connectionURL="jdbc:mysql://localhost/users"
                        connectionName="connect_user"
                        connectionPassword="connect_pass"
                        userTable="auth_users"
                        userNameCol="username"
                        userCredCol="password"
                        userRoleTable="auth_roles"
                        roleNameCol="rolename"/>
                </Context>
            </Host>
        </Engine>
    </Service>
</Server>
```

The `JNDIRealm` defines a `Realm` that provides an interface with an LDAP directory. Access to the `JNDIRealm` is via a JNDI driver.

The `JNDIRealm` contains the following attributes:

- `connectionName` (optional)
- `connectionPassword` (optional)
- `connectionURL` (required)
- `contextFactory` (optional)
- `roleBase` (optional)
- `roleName` (optional)
- `roleSearch` (optional)
- `userBase` (optional)
- `userPassword` (optional)
- `userPattern` (optional)
- `userRoleName` (optional)
- `userSearch` (optional)
- `userSubtree` (optional)

The `connectionName` and `connectionPassword` attributes are the username and password for a particular user that may be needed to access the LDAP directory. A `connectionPassword` is required if a connectionName is provided. The connectionName attribute is not required if anonymous access is supported.

The connectionURL attribute is the URL passed to the JNDI driver to define the connection to the directory.

The contextFactory attribute defines the fully qualified Java class name of the factory used to provide the JNDI InitialContext. If the attribute is not defined, the default context factory used is the standard JNDI LDAP provider.

The roleBase attribute is the root directory for performing searches for roles. The default is the top-level of the directory and is used if the roleBase attribute is not defined.

The roleName and userRoleName attributes are used to select roles from the LDAP directory. The roleName is used with the roleSearch attribute to filter out the roles for the user. The userRoleName defines the name of an LDAP attribute in the user directory entry that can contain a list of roles for that user. If the roleName attribute is not defined, then no role searching is performed, and the roles is located using the userRoleName.

The roleSearch attribute is an LDAP filter to locate the roles for a user. The depth of the search is controlled by the roleSubtree attribute. If the roleSearch attribute is not defined then roles are located within the user directory entry using the userRoleName attribute.

The roleSubtree attribute determines if the roleSearch should descend the subtree of roleBase when searching for role entries. The default value is false, which means only the top level will be searched..

The userBase attribute is the root directory for performing searches for roles. The default is the top-level of the directory and is used if the userBase attribute is not defined.

The userPassword attribute is used when connecting to the LDAP directory to perform authentication. If the userPassword is defined, the LDAP driver connects to the LDAP directory with the connectionName and connectionPassword and retrieve the corresponding value for comparison.

The userPattern attribute is a LDAP filter for identifying the distinguished name of the user directory entry. This attribute can be used as an alternative to the userSearch, userBase, and userSubtree attributes when the distinguished name of a user contains the username.

The userSearch, userBase, and userSubtree attributes are the same as the role equivalents but used for identifying the user, and not the role.

An example of using the JNDIRealm follows:

```
<Server port="8005" shutdown="SHUTDOWN" >
    <Service name="Standalone" >
        <Connector
            className="org.apache.coyote.tomcat4.CoyoteConnector"
            port="8080"  />
        <Engine name="Standalone" defaultHost="localhost" debug="99">
            <Host name="localhost" appBase="webapps" debug="0">
                <Context docBase="ROOT" path="" reloadable="true" >
                    <Realm className="org.apache.catalina.realm.JNDIRealm"
                        connectionURL="ldap://localhost:389"
                        userPattern="uid={0},ou=people,dc=mycompany,dc=com"
```

```
                    roleBase="ou=groups,dc=mycompany,dc=com"
                    roleName="cn"
                    roleSearch="(uniqueMember={0})" />
            </Context>
        </Host>
    </Engine>
  </Service>
</Server>
```

The Realm element may be contained in the following elements:

- Engine
- Host
- Context

Like the Logger, the Realm elements are hierarchical, and a Realm is inherited at a lower level container unless explicitly overridden.

The Realm element contains no elements.

Resources

The Resources element describes the static resources of the Web application. These are the HTML pages, images, JSP pages, and other static files. The use of the Resources element allows the Web application to be deployed to a non-filesystem environment. This could be a database, a WAR file, or any other form of storage.

Of course, a Web application deployed to a non-filesystem environment cannot attempt to directly access the file system via an explicit path, but instead must use the methods such as ServletContext.getResourceAsStream() to access the static resources.

All implementations of the Resources element has the following attribute:

- className (optional, default is the standard implementation)

The standard implementation of the Resources element is the org.apache.naming.resources.FileDirContext and contains these additional attributes:

- cached (optional)
- caseSensitive (optional)
- docBase (optional)

The className is the Java class implementing the Resources to be utilized. This class must implement the javax.naming.directory.DirContext Java interface.

The cached attribute indicates if static resources loaded from the Web application may be cached. Setting cached to true indicates that Tomcat may cache static resources. The default value of the cached attribute is true.

The caseSensitive attribute is used in the Windows environment to control how Tomcat identifies and loads static resources. Setting caseSensitive to true indicates that static resources will be identified in a case sensitive manner. The default value of caseSensitive is true.

The `docBase` attribute is the same as the `docBase` attribute for a Context element.

The `Resources` element is contained in the `Context` element:

The `Resources` element contains no elements.

Valve

The `Valve` element represents an in-line processing function that operates as part of the container request pipeline. `Valves` can be used to perform many functions, and in many ways are quite similar to a `Filter` as described in the Servlet Specification.

The default installation of Tomcat provides the following `Valves`:

- `AccessLogValve`
- `RemoteAddressValve`
- `RemoteHostValve`
- `RequestDumperValve`
- `SingleSignOn` valve

AccessLogValve

The `AccessLogValve` is used to create log files in the same format as access log files created by Web servers. The log files created can then be processed by any of the standard Web log processing tools.

The `AccessLogValve` can be contained in the following elements:

- `Engine`
- `Host`
- `Context`

The configuration of the `AccessLogValve` is very similar to the configuration of a `Logger`. The configurable attributes are as follows:

- `className` (required)
- `directory` (optional)
- `pattern` (optional)
- `prefix` (optional)
- `resolveHosts` (optional)
- `suffix` (optional)

The `className` attribute specifies the Java class to be used for this valve. To use the `AccessLogValve` the `className` must be `org.apache.catalina.valves.AccessLogValve`.

The `directory`, `prefix`, and `suffix` attributes are identical to the `Logger` attributes of the same name.

The `pattern` attribute configures the format of the message logged to the access log. The valid options for the pattern attribute follow:

- %a, the remote IP address
- %A, the local IP address
- %b, the number of bytes sent (uses '-' if zero)
- %B, the number of bytes sent
- %h, the remote host name, or IP address if resolveHosts is false
- %H, the request protocol
- %l, the remote logical username from identd
- %m, the request method
- %p, the local port on which this request was received
- %q, the query string including a ? if it exists
- %r, the first line of the request
- %s, the HTTP status code of the response
- %S, the user session ID
- %t, the date and time in common log format
- %u, the authenticated remote user (uses - if none)
- %U, the requested URL path
- %v, the local server name

There are two predefined logical names for patterns. These are:

- common, defined as %h %l %u %t %r %s %b
- combined, defined as %h %l %u %t %r %s %b Referer User-Agent

The default value for the pattern attribute is common.

The resolveHosts attribute controls the format of the %h in the logging messages. If the resolveHosts attribute is set to true the hostname of the remote host requesting access is resolved via DNS lookups.

Caution

Performing DNS lookups on each request may adversely impact performance on a heavily loaded system. It is recommended that the resolveHosts attribute is set to false on a production system.

An example of using the AccessLogValve follows:

```
<Server port="8005" shutdown="SHUTDOWN" >
    <Service name="Standalone" >
        <Connector
            className="org.apache.coyote.tomcat4.CoyoteConnector"
            port="8080"  />
        <Engine name="Standalone" defaultHost="localhost" debug="99">
            <Host name="localhost" appBase="webapps" debug="0">
```

```
                <Valve
                    className="org.apache.catalina.valves.AccessLogValve"
                    prefix="LOCALHOST_access." suffix=".log"
                    pattern="combined"/>
                <Context docBase="ROOT" path="" reloadable="true" />
            </Host>
        </Engine>
    </Service>
</Server>
```

RemoteAddressValve

The RemoteAddressValve implements a filter that can be used to allow or deny access to an Engine, Host, or Context based on a list of IP addresses.

The RemoteAddressValve can be contained in the following elements:

- Engine
- Host
- Context

The RemoteAddressValve contains the following attributes:

- allow (optional)
- className (required)
- deny (optional)

The allow and deny attributes are a comma-separated list of regular expression patterns that are used to filter the remote IP address. If the allow attribute is set, then the IP address must match for the request to be processed, otherwise all requests are accepted unless the IP address matches the deny attribute pattern.

If the deny attribute is set then any requests from IP addresses that match the patterns will not be processed. If the deny attribute is not set then the allow attribute controls the request filtering.

The className attribute specifies the Java class to be used for this valve. To use the RequestAddressValve the className must be org.apache.catalina.valves.RequestAddressValve.

RemoteHostValve

The RemoteHostValve is similar to the RemoteAddressValve, however the pattern and request matching is done using the remote host name rather than the remote host IP addresses.

An example of using the RemoteAddressValve and RemoteHostValve follows:

```
<Server port="8005" shutdown="SHUTDOWN" >
    <Service name="Standalone" >
        <Connector
            className="org.apache.coyote.tomcat4.CoyoteConnector"
            port="8080"  />
        <Engine name="Standalone" defaultHost="localhost" debug="99">
```

```
            <Host name="localhost" appBase="webapps" debug="0">
                <Valve
                    className="org.apache.catalina.valves.RemoteHostValve"
                    allow="*.thiscompany.com"
                    deny="*.badcompany.com" />
                <Valve
                    className="org.apache.catalina.valves.RemoteAddrValve"
                    deny="10.97.128.*" />
                <Context docBase="ROOT" path="" reloadable="true" />
            </Host>
        </Engine>
    </Service>
</Server>
```

RequestDumperValve

The `RequestDumperValve` is used primarily for debugging Web applications and generates messages to a `Logger`. The `RequestDumperValve` emits information for logging on both the request and response.

The `RequqstDumperValve` can be contained in the following:

- `Engine`
- `Host`
- `Context`

The only attribute that is configured for this valve is the `className`, and that must be set to `org.apache.catalina.valves.RequestDumperValve`.

The information emitted for logging by the `RequestDumperValve` is:

- `authType` (request, response)
- `characterEncoding` (request)
- `contentLength` (request, response)
- `contentType` (request, response)
- `contextPath` (request)
- `cookies` (request, response)
- `header` values (request, response)
- `isSecure` (request)
- `locale` (request)
- `method` (request, response)
- `parameter` values (request)
- `pathInfo` (request)
- `protocol` (request)
- `queryString` (request)

- remoteAddr (request)
- remoteHost (request)
- remoteUser (request, response)
- request URI (request)
- requestedSessionId (request)
- scheme (request)
- serverName (request)
- serverPort (request)
- servletPath (request)
- status (response)

An example of using the RequestDumperValve follows:

```
<Server port="8005" shutdown="SHUTDOWN" >
    <Service name="Standalone" >
        <Connector
            className="org.apache.coyote.tomcat4.CoyoteConnector"
            port="8080"  />
        <Engine name="Standalone" defaultHost="localhost" debug="99">
            <Valve
                className="org.apache.catalina.valves.RequestDumperValve"
                />
            <Logger
              className="org.apache.catalina.logger.FileLogger"
              prefix="ENGINE_log." suffix=".txt"
              timestamp="true" />
            <Host name="localhost" appBase="webapps" debug="0">
            . . . .
            </Host>
        </Engine>
    </Service>
</Server>
```

SingleSignOn

The SingleSignOn valve is a Tomcat provided mechanism for implementing a single sign on for a series of Web applications under a single host. This is an extremely useful Valve for those environments (such as an intranet) where multiple Web applications may service a variety of functions yet all have the same authentication requirements.

The SingleSignOn valve may only be contained in the Host element, and does not have configurable attributes.

When using the SingleSignOn valve, all Web applications must use the same authentication Realm. This requires that the Realm element be configured in the Engine or Host element and not in the Context element because all the Web applications require access to the same Realm.

A user is requested to authenticate when accessing a protected resource on any of the Web applications using the login method defined for the Web application being accessed.

After authentication, the roles assigned to the user are used for resource access management across all of the Web applications without further requests for authentication.

When the user authentication tokens are no longer valid (from closing the browser, letting a session timeout occur) all the user sessions in Web applications will be invalidated and any further attempts to access protected resources will require re-authentication.

An important consideration when using the `SingleSignOn` valve is that the implementation requires the use of HTTP cookies to maintain the session and user identity. This means that the `SingleSignOn` valve can only be used where the clients support cookies.

The `SingleSignOn` valve supports the following attributes:

- ✦ `className` (required)
- ✦ `debug` (optional)

The `className` attribute specifies the Java class to be used for thisvalve. To use the `SingleSignOn` valve the `className` must be `org.apache.catalina.authenticator.SingleSignOn`.

The `debug` attribute has the same meaning and default as all the other `debug` attributes.

An example of using the `SingleSignOn` valve follows:

```
<Server port="8005" shutdown="SHUTDOWN" >
    <Service name="Standalone" >
        <Connector
            className="org.apache.coyote.tomcat4.CoyoteConnector"
            port="8080"  />
        <Engine name="Standalone" defaultHost="localhost" debug="99">
            <Host name="localhost" appBase="webapps" debug="0">
              <Valve
                className="org.apache.catalina.authenticator.SingleSignOn"
              />
            . . . .
            </Host>
        </Engine>
    </Service>
</Server>
```

Special Elements

The special elements are configuration parameters that exist only in specific elements and generally only have a single use or meaning. Some of the special elements duplicate functionality provided in `web.xml`, allowing deployment changes to Web application configuration without modification of the Web application deployment descriptors.

Alias

The `Alias` element provides an alias for a `Host`. Where a system configuration has multiple network names for a single IP address and the Web applications all are shared across those network names, using the Alias element is a simpler configuration option than repeating the Host element for each network name.

The Alias element may only be contained in a Host element, and has no attributes. The Alias element has no contained elements.

An example of using the Alias valve follows:

```
<Server port="8005" shutdown="SHUTDOWN" >
    <Service name="Standalone" >
        <Connector
            className="org.apache.coyote.tomcat4.CoyoteConnector"
            port="8080"  />
        <Engine name="Standalone" defaultHost="sales.thecompany.com" >
            <Host name="sales.thecompany.com" appBase="webapps" debug="0">
                <Alias>technical.thecompany.com</Alias>
                <Alias>management.thecompany.com</Alias>
            . . . .
            </Host>
        </Engine>
    </Service>
</Server>
```

Environment

The Environment element is provided to the Web application deployer to specify values that can be retrieved in the Web application as environment entry resources. The Environment element provides the same visibility to the values as the <env-entry> element in the web.xml for the Web application.

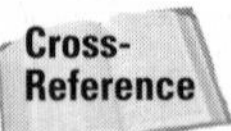

Details about the <env-entry> element can be found in Chapter 3.

The Environment element can be contained in the following:

- ✦ Context,
- ✦ DefaultContext
- ✦ GlobalNamingResources

The Environment element contains the following attributes:

- ✦ description (optional)
- ✦ name (required)
- ✦ override (optional)
- ✦ type (required)
- ✦ value (required)

The description attribute is informational text about the Environment element.

The name, type, and value attributes have the same meaning as the <env-entry-name>, <env-entry-type>, and <env-entry-value> attributes from web.xml. The one notable difference is that within the <env-entry> element the <env-entry-value> is optional, and if it is not provided it must be provided at deployment time. The Environment element is provided to allow for that configuration to occur.

The override attribute controls if an <env-entry> element in the web.xml will override the values provided here. The default value is true, and allows the Web application descriptor to override values in the Environment element.

An example of the use of the Environment element follows:

```
<Server port="8005" shutdown="SHUTDOWN" >
    <Service name="Standalone" >
        <Connector
            className="org.apache.coyote.tomcat4.CoyoteConnector"
            port="8080"  />
        <Engine name="Standalone" defaultHost="localhost" >
            <Host name="localhost" appBase="webapps" debug="0">
                <Context docBase="ROOT" path="" >
                    <Environment
                        name="adminMailAddress"
                        value="admin@thecompany.com"
                        type="java.lang.String"
                        override="false" />
                </Context>
            </Host>
        </Engine>
    </Service>
</Server>
```

Listener

The Listener element provides a mechanism for implementing custom classes that can be notified when changes to the state of containers occur. The Listener element defined in the Tomcat environment is similar in concept to the <listener> elements in Web applications defined by the Servlet Specification.

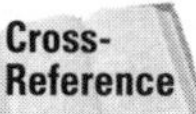

Details about the <listener> element in the Servlet Specification can be found in Chapter 3.

A Listener element can be contained in the following:

- ✦ Context
- ✦ DefaultContext
- ✦ Engine
- ✦ Host

The Listener element must implement org.apache.catalina.LifeCycleListener and may have any attributes required by the custom Listener. Attribute names are mapped to properties in the Java class using standard JavaBean naming conventions.

An example of using a lifecycle Listener for a Host follows:

```
<Server port="8005" shutdown="SHUTDOWN" >
    <Service name="Standalone" >
        <Connector
            className="org.apache.coyote.tomcat4.CoyoteConnector"
            port="8080"  />
        <Engine name="Standalone" defaultHost="localhost" >
            <Host name="localhost" appBase="webapps" debug="0">
                <Listener
                    className="com.thecompany.util.HostListener"
                    debug="99" />
                <Context docBase="ROOT" path="" />
            </Host>
        </Engine>
    </Service>
</Server>
```

Parameter

The `Parameter` element is similar to the `Environment` element in that it provides a Web application deployer the capability to provide configuration to Web applications at deployment time without modifying the WAR. The `Parameter` element defines configuration for the Web application that can be accessed in the same manner as the `<context-param>` element in `web.xml`.

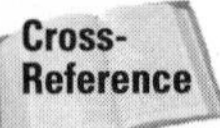

Details on the `<context-param>` element in the Servlet Specification can be found in Chapter 3.

The `Parameter` element can only be contained in the `Context` element.

The `Parameter` element has the following attributes:

✦ `description` (optional)

✦ `name` (required)

✦ `override` (optional)

✦ `value` (required)

The `description` and `override` attributes have the same meaning as the `Environment` attributes of the same name.

The `name` and `value` attributes have the same meaning as the `<param-name>` and `<param-value>` elements in the Web application `web.xml`.

An example of the use of the `Parameter` element follows:

```
<Server port="8005" shutdown="SHUTDOWN" >
    <Service name="Standalone" >
        <Connector
            className="org.apache.coyote.tomcat4.CoyoteConnector"
            port="8080"  />
        <Engine name="Standalone" defaultHost="localhost" >
            <Host name="localhost" appBase="webapps" debug="0">
                <Context docBase="ROOT" path="" >
```

```
                    <Parameter
                        name="winningTeam"
                        value="Kangaroos"
                        override="false" />
                </Context>
            </Host>
        </Engine>
    </Service>
</Server>
```

Resource

The `Resource` element is similar to the `Environment` and `Parameter` elements in that it provides a Web application deployer the capability to provide configuration to Web applications at deployment time without modifying the WAR. The `Resource` element defines configuration for the Web application that can be accessed in the same manner as the `<resource-ref>` element in `web.xml`.

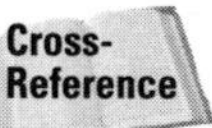

Details on the `<resource-ref>` element in the Servlet Specification can be found in Chapter 3.

The `Resource` element can be contained in the following:

- ✦ `Context`
- ✦ `DefaultContext`
- ✦ `GlobalNamingResources`

The `Resource` element contains the following attributes:

- ✦ `auth` (optional)
- ✦ `description` (optional)
- ✦ `name` (required)
- ✦ `scope` (optional)
- ✦ `type` (required)

The `description` attribute has the same meaning as the `Environment` and `Parameter` attribute of the same name.

The `name`, `type`, `auth`, and `scope` attributes have the same meaning as the `<res-ref-name>`, `<res-type>`, `<res-auth>`, and `<res-sharing-scope>` elements of the `<resource-ref>` element in the Web application configuration `web.xml`.

An example of the use of the `Resource` element follows:

```
<Server port="8005" shutdown="SHUTDOWN" >
    <Service name="Standalone" >
        <Connector
            className="org.apache.coyote.tomcat4.CoyoteConnector"
            port="8080"  />
        <Engine name="Standalone" defaultHost="localhost" >
```

```
            <Host name="localhost" appBase="webapps" debug="0">
                <Context docBase="ROOT" path="" >
                    <Resource
                        description="Corporate Asset Database"
                        name="jdbc/Assets"
                        type="javax.sql.DataSource"
                        auth="Container" />
                </Context>
            </Host>
        </Engine>
    </Service>
</Server>
```

ResourceLink

The ResourceLink element is used in a Context to create a link from a global JNDI resource to the local Context. This ResourceLink is very similar in concept to an alias. A Web application that then performs a JNDI lookup on the ResourceLink will obtain the global resource.

The ResourceLink element can be contained in the following:

✦ Context

The ResourceLink element contains the following attributes:

✦ global (required)

✦ name (required)

✦ type (required)

The global attribute is the name of the JNDI resource in the global JNDI context.

The name attribute is the local name, or alias of the JNDI reference. This is the name the Web application should use to lookup the global JNDI resource.

The type attribute is a fully qualified Java class name representing the class of the global JNDI resource.

An example of the use of the ResourceLink element follows:

```
<Server port="8005" shutdown="SHUTDOWN" >
    <Service name="Standalone" >
        <Connector
            className="org.apache.coyote.tomcat4.CoyoteConnector"
            port="8080"  />
        <Engine name="Standalone" defaultHost="localhost" >
            <Host name="localhost" appBase="webapps" debug="0">
                <Context docBase="ROOT" path="" >
                    <ResourceLink
                        name="jdbc/PoolDB"
                        global="jdbc/PoolDB"
                        type="javax.sql.DataSource" />
```

```
                </Context>
            </Host>
        </Engine>
    </Service>
</Server>
```

ResourceParams

The ResourceParams element is used to configure the resources defined by a Resource element. A ResourceParams element must be configured for every resource name in both the server.xml and also the <resource-ref> and <resource-env-ref> elements in web.xml.

The ResourceParams element can be contained in the following:

- Context
- DefaultContext
- GlobalNamingResources

The ResourceParams element only contains a single attribute, name. The name attribute is required, and must match a corresponding resource defined as a Resource, <resource-ref>, or <resource-env-ref>.

An example of the use of the ResourceParams element follows:

```
<Server port="8005" shutdown="SHUTDOWN" >
    <GlobalNamingResources>
        <Resource
            name="jdbc/PoolDB"
            type="javax.sql.DataSource"
            auth="Container"
            />
        <ResourceParams name="jdbc/PoolDB">
            <parameter>
              <name>factory</name>
              <value>org.apache.commons.dbcp.BasicDataSourceFactory</value>
            </parameter>

            <!-- MySQL dB username and password for dB connections  -->
            <parameter>
              <name>username</name>
              <value>dbpool</value>
            </parameter>
            <parameter>
              <name>password</name>
              <value>dbpool</value>
            </parameter>

            <!-- Class name for JDBC driver -->
            <parameter>
              <name>driverClassName</name>
              <value>com.mysql.jdbc.Driver</value>
            </parameter>
```

```
            <!-- The JDBC connection url for MySQL dB. -->
            <parameter>
              <name>url</name>
              <value>jdbc:mysql://localhost:3306/pooltest</value>
            </parameter>
        </ResourceParams>
    </GlobalNamingResources>
    <Service name="Standalone" >
        <Connector
            className="org.apache.coyote.tomcat4.CoyoteConnector"
            port="8080"  />
        <Engine name="Standalone" defaultHost="localhost" >
            <Host name="localhost" appBase="webapps" debug="0">
                <Context docBase="ROOT" path="" >
                    <ResourceLink
                        name="jdbc/PoolDB"
                        global="jdbc/PoolDB"
                        type="javax.sql.DataSource" />
                </Context>
            </Host>
        </Engine>
    </Service>
</Server>
```

How to Configure Tomcat

This section focuses on using the configuration in scenarios that are likely to occur in day-to-day operation of Tomcat. Some of these relate to development, some to deployment, and some are useful for both.

The examples provided in this section are more comprehensive than the fragments provided previously, and also show more uses of the configuration options to aid in further understanding.

Debugging a Web Application

One of the first tasks that is likely to occur during Web application development is the tracking down and fixing of things that are not working as expected.

First of all, the `logs` directory is where most of the error and access logs will be produced. If in doubt, the configuration of the `Logger` elements in `server.xml` determines the directory for the logs, however this is the default for the standard Tomcat installation.

Tip Sometimes Tomcat fails to start and the console window immediately closes. To find the error messages start a console window manually and execute the command `catalina run`. This displays the errors in the current window.

Tomcat provides a number of ways of configuring the logging and increasing the messages that can be provided for debugging.

The first option is to use the ServletContext log() method to produce messages from your Web application. These messages will be caught and handled by a Logger according to the configuration. The log() method is generally used for long-term logging of information and error messages rather than short-term debugging messages.

Sometimes this sort of debugging is a little more investigative and may require the introduction of the System.out.println() or System.err.println() methods to generate output. This is only half of the solution, as the Context element needs to have the swallowOutput attribute set to true to direct the output generated by the methods to a Logger.

An alternative to this configuration is to use the standard output logger and standard error logger for directing the messages to the appropriate stream. The default Tomcat installation startup scripts redirect standard out and standard error to the logs/catalina.out file.

Tomcat also provides a valve useful for debugging, the RequestDumperValve. This generates a lot of debugging information about the HTTP Request from the client and the HTTP Response generated by Tomcat. Again, the messages produced by the RequestDumperValve need to be collected by a Logger so they will not be lost.

An example server.xml with debugging turned on is shown here. It has the logging directed to multiple files depending on the source of the messages.

```
<Server port="8005" shutdown="SHUTDOWN" >
    <Service name="Standalone" >
        <Connector
            className="org.apache.coyote.tomcat4.CoyoteConnector"
            port="8080"  />
        <Engine name="Standalone" defaultHost="localhost" debug="99">
            <Valve
                className="org.apache.catalina.valves.RequestDumperValve"
            />
            <Logger
              className="org.apache.catalina.logger.FileLogger"
              prefix="ENGINE_log." suffix=".txt" debug="99"
              timestamp="true" />
            <Host name="localhost" appBase="webapps" debug="99" >
                <Logger
                    className="org.apache.catalina.logger.FileLogger"
                    prefix="HOST_log." suffix=".txt" debug="99"
                    timestamp="true" />
                <Context
                    swallowOutput="true" debug="99"
                    docBase="myapp.war" path="/myapp" >
                    <Logger
                        className="org.apache.catalina.logger.FileLogger"
                        prefix="MYAPP_log." suffix=".txt" debug="99"
                        timestamp="true" />
                </Context>
                <Context docBase="ROOT" path="" />
            </Host>
        </Engine>
    </Service>
</Server
```

Automatic Application Deployment

The actual process of Automatic Application Deployment is covered in Chapter 7, however to enable the development process proceed smoothly it is worth investigating the options available.

Cross-Reference

Details of a Context XML configuration suitable for rapid development are covered in Chapter 7 and further in Chapter 10.

The first part of the configuration is to set up the `Host` element to allow Web applications to be deployed without having to modify the `server.xml` for each newly added Web application. The `autoDeploy` attribute controls automatic deployment. When it is set to true, which is the default when Tomcat starts any XML files in the `webapps` directory, any WAR files or directory structures that look like an unpacked WAR file is automatically deployed and has a `Context` with default configuration created without user intervention.

There is additional control over the automatic application deployment in the use of the `Host` attribute. `deployXML` prevents Tomcat from looking for XML files to deploy if set to false.

The preceding configuration only considers deployment when Tomcat is started. It is very often convenient to have Web applications deployed without having to restart the server or to use tools to deploy the Web application. Tomcat can be configured to monitor for new Web applications while running by setting the `liveDeploy` attribute to true.

Caution

WAR files do not automatically expand when there is an existing Web application directory structure of the same name in the `webapps` directory. Using WAR files as a hot-deploy mechanism can be best served by setting the `unpackWARs` attribute in the `Host` element to false. This assists in preventing potential confusion during development and testing when the changes in the newly created WAR file are not loaded by Tomcat.

The following example shows `server.xml` with automatic application deployment turned on. This example explicitly allows all types of automatic deployment and does not allow for WAR files to be automatically expanded.

```
<Server port="8005" shutdown="SHUTDOWN" >
    <Service name="Standalone" >
        <Connector
            className="org.apache.coyote.tomcat4.CoyoteConnector"
            port="8080"  />
        <Engine name="Standalone" defaultHost="localhost" >
            <Host name="localhost" appBase="webapps"
                autoDeploy="true"
                deployXML="true"
                liveDeploy="true"
                unpackWARs="false">
                <Context docBase="ROOT" path="" />
            </Host>
        </Engine>
    </Service>
</Server
```

Keeping Access Logs

Configuring Tomcat to generate Access Logs is a simple process because there is a valve specifically designed for exactly this purpose. This is the `AccessLogValve` and the configuration options are described earlier in the chapter.

The `AccessLogValve` can be configured to provide logs at the `Engine`, `Host`, and `Context` levels of granularity. Simply place the `Valve` configuration at that level and any access that occurs in child containers are logged to that file.

Access logs are sent to a file; however this is one major drawback with the implementation provided by Tomcat. The access logs are "rolled" every day, so in a week seven (7), and in a month thirty (30) log files created. Some Web traffic analysis software is not sophisticated enough to process log files created on a daily basis and expect a log file that is based on the month.

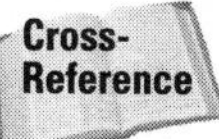

Chapter 18 contains an implementation of a valve, the `MonthlyAccessLogValve`, that modifies the functionality of the `AccessLogValve` to produce log files that are rolled monthly.

The following is an example `server.xml` with access logging enabled. This has the logging directed to multiple files depending on the source of the messages.

```
<Server port="8005" shutdown="SHUTDOWN" >
    <Service name="Standalone" >
        <Connector
            className="org.apache.coyote.tomcat4.CoyoteConnector"
            port="8080"  />
        <Engine name="Standalone" defaultHost="localhost" debug="99">
            <Valve
                className="org.apache.catalina.valves.AccessLogValve"
                prefix="ENGINE_access." suffix=".log"
                pattern="common" />
            <Logger
              className="org.apache.catalina.logger.FileLogger"
              prefix="ENGINE_log." suffix=".txt" debug="99"
              timestamp="true" />
            <Host name="localhost" appBase="webapps" debug="99" >
                <Valve
                    className="org.apache.catalina.valves.AccessLogValve"
                    prefix="LOCALHOST_access." suffix=".log"
                    pattern="%h %t %u %S %r" />
                <Context docBase="ROOT" path="" />
                <Context docBase="myapp.war" path=/myapp" >
                    <Valve
                      className="org.apache.catalina.valves.AccessLogValve"
                      prefix="MYAPP_log." suffix=".txt" debug="99"
                      pattern="combined" />
                </Context>
            </Host>
        </Engine>
    </Service>
</Server
```

Multiple Virtual Hosts

In an environment such as Web hosting, or an internal server that provides multiple services for staff having multiple network names resolving to the same IP address is often desirable. Tomcat supports this configuration by the use of multiple Host elements.

Because the Web applications for each of the virtual hosts are completely independent, it is a simple matter of configuring the Host element to have different appBase directories for each of the hosts. However, it is possible to have multiple hosts sharing the same Web application code bases, limiting the duplication of effort in deploying applications by having the same Web application base directory.

The following is an example of a server.xml configured for multiple virtual hosts. This configuration has three virtual hosts, with server-two and server-three sharing the Web applications.

```
<Server port="8005" shutdown="SHUTDOWN" >
    <Service name="Standalone" >
        <Connector
            className="org.apache.coyote.tomcat4.CoyoteConnector"
            port="8080"  />
        <Engine name="Standalone" defaultHost="www.server-one.org" >
            <Host name="www.server-one.org" appBase="webapps-one" >
                <Context docBase="ROOT" path="" />
                <Context docBase="hello.war" path="/hello" />
            </Host>
            <Host name="www.server-two.org" appBase="webapps-shared" >
                <Context docBase="ROOT" path="" />
                <Context docBase="admin.war" path="/admin" />
            </Host>
            <Host name="www.server-three.org" appBase="webapps-shared" >
                <Context docBase="ROOT" path="" />
                <Context docBase="admin.war" path="/admin" />
            </Host>
        </Engine>
    </Service>
</Server>
```

Configuring Multiple Tomcat Instances

In a development or test environment and even in some deployment environments (such as hosting) it may be useful to not only have multiple virtual hosts, but multiple instances of Tomcat.

Multiple instances of Tomcat are not the same as multiple installations of Tomcat. Having multiple instances uses the same CATALINA_HOME directory containing the core files for running Tomcat, but separate CATALINA_BASE directories for each instance. The advantages of multiple instances of Tomcat include the following.

- ✦ An administrator can start and stop an instance independently
- ✦ The configuration of each instance can be significantly different
- ✦ Provide support for clustering and load-balancing

Tomcat must be installed prior to creating multiple instances. The following instructions rely on a Tomcat installation similar to the installation described in Chapter 2.

Configuring multiple instances of Tomcat is a simple matter of performing the following tasks:

1. Create a new directory structure for the second instance. For this installation, the root directory will be at `c:\tomcat-two`.

   ```
   mkdir c:\tomcat-two
   ```

2. Create the subdirectories needed for the second instance.

   ```
   cd c:\tomcat-two

   mkdir conf
   mkdir logs
   mkdir webapps
   mkdir work
   mkdir temp
   ```

3. Copy the default configuration directory files `web.xml` and `catalina.policy`.

   ```
   copy c:\tomcat\conf\web.xml c:\tomcat-two\conf
   copy c:\tomcat\conf\catalina.policy c:\tomcat-two
   ```

4. Set the environment variable `CATALINA_BASE` to the second instance

   ```
   set CATALINA_BASE=c:\tomcat-two
   ```

5. Create a new `server.xml` for the second instance. This can be a completely new file or a copy of the initial installation that is modified for the new instance. In this example it is appropriate to create a minimal `server.xml` specifically to run just the default Web application.

The important change in the `server.xml` file is to the `Service` element that will receive the `shutdown` command and to the `Connector` element if multiple instances of Tomcat are to be operating simultaneously.

The default `server.xml` has the following values:

```
<Server port="8005" shutdown="SHUTDOWN" >
    <Service name="Standalone" >
        <Connector
            className="org.apache.coyote.tomcat4.CoyoteConnector"
            port="8080"  />
        . . . .
        <Engine name="Standalone" defaultHost="localhost" >
            . . . .
        </Engine>
    </Service>
</Server>
```

Change the server port attribute to 8006 and change the connector port attribute to 8081. Configure the single `Context` resulting in the following `server.xml`.

```
<Server port="8006" shutdown="SHUTDOWN" debug="0" >
    <Service name="Apache Tomcat Bible #2" debug="0" >
        <Connector
            className="org.apache.coyote.tomcat4.CoyoteConnector"
            port="8081" />
        <Engine name="Standalone" defaultHost="localhost" debug="0" >
            <Logger
                className="org.apache.catalina.logger.FileLogger"
                prefix="ENGINE_log." suffix=".txt"
                timestamp="true" />
            <Host name="localhost" appBase="webapps" >
                <Context docBase="ROOT" path="" />
            </Host>
        </Engine>
    </Service>
</Server>
```

Note This instance of Tomcat has none of the default Web applications such as the examples, the documentation, or the manager and administration applications. This version of the configuration is as simple as possible.

You need an installed Web application to test this installaction, so copy the ROOT Web application from the Tomcat installation directory.

```
mkdir c:\tomcat-two\webapps\ROOT
xcopy /S c:\tomcat\webapps\ROOT c:\tomcat-two\webapps\ROOT
```

Finally, startup Tomcat using the `startup` command:

```
startup
```

This displays the configuration of the environment in the current window as shown in Figure 8-2.

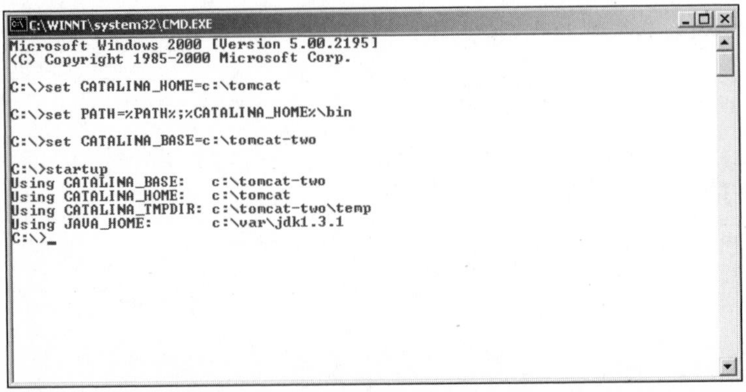

```
C:\WINNT\system32\CMD.EXE
Microsoft Windows 2000 [Version 5.00.2195]
(C) Copyright 1985-2000 Microsoft Corp.

C:\>set CATALINA_HOME=c:\tomcat

C:\>set PATH=%PATH%;%CATALINA_HOME%\bin

C:\>set CATALINA_BASE=c:\tomcat-two

C:\>startup
Using CATALINA_BASE:   c:\tomcat-two
Using CATALINA_HOME:   c:\tomcat
Using CATALINA_TMPDIR: c:\tomcat-two\temp
Using JAVA_HOME:       c:\var\jdk1.3.1
C:\>_
```

Figure 8-2: Starting the second instance of Tomcat

Notice how the CATALINA_BASE directory is configured to the new directory structure that has just been created. The `startup` command has also opened another window that should look like Figure 8-3.

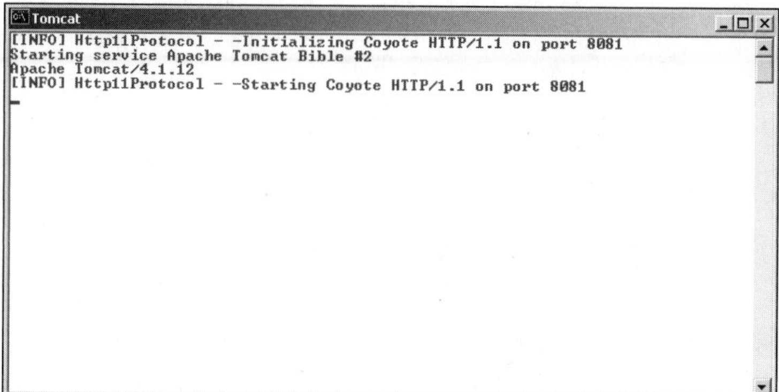

Figure 8-3: Console log of the second instance of Tomcat

Notice how the Coyote HTTP/1.1 Connector is listening on 8081 and not 8080. To see the results of the test, open the URL `http://localhost:8081/` in a Web browser. The results should look like Figure 8-4.

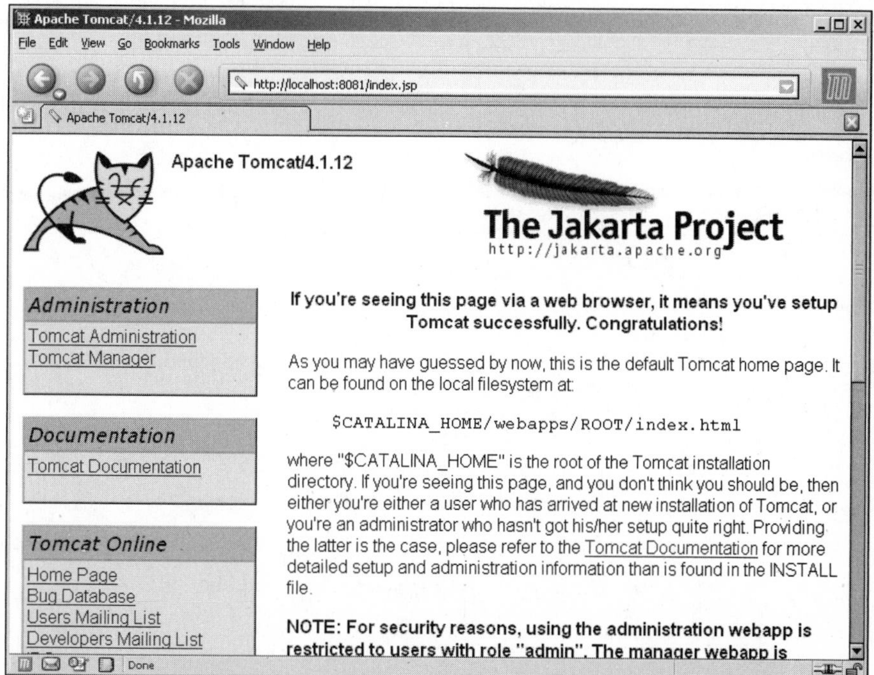

Figure 8-4: Opening the default Web application on the second Tomcat instance

To shutdown Tomcat use the same command window where the `startup` command was issued and enter the following command:

```
shutdown
```

The Tomcat console window should disappear as Tomcat shuts down. The setting of `CATALINA_BASE` can be performed in a batch file or configured in a shortcut so that the second instance can be started by double-clicking the shortcut.

Creating a Shortcut for the Second Instance

To configure the shortcut, create a copy of the shortcut created during installation in Chapter 2 and rename it `tomcat2`.

Right-click the `tomcat2` shortcut and select the Properties menu item. This displays a dialog box similar to that shown in Figure 8-5.

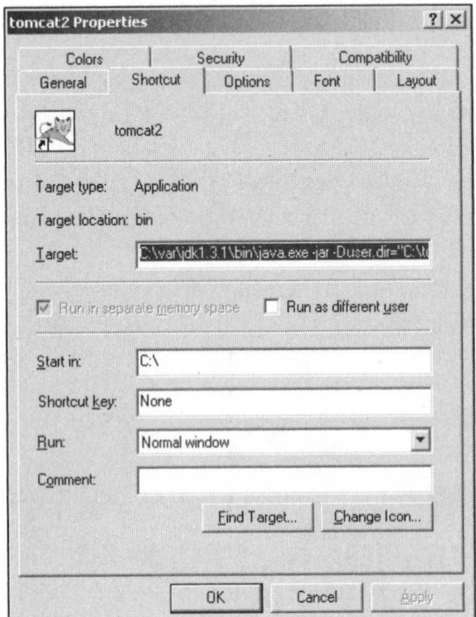

Figure 8-5: tomcat2 shortcut properties

The `Target` property contains the command that will be executed when the shortcut is run. The original value of the property is:

```
C:\var\jdk1.3.1\bin\java.exe -jar -Duser.dir="C:\tomcat"
"C:\tomcat\bin\bootstrap.jar" start
```

To add the new `CATALINA_BASE` into the shortcut, add in the following:

```
-Dcatalina.base="c:\tomcat-two"
```

Following the `-jar` option. The new `Target` property now should be:

```
C:\var\jdk1.3.1\bin\java.exe -jar -Duser.dir="C:\tomcat" -
Dcatalina.base="c:\tomcat-two" "C:\tomcat\bin\bootstrap.jar" start
```

Configuring Tomcat with SSL

An important consideration in developing Web applications is the security of the information passing from the client browser to the server. This information can be encrypted using the Secured Sockets Layer (SSL).

An additional benefit gained in using SSL is that the server (and optionally the client) is authenticated. This gives the user the confidence that the Web site they are accessing is owned and operated by the organization that it claims to be.

This section covers the installation of the additional software required to provide the classes required for SSL, and the configuration necessary to enable an SSL connector.

Download and Installation

The software required for SSL is the Java Secure Sockets Extension (JSSE). Any version above or including 1.0.2 is required for the Tomcat installation. The current version can be downloaded from `http://java.sun.com/products/jsse`.

Note JDK 1.4 has JSSE bundled with the distribution, so no further downloads or installation are necessary. Ignore the rest of this section and skip directly to the Creating Certificates step.

On the JSSE home page, select the link `JSSE 1.0.3_01` to proceed. The link will continue to the 1.0.3 version page. Scroll to the bottom of the page where the software and documentation can be downloaded.

Choose the version suitable for your location (either the US/Canada or global version).

Note Unfortunately this software is downloaded from the Sun Download Center which requires a login to access the resources. The good news is that registration is completely free and it's only a minor hassle. If you happen to be reading this before you start the download, then create a login first; it will be easier than trying to do it as part of the download.

If you are following the instructions and reading at the same time, you might have to restart the process after registering.

Read the license agreement displayed, and if you agree with the conditions, then select the radio button Yes and press the Continue button. You need to agree with the license conditions to download the software.

Select the link

```
Java(TM) Secure Socket Extension (JSSE) (jsse-1_0_3_01-gl.zip)
```

and save the file to the computer.

Extract the `jsse-1_3_3_01-gl.zip` to `c:\`. This creates a directory `jsse1.0.3_01`, and subdirectories. There are two ways to install the JSSE. The first is to copy the files from `c:\jsse1.0.3_01\lib`:

- ✦ `jcert.jar`
- ✦ `jnet.jar`
- ✦ `jsse.jar`

into the Java extensions directory (c:\jdk1.3.1\jre\lib\ext). This creates an installed extension to the Java installation and makes it available to all applications using Java on the computer. That might not be what is desired, so the alternative is to create an environment variable JSSE_HOME that points to the unpacked zip file.

To create the environment variable type the following command in a console window:

```
set JSSE_HOME=c:\jsse1.0.3_01
```

Creating Certificates

Using the SSL protocol requires the creation of public and private keys, and the keys and information about the server require signing by a trusted third-party to create a certificate. This certificate is then used to verify to the client browser that all is well on the server and that it can be trusted to be the server it claims to be.

Having a certificate does not mean that the business operating the site is trustworthy, or that there are any guarantees about the merchandise being sold or the privacy of any information that is stored on the server.

The use of the word trust in these circumstances is very narrow in definition and only means that a third party has performed some validation (in same cases this might be close to none) and that the information has not changed from when the third part signed the certificate.

Typically this process is performed by a third-party certificate authority (CA) such as Verisign or Thawte. However, that costs money and fortunately there is a free alternative provided in the Java distribution. Using the Java keytool, the same result can be achieved, which is suitable for testing this functionality.

The following command creates a new keystore in the Tomcat home directory (where the keys and certificates are held) and a self-signed certificate using a keypair based on the RSA algorithm.

```
c:\jdk1.3.1\bin\keytool -genkey -alias tomcat -keyalg RSA -keystore
c:\tomcat\keystore
```

This command pauses while setting up then prompts for the keystore password. To maintain consistency with the installation in Chapter 2, the passwords used in the example will be simple, but installations that require a greater degree of security should choose better passwords.

Enter the password: secret at the prompt.

During the certificate generation questions are asked to provide the information to be included in the certificate. This information is displayed to the client when a certificate is viewed, so choose appropriate values for your organization. These values are just text, so don't be overly concerned if you make a mistake, or if it is incorrect. For the purposes of this example the default values are satisfactory.

The keytool processes the information and then prompts for the password for the private key. This must be the same as the key store password provided previously; pressing the Enter key selects this as the default option.

Now check that the key store has been created by listing the directory c:\tomcat. The listing should look similar to that shown in Figure 8-6.

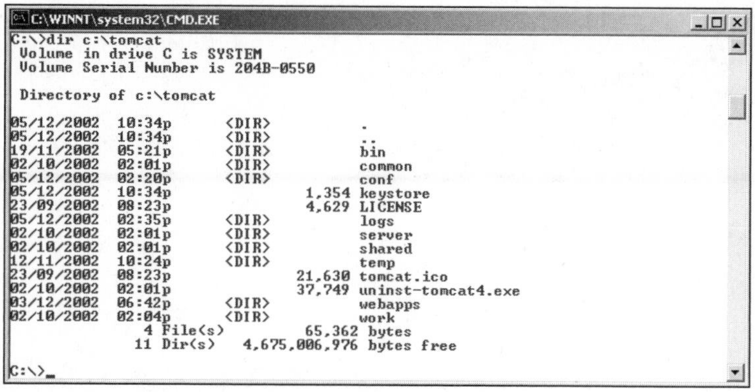

```
C:\WINNT\system32\CMD.EXE
C:\>dir c:\tomcat
 Volume in drive C is SYSTEM
 Volume Serial Number is 204B-0550

 Directory of c:\tomcat

05/12/2002  10:34p      <DIR>          .
05/12/2002  10:34p      <DIR>          ..
19/11/2002  05:21p      <DIR>          bin
02/10/2002  02:01p      <DIR>          common
05/12/2002  02:20p      <DIR>          conf
05/12/2002  10:34p               1,354 keystore
23/09/2002  08:23p               4,629 LICENSE
05/12/2002  02:35p      <DIR>          logs
02/10/2002  02:01p      <DIR>          server
02/10/2002  02:01p      <DIR>          shared
12/11/2002  10:24p      <DIR>          temp
23/09/2002  08:23p              21,630 tomcat.ico
02/10/2002  02:01p              37,749 uninst-tomcat4.exe
03/12/2002  06:42p      <DIR>          webapps
02/10/2002  02:04p      <DIR>          work
               4 File(s)         65,362 bytes
              11 Dir(s)   4,675,006,976 bytes free

C:\>_
```

Figure 8-6: Listing showing the created keystore

The next step is to enable the SSL Connector element in the `server.xml`.

Configuration

The default installation of Tomcat has an SSL Connector preconfigured in the `server.xml` file. It is enclosed in XML comments to prevent the configuration from being active, so to enable the connector remove the XML comments and configure the connector and enclosed factory to match the values as shown previously.

The only attributes that should need addition are shown below in bold.

```
<!-- Define a SSL Coyote HTTP/1.1 Connector on port 8443 -->
<Connector className="org.apache.coyote.tomcat4.CoyoteConnector"
           port="8443" minProcessors="5" maxProcessors="75"
           enableLookups="true"
           acceptCount="10" debug="0" scheme="https" secure="true"
           useURIValidationHack="false">
 <Factory className="org.apache.coyote.tomcat4.CoyoteServerSocketFactory"
          clientAuth="false" protocol="TLS"
          keystoreFile="c:\tomcat\keystore"
          keystorePass="secret"
          />
```

Finally, test the configuration changes.

Testing

With the configuration complete, it is a matter of starting up Tomcat and browsing to the URL `https://localhost:8443/`.

Starting Tomcat should produce output in the console similar to that shown in Figure 8-7.

The difference between this startup and previous configurations is that there is now a second connector listening for connections, this time on port 8443.

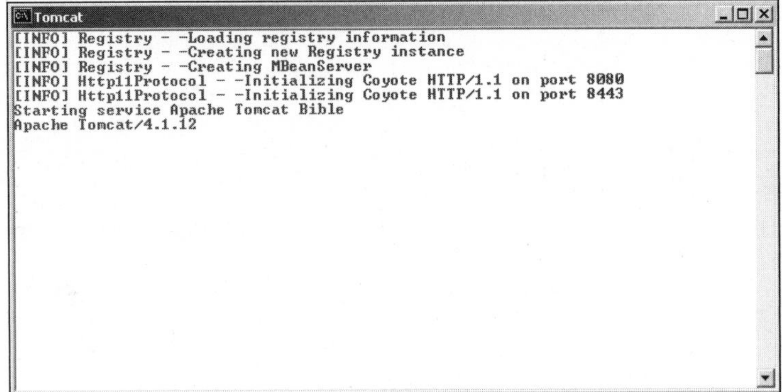

Figure 8-7: SSL Connector on port 8443

If Tomcat fails to start, displaying errors such as "Can't find any SSL implementation," that probably means the `JSSE_HOME` is not set correctly, or that the JAR files were not copied into the extension directory.

Opening the URL `http://localhost:8443/` should eventually display results similar to those shown in Figure 8-8.

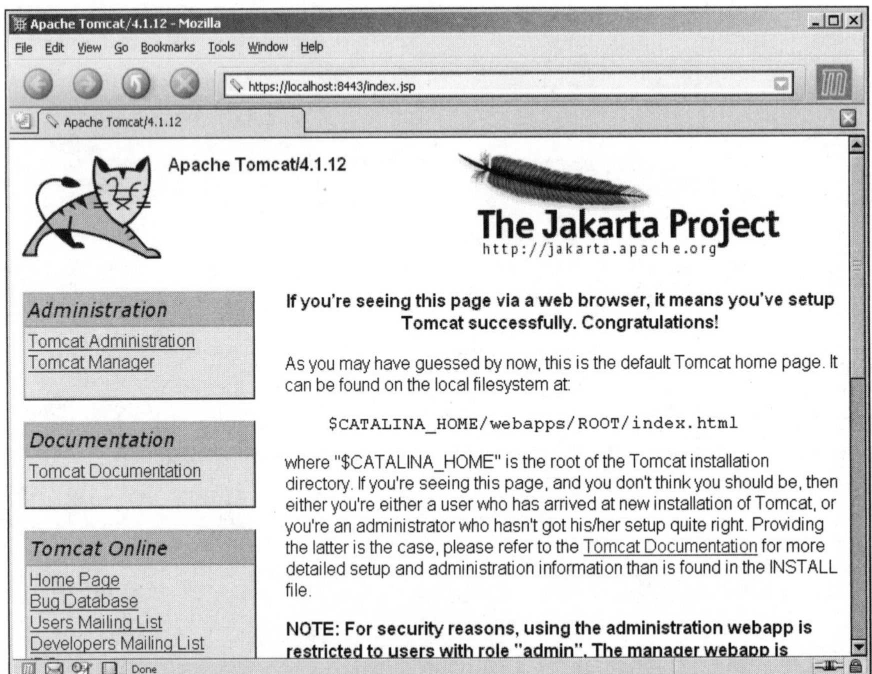

Figure 8-8: Default Web application viewed over SSL

It is highly likely that accessing the URL will cause a number of warning dialog boxes to be shown. This is expected because the certificate used for the SSL connector has been created in a way that the browser cannot determine that the certificate is valid. For this process to work seamlessly the certificate needs to be signed by a Certificate Authority (such as Verisign) known to the browser, or the browser must be configured to permanently recognize the authority of the certificate.

To continue and view the page, press OK when prompted to accept the certificate. This is suitable under these conditions, but if it happens when browsing unknown Web sites make sure to check the validity of the certificates prior to accepting them.

Examples of the dialog boxes for Mozilla and Internet Explorer are shown in Figures 8-9 and 8-10.

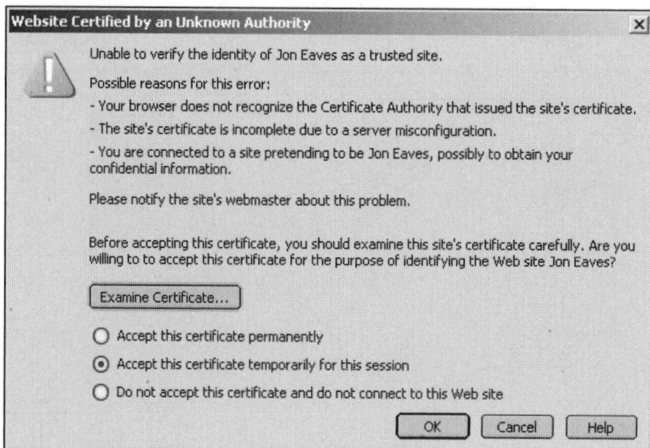

Figure 8-9: Mozilla warning dialog box

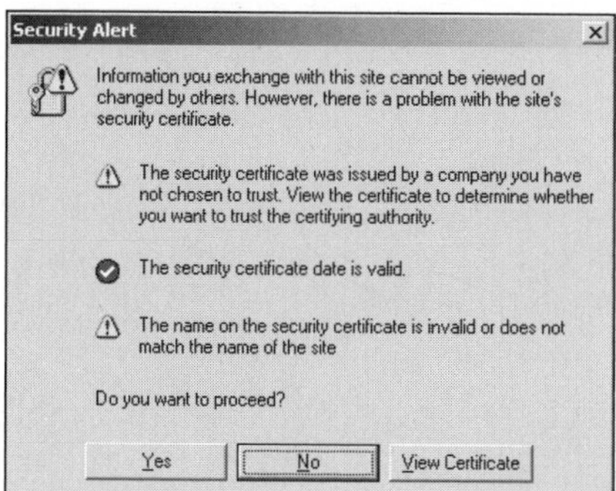

Figure 8-10: Internet Explorer warning dialog box

Summary

This chapter has covered the configuration of Tomcat by examining the structure of the `server.xml` configuration file. This examination was followed by a series of guides for the configuration of Tomcat to meet the most common scenarios.

If modifying a configuration file manually seems like hard work, the next chapter should provide considerable relief, because Chapter 9 covers the administration of Tomcat using the Administration application and operation of Tomcat using the Manager application.

✦ ✦ ✦

Using the Administration and Manager Applications

✦ ✦ ✦ ✦

In This Chapter

Using the Administration Tool

Understanding the Web Manager Application

✦ ✦ ✦ ✦

This chapter examines the use of the Tomcat Administration Tool and the Web Manager Application.

These Web-based applications provide a graphical interface to many of the configuration options for Tomcat and the run-time management of the Tomcat server.

The chapter starts with the pre-requisites for running the tools examining both the Tomcat configuration and the components required.

Next we shall examine the Tomcat Administration Tool and how to use the interface to access the configuration options.

Finally this chapter examines how to use the Web Application Manager to manage the Tomcat server during operation.

Introduction

The Tomcat Administration Tool has been developed to allow management of the Tomcat server from a remote location using a graphical interface. The Administration tool provides access to the configuration options in `server.xml` and the local user database stored in `tomcat-users.xml` for an entire server.

Note This Chapter focuses on the functionality provided by Tomcat in the default configuration. This is most relevant to the choice of Realm that the Administration Tool and Management Application will use for authentication. For convenience, all the examples refer to the `tomcat-users.xml` file as the repository of the user authentication information.

The Web Manager Application has been developed as a simple graphic interface utilizing the existing manager interface. The manager interface is the interface used by the Tomcat Ant tasks and can be used as a purely URL driven tool by sending a series of formatted

URLs to the Web application. The HTML interface provides a simpler interface for starting, stopping, reloading, and installing Web applications for a particular Host.

The Tomcat Ant tasks are described in detail in Chapter 5.

Prerequisites

The Tomcat Administration Tool and the Web Manager Application are both Web applications and need to be configured appropriately for correct operation of the tools.

The Tomcat Administration Tool needs to be configured for each instance of Tomcat that is running. The Administration Tool is capable of managing multiple hosts across an entire server from a single install.

The Web Manager Application must be installed on each Host that requires management.

Configuration

The `server.xml` must contain (at a minimum) the following elements shown in bold in Listing 9-1.

Listing 9-1: Administration Tool server.xml

```
<Server port="8005" shutdown="SHUTDOWN" debug="0" >
    <Listener
className="org.apache.catalina.mbeans.ServerLifecycleListener"
        />

    <Listener
className="org.apache.catalina.mbeans.GlobalResourcesLifecycleListener"
        />

    <GlobalNamingResources>
        <Resource
            name="UserDatabase"
            scope="Shareable"
            type="org.apache.catalina.UserDatabase"
            auth="Container"
            description="User database that can be updated and saved" />

        <ResourceParams name="UserDatabase">
            <parameter>
                <name>factory</name>
                <value>
```

```
                org.apache.catalina.users.MemoryUserDatabaseFactory
            </value>
        </parameter>
        <parameter>
            <name>pathname</name>
            <value>conf/tomcat-users.xml</value>
        </parameter>
    </ResourceParams>
</GlobalNamingResources>

<Service name="Apache Tomcat Bible" debug="0" >

    <Connector
        className="org.apache.coyote.tomcat4.CoyoteConnector"
        port="8080" />

    <Engine name="Standalone" defaultHost="localhost" >

        <Realm
            className="org.apache.catalina.realm.UserDatabaseRealm"
            resource="UserDatabase" validate="true" />

        <Host name="localhost" appBase="webapps" >
            <Context docBase="ROOT" path="" />
        </Host>
    </Engine>
</Service>
</Server>
```

The Manager Application works effectively with the `server.xml` shown in Listing 9-1, however the Manager Application only requires a Realm to be added to cover the Hosts that will be using the Manager Application.

Cross-Reference For more information on Realms and their use in securing a Tomcat installation see Chapter 12.

The next step is to ensure that the Administration Tool `admin.xml` and the Manager Application `manager.xml` is installed in the `webapps` directory of each Tomcat server instance.

Note The context.xml files for the Administration Tool and the Manager Application is the default configuration of Tomcat. In a production system these may be incorporated into the `server.xml` for the server instance if circumstances demand it.

The `admin.xml` contains the XML in Listing 9-2.

Listing 9-2: admin.xml

```
<Context path="/admin" docBase="../server/webapps/admin"
        debug="0" privileged="true">

    <Valve
        className="org.apache.catalina.valves.RemoteAddrValve"
        allow="127.0.0.1"/>

    <Logger
        className="org.apache.catalina.logger.FileLogger"
        prefix="localhost_admin_log." suffix=".txt"
        timestamp="true"/>
</Context>
```

The Valve and the Logger are disabled by default, and can be uncommented to provide restricted access to the Administration Tool, and to provide logging.

The `manager.xml` contains the XML in Listing 9-3.

Listing 9-3: manager.xml

```
<Context path="/manager" docBase="../server/webapps/manager"
        debug="0" privileged="true">
    <ResourceLink name="users" global="UserDatabase"
        type="org.apache.catalina.UserDatabase"/>
</Context>
```

The ResourceLink element is used to select the UserDatabase that contains the usernames, passwords, and roles.

If the Administration Tool is not required, then the elements highlighted in bold in Listing 9-1 can be removed, and the Realm replaced with the following Realm element.

```
<Realm className="org.apache.catalina.realm.MemoryRealm" />
```

The ResourceLink can be removed from the `manager.xml` under these circumstances.

Caution If the Administration Tool and the Manager Application are installed in other Tomcat instances other than the initial install, then the `docBase` attribute must be modified to reflect the full path to the Web applications, or the Web applications must be copied into each Tomcat instance.

Finally, the `tomcat-users.xml` file must contain usernames and roles for accessing the Web applications. To use the Administration Tool a user with the role `admin` must be configured and to use the Manager Application a user with the role `manager` must be configured.

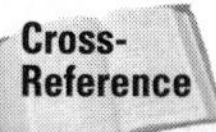

Details about configuring the users required to access the administration Web applications can be found in Chapter 2.

Tomcat Administration Tool

The Tomcat Administration tool is a Web application with a graphical interface that provides access to the Tomcat configuration files.

The configuration files that can be manipulated via the Administration tool are the `server.xml` and `tomcat-users.xml`.

The Administration tool can add, modify, and delete the `server.xml` elements. Details about the possible elements and the attributes associated with each element can be found in Chapter 8.

Using the Administration Tool

The first step in using the Administration tool is to open the URL in a browser. The default installation of Tomcat has this Web application configured at:

```
http://localhost:8080/admin
```

When the Tomcat Administration Tool modifies the `server.xml` file, it does not retain the original formatting of the file and it does not retain any commented out elements in the file. This generally means that the administrator will make a decision between manually managing the `server.xml` and using the Administration Tool.

The rewritten `server.xml` will write the attributes for each element to the file, creating a verbose and relatively confusing file. However all is not lost; the Administration Tool saves a copy of the original `server.xml` by appending a date stamp so any elements that are inadvertently lost can be easily recovered.

This should result in a screen like that shown in Figure 9-1.

To access the Administration tool enter the Administration user configured when Tomcat was installed.

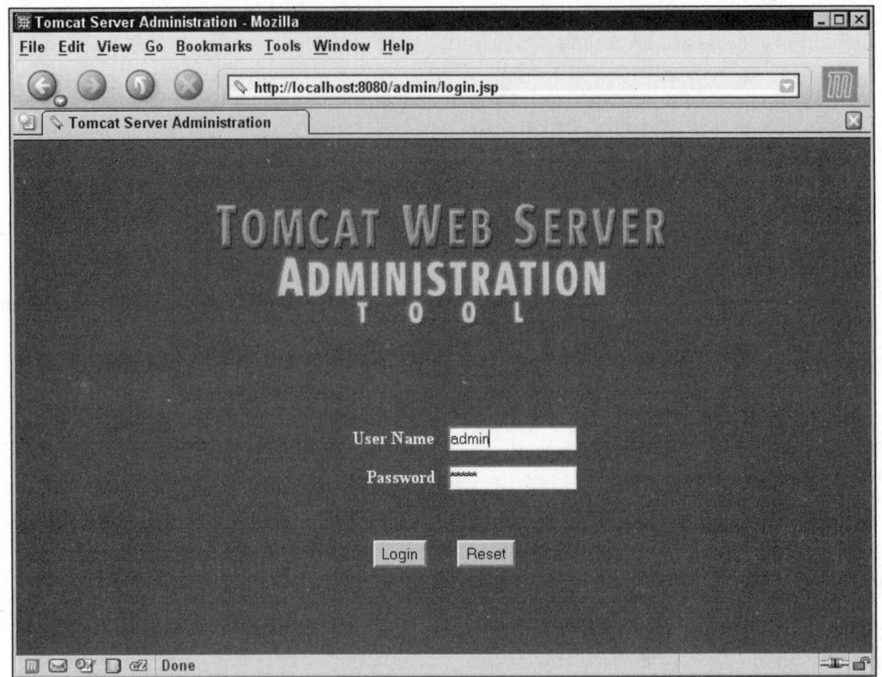

Figure 9-1: Login screen

The Administration user is a user that has the role of "admin" in the file `CATALINA_BASE/conf/tomcat-users.xml`. The authentication information configured for the Administration Tool in Chapter 2 is `admin` for both the username and the password.

If the username and password are correct for the Administration user then the main Administration screen is displayed, as shown in Figure 9-2.

If the username and password do not match a valid user from the `UserDatabaseRealm` then the Administration Tool displays an error: "Invalid username or password." However, if the username and password do match a valid user, but the user is not in the admin role, then the server responds with an "HTTP Error 403–Access to the requested resource is denied."

On the main screen of the Administration tool there are three frames. The first is the *static title* frame. This frame contains the name of the tool and the Commit Changes and Logout buttons. The Commit Changes button is used to write the changes made to the configuration to the `server.xml` file.

The configuration changes made using the Administration Tool are made to the in-memory configuration objects for Tomcat. These changes are not saved permanently unless the Commit Changes button is pressed. This then creates a time-stamped backup copy of `server.xml` and writes out the new configuration.

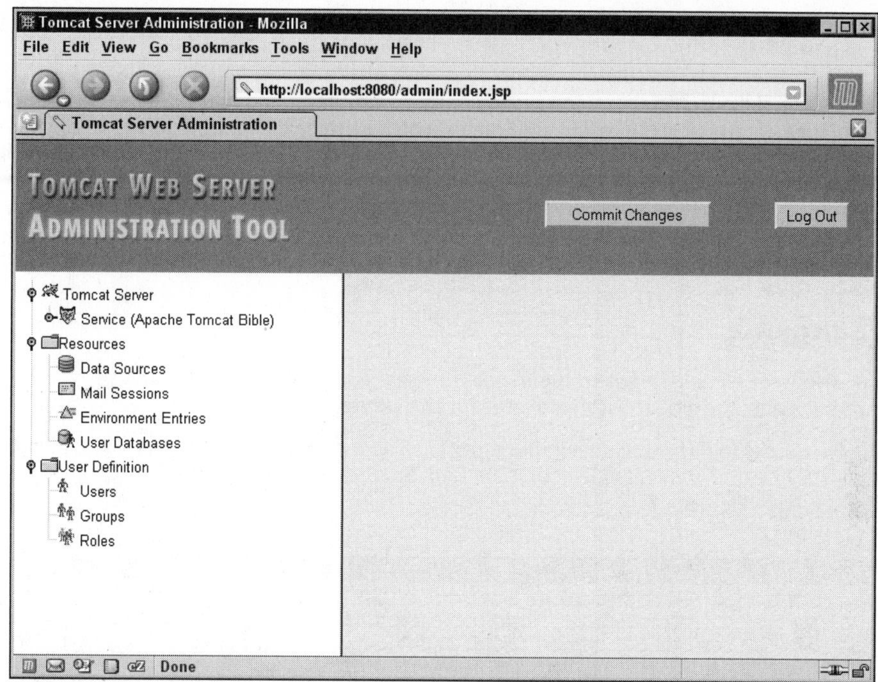

Figure 9-2: Main screen

The Logout button invalidates the current login and displays the Login screen shown in Figure 9-1.

The second is the left -side navigation frame. The navigation of the application is organized as a tree structure representing the configuration and containment structure of `server.xml`. The branches of the tree can be opened and closed, displaying the elements contained in the branch. Elements are selected by clicking the name of the element or the corresponding icon.

The navigation frame is divided into three logical groups. The top group is the navigation tree for the structure of the Tomcat Server. The middle group is the navigation tree for the Global Naming Resources element in the Tomcat Server. The bottom group is the navigation for the `tomcat-users.xml` file.

Note

The Resources and User Definition folders are not selectable, however the elements contained in these folders may be selected by clicking the name or icon.

The third and final group is the main content frame. This frame is blank when the main screen is initially loaded, as shown in Figure 9-2, but when navigation items are selected, or actions performed, the content frame is changed to show the requested information, as can be seen in Figure 9-17.

The content frame for elements has a drop-down list titled "Available Actions" that contains the actions that can be performed with this element. Generally these actions are adding and removing any elements that are directly contained within the current element. For example, the `Server` element can only create and delete `Service` elements, while the `Host` element can create an `Alias`, `Logger`, `DefaultContext`, `Context`, and `Valve`.

Similarly, those elements that do not contain other elements will not have any actions in the drop-down list.

Many of the configuration and available actions are similar and rather than show examples of every possible permutation and combination the examples highlight the more complex or interesting options, or highlight where an option may differ significantly from other elements within the navigation group.

The following sections step through the navigation items and the configuration options that are accessible from each item, starting with the Resources element.

Resources

The resources element maps to the `GlobalNamingResources` element in the `server.xml` and represents the global JNDI resources for the server.

The Resources folder is not selectable other than as a container to contract and expand showing the other elements. Selecting the Data Sources elements displays a screen similar to that shown in Figure 9-3.

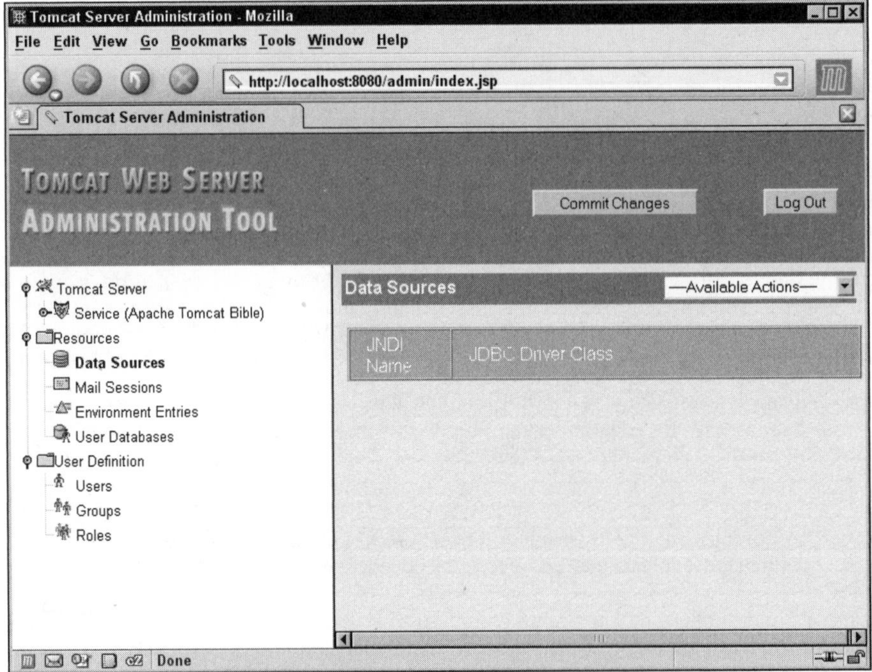

Figure 9-3: Data sources configuration

The Data Sources configuration dialog box has two actions; the ability to create a Data Source, and to delete a Data Source. Selecting Create New Data Source from the drop-down list displays a screen similar to that shown in Figure 9-4.

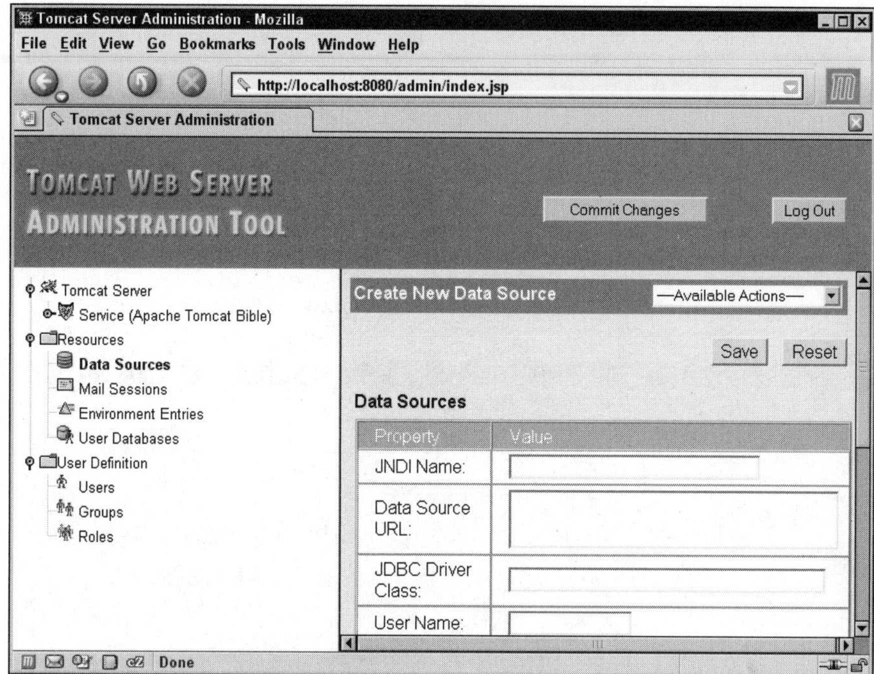

Figure 9-4: Creating a new data source

The data source creation screen provides the capability to enter the resource parameters as well as the definition for the resource. Fill in the table with the fields in Table 9-1 and press Save.

Remember, this does not save the configuration information permanently. To do that the Commit Changes button must be pressed after pressing Save.

Table 9-1: PoolDB JNDI Data Source

Property	*Value*
JNDI Name	`jdbc/PoolDB`
Data Source URL	`jdbc:mysql://localhost:3306/ pooltest?autoReconnect=true`
JDBC Driver Class	`com.mysql.jdbc.Driver`

Continued

Table 9-1 *(continued)*

Property	***Value***
User Name	`dbpool`
Password	`dbpool`
Max Active Connections	`100`
Max Idle Connections	`30`
Max Wait for Connection	`10000`
Validation Query	`<empty>`

Entering the data in Table 9-1 creates the JNDI entry shown in Figure 9-5.

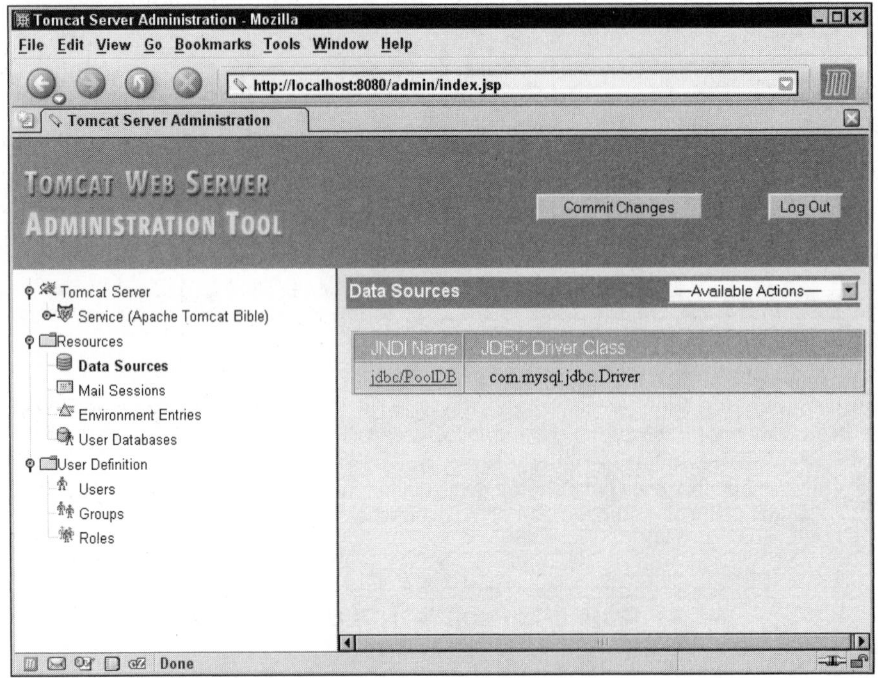

Figure 9-5: Created Data Source

The Data Source screen now shows a list of the data sources available. To edit or view a Data Source, select the data source by clicking on the link in the JNDI Name column. This displays a screen similar to that shown in Figure 9-6.

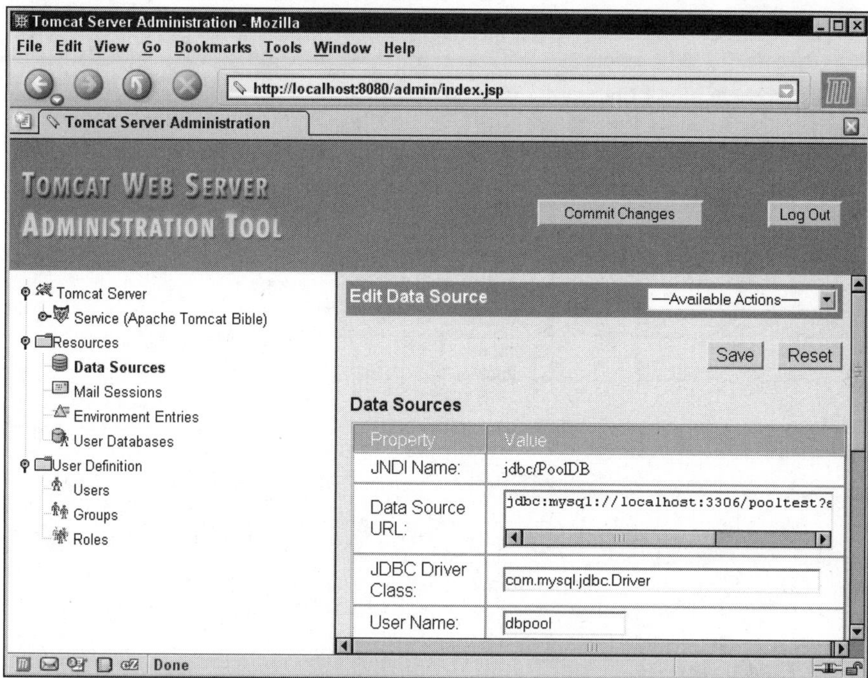

Figure 9-6: Edit jdbc/PoolDB Data Source.

The Mail Sessions, Environment Entries, and User Databases navigation items provide very similar functionality, as can be seen for adding an Environment Entry in Figure 9-7 and selecting a User Database in Figure 9-8.

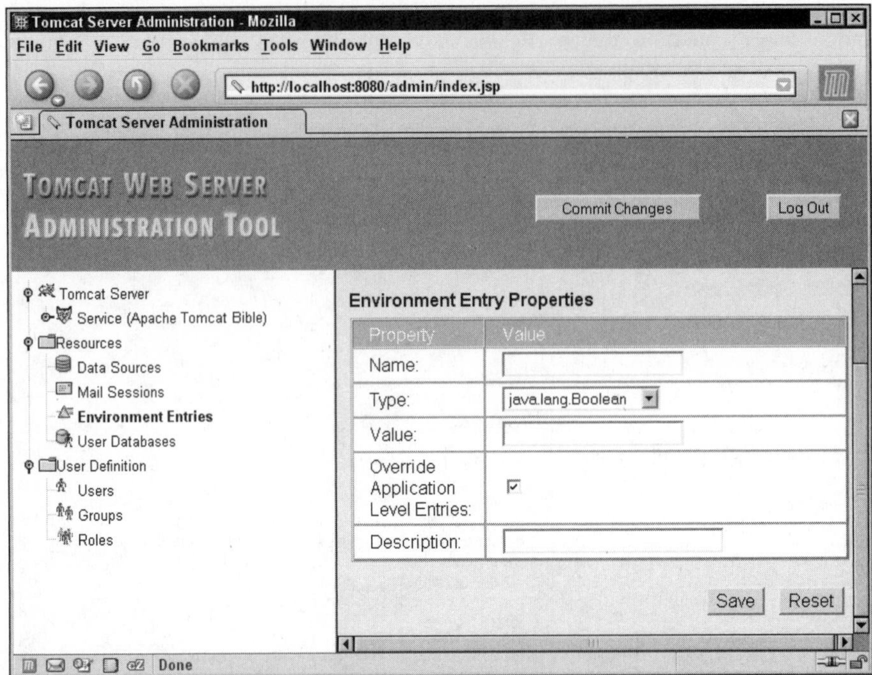

Figure 9-7: Adding Environment Entries

User Definition

The User Definition section uses the `UserDatabase` Realm to add, modify, and delete user authentication information.

Caution

Unlike the Server and Resources sections of the configuration, the User Definition elements do not need to have Commit Changes pressed to save the changes to the authentication information store. As soon as the Save button is pressed, the modification are made permanent. Also, there is no backup kept of the old authentication data, so any mistakes editing the user authentication data are compounded.

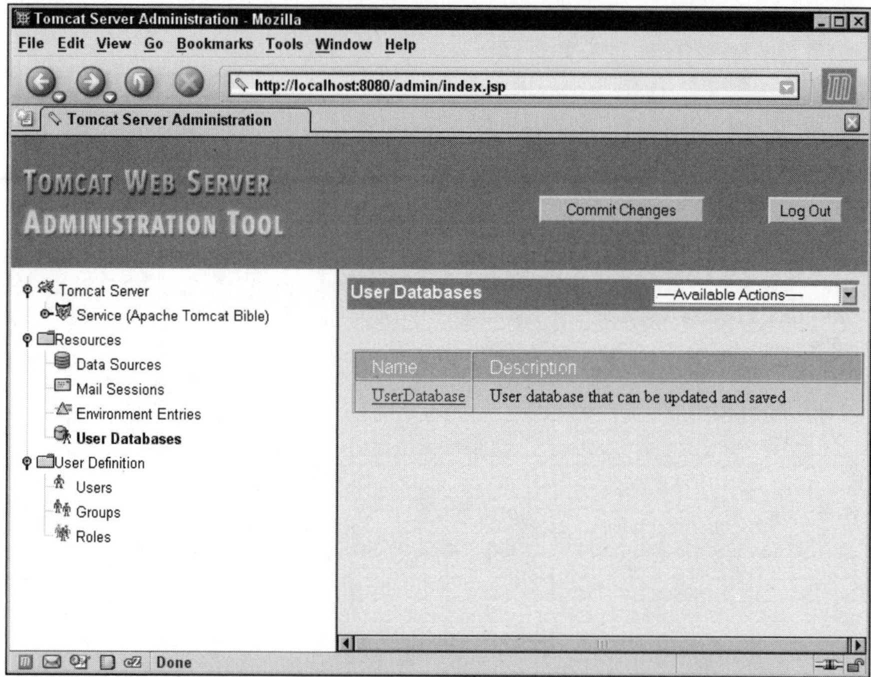

Figure 9-8: User Database selection screen

The User Definition section contains three elements:

✦ Users

✦ Groups

✦ Roles

For authentication purposes only the Users and Roles are important, but the addition of the Groups administration provides a powerful tool for creating various classifications of Users. Put simply, a group is a collection of one or more roles. A user can then have a group assigned instead of (and as well as) individual roles.

This gives an administrator much greater flexibility over assigning authentication information to users. With one change all the users in the group "staff" can have access to a new Web application allowed, or denied. Using just roles would require modifying each user, a time-consuming and error-prone task.

Selecting the Users navigation item displays the Users List Screen shown in Figure 9-9.

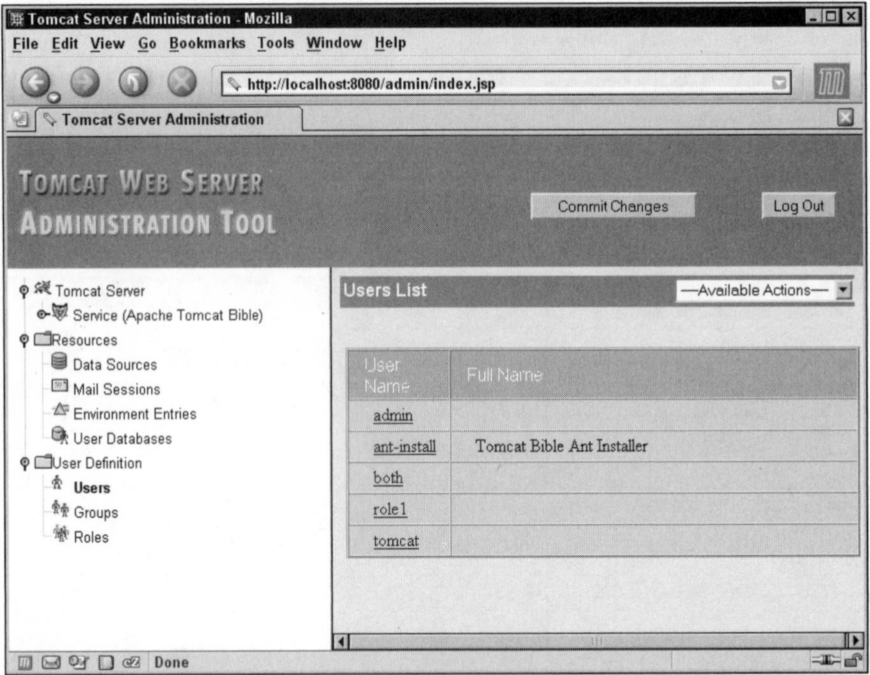

Figure 9-9: Users list

The actions available to manage the Users are to create, edit, and delete users. To edit a user, click the link in the User Name column; a screen similar to Figure 9-10 is displayed.

The user edit screen provides the capabilities to change the properties of the user, and modify the group and role membership of the user. Pressing Save modifies the `tomcat-users.xml` file.

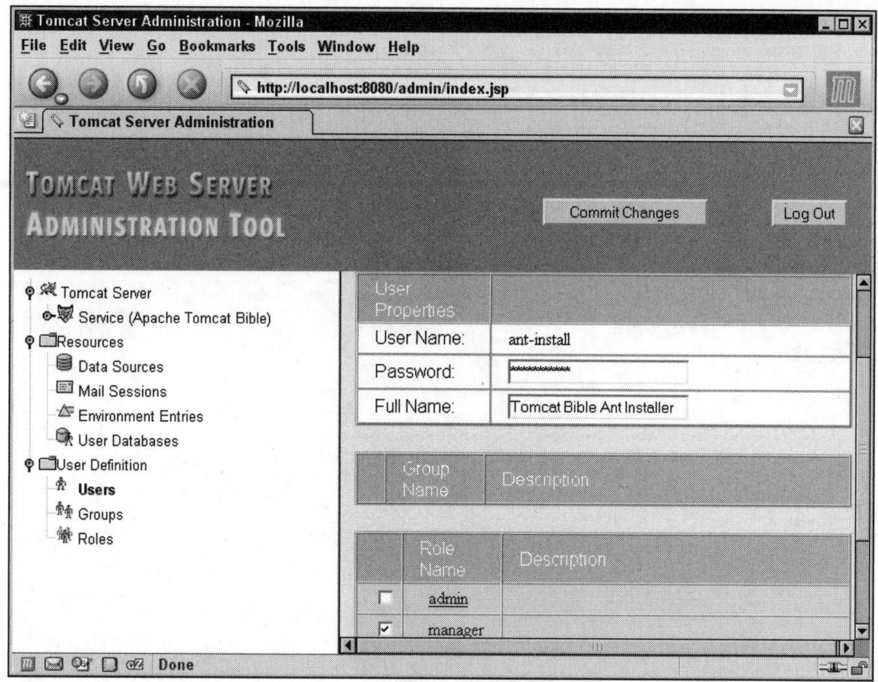

Figure 9-10: Editing a user

The Available Actions drop-down in the Users add, edit, and delete screens displays different information, and at times inappropriate options. Within editing a user, the Available Actions has the action to Delete Existing Users. Fear not, the action refreshes the screen and displays a delete page, and does not delete the current page.

The Group administration functionality is accessed by selecting the Groups navigation item. This displays a default Group List screen. To add a new group, select Create New Group from the Available Actions drop-down list. This displays a screen similar to that shown in Figure 9-11.

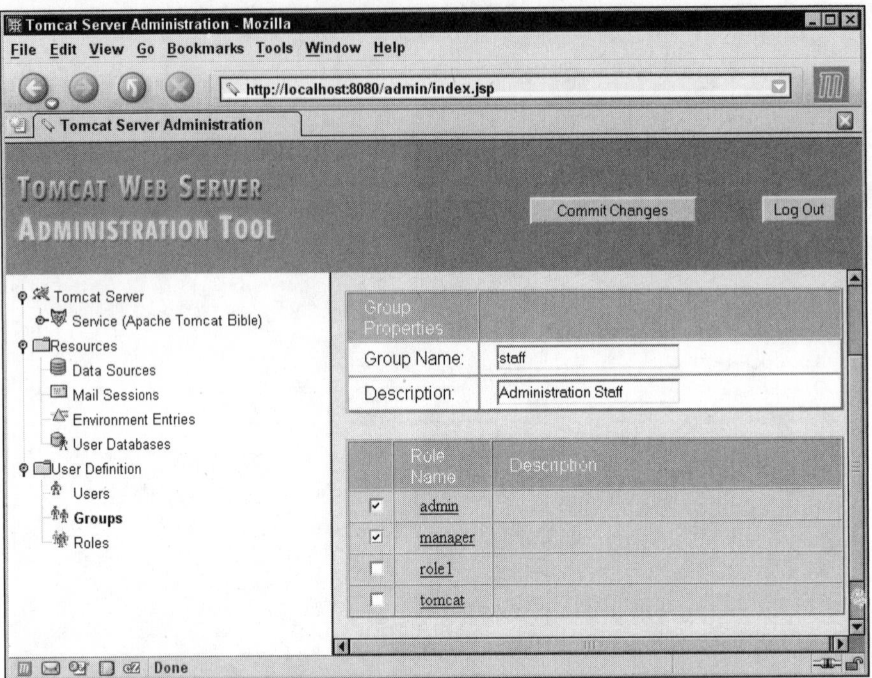

Figure 9-11: Adding a new group

Figure 9-11 shows the addition of a group staff that consists of the Roles admin and manager. Once saved, this group can then be added to existing users, or during the creation of a new user, as shown in Figure 9-12.

The final navigation item in the User Definitions section is Roles. The Roles item administers the authentication roles available within the Realm. As with the other elements in the User Definition section, the actions available are to create a new role, to edit an existing role, to list all the available roles, and to delete roles.

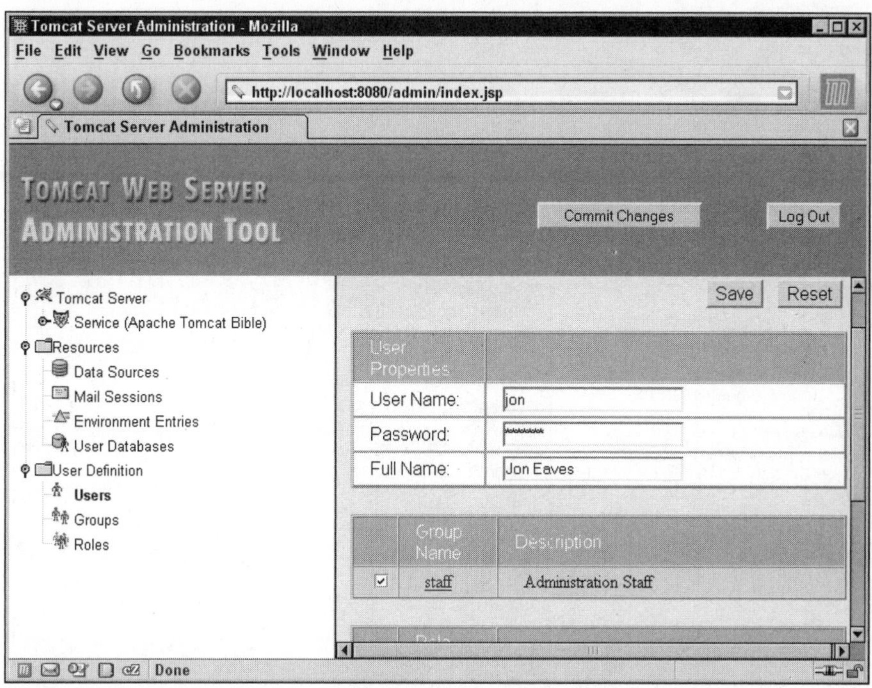

Figure 9-12: Adding a new user with a group

Server

The first navigation item is the `Server` element for the Tomcat instance. Selecting the Tomcat server displays a screen similar to that shown in Figure 9-13.

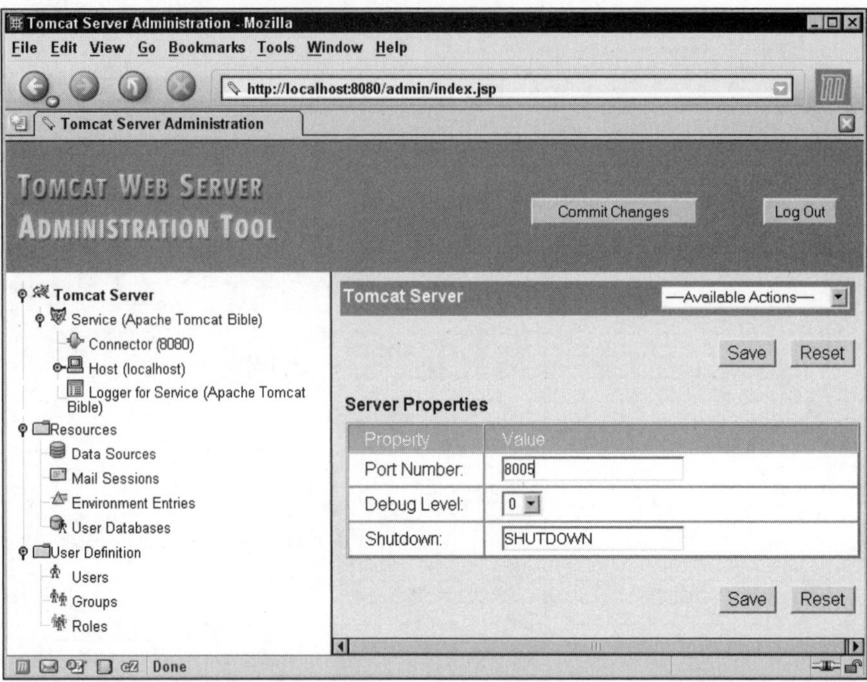

Figure 9-13: `Server` element

The content frame displays the attributes that are editable for the `Server` element, and the Save button applies the changes in the form to the in-memory copy of the `Server` element.

The `Server` element can create and delete `Service` elements. To create a service select the "Create New Service" from the Available Actions. This displays an empty HTML form in the content frame that contains fields for the attributes of the `Service` element and the associated Engine. The screen should look similar to that shown in Figure 9-14.

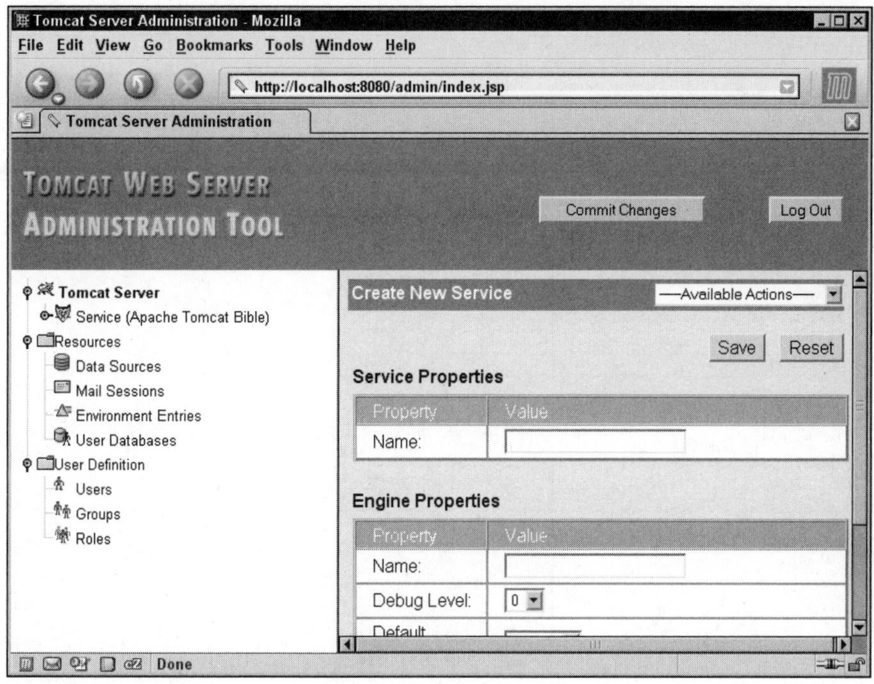

Figure 9-14: Creating a new service

The fields displayed represent the attributes available for these elements. Entering data in the fields and pressing the Save button results in a screen similar to that shown in Figure 9-15.

Note

The Administration tool can only manage the configuration of the standard Tomcat elements. Any elements that are not part of the default Tomcat installation can not be managed. This means the new elements created in Chapter 18 cannot be added using this tool and only can be included by manual editing of `server.xml`. This limitation may be addressed in future releases of Tomcat.

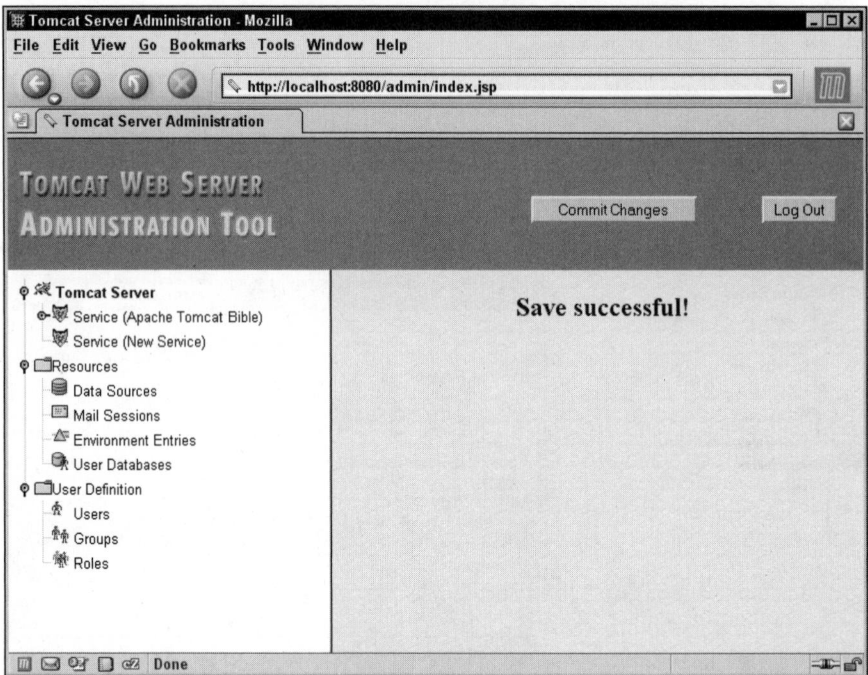

Figure 9-15: New service added to Server

The only other action available to the `Server` element is to delete the service. To return to the content frame with the Available Actions drop-down list, select the `Server` element on the navigation frame.

To delete the newly added service, select Delete Existing Services from the list and a screen similar to that shown in Figure 9-16 should be displayed.

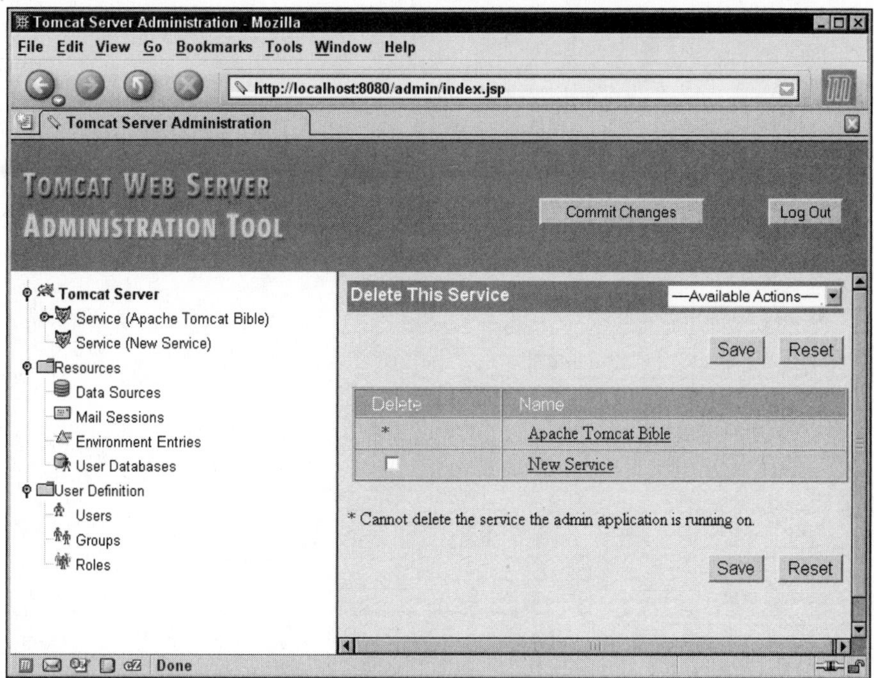

Figure 9-16: Delete service list

The delete service list shows a list of the available services, with a checkbox beside each service that can be deleted. The service that is running the Administration tool cannot be deleted. Selecting a checkbox and pressing Save removes the service from the server and all the elements that the service contains. Any `Hosts`, `Loggers`, `Connectors`, and other elements defined for the service will also be deleted.

Within the `Server` element are the `Service` elements. Selecting a `Service` element displays a screen similar to that shown in Figure 9-17.

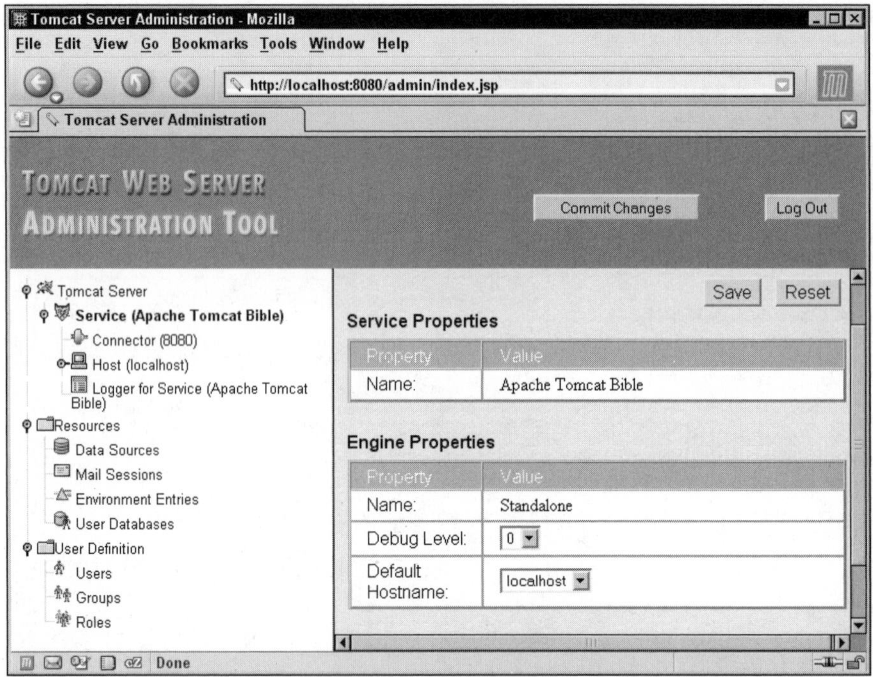

Figure 9-17: `Service` and `Engine` properties

The service administration also can modify the properties of the Engine that is contained within the service. The `Service` element contains many of the functional elements in the Tomcat configuration so the list of available actions is quite extensive. Within a service, the following actions may be performed:

- ✦ Create/Delete Connector
- ✦ Create/Default Context
- ✦ Create/Delete Host
- ✦ Create/Delete Logger
- ✦ Create/Delete Valve

There is no Delete Default Context option, nor is there the ability to Create or Delete a Realm at this point in the hierarchy. If a Realm is configured manually in `server.xml` within the Engine, the Realm will be available for modification within the Service administration elements.

The configuration of the Default Context and Host are similar to previous configuration screens in that they display the attributes of the elements in `server.xml` to be either created new, or modified.

The Connector, Logger, and Valve configuration are more sophisticated because these elements have different attributes depending on the implementation of the class of the element in the configuration.

For these elements it is quite important to select the Type option first. Because the screen is refreshed to display the correct attributes when the Type element is changed, any modifications made to the attributes will be lost.

Using the creation of a Valve as an example of this, Figure 9-18 shows the creation of an `AccessLogValve`. Pay attention to the number of names of the attributes available to the `AccessLogValve` element.

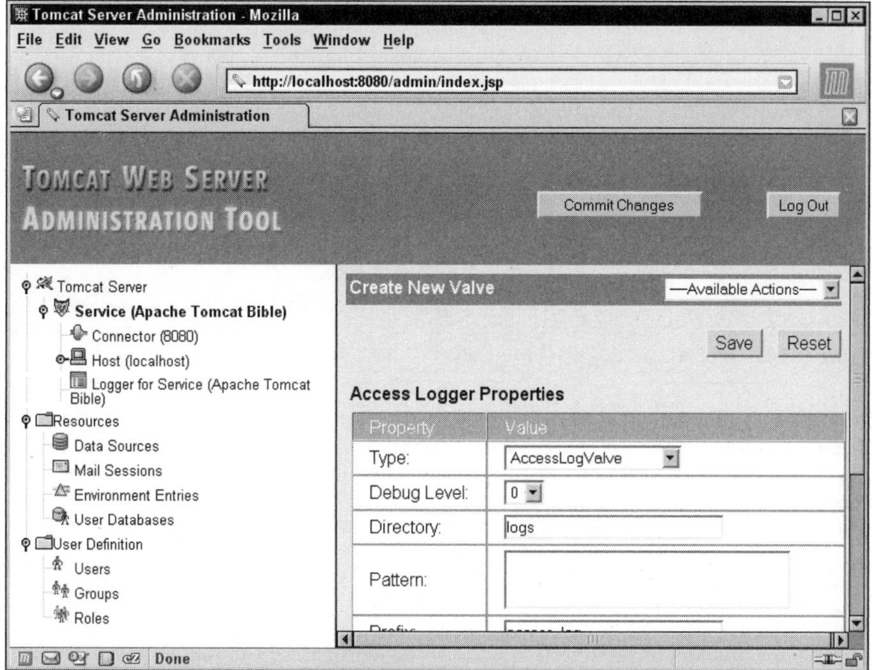

Figure 9-18: Creating an `AccessLogValve`

As a contrast, changing the `Type` property using the drop-down list to `SingleSignOn` displays a screen similar to that shown in Figure 9-19.

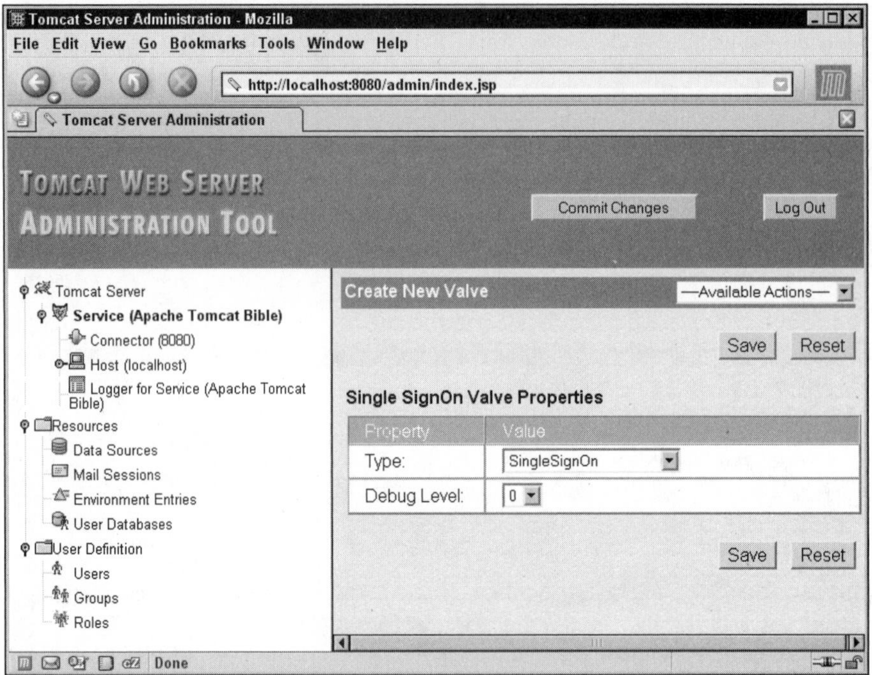

Figure 9-19: Creating a `SingleSignOn` valve

The `Host` element contained in the service is also a container. The `Host` element contains all the contexts for the Web applications installed on the `Host`, as shown in Figure 9-20. With functionality similar to the service, the `Host` element provides an extensive range of actions. Selecting the `Host` element from the navigation frame provides access to the following actions:

✦ Create/Delete Alias

✦ Create/Delete Logger

✦ Create/Delete Context

✦ Create/DefaultContext

✦ Create User Realm

✦ Create/Delete Valve

✦ Delete this Host

As with the service there is the action to create a `DefaultContext`, but not the action to delete it. This list of actions also contains Delete this Host; a similar entry occurs in a Context, but not in the other elements. Delete this Host is a shortcut to the Delete Host action from the service with the current Host already selected for deletion.

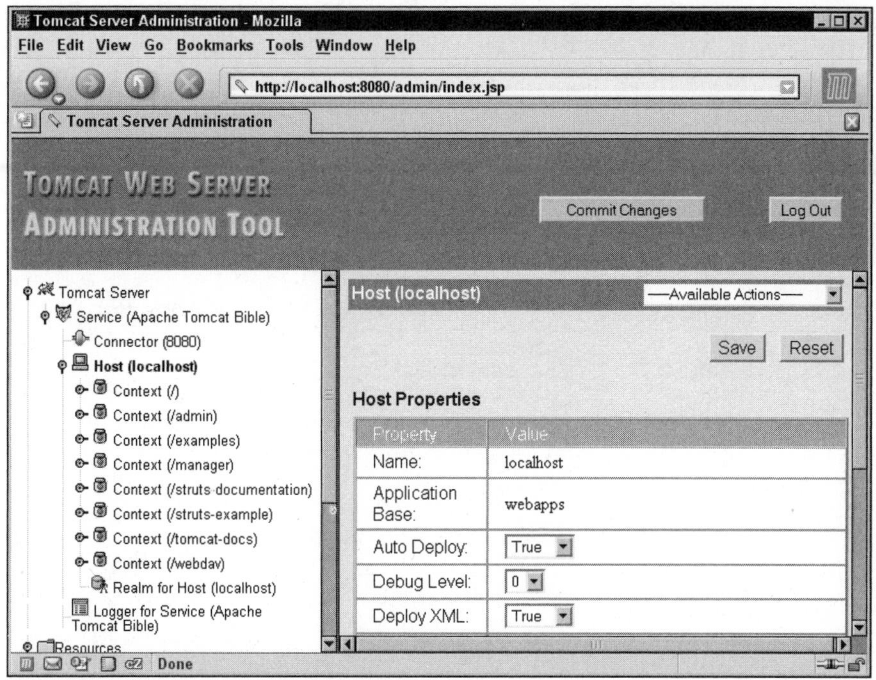

Figure 9-20: List of `Context` elements in a Host

The `Context` element, like the Host and service, contains other elements, and these can be managed using the actions assigned to the `Context`. To manage a `Context`, select the `Context` in the navigation frame and expand the `Context` as shown in Figure 9-21.

The `Context` provides access to the following actions:

✦ Create/Delete Logger

✦ Create/Delete User Realm

✦ Create/Delete Valve

✦ Delete this Context

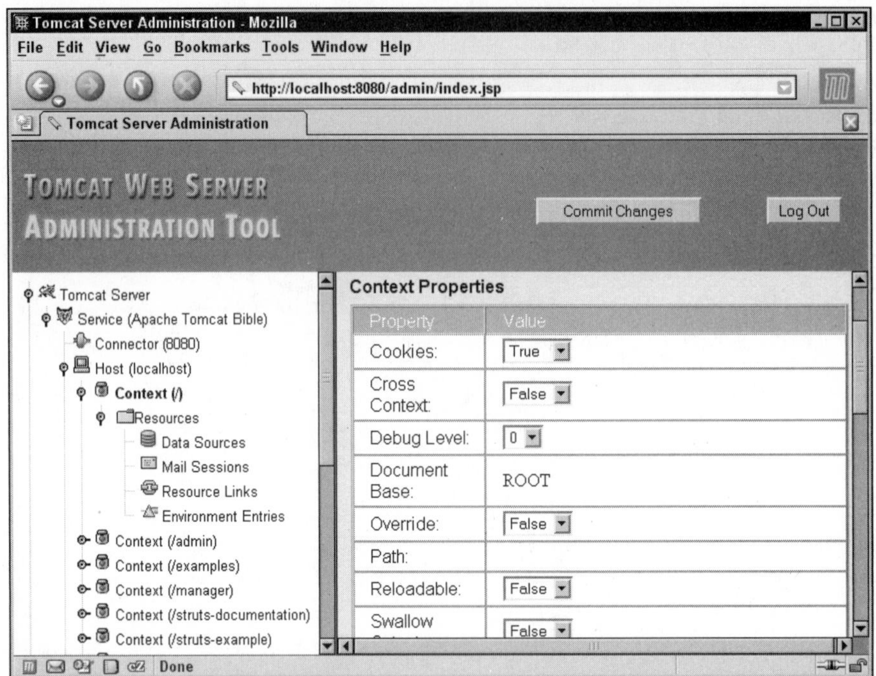

Figure 9-21: `Context` properties and expanded `Context` elements

The expanded `Context` contains a set of Resources that have been configured specifically for this Context. The Data Sources, Mail Session, and Environment Entries are the same as the Resources of the same name in the `GlobalNamingResources` element.

The additional item is the `ResourceLink`. This element provides a means of linking to a global JNDI resource in the configuration. The Web application can then use the name attribute specified in the ResourceLink to obtain a reference to the global JNDI resource.

Summary

The Application Tool is constantly under development and with each new release of Tomcat additional features are added. The Tomcat developers have managed to provide an extremely easy to use and functional graphical interface for administrators to configure Tomcat without having to resort to manual editing of `server.xml`. At present there are some features (such as custom elements) that must be configured by manually editing `server.xml`, however the power gained from the ability to remotely configure a Tomcat server is a feature that should not be ignored.

Manager Application

The Manager Application provides the run-time control over the Web applications running on a Tomcat Server Host. The Manager Application is a Web application that is installed on each host to be managed and can be accessed via direct HTTP commands or an HTML interface.

HTTP commands are direct URL references and can be issued in the browser "URL location" window. There is an extremely limited interface directly using the browser. The HTML interface is a more traditional Web-based interface with a management console look-and-feel.

The direct HTTP interface can be accessed via a browser; however it is more common to use custom tools such as the Tomcat Ant Tasks to access this interface and the use of the HTTP interface via a browser is becoming less popular with the implementation of the HTML interface. However, the HTTP manager interface has some features that are not implemented in the HTML interface. These are discussed later in the chapter.

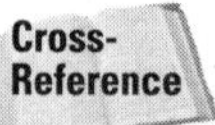

The Tomcat Ant Tasks are described in Chapter 5.

The HTML interface is a simplified management console that provides a fairly thin wrapper over the HTTP interface and this will become obvious when viewing the URLs generated while using the application.

The Tomcat Manager Application is also identified as the Tomcat Web Application Manager within the Web application. Both uses are correct, however to be strictly correct the title of the Web application probably should be Tomcat Web Application Manager Application, but that is probably too much of a mouthful for anybody, so Manager Application or Web Application Manager may be used. For consistency we only use the term Manager Application in this chapter.

Using the Manager Application

The first step in using the Manager Application is to open the URL in a browser. The default installation of Tomcat has this Web application configured at:

```
http://localhost:8080/manager/html
```

The HTML version of the Manager Application is at the preceding URL. The Manager Application can be accessed directly at http://localhost:8080/manager.

This should result in a screen as shown in Figure 9-22. The Manager Application is secured using Basic Authentication and the username and password used is the same credentials as used in the Ant tasks and configured during installation.

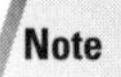

The authentication information configured for the Manager Application in Chapter 2 is "ant-install" for both the username and the password.

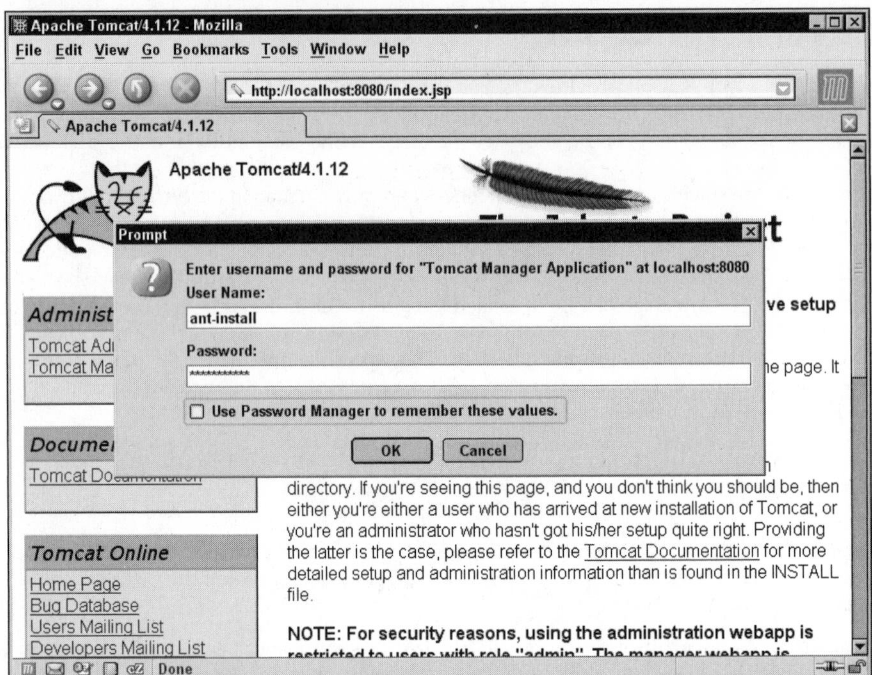

Figure 9-22: Manager Application login

If login is successful, the Manager Application list is displayed as shown in Figure 9-23. This is the only screen for the Manager Application and the information provided on the page covers all the functionality available from the Web application.

The main areas on the list screen are:

- ✦ Message display
- ✦ Application list
- ✦ Install form
- ✦ Server information (not shown in Figure 9-23)

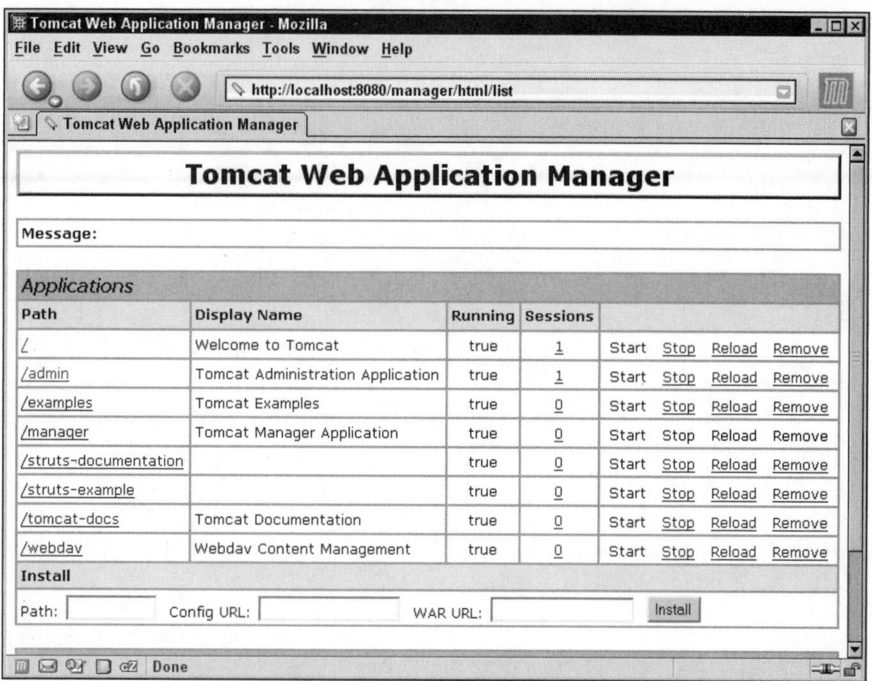

Figure 9-23: Manager Application list

The Message Display area contains confirmation and error messages that are results from actions performed in the Application list or the Install form.

The Server information displays information about the installation of Tomcat. The fields shown are; Tomcat Server Version, JVM Version, JVM Vendor, Operating System Name, Operating System Version, and Operating System Architecture.

The Application list contains a list of all the Web applications currently installed on the Tomcat Server. This area is used to control the activities of the Web applications by using the Start/Stop/Reload and Remove links in the table.

To demonstrate the use of the Manager Application, click the Stop link of the Web application with a Path of "/". This displays a page similar to that shown in Figure 9-24.

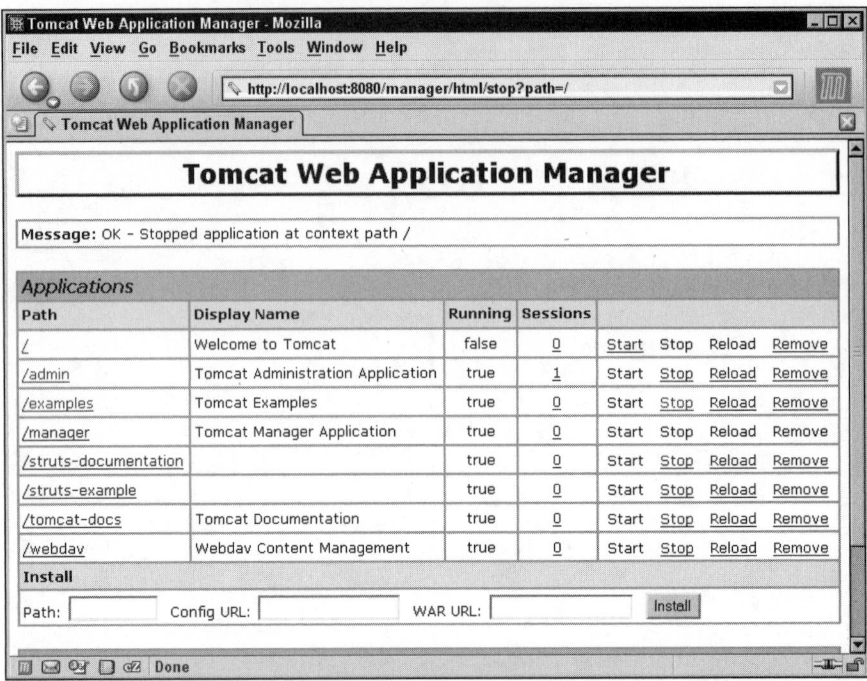

Figure 9-24: Stopping the Web application

The Message area has indicated that the application has stopped successfully; the Running column in the Applications list has the running state of the Web application as false and the Start link can now be accessed, but the Stop and Reload links are no longer available.

Pay close attention to the URL in the Web browser where the command information is displayed. Pressing reload causes that URL to be reloaded and hence re-run the command. This almost always results in some sort of an error. Unfortunately there is no convenient way to return to the list screen where the URL does not contain a command other than editing the browser URL.

The Manager Application does not change any persistent state in the Tomcat configuration. The application merely is a run-time tool for managing the Web applications on the Host. This is often used to Reload Web applications or take them out of service (with Remove) during a development phase. Restarting the Tomcat server starts any stopped Web applications. Removed Web applications will re-appear and installed Web applications will be removed. Other activities must be performed to permanently change the configuration of the Tomcat server.

The Install form provides the functionality to install Web applications using either an XML file containing a Context element or a WAR file (packed or unpacked). Unfortunately, the mechanism for performing this activity is quite cumbersome and error prone and sadly the error reporting mechanisms are very primitive.

The form fields in the Install form are:

✦ Path

✦ Config URL

✦ WAR URL

The Path form represents the context path for the Web application, the Config URL represents the path to a Context XML file, and the WAR URL represents a path to the WAR.

The WAR URL format is somewhat complicated because it can process a packed WAR and an unpacked WAR file. Using the HelloWorld application developed in Chapter 7 as an example of installation, Table 9-2 describes the data to be entered into each field. Make sure that the Web application has been compiled and a jar file created.

Table 9-2: Installing a Web Application

Path	*Config URL*	*WAR URL*
`/hello`	`file:c:\devel\hello\build\WEB-INF\context.xml`	`<blank>`
`/hello`	`<blank>`	`file:c:\devel\hello\build`
`/hello`	`<blank>`	`jar:file:c:\devel\hello\dist\hello-0.1-dev.war!/`

Caution Don't forget to use the Remove option after each successful install or an error will occur. Pay close attention to the URL for the packed WAR; the `"!/"` at the end of the URL is very important.

It would be very nice at this point if the screen displayed what is shown in Figure 9-25, however in the version of Tomcat installed in Chapter 2 there appears to be a minor defect. It is highly likely that after typing in the URLs in Table 9-2 a message such as:

```
FAIL - Encountered exception java.net.MalformedURLException: no protocol:
```

will be displayed. To get a sense of achievement and install the Web application we can resort to a little URL manipulation.

The error appears to be caused by an over-zealous checking of blank parameters in the HTML Manager Application. So, to get around the problem, just remove all the query parameters that have no value. For the second example, the original URL looks something like:

```
http://localhost:8080/manager/html/install?path=&installPath=%2Fhello&installCon
fig=&installWar=file%3Ac%3A%5Cusr%5Cdevel%5Cbuild
```

Remove the `path=&` and `installConfig=&` from the URL to be left with:

```
http://localhost:8080/manager/html/install?path=&installPath=%2Fhello&installWar
=file%3Ac%3A%5Cusr%5Cdevel%5Cbuild
```

Then press return and the screen should look like Figure 9-25.

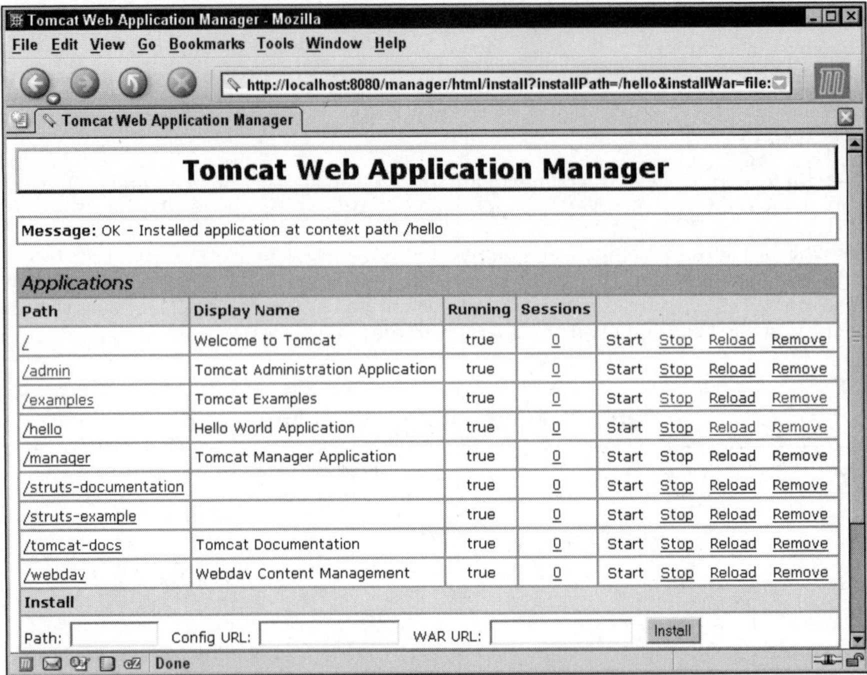

Figure 9-25: HelloWorld application installed

That concludes the features available through the HTML Manager interface, however there are some other features that are useful that can be directly accessed through the HTTP interface.

Features Missing in the HTML Interface

The HTML Manager interface is built on top of the Manager Application. The Manager Application does not provide the same user friendly environment to manage the Tomcat installation, but does provide some additional functionality that cannot be accessed via the HTML Manager interface.

This section contains information about the additional features provided by the Manager interface.

Deploy and Undeploy

At present the deploy feature is only available through the Ant Task interface, however alternative Management Applications may see fit to implement the interface to provide all the functionality in a single tool.

The deploy feature is available at the URL

```
http://localhost:8080/manager/deploy?path=/foo
```

to upload a WAR file for deployment. However this feature requires the use of an HTTP PUT and therefore an external tool to provide the file for deployment.

Upon receipt of the WAR file the Manager Application installs the Web application into the application base directory of the appropriate Host and starts it on the context path specified.

Global Resources

The `GlobalNamingResources` element contains the JNDI resources available to Web applications installed on the server. To obtain a list of the resources use the following URL:

```
http://localhost:8080/manager/resources[?type=xxxxx]
```

The optional parameter, type, is a fully qualified Java class name of the resource type to be returned. If the parameter is not specified all the available resources will be returned.

This displays a list similar to the following:

```
OK - Listed global resources of all types
jdbc/PoolDB:org.apache.commons.dbcp.BasicDataSource
UserDatabase:org.apache.catalina.users.MemoryUserDatabase
```

Security Roles

The security role names and the associated descriptions that are available from the `UserDatabase` resource linked to the Web application for the Manager Application can be displayed by using the following URL:

```
http://localhost:8080/manager/roles
```

This displays a list similar to the following:

```
OK - Listed security roles
admin:
manager:
role1:
tomcat:
```

As can be determined from the preceding examples the HTTP Manager Application interface was not designed to be easily used directly, but provides a framework for third-party tools such as the Ant tasks to manage the Tomcat server.

Summary

In this chapter we have configured and stepped through the functionality provided by the Tomcat Administration Tool and the HTML interface for the Manager Application.

These two tools provide a management interface into the Tomcat server that enables remote administration to be performed easily and with less likelihood of errors. These tools are not as important to developers with Tomcat installed locally, however their value in a live deployment environment increases dramatically especially if the servers are remote.

✦ ✦ ✦

CHAPTER 10

Creating a Real Application

In This Chapter

Defining the Application

Planning the System and Application Architecture

Setting up a Development Environment

Using an MVC Architecture to Develop the Application

Deploying and Running the Application Using Tomcat

Now it's time to use some of the skills learned so far by creating a real application. This chapter leads you through designing and implementing an application to solve a real world problem for a fictional organization, given a realistic set of requirements.

First and foremost you need to design the application to solve the problem at hand. This is done using a number of common design methods, notably:

- Use cases
- Constraints
- Entity Relationship Diagram

Note

These methods are well documented in many books and on the Internet. In the context of this application no real knowledge of them is required.

You will then be in a position to set up your development environment, using Ant and MySQL.

Next we will plan how to implement the application using the Model View Controller architecture.

Cross-Reference

See Chapter 1 for a description of the Model-View-Controller (MVC) Architecture.

With an MVC architecture in mind the structure and relationships between our JSP pages, our classes and our database schema are discussed, as well as how they interact to solve the business problem at hand.

The chapter then leads you through actually developing parts of the application and deploying it to a Tomcat server. The application is developed, calling on Ant scripts to build and package the files appropriately.

Security-related aspects deliberately have not been discussed in this chapter. For details about how this Web application is secured see Chapter 12.

From the download available for this chapter install and get the example application we develop here running on your own system, then follow its development throughout this chapter. Reading this chapter while doing this will enhance your understanding.

Tomcat Cinemas

Congratulations! You've secured a massively lucrative contract to implement a booking system for Tomcat Cinemas. Cathy Simpson, your client, who manages Tomcat Cinemas, has a fairly well-defined set of requirements (no really, you're not dreaming) and a realistic timeframe for achieving a solution (okay, maybe you are dreaming).

Tomcat Cinemas operate at a single location and requires a system to allow both customers browsing the Internet and staff at the cinema to book and pay for tickets, as well as provide simple scheduling information for film showings. Cathy says she also needs some reports to help her with the day-to-day running of the cinema.

Requirements

In your discussions with Cathy a set of requirements has been decided upon. These requirements are used to define the actors involved and how they interact with various parts of the system: our Use Cases.

Note In the context of this example application we don't mean an actor in one of the films showing at Tomcat Cinemas. Instead we mean an entity or agent that interacts with the system we are designing, for example, a customer booking cinema seats is an actor in the system.

So, onto the requirements. Cathy has done the right thing and worked out broadly what she wants the system to do and achieve.

1. Tomcat Cinemas administrators can use the system to add, modify, or disable a theatre.
2. Tomcat Cinemas administrators can use the system to add, modify, or disable a film.
3. Customers can book tickets on the Internet.
4. Using a different interface (screen) to Web based customers; Tomcat Cinema's staff can sell tickets "over the counter" (We will call this the Front Desk).
5. Tomcat Cinemas can use the system to schedule what films will show in each of their theatres.
6. Tomcat Cinemas can use the system to schedule showings at various times throughout the day.
7. Customers who book over the Internet can pay by credit card.
8. Customers who have booked over the Internet can pick up their tickets at the counter by quoting their credit card number.
9. Potential customers on the Internet can view the schedule of movies to be shown for the remainder of the current day.

10. Tomcat Cinemas management wants to know how many seats are remaining for showings.

11. Tomcat Cinemas management need to know the time remaining for a Showing currently running.

12. Tomcat Cinemas management needs a report showing how many of their tickets were purchased over the counter, or over the Internet.

13. Ticket prices are based on the type of Theatre in which the showing is held.

Based on these requirements you discuss the details of the application with Cathy and learn of various definitions and constraints that we must be aware of when building the application.

Definitions

From the analysis and the preceding requirements we can identify some key ingredients in the problem we are trying to solve.

- **Film:** Not much definition required here. Tomcat Cinemas show films as their core business; let's leave it at that.
- **Theatre:** A theatre is a room where films are shown. A theatre can be one of three levels of "luxury." (We'll refrain from calling these classes of theatres to avoid any misunderstandings.) A theatre also has a certain capacity; we can't have people sitting in the aisles!
- **Showing:** A showing is a scheduled screening of a film in a theatre.
- **Booking:** Is a reservation a customer makes to have a seat or seats in the showing of a film.
- **Price:** A price is a mapping between a theatre type and a price per ticket for showings in that theatre.
- **User:** A user or actor of the system. There are a number of types of actors in this context:
  - **Administrator:** A staff member of Tomcat Cinemas with administrative privileges.
  - **Staff:** A member of Tomcat Cinemas staff.
  - **Web Customer:** A largely anonymous user who interacts with Tomcat Cinema's Web site.

Constraints

Typically the analysis of a business problem highlights various constraints that define how a system must or must not work. These are semantic issues that further define the processes that are built into the application.

The following are the constraints that you discover after talking with Cathy about her requirements.

- Only administrators can add, modify, or delete showings, theatres, or films.
- A theatre cannot be edited if there are today or future scheduled showings to run in it.
- A film cannot be edited if there are today or future scheduled showings for it.
- A showing cannot be deleted if there are bookings for it.
- A showing cannot be modified.
- Administrators cannot login to the system remotely, in other words, from the Internet.
- Only staff can use the "over-the-counter" (Front Desk) interface.
- Bookings are made by cash or credit card.
- Each staff member must be identified separately.
- Each showing is entered separately.
- Films start on the hour, for example, 9:00 a.m., 10:00 a.m.
- A staff member cannot be logged onto the system more than once.
- The earliest showing during a day is 8:00 a.m. The last film shows at 9:00 p.m.
- A booking cannot be cancelled once made.
- Staff must use the logout facility when leaving the application.
- The longest film is 2.5 hours.
- The Web interface where customers book their tickets only allows credit card sales.
- The Web interface must be secured using SSL.
- Bookings must be made on the day of the showing.
- A booking cannot be made for a showing that has started.
- Ticket prices are based on the theatre in which the showing is held.
- A showing cannot be scheduled in a disabled theatre.
- A showing cannot be scheduled for a disabled film.

From the requirements and the list of constraints we can flesh out a more detailed view of how the system will function using use cases.

Use Cases

A *use case* is simply a description of a particular interaction with the system, which results in some type of value. Typically use cases are accompanied by a diagram showing how an actor or actors interact with the system, as well as wire frame "storyboards" to show the interface that is used in the interaction.

Diagrams and storyboards are beyond the scope of this book, but interested readers should search the Internet for a more detailed description of how use cases and their associated documents work.

Describing the use cases clarifies the areas where the application must functionally fulfill a business purpose. The actual process of defining each use case allows us as developers to better understand and meet the customer's requirements.

For the purposes of the Tomcat Cinemas application we will list each use case and describe it briefly. By carefully reading each it becomes clear how the preceding constraints define rules for how the use cases are implemented.

After days and nights toiling over the preceding requirements and detailing the different constraints, the following list of eight use cases has been agreed upon.

Use Case 1: Administrator Adds, Modifies, or Disables a Theatre

This use case illustrates the ability of a certain level of user to add, modify, or disable a theatre's record. For instance, if a new theatre within Tomcat Cinemas is built, an administrator can add it to the system for use. In a similar way, if a theatre is renovated to increase capacity, its record can be modified to reflect this. While these renovations are occurring an administrator may want to temporarily disable a theatre's record so showings cannot be scheduled there.

The administrator chooses to list all the theatres in the system by clicking an appropriate link in the menu. A list appears showing details of each theatre. For each theatre in the list the option to modify that theatre is available. There is also a link to add a new theatre.

Selecting to modify an existing theatre takes the administrator to a form with all the selected theatre details populated. One of these items is the option to disable the theatre (Active or Inactive). Once the details have been modified, pressing save updates the record in the database, and returns the administrator to the theatre list.

Selecting to add a new theatre displays a similar form as that mentioned previously, however the form is not pre-populated. Once the details have been entered, pressing save inserts the new theatre in the database and takes the administrator to the theatre list.

If the administrator enters information in a form that violates a validation rule, pressing save merely refreshes the form view with any error messages displayed above the form.

Use Case 2: Administrator Adds, Modifies, or Disables a Film

This Use Case 2 is similar to Use Case 1 in that only certain users can add, modify, or disable films in the system. As films become available to Tomcat Cinemas they need to be added to the system, and if an error is made during this add, the modify facility can allow this to be rectified. Unlike theatres, films stop showing eventually and must therefore be disabled from the system.

In a similar way to theatres, the administrator chooses to list the films currently in the system. A list appears showing all films and their details. For each film in the list there is an option to modify its details. There is also a link to add a new film to the system.

The add and modify functionality for films works in much the same way as theatres.

Use Case 3: Administrator Creates or Deletes a Showing of a Film

The goal of this use case is to depict how an administrator can add or delete showings.

From the menu the administrator chooses to list showings currently scheduled in the system. The administrator can choose to list showings for today only, showings on all days or showings currently running.

For each showing listed there is the option to 'query' a showing. Clicking on this link shows details for the showing. An option exists to remove a future showing if there are no bookings associated with it. Clicking on this link takes the user to a screen asking them to confirm the removal from the system. Answering yes removes the showing and takes the user to the showing list. Answering no returns the user to the query page.

There is also the option to create a new showing. If this option is selected the administrator is presented with a form asking for details of the showing. Once the details have been entered, the user submits the form and validation takes place. Validation primarily checks that the date and time of the showing does not conflict with other showings for the chosen theatre. If validation errors occur the form is displayed with the last selected values entered and messages at the top of the screen describing the problem. If there are no validation errors found the transaction completes and the user is returned to the showing list.

Use Case 4: Administrator/Staff Member Queries a Showing

From a list of showings Administrators or Staff Members are able to query the status of showings in the system.

From a list of showings the Administrator or Staff Member select 'Query' for a particular showing and is presented with current information relating to this showing including:

- The film being shown.
- The theatre.
- The starting date and time.
- The duration.
- The ending date and time.
- The time remaining (if the showing has started, this will count down).
- The number of bookings.
- The seats remaining.

Use Case 5: Staff Member Makes a Booking

Use Case 5 describes how staff record a booking for a given showing in return for cash or credit card payment from the customer. Typically this would occur "over the counter."

By selecting the option to make a booking against a showing in the list described in Use Case 7, the staff member is presented with a form asking for details of the booking. The screen shows details of the showing selected for the booking such as the price per ticket, and the time and date of the showing. For payment of the booking the staff member can select either cash or credit card. If cash is selected, details of the customer and their credit card details are not required. If credit card is selected these details are required to complete the transaction.

Once the details of the booking have been entered, the staff member would click the continue button. If a credit card was used, the transaction would either be approved or declined, and the transaction would complete. For a cash transaction the amount to be collected from the customer is displayed on the screen.

If there are validation problems such as 0 seats being booked, or more seats being booked than are available, the errors are displayed on the form page.

Use Case 6: Web Customer Makes a Booking

Web customers also can make bookings, however, they achieve it through a different interface. This interface only provides one payment method, credit card.

Choosing to make a booking presents the user with a simple form asking for details such as the number of seats required and the customer's credit card details. If the showing selected is sold out a message to this effect will appear instead of the form. If the form is submitted and the credit card is approved the customer is asked to take their credit card number to Tomcat Cinemas to pick up their tickets.

Use Case 7: User Lists Showings Remaining for Today

Use Case 7 defines how both a Web customer and a member of staff can view a list of the remaining showings available at Tomcat Cinemas today. From this list the Web customer can choose to make a booking against a particular showing (see Use Case 6), or, under the over the counter (Front Desk) interface, the staff member can select a showing to make a booking against (Use Case 5) or query a showing (Use Case 4).

Use Case 8: Web Customer Picks up Ticket at Tomcat Cinemas

Once a Web customer has booked seats in a showing, they must have some way of retrieving the physical ticket from Tomcat Cinemas. After they have booked they are told to quote their credit card number when they pick up their tickets.

When the user appears at the counter a staff member can type in the provided credit card number and check details of the booking. A tick box is provided allowing the staff member to record that this booking has been "picked up." This functionality is not implemented in this chapter; it is left as an exercise for the reader.

A Recap

Now that the use cases have been identified let's recap. So far we have:

- Gathered our requirements from the client
- Defined important entities and actors within the system
- Identified key constraints that affect how the system will work
- Identified and defined eight use cases representing interactions with our system

With all this achieved we have a pretty solid idea about what our system needs to do to meet Cathy's requirements. Importantly we have identified three interfaces that the system will require:

- Administration interface: This is where administrators can perform admin only functionality.
- Front Desk interface: This is where Tomcat Cinemas staff can list showings remaining for today or to make bookings.
- Web interface: This is where Web customers can list showings remaining for today or to make bookings.

It is now important to design how the system will be built and what structure different components of the architecture will take on.

Database Design

A quick scan over the language used in the preceding discussion reveals a number of central entities that need to be modeled in the application.

Entities

These entities are easy to identify. The following is a list of the entities that are modeled in the database for the application.

- **FILM**: A film needs to be modeled in the application to associate with showings. Therefore a table representing the FILM entity is required.
- **SHOWING**: Very central to the entire system, a SHOWING represents the instance of business value to Cathy. It aggregates a number of BOOKINGs in a THEATRE in order to view a FILM.
- **THEATRE**: A THEATRE clearly represents the place a SHOWING will take place.
- **BOOKING**: A BOOKING represents a customer's reservation to take part in a SHOWING.
- **PRICE**: A PRICE represents the cost per seat in a type of THEATRE.

Relationships

Defining the relationships between these entities can be achieved in a number of ways. Firstly by spelling out in text the exact relationships that exist here:

1. A SHOWING has none or many BOOKINGs: This is logical in that many customers are hopefully going to book to see each SHOWING of a FILM.
2. A BOOKING has one SHOWING. We are defining here that a BOOKING can only relate to one SHOWING of a FILM.
3. A THEATRE has none or many SHOWINGs: It would be disappointing for Cathy if she could only have one SHOWING in one of her THEATREs, ever. We are specifying here that many SHOWINGs are held in any given THEATRE.
4. A THEATRE has a PRICE and a PRICE can have none or many THEATREs
5. A SHOWING has one THEATRE: A SHOWING cannot occur in two THEATREs; it can only occur in one.
6. A SHOWING has one FILM: No double features I'm afraid.
7. A FILM has none or many SHOWINGs: Again, it wouldn't be much fun being in Cathy's business if she could only show a FILM once. Over a period of time, a FILM can appear in many SHOWINGs.

This list shows how various business rules are being brought out via the relationships. A much less verbose way of representing all these entities and their relationships is with an *Entity Relationship Diagram* (ERD). An ERD is, as the name suggests, a graphic model of these relationships and a pro forma for how the database will appear. Figure 10-1 is the ERD for the Tomcat Cinemas application.

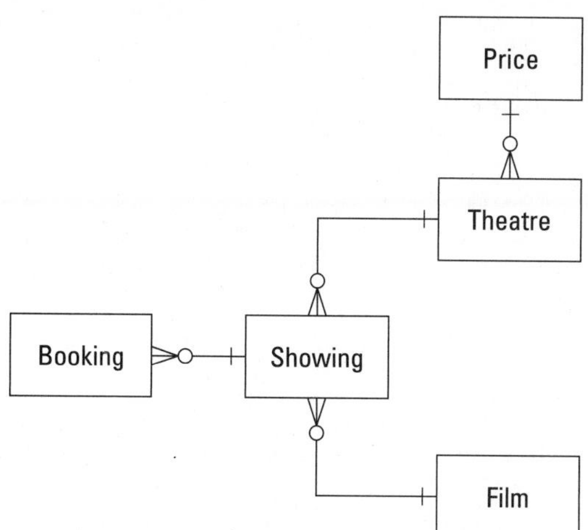

Figure 10-1: An Entity Relationship Diagram for Tomcat Cinemas

Now that the database tables (entities) have been identified, each column of each table needs to be specified. Table 10-1 shows each column, its type and size, and a brief description.

Table 10-1: Tomcat Cinemas Table Structure

Table Name	*Column Name*	*Properties*	*Description*
BOOKING	id	Integer(11), Primary Key, Auto Increment	Uniquely identifies a row in the BOOKING table.
BOOKING	showingId	Integer(11), Foreign Key	Foreign key join to the SHOWING table.
BOOKING	seats	Integer(11), default value: 1	Number of seats in this booking.
BOOKING	bookedVia	varchar(10), Cannot be null	How this booking was made (by Internet or counter).
BOOKING	amount	Integer(11), default value: 0	Cost of booking in cents.
BOOKING	payMethod	varchar(4), cannot be null	Cash or credit card.
BOOKING	cardNo	varchar(10), can be null	Customer's credit card number.
BOOKING	name	varchar(255), can be null	The name of a credit card paying customer.

Continued

Table 10-1 *(continued)*

Table Name	*Column Name*	*Properties*	*Description*
BOOKING	cardType	varchar(10), can be null	The type of credit card used.
BOOKING	pickedUp	Integer(1), default: 0	Indicates if the customer has collected tickets from a booking made on the Internet.
SHOWING	id	Integer(11), Primary Key, Auto increment	Uniquely identifies a SHOWING.
SHOWING	theatreId	Integer(11), Foreign Key	Foreign Key to the THEATRE table.
SHOWING	filmId	Integer(11), Foreign Key	Foreign Key to the FILM table.
SHOWING	dateTimeStart	Timestamp	The date and time the SHOWING begins.
THEATRE	id	Integer(11), Primary Key, Auto increment	Uniquely identifies a THEATRE.
THEATRE	name	varchar(100)	The common name of the THEATRE.
THEATRE	type	char(1), cannot be null, default: A	Represents the type of theatre: A,B,C.
THEATRE	capacity	Integer(11), default: 10	The capacity in seats of this theatre.
THEATRE	active	Integer(1), default: 1	Whether this theatre is active in the system.
PRICE	theatreType	char(1)	Unique, represents the type of theatre this price applies to.
PRICE	amount	Integer(11), default: 0	The amount per ticket for this theatre type.
FILM	id	Integer(11), Primary Key, Auto increment	Uniquely identifies a FILM.
FILM	name	varchar(255), cannot be null	The name of the film.
FILM	length	Integer(11), default: 0	The length of the film in minutes.
FILM	active	Integer(1) default: 1	Whether this theatre is active in the system. Used for logical deletion.

Planning the structure of your tables (as outlined in Table 10-1) is important, as you must ensure that each relationship is catered for and that all the requirements can be satisfied with the system's data in this form.

Typically the design of an application such as Tomcat Cinemas would be a more lengthy process with more depth than what we can print here. You are encouraged to specify more in the application than is listed above, then to try to integrate these new areas into the application.

Setting up the Development Environment

The development environment consists of two distinct areas: the source tree (which includes more than just the source; it may include library jar files needed for compiling as well as database scripts, compiled classes, and so on) and the Tomcat server. For the purposes of development of this application, the Tomcat server points at the build directory within the development environment. However, when the application is formerly deployed to another (or the same) server, the Ant script is used differently to package the application in a specific way.

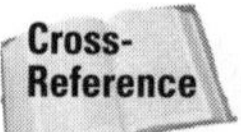

Chapter 5 deals almost exclusively with using Ant. This chapter assumes you have read and understood those concepts.

This section simply walks you through creating the development environment for the application. Were you to install the application from this chapter's download available on the Wiley site, most of the following tasks would be done already. You would still need to walk through the database setup steps and ensure the settings are consistent with your environment.

Directory Structure

The directory structure shown in Figure 10-2 should be used to develop the application.

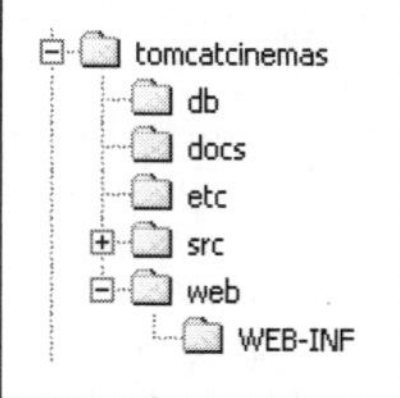

Figure 10-2: Source tree structure

The directory structure illustrated in Figure 10-2 shows the following base directories:

✦ `db`: The db directory stores database scripts that rebuild or populate the database.

✦ `docs`: Javadoc output is placed here.

✦ `etc`: Any other files that need to be placed in this structure.

✦ `src`: The top-level container for Java files (in their package structure).

✦ `web`: JSP, HTML, and image files are stored here.

✦ `web/WEB-INF`: Houses the `web.xml` for packaging of the application.

The Ant `build.xml` file resides in the directory above all these directories.

Package Structure

The src directory described houses the Java files. It's important to plan this structure so that it can handle expansion and flexibility later on. The package structure for this application is:

```
bible.tomcat.tccinemas
bible.tomcat.tccinemas.servlet
bible.tomcat.tccinemas.util
```

Therefore, the src path in the development environment appears as shown in Figure 10-3.

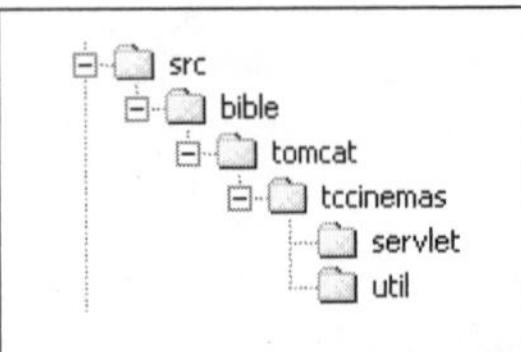

Figure 10-3: The src directory containing the correct package structure directories

Java files are placed in these directories when they are created during the development of the application. The Ant script compiles from this directory into a new directory, tomcatcinemas/build/WEB-INF/classes. The build directory represents the deployed version of the application that Tomcat refers to when it runs.

Setting up the Database

In the download available for this chapter is the Tomcat Cinemas application. Within this project under the db directory are some SQL files that can now be made use of. MySQL will now be administered in the same way as previously, using the command line.

Chapter 2 describes how to get MySQL running. If you haven't yet done this and are unfamiliar with MySQL, you should read that section before going on.

The MySQL Web site (www.mysql.com) provides access to some excellent GUI tools to use with MySQL. Tools such as MySQL Control Center and phpMyAdmin enable you to perform almost any action on a MySQL database that the native command line provides.

Logging into MySQL is required to run the commands. Open up a DOS prompt and type the following:

```
mysql -u <root user name> -p
```

Press Enter; the application will prompt for a password. Enter the administrator password you nominated when you first installed MySQL then press Enter. If you entered the details correctly you should be faced with a command prompt much like that shown in Figure 10-4:

Once logged in, SQL scripts and MySQL commands can be executed. The scripts about to be run establish the database for Tomcat Cinemas and populate it with the correct tables, then create a specific user for the application.

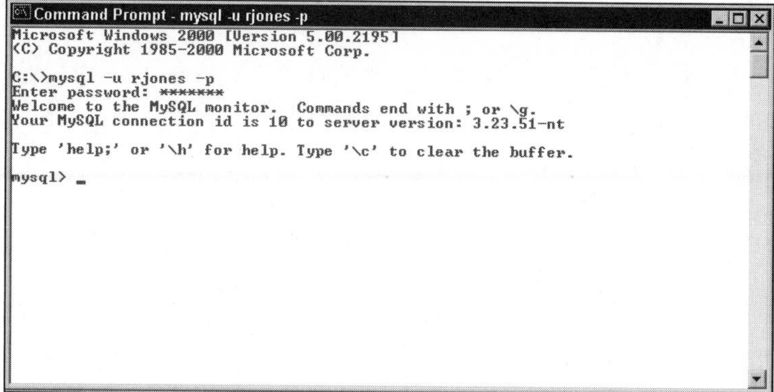

Figure 10-4: MySQL Command Prompt after logging in as the administrator

For convenience assume that your downloaded `tomcatcinemas` project resides at:

```
C:\work\book\tomcatcinemas
```

At the MySQL command prompt type the following line:

```
mysql> source c:\work\book\tomcatcinemas\db\create_database.sql
```

Press enter. MySQL will likely respond with the line:

```
Query OK, 1 row affected (0.00 sec)
```

Congratulations; you have now created your `tomcatcinemas` database. Creating some tables is the next step. To do this type the following:

```
mysql> source c:\work\book\tomcatcinemas\db\create_tables.sql
```

MySQL should respond with a similar message as before. To ensure that the tables have been created type the following in the MySQL command prompt:

```
mysql> use tomcatcinemas;
```

Press Enter. MySQL will respond that the Database has changed. Then type:

```
mysql> show tables;
```

Press Enter. If all has gone well MySQL will list the tables in the `tomcatcinemas` database, as shown in Figure 10-5.

There are other commands that can be typed here to verify the structure of each table, such as:

```
mysql> describe booking;
```

This command prints out the structure of the booking table. The output should appear as shown in Figure 10-6.

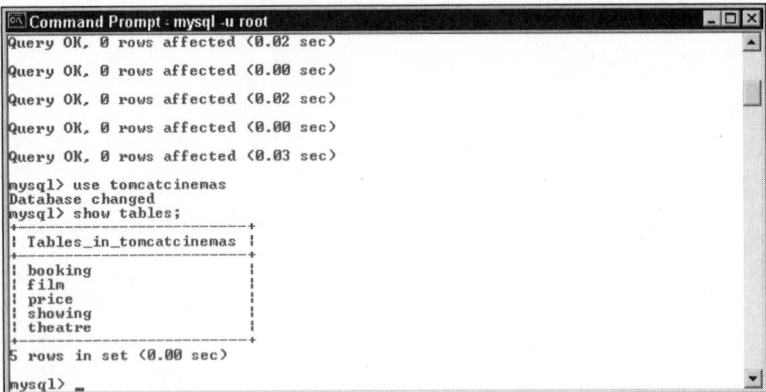

Figure 10-5: MySQL console listing tables created within the `tomcatcinemas` database

```
Command Prompt - mysql -u root
| film                    |
| price                   |
| showing                 |
| theatre                 |
+-------------------------+
5 rows in set (0.00 sec)

mysql> describe booking;
+------------+--------------+------+-----+---------+----------------+
| Field      | Type         | Null | Key | Default | Extra          |
+------------+--------------+------+-----+---------+----------------+
| id         | int(11)      |      | PRI | NULL    | auto_increment |
| showingId  | int(11)      |      |     | 0       |                |
| seats      | int(11)      |      |     | 1       |                |
| bookedVia  | varchar(10)  |      |     |         |                |
| amount     | int(11)      |      |     | 0       |                |
| payMethod  | varchar(4)   |      |     |         |                |
| cardNo     | varchar(10)  | YES  |     | NULL    |                |
| name       | varchar(255) | YES  |     | NULL    |                |
| cardType   | varchar(10)  | YES  |     | NULL    |                |
| pickedUp   | int(11)      |      |     | 0       |                |
+------------+--------------+------+-----+---------+----------------+
10 rows in set (0.00 sec)

mysql> _
```

Figure 10-6: MySQL console showing the structure of the booking table

Now that the tables have been created, some example data can be inserted. Run the `insert_data.sql` file in the way described previously.

A user that our application will utilize to access the database can now be created. Again there is a convenient script located in the `\tomcatcinemas\db` directory called `create_user.sql`. Execute this file in the same way. The user created is called `tccinemaUser` with a default password of `password`. This user only has access to the `tomcatcinemas` database.

Create a new context

To let Tomcat know about the application being set up, a new context is required.

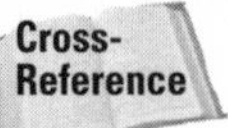

For a description of how contexts are defined within Tomcat, refer to Chapter 8. Chapter 7 also illustrates the use of a template `context.xml` file.

Create a file called `template.context.xml` and place it in the project's root directory, in other words, at the same level as the source directory. Add the following lines shown in Listing 10-1 to the file:

Listing 10-1: template.context.xml file

```
<Context
debug="5"
displayName="Tomcat Cinemas Application"
docBase="@context.docbase@"
path="@context.path@"
reloadable="true"
useNaming="true" >
<Loader checkInterval="1" />
</Context>
```

These lines create a template for how the context will look when it is installed. The next section is required to complete this process.

Create web.xml

Create a file called `web.xml` and place it in the `web/WEB-INF` directory of the application directory structure. Then add the following to this file:

Listing 10-2: Web.xml for Tomcat Cinemas

```
<?xml version="1.0" encoding="ISO-8859-1" ?>

<!DOCTYPE web-app
  PUBLIC "-//Sun Microsystems, Inc.//DTD Web Application 2.3//EN"
  "http://java.sun.com/dtd/web-app_2_3.dtd" >

<web-app>
    <icon>
    </icon>
    <display-name>Tomcat Cinemas Application</display-name>
    <description>
        This is the Tomcat Cinemas Application
    </description>
</web-app>
```

For a full description of `web.xml` refer to Chapter 3 of this book.

Setting up Ant for Tomcat Cinemas

Ant will be used extensively in developing this application. This includes using Ant to communicate with the Tomcat server to perform certain administrative functions.

This chapter discusses the use of Ant in the context of this application only. For a more thorough explanation on working with Ant and Tomcat make sure you read Chapter 5. It is assumed you have followed the instructions to integrate Ant with the Tomcat manager application, as described in Chapter 2.

To set up Ant for the Tomcat Cinemas application, follow these steps:

1. Get a build.xml file

The accompanying download for this chapter contains the appropriate `build.xml` file to use when building this application. Place this file in the `/tomcatcinemas/` directory of your development directory structure.

2. Create a build.properties file

Create a file called `build.properties` and place it in the user's home directory. Open this file up for editing and enter the following lines:

```
manager.password=<password>
manager.username=<user name>
manager.url=<url to access manager application>
catalina.home=<full path to tomcat installation>
```

You should have remembered the manager application's user name and password from when you installed Tomcat. The `manager.url` property would be something like `http://localhost:8080/manager` and the full path to the Tomcat installation would be along the lines of `C:/Tomcat`, for instance, where you installed Tomcat. (Note the /.)

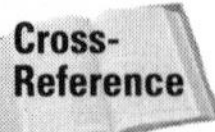

Refer to Chapter 5 for a brief explanation of how to establish where the User home directory is via Ant's `user.home` property.

You will use the `build.xml` file, via Ant, to build the application. The `build.xml` file uses `build.properties` to find the installation of Tomcat and communicate with its manager application.

Database Connectivity

We're not quite done yet! The application must of course communicate with the database via a JDBC driver. In this book we use the MySQL JDBC driver, Connector/J, which can be downloaded from `www.mysql.com` under Products. We use version 2.0.14 in this application.

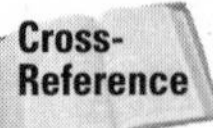

Chapter 2 explains how to install and configure the driver that is used in this application. If you haven't already done so, you should read that chapter now.

For our application to communicate with MySQL, using the specified driver, we need to make some minor modifications to the `template.context.xml` file we created earlier. In doing this we are configuring the correct user, password, and driver for a connection to the database. We also give this resource a unique name that can be referenced by the `web.xml` file as well as internally in our application.

The following lines should be added between the `<Context...></Context>` tags of the `template.context.xml` file:

Listing 10-3: Addition to template.context.xml

```
<Resource name="jdbc/TomcatCinemasDb" auth="Container"
type="javax.sql.DataSource"/>
<ResourceParams name="jdbc/TomcatCinemasDb">
```

```
<parameter>
  <name>username</name>
  <value>tccinemaUser</value>
</parameter>
<parameter>
  <name>password</name>
  <value>password</value>
</parameter>
<parameter>
  <name>driverClassName</name>
  <value>com.mysql.jdbc.Driver</value>
</parameter>
<parameter>
  <name>url</name>
  <value>jdbc:mysql://localhost/tomcatcinemas</value>
</parameter>
<parameter>
  <name>maxActive</name>
  <value>100</value>
</parameter>
<parameter>
  <name>maxIdle</name>
  <value>10</value>
</parameter>
</ResourceParams>
```

These lines may need to be configured slightly to suit your particular installation of MySQL. For instance, the location of the database and its name are defined in the `url` parameter, and the username and password of the Tomcat user are defined here also. If you used anything other than what was in the database scripts provided, you need to modify these parameters accordingly.

Note Note how the database name is defined in the URL parameter. When we deploy this application, the actual production system may have a different database name, like `bookingsystem` or something. As long as the tables are in there, it doesn't matter what name we put here. You can see from this how placing configuration information outside of the application is so powerful.

As part of the Data Source set up you also need to make an equivalent change to the `web.xml` file we created earlier. The changes have been bolded in the following listing:

Listing 10-4: **Web.xml file with reference to resource**

```
<?xml version="1.0" encoding="ISO-8859-1" ?>
<!DOCTYPE web-app
  PUBLIC "-//Sun Microsystems, Inc.//DTD Web Application 2.3//EN"
  "http://java.sun.com/dtd/web-app_2_3.dtd" >
```

Continued

Listing 10-4 *(continued)*

```
<web-app>
    <icon>
    </icon>
    <display-name>Tomcat Cinemas Application</display-name>
    <description>
        This is the Tomcat Cinemas Application
    </description>
     <resource-ref>
      <description>
        Resource reference
      </description>
      <res-ref-name>
        jdbc/TomcatCinemasDb
      </res-ref-name>
      <res-type>
        javax.sql.DataSource
      </res-type>
      <res-auth>
        Container
      </res-auth>
    </resource-ref>
</web-app>
```

Once this is completed you're almost ready to go.

Final Steps

We now need to execute an Ant task that prepares our context to be included by Tomcat. This task is defined in the `build.xml` file we created earlier.

Start up an instance of Tomcat and run the following command from a command prompt in the same directory you placed the `build.xml` file (all the Ant commands we run will be from this directory). This command is run using the following:

```
ant context
```

Once you have run this, your command prompt should look something like the one shown in Figure10-7.

Caution If you specified an incorrect `manager.url` property in your `build.properties` file running `ant context` will throw a `java.net.ConnectException`.

As you can see from Figure 10-7, this task actually runs three tasks for us:

- ✦ `prepare`. Takes the `template.context.xml` file created earlier and from this and creates a `context.xml file` in your `web/WEB-INF` directory.
- ✦ `compile`: Compiles any files placed within our source tree.
- ✦ `context`: Communicates with the running Tomcat server to create a context called `tomcatcinemas`.

```
F:\work\book\tomcatcinemas>ant context
Buildfile: build.xml

prepare:
     [copy] Copying 1 file to F:\work\book\tomcatcinemas\build\WEB-INF

compile:

context:
  [install] OK - Installed application from context file file:///F:\work\book\to
mcatcinemas/build/WEB-INF/context.xml


BUILD SUCCESSFUL
Total time: 3 seconds
F:\work\book\tomcatcinemas>_
```

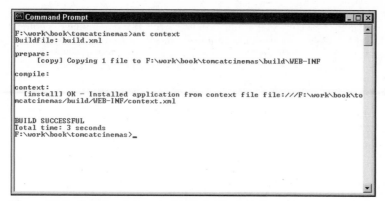

Figure 10-7: Running Ant context task for Tomcat Cinemas

Caution You need to run the `ant context` task each time the server is restarted. However if you make a change to a Java file, the context can be reloaded by using the `reload` target in the Ant script, without restarting the server.

Now that we have created all these files, changed them, and run some strange commands, how do we know if it all worked? Well we're going to execute another command to see if Tomcat knows about the new context. Run the list task in Ant (with the Tomcat server running) as:

```
ant list
```

This reveals if Tomcat considers the context to be running. The resulting output should look like the following, shown in Figure 10-8:

```
F:\work\book\tomcatcinemas>ant list
Buildfile: build.xml

list:
     [list] OK - Listed applications for virtual host localhost

     [list] /tomcatcinemas:running:0:F:\work\book\tomcatcinemas/build

     [list] /manager:running:0:../server/webapps/manager

     [list] /examples:running:0:examples

     [list] /tomcat-docs:running:0:F:\java\Tomcat4_1_12\webapps\tomcat-docs

     [list] /webdav:running:0:F:\java\Tomcat4_1_12\webapps\webdav

     [list] /admin:running:1:../server/webapps/admin

     [list] /:running:0:F:\java\Tomcat4_1_12\webapps\ROOT

BUILD SUCCESSFUL
Total time: 1 second
F:\work\book\tomcatcinemas>_
```

Figure 10-8: Results Ant list task showing the `tomcatcinemas` context as an application

If you can see `/tomcatcinemas` in the list then your context has been instantiated within Tomcat successfully. Notice that the line also points to the build directory. Your's should too. This is where Tomcat looks to get its files and resources from your development environment.

If you are installing the application from the download for this chapter, you should walk through the above steps to ensure everything is in its correct place. Running the context command will have hopefully compiled and deployed the application correctly, and you should now be able to browse to `http://<servername>:<port>/tomcatcinemas/admin` where `servername` and `port` are values appropriate for your installation of Tomcat.

Progress Report

We have now completed setting up our development environment for the Tomcat Cinemas project. We have:

- Created our source tree directory structure.
- Created our package structure for Java source files.
- Set up the database in MySQL by running the scripts included in the download available for this book.
- Created a `template.context.xml` file to define a context for Tomcat Cinemas.
- Created a `web.xml` file and placed it in our `web/WEB-INF` directory.
- Copied `build.xml` file and created its accomplice, `build.properties`, and placed them within the root directory of our project environment and the users home directory respectively.
- Modified `template.context.xml` and `web.xml` to include a Data Source pointing to the Tomcat Cinemas database in MySQL.
- Run the Ant task `context` in order to create a `context.xml` file in the `web/WEB-INF` directory and inform Tomcat of the new context we have created.

We are now ready to begin actually planning how the application will be structured using the MVC Model 2 architecture described in Chapter 1.

Model View Controller (Model 2) Architecture

Chapter 1 introduced the MVC architecture as a way of developing applications such as this one. Chapter 7 implemented a small application to illustrate. However, the implementation here involves more parts, allowing us to cater for its increased sophistication. For instance, having the database available means we must provide a means for it to be manipulated in a way that provides for the functionality of the application. This application will also make more use of validation techniques with the increased user input. As a result, our implementation for Tomcat Cinemas will use the following components:

- **Value Object** (Model): The value objects in our application correspond directly to our major database entities. For example, we will create a `BookingValue` value object that models the structure of the `Booking` entity in the database.
- **Handler** (Model): We will also create a series of handlers to deal with interactions of the application with the database. Typically there is one handler for each main entity or value object in the application, however we will also implement an extra handler to provide for logic requirements that span across multiple entities. A handler's role is to functionally manipulate the relationship between actions executed in the servlet and our value objects. For instance, we will have a `BookingHandler` class that will be responsible for creating, modifying, and listing `BookingValue` objects.

✦ **Servlet** (Controller): Our servlets will correspond functionally to the application and use handlers to manipulate value objects and provide JSP files with the appropriate resources to provide views to the user.

✦ **JSP** (View): The JSP files will be selectively included by the servlets to provide a view of the application.

Figure 10-9 illustrates this relationship together with the corresponding flow through the application:

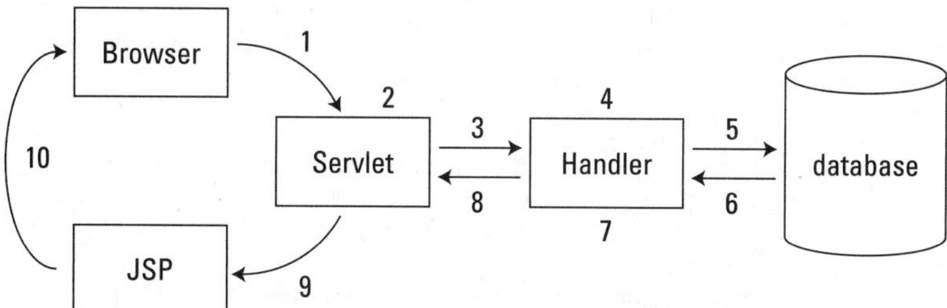

Figure 10-9: Application Flow

For the purposes of this walkthrough assume the user is attempting to view a list of theatres.

1. The browser makes a request to the specific servlet.
2. The servlet interrogates the contents of the request and determines the appropriate action to take. In this case it would be something like: `listTheatres`.
3. The servlet calls the appropriate handler (`TheatreHandler`) to get a `Collection` of `TheatreValue` objects.
4. The handler receives the request for the list of `TheatreValue` objects.
5. The handler executes its connection to the database with the appropriate SQL command.
6. In response to its SQL command the handler receives a `ResultSet` object from the JDBC driver (via the database), representing a list of rows from the Theatre table.
7. The handler packages the result set into a `Collection` of `TheatreValue` objects.
8. The `Collection` of `TheatreValue` objects is passed to the servlet.
9. The servlet receives the `Collection` and allocates it to the scope of an appropriate JSP file.
10. The JSP file generates the appropriate HTML to display in the browser as part of the server's response.

Now that we know the structure of the application we can begin to put pen to paper (so to speak) and start coding!

Beginning Development

Before we launch into specific functionality for the Tomcat Cinemas application, we need to establish some key components of the application, value objects, handlers and servlets. It is not possible to fully list the source code for all these components so you will only find an example of a value object and handler listed in this chapter. Individual methods of handlers and value objects may be referenced in the coming discussions and so for a comprehensive picture of the development of this application it is highly recommended that you download the full application from the Wiley Web site and follow the development with the complete source code available to you.

Value Objects

As mentioned before, our value objects are the application's representation of the real thing, their properties being mapped to the database in a logical fashion. Our value objects are very simple beans. They represent the data stored, or about to be stored, and very little else. They are merely an organized data structure for the application. These objects have a set of private properties, each of which can be set or get via two methods.

Constructing a value object is accomplished in such a way that is convenient for the application. For instance we may want to build a value object as a result of a query on the database. For this we provided a `ResultSet` constructor. A `ResultSet` object is simply a listing of records found as a result of an SQL transaction against the database. It is therefore convenient to use this to construct an instance of a value object. Two other constructors are also provided, one to create a value object with the default values, in other words, a blank constructor, and another, which is fully parameterized, allowing the developer to specify its full value at construction.

Note There is no value object implemented for prices. Prices merely represent reference data for the application to function and there is no requirement for this information to be changed via the application. It is placed in the database and not hard coded in the application for convenience and flexibility. Therefore, should prices need to be changed in the future, the database can be changed directly and the application will behave as desired.

Each value object may also have various helper methods that make conversion from a typical parameter type to the corresponding property type a little easier.

Listing 10-5 contains the source code for one of the value objects, `FilmValue`. To create this object, create a file called `FilmValue.java` and place it in the `src/bible/tomcat/tccinemas/` directory of the application source tree, then add the following:

Listing 10-5: FilmValue Object

```
package bible.tomcat.tccinemas;
import java.sql.*;
import java.util.ArrayList;

public class FilmValue
{
    private long _id = 0;
    private String _name = "";
    private int _length = 0;
    private boolean _active = true;

    public FilmValue()
```

```
{
}
public FilmValue(long id, String name, int length, boolean active)
{
    setId(id);
    setName(name);
    setLength(length);
    setActive(active);
}

public FilmValue(ResultSet rs)
    throws java.sql.SQLException
{
    setId(rs.getLong("id"));
    setName(rs.getString("name"));
    setLength(rs.getInt("length"));
    setActive(rs.getBoolean("active"));
}

//setters
public void setId(long id)
{
    _id = id;
}

public void setName(String name)
{
    _name = name;
}

public void setLength(int length)
{
    _length = length;
}

public void setActive(boolean active)
{
    _active = active;
}

public void setActive(int active)
{
    _active = (active == 1 ? true : false);
}

//getters
public long getId()
{
    return _id;
}
```

Continued

Listing 10-5 *(continued)*

```
    public String getName()
    {
        return _name;
    }

    public int getLength()
    {
        return _length;
    }

    public boolean getActive()
    {
        return _active;
    }

    public void validate()
        throws ValidationException
    {
        ArrayList errors = new ArrayList();

        if((_name == null) || _name.length() < 1)
        {
            errors.add("Name cannot be empty");
        }

        if((_name != null) && _name.length() > 255)
        {
            errors.add("Name cannot be more than 255 characters long");
        }

        if(_length < 1)
        {
            errors.add("A film cannot be less than 1 minute in length");
        }
        else if(_length > 150)
        {
            errors.add("A film cannot be over 2.5 hours long");
        }

        if(errors.size() > 0)
        {
            ValidationException ve = new ValidationException();
            ve.setErrors(errors);
            throw ve;
        }
    }
}
```

The third constructor listed takes a `ResultSet` object as its only parameter, then populates the value object directly. Most of the remaining methods of the class are dedicated to setting and getting the individual properties.

Each value object in our application uses much the same structure. You will find the `ResultSet` constructor especially convenient when we develop our handlers. By including this constructor we can pass our `ResultSet` object from the database query and populate `FilmValue` objects directly.

The last method shown in the Listing 10-5 is the `validate` method. We call this method from the handler to ensure that the structure of the data we have received is legitimate. It throws a `ValidationException`. This is an exception we have invented to suit our purposes, as it contains a convenient list that allows us to add error text as the validation errors arise.

Creation of the `ValidationException` class is left as an exercise for the reader. In short you need to create an exception class with an internal `ArrayList` that can hold error messages. The class also needs to provide methods to add and retrieve error messages as required by the application. You can see the full source code for the `ValidationException` class by referring to the download for this chapter from the Wiley Web site.

We will see the `ValidationException` used more in the servlets. The `validate` method in the value object does not represent the entire set of validation checks we are running against instances of this object. Rather, these limited validation rules only check for missing or oversized values. Validation concerning business rules and constraints are dealt with in the handler.

Note You will notice in the `validate()` method of the `FilmValue` object that we add hard coded Strings (the error messages) to the `ValidationException` before throwing it. If we wanted to change the wording of one of these error messages we would have to make the change and then recompile the class. To avoid this situation, the error messages could be placed in a `messages.properties` file and this file then placed within the application's CLASSPATH. These messages could then be referenced and obtained via a key and then added to the `ValidationException`. Improving the application in this way is left as an exercise for the reader.

Other value objects in the application are:

- `BookingValue`
- `ShowingValue`
- `TheatreValue`

These value object classes all reside in the `bible.tomcat.tccinemas` package.

As Figure 10-9 suggests, our value objects will be tossed around the application from handler all the way forward to the JSP page. They are the mobile structure of our data.

As most of the value objects are the same, developing those remaining is left as an exercise for the reader. Or you can download the application in its entirety from the Wiley Web site.

Now that we have a set of objects that represent our main entities, we need some tools to manipulate them. This is where our handlers come into the picture.

Handlers

Our handlers are where the database interacts with the application or where some processing is completed to provide logic for the application. They are not concerned with how the application flows or which forms are presented on which JSP page. They are mostly focused on acting as a join between the database and the application.

Messages sent to handlers are simple requests: "save this," "get me these," "update this object." In response the handler replies with the desired result of the request; "Here's a collection of objects," "Yes, I've updated that object" or with errors: "I can't update this, there are errors, here are the errors."

Subclass Our Main Handlers

Because our handlers will all need access to common resources, such as database connections and some methods, it is logical to subclass a top-level handler (let's call it `Handler`) into our specific handler implementations on an entity basis. This is illustrated in Figure 10-10.

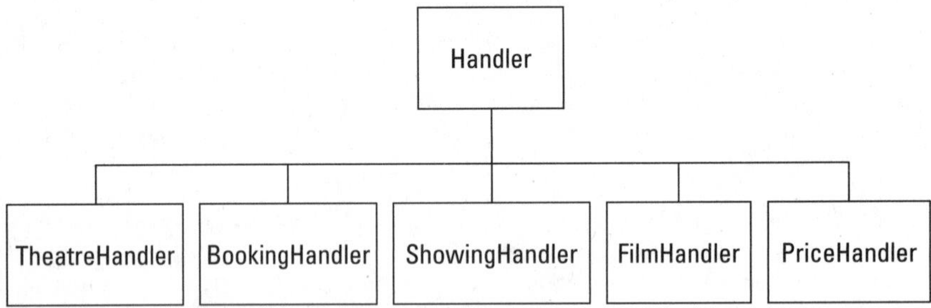

Figure 10-10: Top-level `Handler` object and subclasses

As you can see in Figure 10-10, each entity has its own specific handler. Each handler has access to the resources provided by the top-level object, `Handler`. One such resource is a database connection. Listing 10-6 shows the code for the top level `Handler` class and the `Connection` object it provides. To create this class create a file called `Handler.java` and place it in the `src/bible/tomcat/tccinemas/` directory of the application source tree, then enter the following code:

Listing 10-6: Handler Class

```
package bible.tomcat.tccinemas;

import java.sql.*;
import javax.sql.DataSource;
import javax.naming.*;

public abstract class Handler
{
    private DataSource _ds = null;
```

```
    public Handler()
    {
        init();
    }

    protected void init()
    {
        try
        {
            Class.forName("com.mysql.jdbc.Driver").newInstance();
            Context initCtx = new InitialContext();
            Context envCtx = (Context) initCtx.lookup("java:comp/env");
            _ds = (DataSource)envCtx.lookup("jdbc/TomcatCinemasDb");
        }
        catch(javax.naming.NamingException ne)
        {
            ne.printStackTrace();
        }
        catch(ClassNotFoundException cnfe)
        {
            cnfe.printStackTrace();
        }
        catch(InstantiationException ie)
        {
            ie.printStackTrace();
        }
        catch(IllegalAccessException iae)
        {
            iae.printStackTrace();
        }
    }

    protected Connection getConnection()
        throws java.sql.SQLException
    {
        return _ds.getConnection();
    }
}
```

The code related to the database connection has been bolded. Let's step through the following code fragments.

```
Context initCtx = new InitialContext();
```

This line creates a new `Context` object using its blank constructor.

```
Context envCtx = (Context) initCtx.lookup("java:comp/env");
```

We then initialize a new context representing our Tomcat Server environment by using the first context to look it up. This gives us our environment context.

```
_ds = (DataSource)envCtx.lookup("jdbc/TomcatCinemasDb");
```

We then give our DataSource object a value by using the environment context to lookup the DataSource resource we specified in the template.context.xml file. Think of the DataSource as a database connection waiting to be sought and used.

Our subclasses now have access to this getConnection() method in Handler. They will use this as they execute commands on the database.

An Example Handler

Like value objects, all our handlers are largely structured in the same way. The following types of methods are therefore implemented in each:

1. create: Methods that create a new row(s) in the database.
2. update: Methods that update an existing row(s) in the database.
3. get object: A method to get an individual version of the object, such as a single showing in the database.
4. get objects: Methods that retrieve a listing of rows based on certain parameters.

In developing the application we may create more methods in particular handlers to cater for specific functionality, however, these are the basic type of methods used.

Note It is assumed that the reader has an understanding of how Java works with databases.

Listing 10-7 shows the code for the FilmHandler in its entirety. To create this class, create a file called FilmHandler.java with the contents of Listing 10-7 and place it in the src/bible/tomcat/tccinemas/ directory of the application source tree:

Listing 10-7: FilmHandler Object

```
package bible.tomcat.tccinemas;

import java.sql.*;
import java.sql.Timestamp;
import java.util.ArrayList;
import java.util.Date;
import bible.tomcat.tccinemas.util.*;

public class FilmHandler
    extends Handler
{
    public FilmHandler()
    {
        super();
    }

    protected FilmValue create(FilmValue filmValue)
        throws SQLException,ValidationException
    {
        StringBuffer sql = new StringBuffer();
```

```
        sql.append("INSERT INTO film (name,length,active)");
        sql.append(" VALUES (?,?,?)");

        Connection conn = getConnection();
        PreparedStatement ps = conn.prepareStatement(sql.toString());

        ps.setString(1,filmValue.getName());
        ps.setInt(2,filmValue.getLength());
        ps.setBoolean(3,filmValue.getActive());
        ps.executeUpdate();

        ps.close();
        conn.close();

        return filmValue;
    }

    protected FilmValue update(FilmValue filmValue)
        throws SQLException, ValidationException
    {
        StringBuffer sql = new StringBuffer();
        sql.append("UPDATE film SET name=?,length=?,active=?");
        sql.append(" WHERE id=?");

        Connection conn = getConnection();
        PreparedStatement ps = conn.prepareStatement(sql.toString());

        ps.setString(1,filmValue.getName());
        ps.setInt(2,filmValue.getLength());
        ps.setBoolean(3,filmValue.getActive());
        ps.setLong(4,filmValue.getId());

        ps.executeUpdate();

        ps.close();
        conn.close();

        return filmValue;
    }

    public FilmValue getFilm(long id)
        throws SQLException
    {
        FilmValue rv = null;
        String sql = "SELECT * FROM film WHERE id=?";
        Connection conn = getConnection();
        PreparedStatement ps = conn.prepareStatement(sql);

        ps.setLong(1,id);
        ResultSet rs = ps.executeQuery();
```

Continued

Listing 10-7 *(continued)*

```
        if(rs.next())
        {
            rv = new FilmValue(rs);
        }

        ps.close();
        rs.close();
        conn.close();

        return rv;
    }

    public ArrayList getFilms(boolean activeOnly)
        throws SQLException
    {
        ArrayList rv = new ArrayList();
        String sql = "";

        if(activeOnly)
        {
            sql = "SELECT * FROM film WHERE active=1";
        }
        else
        {
            sql = "SELECT * FROM film";
        }

        Connection conn = getConnection();
        Statement stmt = conn.createStatement();
        ResultSet rs = stmt.executeQuery(sql);

        while(rs.next())
        {
            rv.add(new FilmValue(rs));
        }

        rs.close();
        stmt.close();
        conn.close();

        return rv;
    }
}
```

Let's walk through the methods of `FilmHandler` one by one.

```
public FilmHandler()
```

This is a simple constructor that calls the constructor of its parent class, `Handler`.

```
protected FilmValue create(FilmValue filmValue)
    throws SQLException,ValidationException
```

This is the method we use to create rows in the film table in the database. It returns the created `FilmValue` object. One way to enhance this would be to have the newly created value's `id` number also in the object. However, this would in most cases tie us to the database we are using because such operations generally vary between database products and drivers.

This method is protected as we don't want objects from outside the package `bible.tomcat.tccinemas` executing it. Instead, calls to `create` will be through the `BusinessHandler` explained further on.

```
protected FilmValue update(FilmValue filmValue)
    throws SQLException, ValidationException
```

This is similar to the previous method, except here we are updating a row in the film table.

```
public FilmValue getFilm(long id)
    throws SQLException
```

We use this method to retrieve an individual `FilmValue` object by passing the `id` number of the object required. We would therefore use this method when we start to edit a `FilmValue` object.

```
public ArrayList getFilms(boolean activeOnly)
    throws SQLException
```

When we are presenting a list of films this method is used. The `boolean` parameter allows the specification of including only the active films. A false value would include all films regardless. For example, parameters like this come in handy when developing the JSP page to create a new showing. To create a showing a list of films is required, however this list shouldn't include any films that are not active.

Note `java.sql.PreparedStatement` objects are generally considered good practice and using the `java.sql.Statement` object is considered '"not as good" practice. There are various performance and convenience advantages to using `PreparedStatement`.

There are associated handlers for each of the entities we have discussed in the application:

- `ShowingHandler`
- `BookingHandler`
- `TheatreHandler`
- `FilmHandler`
- `PriceHandler`

The source files for all these handlers reside in the `src/bible/tomcat/tccinemas` directory of the source tree.

As the basic structure for these handlers is basically the same for each (with the exception of the `PriceHandler`), developing the remaining handlers is left as an exercise for the reader. You can also download the entire application from Wiley's Web site.

PriceHandler

We will use `PriceHandler` in the application to determine the appropriate per ticket price for bookings to theatres. The application does not require the ability to create new instances of prices, or to edit individual prices. Therefore the methods implemented in this class will only service look up type requests. For instance if we want to know the per-ticket price of a booking in Theatre A, the `PriceHandler` would determine Theatre A's type, and then do an appropriate lookup on the `PRICE` table and return an appropriate figure. You will notice that no value object is implemented for prices. The signatures for the two `PriceHandler` methods implemented are:

```
public int getPriceForTheatre(TheatreValue tv)
        throws SQLException

public int getPriceForTheatre(String type)
        throws SQLException
```

The method `getPriceForTheatre(TheatreValue)` calls the second method but with the type of Theatre it was passed. This on forwarding of the method call provides flexibility in that if there is a situation where no `TheatreValue` is available to make the `PriceHandler` call, however we have a theatre type only, the required pricing data can still be obtained by calling the second method directly. You will notice other examples of this technique throughout the applications code. The `PriceHandler.java` file resides in the `src/bible/tomcat/tccinemas` directory of the source tree.

Types of Handlers

When developing this type of application it is important to consider the types of handlers we are implementing and how *interaction between* those handlers should occur.

This is brought out when we consider the type of entity that each handler may represent. For instance the `FilmHandler` only deals with films, and the `TheatreHandler` only deals with theatres. However the `BookingHandler` deals with an entity that is itself an aggregate of booking information with a direct relationship to a showing. And the `ShowingHandler` deals with an entity that is an aggregate of showing information with relationships to a film and a theatre.

This situation imposes a hierarchy of handlers that dictates how calls from one handler to another can take place.

- ✦ `FilmHandler`, `TheatreHandler` and `PriceHandler`
- ✦ `ShowingHandler`
- ✦ `BookingHandler`

Generally speaking calls from one handler to another can go up this list. `BookingHandler` can make calls to the `ShowingHandler`, where as the `ShowingHandler` should not call on `BookingHandler`. And the `FilmHandler`, `TheatreHandler` and `PriceHandler` should not rely on any other handlers in the system.

Often there will be cases where functionality in the application will require the input of handlers that would otherwise infringe on this rule.

For instance if you need to check how many seats are available in a showing, you may decide to place a method for this requirement in the ShowingHandler. If you think about our description of the application so far you will see that solving this requirement will require the use of the BookingHandler and the TheatreHandler, whilst referencing the details of a ShowingValue the method is passed. Therefore the ShowingHandler would now be reliant on the BookingHandler and the TheatreHandler. This breaks the hierarchy above.

To avoid this interdependence we can implement the use of a BusinessHandler (residing in the bible.tomcat.tccinemas package) to perform the logic required, and keep the structure imposed by this hierarchy consistent with the rules set out above. The BusinessHandler simplifies a business rule by calling all the necessary low-level handlers.

A Special Case: BusinessHandler

The BusinessHandler in a way acts as a kind of façade, fielding requests from the servlets that require the use of more than one handler or that require some sort of preliminary processing such as validation. This extends to otherwise simple operations such as updating a theatre. For instance to make a theatre inactive we need to ensure that there are no showings allocated to it—functionality from the ShowingHandler is therefore required. Therefore we need to use the BusinessHandler to forward the call through to the TheatreHandler, performing some validation on the way by checking if there are any showings allocated. In making this request through BusinessHandler, we can also ensure that the validate method of the TheatreValue is called and any validation errors found are thrown back to the calling servlet before the update method of the TheatreHandler is invoked.

If you recall the FilmHandler we described earlier, the update and create methods were protected, they cannot be called directly by the servlet (the servlet will reside in the bible.tomcat.tccinemas.servlet package). Instead the BusinessHandler is used to forward calls through to them and provide some extra processing along the way.

As an example the following is a fragment from the BusinessHandler that shows the class definition and the method that acts as a façade to the create method of the FilmHandler.

```
package bible.tomcat.tccinemas;
...
public class BusinessHandler
{
    ...
    public static FilmValue createFilm(FilmValue filmValue)
        throws SQLException, ValidationException
    {
        filmValue.validate();
        FilmHandler fh = new FilmHandler();
        return fh.create(filmValue);
    }
    ...
}
```

We will see the BusinessHandler being used for many such operations in this application.

BusinessHandler is not represented in Figure 10-10, as it does not extend the Handler class. To see the methods implemented in BusinessHandler download the complete application from Wiley's Web site.

Servlets

Servlets control the flow of our application. They take a request from the browser and determine the appropriate action to take. This may include collecting lists of objects, executing updates, creating objects or simply redirecting to another part of the application. They then pass objects required for display to the JSP pages they include. We can see therefore that servlets become the controller portion of our MVC implementation. JSP pages on the other hand fulfill the view part of the MVC.

Like handlers, there are various common methods that are useful to all servlets. Therefore it is convenient to create a parent class that the remaining servlets will be subclasses of; this parent class is the Controller servlet.

For this application the functionality controlled by each of the remaining servlets can be broken up in any number of ways. We have decided to map the servlet structure broadly to the use cases in the system. For instance, some of the use cases deal with an administrator's use of the system. The AdminController servlet deals with all administrative functionality in the system such as adding and modifying films, theatres, and showings. Figure 10-11 shows the class structure of our servlets:

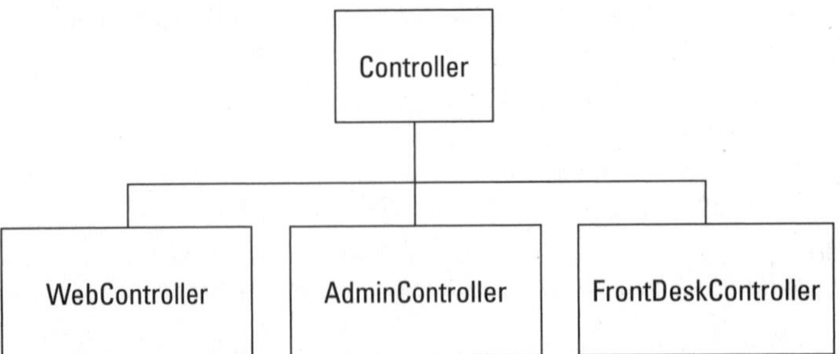

Figure 10-11: Class structure of servlets

The class structure in Figure 10-11 shows the break up of the application's servlets by functionality in the application. Each servlet is described in detail below:

- ✦ Controller: (Controller.java) The top-level servlet is declared as abstract because it will never be directly instantiated by the server. It contains methods that are used by all the child servlets, including standard servlet methods such as destroy(), init(), and doGet() that are simply inherited to the following classes. Because we want to deal with all requests in much the same way, regardless of whether they are GET requests or POST requests, our doGet() method simply passes control onto the doPost() method within the following classes. This servlet also contains a commonly used method for including our JSP pages, which typically occurs as the output of one the actions in each servlet. This method is called performInclude.

✦ **`WebController`:** (`WebController.java`) The `WebController` servlet deals with interactions that involve users on the Internet making bookings and viewing the list of available showings.

✦ **`AdminController`:** (`AdminController.java`) The `AdminController` handles system interactions that administrators perform, such as creating and editing Films and Theatres or creating Showings.

✦ **`FrontDeskController`:** (`FrontDeskController.java`) The `FrontDeskController` deals with interactions that a staff member of Tomcat Cinemas will partake in, such as creating bookings.

All servlets reside in the `bible.tomcat.tccinemas.servlet` package. Having our servlets structured in this way provides for future security and authentication requirements that the application might require.

Registering a Servlet with Tomcat

Once we have built a servlet, or we need to test some functionality in it, we need to tell Tomcat. As you learned in Chapter 3, this is simply a matter of adding a couple of entries to your application's `web.xml` file (located in `web/WEB-INF`). The `web.xml` entry for the `AdminController` is found in Listing 10-8.

Listing 10-8: Web.xml entry for AdminController Servlet

```
......
    <servlet>
        <servlet-name>admin</servlet-name>
        <description>
            Admin Controller Servlet
        </description>
        <servlet-class>
            bible.tomcat.tccinemas.servlet.AdminController
        </servlet-class>
    </servlet>
......
    <servlet-mapping>
        <servlet-name>admin</servlet-name>
        <url-pattern>/admin</url-pattern>
    </servlet-mapping>
......
```

Cross-Reference

Go back to Chapter 3 to find out what the individual entries in `web.xml` mean.

Once you have developed, or at least have a starting point, for each servlet, add entries such as this to the `web.xml` file.

performInclude in the Controller Servlet

As mentioned before, the parent servlet, `Controller`, provides an important method to be used in all the subclass servlets. This method is displayed in Listing 10-9 within our starting shell of the `Controller` servlet, and then explained. To create the `Controller` servlet, create a file called `Controller.java` and place it in the `src/bible/tomcat/tccinemas/servlet` directory of the source tree.

Listing 10-9: Controller servlet shell

```
package bible.tomcat.tccinemas.servlet;

import javax.servlet.*;
import javax.servlet.http.*;
import java.io.*;
import java.sql.SQLException;
import java.util.ArrayList;
import java.util.Date;
import bible.tomcat.tccinemas.*;
import bible.tomcat.tccinemas.util.*;

public abstract class Controller
    extends HttpServlet
{
    protected final String ADMIN_MENU_PAGE = "menu.jsp";

    public void init(ServletConfig config)
        throws ServletException
    {
        super.init(config);
    }

    public void destroy()
    {
    }

    protected void doGet(HttpServletRequest request,
                         HttpServletResponse response)
        throws ServletException, java.io.IOException
    {
        doPost(request,response);
    }

    protected void performInclude(String incPath,
                                  HttpServletRequest req,
                                  HttpServletResponse res)
        throws ServletException, IOException
    {
```

```
        if (incPath != null)
        {
            req.setAttribute("servletPath", getFullServletPath(req));
            RequestDispatcher rd = req.getRequestDispatcher(incPath);
            rd.include(req, res);
        }
    }

    protected String getFullServletPath(HttpServletRequest req)
    {
        String servlet = req.getServletPath();
        String ctxPath = req.getContextPath();
        return (ctxPath + servlet);
    }
}
```

As mentioned before the `Controller` servlet will house methods used by more than one of the subclass servlets in this application, amongst these methods are the standard servlet methods `doGet()`, which simply passes the request and response objects onto the child servlet's `doPost()` method. The `init()` and `destroy()` methods are also found here.

The exact purpose of the `performInclude` method will become clearer as we discuss the instantiated servlets themselves. This method receives three parameters, the familiar request and response objects and a string, `incPath`, which represents the JSP page we will be including.

After checking that `incPath` is not null, in other words, that there is a JSP page specified, the path of the servlet we are using is added to the request so we can access it in the JSP page. As we shall see later on we can access this string in the JSP page via the variable name `servletPath`. This value is constructed via the method `getFullServletPath()` which appears below the `performInclude` method in the Listing. The `performInclude` method then begins its important job of including the JSP page we have specified.

`RequestDispatcher` is designed to pass requests onto other resources such as servlets or JSP pages. Behind the scenes the object is created by the servlet container, in our case Tomcat, as a wrapper around the resource it is sending the request too[1]. Before we call this method (`performInclude`) our servlet will have added other resources to the request object so they can be included on the next JSP page. For example we may need to place a `Film Value` object as a resource for display on a JSP page. It is these resources we are forwarding to the JSP page via the `RequestDispatcher`. Figure 10-12 attempts to visualize this process for you.

Passing resources to the JSP page for a particular task is an important concept to understand. It is used frequently in this application.

As the application expands, the `Controller` servlet houses other methods that are used by more than one servlet. For instance, when we need a list of showings, the child servlets require a common method to get such lists. This method is placed in the `Controller` servlet so it can be accessed by the servlets below.

---

[1] javax.servlet. Request Dispatcher javadoc entry, J2EE 1.3

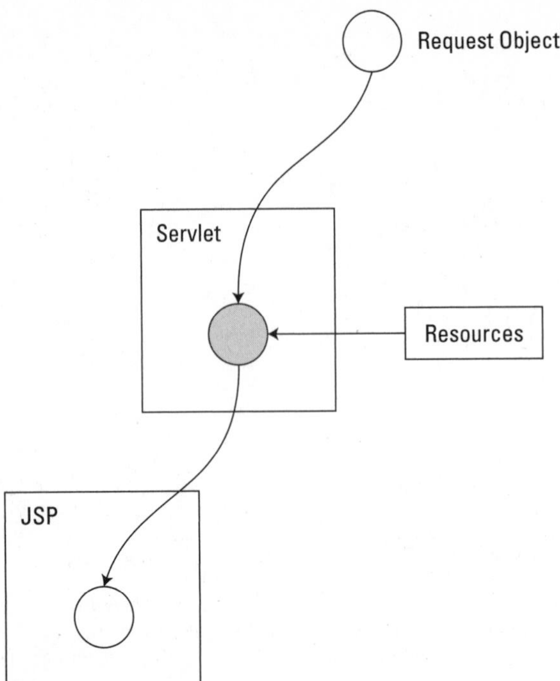

Figure 10-12: `RequestDispatcher` passing resources previously added to the `request` object to the JSP page

Implementing Administrative Functionality

With our `Controller` servlet, handlers and value objects established we can now begin implementing some of the functionality required by the administrative areas of the application.

Adding a Theatre

`AdminController` deals with many interactions in this application, and many of them follow a similar pattern but utilize different resources and pass their information on to different JSP pages. We are going to start with the shell of our `AdminController` and then add the functionality for a simple interaction: adding a new theatre. To create the `AdminController` servlet, create a file called `AdminController.java` and place it in the `src/bible/tomcat/tccinemas/servlet` directory of the application source tree, then enter the code in Listing 10-10:

Listing 10-10: Shell for AdminController servlet

```
package bible.tomcat.tccinemas.servlet;

import javax.servlet.*;
import javax.servlet.http.*;
import java.io.*;
import java.sql.SQLException;
import java.util.ArrayList;
import java.util.Date;
import bible.tomcat.tccinemas.*;
import bible.tomcat.tccinemas.util.*;

public class AdminController
    extends Controller
{
    protected void doPost(HttpServletRequest request,
                          HttpServletResponse response)
        throws ServletException, java.io.IOException
    {
        response.setContentType("text/html");
        PrintWriter out = response.getWriter();
        HttpSession thisSession = request.getSession(true);
        String action = request.getParameter("action");
        String incPath = ADMIN_MENU_PAGE;

        if(action == null)
        {
            action = "menu";
        }

        if(action.equals("menu"))
        {
            incPath = ADMIN_MENU_PAGE;
            request.setAttribute("title",
                          "Tomcat Cinemas Administration Menu");
        }
        else if(action.equals("addTheatre"))
        {

        }
        request.setAttribute("action",action);
        performInclude(incPath,request,response);
    }
}
```

See Listing 10-8 to see how to register this servlet in `web.xml`.

The class begins with the familiar package declaration and essential imports. Because we have relegated all the other standard servlet methods to the `Controller` class, only the `doPost()` method remains in this child object. The `doPost()` method begins by setting up some preliminary items that may be required as we traverse through the flow of the servlet:

```
response.setContentType("text/html");
PrintWriter out = response.getWriter();
HttpSession thisSession = request.getSession(true);
String action = request.getParameter("action");
String incPath = ADMIN_MENU_PAGE;
```

Firstly the type of response we are expecting to output is established with `response.setContentType("text/html");`. The servlet then establishes an object, `PrintWriter`, in case we wish to print output directly from the servlet.

The servlet then acquires the user's current session object. This will be useful if and when we add some session-based variables such as persistent authentication information.

We then set up two strings that will be used throughout the flow control of the rest of the servlet, `action` and `incPath`. `action` represents the task to be performed by the servlet and `incPath` represents the JSP page we wish to include as a result of the `action`. The constant `ADMIN_MENU_PAGE` is initialized in Listing 10-9 above, it is a property of the `Controller` servlet and equates to `menu.jsp`. Remember that throughout this application all JSP pages are referenced in this way. As functionality is added, remember to add a reference to JSP pages in this manner to the `Controller` servlet.

This `menu.jsp` described above is simply a list of links to various parts of functionality that this servlet provides, as shown in Figure 10-13.

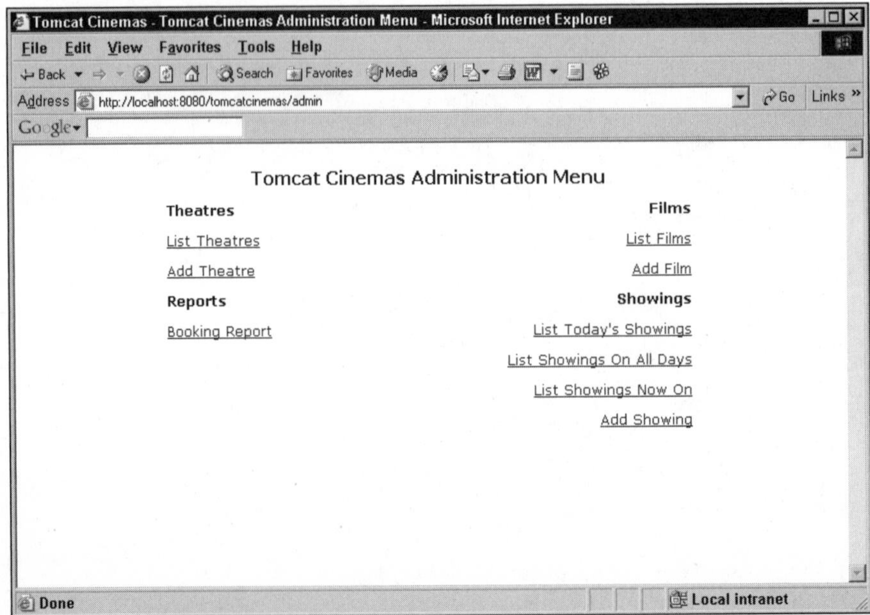

Figure 10-13: Administration menu of Tomcat Cinemas

Going back to the code in Listing 10-10, the action is passed to the servlet in the request, for instance `?action=<some action>`. A default action is usually provided if one is not found. The default action for the `AdminController` is `menu`, which shows the Administration Menu.

The menu is, not surprisingly, a single page listing the actions the administrator can complete, and linking appropriately to each. If you have set up the application from this chapter's download, you should be able to see this screen by browsing to: `http://localhost:8080/tomcatcinemas/admin`. Remember to change the host and port as appropriate for your environment.

Going back to Listing 10-10, the servlet then begins what will eventually be a large `if.. else if...` statement that decides on the activities to happen when each action is executed. In our case the only action that will result in anything so far is the `menu` action, the first block within the `if` statement:

```
if(action.equals("menu"))
{
...
```

For the purposes of this walkthrough we are going to build up the block inside the `add Theatre` action so that we can show the Add Theatre form page correctly. This part of the `if` statement shown originally in Listing 10-10 beneath the `menu` action, should now appear as:

```
...
else if(action.equals("addTheatre"))
{
    incPath = doAddTheatre(request,response, new TheatreValue());
    request.setAttribute("errors",new ArrayList());
}
...
```

As you can see, the value for `incPath` is assigned to the result of a method called `doAddTheatre(request,response,newTheatreValue())`. We will be implementing many such methods to deal with the specifics of each particular action. Typically these `do<Something>` methods perform these types of tasks:

- ✦ Adding resources to the request.
- ✦ Deciding on the JSP page to allocate.
- ✦ Perform some action against the database.

The `doAddTheatre()` method of the `AdminController` follows:

```
...
private String doAddTheatre(HttpServletRequest req,
                            HttpServletResponse res,
                            TheatreValue tv)
{
    String rv = ADMIN_ADD_THEATRE_PAGE;
    req.setAttribute("title","Add New Theatre");
    req.setAttribute("theatreValue",tv);
    return rv;
}
...
```

<jsp:useBean..../>

You may be wondering what happens when one of the `<jsp:useBean.../>` entries attempts to instantiate an object that has not been added to the request. If no such object can be found in the request, the missing object's default blank constructor is used to create one in its place. In cases where no such default constructor exists, for instance `java.lang.Boolean`, a `java.lang.InstantiationException` is thrown.

Add this method to the `AdminController` servlet now. Walking through this method tells us that the JSP page to be used is `ADMIN_ADD_THEATRE_PAGE` (`addTheatre.jsp` located in the `web/` directory). You would define this variable alongside the `ADMIN_MENU_PAGE` initialization in the `Controller` servlet. The method then adds two attributes to the `request` object as resources for the JSP page. These are given aliases that the JSP page can instantiate these objects as. The first is the title of the JSP page, the second is a default `TheatreValue` object. For now ignore the `TheatreValue`; its significance will appear soon.

Returning to the `addTheatre` action in the `if` block from above, another attribute is added to the request, an empty `ArrayList` to display errors in the JSP page. As we haven't encountered any errors yet, the list is empty and the JSP page will display no errors. The flow of the program then falls out of the `if` block and calls `performInclude` to effectively show the chosen JSP page to the browser. We can now step forward to the JSP page that this interaction relies on: `addTheatre.jsp`.

`addTheatre.jsp` will contain a simple form for entering theatre details. Above the form is an area where errors are displayed when incorrect information is entered in the form.

Create a file called `addTheatre.jsp` in the `web/` directory of the source tree. Within this file the first order of business is to import the required Java packages and instantiate the objects the page can use from the request it has just received. Listing 10-11 shows how this is achieved within the JSP page:

Listing 10-11: **Start of addTheatre.jsp**

```
<%@ page import = "java.util.*" %>
<%@ page import = "bible.tomcat.tccinemas.*" %>

<jsp:useBean id="title" class="java.lang.String" scope="request"/>
<jsp:useBean id="action" class="java.lang.String" scope="request"/>
<jsp:useBean id="errors" class="java.util.ArrayList" scope="request"/>
<jsp:useBean id="servletPath" class="java.lang.String" scope="request"/>
<jsp:useBean id="theatreValue" class="bible.tomcat.tccinemas.TheatreValue"
scope="request"/>
...
```

Note that the `id` parameter values match the aliases used when we added each object or attribute to the request. We can use these objects like we would use any type of object within the JSP page.

Once these are declared the main html/jsp body of the page can be started. After outputting the title String in the page's <title></title> tag, the JSP page iterates through any contents of the ArrayList errors. Remember the validate() method in the value object? It throws a homemade exception called ValidationException that contains an ArrayList of error messages. It is this ArrayList we may pass to this page if the user enters incorrect information in our form. The errors are presented in the following code in the JSP page. You will find code like this in most if not all the forms in this application:

```
...
<ul>
    <%for(int i=0; i < errors.size(); i++)
    {
        String msg = (String)errors.get(i);
    %>
        <li><%=msg%></li>
    <%
    }
    %>
</ul>
...
```

Below the errors listing, the form display begins. Within the add theatre form (addTheatre.jsp) we have a hidden form element called action, which, as you can guess, specifies the action to be executed when the form is submitted. The form declaration and this hidden element are as follows:

```
...
<form action="<%=servletPath%>" method="post">
<input type="hidden" name="action" value="addTheatreExe">
...
```

The servletPath variable translates to the path at which the servlet resides. This value was determined within the performInclude method in the Controller servlet. If you view the source of the page in your browser, the HTML appears as:

```
...
<form action="/tomcatcinemas/admin" method="post">
<input type="hidden" name="action" value="addTheatreExe">
...
```

We then display the form, using the TheatreValue to populate the fields with the appropriate values. The HTML/JSP for the name field follows:

```
...
<tr>
    <td><font face="verdana" size="2">Name</font></td>
    <td><input type="text" name="name" size="30" maxlength="100"
value="<%=theatreValue.getName()%>"></td>
</tr>
...
```

We repeat this for each of the editable components of a theatre. For instance we create a select list HTML component for the theatre type property with the following:

```
<tr>
    <td><font face="verdana" size="2">Type</font></td>
    <td><select name="type">
    <option value="A"
    <%=("A".equals(theatreValue.getType()) ? " selected" : "")%>>A
    </option>
    <option value="B"
    <%=("B".equals(theatreValue.getType()) ? " selected" : "")%>>B
    </option>
    <option value="C"
    <%=("C".equals(theatreValue.getType()) ? " selected" : "")%>>C
    </option>
    </select>
    </td>
</tr>
```

Note that each of the form elements has its value set to the equivalent `get` method in the object we are displaying. This ensures that were this form to be submitted and presented again with validation errors, the values would remain in the form's elements. Having a `TheatreValue` available for this page, on its first blank loading or its subsequent validation error loading ensures that the form elements represent the value of the object. This is the reason we added a `new TheatreValue()` as a new attribute to the request in the `doAddTheatre` method listed above.

When you have added form elements for each of the editable properties of a theatre, including name, type, capacity, and whether the theatre is active or inactive, we should be ready to build what we have created so far and view it in the browser. If you need help with the remaining form elements refer to the accompanying download for this chapter.

The First Build

Once the preceding code has been added to `AdminController.java` and `addTheatre.jsp` (in your `web/`directory) and the servlet is specified in the `web/WEB-INF/web.xml` file, you can actually compile a part of the application. You may have compiled using Ant already. We include instructions only at the end of the first piece of functionality, however you will need to use Ant in this way to compile and run the application as development progresses. If you haven't already, start up an instance of Tomcat and run the following command in the command prompt:

```
> ant context
```

You need to run this task each time the server is restarted. As explained previously, this invokes your context in the server from what was defined in the `template.context.xml`.

From now on until the next time the server is restarted you can just use the `ant compile` task to make your changes available to Tomcat. Remember, if you change Java files (not JSP or HTML files) you need to either restart the server (and then run `ant context` again), or simply run `ant reload`—this reloads the `tomcatcinemas` context and your changed Java files become available. The output of `ant reload` is shown in Figure 10-14.

If everything has compiled correctly you should now be able to see some output in your browser. Point your favorite browser to the following address:

```
http://<servername>:<port>/tomcatcinemas/admin?action=addTheatre
```

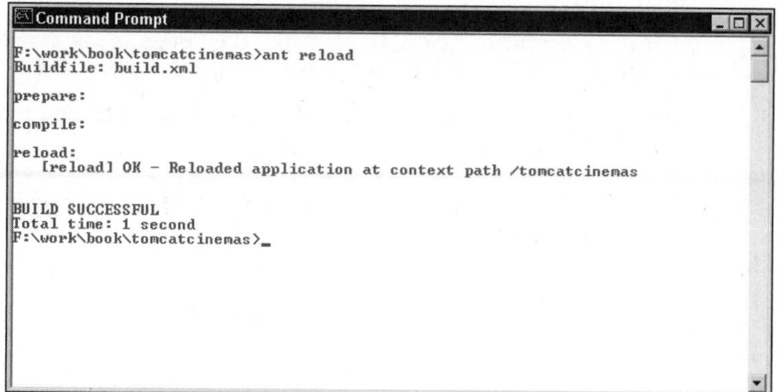

Figure 10-14: Ant reload task output

Where `<servername>` is the address of your server (for example, `localhost`) and `<port>` is the port your server is running on (`8080`). Or if you have downloaded the application and got it running you can simply use the Administration menu.

Hopefully you should have something resembling the form shown in Figure 10-15.

So far we have completed a simple action that sets up the ability to add a theatre by providing the appropriate form. Our task now is to make sure that when this form is submitted the application actually adds a theatre. This will be our `addTheatreExe` action.

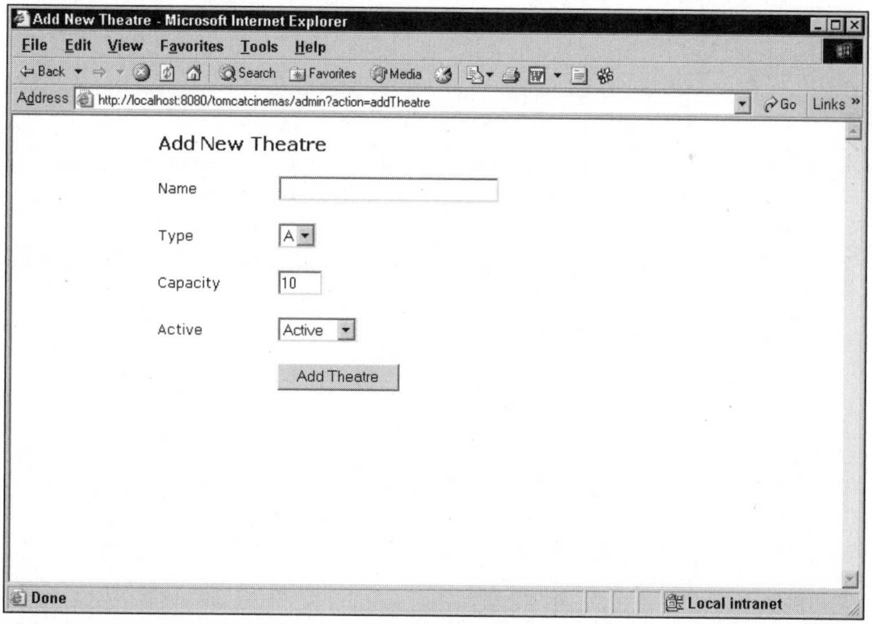

Add New Theatre - Microsoft Internet Explorer
Address http://localhost:8080/tomcatcinemas/admin?action=addTheatre

Add New Theatre

Name

Type A

Capacity 10

Active Active

Add Theatre

Figure 10-15: The `addTheatre.jsp` page appearing after an `addTheatre` action is executed

Once the user has added some details to the form and it is submitted we follow control of the process to the `AdminController` servlet once again (remember the form's action parameter is set to the servlet itself). This time, however, we have a new action, `addTheatreExe`.

Add the `addTheatreExe` action to the `AdminController` servlet as shown in Listing 10-12.

Listing 10-12: addTheatreExe Action in AdminController

```
...
else if(action.equals("addTheatreExe"))
{
    TheatreValue tv = getTheatreFromRequest(request);
    try
    {
        tv = doAddTheatreExe(request,response,tv);
        response.sendRedirect(getFullServletPath(request)
            + "?action=listTheatres");
        return;
    }
    catch(ValidationException ve)
    {
        incPath = doAddTheatre(request,response,tv);
        request.setAttribute("errors",ve.getErrors());
    }
}
...
```

Our first task in this action is to construct a `TheatreValue` object from the contents of the form that was just submitted. This action therefore relies on the `getTheatreFromRequest (request)` method to do this. This method is added to `AdminController` as shown in Listing 10-13.

Listing 10-13: getTheatreFromRequest Method in AdminController

```
    ...
    private TheatreValue getTheatreFromRequest(HttpServletRequest req)
    {
        TheatreValue rv = new TheatreValue();
        rv.setName(req.getParameter("name"));
        rv.setType(req.getParameter("type"));
        rv.setActive(("true".equals(req.getParameter("active")) ? true :
false));
        rv.setCapacity(NumberUtil.toInt(req.getParameter("capacity")));
        return rv;
    }
    ...
```

This method constructs the new `TheatreValue` object from the contents of the form, using the set methods defined in this value object.

Note You will note in Listing 10-13 we use a class called `NumberUtil` to convert the capacity figure from the request (which is a `String`) to an `int` before setting this property in the value object. `NumberUtil` is a class we have created to perform such actions, you can implement this class yourself or have a look at the `bible.tomcat.tccinemas.util.NumberUtil` class in the application download for this chapter, available from the Wiley Web site.

It is then returned to the main flow of the servlet. Once we have a `TheatreValue` object, our action code actually executes the database add by calling on `doAddTheatreExe(request, response,tv)` and passing the newly formed `TheatreValue` object. As we shall see, executing this method may throw a `ValidationException`. A `ValidationException` is an `Exception` object we have created to suit our circumstances. It enables us to store a list of messages that need to be displayed to the user. These messages are typically created when we call the `validate` method on a value object, in the servlet when we are verifying some other part of the user's input, or in the handler itself when more complicated rules need to be tested. We will see an example of this soon. The `doAddTheatreExe` method is added to `AdminController` as follows:

Listing 10-14: doAddTheatreExe Method in AdminController

```
...
private TheatreValue doAddTheatreExe(HttpServletRequest req,
                                     HttpServletResponse res,
                                     TheatreValue tv)
    throws ValidationException
{
    try
    {
        BusinessHandler bh = new BusinessHandler();
        tv = bh.createTheatre(tv);
    }
    catch(SQLException sqle)
    {
        sqle.printStackTrace();
    }
    return tv;
}
...
```

This method simply attempts to create a new theatre in the database with the new representation of our `TheatreValue` using the `BusinessHandler`. The `createTheatre` method of `BusinessHandler` calls `validate()` on the value object, hence the thrown exception. The following is the `createTheatre` method from `BusinessHandler`:

```
...
public static TheatreValue createTheatre(TheatreValue theatreValue)
    throws SQLException, ValidationException
{
    theatreValue.validate();
    TheatreHandler th = new TheatreHandler();
    return th.create(theatreValue);
}
...
```

You can see how the BusinessHandler is used in this sense to proxy the call through to the TheatreHandler in order to add the new theatre to the database.

Should a ValidationException be thrown, control is returned to the catch block in the addTheatreExe action of the servlet:

```
catch(ValidationException ve)
{
    incPath = doAddTheatre(request,response,tv);
    request.setAttribute("errors",ve.getErrors());
}
```

Caution Notice that throughout the code in this application we suppress any java.sql.SQLException that is potentially thrown by not acting on them in the servlet methods. This is not good practice, but has been done in this way to reduce the clutter in the main flow of the servlet. It would be better to catch and deal with the exception within the main flow of the servlet, in other words, in the if.. else if statement in doPost() on an action-by-action basis. A consistent error page would then be used to display to the user when a SQLException has occurred. You should bear this in mind when you are debugging—remember to look at the Tomcat console if something just doesn't seem to be working.

As you can see, doAddTheatre is executed again (this time with the value of the Theatre from the request rather than a blank object) and the errors from the exception are added to the request. Accordingly, the add page (addTheatre.jsp) is displayed again with the offending values in each of the form elements and showing the errors that were found, as shown in Figure 10-16.

The error-inputting user keeps on this cycle until a valid theatre value has been formed and the create method in the handler can be executed fully. In this case the user is redirected back to the list page:

```
...
try
{
    tv = doAddTheatreExe(request,response,tv);
    response.sendRedirect(getFullServletPath(request)
        + "?action=listTheatres");
    return;
}
...
```

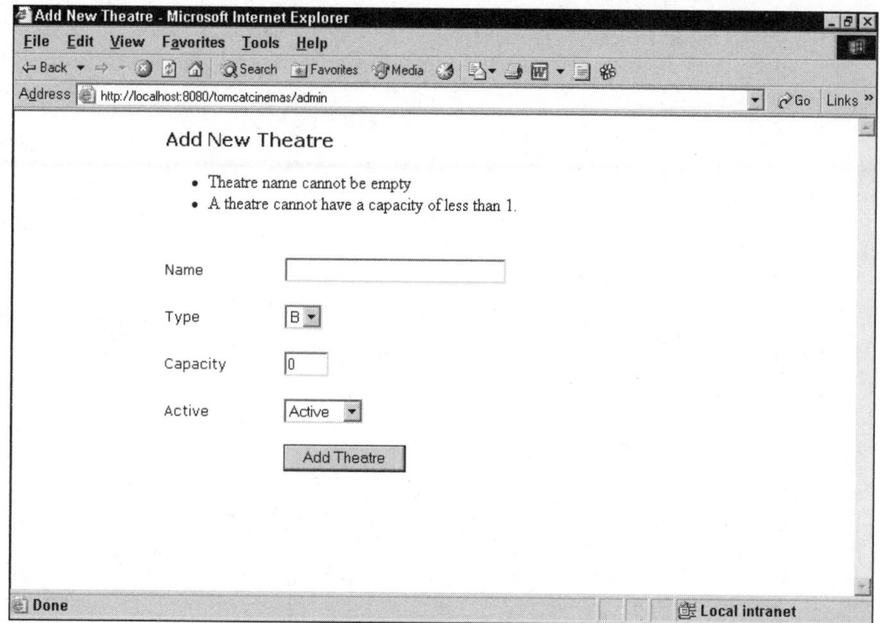

Figure 10-16: The Add Theatre form displayed with errors after incorrect values were submitted

This completes the cycle for adding a simple value within the application. The same is applied to the other entities with varying complexity. Notice that when a value is successfully added we call `response.sendRedirect ("admin?action=listTheatres");` redirecting the user to another action in the servlet. We are now going to walkthrough adding this action to the `AdminController` so you can see a list of the added theatres.

Listing Theatres

For listing theatres the action we need to add to the `AdminController` is simple to implement. We need a single action that passes a list of `TheatreValue` objects to the JSP page, where it can be iterated through and displayed.

We start by adding a `listTheatres` action to the main flow of the `AdminController` servlet:

```
else if(action.equals("listTheatres"))
{
    incPath = doListTheatres(request,response,false);
}
```

This action simply calls a new method for the servlet called `doListTheatres`, passing the `request` and `response` objects and returning the value that `incPath` should be. The code for this method is shown in Listing 10-15.

Listing 10-15: doListTheatres in AdminController

```
private String doListTheatres(HttpServletRequest req,
                              HttpServletResponse res,
                              boolean activeOnly)
{
    String rv = ADMIN_LIST_THEATRE_PAGE;

    try
    {
        TheatreHandler th = new TheatreHandler();
        req.setAttribute("theatres",th.getTheatres(activeOnly));
        req.setAttribute("title","List Theatres");
    }
    catch(SQLException sqle)
    {
        sqle.printStackTrace();
    }
    return rv;
}
```

Add this method to the `AdminController` now.

This method gets an `ArrayList` of `TheatreValues` from the `TheatreHandler` and adds it to the `request` object as a resource to be passed to the JSP page. It then returns the appropriate JSP page to be used. As we have our list of objects, control is passed to the JSP page (`listTheatres.jsp`). Remember that the reference `ADMIN_LIST_THEATRE_PAGE` needs to be defined in the `Controller` servlet:

```
protected final String ADMIN_LIST_THEATRE_PAGE = "listTheatres.jsp";
```

To create this JSP page, create a file called `listTheatres.jsp` and place it in the `web/` directory of the application source tree. This JSP page begins with the following directives and instantiations:

```
<%@ page import = "java.util.*" %>
<%@ page import = "bible.tomcat.tccinemas.*" %>

<jsp:useBean id="title" class="java.lang.String" scope="request"/>
<jsp:useBean id="action" class="java.lang.String" scope="request"/>
<jsp:useBean id="servletPath" class="java.lang.String" scope="request"/>
<jsp:useBean id="theatres" class="java.util.ArrayList" scope="request"/>
```

Notice the `ArrayList` that has been included here. This is the `ArrayList` we added to the `request` object in the servlet from `doListTheatres`.

We then need to iterate through this `ArrayList` to display the theatres we have in the system. The details of each theatre are displayed in the list. At the end of each row, a link to edit the object is provided. This links to an action in the servlet called `editTheatre`. The iteration code, after the column headings appears as:

```
<%for(int i=0; i < theatres.size(); i++)
{
    TheatreValue tv = (TheatreValue)theatres.get(i);
%>
    <tr>
        <td><%=tv.getId()%></td>
        <td><%=tv.getName()%></td>
        <td><%=tv.getType()%></td>
        <td><%=tv.getCapacity()%></td>
        <td><%=tv.getActive()%></td>
        <td>
<a href="<%=servletPath%>?action=editTheatre&id=<%=tv.getId()%>"
target="_self">Edit</a></td>
    </tr>
<%}%>
```

Some formatting has been removed from this code for clarity. You can see how each `TheatreValue` is obtained from the `ArrayList` and its properties are displayed. Add this code and a heading for each column to the `listTheatres.jsp` page.

At the end of the list is a link to add a new theatre (`addTheatre` action) and another link to display the menu. Figure 10-17 shows this list in the browser:

We now have a list of the active theatres in the system, each linking to the edit theatre functionality. With a slight variation on our add theatre code we can simply implement the functionality for editing a theatre.

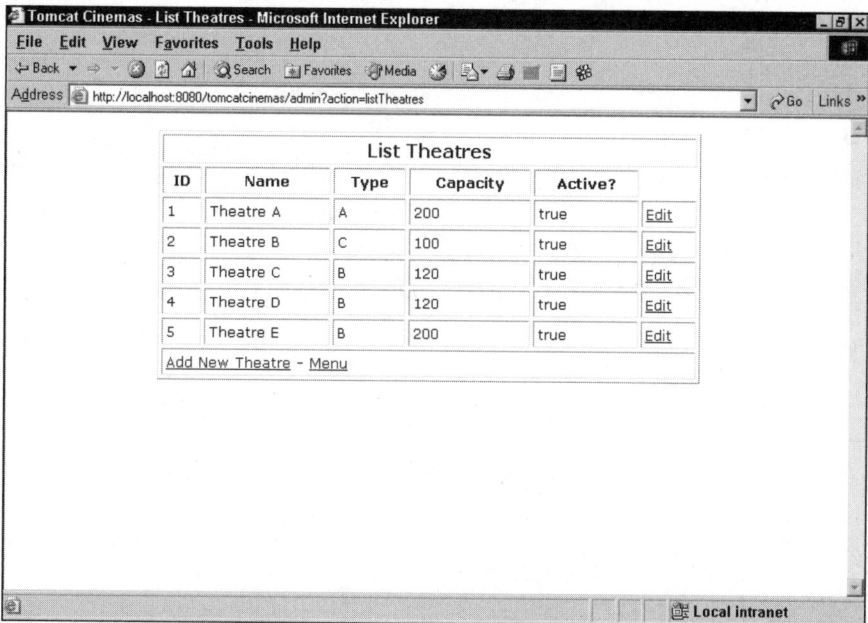

Figure 10-17: Listing theatres

Editing a Theatre

We now need to implement edit functionality for theatres. Clicking on Edit in the list in Figure 10-17 executes a new action in our `AdminController` servlet: `editTheatre`. An example link would appear as:

```
/tomcatcinemas/admin?action=editTheatre&id=6
```

The `id` number parameter being the unique `id` for this theatre.

So that this link executes correctly we add a the new action to `AdminController` called `editTheatre` with the following code:

```
...
else if(action.equals("editTheatre"))
{
   incPath = doEditTheatre(request,response,null);
   request.setAttribute("errors",new ArrayList());
}
...
```

Our `do<Action>` method, `doEditTheatre`, (you can see the pattern by now) performs the necessary functions for setting up the edit page, it resides in the `AdminController`, as shown in Listing 10-16.

Listing 10-16: doEditTheatre in AdminController

```
private String doEditTheatre(HttpServletRequest req,
                             HttpServletResponse res,
                             TheatreValue tv)
{
    String rv = ADMIN_EDIT_THEATRE_PAGE;
    try
    {
        if(tv == null)
        {
            long id = Long.parseLong(req.getParameter("id"));
            TheatreHandler th = new TheatreHandler();
            tv = th.getTheatre(id);
        }
        BusinessHandler bh = new BusinessHandler();
        req.setAttribute("canEdit",
                     new  Boolean(!(bh.hasTodayOrFutureShowings(tv))));
        req.setAttribute("title","Edit Theatre");
        req.setAttribute("theatreValue",tv);
    }
    catch(SQLException sqle)
    {
        sqle.printStackTrace();
    }
    return rv;
}
```

Again, we firstly decide on the page this section of functionality will use, ADMIN_EDIT_THEATRE_PAGE (editTheatre.jsp in the web/ directory). We then test the TheatreValue passed to the method for null. Notice in calling this method that we deliberately passed a null object in place of the TheatreValue. The full reason for this is explained when we examine our return trip for editTheatreExe. For now just accept that it indicates that we don't have a theatre yet, and we need one from the database. As such, the id parameter in the request is passed to the TheatreHandler to get a copy of the object from the database. This is then added to the request along with the title of the page. Notice also the call to the BusinessHandler in setting up a Boolean to be sent to the JSP page. This allows us to tell from the JSP page if the theatre can be edited. Remember one of the constraints we described earlier on was that only theatres that didn't have showings allocated in the future could be edited. The JSP page will use this Boolean object in order to decide if the edit theatre form that is displayed can be submitted and the theatre edited. Adding this method (hasTodayOrFutureShowings) to BusinessHandler is left as an exercise for the reader, or just refer to the source in the application download for this chapter.

In turn, control passes to the JSP page (editTheatre.jsp), which has an almost identical structure to addTheatre.jsp, the only difference being that with editing, a hidden field is required to store the value of the theatre's id number. Therefore the JSP directives, useBean entries and hidden form fields appear as:

```
<%@ page import = "java.util.*" %>
<%@ page import = "bible.tomcat.tccinemas.*" %>

<jsp:useBean id="title" class="java.lang.String" scope="request"/>
<jsp:useBean id="action" class="java.lang.String" scope="request"/>
<jsp:useBean id="servletPath" class="java.lang.String" scope="request"/>
<jsp:useBean id="errors" class="java.util.ArrayList" scope="request"/>
<jsp:useBean id="theatreValue" class="bible.tomcat.tccinemas.TheatreValue"
scope="request"/>
<jsp:useBean id="canEdit" class="java.lang.Boolean" scope="request"/>
...
<form action="<%=servletPath%>" method="post">
<input type="hidden" name="action" value="editTheatreExe">
<input type="hidden" name="id" value="<%=theatreValue.getId()%>">
...
```

Create this JSP page with these entries in the web/ directory of the application source tree. The rest of this page is the same as in addTheatre.jsp page, with errors being iterated and property values stored in the TheatreValue being prepopulated in the form.

When the form is submitted we again pick up the flow in the AdminController editTheatreExe action, as shown in Listing 10-17.

Listing 10-17: editTheatreExe action in AdminController

```
...
else if(action.equals("editTheatreExe"))
{
    TheatreValue tv = getTheatreFromRequest(request);
```

Continued

Listing 10-17 *(continued)*

```
            try
            {
                tv = doEditTheatreExe(request,response,tv);
                response.sendRedirect(getFullServletPath(request)
                    + "?action=listTheatres");
                return;
            }
            catch(ValidationException ve)
            {
                incPath = doEditTheatre(request,response,tv);
                request.setAttribute("errors",ve.getErrors());
            }
        }
        ...
```

If you are creating the application you should add this action to the AdminController servlet. Again this action fairly closely represents the addTheatreExe action described earlier, however we need to make a slight change to the getTheatreFromRequest. Remember, now we need to get the id number from the form for the value object to be properly structured for updating. We modify our getTheatreFromRequest method to appear as shown in Listing 10-18. The bolded code has been added.

Listing 10-18: getTheatreFromRequest in AdminController

```
    private TheatreValue getTheatreFromRequest(HttpServletRequest req)
    {
        TheatreValue rv = new TheatreValue();

        if("editTheatreExe".equals(req.getParameter("action"))
        {
            rv.setId(NumberUtil.toLong(req.getParameter("id")));
        }
        rv.setName(req.getParameter("name"));
        rv.setType(req.getParameter("type"));
        rv.setActive(("true".equals(req.getParameter("active")) ? true :
false));
        rv.setCapacity(NumberUtil.toInt(req.getParameter("capacity")));
        return rv;
    }
```

Once we have a value object representing what the user entered in the form we can continue examining the editTheatreExe action code. The new object is passed (along with request and response objects) to the doEditTheatreExe method in the AdminController. Again this method is similar to the doAddTheatreExe method described in the previous section, however here we are executing the updateTheatre() method of the BusinessHandler. This method in BusinessHandler checks to see if the theatre being edited has any showings allocated today or in the future with a call to the hasTodayOrFutureShowings method. This may seem a little redundant given we performed the same check when presenting the JSP page for the edit theatre form, however between the time the form was presented, and the time the form was submitted, a showing may have been allocated for this theatre. The updateTheatre method of the BusinessHandler is shown in Listing 10-19 below:

Listing 10-19: updateTheatre in BusinessHandler

```
public static TheatreValue updateTheatre(TheatreValue theatreValue)
    throws SQLException, ValidationException
{
    theatreValue.validate();

    if(hasTodayOrFutureShowings(theatreValue))
    {
        ValidationException ve = new ValidationException();
        ve.add("Theatre has today or future showings and "
               + "cannot be edited");
        throw ve;
    }

    TheatreHandler th = new TheatreHandler();
    return th.update(theatreValue);
}
```

If no ValidationException has been thrown, the TheatreValue is passed to the TheatreHandler's update method for the update to occur in the database.

If the update completes successfully the user is transferred to the theatre list (as you can see in listing 10-17). The logic also reacts in a similar fashion to addTheatreExe when a ValidationException is found. The doEditTheatre method is called again, however using the newly formed object, not a null, to be added to the request object and again displayed in the same form with the associated errors displayed. Figure 10-18 shows the edit form with errors:

This completes the description of adding, listing and editing theatres. We now turn our attention to an important piece of functionality to satisfy one of Cathy's requirements, reports.

Reports

Tomcat Cinemas management requires two reports to be available through the application:

- A report showing the number of bookings made via the Web and over the counter.
- A report showing the finishing time of remaining showings currently running.

We are going to walk through implementing the first report. The second report will form part of the listing of showings and can be seen in the download of the full application from Wiley's Web site.

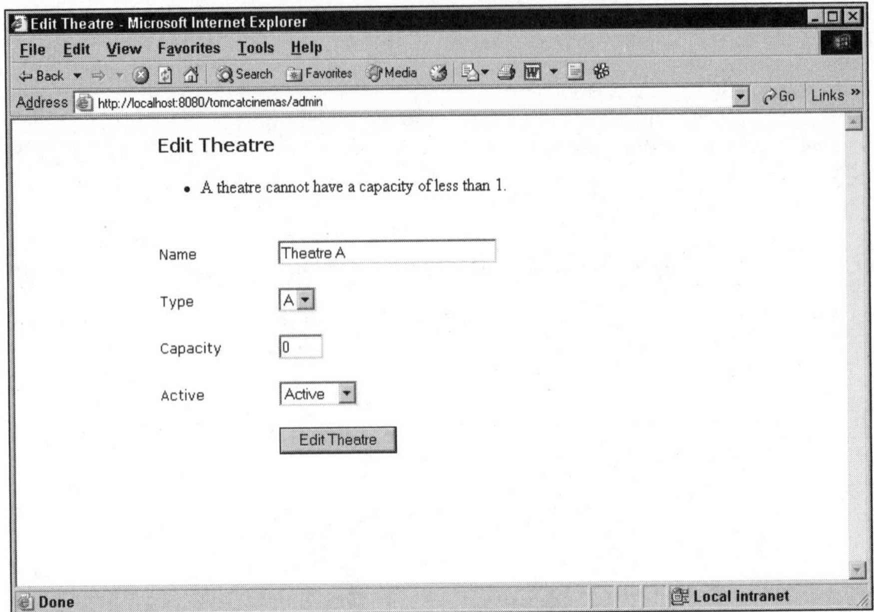

Figure 10-18: Edit Theatre with errors

To fulfill this requirement we need to add a new method to `BookingHandler` to get the data we are going to display. The action for this report needs to be added to the `AdminController` as well as its accompanying `do<Action>` method. We also need to create a simple JSP page to display these items, `bookingsReport.jsp`.

BookingHandler addition

This new method for `BookingHandler`, `getBookingCount(String type)`, returns an integer representing the number of bookings received via the chosen method. The code listing for this method is shown in Listing 10-20.

Listing 10-20: getBookingCount in BookingHandler

```
public int getBookingCount(String type)
    throws SQLException
{
    String sql = "SELECT COUNT(*) as result FROM booking WHERE "
                 + "bookedVia=?";
    Connection conn = getConnection();
    PreparedStatement ps = conn.prepareStatement(sql);
    ps.setString(1,type);

    ResultSet rs = ps.executeQuery();
    int rv = 0;
    if(rs.next())
    {
```

```
            rv = rs.getInt("result");
        }

        ps.close();
        rs.close();
        conn.close();

        return rv;
    }
```

To receive a valid value we obviously need to pass this method a string representing the type of booking, WEB or COUNTER. The method is implemented in this way to save us from coding two identical methods that do exactly the same thing.

New Action and Method for AdminController

With any new functionality we typically add a new action to the servlet. The action added for this report is called bookingReport. It is defined in the AdminController servlet as:

```
else if(action.equals("bookingReport"))
{
    incPath = doBookingReport(request);
}
```

As you can see, this action calls a new method in AdminController that sets up the result of the action and assigns the correct JSP page. This method is called doBookingReport and calls BookingHandler's getBookingCount for each source of bookings and passes the results to the request object. It also adds the title for our report page, as shown in Listing 10-21.

Listing 10-21: doBookingReport in AdminController

```
private String doBookingReport(HttpServletRequest req)
{
    BookingHandler bh = new BookingHandler();
    int web = 0;
    int counter = 0;

    try
    {
        web = bh.getBookingCount("WEB");
        counter = bh.getBookingCount("COUNTER");
    }
    catch(SQLException sqle)
    {
        sqle.printStackTrace();
    }
    req.setAttribute("webCount",new Integer(web));
    req.setAttribute("counterCount",new Integer(counter));
    req.setAttribute("title","Booking Report");
    return ADMIN_BOOKING_COUNT_REPORT;
}
```

Note that the ints we are adding to the request object are converted to object Integers first. The setAttribute method of the request object can only accept objects, not primitives.

Finally, this new method returns the name of the page to incPath in the main flow of the servlet. The JSP page is displayed, bookingsReport.jsp, which simply prints out these values. Create a file called bookingsReports.jsp in the web/ directory of the application source tree now. This file will begin with the following imports and instantiations:

```
<%@ page import = "java.util.*" %>
<%@ page import = "bible.tomcat.tccinemas.*" %>


<jsp:useBean id="title" class="java.lang.String" scope="request"/>
<jsp:useBean id="action" class="java.lang.String" scope="request"/>
<jsp:useBean id="servletPath" class="java.lang.String" scope="request"/>
<jsp:useBean id="webCount" class="java.lang.Integer" scope="request"/>
<jsp:useBean id="counterCount" class="java.lang.Integer" scope="request"/>
```

Add these entries to the bookingsReport.jsp file now, noting the webCount and bookingCount Integer objects that will be used when we display the report to the user. The code to display these values is added as follows:

```
...
<tr>
    <td>Bookings made via the web:</td>
    <td><%=webCount.toString()%></td>
</tr>
<tr>
    <td colspan="2"> </td>
</tr>
<tr>
    <td>Bookings made over the counter:</td>
    <td><%=counterCount.toString()%></td>
</tr>
...
```

Some formatting has been removed from the above code for clarity. You can see how this very simply interaction displays the required report to the user.

Implementing Other Administration Functionality

It is not practical to step through all the interactions that take place within the AdminController. This section is a brief outline of the remaining interactions not discussed previously. You should examine the download of the application from Wiley's Web site to see how these sections have been developed.

Add Showings

Showings represent a more complicated entity than films or theatres. As showings are central to the application there are lots of logical rules that are more complex to implement or are fairly easy to overlook. For instance, when creating a showing it is important that time collisions with other showings in the same theatre do not take place. To implement this interaction validation is managed via the createShowing method in the BusinessHandler, for instance, to ensure that showings do not collide. It is also important to note that you cannot add a showing for an inactive film or theatre.

Adding a showing displays a simple form requiring the selection of a film and a theatre. The form also requires the selection of a date and time for the showing to take place. The Add Showing screen that has been implemented is shown in Figure 10-19.

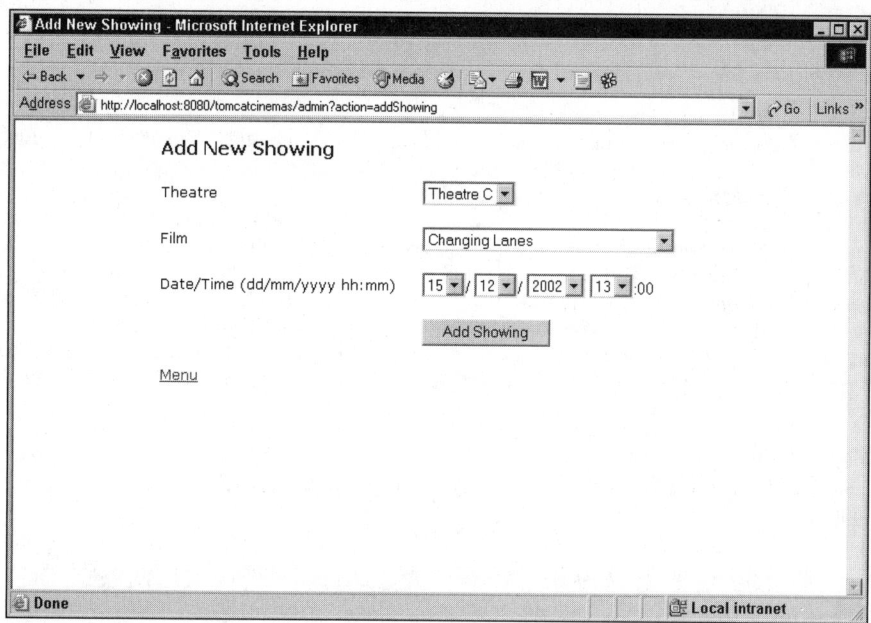

Figure 10-19: The Add New Showing screen in the Administration section

It is recommended the full application be downloaded from Wiley's Web site to see how adding a new showing is implemented.

Listing Showings

Administrative staff will require the ability to view lists of showings that have been scheduled. To service this requirement the `ShowingHandler` will require certain methods to ensure that such lists can be created. `ShowingHandler` will require the following methods:

- `getShowings()` — Returns all showings regardless of time or date.
- `getShowingsByDate(Date)` — Returns all the showings on the given date.
- `getFutureShowings()` — Returns all showings in the future.
- `getShowingsFutureToday()` — Returns all showings remaining for today.
- `getShowingsCurrentlyRunning()` — Returns showings that are currently running.

All these methods will return an `ArrayList` of `ShowingValue` objects to be displayed. In addition to these methods in `ShowingHandler`, a method will be implemented in the `Controller` to service the showing list requirements of all three interfaces, Admin, Front

Desk and Web. When we examine Front Desk and Web interface functionality further on in the chapter the process for listing showings will be explained in more detail.

Implementing the methods listed above in `ShowingHandler` and development of listing showings in the administrative interface is left as an exercise for the reader or the implemented source code can be examined in the download for this chapter from Wiley's Web site.

Query Showing

This functionality is discussed in the next section when we implement the front desk interface.

Delete Showing

When a showing is queried under the administrative interface and there are no bookings allocated to it, the option exists to delete that showing. Clicking this option from the query showing screen asks the user to confirm they wish to delete the showing. If they choose yes the showing is deleted from the system. Choosing no takes the user back to the query screen. This functionality requires some additions to be made to the `ShowingHandler` and `BusinessHandler`, as well as new actions and methods for `AdminController`. As a central Query Showing JSP page is used for the Administration interface and the Front Desk interface, some mechanism must be established to notify this page if the Delete Showing option is to appear. Implementation of this functionality is not explained in this chapter, it is left as an exercise for the reader, or you can look at the source code for this chapter available from the Wiley Web site.

Add/Edit/List Films

This set of functionality is very similar as that for theatres. The Add Film screen is shown in Figure 10-20.

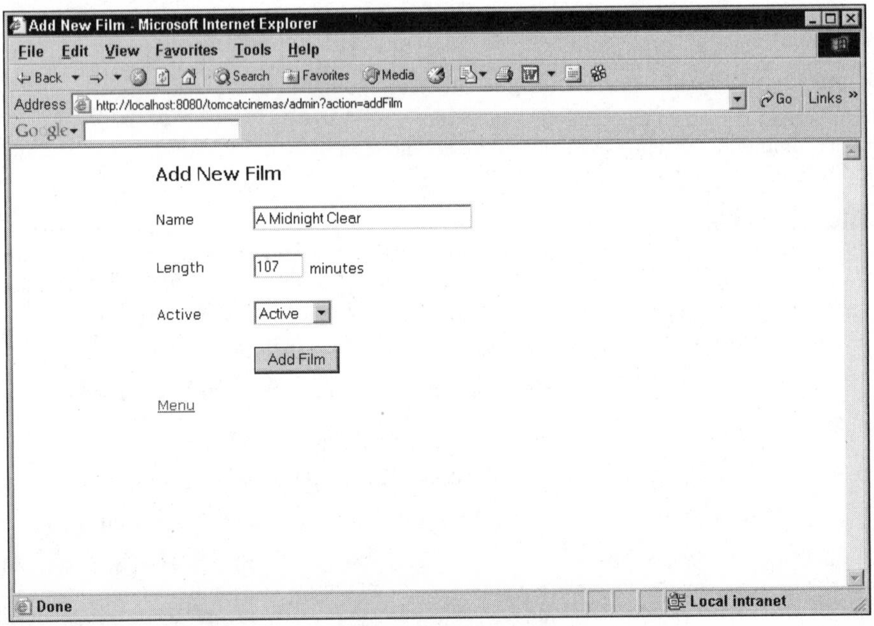

Figure 10-20: Add New Film in the Administration section

Application Progress Report

So far we have achieved the following in the application:

- ✦ Implemented the basic value objects and handlers.
- ✦ Implemented the basic structure for some of the actions within the servlets.
- ✦ Implemented the interaction between a JSP page and a servlet.
- ✦ Added methods to handlers to cater for functionality.
- ✦ Looked at the way the `BusinessHandler` assists in processing logic and validation.
- ✦ Walked through some of the sections required for the administration section of the application.

We are now ready to expand the application to cater for use cases that apply to Front Desk staff and customers on the Internet.

Implementing Front Desk Functionality

Now that we have completed the administrative functionality required in the system we can turn our attention to the requirements of the Front Desk. Remember, here we are dealing with Tomcat Cinema's staff, who use the system to accept bookings over the counter as well as to perform some simple queries on showings.

You will have noticed that the functionality for the Front Desk is similar to that for the customers interacting with Tomcat Cinemas over the Internet. Both sections require the ability to view a list of showings and to make bookings against those showings. To facilitate an explanation of this we will explain the implementation of the Front Desk functionality, whilst the explanation of the Web functionality in the next section will only highlight the differences between the two areas.

FrontDeskController servlet

To implement the Front Desk functionality we create a new servlet called `FrontDeskController`. Create a new file called `FrontDeskController.java` in the `tomcatcinemas/src/bible/tomcat/tccinemas/servlet/` directory of the source tree.

We will begin with the shell of this servlet and add actions and methods to fulfill the functionality. Listing 10-22 shows a beginning outline of this servlet.

Listing 10-22: FrontDeskController servlet shell

```
package bible.tomcat.tccinemas.servlet;

import javax.servlet.*;
import javax.servlet.http.*;
import java.io.*;
import java.sql.SQLException;
import java.util.*;
```

Continued

Listing 10-22 *(continued)*

```
import bible.tomcat.tccinemas.*;
import bible.tomcat.tccinemas.util.*;

public class FrontDeskController
    extends Controller
{
    protected void doPost(HttpServletRequest request,
                          HttpServletResponse response)
        throws ServletException, java.io.IOException
    {
        response.setContentType("text/html");
        PrintWriter out = response.getWriter();
        HttpSession thisSession = request.getSession(true);
        String action = request.getParameter("action");
        String incPath = null;

        if(action == null)
        {
            action = "listBookableShowings";
        }

        if(action.equals("listBookableShowings"))
        {
            //nothing yet
        }
        request.setAttribute("action",action);
        performInclude(incPath,request,response);
    }
}
```

Notice in this servlet that we have set up a default action to be executed, `listBookableShowings`. This action will display to the staff member a list of showings that can have bookings made against them.

In creating this servlet we also need to register its presence with Tomcat. Open the `web/WEB-INF/web.xml` file in your application's source tree and add the following servlet definition under the `AdminController` definition:

```
<servlet>
     <servlet-name>frontdesk</servlet-name>
     <description>
         Front Desk Controller Servlet
     </description>
     <servlet-class>
     bible.tomcat.tccinemas.servlet.FrontDeskController
     </servlet-class>
</servlet>
```

Then add the following servlet mapping underneath the AdminController servlet mapping:

```
<servlet-mapping>
    <servlet-name>frontdesk</servlet-name>
    <url-pattern>/frontdesk</url-pattern>
</servlet-mapping>
```

Now that the servlet is created and registered with Tomcat we can add the functionality for the default action in the servlet, listBookableShowings. Remember during this discussion we will be making references to similar functionality in the Web customer interface and how we can cater for both areas in our implementation.

List Showings

Our front desk staff need to have a list of showings that customers can make bookings against. To get started we need to add some appropriate action code to the servlet so that something happens when the default action is executed. Add the following to the listBookableShowings action in the FrontDeskController servlet:

```
if(action.equals("listBookableShowings"))
{
    incPath = doListShowings(request,response,4,SOURCE_FD);
}
```

The addition has been bolded. You can see that we are making a call to a new method called doListShowings, the result of which provides us with a value for incPath, our JSP page reference. The call to this method includes the request and response objects as well as two other parameters we will explain next.

doListShowings is a method that will service providing lists of showings for all three interfaces in this application, administration, Front Desk and Web. It must therefore know two things during each call: who is calling it (which servlet) and which list is required (bookable showings, all showings, etc). This leads us to the last two parameters in the call made to this method above. The first, in this case 4, refers to the type of list required to be displayed, and the second, SOURCE_FD indicates who is making the call to doListShowings. This parameter will decide which JSP page should be returned as appropriate for the calling interface.

As the doListShowings method will be used by all three areas of the application, it makes sense to place this method in the Controller servlet. Open the Controller servlet and add the following method:

Listing 10-23: doListShowings in Controller servlet

```
protected String doListShowings(HttpServletRequest req,
                                HttpServletResponse res,
                                int type, int source)
{

    ShowingHandler sh = new ShowingHandler();
    FilmHandler fh = new FilmHandler();
    TheatreHandler th = new TheatreHandler();
```

Continued

Listing 10-23 *(continued)*

```
ArrayList list = new ArrayList();
ArrayList films = new ArrayList();
ArrayList theatres = new ArrayList();
String title = "";

try
{
    if(type == 1)
    {
        list = sh.getShowingsByDate(new Date());
        title = "All Showings Today";
    }
    else if(type == 2)
    {
        list = sh.getShowings();
        title = "All Showings";
    }
    else if(type == 3)
    {
        list = sh.getShowingsCurrentlyRunning();
        title = "Showings Now Running";
    }
    else if(type == 4)
    {
        list = sh.getShowingsFutureToday();
        title = "Shows Remaining Today";
    }

    //need some reference data too..
    films = fh.getFilms(false);
    theatres = th.getTheatres(false);
}
catch(SQLException sqle)
{
    sqle.printStackTrace();
}

//add them to the request.
req.setAttribute("title",title);
req.setAttribute("showings",list);
req.setAttribute("films",films);
req.setAttribute("theatres",theatres);

String rv = "";

if(source == SOURCE_ADMIN)
{
    rv = ADMIN_LIST_SHOWING_PAGE;
}
```

```
        else if(source == SOURCE_FD)
        {
            rv = FD_LIST_SHOWING_PAGE;
        }
        else if(source == SOURCE_WEB)
        {
            rv = WEB_SHOWING_PAGE;
        }
        else
        {
            rv = WEB_SHOWING_PAGE;
        }

        return rv;
    }
```

You will notice references to various constants for pages and source indicators, therefore it is important to add the following to the top of the `Controller` servlet as well:

```
public abstract class Controller
    extends HttpServlet
{
    ...
    protected final String ADMIN_LIST_SHOWING_PAGE = "listShowings.jsp";
    protected final String FD_LIST_SHOWING_PAGE = "fdListShowings.jsp";
    protected final String WEB_SHOWING_PAGE = "webListShowings.jsp";
    protected final int SOURCE_ADMIN = 1;
    protected final int SOURCE_FD = 2;
    protected final int SOURCE_WEB = 3;
    ...
}
```

The added lines have been bolded. These will fit alongside the other page constants added from other parts of the application.

Listing 10-23 starts by declaring the various handlers and lists that will be required for the JSP page to display a list of showings. The `ArrayList list` will contain the list of `ShowingValues` for the JSP page. The `ArrayList films` will contain a list of films to be passed to the JSP page and the `ArrayList theatres` will contain a list of theatres to be passed to the JSP page. These last two `ArrayLists` will allow us to display a film or theatre name in the showing list rather than just the `id` number of the film or theatre from the `ShowingValue`. We will see how these are used further when we examine the JSP page.

The `ArrayList list` is populated with a list of showings based on the value of the `type` parameter of the method. In the case of our `FrontDeskController` type 4 has been indicated, therefore the lines:

```
else if(type == 4)
{
    list = sh.getShowingsFutureToday();
    title = "Shows Remaining Today";
}
```

are run. Therefore the list ArrayList is assigned the value of the getShowingsFutureToday() method of the ShowingHandler. getShowingsFutureToday() uses other methods in the ShowingHandler to provide a list of ShowingValue's that remain for the rest of the current day, as shown in Listing 10-24. The methods called by this method in ShowingHandler can be seen in the full source code download for this chapter from Wiley's Web site.

Listing 10-24: **getShowingsFutureToday in ShowingHandler**

```
public ArrayList getShowingsFutureToday()
    throws SQLException
{
    ArrayList master = getShowingsByDate(new Date());
    ArrayList rv = new ArrayList();
    Date now = new Date();

    for(int i=0; i < master.size(); i++)
    {
        ShowingValue sv = (ShowingValue)master.get(i);

        if(sv.getDateTimeStart().getTime() >= now.getTime())
        {
            rv.add(sv);
        }
    }
    return rv;
}
```

Once an appropriate list of ShowingValue's has been retrieved, the ArrayLists gathered are added to the request object in the usual way to be accessed as resources in the JSP page. The doListShowings method then attempts to assign an appropriate JSP page to be returned to the servlet. This value is dependent on the value of the source parameter passed to this method. In the case of our FrontDeskController call to this method, SOURCE_FD was passed so that the following would be assigned as the return value for doListShowings:

```
else if(source == SOURCE_FD)
{
    rv = FD_LIST_SHOWING_PAGE;
}
```

Once this value is assigned rv is returned to the main flow of the FrontDeskController servlet and control is then passed to the JSP page, in this case fdListShowings.jsp.

We can now turn to creating a JSP page to list these showings we have collected, in a way appropriate for the front desk interface. Create a file called fdListShowings.jsp in the web/ directory of the application source tree.

This new JSP page begins with various page directives and instantiations for the objects we require. Add the following to the top of the JSP page you created:

```
<%@ page import = "java.util.*" %>
<%@ page import = "bible.tomcat.tccinemas.*" %>
<%@ page import = "bible.tomcat.tccinemas.util.DateUtil" %>

<jsp:useBean id="title" class="java.lang.String" scope="request"/>
<jsp:useBean id="action" class="java.lang.String" scope="request"/>
<jsp:useBean id="servletPath" class="java.lang.String" scope="request"/>
<jsp:useBean id="theatres" class="java.util.ArrayList" scope="request"/>
<jsp:useBean id="films" class="java.util.ArrayList" scope="request"/>
<jsp:useBean id="showings" class="java.util.ArrayList" scope="request"/>
```

You can see the aliases (`id` attributes) matching the objects we placed in the `request` object within the `doListShowings` method of the `Controller` servlet. Once these are established we need to iterate through the list of showings we have retrieved. In doing so we also wish to display the name of the film that each showing has been scheduled to show and the name of the theatre it will be shown in. If you think about the `ShowingValue` objects we are about to list, they only contain `id` references to films and theatres. This is where the `ArrayList`s of films and theatres comes in handy. We can find the name of the film or theatre referenced by each `ShowingValue` by querying the lists of films and theatres as we go. Add the following list iteration code to the `fdListShowings.jsp` page:

Listing 10-25: **showing list in fdListShowings.jsp**

```
<tr>
    <th><b>ID</b></th>
    <th><b>Theatre</b></th>
    <th><b>Film</b></th>
    <th><b>Start</b></th>
    <th><b>Duration</b></th>
    <th><b>End</b></th>
    <th<b>Options</b></th>
</tr>
<%for(int i=0; i < showings.size(); i++)
{
        ShowingValue sv = (ShowingValue)showings.get(i);
        TheatreValue thisTheatre = new TheatreValue();
        FilmValue thisFilm = new FilmValue();

        for(int j=0; j < theatres.size(); j++)
        {
            TheatreValue tmp = (TheatreValue)theatres.get(j);
            if(tmp.getId() == sv.getTheatreId())
            {
                thisTheatre = tmp;
                break;
            }
        }
```

Continued

Listing 10-25 (continued)

```
        for(int j=0; j < films.size(); j++)
        {
            FilmValue tmp = (FilmValue)films.get(j);
            if(tmp.getId() == sv.getFilmId())
            {
                thisFilm = tmp;
                break;
            }
        }
%>
    <tr>
        <td><%=sv.getId()%></td>
        <td><%=thisTheatre.getName()%></td>
        <td><%=thisFilm.getName()%></td>
        <td><%=DateUtil.format(sv.getDateTimeStart())%></td>
        <td<%=thisFilm.getLength()%> mins</td>
        <td><%=DateUtil.format(DateUtil.addMinutes(sv.getDateTimeStart(),
    thisFilm.getLength()))%></td>
        <td>
<a href="<%=servletPath%>?action=detailShowing&id=<%=sv.getId()%>"
target="_self">Query</a> -
<a href="<%=servletPath%>?showingId=<%=sv.getId()%>&action=makeBooking"
target="_self">Book</a>
        </td>
    </tr>
<%
}
%>
```

Some formatting has been removed from this listing for clarity. You can see in this code how a `FilmValue` and `TheatreValue` are matched with each `ShowingValue` as the iteration progresses, this allows an appropriate film and theatre name to be presented in the list. If everything is working correctly here the list displayed should look something like Figure 10-21 below:

You will notice at the end of each item in this list there are two links. The first is to query that particular showing and the second is to make a booking against that showing. We will explain querying a showing next.

Note Within the `bible.tomcat.tccinemas.util` package of the application download you will find a class called `DateUtil` that we have created to help with some of the date semantics that occur through the application. This is used to a large extent for dealing with showings. For example, the end date and time needs to be provided for each showing in the list. To do this we add a method to `DateUtil` called `addMinutes`. This method receives a date, in our case representing the start date for the showing, and an integer for the number of minutes to add. This will represent the length of the film. `DateUtil.addMinutes` returns a new `Date` class representing the passed date with the minutes added. We use this in the query `Showing` page to show the expected ending time of each showing.

The rest of the methods in `DateUtil` are used to convert between `java.sql.Timestamp` (the date representation in the database) and `java.util.Date`, and vice versa. DateUtil provides some other useful methods used within this application. When you come across them in the source code we recommend having a look at DateUtil.

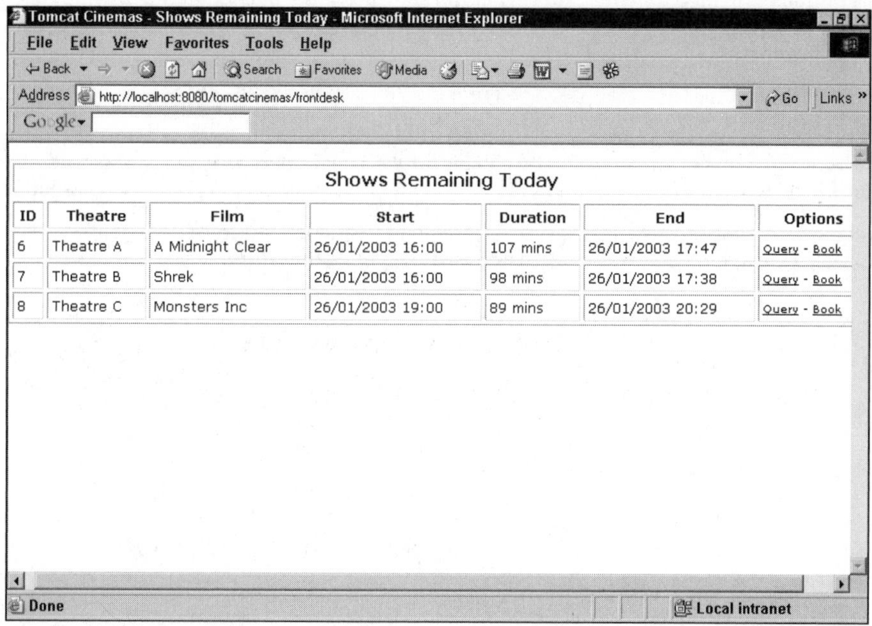

Figure 10-21: List of showings from the Front Desk Interface

Query Showing

From the showing list presented in Figure 10-21 above, Front Desk staff are able to query an individual showing to see specific details. These details include:

- ✦ The showing (ShowingValue) being queried.
- ✦ The film (FilmValue) allocated to this showing.
- ✦ The theatre (TheatreValue) allocated to this showing.
- ✦ Seats remaining: An Integer representing the number of seats remaining for this showing.
- ✦ Bookings for Showing: An integer representing the number of bookings that have been allocated to this showing.
- ✦ Time remaining: An Integer representing the number of minutes remaining for this showing.
- ✦ Can delete: A `Boolean` indicating if this showing can be deleted. In the administrative interface, showings can be deleted if they do not have any bookings. In the Front Desk interface, this should always be false.

Implementation of this functionality is left as an exercise for the reader. You can also download the complete application from the Wiley Web site to see how we have implemented it.

Make Bookings

Our front desk staff need to be able to add bookings to the system. You will notice that one of the options provided for each showing in the showing list explained in the previous section is to add a booking, the `makeBooking` action. Clicking on this list in the showing list requests the following URL:

```
/tomcatcinemas/frontdesk?showingId=17&action=makeBooking
```

This is the functionality the Front Desk staff will use to take a customer's booking to attend a showing. We must ensure here that we cater for Web customers who make bookings, much like we did when we implemented the List Showings functionality in the previous section.

Adding a booking is a two-action process we need to add to the `FrontDeskController` servlet. The action code you need to add is shown in Listing 10-26.

Listing 10-26: makeBooking and makeBookingExe actions in FrontDeskController

```
...
else if(action.equals("makeBooking"))
{
    incPath = doMakeBooking(request,response,
                            new BookingValue(),SOURCE_FD);
}
else if(action.equals("makeBookingExe"))
{
    BookingValue bv = getBookingValueFromRequest(request,true);
    try
    {
        incPath = doMakeBookingExe(request,response,bv,SOURCE_FD);
    }
    catch(ValidationException ve)
    {
        incPath = doMakeBooking(request,response,bv,SOURCE_FD);
        request.setAttribute("errors",ve.getErrors());
    }
}
...
```

From the URL above you can see that the `makeBooking` action is called so we can see that this action sets up our make booking process for the user. We therefore need a new method in the `Controller` servlet called `doMakeBooking`. `doMakeBooking` will cater for requests in this way from the front desk interface and the Web interface. In our call from `FrontDeskController` (Listing 10-26) above we can see that `SOURCE_FD` is used to indicate from where this call arises.

This action serves to present to the user a form to make a booking for the chosen showing. This will include collecting the number of seats to book and the customer's details.

The `doMakeBooking` method needs to be added to the `Controller` servlet as follows:

Listing 10-27: doMakeBooking in Controller servlet

```
protected String doMakeBooking(HttpServletRequest req,
                               HttpServletResponse res,
                               BookingValue bv,
                               int source)
{
    String rv = "";
    if(source == this.SOURCE_FD)
    {
        rv = FD_MAKE_BOOKING_PAGE_1;
    }
    else if(source == this.SOURCE_WEB)
    {
        rv = WEB_MAKE_BOOKING_PAGE_1;
    }

    FilmHandler fh = new FilmHandler();
    ShowingHandler sh = new ShowingHandler();
    BusinessHandler bh = new BusinessHandler();
    TheatreHandler th = new TheatreHandler();
    PriceHandler ph = new PriceHandler();
    FilmValue film = new FilmValue();
    TheatreValue theatre = new TheatreValue();
    ShowingValue showing = new ShowingValue();
    int pricePerSeat = 0;

    try
    {
       showing =
       sh.getShowing(NumberUtil.toLong(req.getParameter("showingId")));
       film = fh.getFilm(showing.getFilmId());
       theatre = th.getTheatre(showing.getTheatreId());
       pricePerSeat = ph.getPriceForTheatre(theatre);
    }
    catch(SQLException sqle)
    {
        sqle.printStackTrace();
    }

    int seatsRemaining = bh.getSeatsRemainingInShowing(showing);
    req.setAttribute("seatsRemaining",new Integer(seatsRemaining));
    req.setAttribute("title","Make Booking Step 1");
```

Continued

Listing 10-27 *(continued)*

```
        req.setAttribute("film",film);
        req.setAttribute("pricePerSeat",
                         NumberUtil.getFormattedAmount(pricePerSeat));
        req.setAttribute("showing",showing);
        req.setAttribute("thisBooking",bv);

        return rv;
    }
```

The JSP page references in this method will need to be added as constants in the same way we added the list JSP pages in the list showings explanation, for instance:

```
protected final String FD_MAKE_BOOKING_PAGE_1 = "fdMakeBooking-1.jsp";
protected final String WEB_MAKE_BOOKING_PAGE_1 = "webMakeBooking-1.jsp";
```

The method in Listing 10-27 decides which of these pages to use based on the `source` parameter passed; in the case of the `FrontDeskController` this is `FD_MAKE_BOOKING_PAGE_1`. The remainder of this method gathers the required information for the booking form to be presented such as the chosen showing, the chosen film and theatre and the price per seat.

You will also notice in Listing 10-27 various other methods in `BusinessHandler` and `PriceHandler` that are used. To see how these methods are implemented you will need to refer to the full source code for this application available from the Wiley Web site.

Once the resources have been correctly gathered and added to the `request` object, the appropriate JSP page reference is returned to the main flow of the servlet and presented to the user. For this to occur correctly we need to create a new JSP page to display the booking form for Front Desk interface users.

Create a file called `fdMakeBooking-1.jsp` in the `web/` directory of the application source tree. Add the following code to the start of the JSP page to cater for the objects we need to import and instantiate:

```
<%@ page import = "java.util.*" %>
<%@ page import = "bible.tomcat.tccinemas.*" %>
<%@ page import = "bible.tomcat.tccinemas.util.*" %>

<jsp:useBean id="title" class="java.lang.String" scope="request"/>
<jsp:useBean id="action" class="java.lang.String" scope="request"/>
<jsp:useBean id="servletPath" class="java.lang.String" scope="request"/>
<jsp:useBean id="showing"
    class="bible.tomcat.tccinemas.ShowingValue" scope="request"/>
<jsp:useBean id="seatsRemaining"
    class="java.lang.Integer" scope="request" />
<jsp:useBean id="thisBooking"
    class="bible.tomcat.tccinemas.BookingValue" scope="request"/>
```

```
<jsp:useBean id="film"
    class="bible.tomcat.tccinemas.FilmValue" scope="request" />
<jsp:useBean id="pricePerSeat" class="java.lang.String" scope="request" />
<jsp:useBean id="errors" class="java.util.ArrayList" scope="request" />
```

We can now begin displaying the booking form. To do so we need to define the HTML form tag and add some hidden fields:

```
<form action="<%=servletPath%>" method="post">
<input type="hidden" name="action" value="makeBookingExe">
<input type="hidden" name="bookedVia" value="COUNTER">
<input type="hidden" name="showingId" value="<%=showing.getId()%>">
```

These lines declare the form we are displaying as well as provide hidden fields for:

- ✦ The action that will be executed when this form is submitted.
- ✦ The `bookedVia` indicator so that we can tell that this booking is made via the Front Desk.
- ✦ The `showingId` of the showing we are booking for.

Before displaying the form elements we need to display any errors that have been passed in the request:

```
<ul>
    <%for(int i=0; i < errors.size(); i++)
    {
        String msg = (String)errors.get(i);
    %>
        <li><%=msg%></li>
    <%
    }
    %>
</ul>
```

We then need to add code to present some information to the user to confirm that they are making a booking for the correct showing as well as other details such as the seats remaining and the price per seat:

```
<tr>
    <td><b>Selected film:</b></td>
    <td><%=film.getName()%></td>
</tr>
<tr>
    <td><b>Start time:</b></td>
    <td><%=DateUtil.format(showing.getDateTimeStart())%></td>
</tr>
<tr>
    <td<b>Seats Remaining:</b></td>
    <td><%=seatsRemaining.intValue()%></td>
</tr>
```

```
<tr>
    <td><b>Price Per Seat:</b></td>
    <td>$<%=pricePerSeat%></td>
</tr>
```

We can then add code to present the actual elements of the booking form itself. As this is the Front Desk interface we must cater for credit card and cash bookings, therefore our first element is a radio button selection to choose either cash or credit card:

```
...
<input type="radio" name="payMethod"
<%if("CASH".equals(thisBooking.getPayMethod())){%>
   checked
<%}%> value="CASH">
...
<input type="radio" name="payMethod"
<%if("CARD".equals(thisBooking.getPayMethod())){%>
 checked
<%}%> value="CARD">
...
```

Note When we implement the Web interface for making a booking, we will hard code 'CARD' as the payment method, because all bookings made via the Web interface are by credit card.

Once the payment method has been established we can add elements for the number of seats required, the customers name, the credit card number and the type of credit card being used:

```
<input type="text" name="seats" maxlength="3" size="5"
       value="<%=thisBooking.getSeats()%>">
...
<input type="text" name="name" size="20" maxlength="100"
       value="<%=thisBooking.getName()%>">
...
<input type="text" name="cardNo" size="20" maxlength="17"
       value="<%=thisBooking.getCardNo()%>">
...
<select name="cardType"><option value=""></option>
    <option value="VISA"
<%if("VISA".equals(thisBooking.getCardType())){%>
 selected<%}%>>Visa</option>
        ...
        </select>
```

When complete, this form should look something like Figure 10-22 below:

When this form is submitted the `makeBookingExe` action is executed. You can see this action defined in the `FrontDeskController` in Listing 10-26.

If you look at Listing 10-26 you can see that the `makeBookingExe` action firstly gathers a `BookingValue` from what has been submitted in the form via the `getBookingValueFromRequest` method. We add this method to the `Controller` servlet as per Listing 10-28 below:

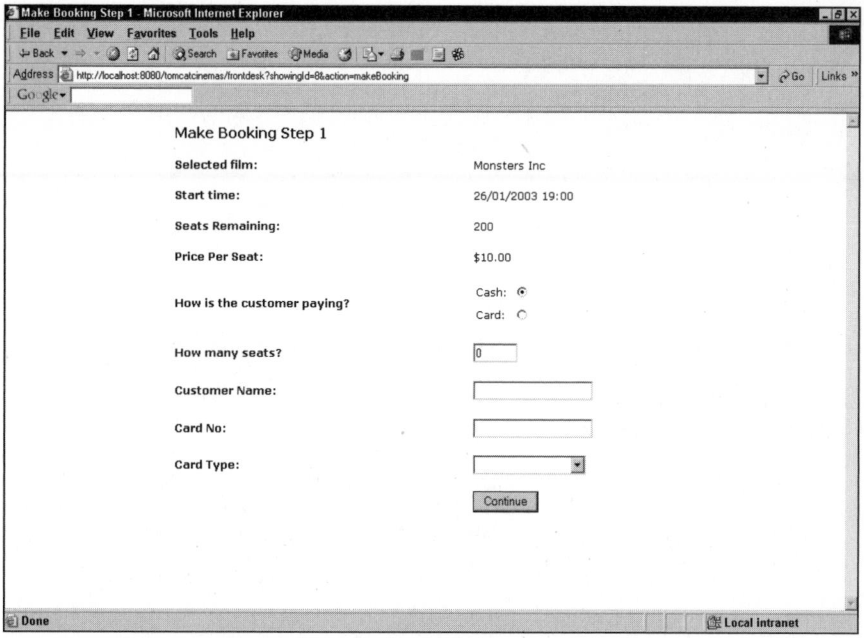

Figure 10-22: Front desk view of making a booking

Listing 10-28: getBookingValueFromRequest in Controller servlet

```
protected BookingValue getBookingValueFromRequest
                        (HttpServletRequest req, boolean counter)
{
    BookingValue rv = new BookingValue();
    BookingHandler bh = new BookingHandler();

    try
    {
        rv.setShowingId(
            NumberUtil.toLong(req.getParameter("showingId")));
        rv.setBookedVia(req.getParameter("bookedVia"));
        rv.setCardNo(req.getParameter("cardNo"));
        rv.setCardType(req.getParameter("cardType"));
        rv.setName(req.getParameter("name"));
        rv.setPayMethod(req.getParameter("payMethod"));
        rv.setSeats(NumberUtil.toInt(req.getParameter("seats")));
        rv.setAmount(bh.getAmountForBooking(rv.getShowingId(),
                    rv.getSeats()));
        rv.setPickedUp(counter);
```

Continued

Listing 10-28 *(continued)*

```
        }
        catch(SQLException sqle)
        {
            sqle.printStackTrace();
        }
        return rv;
    }
```

This method collects all the details that were submitted in the booking form and creates a `BookingValue` to be validated and potentially added to the database. The new `BookingValue` is returned to the servlet and passed to a new method called `doMakeBookingExe`.

Note

The credit card validation implemented in this application only tests for the length (exactly 10 characters) of the entry. Enhancing this is a task you could undertake yourself to better understand how the validation works and what is involved in validating a credit card. As a hint, do a search for 'Luhn formula' on the Internet.

The `doMakeBookingExe` method is added to the `Controller` servlet as per Listing 10-29 below:

Listing 10-29: **doMakeBookingExe in Controller servlet**

```
    protected String doMakeBookingExe(HttpServletRequest req,
                                      HttpServletResponse res,
                                      BookingValue bv,
                                      int source)
        throws ValidationException
    {
        try
        {
            BusinessHandler bh = new BusinessHandler();
            bh.createBooking(bv);
        }
        catch(SQLException sqle)
        {
            sqle.printStackTrace();
        }
        String rv = "";

        if(source == SOURCE_FD)
        {
            rv = FD_MAKE_BOOKING_PAGE_2;
        }
        else if(source == SOURCE_WEB)
```

```
        {
            rv = WEB_MAKE_BOOKING_PAGE_2;
        }
        req.setAttribute("thisBooking",bv);

        return rv;
    }
```

Two extra JSP references will need to be added to the `Controller` servlet for this method to function:

```
protected final String FD_MAKE_BOOKING_PAGE_2 = "fdMakeBooking-2.jsp";
protected final String WEB_MAKE_BOOKING_PAGE_2 = "webMakeBooking-2.jsp";
```

This method attempts to add the `BookingValue` to the database via the `BusinessHandler`. In this capacity the `BusinessHandler` acts as a kind of façade to validate the `BookingValue` before passing it onto the `BookingHandler`. The `createBooking` method of the `BusinessHandler` is as follows:

Listing 10-30: createBooking in BusinessHandler

```
    public static synchronized BookingValue
        createBooking(BookingValue bookingValue)
        throws SQLException, ValidationException
    {
        bookingValue.validate();
        checkSeatsAvailable(bookingValue.getSeats(),
                            bookingValue.getShowingId());

        //simulates a credit card decline, entering a card
        //number starting with 999 triggers this off.
        if(bookingValue.getPayMethod().equals("CARD")
           && bookingValue.getCardNo().startsWith("999"))
        {
            ValidationException ve = new ValidationException();
            ve.add("The credit card was declined");
            throw ve;
        }

        BookingHandler bh = new BookingHandler();
        return bh.create(bookingValue);
    }
```

This method may throw a `ValidationException` from the validate method of the `BookingValue`, or the `checkSeatsAvailable` method of `BusinessHandler`. This method checks to see if the `BookingValue` is for an available number of seats for this showing. You will notice that this method is *synchronized*. This means that only one thread can execute this method at any one time. This ensures that we avoid the situation where two users are competing for the final seats in a showing and they both get the last ticket.

`createBooking` then has some simulation code for a declined credit card. For instance if the credit card typed in begins with "999" the transaction will be declined for illustration purposes. Finally the `BookingHandler`'s `create` method is called for the `BookingValue` to be added to the database.

Returning to the servlets action code (Listing 10-26) if a `ValidationException` is thrown, the `doMakeBooking` method is called again and the booking form is displayed with an appropriate error. If no `ValidationException` is thrown we return back to the flow of the `doMakeBookingExe` method in Listing 10-29. In this case the appropriate JSP file is then retrieved, `fdMakeBooking-2.jsp`.

This JSP page simply presents some confirmation information based on the booking that was made, such as the amount charged. Development of this page is left as an exercise to the reader.

Other Front Desk Functionality

A section of functionality we will not be describing here in any great detail is the ability for Web customers to pick up their tickets from Front Desk staff. When the Web customer's booking is made they are told to quote their credit card number at the counter to collect their tickets. When a customer approaches Tomcat Cinemas Front Desk staff with a credit card number a form allows the staff member to enter the credit card number to indicate that the booking has been picked up. If the credit card number identifies a booking that has already been picked up or was sold over the counter, an error will display. Implementing this is left as an exercise for the reader.

Implementing Public Web Functionality

As luck would have it we have implemented much of the code required for implementing the Public Web interface to the application. Therefore to illustrate the implementation of the Public Web functionality we will firstly set up the WebController servlet, then simply highlight the differences between the two sections.

WebController servlet

To implement Web functionality we need to create a new servlet. Create a file called `WebController.java` in the `src/bible/tomcat/tccinemas/servlet` directory of the application directory structure.

Add the following code to this file:

Listing 10-31: WebController servlet

```
package bible.tomcat.tccinemas.servlet;

import javax.servlet.*;
import javax.servlet.http.*;
import java.io.*;
import java.sql.SQLException;
```

```
import java.util.ArrayList;
import java.util.Date;
import bible.tomcat.tccinemas.*;
import bible.tomcat.tccinemas.util.*;

public class WebController
    extends Controller
{
    protected void doPost(HttpServletRequest request,
                          HttpServletResponse response)
        throws ServletException, java.io.IOException
    {
        response.setContentType("text/html");
        PrintWriter out = response.getWriter();
        HttpSession thisSession = request.getSession(true);
        String action = request.getParameter("action");
        String incPath = null;

        if(action == null)
        {
            action = "listBookableShowings";
        }

        if(action.equals("makeBooking"))
        {
            incPath = doMakeBooking(request,response,
                                    new BookingValue(),SOURCE_WEB);
        }
        else if(action.equals("makeBookingExe"))
        {
            BookingValue bv = getBookingValueFromRequest(request,false);
            try
            {
                incPath = doMakeBookingExe(request,response,bv,SOURCE_WEB);
            }
            catch(ValidationException ve)
            {
                incPath = doMakeBooking(request,response,bv,SOURCE_WEB);
                request.setAttribute("errors",ve.getErrors());
            }
        }
        else if(action.equals("listBookableShowings"))
        {
            incPath = doListShowings(request,response,4,SOURCE_WEB);
        }
        request.setAttribute("action",action);
        performInclude(incPath,request,response);
    }
}
```

You can see that the structure of this file is almost identical to the FrontDeskController servlet. That is except for the SOURCE_WEB parameters passed to the methods we established in the previous section to indicate that the JSP page required is the Web version.

Once you have created this file we need to register the servlet with Tomcat in the usual fashion. Open the web/WEB-INF/web.xml file and add the following servlet definition beneath the FrontDeskController definition:

```
<servlet>
    <servlet-name>web</servlet-name>
    <description>
        Web Controller Servlet
    </description>
    <servlet-class>
        bible.tomcat.tccinemas.servlet.WebController
    </servlet-class>
</servlet>
```

Then add the following servlet mapping beneath the FrontDeskController servlet mapping:

```
<servlet-mapping>
     <servlet-name>web</servlet-name>
     <url-pattern>/web</url-pattern>
</servlet-mapping>
```

Once this servlet is established, it can be accessed via the following URL:

```
/tomcatcinemas/web
```

Executing the URL in this fashion will execute the default action for this servlet, which, like the FrontDeskController, is the listBookableShowings action.

List Showings

The only required change for the Web version of List Showings is the removal of some items from the list:

- ✦ Remove the Query option for each showing.
- ✦ Remove the Theatre name for each showing.
- ✦ Remove the theatres ArrayList iteration.
- ✦ Remove the theatres useBean instantiation.
- ✦ Remove the end time and date for each showing.

Therefore we can simply copy the fdListShowings.jsp file and create a new file called webListShowings.jsp. Then apply the above changes to this file. This is the only change required to get the Web interface showing list working. Once completed the Web showing list should appear as shown in Figure 10-23.

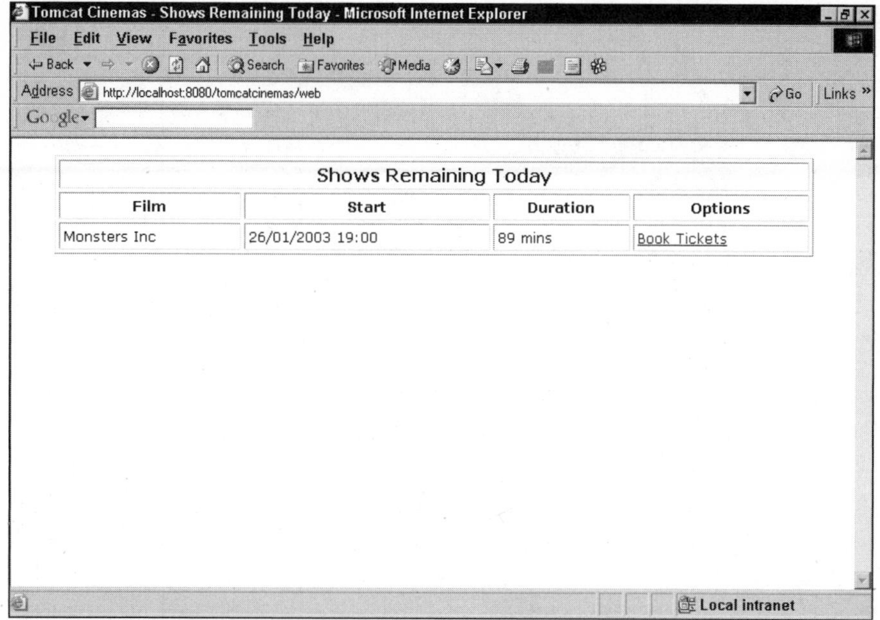

Figure 10-23: Showings list in `WebController` for Web customers

Make Bookings

The bookings functionality of the Web interface is also slightly cut down. The Front Desk booking files can be copied and renamed to the Web interface versions. Create copies of `fdMakeBooking-1.jsp` and `fdMakeBooking-2.jsp` called `webMakeBooking-1.jsp` and `webMakeBooking-2.jsp` respectively.

The `webMakeBooking-1.jsp` file can then be modified in the following ways. Remember this is the form page for making a booking:

✦ Remove the radio button selection for cash or credit card and add a hidden field indicating that all transactions are by card, for instance:

```
<input type="hidden" name="payMethod" value="CARD">
```

✦ Change the `bookedVia` hidden field to indicate that the booking is coming from the Web, for instance:

```
<input type="hidden" name="bookedVia" value="WEB">
```

✦ Remove the seats remaining information from the display.

✦ Use the `seatsRemaining` variable to provide a message to the user if there are no seats available.

The Web version of the booking screen should then appear something like Figure 10-24 below:

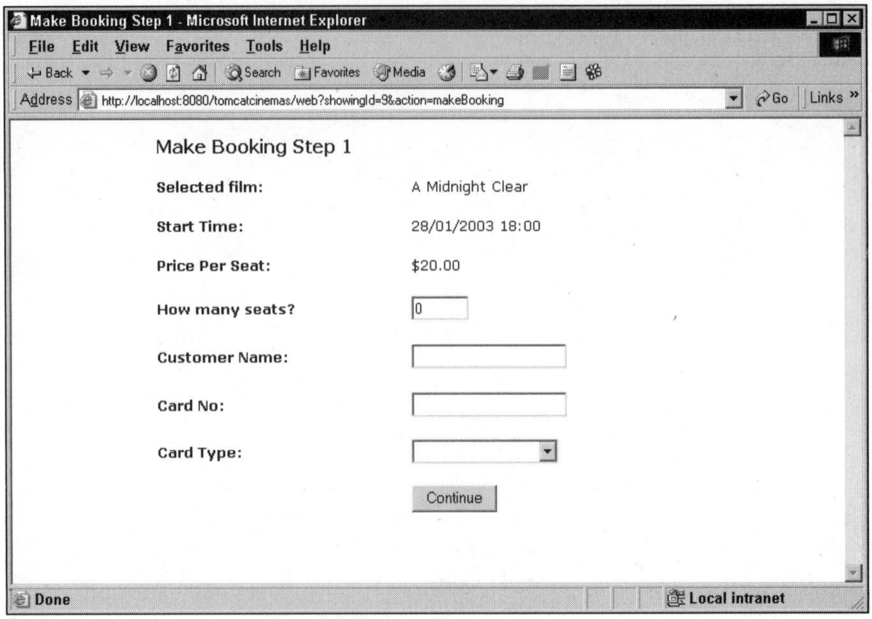

Figure 10-24: Make Booking screen in the Web Interface

The `webMakeBooking-2.jsp` file can then be modified. This page is the confirmation page once a booking has gone through. Simply change this file to display the amount charged to the customer's credit card and include instructions for picking up tickets at Tomcat Cinemas.

These are the only changes required to implement Web functionality based on the code we implemented for the Front Desk.

This concludes our walkthrough development of the Tomcat Cinemas application. We recommend looking closely at the source code for this chapter from the download available at Wiley's Web site.

Other Techniques

The application discussed in this chapter has been built in a particular way. There are various other structures that could be employed to arrive at a similar solution. One such method is to employ a framework. A framework is simply the infrastructure for building the application in a certain way. One example of a framework that would suit this application is Struts.

Struts

Struts is a framework from Jakarta that provides for the development of MVC-based applications. Struts provides the controller portion of MVC and works with other technologies such as JSP (view) and various database connection methods (model) to help deliver a robust and properly architected application. You can read more about Struts in Chapter 13. In Chapter 13 we will take a look at one portion of functionality from the application in this chapter and implement it using Struts.

Packaging the Application

Once development of the application has been completed, and it has passed some form of testing standard, we can now look at packaging the application into a WAR file.

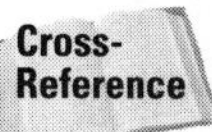

Creating and deploying a WAR file is discussed in more detail in Chapter 7.

Creating a WAR file of our application is very easy using our Ant script. Simply run the following commands:

```
> ant clean dist
```

This command reconstructs the entire build directory including recompiling all Java files. It will then create `JavaDocs` for the entire application, creating a `docs` directory within the dist directory. Then using the build directory as its source, it packages up all classes, JSP files and descriptors into a WAR file and places it at `tomcatcinemas/dist`. The output in the command prompt looks as shown in Figure 10-25.

```
Command Prompt
F:\work\book\tomcatcinemas>ant clean dist
Buildfile: build.xml

clean:
   [delete] Deleting directory F:\work\book\tomcatcinemas\build
   [delete] Deleting directory F:\work\book\tomcatcinemas\dist

prepare:
    [mkdir] Created dir: F:\work\book\tomcatcinemas\build
    [mkdir] Created dir: F:\work\book\tomcatcinemas\build\WEB-INF
    [mkdir] Created dir: F:\work\book\tomcatcinemas\build\WEB-INF\classes
     [copy] Copying 24 files to F:\work\book\tomcatcinemas\build
     [copy] Copying 1 file to F:\work\book\tomcatcinemas\build\WEB-INF
    [mkdir] Created dir: F:\work\book\tomcatcinemas\build\WEB-INF\lib

compile:
    [javac] Compiling 22 source files to F:\work\book\tomcatcinemas\build\WEB-IN
F\classes
     [copy] Copying 2 files to F:\work\book\tomcatcinemas\build\WEB-INF\classes

javadoc:
    [mkdir] Created dir: F:\work\book\tomcatcinemas\dist\docs\api
  [javadoc] Generating Javadoc
  [javadoc] Javadoc execution
  [javadoc] Loading source files for package bible.tomcat.tccinemas...
  [javadoc] Loading source files for package bible.tomcat.tccinemas.servlet...
  [javadoc] Loading source files for package bible.tomcat.tccinemas.test...
  [javadoc] Loading source files for package bible.tomcat.tccinemas.util...
  [javadoc] Constructing Javadoc information...
  [javadoc] Standard Doclet version 1.4.0

  [javadoc] Building tree for all the packages and classes...
  [javadoc] Building index for all the packages and classes...
  [javadoc] Building index for all classes...

dist:
      [jar] Building jar: F:\work\book\tomcatcinemas\dist\tomcatcinemas-0.1-dev.
war

BUILD SUCCESSFUL
Total time: 8 seconds
F:\work\book\tomcatcinemas>_
```

Figure 10-25: `ant clean` and `dist` tasks run to create a WAR file of the application.

Once you have your WAR file you can read about how to deploy it in Chapter 7. Remember that when deploying the application all the contents of the `template.context.xml` must be found in the application's destination environment. This includes the resource and resources parameters we added to facilitate database connectivity.

Summary

What we have discussed in this chapter is merely an example of one way to implement an application. The techniques used in this chapter are far from definitive, however they give you an understanding on how to structure your application in a smart way; a way that will provide for growth and flexibility.

Remember, you can download the entire application (as well as most of the other source code in this book) from Wiley's Web site.

✦ ✦ ✦

Debugging

In This Chapter

This chapter is concerned with debugging Web applications. The chapter first defines what it is that debugging strives to achieve. It then delves into some techniques and tools that developers use to accomplish this.

As the discussion illustrates, debugging is as much a technique that a developer learns through experience as programming itself, and indeed being good at programming can make the process of debugging that much simpler and more effective. A well-designed application allows the programmer to easily identify paths that may be causing problems and also allows the easy (or relatively pain free) resolution of that problem.

Of course, debugging does not just extend to syntax or logical errors within an application, it can also relate to the development environment itself. Understanding the development environment is therefore of critical importance in trying to track down and fix problems.

While this chapter is broadly structured around not using an IDE to do debugging and using an IDE to debug, both form part of the *process* of debugging.

To illustrate the use of specific tools in debugging we have drawn on the use of the two IDEs explained in Chapter 6.

What Is Debugging?

Debugging is the process of investigation that a developer goes through to find the cause of a problem. This problem may be related to the logical flow of the code, the data that the application uses, or in the environment that the application runs in. These are all considerations that the developer must take into account when he or she tries to solve a problem.

Types of Problems

We can broadly divide the myriad of potential problems that can arise in software development into application problems and environment problems. Application related problems reflect some sort of problem that occurs in the code of the application, whereas environment problems can relate to the server itself or in some other resource the application may use. This could extend as far as the operating system or a network.

In this chapter we focus entirely on application-related problems.

Application Related Problems

As mentioned before, application related problems could be caused by some type of flaw within the code of the application. The problem can arise at compile time or runtime, or even both as in the case of Java Server Pages.

Compile time errors are immediately apparent to the programmer because an error is displayed in the console or on the browser. Compile errors usually relate to a syntax error in the code, a missing variable, variables falling out of scope, and so on.

A program may compile, as in it is syntactically correct, however when the application is run, one or many scenarios can cause an error to occur or a part of the program solves the problem it was built to solve incorrectly. We would call this a logical error. This type of error may be due to user input, flawed logic, or a million other reasons.

Programmers become good at identifying problems in an application through experience and the use of various techniques. In this chapter we can't really give you the experience to become good at debugging applications, but we can show you some of the tools and techniques that experienced programmers use.

Debugging without an IDE

Some programmers will tell you that "real men don't use IDEs." While not being locked into a certain development environment does have its advantages, programmers who don't use IDEs must rely on other techniques for debugging their applications. These other techniques may involve:

- Print statements
- Application logging tools
- Java debugging tools
- Profiling
- Assertions
- Documentation
- Using revision control.
- Looking at code
- Walking away from the problem
- Getting someone else to look at the code
- When the data is the problem

We will now look at these techniques, then look at ways to debug Java Server Pages without the use of an IDE.

Print Statements

Placing millions of print statements in your code is less than fun. It's tedious, boring, and involves lots of typing. But with these disadvantages comes a lot of flexibility that IDE-based tools cannot compete with.

To illustrate the use of print statements let's look at a simple code fragment:

```
int errorCauser = 10;

for(int i=1;i < 10; i++)
{
   errorCauser = i % errorCauser;
}
```

Rest assured that the variable `errorCauser` does cause an error. It eventually causes a divide by zero error because it is assigned the result of `i %errorCauser` (or `i modulus errorCauser`) and therefore becomes zero eventually.

If the code fragment were in a servlet, any error would not be apparent until the servlet was run. Upon browsing to the servlet it would result in the Exception shown in Figure 11-1.

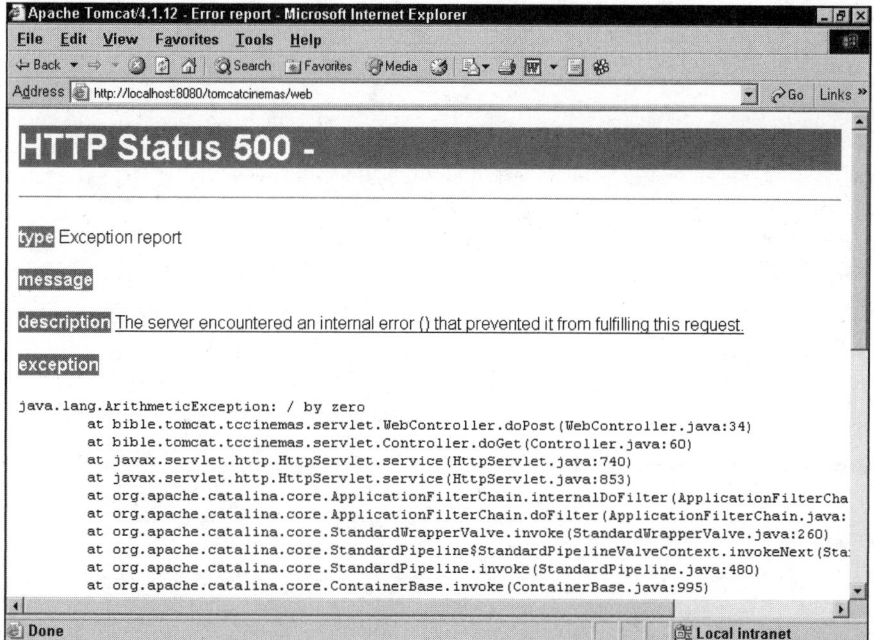

Figure 11-1: Servlet runtime error

The `/ by zero` hint in the exception description provided by Tomcat, together with the line number, would guide the developer to the line that was causing the problem.

If we were developing code like this that we thought worked correctly (although we probably wouldn't call a variable `errorCauser`!) it is possible that the connection between this variable being reduced and the divide by zero error would not be clear to the programmer until the value of the variables could be seen.

We can remedy this by placing some simple `System.out.println` statements around the code to output the relevant values as they are being processed. The resulting code would look like the following:

```
int errorCauser = 10;
for(int i=1;i < 10; i++)
{
    System.out.println("before op");
    System.out.println("value of i: " + i);
    System.out.println("value of errorCauser: " + errorCauser);
    System.out.println("");

    errorCauser = i % errorCauser;

    System.out.println("after op");
    System.out.println("value of i: " + i);
    System.out.println("value of errorCauser: " + errorCauser);
    System.out.println("");
}
```

As you can see, we have placed `System.out.println` statements at the start and end of each run of the `for` loop. When the servlet is executed again, the error would still appear in the browser, but our server console would output the following:

```
before op
value of i: 1
value of errorCauser: 10

after op
value of i: 1
value of errorCauser: 1

before op
value of i: 2
value of errorCauser: 1

after op
value of i: 2
value of errorCauser: 0

before op
value of i: 3
value of errorCauser: 0
```

From this we can see that the error occurred during the third run through the `for` loop. After seeing this output the developer would hopefully realize that the order of the variables in the modulus statement are the wrong way around; the line should in fact read:

```
errorCauser = errorCauser % i;
```

Although this is a very simple and contrived example (there is no real point to this snippet of code) of using print statements to help solve problems, it does illustrate how they can potentially be used in more complex scenarios such as ensuring that certain methods are called, or testing for null objects and so on.

toString()

Every object in Java derives from `java.Object`, and in doing so inherits a `toString()` method. By default this method returns the name of the class as well as a hex representation of the hash code of the object. The Java API documentation states that all subclasses of this object should override this method.

Having a `toString()` method in your own classes allows the contents of the object to be displayed in some way during the debugging process. For instance, the `toString()` method of a simple bean may appear as:

```
.....
public String toString()
{
    StringBuffer sb = new StringBuffer();
    sb.append("Name: " + name + "\n");
    sb.append("Age: " + age + "\n");
    sb.append("Address: " + address + "\n");

    return sb.toString();
}
.....
```

Therefore if this were the `toString()` method on our class, `MyObject`, it could be output to the console with:

```
MyObject mine = new MyObject();
System.out.println(mine.toString());
```

These methods are often laborious to create, especially where there are many member variables, however due to the amount of debugging that may have to occur on larger objects, they are invaluable in the debugging process and therefore worth the extra time to create.

Application Logging Tools

Logging tools offer a more sophisticated debugging mechanism than just print statements within code. Logging tools can be used within code and output debugging statements in different ways, even categorized so that only say critical errors are reported to the console, while informational items are entered in a log file.

Log4j

Log4j (`http://jakarta.apache.org/log4j/`) is an Apache backed tool that provides just this and much more. Log4j can output to many media including:

- File
- Console
- java.io.OutputStream
- java.io.Writer
- A remote server
- A remote syslog (Unix)
- A remote listener (using JMS)
- Windows NT Event Log

The format of these outputs can be customized according to the developer's wishes and its behavior can be modified without recompiling. While there is a certain administrative overhead in integrating Log4j into your application, the power and flexibility of this tool can be a lifesaver in debugging larger applications.

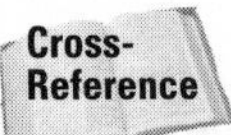

Chapter 17 explains Log4J in more detail.

Servlet Logging

The ServletContext object that is available from within your servlet has a logging facility. This logging facility logs items to a log file in the server. In Tomcat this file is located at: %CATALINA_HOME%/logs. The following code was placed inside the doPost method of a servlet:

```
ServletContext ctx = getServletContext();
ctx.log("this is a log entry");
```

This log entry appears in the log file localhost_log.24-12.2002.log within the preceding directory. A log item can be similarly written to the log files by calling either of the following methods:

```
log(java.lang.String message)
log(java.lang.String message, java.lang.Throwable throwable)
```

This second method allows the developer to write an Exception (or anything that is Throwable) to the log file and provide an appropriate message as well. Therefore the code:

```
ServletContext ctx = getServletContext();
ctx.log("this is a log entry", new ServletException("myexception"));
```

```
Would result in the following being written to the log file:
```

```
...
2002-12-24 17:29:19 this is a log entry
javax.servlet.ServletException: myexception
    at
bible.tomcat.tccinemas.servlet.WebController.doPost(WebController.java:25)
    at bible.tomcat.tccinemas.servlet.Controller.doGet(Controller.java:60)
    at javax.servlet.http.HttpServlet.service(HttpServlet.java:740)
    at javax.servlet.http.HttpServlet.service(HttpServlet.java:853)
    at
...
```

We can see then that this is an alternative method to writing debugging output to the console. The provision of this ability to log statements from the servlet to the log file is part of the Servlet Specification.

Java Logging

With J2SE 1.4 came a new extension to the java.util package in the form of java.util.logging. This package offers similar logging functionality to Log4j discussed in the previous section. One advantage of using this tool over Log4j is its native presence within the Java platform.

Java Debugging Tool

Java Debugger (JDB) is a debugging tool that comes packaged with the JDK. It is possible to start Tomcat in a debugging mode and then attach the JDB tool to the running process to debug Java classes.

Profiling

Profiling is the process of investigating why an application may be running slowly or badly, and using tools to find out where the program may be spending most of its time. Many tools can be employed to do this but probably one of the simplest ways is to time the execution of code by adding more code. For instance, adding a timestamp (`System.currentTimeMillis()`) at certain points in the program's execution allows you to see how long an individual task took to complete. For instance, the following code would print out the difference in time between the first line of the code fragment and the last line. The processing in between involves looping through the numbers 0 to 1,000,000:

```
long start = System.currentTimeMillis();

for(int i=0; i <= 1000000; i++)
{
   //nothing happens in here.
}

long end = System.currentTimeMillis();
long diff = end - start;

System.out.println("the time elapsed was:" + diff);
```

If you run a servlet or JSP page, the text "the time elapsed was:..." and then the result of the difference between start and end times captured would be printed out in the Tomcat console. Around more intensive blocks of code, this type of analysis could identify problems and help with comparing different techniques for improving performance.

More advanced and comprehensive tools such as JProbe and OptimizeIt allow bottlenecks in an application's execution to be identified.

Profiling may also extend beyond the reach of the application code itself and may encompass environmental causes. For instance, a slow network may adversely affect a program that uses a remote data source.

Assertions

Assertions are statements in code that test a certain belief concerning the state of variables or objects. For instance, one assertion may be that a `boolean` variable is true, such as:

```
public boolean myMethod(boolean tested)
{
    if(!tested)
    {
        System.out.println("tested is not true");
    }
    else
    {
```

```
            assert tested; // this will always be true.
        }
        return tested;
    }
```

Assertions are a very powerful technique of quickly discovering problems in code. They prove or disprove a programmer's belief about how the application runs. The preceding example is a very contrived one; we can tell that it will always assert to true. Should an assertion not resolve to true, an `AssertionError` will be thrown. More complex examples attempt to resolve the preconditions that must exist before a piece of code is run, and post conditions test the result of a piece of code.

Pre and Post Conditions

Conditions placed at the start and end of a method, testing for the expected input and expected output, are important in the debugging process. The `assert` statement is excellent for accomplishing this. For instance, suppose we require a method to only accept integer values that are greater than 10 and less than 110. Using assertions to enforce this, the code would appear as:

```
private void processVariable(int variable)
{
    assert variable > 10 && variable < 110 : variable;
    ....
}
```

You should only test the parameters of a non-public method in this way, because a public method should always check that the parameters it receives are within acceptable bounds.

The preceding example is a pre-condition to the remaining processing that the method holds. A post condition would test the return value of a method in a similar way. For instance:

```
public int getResult()
{
    assert result > 1000 && result < 15000 : result;
    return result;
}
```

This example tests that the returning value, `result`, will be greater than 1000 and less than 15000.

Class Invariant

If we have a class that holds a set of values that all must be within certain ranges before the instance of the object is considered to be in a certain state, a class invariant is used to provide a test to see if these apply. For instance, suppose we have a `SpaceShuttle` object whose values must be okay before a launch can proceed. A method such as `canLaunch` would be as follows:

```
public boolean canLaunch()
{
    boolean rv = true;

    if(_fuel < 200000)
    {
        rv = false;
```

```
        }

        if(_sizeOfCrew < 2 || _sizeOfCrew > 5)
        {
            rv = false;
        }
        return rv;
    }
```

This type of method can then be used in an `assert` statement to ensure that the value of the `SpaceShuttle` object is okay, for example:

```
assert ss.canLaunch();
```

Where `ss` represents an instance of the `SpaceShuttle` object.

Assertions were added to Java in JDK 1.4.0. For more information on developing, compiling, and running classes containing `assert` statements, please consult the Sun Documentation.

Documentation

Programmers love commenting their code. Okay, maybe I'm lying there, but programmers debugging a piece of code actually do love comments. Comments are an important component of any piece of mildly complex code, and the more complex the code, the more likely someone is going to have to debug it at some stage. A well-phrased comment at just the right place can save a developer hours of time trying to figure out why something was done the way it was.

Other forms of documentation also can help in the debugging process by shedding light on the application and its intended environment. Specifications, whether written to describe the larger architectural implementation or low-level algorithms, can prime a developer fresh to the project with important information.

Revision Control

Source control is every developer's best friend, not only because of the many conveniences of versioning and branching, but also because differences between versions may point to the cause of bugs.

As an example, many source control systems allow the programmer to perform a *diff* (view the differences) between two versions of a file in the code repository. For instance, if a bug's behavior can be tracked to version 1.5 of a file, or a release of many files, but not in 1.4, the differences between these two versions can be output and analyzed. While this may not solve any problems directly, it will point the programmer in the right direction and make his or her investigation a lot more informed.

Looking at Code

It may sound obvious but sitting quietly and reading through code, maybe with a pen and piece of paper available, is an effective method of debugging a piece of code.

Walking Away

What? Walk away from the computer when there is an error?! This is one of those "things-you-learn-through-experience" items we mentioned. Often a developer will have his or her head so buried in the problem and a set of potential (and maybe incorrect) solutions, that hours can be wasted effectively getting nowhere. This is where walking away from the problem domain and thinking about other things can help dramatically.

Pragmatically, this doesn't have to mean physically walking away from the computer, it may just mean fixing another bug, or doing something besides fixing *that* problem. This might all sound a bit magical but more often than not, it works.

Getting Someone Else to Look at the Code

This is related to the previous item. When a programmer has a preset idea of how the problem *must* be solved, a set of fresh eyes must take a different perspective. A new person to the problem must learn the intricacies of what the code is doing. In doing this, they will often consider other possibilities to a potential solution.

When the Data Is the Problem

Applications that use data rely on the integrity of that data to perform their job. Unless the program is 100 percent bullet proof, there are invariably times when the structure of the data that the program uses is not in the exact form it expects. In programs that have not been designed or implemented to deal with this, the problem being experienced may be attributed to bad data. This can apply equally to databases, delimited text files and so on.

This concludes a brief list of debugging techniques used by developers when not using an IDE. All developers will use at least a sub set of these throughout their career. There are countless other methods for finding an error within the code of an application, certainly more than the scope of this book allows. We will conclude this section with a brief discussion concerning the debugging of JSP pages.

Debugging Java Server Pages

Debugging JSP is difficult and at times frustrating. Unfortunately, the error messages provided by the JSP engine are not entirely simple to decipher.

As you know, the first time a JSP page is accessed the container may have to compile it. The output of this compile is a servlet within the server's work directories. In Tomcat this directory resides at: `%CATALINA_HOME%/work/standalone/<HOST NAME>/<CONTEXT NAME>`. You will see in this directory some `.java` files representing the JSP pages within this context. Each has a corresponding `.class` file, being the compiled version.

With this knowledge our ability to debug a simple JSP error easily is increased. Often the error messages that display in the browser point to this `.java` file with a corresponding line number. For instance, if we placed the same code as in the Print statement example within a new JSP page (`MyJSP.jsp`), in addition to the servlet exception we witnessed earlier, there would be a root cause below it, pointing to the Java file that was generated. The JSP page therefore appears as:

```
<%
int errorCauser = 10;

for(int i=1; i < 10; i++)
{
    errorCauser = i % errorCauser;
}
%>
```

And the corresponding root cause explanation that appears in the browser would appear as shown in Figure 11-2.

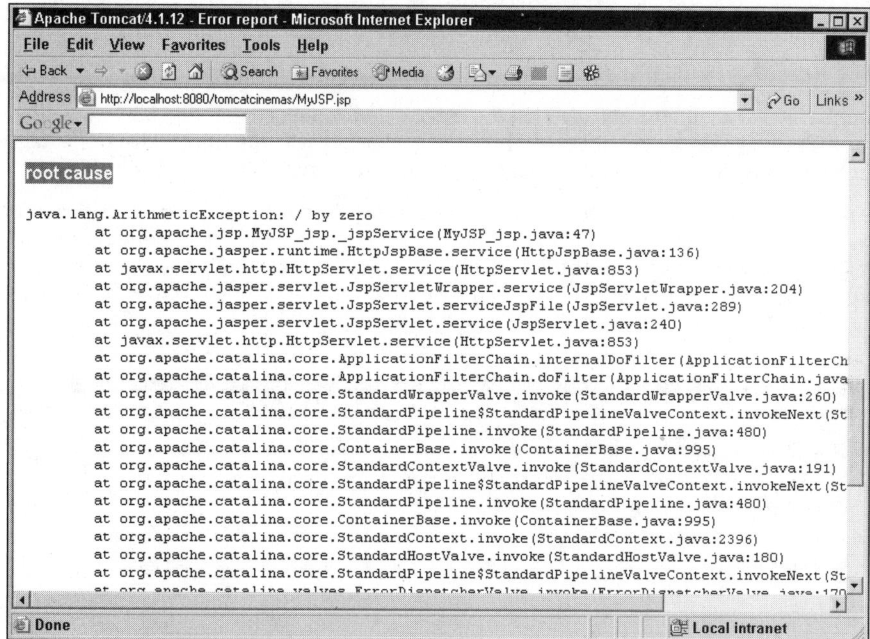

Figure 11-2: Root cause to JSP error

You can see from Figure 11-2 that a name similar to the JSP page name appears in the exception, `MyJSP_jsp.java`, and a line number is provided, 47.

This file is the generated servlet version of our JSP page and resides in the work directories of Tomcat. Going to line47 reveals the now infamous `errorCauser = i % errorCauser;` line. This is a run-time error in the JSP page; the page compiled correctly, yet failed when it was executed. By looking at the generated Java file you can more or less decipher the problem that the program has run into, together with the message of the exception (in this case a `java.lang.ArithmeticException`) thrown.

Often the code that is generated corresponding to the JSP page will not be very easy to read. This is more the case when there are a lot of `<%=someVariable%>` items interspersed throughout the code. In generating the servlet the server replaces these with `out.print` statements. Lots of these fragments mixed with other Java statements can make the code more convoluted and difficult to read.

The preceding example is a very simple one, and the error produced by the server is actually fairly clear. More difficult problems to debug include syntactical errors in the JSP tag syntax. For instance if the line:

```
<jsp:forward page="someFile.jsp" >
```

(Yes, there is a deliberate error placed here) were placed in a JSP page, for our page to forward the request to `someFile.jsp`, the resulting error would be at best cryptic. This line results in: `org.apache.jasper.JasperException: Unable to compile class for JSP`. And the root cause is a: `java.lang.ArrayIndexOutOfBoundsException`. Not very helpful. The error is caused by some invalid XML syntax in this code, and should read:

```
<jsp:forward page="someFile.jsp" />
```

That's right, that simple missing / on the end caused so much trouble. This is a compile time error. The container could not compile the page due to the error. Knowledge of JSP tag syntax together with a keen eye, is a distinct advantage in debugging these types of problems.

A similarly difficult problem to resolve is the absence of closing curly brackets in embedded Java code. This has the effect of disturbing the generation of the corresponding servlet. For instance, if we removed the closing } in the `errorCauser` example's `for` loop shown previously, the resulting compile errors would point to a `catch` statement that was missing a corresponding `try` block. The result of this appears in Figure 11-3:

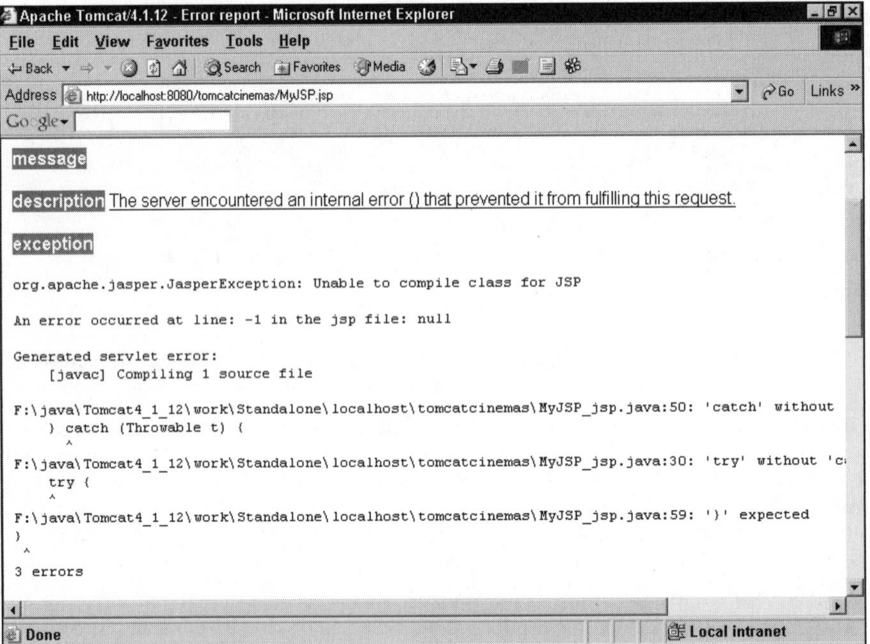

Figure 11-3: JSP compile error

If we examine the code surrounding lines 50, 30, and 59 it points to the beginning of a `catch` block within the generated code. Within a more complicated page with a larger group of content within the try block of the code, only very careful examination would reveal the cause of the error.

When a JSP page is full of logic, `include` files and JSP Tag entries, debugging complexity increases exponentially. This is one of the reasons why good design is paramount to make working with the application all the more stress free. For instance a well-executed MVC architecture would render the JSP pages only to print out content and variables, with little or no logic required.

Error Page

It is possible to identify a specific JSP page to be displayed in the case of an error. This is achieved by adding the following page directive to the top of the error page (called `error.jsp`).

```
<%@ page isErrorPage="true" %>
```

Doing this allows an implicit object, `exception`, to be referenced as the exception that has caused the error to occur.

Files that may cause an exception have the following directive directing errors be sent to the nominated error page:

```
<%@ page errorPage="error.jsp"  %>
```

Whenever an exception occurs in this page, the `error.jsp` file is displayed. With the `isErrorPage="true"` page directive the error page can capture the stack trace and perform some display or logic. This may assist with debugging by having a uniform presentation of JSP errors, or performing some sort of notification or logging mechanism when an error occurs.

Precompiling Java Server Pages

One additional way of debugging a JSP without having to deploy to a server and have it compile the page on the first load is to pre-compile the page before hand. Like `javac` is a compiler for `.java` files, `jspc` is a compiler for JSP files. You can execute `jspc` from the command line on your JSP files. Using `jspc` with Ant is explained in Chapter 5.

Debugging with an IDE

The previous section discussed the process of debugging without using an IDE and therefore focused more on techniques, rather than tools. This section focuses entirely on debugging using an IDE.

In Chapter 6 we discussed using two IDEs for Web application development. This section again focuses on those same IDEs but in a purely debugging sense. Both have some very useful debugging tools for us to make use of.

Those who have used IDEs before will be familiar with the basic concepts of debugging, however some readers may not, and so some definitions are required before we get started:

✦ **Breakpoint:** A breakpoint is the position in the code where you would like the execution of the program to wait for further instructions.

✦ **Step:** After a breakpoint has been hit, the programmer would use step to "step" through the lines of code following, one by one. Using step follows the logic of the code, and will therefore loop where there are looping structures and so on.

✦ **Continue:** Continue begins execution of the program again.

✦ **Watch:** A watch is similar to the print statements we used before. Adding a watch means you add a watch to a variable, thereby checking its value as you step through the code. If the value of the variable changes in the program the Watch reflects this change appropriately.

We expand on these definitions further in the coming discussion, however as a learning exercise you are encouraged to use the IDEs yourself.

Debugging with SunONE Studio

For the purposes of this discussion we use the same Web Module created in the Internal Tomcat Server discussion of SunONE Studio in Chapter 6, `MyWebApp`. During that discussion we created a simple JSP page, `MyJSP`, and a servlet called `MyServlet`. We are going to use these files to illustrate debugging of JSP files within the context of a Web application. These concepts are very much the same were we to be using a non-Web application.

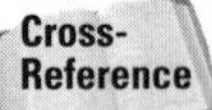

It is recommended that you read Chapter 6 to become familiar with SunONE Studio. This section refers to files and environments previously established in Chapter 6.

Debugging JSP in SunONE Studio

SunONE Studio integrates debugging for JSP files by matching the resulting servlet of a JSP file, line for line, with the JSP file itself. In SunONE Studio you can add breakpoints and watches into a JSP file and then step through the code to pick up any logical errors.

Let's start by using the same code that we used in the non-IDE debugging example from the previous section. Copy this code into the `MyJSP.jsp` file from the Chapter 6 Web Module, MyWebApp, we created. The contents of your MyJSP.jsp file in SunONE Studio Web Module should now appear as:

```
...
<%
int errorCauser = 10;

for(int i=1; i < 10; i++)
{
    errorCauser = i % errorCauser;
}
%>
...
```

We will use the debugger in SunONE Studio to determine the number of loops our problem code will be able to execute before the divide by zero error occurs. To achieve this we are going to add two watches to debug with, one for the `i` variable and one for the `errorCauser` variable.

Add a watch by highlighting the name of the variable in the code and selecting `Debug > Add Watch...`. A small dialog box will confirm that you wish to add a watch to the variable selected. Do this for both the `errorCauser` variable and for `i`.

Now we need to tell the execution process to pause where we want it to. Place the cursor on the line where the `errorCauser` variable is declared and initialized. From the menu select `Debug > Add Breakpoint`. A red line will appear on the Editor window indicating a Breakpoint at this stage. A breakpoint means that for debugging purposes, halt execution at this line and await instructions. This allows us to step through the remaining lines of code so that we can see variables with a watch attached changing their value.

When placing a breakpoint in the source code, make sure you position it on a line that has code. Adding a breakpoint to a line without code does not work.

We can now start the IDE's debugging process. Go to the Debug menu and select Start. The server starts in the usual way and the Workspace changes to debugging. A new browser appears and your source code is displayed with a green line indicating where the execution point currently is; it's all happening!

Your (now very busy) screen should look like Figure 11-4:

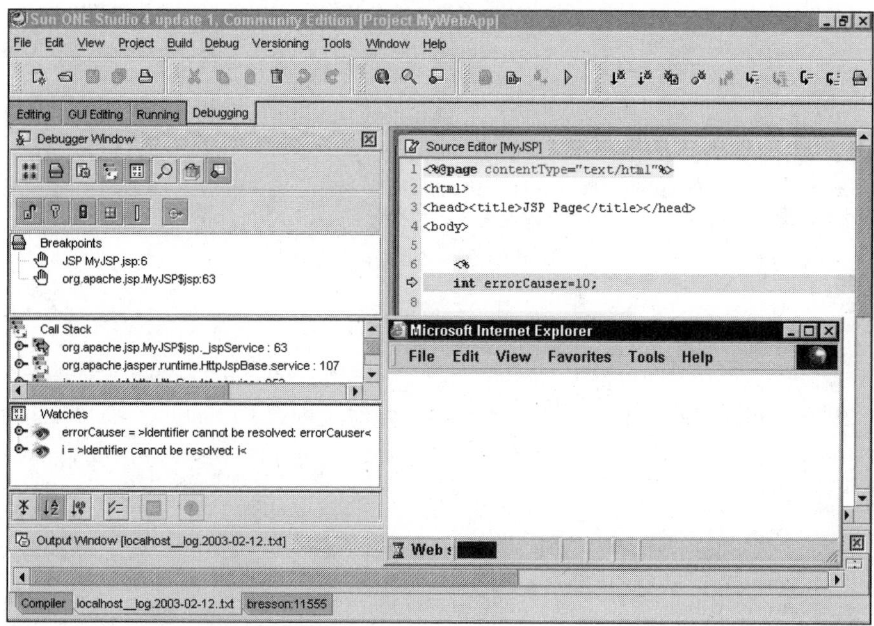

Figure 11-4: Debugging a JSP file has started.

Now go to the Debug menu again and click Step into. This moves the execution point to the next line of code (find the step into button in the button menu to make this easier, or simply press the F7 key on your keyboard), which is the `for` loop initialization. Press it again and the execution point moves to the `errorCauser` line where the error will occur soon. Note now in the Watches window of the Debugger window that our watches have values. Watch these values as you continue to step through the code. Once the end of the `for` loop is reached it loops around again, following the logic in the page. Keep going until the error is found; the output window at the base of the screen will show the exception. Note that the value of the `i` watch is 3 and the `errorCauser` watch is 0. We can therefore determine that the loop fails on the third round at the `errorCauser = i % errorCauser` line.

Note

There are a few different types of `Step` commands available. Their usage is not pertinent to the current example, however they generally refer to the IDE's debugging behavior when methods are called from the within the code being debugged. The SunONE Documentation explains their differences.

This feature of being able to step through the code inside the JSP file itself is important. Other IDEs may only allow these debugging tools to be used on the generated servlet code. SunONE Studio also enables you to step through the JSP file *and* the generated servlet and add breakpoints and watches to both.

Figure 11-4 shows various windows open while this debugging process is occurring. While the code and the current step position are displayed in the right panel, the left panels show various types of information that should be changing as we step through the program.

✦ The first left panel in Figure 11-4 shows the Breakpoints list. This lists the breakpoints we have created in the source code we are stepping through currently.

✦ The second left panel in Figure 11-4 shows the hierarchy of methods called from within the program. This is the *Call Stack*.

✦ The third left panel in Figure 11-4 shows the current status of any watches you have added, as well as their current value.

These are just the panels viewable in Figure 11-4. Other panels can be added to this view, such as:

✦ **Variables View:** Lists the current variables in scope.

✦ **Classes View:** Shows the hierarchy of all classes loaded in the code being debugged.

✦ **Threads View:** Shows the threads the currently debugged program has created so far.

The way the debugger in SunONE behaves when debugging a JSP file can be configured by going to `Options > Debugging and Executing > JSP & Servlets`. Here you can tell the debugger to skip static (HTML) lines in the JSP file, and which browser to use when it starts.

Once you have completed the debug process you can select `Debug > Finish`, and the debug process will end. It should be noted that all Java programs could make use of the debug process in SunONE Studio in this way. We have chosen to illustrate this in the context of a JSP page, given the focus of the book.

Compile Errors in JSP Files

It is possible to compile JSP pages before they arrive within the context of the server. As mentioned before, the ability to do this allows JSP files to be analyzed for correctness before they are viewed in a browser.

The following steps show you how to compile this file and view any errors it may contain within the IDEs standard output. Take the file we have been debugging previously and add a deliberate error to the `for loop` declaration. Change the `for loop` declaration to appear as:

```
for(int i; i < 7; i++)
```

As you can see, the `int i`, has not been properly initialized. Right-click the file within the Explorer view of the editing workspace and select Compile. The SunONE Studio interface should look similar to Figure 11-5:

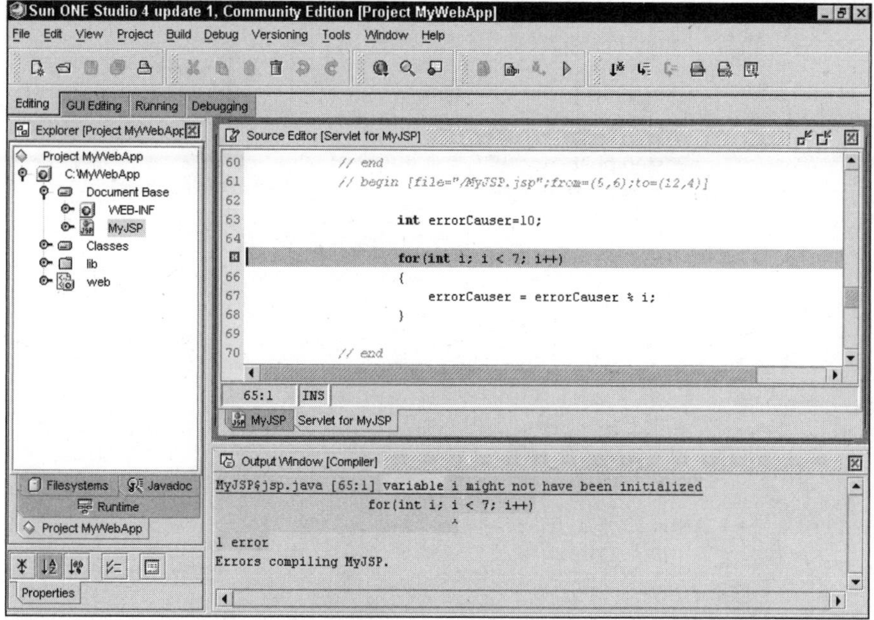

Figure 11-5: Compile errors in a JSP file.

When compile is selected the output window displays the error we deliberately entered into the code. The title of the error is highlighted to hot link to the place in the code where the error was found. When you double-click this link the line of code in error is highlighted within the JSP page's corresponding servlet. Notice two files in the editor view in Figure 11-5. The active file is the servlet; the inactive file is our JSP page. Once we correct the error and recompile the page, the output windows should display "Finished MyJSP." If all has gone correctly and there are no errors apparent in the output window we can execute the file to display in the browser by right-clicking the file and selecting Execute. This starts the Internal Tomcat Server (if required) and displays the JSP page in the browser. If you fixed the MyJSP file to have the error line as `errorCauser = errorCauser % i;` and not `errorCauser = i % errorCauser;`, the page should finish executing without error.

Http Monitor

The HTTP Monitor is available by default when you debug your application, but you can access this tool at any time by selecting `Debug > HTTP Monitor`. This tool monitors all HTTP information being processed by the server. If you click through its tabs you will see the type of information it stores as you execute code from within your project. One super cool feature is the ability to replay particular requests to the server to see their effects. This enables you to reproduce particular errors exactly as they occurred at that particular request.

From some initial requests to the `MyJSP` page on the internal server, the requests that are used are recorded in the HTTP Monitor, as shown in Figure 11-6:

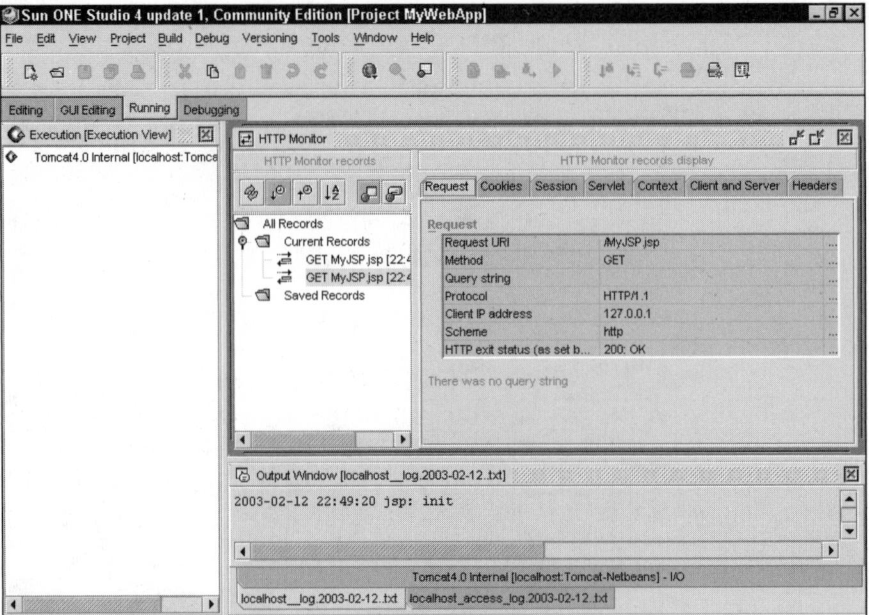

Figure 11-6: HTTP Monitor

The list of `GET MyJSP.jsp` items in the main window shows different HTTP GET requests made to the Internal server in displaying this page. If you right-click one of these items you would see options to replay this request. Selecting one of these again displays the page in the same way the original request was made. The debugging and testing possibilities of this kind of tool are virtually endless.

The preceding examples used a JSP page to illustrate debugging features of SunONE Studio, however the same functionality can be used for servlets created in the Web Module. The process you would go through to do this is very similar.

There is obviously more to debugging with SunONE Studio than can be printed here, however the preceding discussion gives you some insight into the power of SunONE Studios and its ease of use with respect to debugging Web applications.

Debugging with the Eclipse Platform

The remaining section of this chapter deals with debugging a Web application using the Eclipse Platform. Eclipse has the ability to use different plug-ins to allow integration with Tomcat. The debugging process is therefore different depending on which plug-in is being used.

In this section we have chosen two plug-ins and shown the debugging process under these environments. Some of the concepts explained in the SunONE section are the same as for Eclipse.

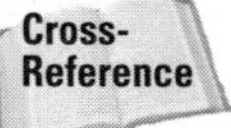

Chapter 6 explains the use of the Eclipse Platform. It is recommended that you are familiar with the Eclipse Platform, and have completed the sample application before proceeding.

Tomcat 4.x Patch for JSP Debugging

JSP compilation using Jasper generates servlet source and class files under the work directory `C:\tomcat\work`, unless the `workDir` argument is explicitly specified within the context definition in `server.xml`.

In Tomcat 4.x, these servlets are always placed in the `org.apache.jsp` package irrespective of the location of the page within the Web application's root. For example, a JSP file placed in the document root of the Web application will be compiled into a servlet with a package declaration of `org.apache.jsp`. The same package declaration will also be applied to servlets generated from JSP files located within subdirectories under the document root.

The Eclipse Java Builder does, however require that source files be located in directories corresponding to their package structure. Therefore, a class with package declaration `bible.tomcat` must reside in a `bible\tomcat` directory within the source tree. The Eclipse Java Builder is less lenient than `javac` command distributed with Sun's JDK.

A problem arises when Eclipse's Java Builder is required to compile servlet classes generated by Jasper for debugging purposes. The files generated by Jasper are not placed in a directory structure corresponding to the package structure.

Eclipse works around this problem by explicitly specifying a working directory in the Web applications context, in which generated files are to be placed. This working directory is specified to include the package directory structure required by the Eclipse Java Builder. An example working directory is shown can be found at this Web site: `C:\eclipse\workspace\project\work\org\apache\jsp`.

However, this workaround is not sufficient. Within the Web application document root there may be various subdirectories, for example `foo`. JSP files within the `foo` subdirectory will be compiled and placed into a directory named `foo` under the working directory. Eclipse is unable to compile the generated servlet source due to a mismatch between the package name, `org.apache.jsp`, and the location of the code in the source tree. Java Builder generates the following error:

```
The declared package does not match the expected package org.apache.jsp.foo
```

The Tomcat 4.x patch for JSP debugging fixes this problem by appending the subdirectory name to the package declaration. In this case, the servlet source has the following declaration:

```
package org.apache.jsp.foo;
```

Eclipse's java builder successfully compiles the generated servlet, enabling debugging to take place using the built-in debug tool.

Download

To allow debugging with the Sysdeo Eclipse Tomcat Launcher and the Lomboz plug-in it is necessary to download a patch for the Tomcat server. This patch fixes a known problem with Tomcat described in the Tomcat 4.x Patch for JSP Debugging section.

The patch may be downloaded from `http://www.sysdeo.com/eclipse/tomcatPlugin.html`. Select the patch corresponding to the version of Tomcat you are using: `jasperDebugPatchV4.1.12.zip`, and when prompted save the file to disk.

Installation

The JSP debugging patch must now be applied to the Tomcat server. Extract the `jasperDebugPatchV4.1.12.zip` file downloaded previously to `C:\tomcat\common\classes`. It will create the directory `C:\tomcat\common\classes\org\apache\jasper` and subdirectories.

JDK 1.4.x is recommended for debugging with Eclipse because it supports the hot code replacement feature. However, throughout this chapter JDK 1.3.1 is used to retain consistency with the rest of the book. Without a 1.4.x JDK the Eclipse Platform cannot hot swap code from the development environment straight into the in process Tomcat, requiring Tomcat to be restarted.

Caution

Unless you recompile all JSP pages after applying this patch, a `HTTP 500: Internal Server Error` may be displayed when viewing a JSP. This is a result of the patched version of Tomcat attempting to load for generated servlets with invalid package declarations. To avoid these errors, stop the Tomcat server and delete the contents of the `C:\tomcat\work` directory. If you have custom work directories specified in any contexts within `C:\tomcat\conf\server.xml`, be sure to delete those as well. Upon startup, any subsequent requests will compile JSPs into servlets with valid package declarations, and the page will display correctly.

Debugging with the Sysdeo Tomcat Plug-in

Typically, debugging of servlets is difficult. Developers resort to logging debug output to standard out, or using a logging framework like log4j. However, with the use of Eclipse and the Tomcat Launcher plug-in, it is possible to actively debug the servlets and JSP with the use of a fully featured debugging tool.

Using eclipse, the following steps explain how to debug the Tomcat project created in Chapter 6. The described steps focus on JSP debugging. Servlet debugging follows a similar procedure, with some of the steps omitted.

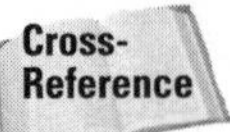

The Tomcat project setup is explained in the Sysdeo Eclipse Tomcat Launcher section of Chapter 6.

Although JSP debugging is supported, the facility to directly step through JSP source code is not supported. Unfortunately, it is only possible to step through the servlet source code generated from the JSP.

If necessary, start the Tomcat server using the Start Tomcat button on the toolbar or select `Tomcat>Start Tomcat` from the menu.

If it is not already displayed, open the Java Perspective on your Eclipse workbench.

It is essential for JSPs that Tomcat pre-generates the servlet before debugging can commence. If you haven't already done so open `http://localhost:8080/hello/HelloWorldJSP.jsp` in your favorite browser.

When a user requests a JSP in a browser, Tomcat generates a servlet in the context's working directory. As you may have seen in Chapter 6, the context created for the Tomcat project specifies a working directory located in `C:\eclipse\workspace\hello\work\org\apache\jsp`. All generated servlet source code and object files are placed in the working directory.

To see the files generated by Tomcat it is necessary to refresh the Package View in the Java Perspective. Right-click the project name "hello" and select Refresh from the pop-up menu.

After the Package View is refreshed and the work directory is expanded, a generated servlet generated named `HelloWorldJSP_jsp.java` should be displayed as shown in Figure 11-7.

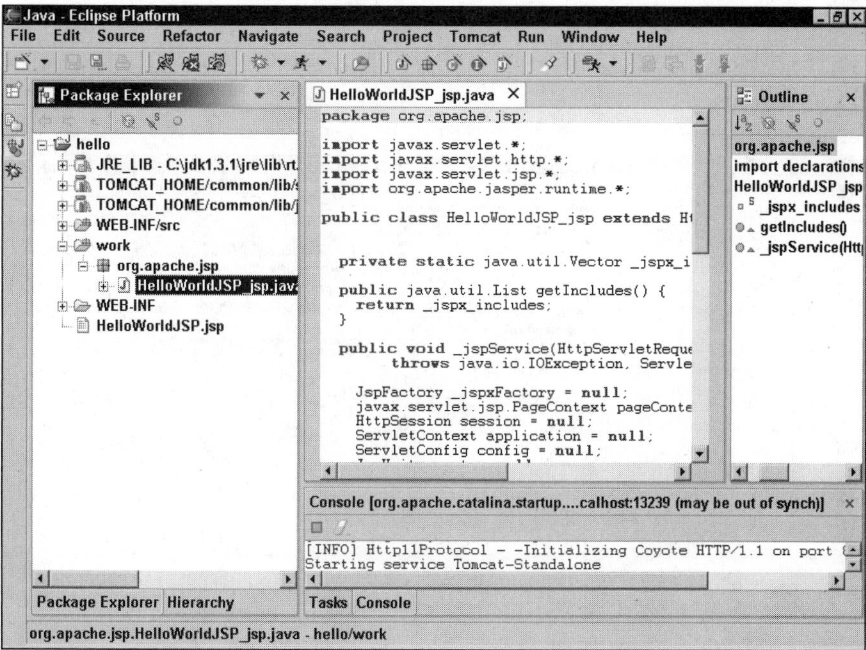

Figure 11-7: Generated servlet source in the project's work directory

Double-click `HelloWorldJSP_jsp.java` in the package View to open the generated servlet in the Eclipse Text Editor.

To debug the page, a breakpoint should be set to suspend execution of the program so it can be analyzed in the Debugger Perspective. Set a breakpoint on line 42 of `HelloWorldJSP_jsp.java`. by double-clicking the vertical ruler, next to the line of source:

```
String helloMessage = "Hello World!";
```

Once the breakpoint has been set, the JSP needs to be rerun. Open `http://localhost:8080/hello/HelloWorldJSP.jsp` in your favorite browser. Notice this time that no response is returned. Due to the suspended execution of the JSP, the browser appears to hang.

When you switch back to Eclipse, the Debug Perspective is already opened and the Text Editor view highlights the current point of execution in the source code.

Using the top-right View, the user can navigate through variables, breakpoints, expressions, or display the results of hand-written expressions. For a more detailed description of the features of the debugging tool, please refer to the Eclipse User Guide.

Notice that the servlet execution has been suspended just before the breakpoint. Therefore, there is no reference to `helloMessage` in the Variables View.

If we step through to the next line of code by clicking the Step Over button on the Debug View toolbar, or select `Run>Step Over` from the menu, you will see the next line of code highlighted. The Variables View will also show the value of the variable, `helloMessage= "HelloWorld!"`, shown in Figure 11-8. Alternatively, the user may explicitly inspect the variable by highlighting the entire variable name in the source code, right-clicking, and selecting Inspect from the pop-up menu. The properties of the variable are displayed in the Expressions View.

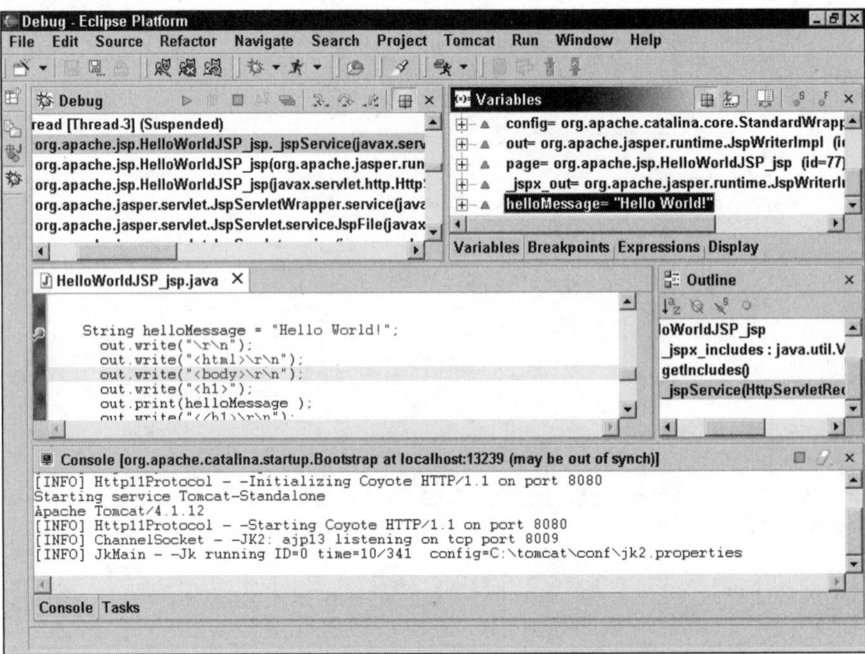

Figure 11-8: Variable View in debug perspective

Through the Variables View it also is possible to change the values of the variable at runtime. Double-clicking the `helloMessage` variable opens an editable text field; in the text field, replace `"Hello World!"` with `"G'Day world!"` and press enter to commit the changes.

Once sufficient debugging has taken place, normal execution of the program can resume by selecting Resume from the Debug View toolbar, or selecting `Run>Resume` from the menu. The execution of the servlet will resume, and after completion a response is returned to the browser, displaying the results of the test.

The result displayed in the browser reflects the changes made to the `helloMessage` variable in the debugger. In this case "`G'Day World!`" should be displayed.

Note

Debugging servlets is just like the steps outlined for debugging JSP, however breakpoints can be set directly in the servlet source code, because pre-generation of servlets is not necessary.

Upon completion of debugging the JSP request, the Debugging Perspective may be closed. At this point the developer may make any necessary changes made to the source code using the Java Perspective. Assuming the Tomcat server is left running and at least one breakpoint exists, debugging another session for `HelloWorldJSP.jsp` is as simple as opening the URL `http://localhost:8080/hello/HelloWorldJSP.jsp` in a browser.

Caution

Be careful not to terminate the process. This will stop the Tomcat server.

Debugging with the Lomboz Tomcat Plugin

With some minor modifications to the Lomboz J2EE project developed in Chapter 6, debugging is also possible using the Lomboz plug-in. It is essential that a working version of the hello Lomboz J2EE project has been set up prior to commencing this section.

Cross-Reference

The Lomboz J2EE project setup is explained in the Lomboz J2EE Plug-in section of Chapter 6.

Note

Like the Sysdeo, debugging from within the JSP file is not supported; the generated servlet must be used to debug.

If it is not already displayed, open the Java Perspective on your Eclipse workbench.

Stop the Tomcat server if it is already running. Click on the Lomboz J2EE View, and under the Container named hello, right click on the Tomcat server entry. Select Stop Server from the pop-up menu to stop the Tomcat server.

It is essential to undeploy any previous versions of the application before proceeding. Applications deployed using WAR files may interfere with the debugging process. Right click on the hello Container and select Undeploy from the pop-up menu. A dialog will appear while the plug-in is removing the WAR file and the expanded context from the `C:\tomcat\webapps` directory.

Note

During the project setup explained in Chapter 6, the project's build path should include the jasper runtime libraries. If this is not the case the Lomboz plug-in will be unable to debug JSPs.

To check the project's build path right click on the project in the Package Explorer View and select Properties from the pop-up menu. In the Properties for hello dialog select Java Build Path from the left pane. In the right pane a tabbed panel should be displayed, click the Libraries tab to include internal and external JAR files and classpaths into the build path. Check the JAR `TOMCAT4/common/lib/jasper-runtime.jar` is included in the build path.

If `jasper-runtime.jar` not included in the build path it may be added using the Add Variable feature. Clicking the Add Variable button displays a list of pre-defined variables. Click on `TOMCAT4`, and then press the Extend button. A Variable extension dialog box will appear. In the variable extension select `common/lib/jasper-runtime.jar` from the menu and press OK to add the library to the build path.

To successfully debug JSPs, the Tomcat context in Listing 11-1 is configured to generate servlets within the Eclipse workspace. The `workDir` argument specifies that all servlets generated from JSPs are to be placed underneath the Eclipse workspace in the `j2src` directory. The `docBase` is also configured to point directly at the development area in the Eclipse workspace. Add the context in Listing 11-1 into your `C:\tomcat\conf\server.xml file`.

Listing 11-1: server.xml (fragment)

```
...
<Context path="/hello"
    docBase="C:\eclipse\workspace\hello\hello"
    workDir="C:\eclipse\workspace\hello\j2src\org\apache\jsp" />
...
```

Start server in debug mode, without deploying the Container. In the Lomboz J2EE View, right click on the Tomcat server and select Debug Server from the pop-up menu.

Caution Deploying the container will generate a WAR file and deploy it into the `webapps` directory of the Tomcat server. This may interfere with the manual context configured in Listing 11-1.

Caution It is essential for JSPs that Tomcat pre-generates the servlet before debugging can commence. If you haven't already done so open `http://localhost:8080/hello/HelloWorldJSP.jsp` in your favorite browser.

When a user requests a JSP in a browser, Tomcat generates a servlet in the context's working directory. As you may have seen earlier, the context created for the Tomcat project specifies a working directory located in `C:\eclipse\workspace\hello\jspsrc\org\apache\jsp`. All generated servlet source code and object files are placed in the working directory.

To see the files generated by Tomcat it is necessary to refresh the Package View in the Java Perspective. Right-click the project name `"hello"` and select Refresh from the pop-up menu.

After the Package View is refreshed and the work directory is expanded, a generated servlet named `HelloWorldJSP_jsp.java` should be displayed as shown in Figure 11-9.

Double click `HelloWorldJSP_jsp.java` in the package View to open the generated servlet in the Eclipse Text Editor.

To debug the page, a breakpoint should be set to suspend execution of the program so it can be analyzed in the Debugger Perspective. Set a breakpoint on line 42 of `HelloWorldJSP_jsp.java`. by double-clicking the vertical ruler, next to the line of source:

```
String helloMessage = "Hello World!";
```

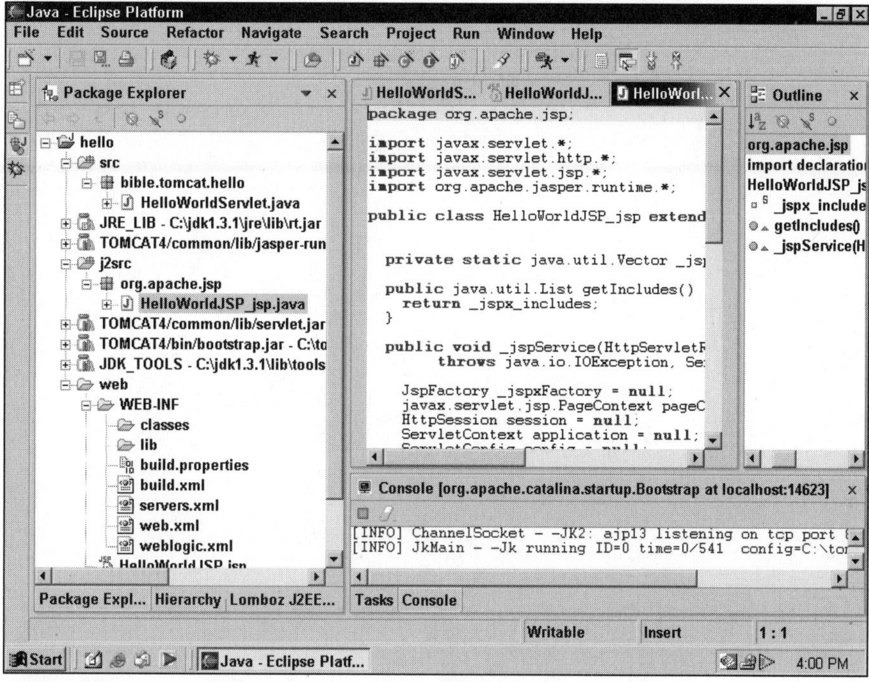

Figure 11-9: Generated servlet source in the project's j2src directory

Summary

The discussions in this chapter have extended from debugging techniques that programmers use in their everyday work to using the specific features of IDEs to assist in the debugging process. Debugging is a big part of a programmer's work and mentioning every technique and tool available is clearly not possible. As always, good design is the key to good debugging. A well-designed program will allow for the simple resolution of problems with a minimum of fuss and disruption to the development process.

✦ ✦ ✦

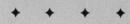

Application Security

CHAPTER 12

In This Chapter

This chapter looks at one of the more challenging areas in Web application development, that of securing the Web application.

The chapter starts with an examination of security in general and different aspects of security that might need to be addressed depending on circumstances.

It is followed by a recap of the security components provided by Tomcat that have already been covered in previous chapters and how they may be applied.

The chapter concludes by implementing security requirements to the Web application developed in Chapter 10.

Aspects of Security

The security of Web applications can be considered to have a number of facets. These relate to different requirements for the Web application and the data that is used by it. There are several sorts of questions that can be used to identify how and what should be secured:

- Who can access the application?
- How can the users be identified?
- Where can the application be accessed from?
- Is any of the application data private?
- Who can add/modify/delete data?

If these questions look like additional requirements for a Web application then that is good, as that is exactly what they are. A common error in building software of all types, not only Web applications, is to try and build the functionality of the software (what it does) and then try to add security later.

This is a path that leads to much pain and suffering for the developers and the users. It is very important to consider the security requirements part of exactly the same process as the functionality requirements and design and build the Web application with all the requirements in mind from the beginning.

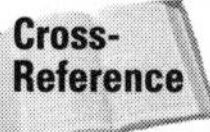

This chapter implements the security requirements covered in Chapter 10.

There are four main aspects relating to security requirements:

- ✦ Authentication
- ✦ Authorization
- ✦ Data integrity
- ✦ Confidentiality

These aspects are covered in more detail in the following sections.

Authentication

Authentication is the proof of identity. The most well known form of authentication is the username and password, however, having a personal key pair and certificate is starting to become more common with the introduction of smart cards to securely hold the keys.

Authentication is used in many applications to attach identity to a session that is accessing a resource. This resource may be protected in some manner. The reason for authentication is to validate if the identity is authorized to access the resource. An example of this is Internet banking or Web-based e-mail.

There also are applications where the resources are not protected and the authentication is used to apply personalization or provide identity for submitted information. Examples of this use include Web-based information services such as Slashdot (`www.slashdot.org`) or Java Developers Connection (`http://developer.java.sun.com`).

The servlet specification provides support for the container to perform authentication via the security-constraint element in the `web.xml` file.

The forms of authentication specified in the servlet specification and provided by Tomcat are:

- ✦ HTTP basic authentication
- ✦ HTTP digest authentication
- ✦ Form-based authentication
- ✦ SSL client authentication

There also is the option to implement a custom authentication solution manually, accessing a user database directly after obtaining user credentials from a form or HTTP request. This can be done as part of the core Web application or implemented as a filter that controls access to resources based on the requests. This chapter focuses on container-provided security and authentication mechanisms.

HTTP basic authentication is the simplest method for a Web application to support. There are no other resources required to be provided by the Web application (other than configuration of the user database) and if the requirement is merely to protect a resource then this provides a quick method for the Web application deployer.

There are three considerable drawbacks with using HTTP basic authentication. The first is that the security of the transmitted information is very poor. The username and password are transferred by the browser for every request and are "protected" by a BASE-64 encoding of the information.

The second drawback is the visual aspects of the authentication dialog box are quite basic, and do not fit in well with the style of many Web applications.

The third drawback is that the use of basic authentication is controlled by the browser, and there is no way to log out the user other than to shut down the browser. This is generally not a particularly acceptable option.

HTTP digest authentication is an extremely similar approach to HTTP basic authentication, the difference being that the information transmitted from the browser to the server does not contain the password, but a digest consisting of the password and some random values. HTTP digest authentication is not commonly used due to lack of support in browsers.

Form-based authentication provides advantages over HTTP basic authentication. The first and most significant from a visual point of view, the form-based authentication uses an HTML FORM element that can be styled to suit a Web application. The second advantage is that form-based authentication is implemented using some form of server-side session tracking and as a result the session can be invalidated and the user can log out, often a very desirable feature.

The final available option is SSL client authentication. This is not just using SSL configured in the server as shown in Chapter 8, but actually having the servlet container verify the authenticity of the client-presented certificates. This is generally not a very attractive option because it requires the users of the system to create and install certificates to use the Web application. In certain specific circumstances (such as an extranet application) it may be a worthwhile authentication mechanism.

It is a very useful technique to implement HTTP basic authentication or form based authentication over HTTPS because this secures the credentials passed between the browser and Tomcat.

Authorization

Authorization is also known as *access control*. Authentication provides the identity of the user accessing the resource, and authorization determines if the user has the permissions to access the resource.

In the servlet specification the authorization model is role based. What this means is that a user is assigned one or more roles and resources can be accessed by authenticated users with the specified role. Roles are a convenient means of providing a set of users with the same access rights. Users can be added or removed from a particular role to change the resources that can be accessed. If new resources are added to the Web application (such as new functionality) then all users that are currently assigned to a particular role can then access the new resource with a single change. This is a preferable position to modifying the access rights to each and every user.

The Tomcat file-based authentication realm has also implemented the concept of groups. A group is a collection of roles and a user may be assigned to a group and to roles, increasing the flexibility of managing the access rights of users.

Tomcat provides access to the authentication and authorization information by using a *Realm*. A Realm provides a mapping between the username, password, and the roles assigned to the user.

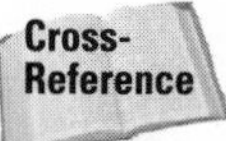

Details on configuring Realms are covered in Chapter 8.

Authorization of access to resources can be performed in two ways. The first is declarative, and this is where the application developer provides elements in the Web application deployment descriptor (`web.xml`) to specify resources that are protected. This is the `security-constraint` element, and provides a URL mapping specifying the resource that is protected and the role required to access the resource.

Caution

> The declarative security model is based only on client initiated requests. Any use of the `RequestDispatcher` to invoke `forward` or `include` methods to resources is not processed by the servlet container and may be used to access otherwise "protected" resources.
>
> Because the Web application developer has complete control over the use of these methods to access resources within the Web application selecting the appropriate mechanisms to implement security within the Web application is an important design consideration.

An example of the `security-constraint` element and the corresponding user and role configuration is shown in Listing 12-1.

Listing 12-1: **Declarative Security Configuration**

```
(in web.xml)
<security-constraint>
      <display-name>Administrators Only</display-name>
      <web-resource-collection>
          <web-resource-name>
              Administration
          </web-resource-name>
          <url-pattern>/admin/*</url-pattern>
          <http-method>GET</http-method>
          <http-method>POST</http-method>
      </web-resource-collection>
      <auth-constraint>
          <role-name>cinema-admin</role-name>
      </auth-constraint>
      <user-data-constraint>
          <transport-guarantee>
              NONE
          </transport-guarantee>
      </user-data-constraint>
  </security-constraint>

(in conf/tomcat-users.xml)
<?xml version='1.0' encoding='utf-8'?>
<tomcat-users>
  <role rolename="cinema-admin"/>
  <user username="jon" password="733t" roles="cinema-admin"/>
</tomcat-users>
```

As can be seen from Listing 12-1, declarative security is controlled at a high-level with a very coarse grained approach to authorizing access to a resource. In many situations this may be suitable, but where authorization forms part of business rules then an alternative mechanism is required.

An example of authorization forming part of the business rules of a system might be preventing access to a resource out of "standard business hours (9.00am to 5.00pm)" or having roles with fine-grained rights such as "can view or modify, but not add or delete records."

To facilitate these requirements, the second style of security model for authorization is available. This is called *programmatic security* and as the name suggests, requires the Web developer to explicitly write code to implement the authorization rules.

Note

Programmatic security requires the implementation of rules within the Java code of the Web application, but still uses the servlet security framework for authentication of the users. If the `security-constraint` elements are not used within the Web application then the following APIs will not contain useful values.

There are three methods used to obtain user and role information when developing programmatic security solutions:

- `String getRemoteUser()`
- `boolean isUserInRole(String role)`
- `Principal getUserPrincipal()`

`getRemoteUser()` returns the username that is currently authenticated, or `null` if the user is not authenticated.

`isUserInRole()` returns true if the currently authenticated user is in the specified role.

`getUserPrincipal()` returns a `Principal` object representing the currently authenticated user, or `null` if the user is not authenticated. The `Principal` object can then be queried using `principal.getName()` to return the current username.

Data Integrity

Data integrity is often a forgotten aspect of security. Data integrity is the property that prohibits changes from occurring in the data during transmission. Basically, whatever the client or server sends, the recipient gets exactly as sent, or can detect that a change has been made.

This is a very important part of Web application security. Imagine what would happen if a purchase of 10 items from a Web site was changed to 100 items without the knowledge of the purchaser.

A Web application developer can do little to impact on the data integrity of information because it is a servlet container responsibility and is provided when HTTPS/SSL connections are used.

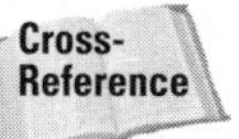

Setting up an SSL connection is described in Chapter 8.

Confidentiality

Confidentiality is generally the only part that most people consider when thinking about security. Confidentiality is the aspect of security that keeps private data private during transmission and is implemented by encrypting the data. Servlet containers provide this functionality by implementing an HTTPS/SSL connection to be used by the Web application.

Confidentiality for many Web applications is not enough because the data may be transmitted secretly, but if there is no authentication or authorization then anybody can access the original data! The converse is certainly true as well. If the authentication information can be easily examined during transmission between the client and server, then authentication is severely compromised.

The confidentiality configuration is performed as part of the declarative security model and is often outside the control of the Web application developer. This may cause issues if the Web application developer requires data to be transmitted confidentially. The `ServletRequest` object provides a method `isSecure()` that returns true if the request was made over a secure channel.

The Web developer can implement code within a Web application either as a filter, or as code within a servlet that can prohibit access to resources unless the request has been performed over a secure channel.

Tomcat Security Components

Tomcat provides a number of components that can form a part of the security configuration for a Web application. Some of these are part of the Tomcat configuration and are specific to Tomcat, while other elements are part of the servlet specification and are appropriate across all Web application servers.

Within the `conf/server.xml` the following elements form part the of the security configuration:

✦ Realm

✦ Connector (SSL)

✦ Valve (`RemoteAddressFilter`, `RemoteHostFilter`)

Cross-Reference

Details about the configuration of these elements in `server.xml` are covered in Chapter 8.

The `Realm` element represents the user authentication model for the Web application. A `Realm` element may be configured at the Engine, Host, or Context level and any Realms configured will be inherited by lower-level containers and may be overridden as desired.

The two most likely Realm elements to be encountered are the `MemoryRealm` and the `JDBCRealm`. `MemoryRealm` is the default Tomcat Realm for providing the authentication and authorization data. `MemoryRealm` is configured via an XML file, by default `conf/tomcat-users.xml`.

Note

The `MemoryRealm` and `UserDatabaseRealm` entries in the default Tomcat configuration file provide the same functionality when used as an authentication realm. The `UserDatabaseRealm` provides additional functionality when used by the Tomcat Administration Tool, and can be updated by the Web-based interface. The `MemoryRealm` provides a "read-only" snapshot of the same information.

The `JDBCRealm` provides access to a user authentication scheme in a relational database that contains the mapping between the users, password, and roles. Generally this requires 3 tables; the first is the user table that contains the username and passwords. The second is the role table that contains the role identifiers and the names. The third is a mapping table that maps the relationships between the user table and the role table.

The `Connector` elements provide the mechanism for requests from clients to be delivered to Tomcat and processed. A Connector can be configured to support the SSL protocol via a Factory element within the Connector. If a CONFIDENTIAL transport guarantee is to be used it is important to configure the HTTP connector attribute `redirectPort` to the correct port number for the new SSL-enabled connector.

Tip

The default Tomcat configuration provides an SSL connector on port 8443, however the standard SSL well-known port number is 443.

Caution

Using the `redirectPort` to switch from the HTTP connector to the SSL enabled connector requires additional configuration that will be described in detail later in the chapter. The startup script for Tomcat needs to be modified to include an additional parameter to provide the `java.net.URL` implementation information about the https `URLStreamHandler`.

The `Valve` element provides two options for IP or host-based security. The `Valves` are the `RemoteAddressFilter` and `RemoteHostFilter`. These can be configured to allow or deny access to a set of resources covered by the `Valve`. The `Valve` can be configured at the Engine, Host, or Context level and will cover all the containers that are at the same level or lower than the `Valve`.

The following elements are configured in the `web.xml` of the Web application.

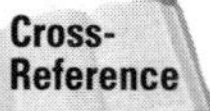

Cross-Reference

Configuration of the Web application elements is covered in Chapter 3.

The main security configuration in the `web.xml` is the `security-constraint` element that defines the resources that are protected. Within the `security-constraint` the `web-resource-collection` defines the resources and the `auth-constraint` defines the role required to access the resources. The `security-constraint` element defines the authorization requirement for the Web application.

In addition to the `security-constraint` element the `login-config` element defines the authentication mechanism for the Web application.

Two other elements in the deployment descriptor provide identification and linking of the roles used in the Web application. The `security-role` element is used to define the roles that are used in the Web application. The `security-role-ref` element defines a linking of a `role-name` used in the code for the Web application, in methods such as `isUserInRole(role)`, to a `role-link`. The `role-link` is the name of the role defined in the Realm.

Tomcat Cinemas Security Requirements

From examining the requirements list in Chapter 10, the following requirements are related to security and are addressed in this chapter. This section examines the requirements and how they may be implemented.

- ✦ Administrators cannot login to the system remotely (from the Internet)
- ✦ Only staff can use the over-the-counter interface
- ✦ Each staff member must be identified separately
- ✦ A staff member cannot be logged onto the system more than once

✦ Staff must use the logout facility when leaving the application

✦ The Web interface must be secured using SSL

Address Access Control

There are two main candidates for implementing this functionality within a Web application. The first is to use the Tomcat built-in Valves, `RemoteAddressFilter`, the second is to implement this functionality as part of the Web application.

It would be advantageous to use the `RemoteAddressFilter` because it requires no additional coding to implement. However, the design of the Web application needs to be different from the results in Chapter 10. The smallest unit of control the `RemoteAddressFilter` can operate on is at a Context (or Web application level). This means that the entire Web application would either be blocked (not very useful for Web bookings!) or the Web application would be split into three distinct applications that are controlled separately.

The implementation of the address access control is performed by developing a Filter than can intercept the requests to the administration application and checking that the IP address of the request is from an appropriate location. Building this functionality as a filter does not directly change the operation of the Web application and this filter may be used on other applications.

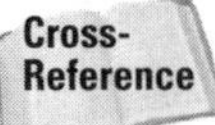

Further information on Filters can be found in Chapter 3.

Staff Authentication

There are two types of internal users for the Web application.

✦ **Administrator:** A staff member of Tomcat Cinemas with administrative privileges.

✦ **Staff:** A member of Tomcat Cinemas staff.

The administrators can access the administrative functionality only. The staff can access the front desk functionality only. This maintains a clear separation of job function, however the flexibility of the authentication and authorization components make changing this behavior a relatively easy task.

The Web application uses declarative security for the administration functionality and for the front desk functionality to force the Tomcat Cinemas internal users to authenticate. All administrator users belong to the "cinema-admin" role, and all staff belong to the cinema-staff role.

To implement this functionality the Web application is configured to use the form based authentication mechanism. This also provides the capabilities to implement the staff identification requirements that cannot be fulfilled using the BASIC or DIGEST authentication schemes.

Staff Identification and Restriction

The requirement to prevent multiple simultaneous logins using the same username is not necessarily common; however it prevents staff members from sharing their authentication information (username and passwords) to other staff members on the same shift. This provides better control for the management of Tomcat Cinemas and better reporting facilities.

More importantly it provides a great example of how to use the declarative security to authenticate users and then perform more fine grained security control using the information from the authenticated users.

To implement this functionality the Web application checks the status of the session to see if the currently authenticated user has been validated and is not currently logged in. If the user is not logged in, information is stored in the session and in the Web application context to identify this user as currently logged in. If the user is already logged in, the current session is abandoned and the login is rejected.

Staff Logout

This requirement is provided to simplify the Web application. If staff members use the logout functionality to exit the application then the Web application can clean up its currently-logged-in-status very easily.

Because HTTP is a stateless protocol and users are users this requirement does not make much sense in the real world. A more sophisticated algorithm to appropriately handle abandoned logins would need to be implemented, however that is beyond the scope of this example.

To implement this functionality the Web application will remove the user from the list of currently-logged-in users and abandon the current session.

Web Customer Access Secured with SSL

The functionality to secure the Web customer access is a fairly common requirement and is provided completely by the Tomcat and Web application configuration.

An SSL Connector is configured and the Web application defines a security constraint over the Web booking resources. The security constraint does not define an `auth` constraint (or the Web customers would have to log in!) but has a transport guarantee of `CONFIDENTIAL`.

If a Web customer accesses the booking servlet using a non-secure (HTTP) protocol then the use of the `CONFIDENTIAL` transport guarantee forces a switch to use a secure transport protocol (HTTPS). If the Web customer is already using HTTPS as the protocol, then no switch is needed.

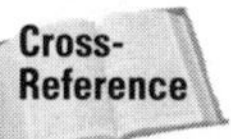

This functionality requires the Tomcat and SSL Connector to be configured. Details about how to perform this configuration can be found in Chapter 8.

Updating Tomcat Cinemas

The following sections work through the requirements and implement the security functionality for Tomcat Cinemas.

The format of each of the sections follows a common template:

- Modifications to the Web application configuration
- Modifications to the Web application code
- Modifications to the Tomcat configuration
- Testing and troubleshooting the modifications

To work with the examples in this chapter it is highly recommended to have worked through the Tomcat Cinemas example in Chapter 10.

The configuration for the development environment and all the code for the application can be found in Chapter 10; only the additions and modifications are shown in this chapter.

Authentication of Administrators and Staff

The first step in implementing the authentication of administrators and staff is to modify the Web application deployment descriptor, `web.xml`, as shown in Listing 12-2. This defines the security constraints and the login configuration for the Web application. These elements need to be inserted into the `web.xml` in the correct order, and these should be inserted after the servlet-mapping elements.

Listing 12-2: **Updating web.xml**

```
. . . .
</servlet-mapping>

<security-constraint>
      <display-name>Front Desk</display-name>
      <web-resource-collection>
          <web-resource-name>Front Desk
          </web-resource-name>
          <url-pattern>/frontdesk/*</url-pattern>
          <http-method>GET</http-method>
          <http-method>POST</http-method>
      </web-resource-collection>
      <auth-constraint>
          <role-name>cinema-staff</role-name>
      </auth-constraint>
      <user-data-constraint>
          <transport-guarantee>
              NONE
          </transport-guarantee>
      </user-data-constraint>
  </security-constraint>
  <security-constraint>
      <display-name>Administrators Only</display-name>
      <web-resource-collection>
          <web-resource-name>
              Administration
          </web-resource-name>
          <url-pattern>/admin/*</url-pattern>
          <http-method>GET</http-method>
          <http-method>POST</http-method>
      </web-resource-collection>
      <auth-constraint>
          <role-name>cinema-admin</role-name>
```

```
        </auth-constraint>
        <user-data-constraint>
            <transport-guarantee>
                NONE
            </transport-guarantee>
        </user-data-constraint>
    </security-constraint>
      <login-config>
          <auth-method>FORM</auth-method>
          <form-login-config>
              <form-login-page>/login.html</form-login-page>
              <form-error-page>/login_err.html
              </form-error-page>
          </form-login-config>
      </login-config>
      <security-role>
          <description>A cinema staff member</description>
          <role-name>cinema-staff</role-name>
      </security-role>
      <security-role>
          <description>A cinema administrator</description>
          <role-name>cinema-admin</role-name>
      </security-role>
```

Listing 12-2 defines the `security-constraint` for the Front Desk and Administration sections of the Web application. The resources that match the `url-pattern` require a user with a role defined in the `auth-constraint`. Both of these sections of the application do not require a transport guarantee.

The `login-config` element defines the `auth-method` and the associated configuration. Because the `auth-method` is `FORM`, the configuration defines the pages the servlet container will use for the login and error pages. These pages can be a static HTML page as shown above, or a JSP page or even a servlet.

Finally the `security-role` elements define the roles that are used by the Web application and map to the role names defined in the authentication realm.

The next step is to update the Web application. The use of the FORM authentication requires a login page and the login error page; these are shown in Listing 12-3 and 12-4. Create these files in the `web` directory where they will be installed with the other Web resources by the build scripts.

Listing 12-3: **login.html**

```
<!DOCTYPE HTML PUBLIC "-//W3C//DTD HTML 4.01 Transitional//EN">

<HTML>
  <HEAD>
    <TITLE>tomcat cinemas</TITLE>
  </HEAD>
```

Continued

Listing 12-3 *(continued)*

```
  <BODY>
  <h1>Tomcat Cinemas Staff Only</h1>
  <p>
  <table>
    <form action="j_security_check" method="post">
      <tr>
         <td>Username</td>
         <td><input type="text" name="j_username"></td>
      </tr>
      <tr>
         <td>Password</td>
         <td><input type="password" name="j_password"></td>
      </tr>
      <tr>
      <p>
         <td align="right"><input type="submit" value="Login"></td>
         <td align="left"><input type="reset"></td>
      </tr>
    </form>
  </table>
  </BODY>
</HTML>
```

The login page uses the custom action (`j_security_check`) and form field names (`j_username, j_password`) defined in the servlet specification.

Listing 12-4: login_err.html

```
<!DOCTYPE HTML PUBLIC "-//W3C//DTD HTML 4.01 Transitional//EN">

<HTML>
  <HEAD>
    <TITLE>Error During Login</TITLE>
  </HEAD>
  <BODY>
      An error occurred during login.
      <p>
      This may be due to insufficient privileges to access
      the desired resource, or due to an incorrect username
      and/or password.
      <p>
      Click on the link below to try again.
  <p>
  <a href="index.html">Return to Index Page</a>
  </BODY>
</HTML>
```

The login error page is quite simple and merely provides an error message and a link to return to the index page of the application.

The next step is to modify the controller servlets to obtain the username of the currently logged in user. This is then displayed as part of the output. Listing 12-5 shows the modifications to the `AdminController`, shown in bold.

Listing 12-5: AdminController.java

```
public class AdminController
    extends Controller
{
    protected void doPost(HttpServletRequest request,
                          HttpServletResponse response)
        throws ServletException, java.io.IOException
    {
        . . . .
        if(action == null)
        {
            action = "menu";
        }

        /*
         * Authentication information !
         */
        String user = request.getUserPrincipal().getName();

        if (action.equals("logout"))
        {
            HttpSession session = request.getSession(true);
            session.invalidate();
            incPath = "/index.html";
        }

        //action decision block
        if(action.equals("menu"))
        {
            incPath = ADMIN_MENU_PAGE;
            request.setAttribute("title",
                                 "Tomcat Cinemas Administration Menu");
            request.setAttribute("user",user);
        }
        else if(action.equals("addTheatre"))
        . . . .
}
```

Examining Listing 12-5, the changes are fairly minor. The username is obtained from the `request` object and a new action logout is defined where the current session is invalidated and the user is then directed to the Web application default page. The username is set as an attribute in the `request` object used in the JSP pages.

The next step is to make some minor modifications to the JSP file for the Administration Menu to display the username and the logout action. These modifications to `menu.jsp` are shown in bold in Listing 12-6.

Listing 12-6: **menu.jsp**

```
<jsp:useBean id="title" class="java.lang.String" scope="request"/>
<jsp:useBean id="user" class="java.lang.String" scope="request"/>
<jsp:useBean id="servletPath" class="java.lang.String" scope="request"/>

<html>
<head><title>Tomcat Cinemas - <%=title%></title></head>
<body>
<table cellspacing="3" cellpadding="4" border="0" width="500" align="center">
<tr>
    <td align="center" colspan="2">
        <font face="verdana" size="3"><b><%=title%></b></font>
    </td>
</tr>
<tr>
    <td align="center" colspan="2">Current User: <%=user%></td>
</tr>
<tr>
    <td align="center" colspan="2">
        <a href="<%=servletPath%>?action=logout">Logout</a>
    </td>
</tr>
<tr>
    <td width="50%">
        <font face="verdana" size="2"><b>Theatres</b></font>
    </td>
    <td width="50%" align="right">
        <font face="verdana" size="2"><b>Films</b></font>
    </td>
</tr>
. . . .
```

That completes the changes for the Administration side of the Web application. Similar changes need to be made to the Front Desk functionality. Listing 12-7 shows the modifications to the `FrontDeskController`, shown in bold.

Listing 12-7: **FrontDeskController.java**

```
public class FrontDeskController
    extends Controller
{
    protected void doPost(HttpServletRequest request,
                          HttpServletResponse response)
```

```
        throws ServletException, java.io.IOException
    {
        response.setContentType("text/html");
        PrintWriter out = response.getWriter();
        String action = request.getParameter("action");
        String incPath = null;

        String user = request.getUserPrincipal().getName();

        if(action == null)
        {
            action = "listBookableShowings";
        }

        if (action.equals("logout"))
        {
            session.invalidate();
            incPath = "/index.html";
        }
        else if(action.equals("listBookableShowings"))
        . . . .
        else if(action.equals("detailShowing"))
        {
            incPath = doDetailShowing(request,response,SOURCE_FD);
        }

        request.setAttribute("user", user);
        request.setAttribute("action",action);
        performInclude(incPath,request,response);
    }
}
```

Listing 12-8 shows the modifications to the associated JSP file shown in bold.

Listing 12-8: fdListShowings.jsp

```
<%@ page import = "java.util.*" %>
. . . .
<jsp:useBean id="showings" class="java.util.ArrayList" scope="request"/>
<jsp:useBean id="user" class="java.lang.String" scope="request"/>

. . . .
<tr>
    <th colspan="7"><font face="verdana" size="3" color="black">
        <b><%=title%></b></font>
    </th>
</tr>
<tr>
```

Continued

Listing 12-8 *(continued)*

```
    <td>Current User: <%=user%></td>
    <td colspan="5">
        <a href="<%=servletPath%>?action=logout">Logout</a>
    </td>
</tr>
<tr>
. . . .
```

The final step in the modifications in this section is to add some users and roles and configure Tomcat to use the `Realm` for this Web application.

Note: This example uses the `MemoryRealm` for the users and roles. There is a `UserDatabaseRealm` configured for the Engine in the default Tomcat installation. This uses exactly the same configuration as a `MemoryRealm` and is provided in the default installation for the Tomcat Administration Tool to add users, groups, and roles.

More details on configuring a `MemoryRealm` can be found in Chapter 8.

Check the `server.xml` for a `MemoryRealm` or `UserDatabaseRealm` for the Engine, and if one does not exist include this element as a component in the Engine.

```
<Realm className="org.apache.catalina.realm.MemoryRealm" />
```

Add the following roles to the `tomcat-users.xml` configuration file.

```
<role rolename="cinema-staff"/>
<role rolename="cinema-admin"/>
```

In addition, add the following users.

```
<user username="boss" password="boss" roles="cinema-admin"/>
<user username="staff1" password="staff1" roles="cinema-staff"/>
<user username="staff2" password="staff2" roles="cinema-staff"/>
```

The modifications to the Web application and the configuration are now complete. It's time to test them!

Start Tomcat and check the logs for errors. Any errors at this stage will be due to the configuration of the Realm, so check the changes for errors.

Compile and build the Tomcat Cinemas application. If any errors occur at this stage, just check that the changes made to the controller servlets were done as shown in Listing 12-5 and 12-7.

Note: Continue to use either Ant or the IDE as the development tool; however it may pay to reexamine Chapters 5 and 6 for any memory-jogging hints on how to perform these tasks.

Install the Web application using the context fragment used in Chapter 10, and check the server logs. This is the most likely time errors will occur because the contents of the `web.xml` file have changed significantly. If the errors indicate a parsing error for the Web application, it probably means there are errors in the newly added `security-constraint`, `login-config` or `security-role` elements. Double-check the changes against Listing 12-2.

Open the URL `http://localhost:8080/tomcatcinemas/` in a browser. This displays the default page shown in Figure 12-1.

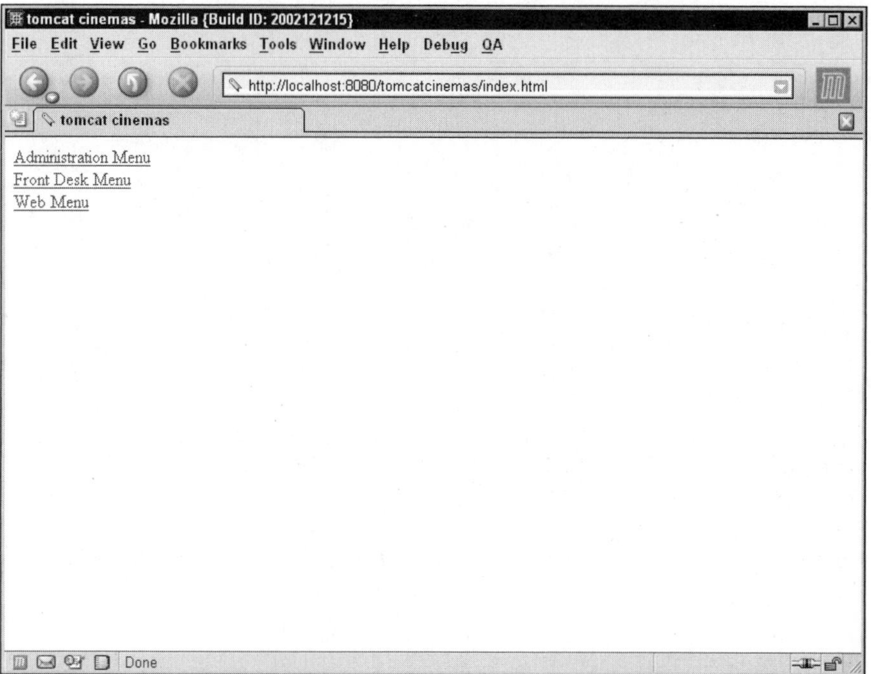

Figure 12-1: Tomcat Cinemas Default Page

Now select the Administration Menu. This displays a login page, as shown in Figure 12-2.

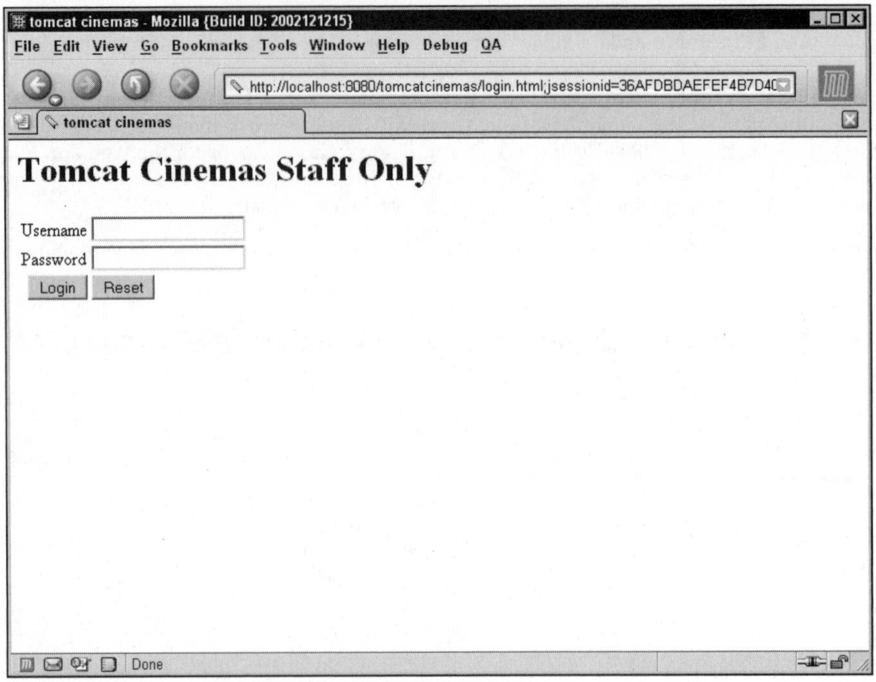

Figure 12-2: Tomcat Cinemas Login Page

Enter the username as boss and password boss. This displays the Administration Menu as shown in Figure 12-3. The Administration Menu now includes the additional functionality with the display of the current user and the logout link.

Click the Logout link and the Web application displays Figure 12-1 again. Try the Front Desk Menu; this time use the details for the staff user. This should display a listing of the shows remaining today.

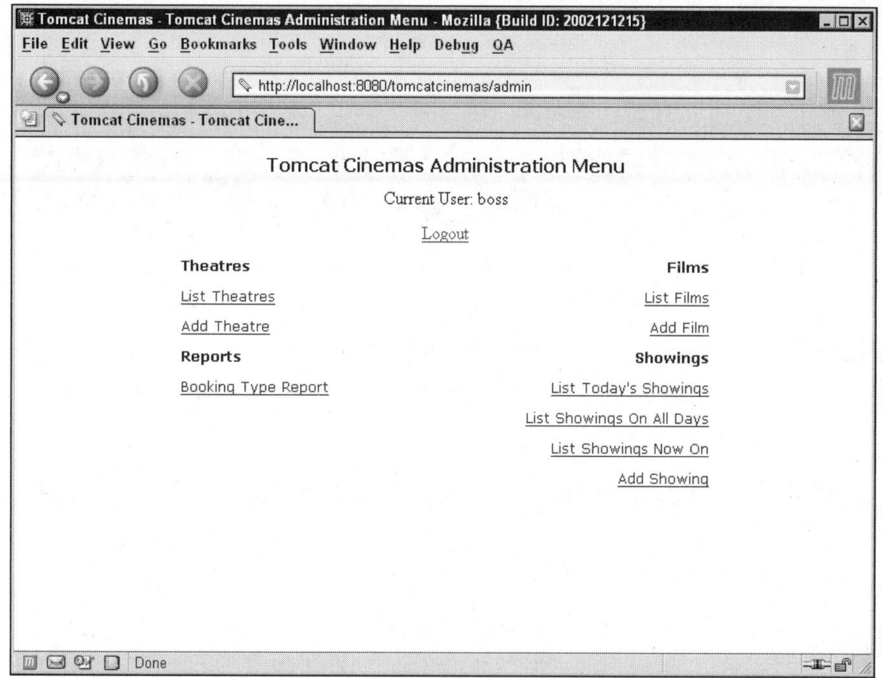

Figure 12-3: Tomcat Cinemas Administration Menu

While logged in as staff1 use the Back button on the browser to return to the Tomcat Cinemas Default Page and select the Administration Menu link. This should display a screen similar to Figure 12-4.

This isn't exactly the most professional looking result, and it's highly likely that users will either attempt to do this deliberately, or as a result of selecting the incorrect link by accident. While not directly related to security functionality we will clean up this error message by using the `error-page` element in `web.xml`. Insert the following element into `web.xml` after the end of the `servlet-mapping` elements:

```
<error-page>
    <error-code>403</error-code>
    <location>/login_err.html</location>
</error-page>
```

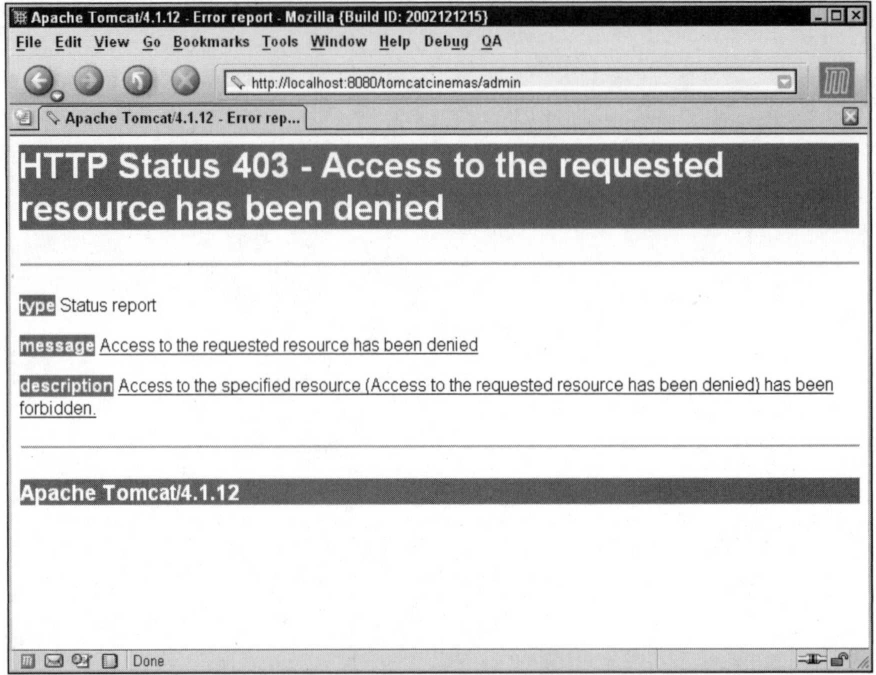

Figure 12-4: Access Denied using the default error report

This configuration re-uses the login error page, which is completely suitable for this purpose. Rebuild the application and reload. Now perform the same sequence of actions:

1. Select the Front Desk Menu from the default page.
2. Login as the staff1 user.
3. Use the Back button on the browser and select the Administration Menu.

This should now display a screen similar to that shown in Figure 12-5.

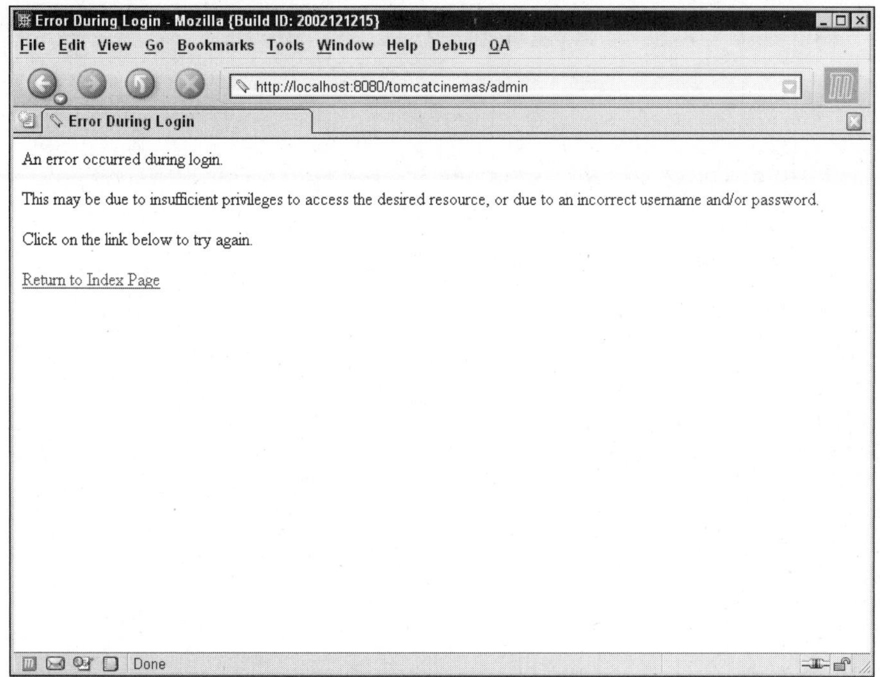

Figure 12-5: Access Denied using a custom error page

The first phase of the implementation of the security requirements to the Tomcat Cinemas Web application is now completed. There is declarative security around the resources that require privileges to access, and administrators and staff members are only able to access the functionality needed for their specific roles.

Address Access Control for Administration

The first step in implementing the access control is to add in the configuration for the filter that will be used. The `filter` and `filter-mapping` elements shown in Listing 12-9 must be added to the `web.xml` deployment descriptor before any of the `servlet` elements.

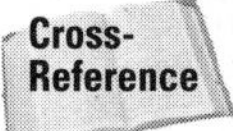

Details about the filter and filter-mapping elements can be found in Chapter 3.

Listing 12-9: Adding Filter Elements to web.xml

```
<filter>
    <filter-name>AccessFilter</filter-name>
    <filter-class>
        bible.tomcat.tccinemas.servlet.AccessAddressFilter
    </filter-class>
    <init-param>
        <param-name>ip-filter</param-name>
        <param-value>127.0.0.1</param-value>
    </init-param>
    <init-param>
        <param-name>error-page</param-name>
        <param-value>/access_err.html</param-value>
    </init-param>
</filter>

<filter-mapping>
    <filter-name>AccessFilter</filter-name>
    <url-pattern>
        /admin
    </url-pattern>
</filter-mapping>
```

The `filter` element contains the configuration parameters for the filter. These are the `ip-filter` and the `error-page`. A filter has a lifecycle similar to a servlet, and these values are used in initialization of the filter.

The `ip-filter` parameter is used as a simple string match to determine if the source of the request is from a valid IP address. The implementation provided uses the `String.startsWith()` to perform the match, so a substring here such as `127.0` would match `127.0.0.1` and `192.168.0` would match any address on that C-class network. Wild cards are not supported, nor are multiple addresses. These enhancements can be added if desired, but would needlessly complicate the example.

The `error-page` parameter is to provide a mechanism for specifying a URL to be displayed when the IP address is not acceptable.

If the `ip-filter` or `error-page` parameters are not defined, then the filter doesn't actually perform any filtering and passes all the requests directly to the application. This is to prevent the Web application from failing when the filter is misconfigured. It would be simple to change this behavior to actually prevent the application from working at all unless the filter has all the parameters defined.

The `filter-mapping` element configures the `filter` to be applied to the administration URL.

The next step is to use the code in Listing 12-10 to create a filter. Create a file in `src\bible\tomcat\tccineams\servlet` called `AccessAddressFilter.java`. This matches the configuration in the `web.xml` in Listing 12-9.

Listing 12-10: AccessAddressFilter.java

```
package bible.tomcat.tccinemas.servlet;

import javax.servlet.*;
import javax.servlet.http.*;
import java.io.*;

public class AccessAddressFilter
implements Filter
{
    private boolean _filter;
    private String _ipFilter;
    private String _errPage;
```

The `init()` method is called when the filter after the filter has been instantiated and is ready for service. As with a servlet the `init()` method can be used to perform the "once-only" tasks associates with the filter. The `destroy()` method is called prior to the filter being removed from service and is used to free any external resources, such as database connections that might have been obtained. The `AccessAddressFilter` is so simple that the `destroy()` method doesn't actually perform any function but is required to satisfy the `Filter` interface.

The `init()` method processes the configuration parameters defined in the `web.xml` and provided they are valid sets the boolean flag `_filter` to true. This flag is used in the `doFilter()` method to determine if filtering should be occurring. Obviously, this functionality could be significantly enhanced to perform more robust checking of the input parameters, however, to keep the example fairly small those have been omitted.

```
    public void init(FilterConfig cfg)
    {
        _ipFilter = cfg.getInitParameter("ip-filter");
        _errPage = cfg.getInitParameter("error-page");
        _filter = true;
        if ((_ipFilter == null) || (_errPage == null))
        {
            _filter = false;
        }
    }

    public void destroy()
    {
        // do nothing
    }
```

The `doFilter()` method is called for each request that matches the `url-pattern` in the associated `filter-mapping` element in the `web.xml`.

The processing obtains the IP address from the `request` object and does a simple string comparison against the configuration value. If the IP address does not match the configuration then the current session is obtained, invalidated, and the response is redirected to the configured error page.

The session is invalidated when the address is invalid due to the use of the form-based authentication. The form-based authentication uses the session to store the authentication and because the servlet container performs that processing before the Web application can process the request, the session is already created before the filter is executed.

If the IP address does match, then the next filter in the chain is invoked. This processing step is required by the servlet specification. The `doFilter()` method must either fill out the response object, or continue the processing in the pipeline.

The next element in the processing pipeline may be another filter, or as it is in this case, a servlet.

```
    public void doFilter(ServletRequest request,
                         ServletResponse response,
                         FilterChain chain)
        throws ServletException, IOException
    {
        RequestDispatcher rd = null;
        if (_filter)
        {
            String remoteIP = request.getRemoteAddr();
            if (!remoteIP.startsWith(_ipFilter))
            {
                if (request instanceof HttpServletRequest)
                {
                    HttpServletRequest hsr = (HttpServletRequest)request;
                    HttpSession session = hsr.getSession(false);
                    if (session != null)
                    {
                        session.invalidate();
                    }
                }
                rd = request.getRequestDispatcher(_errPage);
                rd.forward(request, response);
                return;
            }
        }

        // any other filters in the chain ?
        chain.doFilter(request, response);
    }

}
```

The final step is to create the error page for any illegal accesses. Create a file in the `web` directory called `access_err.html`, containing the code in Listing 12-11.

Listing 12-11: **access_err.html**

```
<!DOCTYPE HTML PUBLIC "-//W3C//DTD HTML 4.01 Transitional//EN">

<HTML>
  <HEAD>
    <TITLE>Error Accessing Administration Menu</TITLE>
  </HEAD>
  <BODY>
  Administration functionality can only be accessed from
  specified internal IP addresses.
  <p>
  Please contact the system administrator if this page
  occurs.
  <p>
  <a href="index.html">Return to Index Page</a>
  </BODY>
</HTML>
```

There is no additional configuration required for Tomcat, so it is simply a matter of recompiling and installing the Web application. As with before, use the context fragment to install the Web application and open the URL `http://localhost:8080/tomcatcinemas/` in a browser. This displays the default page shown in Figure 12-1.

The next step depends on the configuration of the environment that Tomcat and the Web browser is installed. The configuration defined in Listing 12-9 prohibits any access to the administration functionality from any IP address that isn't on the same local machine. This might not be possible in all environments, and if so, change the `ip-filter` parameter in Listing 12-9 to the IP address of the computer that is running the Web browser.

Select the Administration Menu and enter the boss username and password. This should display a screen similar to that shown in Figure 12-3. If this does not occur, and the screen displayed looks like Figure 12-6, then the `ip-filter` configuration for the Web application needs to be changed to allow access.

Provided that the results are similar to Figure 12-3 (the display of the Administration Menu screen) change the `ip-filter` parameter to something completely invalid such as the following:

```
<init-param>
    <param-name>ip-filter</param-name>
    <param-value>INVALID</param-value>
</init-param>
```

Obviously this prevents access from all IP addresses, and because the `AccessAddressFilter` does not perform any checking on the parameters this works very well.

Reload the Web application, open the URL `http://localhost:8080/tomcatcinemas/`, select the Administration Menu option, and enter the boss username and password. This should display the screen shown in Figure 12-6.

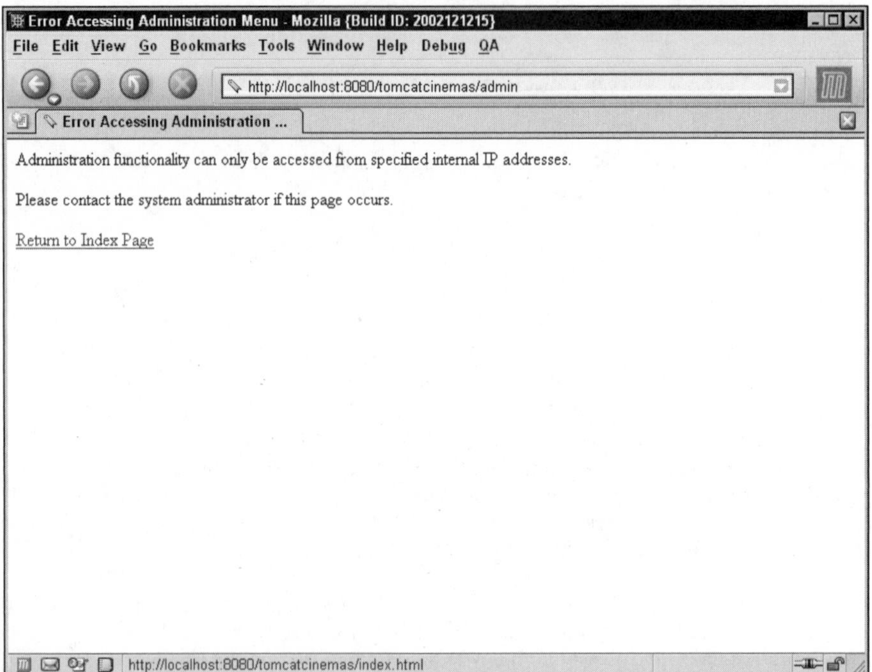

Figure 12-6: Administration Access Denied

The second phase of the implementation of the security requirements to the Tomcat Cinemas Web application is now completed. There is a filter that prohibits access to the Administration Menu unless the request comes from an IP address specified in the filter configuration.

Staff login restrictions

The staff login restrictions are implemented in the `FrontDeskController` servlet, and keep track of the staff that is currently using the system. The logout functionality implemented in an earlier section provides a hook to remove the staff when their shift is completed.

What is required is to implement a Web application-wide store that is updated as staff login and logout. If a staff member is already logged into the Web application, then any further attempts to login will be denied.

The first step is to make the changes to `FrontDeskController.java` as shown in Listing 12-12. The changes to the code are shown in bold.

Listing 12-12: FrontDeskController.java

```
package bible.tomcat.tccinemas.servlet;

. . . .

public class FrontDeskController extends Controller
{
    private final static String USER_KEY = "validatedUser";

    protected void doPost(HttpServletRequest request,
                          HttpServletResponse response)
        throws ServletException, java.io.IOException
    {
        response.setContentType("text/html");
        PrintWriter out = response.getWriter();
        String action = request.getParameter("action");
        String incPath = null;
        HttpSession session = request.getSession(true);

        String user = request.getUserPrincipal().getName();
        boolean loginErr = false;
        if (session.getAttribute(USER_KEY) == null)
        {
            if (validateUser(user))
            {
                session.setAttribute(USER_KEY, user);
            }
            else
            {
                action="logout";
                loginErr = true;
            }
        }
```

The `session` object is used to store a guard value. If the guard value exists in the session then the user validation process has occurred, and there is no need to perform the validation again.

If the validation is successful, the guard value is stored in the session; if the validation is unsuccessful the action is changed to perform a logout of the user.

```
        if(action == null)
        {
            action = "listBookableShowings";
        }

        if (action.equals("logout"))
        {
```

```
            session.invalidate();
            if (loginErr)
            {
                incPath = "/login_err.html";
            }
            else
            {
                invalidateUser(user);
                incPath = "/index.html";
            }
        }
        . . . .
        request.setAttribute("user", user);
        request.setAttribute("action",action);
        performInclude(incPath,request,response);
    }
```

The `validateUser()` and `invalidateUser()` methods are simple wrappers around setting and removing the username from a `HashMap` stored in the servlet context for the Web application.

```
    public synchronized boolean validateUser(String user)
    {
        boolean rv = false;
        ServletContext ctx = this.getServletContext();
        if (ctx != null)
        {
            HashMap map = (HashMap)ctx.getAttribute("loggedInUsers");
            if (map == null)
            {
                map = new HashMap();
                ctx.setAttribute("loggedInUsers", map);
            }
            if (!map.containsKey(user))
            {
                map.put(user,user);
                rv = true;
            }
        }
        return rv;
    }

    public synchronized void invalidateUser(String user)
    {
        ServletContext ctx = this.getServletContext();
        if (ctx != null)
        {
            HashMap map = (HashMap)ctx.getAttribute("loggedInUsers");
            if (map == null)
            {
```

```
                return;
            }
            if (map.containsKey(user))
            {
                map.remove(user);
            }
        }
    }
}
```

There is no additional configuration required for Tomcat, so it is simply a matter of recompiling and installing the Web application. Use the context fragment to install the Web application and open the URL `http://localhost:8080/tomcatcinemas/` in a browser. This displays the default page for the Web application.

Select the Front Desk Menu item and login as the staff1 user with staff1 as the password. This should display a screen similar to that shown in Figure 12-7.

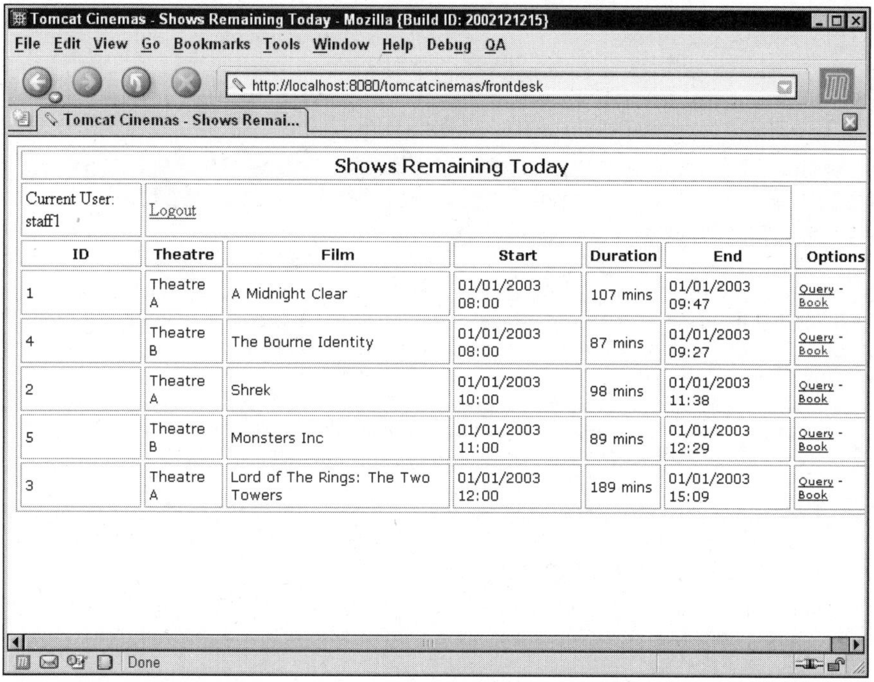

Figure 12-7: staff1 login

Now open another browser window, or use another computer to access the same URL and login as staff2 user with staff2 as the password. This should display a screen similar to that shown in Figure 12-8.

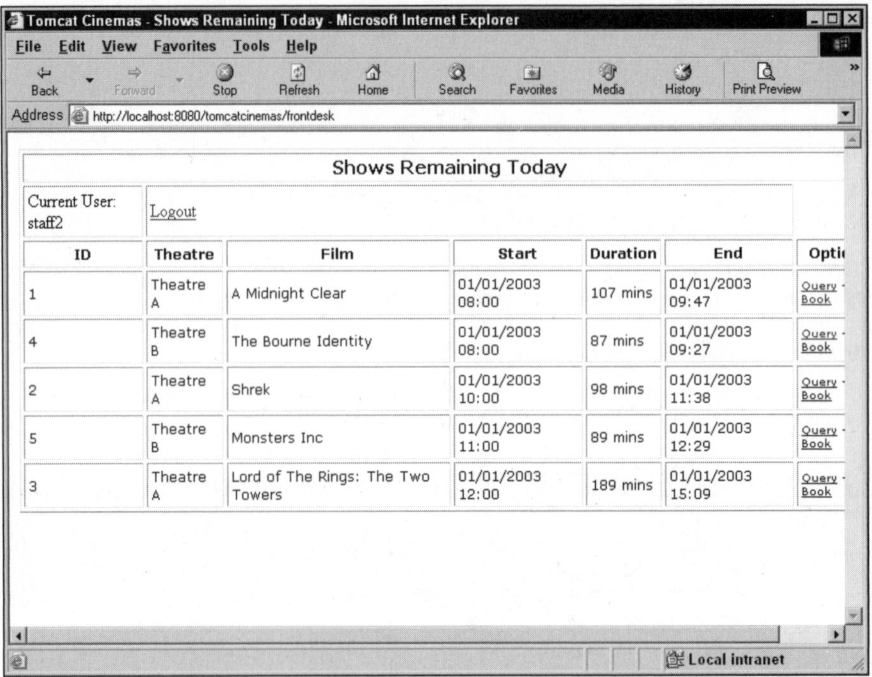

Figure 12-8: staff2 login

If the browser automatically displays the same screen as Figure 12-7 after selecting the Front Desk Menu, the browser is sharing the session information across the same instance of the browser, but with two windows. To continue with the testing, use a different browser, or try a completely separate computer if there is one available.

Mozilla 1.3 shares the session information across windows under Windows 2000, which is why Figure 12-7 uses Mozilla and Figure 12-8 uses Internet Explorer.

Select logout using the browser window for staff1. This returns to the default menu page for the application. Select the Front Desk Menu and login as staff2 with the password of staff2. This should fail and display the screen shown in Figure 12-9.

The third phase of the implementation of the security requirements to the Tomcat Cinemas Web application is now completed. Tomcat Cinemas staff members are restricted to disallow multiple concurrent logins with the same username.

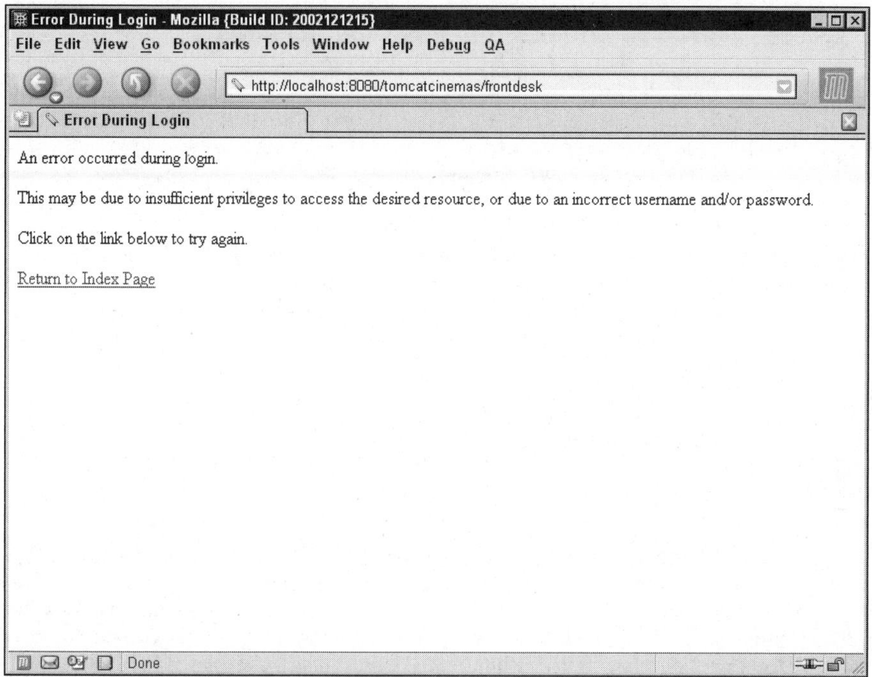

Figure 12-9: Failed staff2 multiple login

In a real world implementation, requiring users to use a logout option to keep the application consistent is not workable, and a more sophisticated mechanism would be implemented to fulfill this requirement.

SSL Configuration

The fourth and final phase in implementing the security requirements is to configure the Web booking functionality to be delivered securely. This protects the customer details as they book their tickets to the showings.

The first task is to add a `security-constraint` to configure the Web application to use a secure transport mechanism when accessing the resources utilized by the Web booking functionality. The `web.xml` file should be modified to include the XML code shown in Listing 12-13.

Listing 12-13: Web Booking Security Modifications

```
<security-constraint>
    <display-name>Web Booking</display-name>
    <web-resource-collection>
        <web-resource-name>Web Booking
        </web-resource-name>
        <url-pattern>/web/*</url-pattern>
        <http-method>GET</http-method>
        <http-method>POST</http-method>
    </web-resource-collection>
    <user-data-constraint>
        <transport-guarantee>
            CONFIDENTIAL
        </transport-guarantee>
    </user-data-constraint>
</security-constraint>
```

The interesting difference between this security constraint and those implemented for the Administration and Front Desk requirements is that there is no `auth-constraint` element. This means that there is no authentication required to access these resources. This is exactly the functionality that is needed, because the Web booking is somewhat cumbersome it required the ticket purchasers to authenticate to purchase tickets.

The Web application uses the credit-card number as the identification between the booking and payment for the tickets on the Web and picking up the tickets at the cinema.

The next task is to configure a secure connector for the Tomcat server, which needs to be performed before to any further configuration can be done.

To configure the secure connector:

1. Download, install, and configure the Java Secure Sockets Extension (JSSE).
2. Create a certificate for the Tomcat server.
3. Configure an SSL Connector in `server.xml`.
4. Test the configuration.

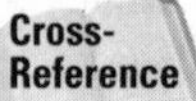

Details on the configuration and testing of the SSL connector are covered in Chapter 8.

To test the configuration with the Tomcat Cinemas application, start Tomcat and open the URL `https://localhost:8443/tomcatcinemas/web` in a browser.

Be careful when typing the URL. It must have https at the front, and the port number must be 8443.

This should display a screen similar to that shown in Figure 12-10.

Note

The browser may display a warning dialog box about the SSL certificate that is used for the Tomcat server. This is normal and can be ignored for the purposes of testing. If a similar warning occurs when browsing unknown Web sites, read the warning carefully and check the properties of the certificate. There may be something untoward occurring.

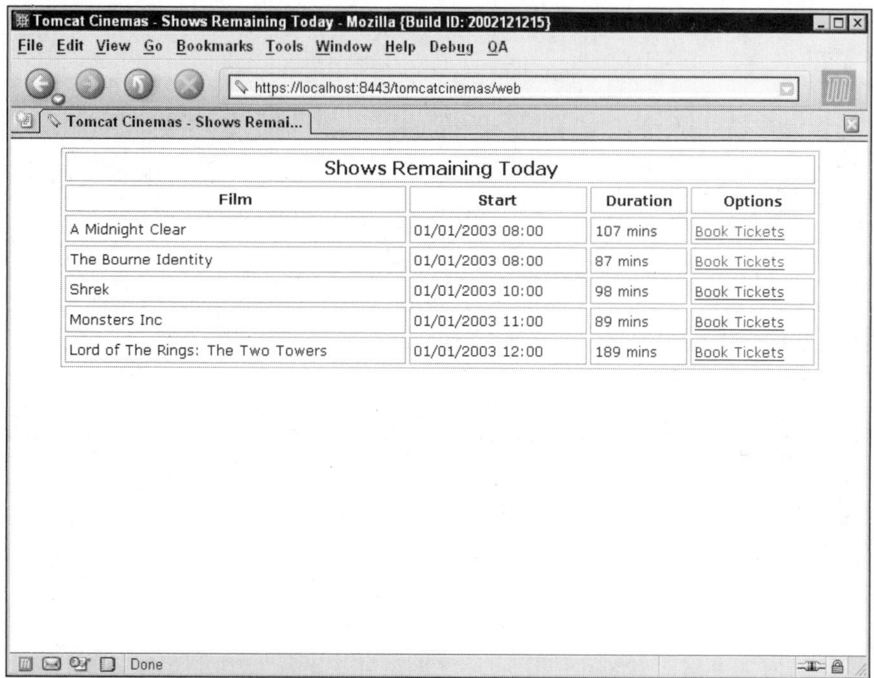

Figure 12-10: Secure Web booking screen

However, the benefits of using the `security-constraint` should allow the redirecting of the request if it is made over an insecure channel. Open the URL `http://localhost:8080/tomcatcinemas` and select the Web Menu option.

This displays a screen similar to those shown in Figure 12-11 and Figure 12-12. Figure 12-11 indicates that there is additional configuration required to automatically redirect to use a secure protocol.

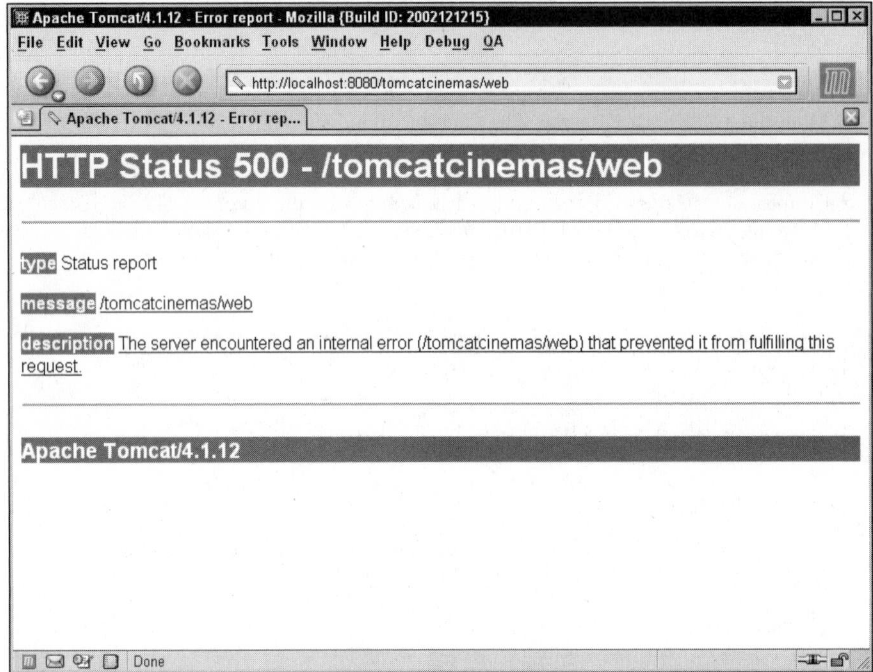

Figure 12-11: Unknown protocol error

If a screen similar to Figure 12-11 occurs, check the Tomcat log files. An exception has been recorded. This exception probably starts with lines similar to the following:

```
java.net.MalformedURLException: unknown protocol: https
at java.net.URL.<init>(URL.java:302)
at java.net.URL.<init>(URL.java:219)
at
org.apache.catalina.authenticator.AuthenticatorBase.checkUserData(AuthenticatorB
ase.java:730)
at org.apache.catalina.authenticator.AuthenticatorBase.invoke(Authentica
torBase.java:490)
. . . .
```

This does look rather fatal, but not all hope is lost; there is a solution to this particular configuration error. This error occurs when Tomcat is performing a redirect to an HTTPS URL. Within the Tomcat authentication code a new URL is constructed, as shown in Listing 12-14:

Listing 12-14: AuthenticatorBase.java

```
// Redirect to the corresponding SSL port
String protocol = "https";
String host = hrequest.getServerName();
. . . .

URL url = null;
try {
    url = new URL(protocol, host, redirectPort, file.toString());
    if (debug >= 2)
        log("  Redirecting to " + url.toString());
    hresponse.sendRedirect(url.toString());
    return (false);
} catch (MalformedURLException e) {
    if (debug >= 2)
        log("  Cannot create new URL", e);
    hresponse.sendError
       (HttpServletResponse.SC_INTERNAL_SERVER_ERROR,
        hrequest.getRequestURI());
    return (false)
}
```

Tip One of the great advantages of using open source software is that finding and fixing errors is made a great deal simpler when the code can be examined to see exactly what is happening. In this particular case it leads directly to the solution.

Examining the Java API for the `java.net.URL`, there is a very important description for the constructor of a `URL` object. When a `URL` object is constructed, a `URLStreamHandler` object is also created to handle the protocol. The `URLStreamHandler` requires any unknown classes to be defined using the system property `java.protocol.handler.pkgs`.

The system property should contain a pipe (`|`) separated list of package names to find the protocol handling classes. This property needs to be defined as follows:

```
java.protocol.handler.pkgs=com.sun.net.www.ssl.internal.www.protocol
```

Note This information and more capabilities of the JSSE can be found in the Java Secure Socket Extension (JSSE) API User's Guide.

To include this as part of the Tomcat runtime, this value must be defined for the JVM. The scripts `catalina.bat` and `catalina.sh` ultimately control the startup and shutdown of Tomcat and need modification to correct this error. These scripts are located in the `bin` directory of the Tomcat installation.

catalina.bat contains a number of commands of the following form near the end of the file:

```
%_EXECJAVA% %JAVA_OPTS% %CATALINA_OPTS% %DEBUG_OPTS%
-Djava.endorsed.dirs="%JAVA_ENDORSED_DIRS%" -classpath "%CLASSPATH%"
-Dcatalina.base="%CATALINA_BASE%" -Dcatalina.home="%CATALINA_HOME%"
-Djava.io.tmpdir="%CATALINA_TMPDIR%" %MAINCLASS% %CMD_LINE_ARGS% %ACTION%
```

catalina.sh contains commands that are similar as follows:

```
"$_RUNJAVA" $JAVA_OPTS $CATALINA_OPTS \
  -Djava.endorsed.dirs="$JAVA_ENDORSED_DIRS" -classpath "$CLASSPATH" \
  -Dcatalina.base="$CATALINA_BASE" \
  -Dcatalina.home="$CATALINA_HOME" \
  -Djava.io.tmpdir="$CATALINA_TMPDIR" \
  org.apache.catalina.startup.Bootstrap "$@" start \
  >> "$CATALINA_BASE"/logs/catalina.out 2>&1 &
```

These are the commands that start the JVM that executes the Tomcat class files, and each of the groups are used to start Tomcat with different options. The simplest option is to modify all of the commands to include the SSL protocol handler definition.

Caution Create a backup of catalina.bat and catalina.sh before starting the modifications.

Modify the commands as follows to include the bold text:

```
%_EXECJAVA% %JAVA_OPTS% %CATALINA_OPTS% %DEBUG_OPTS%
-Djava.protocol.handler.pkgs=com.sun.net.www.ssl.internal.www.protocol
-Djava.endorsed.dirs="%JAVA_ENDORSED_DIRS%" -classpath "%CLASSPATH%"
-Dcatalina.base="%CATALINA_BASE%" -Dcatalina.home="%CATALINA_HOME%"
-Djava.io.tmpdir="%CATALINA_TMPDIR%" %MAINCLASS% %CMD_LINE_ARGS% %ACTION%
```

and

```
"$_RUNJAVA" $JAVA_OPTS $CATALINA_OPTS \
  -Djava.endorsed.dirs="$JAVA_ENDORSED_DIRS" -classpath "$CLASSPATH" \
  -Djava.protocol.handler.pkgs=com.sun.net.www.ssl.internal.www.protocol \
  -Dcatalina.base="$CATALINA_BASE" \
  -Dcatalina.home="$CATALINA_HOME" \
  -Djava.io.tmpdir="$CATALINA_TMPDIR" \
  org.apache.catalina.startup.Bootstrap "$@" start \
  >> "$CATALINA_BASE"/logs/catalina.out 2>&1 &
```

That completes the changes required to the Tomcat configuration to allow the automatic switching to use the HTTPS protocol.

Restart Tomcat to include the changes to the environment and install the Tomcat Cinemas application using the context fragment. Open the URL http://localhost:8080/tomcatcinemas and select the Web Menu option.

This now should display the screen shown in Figure 12-12:

Figure 12-12: Automatic switching to HTTPS protocol

If the screen still looks like Figure 12-11, double-check that the commands modified in `catalina.bat` or `catalina.sh` were the correct commands. If in doubt modify all of the commands to include the protocol handler definition.

Summary

This chapter covered some of the basic background on security topics and how they are relevant to Web applications. It focused on providing a solution to the security requirements for the Tomcat Cinemas Web application.

✦ ✦ ✦

P A R T

IV

Advanced Tomcat Techniques

✦ ✦ ✦ ✦

In This Part

✦ ✦ ✦ ✦

Frameworks

In This Chapter

Learining what a Framework is

Learning about the Struts Framework

Example of Struts Implementation

Understanding Other Frameworks

This chapter examines some frameworks that can be integrated with, or used to develop applications. This examination focuses on Tomcat, but other servlet containers may also be able to make use of these frameworks in a similar way.

A *framework* is simply the outline and surrounding infrastructure for doing something in a certain way.

This chapter is primarily concerned with a Jakarta framework called Struts, however some other frameworks are also briefly discussed.

The chapter begins by defining what a framework is and then describing the Struts framework in detail. The chapter then walks through the implementation of a part of the application built in Chapter 10 using Struts. This section guides you through the installation and configuration portion of the process and then some actual Struts development where the film administration portion of the application is converted to use Struts.

The chapter concludes with a discussion of common features in frameworks and some of the other available frameworks.

What Is a Framework?

A framework is simply the blueprint and infrastructure for doing something in a certain way. In this way a framework could help you build your application (an Application Framework like Struts) or provide unit testing for your application like Jakarta's Cactus framework. These frameworks do not build your application or do your testing, but they provide the basic outline and structure for how your application will be built and how your unit tests will be constructed.

Why Frameworks are Good

Frameworks typically focus on problems that have been solved many times. For instance, MVC Model 2 architecture is something many Web applications will want to apply. This is a problem domain that has been solved over and over again, in many different ways. Struts provides a framework for solving this problem efficiently and with enough flexibility to cover many common scenarios. Using a framework such as Struts means not having to solve this particular problem in your own way for this application.

Frameworks typically use industry proven methods for achieving their goals and in so doing allow applications that make use of them to reduce the time taken for development (read cost!) and increase the quality of the software produced.

The Struts Framework

Struts (`http://jakarta.apache.org/struts/`) is a framework written by Craig R. McClanahan and donated to Apache in 2000. Struts is used for actually building an application in a modular and extensible fashion. This Application Framework promotes the use of the MVC Model 2 architecture by focusing on the controller portion of MVC and integrating with other technologies such as JSP, custom tags, and JDBC to allow for the development of the model and view components.

See Chapter 1 for a definition of MVC architecture and Chapter 10 for a detailed illustration of how an MVC application may be built. It is interesting to compare the methods used in Chapter 10 with those described using Struts in this chapter. Struts will be illustrated in this chapter using parts of the application developed in Chapter 10.

The servlet that Struts provides allows requests from a browser to be routed to an appropriate action for processing and then forwarded onto a designated view page. Figure 13-1 provides a simplified view of this situation:

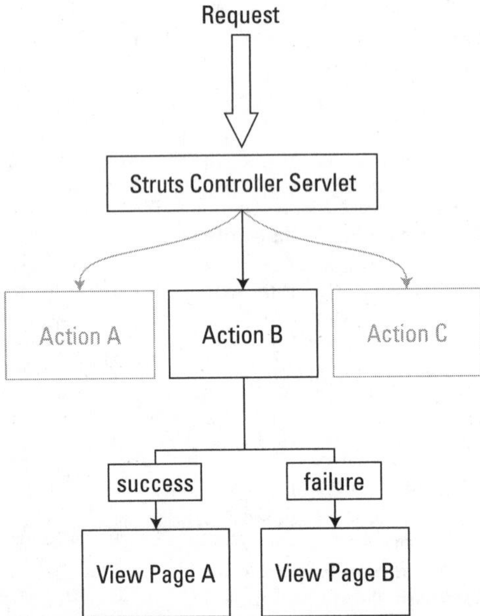

Figure 13-1: Simplified Struts process within an application

A simple data structure called an ActionForm can be used as a transport medium for information between the view page, the servlet, and the action for processing, and utilizing custom tags in the JSP pages. We can map HTML form elements to the values the ActionForm holds.

Figure 13-1 shows a request made to the Struts Controller Servlet (org.apache.struts.action.ActionServlet). Using what is described in the Struts configuration file (struts-config.xml), the servlet is able to instantiate an appropriate Action class (a sub class of org.apache.struts.action.Action). We can see from this that the controller servlet performs much of the "traffic cop" work of the application, determining the next action to take as the application flows.

The behavior of this servlet is determined by ActionMappings defined in the struts-config.xml file. The actions perform some processing that may or may not include the use of a handler or data access object. Based on the result of the action, control can then be forwarded to another resource such as a JSP page or another action to show the results of the processing or for some other means.

A number of potential forwarding targets can be specified (in Figure 13-1 two are specified, one for success and one for failure).

When the servlet instantiates the appropriate Action class, its execute method is invoked and is passed:

✦ Request (HttpServletRequest)

✦ Response (HttpServletResponse)

✦ Action Mapping (ActionMapping)

✦ Action Form (ActionForm)

You will be familiar with the first two being the HTTP request and response objects we have seen previously when working with servlets. The ActionMapping object represents what the servlet (ActionServlet) knows about this instance of the Action class.

The ActionForm represents the data that may be captured from the request and used in processing. In terms of the example in Chapter 10, an ActionForm most closely represents a value object. The ActionForm contains a simple bean structure with various properties, each with an associated get and set method.

In Struts, the ActionForm bean object may also contain methods to provide simple data validation (is this property's value empty or missing, is that property's value too long, and so on) and the ability to load and reset the values it holds. These form-beans can be associated with appropriate actions in the struts-config.xml file.

Struts assists us in dealing with validation problems when a user is entering data using a form. An ActionForm object can implement a validate method that is called before an action on the object (such as creating a new row in a database) is executed. Using custom tags, these errors can then be printed out on the original form page (JSP view component) with the values retained in the form elements. In this way you can see the direct relationship between the ActionForm object and the data presented in the form. We can see an example of this when we implement some of the functionality of Chapter 10's Tomcat Cinemas using Struts.

Struts provides a number of custom tag libs to assist with the presentation of information in this way, broadly, the categories of tags it provides are:

✦ Bean tags: Bean tags are used to display a bean or create new beans.

✦ HTML tags: Used in the rendering of forms (populated with the data in an `ActionForm`) to display information from the application. These are fundamental to using struts in a Web application context.

✦ Logic tags: Tags that provide logic for conditional output and iterative operations.

✦ Nested tags: Allows for the nesting of Struts tags.

✦ Template tags: Useful for the presentation of templates.

✦ Tiles tags: Used to enhance the include functionality provided by Java Server Pages.

Unfortunately we won't be able to illustrate the use of all these categories of tags within this chapter, there are, however many examples on the Internet explaining their usage.

Preparing Tomcat Cinemas to Use Struts

Preparing your development environment to use Struts is fairly straightforward. We will step through the process in the following pages, but remember to refer to the documentation, FAQs, and mailing lists if it doesn't seem to be working. For our purposes we will be using Struts 1.1 Beta 2. The following instructions refer to adding Struts to theapplication developed in Chapter 10's Tomcat Cinemas. Or you can simply get the completed application from the download for this chapter from the Wiley Web site.

1. Follow the instructions for downloading and installing Struts in Chapter 2. Within the Struts directory where the Zip file was unpacked, you will find various jar files, Tag Library Description files and some documentation and example application Web archives (WAR).

2. Copy the `build.xml` file that comes with the download for this chapter from the Wiley Web site, and paste it into the `tomcatcinemas/` directory of your application source tree. Open this `build.xml` file and find the line that reads:

```
<property name="struts.home"
          value="c:/jakarta-struts-1.1-b2" />
```

And change the value to reflect the location you installed Struts.

Behind the scenes, Step 2 configures the `build.xml` file to use the correct directory to:

   a. Include `struts.jar` from the Struts installation in the CLASSPATH for building the application.

   b. Copy `struts.jar` from the Struts installation to the `web/WEB-INF/lib` directory of the build location.

   c. Copy `struts*.tld` files from the Struts installation to the `web/WEB-INF/` directory of the build location.

   d. Copy `commons*.jar` files from the Struts installation to the `web/WEB-INF/lib` directory of the build location.

   e. Copy the `jdbc2_0-stdext.jar` file from the Struts installation to the `web/WEB-INF/lib` directory of the build location.

3. Now open the web.xml file located in the tomcatcinemas/web/WEB-INF/ directory. We are going to add the Struts ActionServlet to this Web application. Add the following servlet description for the Struts controller servlet, ActionServlet:

```
<!-- Action Servlet Configuration -->
<servlet>
 <servlet-name>action</servlet-name>
 <servlet-class>
    org.apache.struts.action.ActionServlet
 </servlet-class>
 <init-param>
   <param-name>application</param-name>
   <param-value>ApplicationResources</param-value>
 </init-param>
 <init-param>
   <param-name>config</param-name>
   <param-value>
       /WEB-INF/struts-config.xml
   </param-value>
 </init-param>
 <init-param>
   <param-name>debug</param-name>
   <param-value>10</param-value>
 </init-param>
 <init-param>
   <param-name>detail</param-name>
   <param-value>10</param-value>
 </init-param>
 <init-param>
   <param-name>validate</param-name>
   <param-value>true</param-value>
 </init-param>
 <load-on-startup>2</load-on-startup>
 </servlet>
```

These parameters are described in the Struts documentation. Of particular note are the application parameter and the config parameter. These refer to configuration files we will create later on.

We are now going to add a servlet mapping for this Struts controller servlet. Add the following servlet mapping to web.xml:

```
<!-- Action Servlet Mapping -->
<servlet-mapping>
    <servlet-name>action</servlet-name>
    <url-pattern>*.do</url-pattern>
</servlet-mapping>
```

Now add the following custom tag declarations to the web.xml file. These directives must appear below the error-page declaration entry and above the database resource reference added in Chapter 10 for Tomcat Cinemas.

```
<!-- Struts Tag Library Descriptors -->
<taglib>
  <taglib-uri>/WEB-INF/struts-bean.tld</taglib-uri>
  <taglib-location>
      /WEB-INF/struts-bean.tld
  </taglib-location>
</taglib>
<taglib>
  <taglib-uri>/WEB-INF/struts-html.tld</taglib-uri>
  <taglib-location>
      /WEB-INF/struts-html.tld
  </taglib-location>
</taglib>
<taglib>
  <taglib-uri>/WEB-INF/struts-logic.tld</taglib-uri>
  <taglib-location>
      /WEB-INF/struts-logic.tld
  </taglib-location>
</taglib>
<taglib>
  <taglib-uri>/WEB-INF/struts-template.tld</taglib-uri>
  <taglib-location>
      /WEB-INF/struts-template.tld
  </taglib-location>
</taglib>
```

These declarations define the custom tags used in Struts so they can be used in our JSP pages.

The final two steps in preparing the development environment for Struts provide for the addition of two new files, `ApplicationResources.properties` and `struts-config.xml`. `ApplicationResources.properties` is a file used to store common values used throughout the application such as messages, titles, and other text. As we develop the Struts portion of the Tomcat Cinemas application we will add values to this file and reference them from within Java files and JSP pages.

`struts-config.xml` defines the behavior of the framework within the application. It includes mappings for actions, form bean, and datasource definitions as well as other information. At this stage we will begin with a shell of this file and add items as the application is developed.

4. Create a blank file called `ApplicationResources.properties` and place it in the `tomcatcinemas/src` directory of the development environment for Tomcat Cinemas. We will use this file to reference properties throughout the Struts portion of the application. An example of an entry in this file would be:

   ```
   film.list.title=List Films
   ```

   As you will see later, we will use such properties to assist in the presentation of the page and assign messages for errors and other information. Having this information separated from the class and JSP files means they are centralized and can be changed more easily.

5. Create a new file in the `tomcatcinemas/web/WEB-INF` directory called `struts-config.xml` and add the following content:

```
<?xml version="1.0" encoding="ISO-8859-1" ?>

<!DOCTYPE struts-config PUBLIC
          "-//Apache Software Foundation//DTD Struts Configuration
1.0//EN"
          "http://jakarta.apache.org/struts/dtds/struts-
config_1_0.dtd">

<struts-config>

<!-- ======= Datasource Definitions =============== -->

   <data-sources>
   </data-sources>

<!-- ======= Form Bean Definitions ================ -->

   <form-beans>
   </form-beans>

<!-- ======= Global Forward Definitions =========== -->

   <global-forwards>
   </global-forwards>

<!-- ======= Action Mapping Definitions =========== -->

   <action-mappings>
   </action-mappings>

</struts-config>
```

As you can tell from the headings as comments we are going to define much of the workings of Struts in the application from this file.

Adding a Datasource

Now that all the pieces are in place to begin developing with the Struts framework we need to add a datasource definition to the `struts-config.xml` file. We could use the data source provided already by the `context.xml` file within our application, however this gives us the opportunity to define this resource completely within the context of Struts. To implement a datasource in this way the `<data-sources></data-sources>` tags in the `struts-config.xml` file should now resemble the following, shown in Listing 13-1:

Listing 13-1: Data-source Definition Added to struts-config.xml

```
<data-source>
    <set-property property="autoCommit" value="true"/>
    <set-property property="description" value="MySQL"/>
    <set-property property="driverClass" value="com.mysql.jdbc.Driver"/>
    <set-property property="maxCount" value="4"/>
    <set-property property="minCount" value="2"/>
    <set-property property="user" value="tccinemaUser"/>
    <set-property property="password" value="password"/>
    <set-property property="url"
value="jdbc:mysql://localhost/tomcatcinemas"/>
</data-source>
```

This entry in the `struts-config.xml` file establishes the requirements for a connection to the database we created in Chapter 10, `tomcatcinemas`. Most of the values specified in this declaration should be familiar to you. Accessing this data source will be described when developing the action classes further on.

Using Struts in Tomcat Cinemas

Now that our environment is ready to utilize the Struts framework we can look at implementing an existing piece of the Tomcat Cinemas functionality to use it. Over the coming pages we will simply add files to illustrate the use of Struts rather than replace the existing files that currently deal with this functionality. For the purposes of this illustration we will develop the Film Administration portions of the application using Struts. The following components will be implemented:

✦ List films currently in the database.

✦ Allow a user to add a new film to the database.

✦ Allow a user to edit a film in the database.

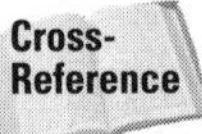

It is assumed you have read Chapter 10, where the Tomcat Cinemas application was described and parts of its functionality were developed.

The security additions applied in Chapter 12 and some of the business rules defined in Chapter 10 for the Tomcat Cinemas application are not included in this example. The aim of this example is to specifically illustrate the use of Struts.

Listing Films

Listing films involves creating a collection of film objects based on the contents of the film table. This "Film" object (a form bean in struts) represents a row in the database. We need to create this film object in a similar way we created the `FilmValue` object in Chapter 10. For our purposes this new object will be called `FilmForm`. This `FilmForm` object contains the properties of a film, access methods such as `get<Property>` and `set<Property>` as well as some extra methods we will use for loading an instance of the object and for validation. This is the ActionForm subclass we described in the introduction to Struts earlier in the chapter.

Create a file called FilmForm.java and place it into the /src/bible/tomcat/tccinemas directory of the Tomcat Cinemas source tree. Add the following package and import statements to this file:

```
package bible.tomcat.tccinemas;

import javax.servlet.http.HttpServletRequest;
import org.apache.struts.action.*;
import java.sql.*;
```

We now need to declare the class FilmForm with the following:

```
public final class FilmForm
    extends ActionForm
```

Our FilmForm object extends a class called org.apache.struts.action.ActionForm. ActionForm is a Java Bean that is used in a corresponding action mapping that will be defined further on.

A quick perusal of the database will show that a film has the following properties that can now be defined in the class:

```
private long id = 0;
private String name = "";
private int length = 0;
private boolean active = true;
```

You can now create set and get methods for these properties.

In addition to the set and get methods there are three more methods that need to be implemented.

The following reset(...) method acts to reset the properties of the bean to their default values:

```
public void reset(ActionMapping mapping, HttpServletRequest request)
{
    this.id = 0;
    this.name = "";
    this.length = 0;
    this.active = true;
}
```

The ActionMapping and HttpServletRequest objects are passed to this method in case some values they hold are pertinent to this reset task. In our case, they are not.

We also add a simple validation method to the FilmForm bean. This method overrides the validate(...) method provided by the ActionForm class. We use this method to offer only simple validation to form input; more complex business logic should be validated in the action class we will create soon. In terms of listing film objects, there is of course no validation required, however this method is required later when we add a new film object or edit an existing value. It is shown in Listing 13-2 for clarity. The validate method is as follows:

Listing 13-2: Validate Method of the FilmForm object

```
public ActionErrors validate(ActionMapping mapping,
                             HttpServletRequest request)
{
    ActionErrors errors = new ActionErrors();

    if((name == null) || (name.length() < 1))
    {
       errors.add("name", new ActionError("error.film.name.missing"));
    }

    if(length < 1 || length > 150)
    {
        errors.add("length",
            new ActionError("error.film.length.size"));
    }
    return errors;
}
```

The framework calls this method implicitly when the properties of the bean are populated and the associated action mapping defines the validate attribute as true.

Notice that we have added some `ActionError` objects to an `ActionErrors` object in this method, in each case specifying a name such as `error.film.name.missing`. This represents some error text that we need to add to the `ApplicationResources.properties` file we created earlier. An example of a value for this property would be "The film must have a name." Therefore the entry in the `ApplicationResources`.properties file would read:

```
error.film.name.missing=The film must have a name<br>
```

The final additional method we add to the `FilmForm` object is for loading the values of the properties from the database. This method is virtually identical to the `ResultSet` constructor we added to the `FilmValue` object in Chapter 10. The method receives a `ResultSet` and sets the values in the bean. Refer to Listing 13-3.

Listing 13-3: Load Method of the FilmForm Object

```
public void load(ResultSet rs)
{
    try
    {
        this.id = rs.getLong("id");
        this.name = rs.getString("name");
        this.length = rs.getInt("length");
        this.active = rs.getBoolean("active");
    }
```

```
        catch (SQLException sqle)
        {
            sqle.printStackTrace();
        }
    }
```

The `FilmForm` object is now complete. In an architectural sense this object forms part of the model component of our MVC model. We now need to add a business logic layer to the application to fulfill the same role as the `FilmHandler` in Chapter 10.

Create a file called `StrutsFilmHandler.java` in the `tomcatcinemas/src/bible/tomcat/tccinemas` directory of the Tomcat Cinemas source tree. The package, import, and class declarations to place in this file are as follows:

```
package bible.tomcat.tccinemas;

import java.sql.*;
import java.util.*;
import bible.tomcat.tccinemas.util.*;

public class StrutsFilmHandler
```

Note

Note that the `StrutsFilmHandler` uses the `bible.tomcat.tccinemas.util` package. This package contains some helpful classes for dealing with dates and numbers. This package was discussed in Chapter 10 and the source files are available in the download for this chapter.

To list a collection of films we need to add a method to this class to provide the list. The `listFilms` method shown in Listing 13-4 achieves this:

Listing 13-4: listFilms Method in StrutsFilmHandler

```
public ArrayList listFilms(Connection cn)
    throws FilmException
{
    PreparedStatement ps = null;
    ArrayList rv = new ArrayList();

    try
    {
        String sql = "SELECT * FROM film";
        ps = cn.prepareStatement(sql);

        if(ps != null)
        {
            ResultSet rs = ps.executeQuery();
```

Continued

Listing 13-4 *(continued)*

```
            while(rs.next())
            {
                FilmForm tmp = new FilmForm();
                tmp.load(rs);
                rv.add(tmp);
            }
        }
    }
    catch (SQLException sqle)
    {
        throw new FilmException(sqle.getMessage());
    }
    finally
    {
        try
        {
            if (ps != null)
            {
                ps.close();
            }
        }
        catch (SQLException sqle)
        {
            sqle.printStackTrace();
        }
    }
    return rv;
}
```

The method we have created in Listing 13-4 is called from the `action` class we create next for listing films. You can see it is passed a `Connection` object and prepares an `ArrayList` of `FilmForm` objects based on a simple `SELECT` query executed against the `Connection`.

Notice an exception used in this file called `FilmException`. `FilmException` is simply an `Exception` we have created to be specific to the application we are developing.

Create a file called `FilmException.java` in the `tomcatcinemas/src/bible/tomcat/tccinemas` directory of the Tomcat Cinemas source tree. The source for this file is found in Listing 13-5:

Listing 13-5: FilmException

```
package bible.tomcat.tccinemas;

public class FilmException
    extends Exception
{
```

```
    public FilmException(String msg)
    {
        super(msg);
    }
}
```

We can now prepare an Action class to deal specifically with the action of listing films. This forms the part of the controller component of the MVC model. It provides the Struts controller servlet with an appropriate action to execute when a list films request is received. Before we create the Action class we must add an appropriate action mapping and form bean definition to the struts-config.xml file created earlier. You should open this file now. It is located in the tomcatcinemas/web/WEB-INF directory.

Within the <form-beans></form-beans> tags of the struts-config.xml file add the following:

```
<!-- Add Film form bean -->
<form-bean
    name="filmForm"
    type="bible.tomcat.tccinemas.FilmForm" />
```

This registers the FilmForm object we created earlier with Struts and allows this form bean to be referenced in an action mapping.

Now enter the following between the <action-mappings></action-mappings> tags of the struts-config.xml file:

```
<!-- List films -->
<action
    path="/listFilms"
    type="bible.tomcat.tccinemas.FilmListAction"
    scope="request"
    validate="false">
    <forward name="success" path="/strutsListFilms.jsp"/>
</action>
```

This entry adds an action mapping to the application and references two files we have yet to create. The first, as a value of the type parameter, bible.tomcat.tccinemas. FilmListAction, is the Action class that will perform the listing action for the controller servlet. The second is the value of the success forward tag, strutsListFilms.jsp. This file actually prints the FilmForm objects on the page for us. We can see here how the action can have various forward eventualities that pass control to JSP pages, building the flow of the application.

If there is a problem with the action, we are going to pass control to another file by referencing an error forward specified in the struts-config.xml file. This forward can be global to the application and used whenever an error is encountered, across any action we implement. We nominate this by adding a global-forward. Within the <global-forward></global-forward> tags in the struts-config.xml file add the following:

```
<forward name="error" path="/strutsError.jsp"/>
```

We reference this and the success forward in the Action class we create next.

We can now create the `Action` class `FilmListAction`. This class extends the class `org.apache.struts.action.Action` from the Struts framework and acts as an adapter between the request from the browser (via the controller servlet) and the business logic class, `StrutsFilmHandler`. It is within this class that we can perform any additional business logic validation that may be required based on the request from the client.

Create a file called `FilmListAction.java` in the `tomcatcinemas/src/bible/tomcat/tccinemas` directory of the Tomcat Cinemas source tree. The package, import, and class definition are as follows:

```
package bible.tomcat.tccinemas;

import java.io.IOException;
import java.lang.reflect.*;
import java.util.*;
import javax.servlet.*;
import javax.servlet.http.*;
import org.apache.struts.action.*;
import org.apache.struts.util.*;

import javax.sql.*;
import java.sql.*;

public class FilmListAction
    extends Action
```

For our purposes we are only going to override one method from the `Action` class it extends, `execute(..)`. This method is called when the action is invoked by the controller servlet. This method is shown in Listing 13-6:

Listing 13-6: **execute Method of FilmListAction**

```
public ActionForward execute(ActionMapping mapping,
                             ActionForm form,
                             HttpServletRequest request,
                             HttpServletResponse response)
    throws IOException, ServletException
{
    StrutsFilmHandler sfh = new StrutsFilmHandler();
    ArrayList rv = new ArrayList();

    DataSource ds = null;
    Connection cn = null;

    try
    {
        ds = getDataSource(request);
        cn = ds.getConnection();

        rv = sfh.listFilms(cn);
```

```
            request.setAttribute("films",rv);
            request.setAttribute("context",request.getContextPath());
        }
        catch(FilmException excp)
        {
            getServlet().log("FilmException", excp);
            return (mapping.findForward("error"));
        }
        catch (SQLException sqe)
        {
            getServlet().log("Connection.process", sqe);
            return (mapping.findForward("error"));
        }
        finally
        {
            try
            {
                if (cn != null)
                {
                    cn.close();
                }
            }
            catch (SQLException e)
            {
                getServlet().log("Connection.close", e);
            }
        }
        return (mapping.findForward("success"));
    }
```

The execute method of the `ListFilmAction` class performs the actual logic for retrieving the list of films. The method is passed the following:

- ✦ `org.apache.struts.action.ActionMapping` object: Represents what the controller servlet knows about the mapping of a request to this `Action` class.
- ✦ `org.apache.struts.action.ActionForm` object: Represents the form bean that may be passed to this action that was specified in the action mapping. In the case of our film list this mapping is not included because we are merely making a request for the list rather than performing some action on an instance of the `form` object. We see this used when we edit or create a new `FilmForm` object.
- ✦ `javax.http.servlet.HttpServletRequest` object: You should already be familiar with this object.
- ✦ `javax.http.servlet.HttpServletResponse` object: You should already be familiar with this object.

The method then instances a `StrutsFilmHandler` object that we created earlier and retrieves a list of `FilmForm` objects in an `ArrayList` using the `listFilms` method. This collection is then added to the request as a resource for accessing in a JSP page. The method then returns a specific mapping based on the success or error status of the action. In the case of an error we have logged the exception to the application's servlet logger and passed the user to the JSP page for an error, in this case the `strutsError.jsp` page. For a success, we have passed control onto another JSP page, `strutsListFilms.jsp`.

This is the file we will create next. This file prints out the collection of `FilmForm` objects in the manner we desire.

Create a file called `strutsListFilms.jsp` in the `tomcatcinemas/web` directory of the Tomcat Cinemas source tree. The declarations for this JSP page are as follows:

Listing 13-7: strutsListFilms.jsp

```
<%@ page language="java"%>
<%@ page import="java.util.*" %>
<%@ page import="bible.tomcat.tccinemas.*" %>
<%@ page errorPage="strutsError.jsp" %>
<%@ taglib uri="/WEB-INF/struts-html.tld" prefix="html" %>
<%@ taglib uri="/WEB-INF/struts-bean.tld" prefix="bean" %>

<jsp:useBean id="films" class="java.util.ArrayList" scope="request"/>
<jsp:useBean id="context" class="java.lang.String" scope="request"/>
```

The page import statements are self-explanatory; we need objects from these packages to fulfill the action and display the results to the user.

The `errorPage` directive means that any error that occurs in running this page will immediately forward the user to the error page specified, in this case `strutsError.jsp`. Create a file called `strutsError.jsp` in the `web/` directory of the application source tree. Have a look at the download for this chapter available from the Wiley Web site to see how this page has been implemented.

The tag lib directives inform the compiler of the location of the relevant tag library descriptor files within the application. Also remember that we specified these tag libs in the `web.xml` file earlier.

The `useBean` entries instantiate the objects we added to the request as resources in the `ListFilmsAction` class earlier. `films` is the `ArrayList` of `FilmForm` objects we will be outputting.

We begin the actual body of the JSP page by printing the title of the page and the column headings for the list we are about to display:

Listing 13-8: strutsListFilms.jsp

```
<html>
<head><title><bean:message key="film.list.title"/></title></head>
<body>
<table cellspacing="3" cellpadding="3" border="1" width="500" align="center">
```

```
<tr>
    <th colspan="6"><b><bean:message key="film.list.title"/></b></th>
</tr>
<html:messages message="true" id="msg" header="messages.listFilms.header"
footer="messages.listFilms.footer">
<li><bean:write name="msg"/></li>
</html:messages>
<tr>
    <th><b><bean:message key="film.prompt.id"/></b></th>
    <th><b><bean:message key="film.prompt.name"/></b></th>
    <th><b><bean:message key="film.prompt.length"/></b></th>
    <th><b><bean:message key="film.prompt.active"/></b></th>
    <th></th>

  </tr>
```

Some formatting has been removed from Listing 13-8 for clarity. Notice entries in this listing such as `<bean:message key="film.list.title"/>`. These are references to properties for the application that we will specify in the `ApplicationResources.properties` file. Properties such as these have been added to most of the text we may want to configure at some stage. Doing so therefore only requires a change to the `ApplicationResources.properties` file, rather than the JSP page directly.

Ignore the `<html:messages...>` tag; this will be explained when the add a new film functionality is added.

The JSP page can now actually print out a list of films with the following listing that loops through the `ArrayList` and displays each property of the `FilmForm` object in turn. At the end of each row is a link to edit each film. We will build the edit functionality last. At the base of the list we will add a link to add a new film. This will be built next. The code to print out the contents of the objects in the `ArrayList` is shown in Listing 13-9:

Listing 13-9: **strutsListFilms.jsp**

```
<%for(int i=0; i < films.size(); i++)
{
        FilmForm ff = (FilmForm)films.get(i);
%>
<tr>
   <td><%=ff.getId()%></td>
   <td><%=ff.getName()%></td>
   <td><%=ff.getLength()%></td>
   <td><%=ff.getActive()%></td>
   <td><a href="<%=context%>/editFilm.do?id=<%=ff.getId()%>"
       target="_self">Edit</a></td>
 </tr>
<%
}
%>
```

Some formatting has been removed from Listing 13-9 for clarity. The result of this action is a list of films displayed in the same way as shown in Chapter 10.

We're almost complete. Our final task to complete this action is to add some properties to the `ApplicationResources.properties` file so that the preceding references will work. Ensure that you add a property for all the `<bean:message.../>` entries you add. Referencing a property in a JSP where the property either doesn't exist or (as most of us do from time to time) is misspelled, will throw an `org.apache.jasper.JasperException` with the message: `Missing Message for key <missing key>`. This is a common error.

Once you have completed this final step it is recommended that you stop Tomcat if it was already started and restart it. Now use the following Ant tasks to compile and deploy the files appropriately, as shown in Chapter 10.

```
>ant clean
>ant context
```

All the files should be compiled and/or copied to the correct position within the build directory of the Tomcat Cinemas development environment. If you point your browser to

```
http://<host>/tomcatcinemas/listFilms.do
```

you can see the result of all our hard work in Figure 13-2, a complete list of the films in the database along the same lines as that presented in Chapter 10.

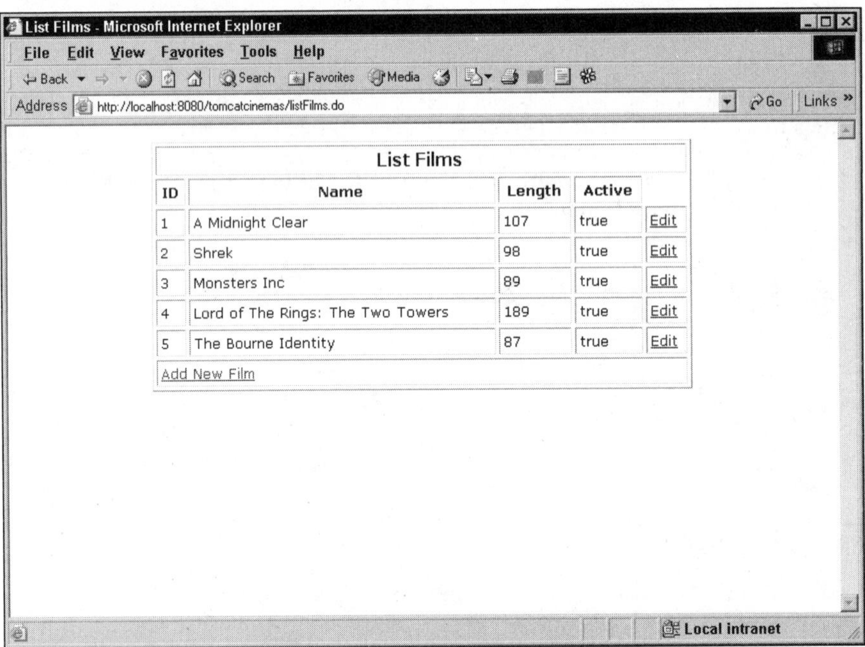

Figure 13-2: List of Films developed under the Struts framework

A Recap

So far we have created the following files for our first implementation of Struts in the Tomcat Cinemas application:

- ✦ struts-config.xml
- ✦ ApplicationResources.properties
- ✦ FilmForm.java
- ✦ StrutsFilmHandler.java
- ✦ FilmListAction.java
- ✦ FilmException.java
- ✦ strutsError.jsp
- ✦ strutsListFilms.jsp

In so doing we have created a list of films much like the list that was developed as part of Chapter 10. We will now turn our attention to adding the functionality to add a new film to the database using the Struts framework.

Add a New Film

By implementing the Add a New Film functionality using Struts, the validation mechanism it provides can be seen in some detail. To complete this functionality the FilmForm object will be used as the representation of the data that is captured from the user in the form. A new Action object will be created to fulfill the flow of the application and call the StrutsFilm Handler to perform the insert into the database using a new method that will be created.

Let's begin by creating a JSP page to display the form in the browser. Create a file called strutsAddFilm.jsp in the tomcatcinemas/web directory of the Tomcat Cinemas source tree.

Add the following lines to the new file:

```
<%@ page language="java" %>
<%@ page import="java.util.*" %>
<%@ page errorPage="strutsError.jsp" %>
<%@ taglib uri="/WEB-INF/struts-bean.tld" prefix="bean" %>
<%@ taglib uri="/WEB-INF/struts-html.tld" prefix="html" %>

<html>
<head><title><bean:message key="film.add.title"/></title></head>
<body>
<table cellspacing=0 cellpadding=0 border=0 align=center width=500>
<tr>
    <td colspan="2"><font face="verdana" size="3"><b><bean:message
key="film.add.title"/></b></font></td>
</tr>

<html:errors/>
```

```
<html:messages message="true" id="msg" header="messages.header"
footer="messages.footer">
<li><bean:write name="msg"/></li>
</html:messages>
```

This file so far appears much the same as the strutsListFilms.jsp file we created in the previous section, with one exception. We have introduced some custom tags that come with Struts. The <html:errors/> tag indicates that any errors that are passed to this page as part of validation in the Action class or the form bean should be displayed here. Below this is a tag that works in a similar way but with messages that may be passed to the page, say to confirm an action has been completed or some other information. The messages.header and messages.footer values refer to properties in the ApplicationResources.properties file to provide some header and footer html around the messages when they are displayed. These were seen in the strutsListFilms.jsp previously.

Moving on with the form itself, the following creates the form and the first element:

```
<html:form action="addFilm">
<tr>
    <td><font face="verdana" size="2">
        <bean:message key="film.prompt.name"/>
    </font></td>
    <td><html:text property="name" size="16"/></td>
</tr>
```

There are a range of custom tags provided to handle all form elements that may be implemented. The <html:form action="addFilm"> tag specifies the beginning of a form in the same way as a traditional HTML <form ...> tag. The action value specifies the Action (we are yet to create) to be executed when the form is submitted.

The page then displays a prompt indicating which form element this is. The key of the <bean:message...> tag is another key reference to a property in the ApplicationResources.properties file. The first form element is then displayed with:

```
<html:text property="name" size="16"/>
```

This displays a text form field for the name property of the FilmForm object. The value of the property attribute in this tag is important, because it must match the name of the property in the FilmForm object.

The remaining elements of the form are shown in Listing 13-10:

Listing 13-10: **strutsAddFilm.jsp**

```
<tr>
    <td colspan="2"> </td>
</tr>
<tr>
    <td><font face="verdana" size="2"><bean:message
key="film.prompt.length"/></font></td>
    <td><font face="verdana" size="2"><html:text property="length" size="16"
maxlength="4"/> minutes</font></td>
```

```
</tr>
<tr>
    <td colspan="2"> </td>
</tr>
<tr>
    <td><font face="verdana" size="2"><bean:message
key="film.prompt.active"/></font></td>
    <td><html:select property="active">
        <html:option value="true">active</html:option>
        <html:option value="false">inactive</html:option>
        </html:select>
    </td>
</tr>
<tr>
    <td colspan="2"> </td>
</tr>
<tr>
    <td> </td>
    <td><html:submit><bean:message key="film.button.add"/></html:submit></td>
</tr>
.........
</html:form>
```

As you can see, the remaining elements of the form use more properties from the `ApplicationResources.properties` file. The only additional HTML custom tags used here are the `html:select` and `html:option` tags for displaying a select list.

Further information about the use of these and other custom HTML tags can be found in the Struts documentation.

The Add Film form should display something like Figure 13-3.

Now that we have a form with which to add new Films, we need an action for it to submit to and perform some work. We start by adding a new `action-mapping` to the `struts-config.xml` file. Between the `<action-mappings>...</action-mappings>` tags add the following action:

```
<!-- Add Film -->
<action
    path="/addFilm"
    type="bible.tomcat.tccinemas.FilmAddAction"
    name="filmForm"
    scope="request"
    validate="true"
    input="/strutsAddFilm.jsp">
    <forward name="success" path="/listFilms.do"/>
    <forward name="failure" path="/strutsAddFilm.jsp"/>
</action>
```

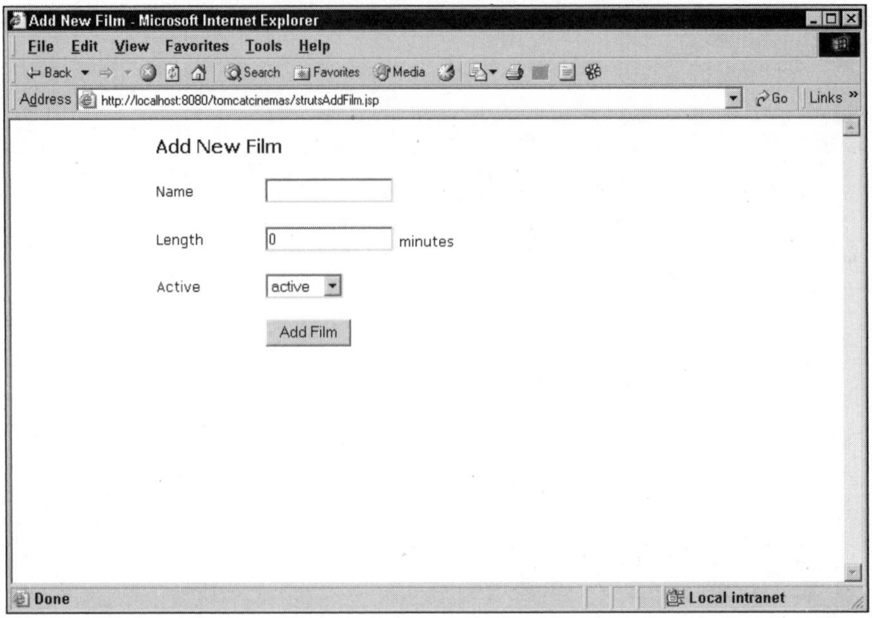

Figure 13-3: Add Film form

This action mapping is a little more interesting than the one we added for the list films action. First of all, the path indicates the URL that this action resides at, within the context of the application. The type indicates the action class to be executed. The name indicates the form-bean to be referenced as part of the execution of this action. Remember that we added a form-bean definition for the `FilmForm` object earlier. The `validate` attribute is set to true and indicates that the `FilmForm` object should be validated before the processing of this action. The `input` attribute indicates where the input for this action is taking place. We have added two forwarding eventualities from this action, one for success and one for failure. The 'success' is executed when the film is successfully added to the database, whereas the 'failure' forward sends the user straight back to the input JSP page when validation errors are found.

The corresponding action class for this declaration, `bible.tomcat.tccinemas.FilmAddAction`, can now be created. Create a file called `FilmAddAction.java` in the `tomcatcinemas/src/bible/tomcat/tccinemas` directory of the Tomcat Cinemas source tree. This action class is much the same as the action class we implemented for listing of films. For illustration purposes we only describe the execute method that actually performs the work. Refer to Listing 13-11.

Listing 13-11: **execute Method of FilmAddAction**

```
public ActionForward execute(ActionMapping mapping,
                             ActionForm form,
                             HttpServletRequest request,
                             HttpServletResponse response)
```

```
        throws IOException, ServletException
    {
        StrutsFilmHandler sfh = new StrutsFilmHandler();
        DataSource ds = null;
        Connection cn = null;

        try
        {
            ActionMessages messages = new ActionMessages();
            ds = getDataSource(request);
            cn = ds.getConnection();

            sfh.addFilm((FilmForm) form, cn);

            messages.add("successMessage",
                         new ActionMessage("film.add.success"));
            request.setAttribute(Action.MESSAGE_KEY, messages);

            if (servlet.getDebug() >= 1)
            {
                servlet.log("Film added successfully");
            }
        }
        catch(FilmException excp)
        {
            getServlet().log("FilmException", excp);
            return (mapping.findForward("error"));
        }
        catch (SQLException sqe)
        {
            getServlet().log("Connection.process", sqe);
            return (mapping.findForward("error"));
        }
        finally
        {
            try
            {
                if (cn != null)
                {
                    cn.close();
                }
            }
            catch (SQLException e)
            {
                getServlet().log("Connection.close", e);
            }
        }
        return (mapping.findForward("success"));
    }
```

Again the StrutsFilmHandler is used, this time to add the new film to the database. We will add the addFilm(...) method for this object next. In the preceding method you can see that the values for the new film have been implicitly passed to this method in the form of an ActionForm object, which needs to be cast to the FilmForm object to be passed to the StrutsFilmHandler.

Once this is successfully executed a new message is added to the request object to display in the next page in the process; in this case the Film List (see the action-mapping definition for this action to see how going to the film list is decided). The property referenced in this method (film.add.success) needs to be added to the ApplicationResources.properties file.

We now need to create the addFilm(...) method of the StrutsFilmHandler to actually store the new film in the database. This method works along similar lines to the listFilms method we created earlier. The addFilm method is displayed in Listing 13-12:

Listing 13-12: addFilm Method of StrutsFilmHandler

```
public void addFilm(FilmForm filmForm, Connection cn)
    throws FilmException
{
    PreparedStatement ps = null;

    try
    {
        String sql = "INSERT INTO FILM (name, length, active)";
        sql = sql + " VALUES (?,?,?)";
        ps = cn.prepareStatement(sql);

        if (ps != null)
        {
            ps.setString(1, filmForm.getName());
            ps.setInt(2, filmForm.getLength());
            ps.setBoolean(3, filmForm.getActive());
            ps.executeUpdate();
        }
    }
    catch (SQLException sqle)
    {
        throw new FilmException(sqle.getMessage());
    }
    finally
    {
        try
        {
            if (ps != null)
            {
                ps.close();
            }
        }
```

```
            catch (SQLException sqle)
            {
                sqle.printStackTrace();
            }
        }
    }
```

This method executes a simple SQL statement against the passed database `Connection` and the new film is added to the `film` table.

The new files and code are now completed for adding a new film to the database. Make sure you have added the appropriate properties to the `ApplicationResources.properties` file to reflect those used in the application. Before running the application to test this new functionality restart Tomcat and re-execute the `ant context` command to compile and deploy the Web application to Tomcat. Once this is completed, point your browser to `http://localhost:8080/tomcatcinemas/strutsAddFilm.jsp`. When the form is loaded enter the details for a new film and press Add Film.

If the addition of the new film was successful, the list of films is displayed (`listFilms` action) along with a comforting message indicating this to the user. This appears as shown in Figure 13-4:

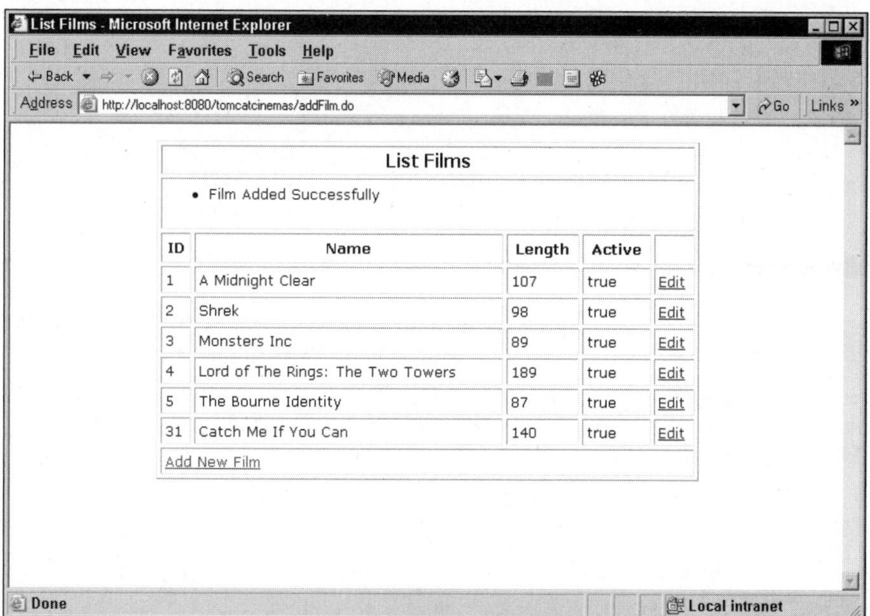

Figure 13-4: Listing films after successful addition of a new film

If some validation error in the `validate` method of the `FilmForm` object was found (remember that for the `action-mapping` for this action we added the parameter `validate="true"`), then the form is redisplayed with the appropriate error messages displayed for the user as shown in Figure 13-5:

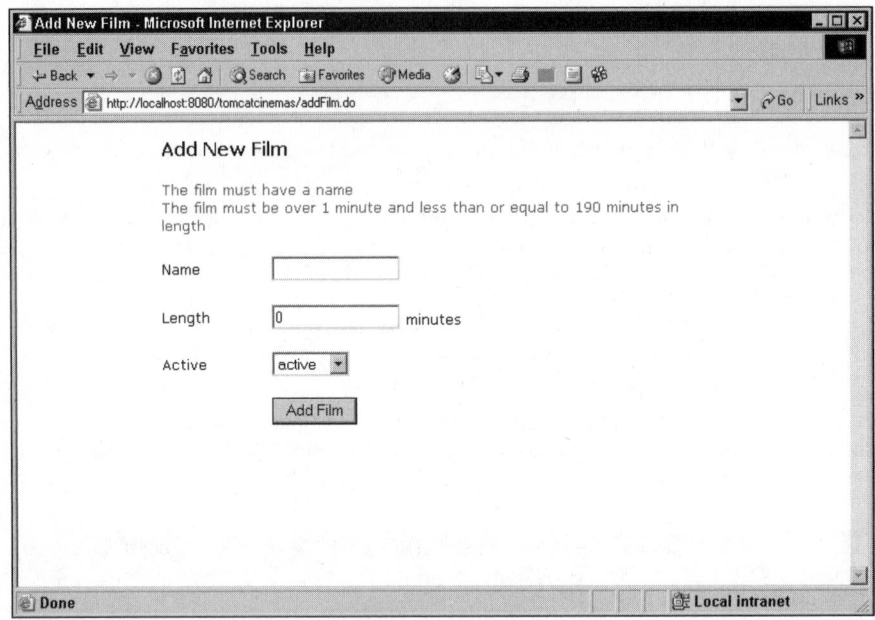

Figure 13-5: Add New Film with validation errors found

If all has worked out correctly, you should now be able to add new films to the database using the Struts framework. Our next task is to provide for the editing of films.

Edit a Film

Implementing the edit film functionality calls for two new actions, the first to retrieve the film to be edited from the database and display it in an appropriate form, the second to actually edit the film with the new values while providing for any validation errors.

Let's begin by specifying the actions required in the `struts-config.xml` file. The following two action-mappings should be added between the `<action-mappings>..</action-mappings>` tags:

```
<!-- Prepare for edit film -->
<action
    path="/editFilm"
    type="bible.tomcat.tccinemas.FilmGetAction"
    name="filmForm"
    scope="request"
    validate="false">
```

```
    <forward name="success" path="/strutsEditFilm.jsp"/>
    <forward name="failure" path="/listFilms.do"/>
</action>
<!-- Edit the film -->
<action
    path="/editFilmExe"
    type="bible.tomcat.tccinemas.FilmEditAction"
    name="filmForm"
    scope="request"
    validate="true"
    input="/strutsEditFilm.jsp">
    <forward name="success" path="/listFilms.do"/>
    <forward name="failure" path="/strutsEditFilm.jsp"/>
</action>
```

The first `action-mapping` provides for actually retrieving the film we are editing. It specifies the class to be executed as the `Action`, `bible.tomcat.tccinemas.FilmGetAction`, which needs to be created. It also specifies the `form-bean` (in the `name` attribute) we added earlier so that this `ActionForm` can be presented in the html form in the edit film page we will create soon. The success forward for this action means that the retrieval was successful and that the edit film JSP page is displayed. In the case of a failure, the list of films is displayed again.

Looking at this mapping it becomes more clear how the different components in Struts are related together to provide the desired interaction.

The second action added actually executes the update of the record in the database or provides some meaningful validation messages to the user. Notice the inclusion of the `input` parameter; this is required to facilitate validation. This mapping also specifies the `form-bean` added earlier in its `name` attribute. The success forward for this action passes control onto the `listFilms` action along with a message confirming that the film has indeed been edited. A failure takes the user back to the edit film form page.

Take particular note of the name parameter in both these actions. The name specified must be used when we get the desired film from the database and its corresponding object is placed in the request as a resource. This is pointed out again when we get to it. Ensuring this is consistent enables the forms properties to be populated automatically when `FilmGetAction` is executed. This name also maps directly to the form bean added earlier. Failing to ensure consistent naming is a major source of errors.

Lets start by creating the `Action` class, `FilmGetAction`. As mentioned previously this action simply retrieves a `FilmForm` object from the database and passes it to the `strutsEditFilm.jsp` file.

Create a file called `FilmGetAction.java` in the `tomcatcinemas/src/bible/tomcat/tccinemas` directory of the Tomcat Cinemas source tree. The package, import, and class declaration statements for this class are identical to the previous actions we have created. Add these to this file now, changing the class name to `FilmGetAction`.

The `execute` statement for retrieving the `FilmForm` object in this class is shown in Listing 13-13:

Listing 13-13: execute Method of FilmGetAction

```
public ActionForward execute(ActionMapping mapping,
                             ActionForm form,
                             HttpServletRequest request,
                             HttpServletResponse response)
    throws IOException, ServletException
{
    StrutsFilmHandler sfh = new StrutsFilmHandler();
    DataSource ds = null;
    Connection cn = null;

    try
    {
        ActionMessages messages = new ActionMessages();
        ds = getDataSource(request);
        cn = ds.getConnection();

        FilmForm ff = sfh.getFilm(request.getParameter("id"), cn);

        if(ff == null)
        {
            messages.add("failureMessage",
                         new ActionMessage("film.get.failure"));
            request.setAttribute(Action.MESSAGE_KEY, messages);
            return (mapping.findForward("failure"));
        }

        request.setAttribute("filmForm",ff);
        messages.add("successMessage",
                  new ActionMessage("film.get.success"));
        request.setAttribute(Action.MESSAGE_KEY, messages);

        if (servlet.getDebug() >= 1)
        {
            servlet.log("Film retrieved successfully");
        }
    }
    catch(FilmException excp)
    {
        getServlet().log("FilmException", excp);
        return (mapping.findForward("error"));
    }
    catch (SQLException sqe)
    {
        getServlet().log("Connection.process", sqe);
        return (mapping.findForward("error"));
    }
    finally
    {
```

```
        try
        {
            if (cn != null)
            {
                cn.close();
            }
        }
        catch (SQLException e)
        {
            getServlet().log("Connection.close", e);
        }
    }
    return (mapping.findForward("success"));
}
```

The structure of this method is similar to previous `Action` classes we have implemented. To retrieve the `FilmForm` object from the `StrutsFilmHandler` we call a new method, `getFilm`. `getFilm(...)` is illustrated next. If a `FilmForm` value is found it is added to the `request` object as a resource to be retrieved in the JSP page. Note that the alias it is given, `filmForm`, is deliberately the same as that specified in the `action-mapping`.

The return values used in the previous method correspond to the `action-mapping` we added to the `struts-config.xml` file. The error mappings use the `global-forward` mapping. The only point of failure in this method is where the object returned from the `StrutsFilmHandler` is null. In this case we can assume that the film requested could not be found. Reading the `action-mapping` for this action, we can tell that the user will be passed back to the film list and see an appropriate message displayed.

Let's now look at the `getFilm(...)` method we have to add to the `StrutsFilmHandler`. This method is passed the `id` parameter from the request that identifies the film being retrieved (remember the link in the films list to edit a film, the parameter passed in the query string was the unique `id` for each film). Inside the method (Listing 13-14), the `id` parameter (a `String`) is converted to a `long` before being passed to the `PreparedStatement` for execution. The `FilmForm` object is loaded with the `ResultSet` and the value returned to the `Action` class. If there was no record found in the `ResultSet` object, a `null` object is returned. All this can be seen in Listing 13-14:

Listing 13-14: **getFilm Method of StrutsFilmHandler**

```
public FilmForm getFilm(String id, Connection cn)
    throws FilmException
{
    PreparedStatement ps = null;
    FilmForm rv = new FilmForm();
    try
    {
        String sql = "SELECT * FROM film where id=?";
        ps = cn.prepareStatement(sql);
```

Continued

Listing 13-14 *(continued)*

```
            if(ps != null)
            {
                ps.setLong(1, NumberUtil.toLong(id));
            }

            ResultSet rs = ps.executeQuery();

            if(rs.next())
            {
                rv.load(rs);
            }
            else
            {
                rv = null;
            }
        }
        catch(SQLException sqle)
        {
            throw new FilmException(sqle.getMessage());
        }
        finally
        {
            try
            {
                if(ps != null)
                {
                    ps.close();
                }
             }
             catch(SQLException sqle)
             {
                 sqle.printStackTrace();
             }
         }
         return rv;
    }
```

Now that we have retrieved a `FilmForm` object we can present the `strutsEditFilm.jsp` page populated with the film's details.

Create a file called `strutsEditFilm.jsp` in the `tomcatcinemas/web` directory of the Tomcat Cinemas source tree. This page will be exactly the same as the `strutsAddFilm.jsp` page, with a few exceptions:

✦ Our `<bean:message...` tags will change to reference properties in the `ApplicationResources.properties` file appropriate for editing, for instance:

```
<bean:message key="film.edit.title"/>
```

✦ The `<html:form` tag will be a changed to:

```
<html:form action="editFilmExe">
```

so that the form submits to the correct action path.

✦ We will add a new element to the form to hold the `id` of the film we are editing, for instance:

```
<html:hidden property="id"/>
```

An easy way to do this is to copy the code from the `strutsAddFilm.jsp` page and copy it into the new `strutsEditFilm.jsp` page, then make the preceding additions and modifications as appropriate. Ensure that the key values for the `<bean:message` tags are added to the `ApplicationResources.properties` file as well. This should complete the code to present the edit form with the details of the film we are editing prepopulated. The form is prepopulated because tags such as:

```
<html:text property="name" size="16"/>
```

map to the `getName()` method of the `FilmForm` object when the page is built.

If you compile and deploy what has been completed so far, making sure you restart or reload Tomcat, you should be able to select a film from the film list (point your browser at: `http://localhost:8080/tomcatcinemas/listFilms.do`) and have the film editing page presented with the chosen film's details in the form. This should appear something like Figure 13-6:

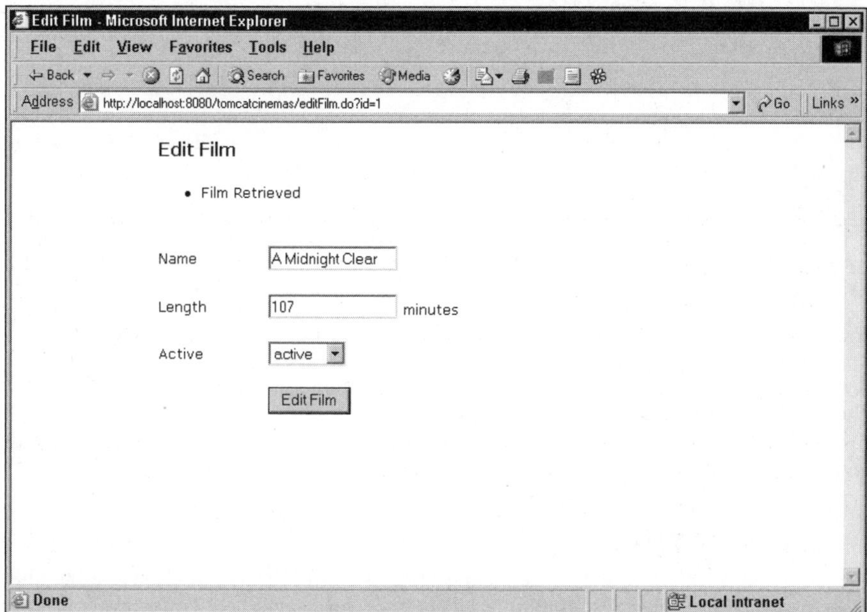

Figure 13-6: Edit Film page

The 'Film Retrieved' message is a little redundant, but it illustrates the use of messages in presenting pages. If you go back to Listing 13-13 you will note that we add this to our `messages` object when we are sure that the Film has been retrieved:

```
messages.add("successMessage", new ActionMessage("film.get.success"));
```

The property `film.get.success` references the text "Film Retrieved" in the `ApplicationResources.properties` file.

Possible problems you may encounter when developing this page are:

- ✦ An exception `javax.servlet.jsp.JspException` with the message: `No getter method for property <property name>`. This would mean that there is a difference between the names of the properties in the `FilmForm` object and the value of the `property` attribute of one of the `<html:..>` form elements in the JSP page. These must be the same.

- ✦ None of the fields in the form are populated. This is possibly due to the `FilmForm` object either not being added to the request object in the Action, in other words:

  ```
  request.setAttribute("filmForm",ff);
  ```

  or the alias assigned in this `setAttribute` call is different from the value of the `form-bean` tag name attribute assigned to this object in the `struts-config.xml` file. Another reason why one of the form elements is not prepopulated is because the value of the `property` attribute in a form element, for example:

  ```
  <html:text property="name" size="16"/>
  ```

  does not match a corresponding property in the `FilmForm` object.

- ✦ An exception `javax.servlet.jsp.JspException` with the message: `Missing message for key: <key name>`. This error means that you have either failed to add a property key to the `ApplicationResources.properties` file and have referenced it in the JSP page, or that the property is simply misspelled in the JSP page.

These are just a few of the errors you could encounter when implementing such functionality. If you are stuck on another error, or the solutions posed here do not fix the problem, consult the Struts documentation or refer to the very active Struts mailing list available from the Jakarta site (`http://jakarta.apache.org/struts/`).

Now that our form is being displayed with the correct values populated, we need a new Action for it to submit to. Remember that we added two actions to the `struts-config.xml` file to implement editing a film; the first retrieves the film for the edit page, the second actually updates the value in the database. This is `FilmEditAction`. In addition to developing this `Action` we also need to add another method to the `StrutsFilmHandler` class to actually perform the database update for the film being edited.

Create a file called `FilmEditAction.java` in the `tomcatcinemas/src/bible/tomcat/tccinemas` directory of the Tomcat Cinemas source tree.

The new class begins with the same package, import, and class declaration statements used in previous actions implemented in this application. The `execute(..)` method of the action is, however, slightly different, calling `StrutsFilmHandler` to update the film being edited, and returning an appropriate `ActionForward` object to assist with the flow of the application. The `execute(..)` method of the `Action` class is shown in Listing 13-15:

Listing 13-15: execute Method of FilmEditAction

```
public ActionForward execute(ActionMapping mapping,
                             ActionForm form,
                             HttpServletRequest request,
                             HttpServletResponse response)
    throws IOException, ServletException
{
    StrutsFilmHandler sfh = new StrutsFilmHandler();
    DataSource ds = null;
    Connection cn = null;

    try
    {
        ActionMessages messages = new ActionMessages();
        ds = getDataSource(request);
        cn = ds.getConnection();

        sfh.editFilm((FilmForm) form, cn);

        messages.add("successMessage",
                     new ActionMessage("film.edit.success"));
        request.setAttribute(Action.MESSAGE_KEY, messages);

        if (servlet.getDebug() >= 1)
        {
            servlet.log("Film edited successfully");
        }
    }
    catch(FilmException excp)
    {
        getServlet().log("FilmException", excp);
        return (mapping.findForward("error"));
    }
    catch (SQLException sqe)
    {
        getServlet().log("Connection.process", sqe);
        return (mapping.findForward("error"));
    }
    finally
    {
        try
        {
            if (cn != null)
            {
                cn.close();
            }
        }
```

Continued

Listing 13-15 *(continued)*

```
            catch (SQLException e)
            {
                getServlet().log("Connection.close", e);
            }
        }
        return (mapping.findForward("success"));
    }
```

This instance of the execute method is very similar to that of the `FilmAddAction` class implemented earlier.

We should now implement the `editFilm(..)` method in the `StrutsFilmHandler` to complete the functionality for editing films. Listing 13-16 shows this method:

Listing 13-16: editFilm Method of StrutsFilmHandler

```
    public void editFilm(FilmForm filmForm, Connection cn)
        throws FilmException
    {
        PreparedStatement ps = null;

        try
        {
            String sql = "UPDATE FILM SET name=?, length=?, active=? WHERE 
id=?";
            ps = cn.prepareStatement(sql);

            if (ps != null)
            {
                ps.setString(1, filmForm.getName());
                ps.setInt(2, filmForm.getLength());
                ps.setBoolean(3, filmForm.getActive());
                ps.setLong(4, filmForm.getId());
                ps.executeUpdate();
            }
        }
     ......
    }
```

The exception handling has been omitted from Listing 13-16 to focus only on the actual database update. The full source code can be found in the source code download for this book available from the Wiley Web site.

One of the business rules for editing a new film has been omitted from this illustration. A film cannot be set to inactive if there are showings scheduled to show it. Adding this validation to the application is left as an exercise for the reader.

Once you have added this method you can compile the application again and test editing a film. Notice that much like the add film functionality, when incorrect input is made validation errors are produced when the `validate` method of the `FilmForm` object is executed, resulting in something like Figure 13-7:

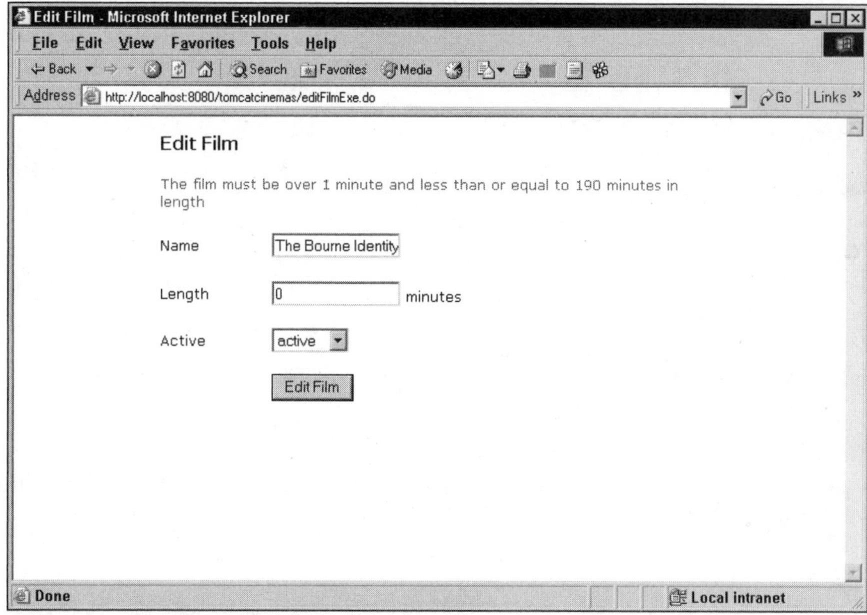

Figure 13-7: Editing a film with validation errors

When correct input is entered into the form and the action is successfully executed, the user is taken to the film list, where a message is displayed confirming a successful edit. This message is made available to the list page because the `EditFilmAction` added the message when the `editFilm` method in `StrutsFilmHandler` was successfully executed. The film list appears as shown in Figure 13-8 when an edit has been completed.

You can see the confirmation message above the column headings.

Our partial implementation of the Tomcat Cinemas application using the Struts Framework is now complete. We have provided the ability to list films from the database, add a new film, and edit the existing films.

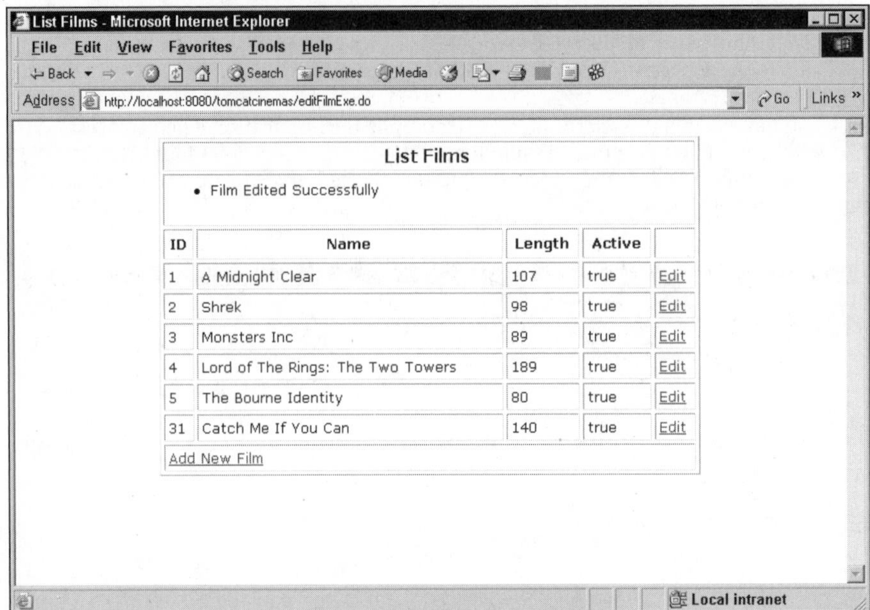

Figure 13-8: Successful edit of a film takes the user to the film list page.

Final Thoughts

While it may take some time for you to completely wrap your head around Struts, the time spent learning is well worth it. The ability to develop an application under a properly structured MVC model is invaluable. In this chapter's example we have barely nudged the full capabilities of Struts.

It is interesting to compare the methods used in developing this section to the structure implemented in Chapter 10. Some similarities can be seen in the responsibilities of the various components, such as the controller servlets and the value objects. Which is better is a matter of opinion. Both solutions offer their own set of pros and cons.

We urge you to explore Struts in greater detail using the plethora or resources on the Internet or in one of the books written about using Struts.

Other Frameworks

Although the Struts project is very popular, it is not the only framework available. Many other Web application frameworks are available, all of which provide some form of best practice when developing Web applications. There is no one best practice and there are many ways to skin a Web application (excuse the pun).

Bear in mind that not all frameworks were created equal, and not all are designed to suit a single purpose. Some Web application frameworks are designed to assist development in one specific area, and others can entirely insulate the developer from the container, creating a completely new programming environment.

When selecting a framework it is essential that a CTO or development team evaluate the product entirely before committing to a technology. To help with the evaluation process the Wafer project was formed, allowing developers to cut to the chase and see an example application implemented in each framework. This enables the evaluating party to more easily analyze the strengths and weaknesses of each framework without the need to rely on marketing hype and data sheets. The Wafer project is currently in the process of developing a prototype WebLog example application, however lots of useful information can be found about these frameworks and others at `www.waferproject.org/`.

The following is a brief discussion of the common features found in Web application frameworks. The chapter then concludes with a brief description of three frameworks that are freely available for you to use in your own applications.

Common Features

Any good framework should provide a set of minimal features. The concepts of templating and the use of a MVC (or equivalent) architecture is common across all the frameworks listed.

Templating

Templating languages are designed to allow a non-programmer to create Views by defining the layout and structure of the document using a template. At runtime templates undergo transformation, combining the template and content to create a finished document.

Many templating tools are available to Web developers. Table 13-1 lists some of the common templating engines that can be used from within a servlet container.

Table 13-1: Templating Languages

Name	*URL*	*Brief Description*
JSP	`http://java.sun.com/products/jsp/`	Java Server Pages can be used to generate dynamic content with embedded Java scriptlets.
JSTL	`http://jakarta.apache.org/taglibs/doc/standard-doc/intro.html`	JSP now supports the Java Standard Tag Library (JSTL). JSP can include XML tags as placeholders for dynamically generated content. The Apache Standard TagLib project is an implementation of the standard tag library.
Velocity	`http://jakarta.apache.org/velocity/`	Velocity is an alternative Java-based template engine supporting templates written in a PHP-like syntax. Velocity also enforces a MVC paradigm by preventing the use of Java code within the template.
XML/XSLT	`www.w3.org/TR/xslt`	Extensible Stylesheet Language Transformation (XSLT) can be used to transform an XML document into HTML, text, or another XML document. XSLT uses the XSL vocabulary to specify formatting.

MVC Architecture

The Model View Controller (MVC), aka Model 2, architecture is a design pattern that has become popular amongst the Web developer community. MVC has come about in response to the inability to separate Web site design from programming logic.

Initial Web applications written in CGI or servlets embedded HTML inline with the programming logic. Technologies such as ASP and JSP took the opposite approach by embedding the programming logic within a HTML document. Both approaches fail to separate the design tasks from programming tasks, which resulted in the inability for designers and programmers to collaborate effectively.

MVC, however, makes a clear distinction between the View and the controller. A Web site designer can create a view in JSP with a minimal amount of presentation logic to generate the desired output. The application programmer takes ownership of the controller, implementing business logic either inside the servlet or communicating with a component-based technology such as EJB. The model acts as an interface between the designer and the programmer, specifying the data structure that is passed between the Servlet and JSP.

A more detailed discussion of MVC can be found at `www.javaworld.com/javaworld/jw-12-1999/jw-12-ssj-jspmvc.html`.

The main role of a framework is to enforce the use of a MVC-like design pattern. Some of the MVC variants are explained in the following sections.

Push

This is the most common method of using MVC. The controller accepts an incoming request; Ant then performs the necessary processing and prepares the model for display. The model is then passed-on (or pushed) to the view for rendering.

The push model is easy for a programmer to understand and implement, and provides tremendous advantages over an inline approach to Web site generation. It is therefore the dominant implementation of MVC, and supported by many templating languages and frameworks.

The approach is, however, very programmer centric, and the template designer cannot makestructural or flow changes to the site without involving the programmer.

Pull

The Pull model takes a different approach; template designers no longer have a model pushed upon them when constructing a view. Instead they have access to an object in the view that allows a template designer to "pull" the model information they require.

The Pull MVC model means screen and form layout changes no longer require a programmer to change the model that is "pushed;" the template designer can simply change the view to use the collection of available objects to make the necessary change. Obviously for this model to be successful there needs to be a well designed and documented API to which the template designers have access.

Examples of Pull MVCs are TagLibs, WebWork, and Tea, the templating component of the TeaServlet framework. A good discussion of Pull versus Push with regard to MVC can be found at: `http://jakarta.apache.org/turbine/turbine-2/pullmodel.html`.

Hierarchical

The Hierarchical MVC (HMVC) pattern creates parent-child MVC layers to add further structure to a Web and client-based GUI development. The HMVC pattern is used by many windowing toolkits.

HMVC adds additional structure to the MVC model such as event handling and application flow support. The concept of layering allows the creation of a foundation layer on which child layers can call upon, hence simplifying application development.

A more detailed overview of HMVC is available from `www.javaworld.com/javaworld/jw-07-2000/jw-0721-hmvc_p.html`.

Other Features

In addition to the common features, some frameworks may include support for other, more advanced features. The following features are contained in more sophisticated frameworks.

Event Handling

Some frameworks go a long way to hide the complexities of the underlying constraints of a Web-based application and provide an event-handling paradigm similar to that provided by a GUI toolkit.

Instead of a controller having to interpret the HTTP request and determine the context of the request, as well as the command executed, the developer wants only to listen for an event and act appropriately when one occurs.

Such an event-handling model significantly reduces the complexity, and size of the Controlling servlet.

Form Validation

The ability to validate form input is a common problem in Web-based systems, and results in the application developer having to develop vast quantities of code to verify the integrity of the data provided by the user. As validation rules are typically duplicated from the database tier, a simple mechanism to maintain the rules is essential.

Frameworks supporting form validation should supply a simple interface to validate input data according to commonly used rules such as pattern matching, length, and range checking. The generated validation code may be implemented on the client-side using JavaScript validating the user input before a request is made to the server. Alternatively the framework may only support server-side validation, where a filter-like implementation will intercept the contents of the request and validate user input before being passed to the controller.

Error Handling

An often-overlooked area of complexity in Web applications is error handling. The code base of an application often increases in size by an order of magnitude when error handling is added. Frameworks supporting this feature should make the process of dealing with errors as trivial as possible.

Error handling may include dealing with server errors, or errors resulting from failed form validation. In either case the framework should handle the application fail-over, show the user a suitable error screen, and assist the user to continue with a transaction with as little disruption as possible.

Security

Some frameworks provide security above and beyond that provided by the servlet container. Such features include a schema to store users, roles, and permissions, and an easy way to administer these details. In addition, the framework should support declarative and implicit access control to the application.

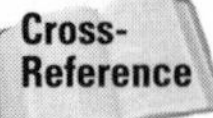

Although many frameworks may support security, some of them will he hard-pressed to compete with the security features of Tomcat described in Chapter 12.

Internationalization

Internationalization, abbreviated to I18n, is often an afterthought when developing Web applications, or something that is left to a later phase of development requiring a complete overhaul of the site.

Frameworks with I18n features should simplify the addition of content and error messages written in different languages, and with different character encoding. In addition, the framework may have the ability to determine the locale of a user based on HTTP headers or user profile information, and generate content in the appropriate language with the appropriate character encoding.

Web Application Frameworks

Table 13-2 lists a number of Web application frameworks available to the developer community.

Table 13-2: Web Application Frameworks

Name	*URL*	*Brief Description*
Barracuda	`http://barracuda.enhydra.org/`	A presentation framework.
Cocoon	`http://xml.apache.org/cocoon/`	An XML publishing framework. Allows the definition of XML documents and the transformations on them for presentation.
SOFIA	`www.salmonllc.com/`	A tool set for developing database-driven Web applications. Has an extensive custom tag library and integration with popular HTML and Java IDEs.
Java Server Faces	`http://java.sun.com/j2ee/javaserverfaces/`	Sun's Web application presentation framework.
Maverick	`http://mav.sourceforge.net/`	An MVC-focused framework.

Name	URL	Brief Description
Struts	http://jakarta.apache.org/struts/	Application framework providing control layer and interaction with view and model components of MVC.
TeaServlet	http://teatrove.sourceforge.net/	Template engine using the Tea language.
Turbine	http://jakarta.apache.org/turbine/	Servlet-based application framework.
WebWork	www.opensymphony.com/webwork/	HMVC Web application framework supporting various view technologies.

A more extensive but by no means complete list of available frameworks can be found at the Wafer project at `www.waferproject.org/`.

In this section we briefly describe three of these frameworks and provide some links for you to investigate:

- ✦ SOFIA
- ✦ Barracuda
- ✦ Turbine

These three frameworks are all open source and can be integrated with Tomcat.

SOFIA

SOFIA was until recently referred to as The JADE Open Framework. SOFIA stands for *Salmon Open Framework for Internet Applications* and describes itself as an open source tool set for building database driven Web applications.

In fulfilling this goal SOFIA integrates with any J2EE compliant container, and on the development side provides for integration with Dreamweaver (HTML/JSP) and IntelliJ IDEA or Eclipse for Java.

SOFIA attempts to remove the tight coupling between an application's user interface and business logic when developing inline JSP with an extensive custom tag library. This custom tag library basically extends HTML, with the resulting tags allowing interaction with the application and its database. In addition, developers can create their own GUI components in Java, allowing for their re-use across the application.

SOFIA utilizes a number of patterns in its architecture, most notably the MVC pattern for the separation of presentation code from business logic. Other patterns include GUI patterns such as those found in Swing and AWT for the presentation of common interface tools such as form elements and data grids. The Observer pattern is also utilized in SOFIA to assist with event handling and the routing of application flow.

SOFIA differentiates itself from other frameworks like Struts with its IDE integration and its ability to interact with Smart View Components in the View component. SOFIA, however, does not support internationalization.

SOFIA has a large amount of documentation available allowing the developer to walk through everything from code examples and video demonstrations to API documents. An active community also provides an interactive free support service on its mailing list.

Commercial support arrangements are also provided to varying levels. There are also training courses available to help developers learn more about using SOFIA in their applications.

SOFIA has been implemented in a number of commercial Web applications.

More information about SOFIA can be found at `www.salmonllc.com/`.

Barracuda

Barracuda is a presentation framework for the building of Web applications and is developed by the same group that releases the Enhydra Java/XML application server.

This framework is actively developed by a small group of committers who develop its main core. Community members are encouraged to contribute to the project by fixing bugs, submitting add-on software, and assisting other users in the Barracuda mailing list.

Barracuda boasts a large volume of documentation, walkthroughs, and tutorials, including UML diagrams. There also are some examples and tutorials available to learn from.

Architecturally Barracuda can be broadly broken down into six key areas that can be used independently or as a whole:

✦ Client Capabilities: Identifying the thin client (browser) capabilities of the request. This information is used to present the apprpropriate response to the client.

✦ Events: Discerning what tasks to perform using Swing-like event model listeners and ensuring they are executed.

✦ Form Mapping and Validation: Maps interface forms to objects and provides for validation of input and business logic.

✦ XMLC (template generation): Generates templates that can be manipulated programmatically (Push MVC).

✦ Localization: Utilizes XMLC template generation, custom Ant tasks, and property files to generate localized views of the application.

✦ Component Model: A hierarchy of components is developed to present the interface. Components render data into the DOM structure. These Barracuda components are structured around the data they present and bound to a part of the DOM structure for presentation.

There are some issues with using Barracuda with J2SE 1.4 centering on the inclusion of some new packages in the J2SE and the addition of the `assert` keyword in the Java language. Refer to the Barracuda site for more information.

More information about Barracuda and Enhydra can be found at `http://enhydra.org/`.

Turbine

Turbine is released by the Apache Foundation's Jakarta Project under the Apache Software License. The latest stable version at time of writing is 2.2. A bug fix release (2.2.1) has not yet been scheduled and 2.3 will be the next feature-adding release.

Turbine is described as a servlet-based framework for building Web applications. It comprises a vast set of tools and APIs for developing these applications. The Turbine framework can be broken down into five modules: Action, Page, Screen, Navigation, and Layout. Actions form the processing flow of the application and the remaining modules interact to produce the required output for the response.

Turbine also provides for Access Control Lists (ACL) and Permissions to control the users interaction throughout the five modules (Turbine Security). Turbine employs a relational database to fulfill this functionality.

Turbine also comes packaged with a set of utility classes that may or may not be helpful in developing your application.

To get started with Turbine it is recommended you download and install the Turbine Development Kit (TDK) available from the Turbine site.

A number of other projects have been decoupled from Turbine; among them are Torque, a database persistence layer, and Fulcrum, a services framework. Fulcrum comprises a number of services that provide for some requirement of an application. For instance, the crypto service allows an application to utilize cryptographic algorithms and the scheduler service provides for the timed execution of certain tasks.

There are two mailing lists (user and developer) available for discussions on Turbine. This together with the documentation found at the Turbine site and the TDK enables you to get going with Turbine.

A number of Web sites have implemented Turbine technology in one form or another, most notably `www.openoffice.org` and `www.netbeans.org`.

You can find out more about Turbine by visiting the Turbine site at `http://jakarta.apache.org/turbine/`.

Summary

The landscape of frameworks you can use to develop your application is very wide, and we have only illustrated a small portion of them. Our walkthrough of Struts, for instance, did not touch on many of its TagLib features. The rich diversity of these frameworks is often overwhelming and it is easy to become too hung up on features when a less feature-rich but well designed and cleanly implemented framework may be the better candidate.

We encourage you to learn more about the frameworks mentioned in this chapter. Using them can be a rewarding learning process and will ultimately make your applications more extensible and robust.

✦ ✦ ✦

SOAP

✦ ✦ ✦ ✦

In This Chapter

SOAP Overview

Apache SOAP

Simple SOAP Service Example

Context-Based SOAP Service Example

Tomcat Cinemas SOAP Service Example

✦ ✦ ✦ ✦

The latest buzzword to grace the developer community is Web services. Put simply, *Web services* are programming interfaces exposed by a remote application, providing application communication over the Web. A Web service provides a programming interface with the use of the *Simple Object Access Protocol* (SOAP); the interface is defined using the *Web Service Description Language* (WSDL). Clients can easily find Web services that are registered using the *Universal Description Discovery Integration* (UDDI) directory service.

Web services have been largely popularized by the Microsoft .NET platform, but Web services have been developed as a W3C standard, in conjunction with industry partners such as Microsoft, IBM, BEA Systems, Sun Microsystems, Oracle, and Hewlett-Packard.

This chapter focuses on the use of SOAP, the protocol behind all Web services. Although technically not a Web service in itself, a SOAP service offers many of the advantages of a Web service without the formality of a WSDL definition or UDDI registration.

WSDL and UDDI lie outside the SOAP specification, and are therefore out of the scope of this chapter. Therefore, to deploy an application as a Web service it will be necessary to explicitly describe the exposed API using WSDL, and manually register the application on a UDDI directory service. Some SOAP implementations offer tools to assist with the deployment of a Web service, however support for WSDL and UDDI is not guaranteed across all implementations. More information about WSDL can be found from reading the WSDL specification `www.w3.org/TR/wsdl12/`. The UDDI specification can be found at `www.oasis-open.org/committees/uddi-spec/tcspecs.shtml`.

The first part of this chapter provides a brief overview of SOAP, and introduces a simple working service example. The remainder of the chapter extends some of the Web applications created in Chapters 7 and 10, exposing them as services. The examples services in this chapter are accessed using a variety of SOAP clients (command-line application, servlet, and J2ME MIDlet) using two client-side SOAP APIs (Apache SOAP and kSOAP from Enhydra.org).

SOAP Overview

Before jumping in and creating an Apache SOAP service, it is important to understand the fundamentals of the protocol; according to the SOAP specification, SOAP is “a lightweight protocol for exchange of information in a decentralized, distributed environment." SOAP 1.1 was originally submitted to the World Wide Web Consortium (W3C) as a *Note*, or a pubic record of an idea. Documentation of the Note is available from `www.w3.org/TR/SOAP`.

SOAP 1.2 has currently reached a *Candidate Recommendation* maturity level within the W3C, the Candidate recommendation document can be found at `www.w3.org/TR/soap12-part0/`. The technical community is free to implement the specification and offer technical feedback before it is promoted to a *Proposed Recommendation*, and then possibly onto a *Recommendation* status. Many SOAP 1.2 implementations are currently underway.

Advantages of SOAP

There are several advantages to using SOAP services on a distributed network over protocols such as RMI, CORBA, and ODBC.

For starters, SOAP is platform and language neutral. The large degree of cooperation between industry heavyweights has meant that there are SOAP extensions for most programming languages, running on a variety of platforms. The result is a collection of loosely coupled systems, running on a heterogeneous network.

RMI is an excellent Java-to-Java communication protocol for homogeneous environments such as J2EE. It is efficient, and allows distributed Java applications to easily invoke remote methods and communicate without the need to marshal and unmarshal data. It is, however, restricted to the Java programming language.

SOAP, compared to CORBA, is a lightweight protocol, and services deployed on SOAP servers do not require any knowledge of the protocol. The same cannot be said for CORBA applications.

ODBC has been used for decades to communicate with distributed database servers, and provides an open and well-defined protocol that nearly all database vendors support. However, modern n-tier applications typically avoid the implementation of business logic on the database server, preferring to develop on a middle tier. Many large corporations are exposing interfaces to legacy database via Web and SOAP services. This clears the way for these systems to be superseded at a later date, without requiring client applications to be modified.

SOAP Concepts

This remainder of this chapter assumes you are familiar with the basic concepts of SOAP. As with any protocol, SOAP defines the method of communication over a network, and also the format of the data transmitted. In addition SOAP provides a higher level of communication between applications using Remote Procedure Calls (RPC).

The concepts of the SOAP Protocol, SOAP Messages, and SOAP RPC are introduced in this section.

Protocol

All communication using SOAP involves a sender and receiver; for each transaction there is to be one sender and one receiver. The sender is the producer of the SOAP message and the receiver consumes the body of the message.

SOAP can be bound on top of other protocols such as HTTP and SMTP. HTTP is an obvious choice because of its ability to easily traverse firewalls. This chapter focuses solely on the binding of SOAP to HTTP.

Message

A SOAP message defines the basic unit of communication between the sender and receiver. A SOAP service is the provisioning of an application that produces and/or consumes SOAP messages.

At the top level of the XML message is a SOAP envelope. The envelope contains one or more header blocks, an indication to the receiver of any special processing that needs to take place on the body of the message. The body node contains the payload of the SOAP message.

If a fault occurs on the sender, a SOAP fault node is added inside the envelope, indicating the error that occurred.

RPC

Remote Procedure Calls (RPC) allow synchronous communication between clients and servers. RPC is not specific to SOAP; it is available in a variety of languages and programming platforms. RPC over SOAP does however offer Remote Procedure calls to be encapsulated in a platform independent way, using XML. RPC provides a request/response method of communication between a client and a server. A client sends a SOAP message, invoking a method, and a SOAP message is returned from the server, containing the response. If SOAP RPC is bound to HTTP, this request/response method of communication is implicitly supported by the underlying protocol. SOAP RPC is not however limited only to HTTP.

The SOAP request contains the service and method names which to invoke, and the response contains a return type contained in the body, or a SOAP fault if an error occurred fulfilling the request.

Object serialization is an essential part of RPC. SOAP senders need to marshal/serialize platform-specific objects into an XML representation of the data structure. The SOAP receiver needs to unmarshal/deserialize the XML to a native object before the message can be processed. RPC uses object serialization to pass method arguments to the server, and forward method return values to the client.

Apache SOAP

Apache SOAP is a sub project of the Apache XML Project; it is an implementation of the W3C Simple Object Access Protocol (SOAP). Apache SOAP is an open source implementation supporting most of the SOAP v1.1 specification.

During the time of writing a follow-on project from Apache SOAP reached maturity, resulting in the release of Apache Axis 1.0. Apache Axis is essentially Apache SOAP 3.0, but due to the uncertainty of whether XML Protocol working group would call the XML protocol XMLP or SOAP, it was named Axis. Apache Axis is a total rewrite of Apache SOAP, implements most of Version 1.2 of the SOAP specification, and supports generation of a WSDL deployment descriptor from Java code, and vice versa.

Apache SOAP was chosen over Apache Axis due to the maturity of the product and the stability of SOAP 1.1. However, Apache Axis is fast becoming the accepted standard Apache SOAP implementation, surpassing Apache SOAP with adherence to the latest SOAP specifications, compliance with the standard JAX-RPC API for XML-Based RPC, and increased performance. Although, in the near future, readers will be best suited to adopt Apache Axis, the coverage of Apache SOAP will demonstrate the concepts of building a SOAP service, and provide real world examples of SOAP clients. These concepts may be applied to many of the Java-based SOAP implementations available including Apache Axis, however APIs will most certainly differ.

Download

The latest version of the Apache SOAP distribution is available from `http://xml.apache.org/soap/`.

Click on the Download link on the left hand side of the page. This will take you to the main distribution site. To see the distribution files for the latest version click on the `version-2.3.1` link.

Select the zip file `soap-bin-2.3.1.zip`, and when prompted save the file to disk.

Note Apache SOAP requires the following Java libraries to be contained in the classpath.

- ✦ JavaMail API (`mail.jar`)
  `http://java.sun.com/products/javamail/`
- ✦ JavaBeans Activation Framework (`activation.jar`)
  `http://java.sun.com/products/javabeans/glasgow/jaf.html`
- ✦ Java API for XML Processing (JAXP) compatible parser (`xmlParserAPIs.jar` and `xercesImpl.jar`)
  `http://java.sun.com/xml/jaxp/`

Fortunately, Apache Tomcat 4.1.12 already has all the required libraries installed in `C:\tomcat\common\lib` and `C:\tomcat\common\endorsed`.

Installation

Installing the Apache SOAP distribution is as simple as extracting a ZIP file. When it comes to using Apache SOAP with Tomcat on the server-side, there are two ways Apache SOAP can be used: by deploying a Web archive, or integrating SOAP into your Web application.

The simplest way is to deploy the Web archive, but it has some limitations when attempting to create SOAP services from existing Web applications, in which case it is necessary to integrate Apache SOAP with a Web application.

Note Because previous versions of Tomcat included an XML parser prior to Xerces 1.1.2, it was necessary to add `xerces.jar` to the beginning of the Tomcat classpath for the library to be recognized. Tomcat 4.1.12, however, includes Xerces 2, making this step unnecessary.

Client-Side soap applications using Apache SOAP are explored in the Simple SOAP Service Example section.

Extracting the Binary Distribution

Before Apache SOAP can be used with Tomcat it is necessary to extract the distribution to the hard disk.

Extract the `soap-bin-2.3.1.zip` file to the `C:\`. This creates a directory, `C:\soap-2_3_1`, and subdirectories.

The `C:\soap-2_3_1` directory now contains API documentation, user documentation, SOAP libraries, samples, and a SOAP Web Archive. In the rest of this section we explore how Apache SOAP can be used with Tomcat.

Deploying the SOAP Web Archive

Installation of Apache SOAP on Tomcat 4.1.12 is as easy as deploying a WAR file. Simply copy the SOAP Web Archive from `C:\soap-2_3_1\webapps\soap.war` to `C:\tomcat\webapps`, and restart the Tomcat server.

After the Apache SOAP Web Archive has been deployed, open the URL `http://localhost:8080/soap/servler/rpcrouter` to test the installation. The resulting page should look like that shown in Figure 14-1.

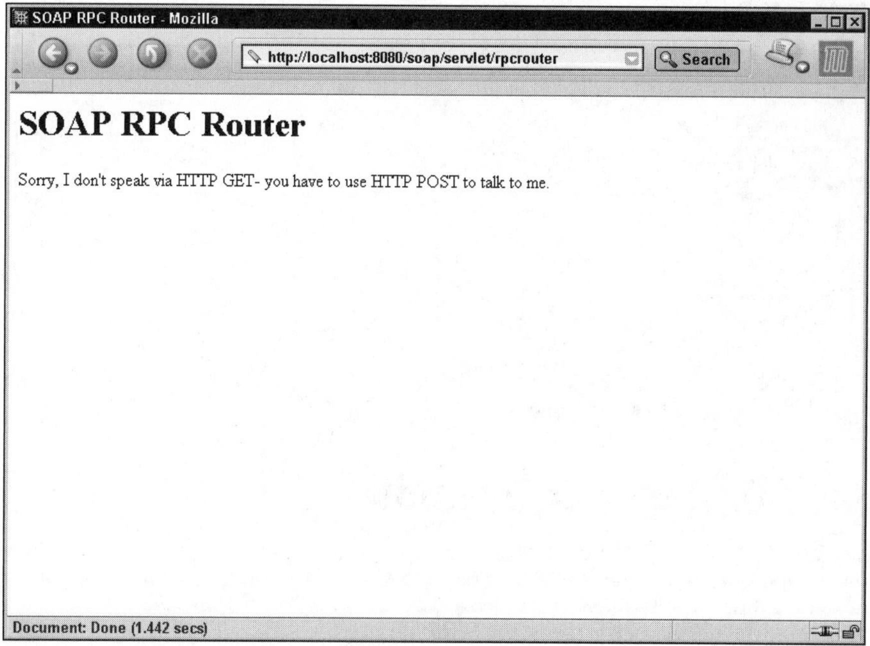

Figure 14-1: Expected output from RPC Router test

Although the test doesn't do anything useful, it does prove that the SOAP RPC Router Serlvet is operational and accepting requests.

Next, open the URL `http://localhost:8080/soap/admin/` in your browser. The page that is displayed enables an administrator to deploy and undeploy SOAP services from the Apache SOAP server. The screen should look like that shown in Figure 14-2.

Congratulations, you now have an operational SOAP server. We will now go ahead and implement a simple SOAP service.

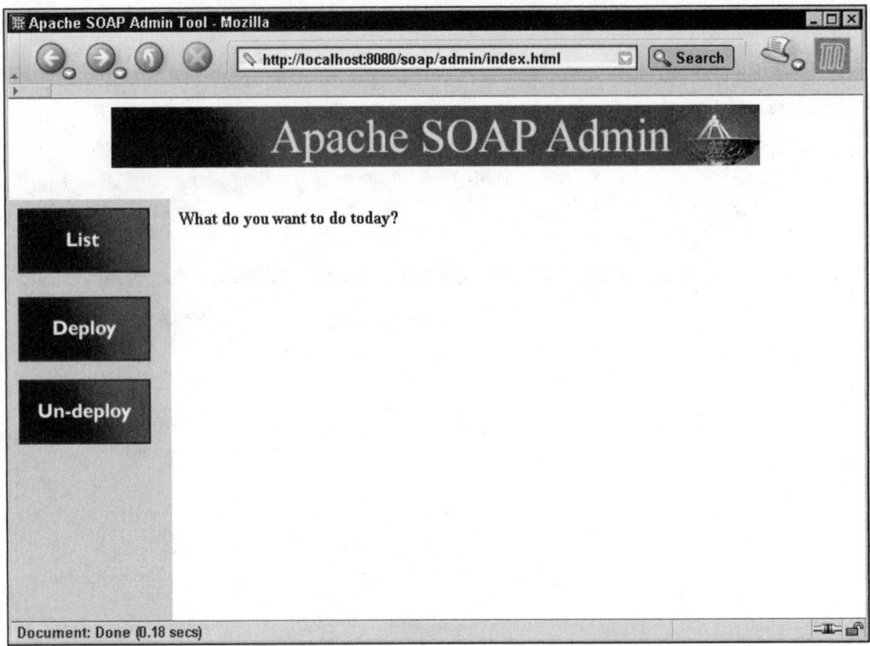

Figure 14-2: Apache SOAP administration client

Simple SOAP Service Example

In this example, a simple SOAP service scenario is presented and implemented using the Apache SOAP server. The SOAP service takes the Hello City application developed in Chapter 7 and extracts the business login into a SOAP service. For the purpose of testing, a command line SOAP client makes use of the SOAP service.

SOAP Service

First, let's jump straight into the SOAP service. Apache SOAP allows almost any class to act as a SOAP service, making its methods available via SOAP Remote Procedure Calls (SOAP-RPC). The development of the SOAP service is the easy part, and depending on your application you may already have methods suitable to expose via a SOAP interface.

Looking at Listing 14-1, the `CityService` class looks like any other Java class, and knows nothing about the SOAP protocol. The source code should reside in the project's `src` directory under the appropriate package name. However simple the class looks, it is in fact the core of our SOAP service. As you will see later, all the effort in creating SOAP services is in the deployment.

The implementation body of `CityService` looks very familiar to the `CityServlet` developed in Chapter 7. Here the business logic has been extracted and then encapsulated in the `getGreeting()` method.

Listing 14-1: CityService.java

```
package bible.tomcat.hello;

import java.io.*;
import java.lang.*;
import java.util.*;

/*
 * A simple SOAP service implementation of the Hello City application.
 *
 * Methods contained in the CityService class may be invoked remotely
 * using SOAP Remote Procedure Calls (SOAP-RPC).
 */
public class CityService
{
    /*
     * getGreeting() provides the body of the SOAP service,
     * and contains all the business logic for the Hello City
     * Web application.
     */
    public String getGreeting(String city)
    {
        /*
         * Check the input.
         */
        if ((city == null) || (city.length() < 1))
        {
            throw new IllegalArgumentException("Please choose a city");
        }

        /*
         * Determine an appropriate greeting for the chosen city.
         */
        String greeting = null;

        if (city.equals("MEL"))
        {
            greeting = "G'day";
        }
        else if (city.equals("PAR"))
        {
            greeting = "Bonjour";
        }
        else if (city.equals("MIL"))
        {
            greeting = "Ciao";
        }

        return greeting;
    }
}
```

SOAP Client

The client-side of a SOAP application is not quite as trivial as the SOAP service. The client must explicitly know how to deal with SOAP requests and responses. The client in Listing 14-2 uses the Apache SOAP client-side API to connect to the Hello City SOAP service running on an Apache SOAP server.

The following code fragment shows how to prepare a Remote Procedure Call (RPC) to the SOAP service. The `setTargetObjectURI()` method specifies the target SOAP service to connect to, and the `setMethodName()` method defines the remote method to invoke. The URI and method name should correspond to the service defined in deployment descriptor. The Configuration section, later in this chapter, will include a discussion of deployment descriptors. The encoding style has been explicitly set to use SOAP Encoding using `setEncodingStyleURI()`. This is the default encoding style.

```
Call call = new Call();
call.setTargetObjectURI(URI);
call.setMethodName(GREETING_METHOD);
call.setEncodingStyleURI(Constants.NS_URI_SOAP_ENC);
```

Registered serializers/deserializers are required for all parameter and return data types. Fortunately, Apache SOAP has pre-defined serializers/deserializers that are available for commonly used Java objects, such as String, Integer, Boolean, and so on. It is therefore not necessary for the Hello City client to register any serializers/deserializers.

The next code fragment explains how method arguments are sent via SOAP to the SOAP service as parameters. A parameter must be declared for each remote procedure argument. Each parameter name and class name should match the corresponding argument name and type in the remote method declaration of Listing 14-1 `CityService.java`.

```
Vector params = new Vector();
params.addElement(
    new Parameter("city", String.class, city, null));
call.setParams(params);
```

Next the client must invoke the RPC, and capture the SOAP response. This is demonstrated in the following code. The `url` parameter passed to the RPC `invoke()` method specifies the endpoint of the SOAP RPC Router servlet, and the SOAP action header. The remote method will be invoked synchronously, and eventually a SOAP response will be returned.

The SOAP action header feature is optional for SOAP clients. Unfortunately the method declaration for `invoke()` implies the `SOAPActionURI` is required.

```
soapActionURI = "";
Response resp = call.invoke(url, soapActionURI);
```

After a response has been returned, the client can then interpret the contents of the SOAP response.

The code in Listing 14-2 implements all the elements explained previously to create a complete SOAP client. The `CityTestClient.java` source should reside in the project's `src` directory under the appropriate package name.

Listing 14-2: CityTestClient.java

```
package bible.tomcat.hello;

import java.io.*;
import java.net.*;
import java.util.*;

import org.apache.soap.*;
import org.apache.soap.rpc.*;

/**
 * A SOAP client to test the Hello City SOAP service. The command-line
 * usage is as follows:
 * <p><code>
 * java CityTestClient &lt;city&gt; &lt;name&gt; &lt;SOAP-router-URL&gt;
 * </code></p>
 * Where: <br>
 * <b>city:</b> is one of the following cities [MEL|PAR|MIL]<br>
 * <b>name:</b> is the users name<br>
 * <b>SOAP-router-URL</b> is the endpoint of the Apache SOAP RPC Router
 */
public class CityTestClient
{
    /*
     * The URI that the SOAP service used to identify itself in
     * the deployment descriptor.
     */
    public static final String URI = "urn:hello_web_service";

    /*
     * The remote method to invoke on the SOAP service. The method
     * name must be one of methods exposed by the SOAP service.
     */
    public static final String GREETING_METHOD = "getGreeting";


    /**
     * Mainline.
     */
    public static void main (String[] args)
    throws Exception
    {
        /*
         * Process the command-line arguments.
         */
        if (args.length != 3)
        {
            System.err.println ("Usage: java " +
```

Continued

Listing 14-2 *(continued)*

```
                CityTestClient.class.getName () +
                " <city> <name> <SOAP-router-URL>");
            System.exit (1);
        }

        String city = args[0];
        String name = args[1];
        URL url = new URL(args[2]);

        /*
         * Build a Remote Procedure Call (RPC).
         */
        Call call = new Call();
        call.setTargetObjectURI(URI);
        call.setMethodName(GREETING_METHOD);
        call.setEncodingStyleURI(Constants.NS_URI_SOAP_ENC);

        /*
         * Declare a RPC parameters
         */
        Vector params = new Vector();
        params.addElement(
                new Parameter("city", String.class, city, null));
        call.setParams(params);


        /*
         * Invoke the RPC.
         */
        Response resp = call.invoke(url, "");

        /*
         * Interpret the SOAP response, or any faults that may have
         * occurred.
         */
        if (resp.generatedFault())
        {
            Fault fault = resp.getFault();
            System.err.println("Generated fault: " + fault);
        }
        else
        {
            Parameter result = resp.getReturnValue();
            String greeting = (String)result.getValue();
            System.out.println(greeting + " " + name);
        }
    }
}
```

Configuration

The deployment descriptor is used to register a SOAP service with the Apache SOAP instance. The deployment descriptor is written as an XML document, and contains information about the services to be exposed to SOAP clients.

Listing 14-3 describes a standard Java class deployment descriptor used to deploy the Hello City SOAP service. The SOAP deployment descriptor is usually named `DeploymentDescriptor.xml` and should be placed in a descriptor directory (for example, `/etc`) under the project work area. The relevant attributes in the deployment descriptor are described as follows:

- **Service-URN:** the `id` attribute of the service element defines the Universal Resource Name of the SOAP service. This name uniquely identifies the SOAP service running on the Apache SOAP instance, and is used by the RPC Router to route requests to the SOAP service implementing class.
- **Provider-Type:** because we are implementing all our SOAP services in Java using simple classes, the provider `type` attribute will always equal "java". It is possible to write SOAP service providers using EJB and BSF Scripts. To read more about these refer to the *Apache SOAP User's Guide.*
- **Provider-Scope:** the lifecycle of the SOAP service class is defined by the `scope` attribute. Valid values for this attribute are "Request" | "Session" | "Application". A request-level scope creates a new SOAP service class or each incoming request. The session-level scope creates a SOAP service class for each user session, and the application-level scope keeps the SOAP service object until the RPC Router servlet is terminated.
- **Provider-Exposed methods:** the methods attribute defines a list of white-space delimited method names to be exposed by the SOAP service. All the methods defined must match method declarations in the implementing class.
- **Provider-Implementing class:** the class attribute of the Java subelement defines the class that implements the SOAP service. All the exposed methods defined previously must be publicly available from within this class. The class can be a simple Java class or a JavaBean.
- **Fault Listener:** the fault listener defined in the deployment descriptor waits for any faults that occur on the server-side, and create a SOAP Fault message containing additional information about the fault or exception. The `DOMFaultListener` is a basic fault handler provided by Apache SOAP, and is suitable for most applications. For more information about the different fault handlers, and how to create custom fault listeners, please refer to the *Apache SOAP User's Guide.*

Listing 14-3: DeploymentDescriptor.xml

```
<isd:service xmlns:isd="http://xml.apache.org/xml-soap/deployment"
 id="urn:hello_web_service">
    <isd:provider type="java"
     scope="Application"
     methods="getGreeting">
```

Continued

Listing 14-3 *(continued)*

```
        <isd:java class="bible.tomcat.hello.CityService"/>
    </isd:provider>
    <isd:faultListener>
        org.apache.soap.server.DOMFaultListener
    </isd:faultListener>
</isd:service>
```

Building and Deploying

SOAP services can be deployed using the Apache SOAP administration client or a client-side service manager application. Both methods use an XML-based deployment descriptor as the primary mechanism to gather information about the SOAP service, explained in the previous Configuration section.

Deploying a SOAP service to the Apache SOAP is not as easy as it is made out in the *Apache SOAP User's Guide*. The default method of deploying the SOAP Web Archive on the Tomcat 4.x server gives rise to particular difficulties with the Tomcat 4 class loader behavior. See the following section, titled "Apache SOAP and Tomcat 4 Class Loaders," for an explanation.

Ant-Based Deployment

Although Apache SOAP provides a Web-based administration tool to deploy SOAP services, in the long run it is easier to automate these SOAP administration tasks within the project's build file.

As you may already have a build file to compile the SOAP service, with a little extra effort it is possible to add SOAP-specific targets, automating the deployment of SOAP services. The build file in Listing 14-4 shows how SOAP targets can be added to a simple Java project's build file.

Caution The following build file in Listing 14-4 is specialized for a standalone Java application, not a Web application. Although it looks very similar to the build files used throughout this book, the Web-specific tasks have been removed, and the destination directory for the compiled classes is `${basedir}/classes`, not `${basedir}/build/WEB-INF/classes`.

The first thing you may notice is the addition of three extra parameters into the File and Directory Names section.

- ✦ **desc.home:** the directory into which deployment descriptors and other configuration files are placed. The SOAP deploy target will look in this directory to find the SOAP deployment descriptor file. The value of the `desc.home` property defaults to `etc`.
- ✦ **soap.url:** the URL of the Apache SOAP RPC Router servlet. The RPC Router is used to remotely deploy SOAP services. The `soap.url` value defaults to `http://localhost:8080/soap/servlet/rpcrouter`.
- ✦ **soap.context:** the location of the Web context the Apache SOAP server is installed under Defaults to `C:\tomcat\webapps\soap`. This property is used to copy classes into the `/soap` context so the Web application classes are available to the SOAP Web application class loader.

Apache SOAP and Tomcat 4 Class Loaders

Tomcat 4 class loaders were introduced in Chapter 3, and the parent-child relationship between class loaders explained. To recap, a Web application class loader attempts to load a class or resource locally **before** delegating the request to a parent class loader. The behavior of Tomcat 4 class loaders is essential to understanding where to place SOAP service classes.

The instructions for installing Apache SOAP server-side under Apache Tomcat are targeted to Version 3.2, and recommend that any of your code that you want to deploy as services be included in the classpath before starting Tomcat. However, the class loader behavior has changed in Tomcat 4, and the contents of the CLASSPATH environment variable are completely ignored by the System class loader.

The question still remains; where do we place the SOAP service so its class files are accessible to the `/soap` Web application? For the `/soap` Web application to have access to the SOAP service, its class files must be included by the local Web application class loader, or one of the parent class loaders. The following class loaders are used by Tomcat 4.x, listed order of execution:

- **Bootstrap:** only the JVM, and system extension classes can reside in the Bootstrap class loader.
- **System:** previously, in Tomcat v3.2, the System class loader would have loaded SOAP services, however the contents of the CLASSPATH are ignored preventing this scenario.
- **Common:** application classes should not be placed in the Common class loader. It is therefore recommended that the SOAP service not reside here.
- **Catalina:** classes and resources in the Catalina class loader are invisible to the Web applications. SOAP service classes definitely cannot be placed here.
- **Shared:** classes in the Shared class loader are accessible by all Web application class loaders. This, however, may not be appropriate, especially in a multi-user environment. If this visibility of the SOAP service to other Web applications is not a problem, place unpacked SOAP service classes in `CATALINA_HOME/shared/classes`, or place a JAR file containing the SOAP service under `CATALINA_HOME/shared/lib`.
- **WebappX:** to include the SOAP service in the local Web application class loader, place unpacked SOAP service classes under `/WEB-INF/classes` of your Web application context, or place JAR files containing the SOAP service under `/WEB-INF/lib`. All SOAP services will therefore reside under the Apache SOAP context.

This therefore leaves us with two options; placing the SOAP service in a folder accessible by the Shared class loader, or placing the SOAP service under the Apache SOAP distribution. Neither solution is particularly elegant, resulting in SOAP service classes residing in an inappropriate context.

However, for the purpose of the Simple SOAP Service Example we will place the SOAP service JAR file under the Apache SOAP context. Don't despair though, a more elegant solution to the class loading problem will be proposed in the Context-Based SOAP Service Example.

If you neglect to make the SOAP service classes available to one of the Tomcat class loaders and simply deploy the Web application using the admin client or the service manager, an error will result while using the SOAP service. The SOAP response to the client will contain a fault, indicating that there was a problem building the SOAP envelope. The fault will contain a `javax.servlet.ServletException` thrown by Tomcat with and an embedded `java.lang.NullPointerException` exception. If you receive such an error, check that the SOAP service class files have been copied to the appropriate class loader directory, and if necessary, restart the Tomcat server.

The External Dependencies and Compilation Classpath section define the additional SOAP libraries that are required by the `CityTestClient` class and the service manager client. Although they are included in the compilation classpath, these classes are not actually used by the SOAP service class.

SOAP depends on the JAXP, Xerces, Java Mail, and Java Activation Framework libraries. For convenience we shall use the versions of these libraries that come bundled with the Tomcat distribution.

Towards the end of the build file in Listing 14-4, three new targets have been defined, all of which use the Apache SOAP service manager client application to deploy, undeploy, and list the Web applications deployed on the SOAP server.

The SOAP targets all contain the soap prefix to avoid a clash with any existing targets in the build file by the same name.

For the purposes of this example only, the SOAP service JAR file is copied by the SOAP deploy task, to the classpath within the `/soap` context. The SOAP undeploy target removes the JAR file when removing the Web application from the SOAP server. For an explanation about why this is done, see the Apache SOAP and Tomcat 4 Class Loaders section earlier in the chapter.

The Tomcat server must be restarted after deploying the SOAP service so that the Apache SOAP server context can load the new SOAP service JAR file.

Finally the Test Targets at the end of Listing 14-4 define the suite of tests to run against the SOAP server. The suite only includes a single `CityTestClient` test case. The test case is run with test data provided as arguments to the Java interpreter.

Listing 14-4: **build.xml**

```
<project name="Hello World SOAP service" default="compile" basedir=".">


<!-- ==================== Property Definitions ====================== -->

  <property file="build.properties"/>
  <property file="${user.home}/build.properties"/>


<!-- =================== File and Directory Names =================== -->

  <property name="app.name"       value="hello_web_service"/>
  <property name="app.version"    value="0.1-dev"/>
  <property name="build.home"     value="${basedir}/classes"/>
  <property name="dist.home"      value="${basedir}/dist"/>
  <property name="docs.home"      value="${basedir}/docs"/>
```

```
  <property name="src.home"      value="${basedir}/src"/>
  <property name="desc.home"     value="${basedir}/etc"/>
  <property name="soap.url"
          value="http://localhost:8080/soap/servlet/rpcrouter"/>
  <property name="soap.context" value="C:/tomcat/webapps/soap"/>


<!--  ==================== Compilation Control Options ================ -->

  <property name="compile.debug"       value="true"/>
  <property name="compile.deprecation" value="false"/>
  <property name="compile.optimize"    value="true"/>


<!-- ==================== External Dependencies ======================= -->

  <property name="soap.jar"
      value="C:/soap-2_3_1/lib/soap.jar"/>

  <property name="jaxp.jar"
      value="C:/tomcat/common/endorsed/xmlParserAPIs.jar"/>

  <property name="xerces.jar"
      value="C:/tomcat/common/endorsed/xercesImpl.jar"/>

  <property name="mail.jar"
      value="C:/tomcat/common/lib/mail.jar"/>

  <property name="jaf.jar"
      value="C:/tomcat/common/lib/activation.jar"/>

<!-- ==================== Compilation Classpath ======================= -->

  <path id="compile.classpath">

    <!-- Include the classes that have been compiled -->
    <pathelement location="${build.home}"/>

    <!-- Include all JAR files that will be included -->
    <pathelement location="${soap.jar}"/>
    <pathelement location="${jaxp.jar}"/>
    <pathelement location="${xerces.jar}"/>
    <pathelement location="${mail.jar}"/>
    <pathelement location="${jaf.jar}"/>

  </path>


<!-- ==================== All Target ================================== -->

  <target name="all" depends="clean,compile"
```

Continued

Listing 14-4 (continued)

```
   description="Clean build and dist directories, then compile"/>


<!-- ==================== Clean Target ================================== -->

  <target name="clean"
   description="Delete old build directory">
    <delete dir="${build.home}"/>
  </target>

<!-- ==================== Compile Target ================================ -->

  <target name="compile" depends="prepare"
   description="Compile Java sources">

    <!-- Compile Java classes as necessary -->
    <mkdir    dir="${build.home}"/>
        <javac srcdir="${src.home}"
               excludes="**/*Servlet.java"
          destdir="${build.home}"
            debug="${compile.debug}"
      deprecation="${compile.deprecation}"
         optimize="${compile.optimize}">
        <classpath refid="compile.classpath"/>
    </javac>

    <!-- Copy application resources -->
    <copy  todir="${build.home}">
      <fileset dir="${src.home}" excludes="**/*.java"/>
    </copy>

  </target>


<!-- ==================== Dist Target =================================== -->

  <target name="dist" depends="compile,javadoc"
   description="Create binary distribution">

    <!-- Copy documentation subdirectories -->
    <mkdir   dir="${dist.home}/docs"/>
    <copy    todir="${dist.home}/docs">
      <fileset dir="${docs.home}"/>
    </copy>

    <!-- Create application JAR file -->
    <jar jarfile="${dist.home}/${app.name}-${app.version}.war"
         basedir="${build.home}"/>

    <!-- Copy additional files to ${dist.home} as necessary -->
```

```
  </target>


<!-- ==================== Javadoc Target ================================ -->

  <target name="javadoc" depends="compile"
   description="Create Javadoc API documentation">

    <mkdir          dir="${docs.home}/api"/>
    <javadoc sourcepath="${src.home}"
                    destdir="${docs.home}/api"
           packagenames="*">
      <classpath refid="compile.classpath"/>
    </javadoc>

  </target>

<!-- ==================== Prepare Target ================================ -->

  <target name="prepare">

    <!-- Create build directories as needed -->
    <mkdir  dir="${build.home}"/>

  </target>


<!-- ==================== Soap Deploy Target ============================ -->

  <target name="soapdeploy" depends="compile"
   description="Deploy a SOAP service to the Apache SOAP server">

    <java classname="org.apache.soap.server.ServiceManagerClient"
     classpathref="compile.classpath" fork="yes" >
       <arg value="${soap.url}"/>
       <arg value="deploy"/>
       <arg  path="${desc.home}/DeploymentDescriptor.xml"/>
    </java>

    <!-- Copy SOAP service JAR to soap context -->
    <mkdir  dir="${soap.context}/WEB-INF/lib"/>
    <copy  file="${dist.home}/${app.name}-${app.version}.war"
          toDir="${soap.context}/WEB-INF/lib"/>

  </target>


<!-- ==================== Soap Undeploy Target ========================== -->

  <target name="soapundeploy"
   description="Undeploy a SOAP service from the Apache SOAP server">
```

Continued

Listing 14-4 (continued)

```
    <java classname="org.apache.soap.server.ServiceManagerClient"
     classpathref="compile.classpath" fork="yes" >
        <arg value="${soap.url}"/>
        <arg value="undeploy"/>
        <arg value="urn:${app.name}"/>
    </java>

    <!-- Remove SOAP service JAR from soap context -->
    <delete
     file="${soap.context}/WEB-INF/lib/${app.name}-${app.version}.jar"/>
  </target>


<!-- ===================== SOAP List Target ========================= -->

  <target name="soaplist"
   description="List installed applications on the Apache SOAP server">

    <java classname="org.apache.soap.server.ServiceManagerClient"
         classpathref="compile.classpath" fork="yes" >
            <arg value="${soap.url}"/>
            <arg value="list"/>
    </java>

  </target>


<!-- ===================== Test Targets ============================= -->

  <target name="test">

      <antcall target="soaptest"/>

  </target>


  <target name="soaptest" depends="compile">

      <java classname="bible.tomcat.hello.CityTestClient"
       classpathref="compile.classpath" fork="yes" >
          <arg value="MEL"/>
          <arg value="Warner"/>
          <arg value="${soap.url}"/>
      </java>

  </target>

</project>
```

Administration Client Deployment

It is also possible to deploy the SOAP service using the Apache SOAP administration client, available at `http://localhost:8080/soap/servlet/rpcrouter`. Clicking the Deploy link displays a Deployment Descriptor Template like the one shown in Figure 14-3.

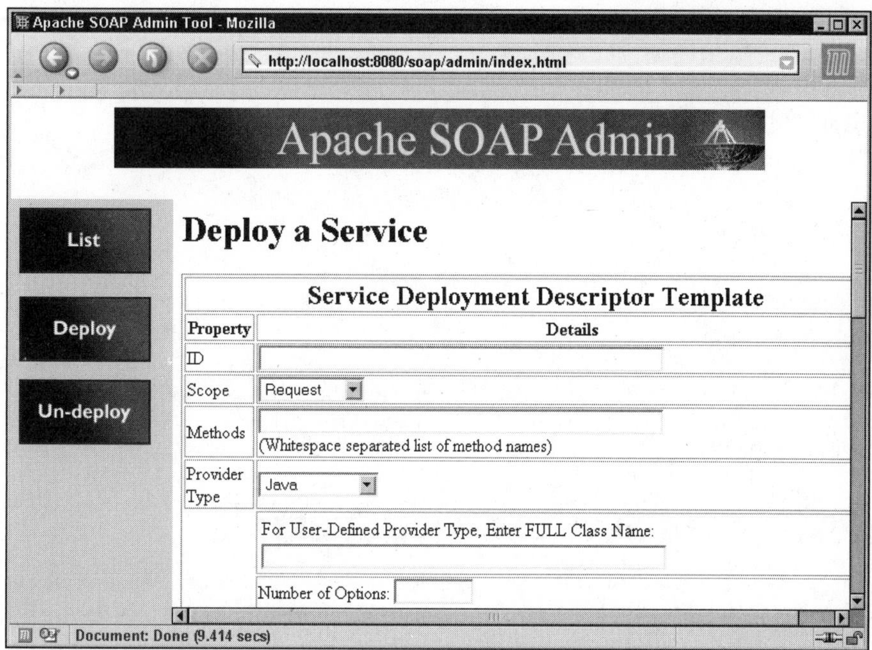

Figure 14-3: Deployment descriptor template in the Apache SOAP admin client

This template structure resembles the deployment descriptor shown previously. After entering all the relevant information and submitting the form the SOAP service is deployed.

If deploying a SOAP service using the admin client, you must manually copy the SOAP service class files under the `/WEB-INF/classes` of the `/soap` context, or place JAR files containing the SOAP service under `/WEB-INF/lib`. After the files have been copied, the Tomcat server must be restarted for the Apache SOAP server to recognize the new class files.

Testing

After deploying the application, testing is easy with the use of the test target included at the end of the build file in Listing 14-4. The `soaptest` target runs the `CityTestClient` class for the city of Melbourne, with the name Warner (that's me!).

It is essential the SOAP service has been deployed to the Apache SOAP server using the `soapdeploy` target, and the Tomcat server restarted for the test to run successfully.

Of course, you could run the CityTestClient class using the command line Java interpreter, however it would be necessary to include all the relevant SOAP classes in the classpath. The complexities of the classpath are taken care of in the build file.

From within the Hello Client SOAP service development directory (in other words, `C:\work\hello_web_service\`) run the `test` target in the build file by issuing the following command:

```
C:\work\hello_web_service\> ant test
```

This invokes the suite of tests, including the `CityTestClient` test class. The output of the test should look similar to the following.

```
Buildfile: build.xml
test:
prepare:
compile:
soaptest:
     [java] G'day Warner
BUILD SUCCESSFUL
Total time: 7 seconds
```

You have now overcome all the hype and successfully implemented a SOAP service. The following section shows the next step: integrating the Hello City SOAP service with the Web application developed in Chapter 7.

Context-Based SOAP Service Example

Using the SOAP server deployed using a Web Archive is useful for very simple applications. Unfortunately this requires SOAP service class files to be manually copied to a class directory within the SOAP server, a rather ugly way to deploy SOAP services.

This method also has severe limitations if the implementing class of the SOAP service actually resides in a separate Web application. In this case the SOAP server residing it its own `/soap` context cannot load classes contained in a separate Web application without duplication of business logic.

Although not a trivial example, the aforementioned scenario is common for existing Web projects adopting SOAP services. This example solves this problem and proposes a better way to integrate SOAP with Web applications.

A more elegant way to deploy SOAP services takes advantage of the Web application structure provided by Tomcat, by including the SOAP library into an existing Web application. This method may result in multiple SOAP servers running on a single instance of Tomcat. However, the benefits of encapsulating the SOAP service and the SOAP server in a single Web application far outweigh the cost of running multiple SOAP servers.

This example shows how the Apache SOAP server can be integrated inside a Web application. For demonstration purposes we will modify the Hello City Web application to make use of the SOAP service created in the previous example.

SOAP Service

This example is based upon the SOAP service created in the Simple SOAP Service Example section. The SOAP service implementing class requires no modification; just import the `CityService.java` file into the `/src` directory of your Web project using appropriate package directories.

SOAP Client

The client to the SOAP service will be the main controlling servlet of the Hello City Web application. Listing 14-5 shows a modified servlet with the business logic removed, and in its place a Remote Procedure Call to the `getGreeting()` method in the Hello City SOAP service.

Like the command-line client used in the previous example, the servlet uses the client-side Apache SOAP API to make the RPC and interpret the SOAP response. Notice that the servlet uses servlet context initialization parameters for the URL of the SOAP server, and the URN and method name of the SOAP service. The values of these parameters are specified in the `web.xml` file defined in the section titled "Configuration."

Listing 14-5: Changing CityServlet.java to utilize a SOAP service

```
package bible.tomcat.hello;

import java.io.*;
import java.net.*;
import java.lang.*;
import java.util.*;

import javax.servlet.http.*;
import javax.servlet.*;

import org.apache.soap.*;
import org.apache.soap.rpc.*;

/*
 * This is the main controlling servlet for the Hello City
 * application.
 *
 * This HttpServlet controls the simple interactions between
 * a form (created by CityForm.jsp) and the results page
 * (created by CityResult.jsp) using the CityService SOAP service
 */
public class CityServlet
extends HttpServlet
{
    public final String FORM_PAGE   = "/CityForm.jsp";
    public final String RESULT_PAGE = "/CityResult.jsp";

    /*
     * These are identifiers used by the FORM_PAGE for the
```

Continued

Listing 14-5 *(continued)*

```
 * form processing.
 */
public final String NAME_FIELD      = "NAME";
public final String CITY_FIELD      = "CITY";

public URL url;
public String uri;
public String methodName;

public void init(ServletConfig sc)
throws ServletException
{
    /*
     * On initialisation, load the static lookup information
     * into the ServletContext for use by the Web application
     * from the Web application files.
     */

    ServletContext ctx = sc.getServletContext();
    Enumeration en = ctx.getInitParameterNames();

    while (en.hasMoreElements())
    {
        String p = (String)en.nextElement();

        if (p.equals("soap.url"))
        {
            try
            {
                url = new URL(ctx.getInitParameter(p));
                ctx.setAttribute("url", url);
            }
            catch (MalformedURLException e)
            {
                throw new ServletException(e.getMessage());
            }
        }

        if (p.equals("soap.uri"))
        {
            uri = ctx.getInitParameter(p);
            ctx.setAttribute("uri", uri);
        }

        if (p.equals("soap.methodName"))
        {
            methodName = ctx.getInitParameter(p);
            ctx.setAttribute("methodName", methodName);
        }
    }
}
```

```
/*
 * Invoke doPost() from doGet(), if ever called.
 */
public void doGet(HttpServletRequest req, HttpServletResponse res)
throws ServletException, IOException
{
    doPost(req, res);
}

/*
 * doPost() provides the body of the servlet controller,
 * and invokes the business logic
 *
 * doPost() is also responsible for determining what page
 * should be displayed.  If the servlet is invoked with no
 * parameters, it is assumed that the request is for the
 * display of the form page.
 */
public void doPost(HttpServletRequest req,
        HttpServletResponse res)
throws ServletException, IOException
{
    String incPath = FORM_PAGE;
    String error = "";

    /*
     * Has the servlet been invoked from the FORM_PAGE ?
     */
    String action = req.getParameter("action");
    if (action != null)  // yes !
    {
        boolean gotError = false;
        incPath = RESULT_PAGE;

        /*
         * Grab the fields (name and city) from the HTTP request
         */
        String name = req.getParameter(NAME_FIELD);
        String city = req.getParameter(CITY_FIELD);

        /*
         * Now calculate the results
         */
        if ((name == null) || (name.length() < 1))
        {
            error = "Please enter a name!";
            gotError = true;
            name = null;
        }

        if ((city == null) || (city.length() < 1))
```

Continued

Listing 14-5 *(continued)*

```
{
    if (gotError)
    {
        error += " and ";
    }
    error += "Please choose a city";
    gotError = true;
}

if (gotError)
{
    incPath = FORM_PAGE;
    req.setAttribute("errorMessage", error);
    performRedirect(incPath, req, res);
    return;
}

// we've got real values, so we'll use them in the JSP
req.setAttribute("theCity", city);
req.setAttribute("theName", name);

/*
 * Build a Remote Procedure Call (RPC).
 */
Call call = new Call();
call.setTargetObjectURI(uri);
call.setMethodName(methodName);
call.setEncodingStyleURI(Constants.NS_URI_SOAP_ENC);

/*
 * Declare RPC parameters.
 */
Vector params = new Vector();
params.addElement(
        new Parameter("city", String.class, city, null));
call.setParams(params);


try
{
    /*
     * Invoke the RPC.
     */
    Response resp = call.invoke(url, "");

    /*
     * Interpret the SOAP response, or any faults that may
     * have occurred.
     */
```

```
                if (resp.generatedFault())
                {
                    Fault fault = resp.getFault();
                    req.setAttribute("errorMessage", fault.toString());
                }
                else
                {
                    Parameter result = resp.getReturnValue();
                    String greeting = (String)result.getValue();
                    req.setAttribute("theGreeting", greeting);
                }
            }
            catch (SOAPException e)
            {
                req.setAttribute("errorMessage", e.getMessage());
            }
        }
        else
        {
        }

        /*
         * Now, we've done our calculations, got some results, or
         * some sort of error, so, let the user know what's been
         * going on !
         */
        performRedirect(incPath, req, res);
    }

    private void performRedirect(String incPath,
            HttpServletRequest req,
            HttpServletResponse res)
    throws ServletException, IOException
    {
        String servletName;
        if (incPath != null)
        {
            servletName = req.getServletPath();
            req.setAttribute("servletPath",
                    req.getContextPath()+servletName);
            req.setAttribute("nameField", NAME_FIELD);
            req.setAttribute("cityField", CITY_FIELD);

            /*
             * Now, forward the results to the appropriate JSP page
             */
            RequestDispatcher rd = req.getRequestDispatcher(incPath);
            rd.forward(req, res);
        }
    }
}
```

Configuration

The Web application configuration is where the integration of the Apache SOAP server happens. Here the RPC Router, the servlet that routes incoming SOAP requests to SOAP services, is defined. This is essentially the server-side component of Apache SOAP.

In Listing 14-6 contains the default Hello City Web application configuration, modified to include necessary servlet initialization parameters, along with the Apache-SOAP RPC Router servlet declaration and URL mapping.

The `context-param` element defines three servlet context initialization parameters; these parameters are used within the `ClientServlet` class at runtime. The individual parameters follow:

- `soap.url`: specifies the endpoint of the SOAP RPC Router servlet.
- `soap.urn`: specifies the unique name of target SOAP service to connect to.
- `soap.methodName`: defines the remote method provided by the SOAP service which to invoke.

The `servlet` and `servlet-mapping` elements define the `org.apache.soap.server.http.RPCRouterServlet` class and maps it to the `/servlet/rpcrouter` URL underneath the Web application context. The `RPCRouterServlet` class is included in the Apache SOAP client-side JAR file, and is made available to the Web application during the deployment process.

Listing 14-6: **Updated web.xml**

```
<?xml version="1.0" encoding="ISO-8859-1" ?>

<!DOCTYPE web-app
  PUBLIC "-//Sun Microsystems, Inc.//DTD Web Application 2.3//EN"
  "http://java.sun.com/dtd/web-app_2_3.dtd" >

<web-app>
    <icon>
    </icon>
    <display-name>Hello World Application</display-name>
    <description>
        This is the simple Hello World! application
    </description>

    <context-param>
        <param-name>soap.url</param-name>
        <param-value>
            http://localhost:8080/hello_web_service/servlet/rpcrouter
        </param-value>
        <description></description>
    </context-param>
    <context-param>
        <param-name>soap.uri</param-name>
        <param-value>urn:hello_web_service</param-value>
        <description></description>
    </context-param>
```

```
    <context-param>
        <param-name>soap.methodName</param-name>
        <param-value>getGreeting</param-value>
        <description></description>
    </context-param>

    <servlet>
        <servlet-name>rpcrouter</servlet-name>
        <display-name>Apache-SOAP RPC Router</display-name>
        <description>no description</description>
        <servlet-class>
            org.apache.soap.server.http.RPCRouterServlet
        </servlet-class>
        <init-param>
            <param-name>faultListener</param-name>
            <param-value>
                org.apache.soap.server.DOMFaultListener
            </param-value>
        </init-param>
    </servlet>

    <servlet>
        <servlet-name>city</servlet-name>
        <description>
            The Hello City! Servlet
        </description>
        <servlet-class>
            bible.tomcat.hello.CityServlet
        </servlet-class>
    </servlet>

    <servlet-mapping>
        <servlet-name>rpcrouter</servlet-name>
        <url-pattern>/servlet/rpcrouter</url-pattern>
    </servlet-mapping>

    <servlet-mapping>
        <servlet-name>city</servlet-name>
        <url-pattern>/city</url-pattern>
    </servlet-mapping>

    <welcome-file-list>
        <welcome-file>index.jsp</welcome-file>
    </welcome-file-list>

    <error-page>
        <error-code>404</error-code>
        <location>/city</location>
    </error-page>

</web-app>
```

As the SOAP service has not changed, neither has the deployment descriptor. The same `DeploymentDescriptor.xml` file used in the Simple SOAP service can be included in the Web project under the `/etc` directory.

The Ant script in the next section looks in the `/etc` directory for the deployment descriptor when deploying the SOAP service.

Building and Deploying

Deployment of the SOAP service follows the same process as defined in the Ant-Based Deployment section under the Simple SOAP Service Example. This process involves defining a deployment descriptor, and deploying the SOAP service class files to the Apache SOAP server using an Ant build script.

Because the deployment of the Web application (acting as a SOAP client) requires a build file, this section focuses on the addition of SOAP deploy targets to the build file, and does not cover the Apache SOAP admin client. In describing the build file we focus on the differences between the default Hello City build file in Chapter 7 and that shown in Listing 14-7.

The first thing you may notice in Listing 14-7 is the addition of the extra `desc.home` parameter into the File and Directory Names section, which defines the directory into which deployment descriptors and other configuration files are placed.

Caution The `soap.url` property must be defined outside the build file. Add a property to your project's build.properties file with the location of the Apache SOAP RPC router after the project has been deployed. The property definition should look like:

```
soap.url=\
  http://localhost:8080/context/servlet/rpcrouter
```

Note The SOAP service is loaded with the same class loader as the SOAP server so the `soap.context` property is no longer required.

The External Dependencies and Compilation Classpath elements in Listing 14-7 define the additional SOAP library that is required by the `CityServlet` class and the service manager client. Although they are included in the compilation classpath, these classes are not actually used by the SOAP service class.

Tip Because the JAXP, Xerces, Java Mail, and Java Activation Framework libraries are loaded by the Tomcat Common class loader, it is not necessary to explicitly include them in the External Dependencies section.

The SOAP client-side JAR file contains not only the client side API, but also the RPC Router servlet. By including the SOAP client-side JAR file in the WAR file, the Web application can run its own SOAP server, and at the same time allow servlet classes to act as SOAP clients. The prepare target copies all the external SOAP dependency, to the `${build.home}/WEB-INF/lib` directory, where it will be included in the resulting context or WAR file.

Note Unless the administration JSP pages contained in `C:\soap-2_3_1\webapps\soap\admin` are explicitly included in the `${web.home}` directory of your Web application, the administration console will not be available.

At the end of the build file, three new targets have been defined, all of which use the Apache SOAP service manager client application to deploy, undeploy, and list the Web applications deployed on the SOAP server. The `soapdeploy` target relies on the SOAP deployment descriptor to be available from `${desc.home}/DeploymentDescriptor.xml`.

The SOAP targets all contain the "soap" prefix to avoid a clash with any existing targets in the build file by the same name.

The Tomcat server must be restarted after deploying the SOAP service so that the Apache SOAP server context can load the new SOAP service JAR file.

Listing 14-7 contains the complete Web application and SOAP service build file for the Hello City application.

Listing 14-7: build.xml

```
<project name="Hello World SOAP service" default="compile" basedir=".">


<!-- ==================== Property Definitions ====================== -->

  <property file="build.properties"/>
  <property file="${user.home}/build.properties"/>


<!-- ================== File and Directory Names ==================== -->

  <property name="app.name"      value="hello_web_service"/>
  <property name="app.path"      value="/${app.name}"/>
  <property name="app.version"   value="0.1-dev"/>
  <property name="build.home"    value="${basedir}/build"/>
  <property name="dist.home"     value="${basedir}/dist"/>
  <property name="docs.home"     value="${basedir}/docs"/>
  <property name="src.home"      value="${basedir}/src"/>
  <property name="web.home"      value="${basedir}/web"/>
  <property name="desc.home"     value="${basedir}/etc"/>


<!-- ================= Custom Ant Task Definitions ================== -->

  <taskdef name="install" classname="org.apache.catalina.ant.InstallTask"/>
  <taskdef name="list"    classname="org.apache.catalina.ant.ListTask"/>
  <taskdef name="reload"  classname="org.apache.catalina.ant.ReloadTask"/>
  <taskdef name="remove"  classname="org.apache.catalina.ant.RemoveTask"/>

  <taskdef name="deploy"    classname="org.apache.catalina.ant.DeployTask"/>
  <taskdef name="undeploy"  classname="org.apache.catalina.ant.UndeployTask"/>
```

Continued

Listing 14-7 *(continued)*

```
  <target name="deploy" description="Deploy web application">
      <deploy
          url="${manager.url}"
          username="${manager.username}"
          password="${manager.password}"
          path="${app.path}"
          war="file:///${dist.home}/${app.name}-${app.version}.war"/>
  </target>

  <target name="undeploy" description="Undeploy web application">
      <undeploy
          url="${manager.url}"
          username="${manager.username}"
          password="${manager.password}"
          path="${app.path}"/>
  </target>

<!--  ==================== Compilation Control Options ================ -->

  <property name="compile.debug"       value="true"/>
  <property name="compile.deprecation" value="false"/>
  <property name="compile.optimize"    value="true"/>


<!-- ==================== External Dependencies ====================== -->

<!-- External dependency -->
  <property name="soap.jar"
      value="C:/soap-2_3_1/lib/soap.jar"/>


<!-- ==================== Compilation Classpath ====================== -->

  <path id="compile.classpath">

    <!-- Include all JAR files that will be included in /WEB-INF/lib -->
    <pathelement location="${soap.jar}"/>

    <!-- Include all elements that Tomcat exposes to applications -->
    <pathelement location="${catalina.home}/common/classes"/>
    <fileset dir="${catalina.home}/common/endorsed">
      <include name="*.jar"/>
    </fileset>
    <fileset dir="${catalina.home}/common/lib">
      <include name="*.jar"/>
    </fileset>
    <pathelement location="${catalina.home}/shared/classes"/>
    <fileset dir="${catalina.home}/shared/lib">
      <include name="*.jar"/>
    </fileset>
```

```
  </path>


<!-- ==================== All Target ================================== -->

  <target name="all" depends="clean,compile"
   description="Clean build and dist directories, then compile"/>


<!-- ==================== Clean Target ================================ -->

  <target name="clean"
   description="Delete old build and dist directories">
    <delete dir="${build.home}"/>
    <delete dir="${dist.home}"/>
    <delete dir="${basedir}/gensrc"/>
  </target>


<!-- ==================== Compile Target ============================== -->

  <target name="compile" depends="prepare"
   description="Compile Java sources">

    <!-- Compile Java classes as necessary -->
    <mkdir    dir="${build.home}/WEB-INF/classes"/>
    <javac srcdir="${src.home}"
          destdir="${build.home}/WEB-INF/classes"
            debug="${compile.debug}"
      deprecation="${compile.deprecation}"
         optimize="${compile.optimize}">
        <classpath refid="compile.classpath"/>
    </javac>

    <!-- Copy application resources -->
    <copy  todir="${build.home}/WEB-INF/classes">
      <fileset dir="${src.home}" excludes="**/*.java"/>
    </copy>

  </target>

  <target name="webinc" >
      <mkdir dir="${basedir}/gensrc" />
          <exec
              executable="${catalina.home}/bin/${catalina.jspc}"
              failonerror="true"
              vmlauncher="true"
              dir="${basedir}" >
              <arg line="-d gensrc -webapp web -webinc web.inc" />
          </exec>
  </target>
```

Continued

Listing 14-7 (continued)

```
  <!-- ==== jspc target ==== -->
  <target name="jspc" depends="webinc, compile, prepare"
      description="Invoke Jasper JSP compiler" >
      <mkdir dir="${basedir}/gensrc" />

      <javac
          srcdir="${basedir}/gensrc"
          destdir="${build.home}/WEB-INF/classes" >
          <classpath refid="compile.classpath" />
      </javac>

      <!-- remove any *.jsp files in the build directory -->
      <delete>
          <fileset dir="${build.home}" includes="**/*.jsp" />
      </delete>
  </target>


<!-- ==================== Dist Target ================================= -->

  <target name="dist" depends="compile,javadoc"
   description="Create binary distribution">

    <!-- Copy documentation subdirectories -->
    <mkdir   dir="${dist.home}/docs"/>
    <copy    todir="${dist.home}/docs">
      <fileset dir="${docs.home}"/>
    </copy>

    <!-- Create application JAR file -->
    <jar jarfile="${dist.home}/${app.name}-${app.version}.war"
         basedir="${build.home}"/>

    <!-- Copy additional files to ${dist.home} as necessary -->

  </target>

  <target name="jar" >

    <mkdir   dir="${dist.home}/docs"/>
    <copy    todir="${dist.home}/docs">
      <fileset dir="${docs.home}"/>
    </copy>

    <jar jarfile="${dist.home}/${app.name}-${app.version}.war"
         basedir="${build.home}"/>

  </target>
```

```
<!-- =================== Install Target ============================== -->

  <target name="install" depends="compile"
   description="Install application to servlet container">

    <install url="${manager.url}"
        username="${manager.username}"
        password="${manager.password}"
            path="${app.path}"
             war="file://${build.home}"/>

  </target>


  <target name="context" depends="compile"
      description="Install to container using context.xml">

      <install url="${manager.url}"
          username="${manager.username}"
          password="${manager.password}"
          path="${app.path}"
          config="file:///${build.home}/WEB-INF/context.xml"/>
  </target>


<!-- =================== Javadoc Target ============================== -->

  <target name="javadoc" depends="compile"
   description="Create Javadoc API documentation">

    <mkdir          dir="${dist.home}/docs/api"/>
    <javadoc sourcepath="${src.home}"
               destdir="${dist.home}/docs/api"
          packagenames="*">
      <classpath refid="compile.classpath"/>
    </javadoc>

  </target>


<!-- ===================== List Target =============================== -->

  <target name="list"
   description="List installed applications on servlet container">

    <list    url="${manager.url}"
        username="${manager.username}"
        password="${manager.password}"/>

  </target>
```

Continued

Listing 14-7 *(continued)*

```
<!-- =================== Prepare Target ============================== -->

  <target name="prepare">

    <!-- Create build directories as needed -->
    <mkdir  dir="${build.home}"/>
    <mkdir  dir="${build.home}/WEB-INF"/>
    <mkdir  dir="${build.home}/WEB-INF/classes"/>


    <!-- Copy static content of this Web application -->
    <copy todir="${build.home}">
      <fileset dir="${web.home}"/>
    </copy>

    <!-- Create a context file if required -->
    <filter token="context.docbase" value="${build.home}" />
    <filter token="context.path" value="${app.path}" />
    <filter token="context.appname" value="${app.name}" />
    <copy todir="${build.home}/WEB-INF" filtering="true" >
        <fileset dir="${basedir}">
            <present present="srconly" targetdir="${basedir}">
                <mapper type="glob" from="template.*" to="*" />
            </present>
        </fileset>
        <mapper type="glob" from="template.*" to="*" />
    </copy>

    <!-- Copy external dependencies as required -->
    <mkdir  dir="${build.home}/WEB-INF/lib"/>
    <copy todir="${build.home}/WEB-INF/lib" file="${soap.jar}"/>

    <!-- Copy static files from external dependencies as needed -->
    <!-- *** CUSTOMIZE HERE AS REQUIRED BY YOUR APPLICATION *** -->

  </target>


<!-- =================== Reload Target ============================== -->

  <target name="reload" depends="compile"
   description="Reload application on servlet container">

    <reload url="${manager.url}"
       username="${manager.username}"
       password="${manager.password}"
           path="${app.path}"/>

  </target>
```

```
<!-- ==================== Remove Target ================================ -->

  <target name="remove"
   description="Remove application on servlet container">

    <remove url="${manager.url}"
       username="${manager.username}"
       password="${manager.password}"
           path="${app.path}"/>

   </target>


<!-- ==================== Soap Deploy Target ========================== -->

  <target name="soapdeploy" depends="compile"
   description="Deploy a SOAP service to the Apache SOAP server">

        <java classname="org.apache.soap.server.ServiceManagerClient"
         classpathref="compile.classpath" fork="yes" >
            <arg value="${soap.url}"/>
            <arg value="deploy"/>
            <arg  path="${desc.home}/DeploymentDescriptor.xml"/>
        </java>

  </target>


<!-- ==================== Soap Undeploy Target ======================== -->

  <target name="soapundeploy"
   description="Undeploy a SOAP service from the Apache SOAP server">

    <java classname="org.apache.soap.server.ServiceManagerClient"
     classpathref="compile.classpath" fork="yes" >
        <arg value="${soap.url}"/>
        <arg value="undeploy"/>
        <arg value="urn:${app.name}"/>
    </java>

  </target>


<!-- ====================== SOAP List Target ========================== -->

  <target name="soaplist"
   description="List installed applications on the Apache SOAP server">

    <java classname="org.apache.soap.server.ServiceManagerClient"
      classpathref="compile.classpath" fork="yes" >
        <arg value="${soap.url}"/>
        <arg value="list"/>
```

Continued

Listing 14-7 *(continued)*

```
    </java>
  </target>
</project>
```

Before testing the new Hello City Web application (with an embedded SOAP service) the Web application must be deployed in the usual fashion using the `install`, `context`, or `deploy` Ant targets. Afterward, the SOAP service must be deployed using the `soapdeploy` target. Restart the server after deploying for the SOAP service classes to be recognized by the SOAP server.

Testing

After deploying the Web application, it is necessary to test the embedded SOAP server. Open the URL `http://localhost:8080/hello/servlet/rpcrouter` in your favorite Web browser. Just like the test in the section titled "Deploying the SOAP Web Archive", earlier in the chapter, the screen shown in 14-1 should be displayed.

To test the new Hello City Web application open the URL `http://localhost:8080/hello/`. The resulting functionality should resemble the original Hello City Web application.

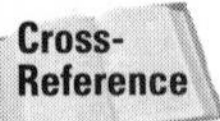

See the "Testing Hello City!" section in Chapter 7.

The Hello City Web application has now been modified to make use of a SOAP service. You can see how business logic can be extracted from the servlet and provided by a remote service. This service also has the added advantage of being available to many clients. We explore the use of different SOAP clients in the next section.

Tomcat Cinemas SOAP Service Example

The Tomcat Cinemas Web application developed in Chapter 10 is a good example of a typical Web-based business application. However, not all interactions with a business system are suited to the Web. Sometimes other clients, or even other systems, need to use the functionality provided by the business system.

In the case of Tomcat Cinemas, it may be decided that a Web-based front desk application is not suitable, and a client-side application is required to operate the till in addition to creating customer bookings. As a result, a thick-client application needs to be developed. A natural choice for developing such an application would be C++, due to its ability to interact at a low-level with hardware such as a till drawer.

Introducing another client into a distributed system poses an interesting question. How do we leverage our existing business logic? As discussed in the introduction to this chapter, technologies such as EJB and RMI are not appropriate because of the lack of a Java-based client, and using direct database access using ODBC means a large portion of the business logic needs to be replicated. The most appropriate method of making the Tomcat Cinemas application available over a heterogeneous network is to expose the required functionality as a SOAP service.

The use of SOAP also opens up other possibilities, one of which is the use of wireless devices to connect to the Tomcat Cinemas SOAP service. Along with the host of client-side SOAP APIs available, there are lightweight SOAP APIs that are targeted to wireless devices such as mobile handsets.

One of which is kSOAP, a lightweight SOAP API designed to run on the J2ME platform. As many mobile devices are J2ME enabled, this is a perfect opportunity to expose selected components of the Tomcat Cinemas application, and make them available over a wireless network.

The remainder of this chapter focuses on developing a J2ME application (MIDlet) that uses the kSOAP API to communicate with a Tomcat Cinemas SOAP service. For the purposes of this demonstration, only a small portion of the Tomcat Cinemas functionality is exposed via a SOAP service to a kSOAP client. The functionality includes the ability to view a list of movies showing on the current day. The ability to book tickets to the showing is deemed out-of-scope.

Prerequisites

As many readers do not have access to a J2ME enabled mobile device, it is necessary to download the J2ME Wireless Toolkit to try out the following examples. Even if you are lucky enough to have a J2ME device in your possession, the Wireless Toolkit is essential to build and package J2ME MIDlets before they can be deployed to a device.

Another prerequisite to J2ME SOAP development is the kSOAP library. In this section you download the kSOAP library and run interoperability tests between the kSOAP client and the Apache SOAP server.

J2ME Wireless Toolkit

The J2ME wireless toolkit contains a reference implementation of the Mobile Information Device Profile (MIDP), combined with the Connected Limited Device Configuration (CLDC). The toolkit also provides a developer with a lightweight IDE for building and packaging MIDlets, and an emulation environment to test J2ME applications.

The J2ME Wireless Toolkit to develops and tests a Tomcat Cinemas J2ME SOAP client.

Download

The J2ME Wireless Toolkit is available from `http://java.sun.com/j2me/`. Click the J2ME downloads tab and select the link for the J2ME Wireless Toolkit 1.0.4.

On the J2ME Wireless Toolkit page scroll down to the Downloads section and select J2ME Wireless Toolkit 1.0.4_01 for Windows. Click the Continue button on the next page; a Binary Code License Agreement is displayed. Read the License Agreement and press Accept to continue to the Download page. Chose to download the toolkit via HTTP or FTP by clicking the respective button, and when prompted save `j2me_wireless_toolkit-1_0_4_01-bin-win.exe` to disk.

Installation

Run the installer by double clicking the downloaded file `j2me_wireless_toolkit-1_0_4_01-bin-win.exe`. The installer extracts the necessary files to start the installation process. When this is completed a welcome screen is shown; click Next to continue the installation.

The Binary Code License Agreement is then displayed. Once you have read the agreement, click Yes to proceed.

The installer then detects the location of the JDK. If the instructions in Chapter 2 were followed correctly the Java Virtual Machine Location is set to `C:\jdk1.3.1`. If this is correct, press Next, otherwise click Browse to find the location of the JDK you wish to use to run the J2ME Wireless Toolkit.

The next step is to choose a destination folder. The J2ME Wireless toolkit will be installed under the folder `C:\WTK104` as shown in Figure 14-4. Leave the destination folder as is, and press Next to proceed.

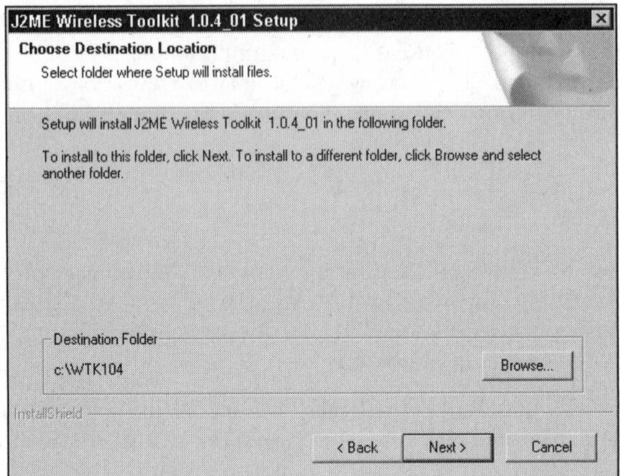

Figure 14-4: Choosing a destination folder for the J2ME Wireless Toolkit installation

The installer then prompts for a program folder location in which to place the Wireless Toolkit in the Start menu. The default location should be adequate; press Next to continue.

A confirmation screen is displayed. Check the installation details, and click Next to proceed with the installation.

Once the installation is complete, click the Finish button to exit the installer. The J2ME Wireless Toolkit can now be used to develop application for wireless devices.

Configuration

The Wireless Toolkit can be configured using the preferences console. To open the Wireless Toolkit preferences select `J2ME Wireless Toolkit 1.0.4_01>Preferences` from the Start menu. The preferences console should look similar to Figure 14-5.

The default preferences are sufficient to run the examples in this chapter. However, if your workstation is located behind a proxy, you may have to configure the HTTP proxy hostname and port number to connect to remote SOAP servers; see Figure 14-5.

It is also possible to set various debugging options in the toolkit by selecting the Tracing tab, and selecting the required trace output. This output will appear in the KToolbar console.

The device emulator to test applications under can be set by selecting `J2ME Wireless Toolkit 1.0.4_01>Default Device Selection` from the Start menu. A range of different mobile device emulators is available from the drop-down list as shown in Figure 14-6. Select the desired device and press OK to make it active.

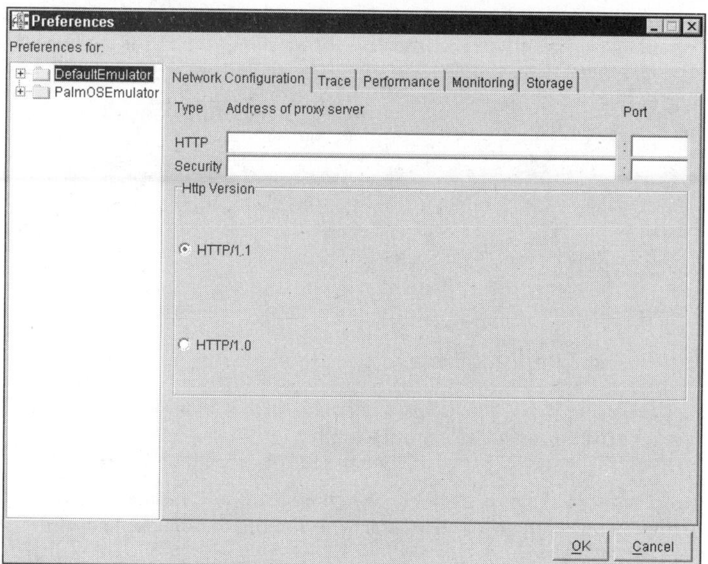

Figure 14-5: J2ME Wireless Toolkit Preferences

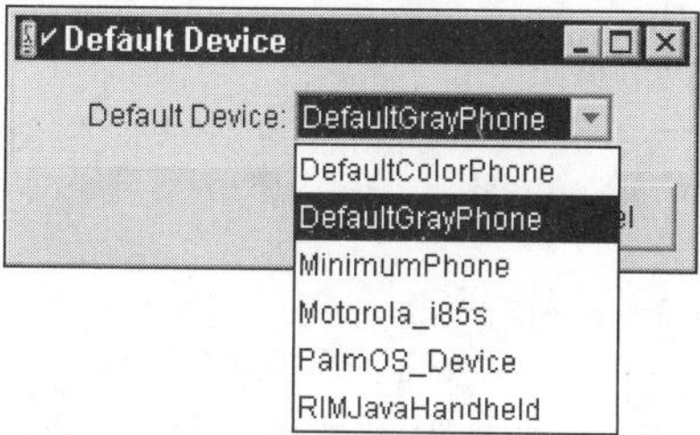

Figure 14-6: Device emulator selection

The J2ME Wireless Toolkit installation can now be tested.

Test

To test the Wireless Toolkit installation, run one of the sample applications that come with the distribution. The sample application will attempt to make a HTTP connection to the Tomcat server running on port 8080.

Caution Tomcat should be running with a valid Root context for the test to complete successfully. Attempt to open the URL `http://localhost:8080/index.jsp` in a browser before proceeding.

To run the sample application start the KToolbar by selecting `Wireless Toolkit 1.0.4_01>KToolbar` from the Start menu. The KToolbar is the lightweight IDE that can be used to build and package J2ME applications.

To open one of the J2ME samples click Open Project from the toolbar, or `File>Open Project...` from the menu. A dialog box like the one shown in Figure 14-7 is displayed.

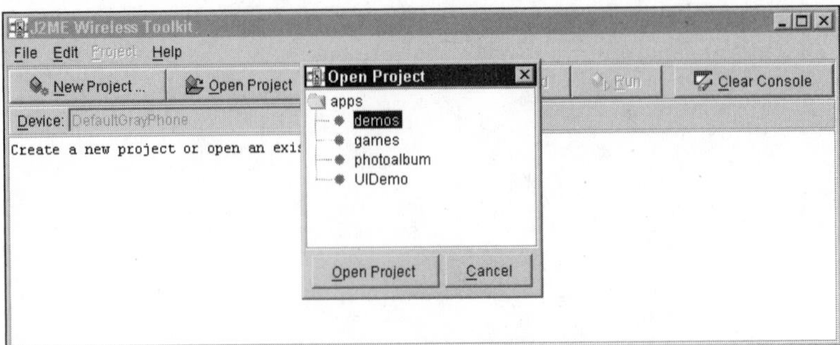

Figure 14-7: Opening an existing project using the KToolbar

Select the demos project and click Open Project. The console should indicate that the demos project was loaded. Press Run on the toolbar to start the sample demos application.

Running a MIDlet opens a device emulator like that shown in Figure 14-8. The exact device may differ depending on the default device selection chosen in the Configuration section. Select HTTP from the list of applications to launch by clicking the emulator thumb pad. Click the right-hand soft key to launch the application. The right-hand soft key can be found under the Launch label on the lower-right corner of the display.

The HTTP demo application is launched, and the HTTP demo can be used to connect to a HTTP server and display the response as HTML on the emulator display. Now it is time to use the HTTP demo to connect to the Tomcat server.

Open the Menu by clicking the right-hand soft key. From the menu use the thumb pad to select item named "Choose" from the menu. Press the center of the thumb pad to select the menu item.

You are prompted to choose a URL to display. Press Add using the left-hand soft key; this adds a URL to the list. In the input box key in `http://localhost:8080/index.jsp` press OK using the right-hand soft key.

Tip

You can type into an input box using the keyboard. Typing on the keyboard brings the input box to fill the entire display. Once typing has been completed, press the center part of the thumb pad to take you back to the original input screen.

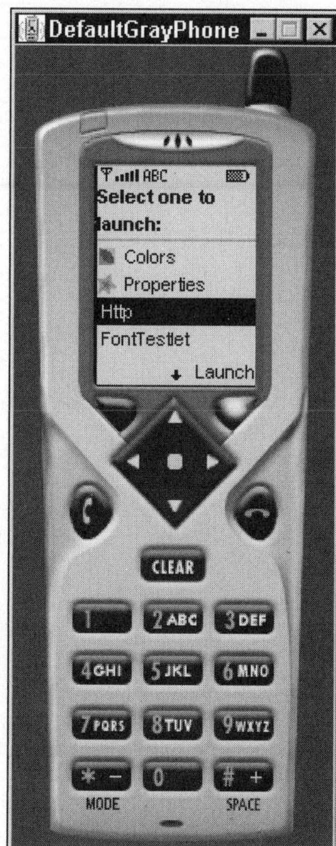

Figure 14-8: J2ME demos launcher

Scroll to the bottom of the list and select the newly added URL (`http://localhost:8080/index.jsp`) using the thumb pad to scroll, and the center of the thumb pad to select. Press OK using the right-hand soft key to proceed.

The display now shows the selected URL along with some instructions. Go to the menu and select Get. This sends an HTTP GET request to Tomcat.

A truncated HTML response should be shown on the emulator display; see Figure 14-9 for an example.

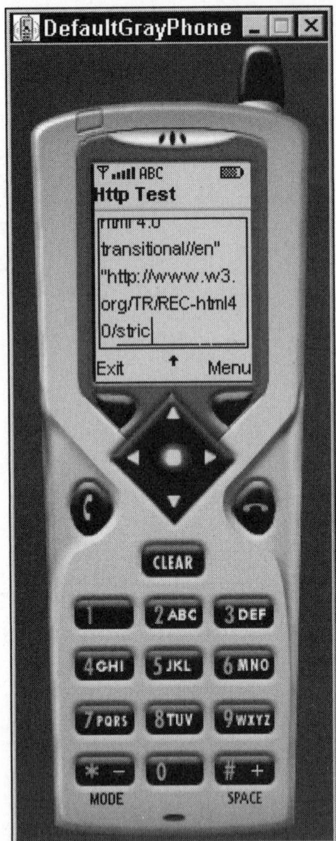

Figure 14-9: HTML response from the Tomcat server

A HTML response shown in the emulator demonstrates that the J2ME MIDlet can successfully make a HTTP connection to the Tomcat server. This test is essential before attempting to communicate via SOAP using HTTP.

If the test was unsuccessful a `java.io.IOException` will most likely be displayed in the emulator. If this is the case, check that the Tomcat server is running on port 8080, and that you can successfully navigate to the URL using a Web browser. If there is still a problem try setting the HTTP proxy as explained in the earlier section in this chapter titled "Configuration," and as a last resort, downgrade to HTTP Version HTTP/1.0 using the J2ME Wireless Toolkit Preferences.

To close the emulator, press the power button on the phone; alternatively close the window as you would normally.

kSOAP

The kSOAP project provides a lightweight SOAP API implemented from the ground up for the limited constraints of mobile devices. kSOAP may sound like an unusual name (J2ME-SOAP or MIDP-SOAP might be more appropriate). The K originates from K virtual machine, or *Kilobyte Virtual Machine* (KVM), the virtual machine that underpins J2ME.

The size of KVM and kSOAP is deigned to be in the order of tens of kilobytes. With such a small download size, each J2ME MIDlet can be packaged with the kSOAP MIDP library included.

kSOAP is developed by Enydra.org, an open source group similar to the Apache Foundation. The Enhydra.org group also hosts the kXML and kObjects projects, a lightweight XML parser, and utility objects suitable for the J2ME platform respectively. kSOAP uses the kXML library for XML parsing and document construction.

Download

kSOAP can be downloaded from `http://ksoap.enhydra.org/`. From the kSOAP project page click the Downloads link located on the left side of the page under the Software heading.

The current version of the kSOAP distribution comes pre-packaged and pre-verified for MIDP. Click on `ksoap-midp.zip` to download the distribution. When prompted, save this file to disk.

The default distribution of kSOAP does not support the encoding of all Java data types like Apache SOAP does. It is therefore necessary to download separate extensions depending on the Java data types you wish to support.

During the course of this example, Java Date objects are transferred as part of a SOAP envelope to encode and decode Java Date values the `MarshalDate` extension is required. Click on the `MarshalDate.java` link to download the source code for the kSOAP optional extension. Save this file to disk; it will be included in the code base of the Tomcat Cinemas J2ME SOAP client later on.

The `MarshalDate` optional extension relies on a utility class available from `http://kobjects.org/`. Open the kObjects site in a browser and navigate to the Utils4ME project. This project includes utility classes appropriate for the requirements of the J2ME platform.

From the Classes Suitable for J2ME and J2SE section of the Utils4ME project, select the `IsoDate.java` link. Save this file alongside `MarshalDate.java`; it also will be included as part of the J2ME SOAP client source code.

Although not used in this example, kSOAP also provides other marshalling classes used for encoding/decoding data types not supported by the base kSOAP library. `MarshalBase64.java` uses a base 64 encoder/decoder to handle base 64 encoded byte arrays. `MarshalHashtable.java` handles the encoding/decoding of Java Hashtables.

Installation

kSOAP is not installed as such; the library is to be included in the J2ME application. This is explained during the course of the Tomcat Cinemas SOAP Service section.

Interoperability Test

There are a number of tools to test the interoperability between SOAP clients and servers. Interoperability testing is an ongoing project, testing the compatible features between different SOAP client and server configurations. More information about the tests used and their results can be found at `www.xmethods.net/ilab/`.

Previously in this chapter, all examples have used the same SOAP library on the client and server side; therefore interoperability was not an issue. However, to gauge the compatibility between the Apache SOAP server and a kSOAP J2ME client, it is essential to run the suite of interoperability tests.

Results of interoperability testing between a kSOAP client and many SOAP servers can be found at `http://ksoap.enhydra.org/software/documentation/round-2-base/index.html`. The kSOAP and Apache SOAP 2.2 results show that all tests ran successfully.

You may want to run the tests yourself, just to make sure. The following steps guide you through setting up and running the SOAPBuilders Interoperability Lab "Round 2" tests.

Download

A pre-packaged kSOAP Interop test client MIDlet is available from `http://midlet.org/`. Open the URL in a browser, and once the site is displayed navigate to the Developer link on the left side of the page.

The list of developer MIDlets should contain the kSOAP Interop Client 1.0.0. Right-click the JAD Download link and save the file `kSOAPInterop.jad` to disk.

Install

Installation is simple, given that the Apache SOAP Web archive comes bundled with a pre-compiled server-side test harness, and the kSOAP Interop Client is pre-packaged as a MIDlet.

Installation of the Apache SOAP interoperability echo test suite is most easily done using the Apache SOAP administration client `http://localhost:8080/soap/admin/`. Fortunately the SOAP Web archive already comes bundled with the sample classes, so it is not necessary to compile the project. The pre-compiled interoperability echo test suite classes can be found in `C:\tomcat\webapps\soap\WEB-INF\classes\samples\interop`.

To deploy the interoperability echo test suite classes as a SOAP service, open the Apache SOAP administration client and click the Deploy link on the left navigation. This opens a deployment descriptor template shown in Figure 14-10.

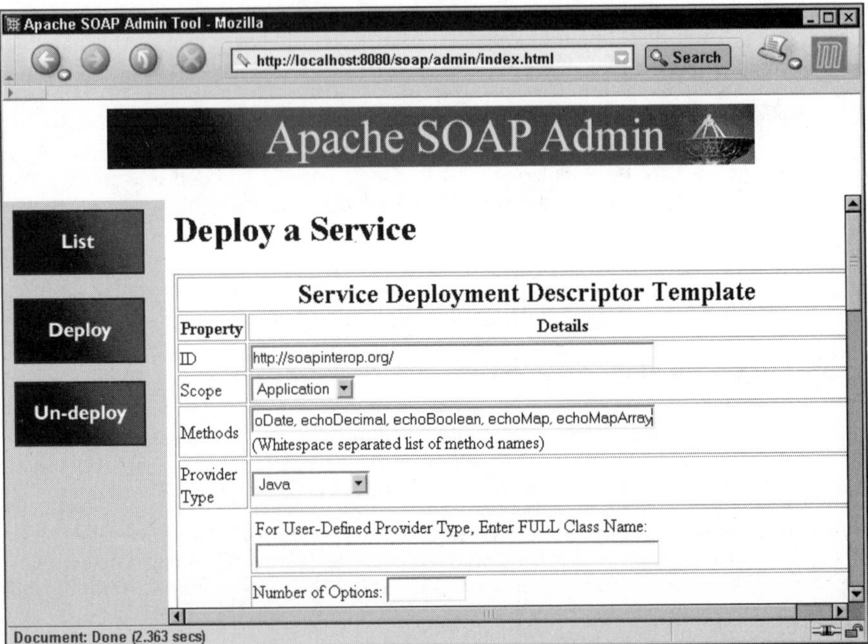

Figure 14-10: Service deployment descriptor template

Fill the template according to Table 14-1, and click Deploy once completed. This deploys the interoperability echo test suite to the Apache SOAP server, and a confirmation message is displayed stating that the service `http://soapinterop.org/` has been deployed.

You may look at the deployment details by clicking the List button on the navigation, and selecting `http://soapinterop.org/` from the list of deployed services.

Table 14-1: Interoperability Test Deployment Descriptor

Property	*Sub-Property*	*Value*
ID		`http://soapinterop.org/`
Scope		Application
Methods		`nop`, `echoInteger`, `echoString`, `echoFloat`, `echoStruct`, `echoIntegerArray`, `echoFloatArray`, `echoStringArray`, `echoStructArray`, `echoVoid`, `echoBase64`, `echoHexBinary`, `echoDate`, `echoDecimal`, `echoBoolean`, `echoMap`, `echoMapArray`
Provider Type		Java
Provider Type	Enter FULL Class Name	n/a
Provider Type	Number of Options	n/a
Provider Type	Key	n/a
Provider Type	Value	n/a
Java Provider	Provider Class	`samples.interop.EchoTestService`
Java Provider	Use Static Class	No
Script Provider	Script Language	n/a
Script Provider	Script Filename	n/a
Script Provider	Script	n/a
Type Mappings	Number of mappings	1
Type Mappings	Encoding Style	SOAP
Type Mappings	Element Type: Namespace URI	`http://soapinterop.org/xsd`
Type Mappings	Element Type: Local Part	`SOAPStruct`
Type Mappings	Java Type	`samples.interop.Data`
Type Mappings	Java to XML Serializer	`samples.interop.DataSerializer`
Type Mappings	XML to Java Deserializer	`samples.interop.DataSerializer`
Default Mapping Registry Class		n/a

The MIDlet does not require any installation; running the `kSOAPInterop.jad` file automatically downloads the necessary MIDlet JAR file from `http://midlet.org`.

Test

Running the tests is simple; double-click the `kSOAPInterop.jad file` and after a short while a J2ME emulator should be displayed with kSOAP Interop in the launcher menu, as shown in Figure 14-11.

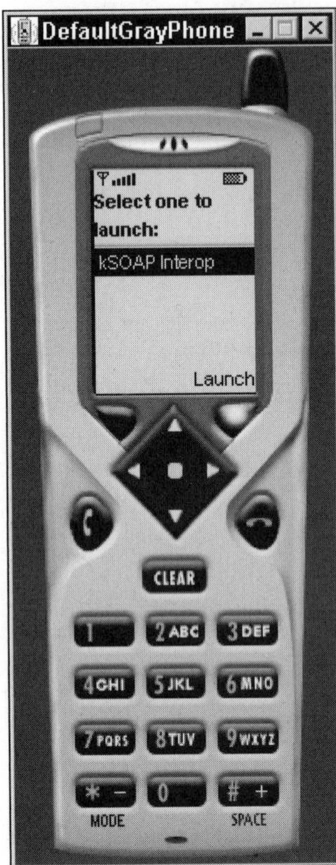

Figure 14-11: kSOAP Interop client running in emulator

Click the Launch soft key to run the application. You are greeted with a kSOAP Interop menu. Highlight the `Specify endpoint` item and press the OK soft key.

In the text box, fill in the endpoint to your Apache SOAP installation. If you deployed the Web archive it will be located at `http://localhost:8080/soap/Servlet/rpcrouter`. Press the OK soft key when you are done.

Tip Once an endpoint has been specified, it is saved in the device record store and accessed at a later stage from the `Select server` menu.

The Interop test now specifies a list of Echo Methods that can be tested against the specified Apache SOAP endpoint.

Make sure the Apache SOAP server is operational before running any of the tests. To run the first test select `String` and press OK. The kSOAP Interop test client attempts to connect to the Apache SOAP server, which then echoes the request parameter back to the client. If the echoed response matches the request, an OK response is displayed like that shown in Figure 14-12.

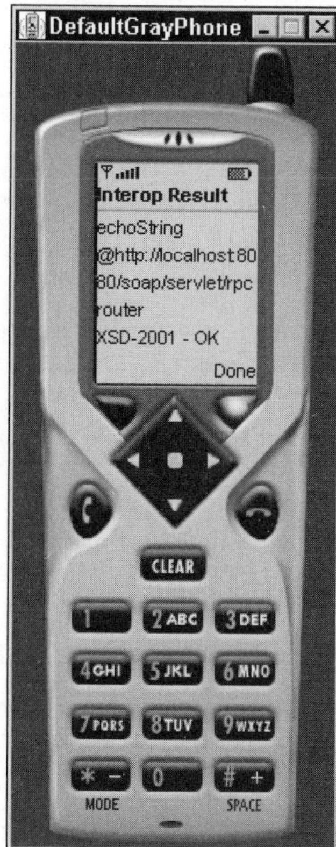

Figure 14-12: Successful Interop result

You may continue and run all the interoperability tests. To exit press the power button on the device emulator, or simply close the window it is running in.

Tomcat Cinemas SOAP Service

The scope of the Tomcat Cinemas SOAP service example is to make the viewing of Showing information available via SOAP. Specifically this includes viewing a list of today's showings, and a drill-down view of a selected showing with detailed information.

From examples in Chapter 10 you can see the business logic to display lists and individual showings already exist in the `ShowingHandler` class. Implementing a SOAP service based on this business logic can be done in two ways; make the existing methods publicly available via SOAP, or create a facade simplifying the access point into the SOAP service.

We use the later method, or creating a facade, when developing the Tomcat Cinemas application available as a SOAP service. This enables greater flexibility, targeting the application to different devices, as subtle changes in behavior and return types can be made without having to change the existing code base. This is especially relevant for de-normalizing the showing data structure for a mobile device, as you will see later in Listing 14-8.

A facade also provides a layer of abstraction over the existing business logic. This means clients to the SOAP service are sheltered from changes made to the underlying system. If, for example, the `ShowingHandler` class changed name to `MovieSessionHandler`, the facade would undergo minor changes but clients that use the facade would remain unchanged.

Now, without any more delay, we shall implement the Tomcat Cinemas SOAP service.

Implementation

As seen previously, a SOAP service only needs to be implemented as a simple java object. In this case the `WebServiceHandler` acts as a facade, providing a single access point to the service, with a de-normalized view of the Tomcat Cinemas data.

First we must define the data structure the SOAP service is to return. Notice that the `Value` objects used in the Tomcat Cinemas application described in Chapter 10 contain identifiers for other `Value` objects. These identifiers are akin to foreign keys in the database. It is therefore up to the Controller servlet to traverse the identifiers to construct a page containing all the relevant data, similar to a database join.

This traversal step is acceptable for a Web application running in a single servlet container, because it only incurs one to two method invocations, but in a distributed system remote method calls should be kept to a minimum. This is especially prevalent over a wireless network.

The solution is to create a de-normalized view of the data. By de-normalizing the data we create a less structured, but more efficient representation of the data. The `Value` object in Listing 14-8 is a de-normalized version of the `ShowingValue` object; it combines all the data from the aggregated objects into a single view. SOAP clients using the Tomcat Cinemas SOAP service do not have to make subsequent remote procedure calls to traverse aggregated objects. All the data required to display showing information should be contained in a single data structure.

`AggregateShowingValue` is very similar to the `ShowingValue` class developed in Chapter 10, however all object identifiers (foreign keys) have been removed, and in their place relevant fields from the aggregated object have been included. Aside from that `AggregateShowingValue` is a normal `Value` object.

The source code for Listing 14-8 should be placed under the source tree in the Tomcat Cinemas Web application project. Place `AggregateShowingValue.java` in the Tomcat Cinemas project, under `src/bible/tomcat/tccinemas`.

Listing 14-8: AggregateShowingValue.java

```
package bible.tomcat.tccinemas;

import java.util.Date;

public class AggregateShowingValue
{
    private long _id;
```

```
private String _theatreName;
private String _filmName;
private Date _dateTimeStart = new Date();
private int _filmLength;

public AggregateShowingValue()
{
}

public AggregateShowingValue(ShowingValue showing,
                             TheatreValue theatre,
                             FilmValue film)
{
    setId(showing.getId());
    setTheatreName(theatre.getName());
    setFilmName(film.getName());
    setDateTimeStart(showing.getDateTimeStart());
    setFilmLength(film.getLength());
}

public AggregateShowingValue(long id,
                             String theatreName,
                             String filmName,
                             Date dateTimeStart,
                             int filmLength)
{
    setId(id);
    setTheatreName(theatreName);
    setFilmName(filmName);
    setDateTimeStart(dateTimeStart);
    setFilmLength(filmLength);
}

//setters

public void setId(long id)
{
    _id = id;
}

public void setTheatreName(String theatreName)
{
    _theatreName = theatreName;
}

public void setFilmName(String filmName)
{
    _filmName = filmName;
}

public void setDateTimeStart(Date dateTimeStart)
{
```

Continued

Listing 14-8 *(continued)*

```
        _dateTimeStart = dateTimeStart;
    }

    public void setFilmLength(int filmLength)
    {
        _filmLength = filmLength;
    }

    //getters

    public long getId()
    {
        return _id;
    }

    public String getTheatreName()
    {
        return _theatreName;
    }

    public String getFilmName()
    {
        return _filmName;
    }

    public Date getDateTimeStart()
    {
        return _dateTimeStart;
    }

    public int getFilmLength()
    {
        return _filmLength;
    }

    public String toString()
    {
        StringBuffer rv = new StringBuffer();
        rv.append("id: " + _id + "\n");
        rv.append("theatre name: " + _theatreName + "\n");
        rv.append("film name: " + _filmName + "\n");
        rv.append("date/time: " + getDateTimeStart() + "\n");
        rv.append("film length: " + getFilmLength() + "\n");
        return rv.toString();
    }
}
```

Next comes the facade, The `WebServicesHandler` class in Listing 14-9 contains methods that will be exposed by the SOAP service. The facade methods call the necessary handler objects and transform the results into de-normalized data structures to be returned via SOAP.

The source code for the `WebServicesHandler` class should be placed alongside the other Tomcat Cinemas handlers in `src/bible/tomcat/tccinemas`, in the project workspace.

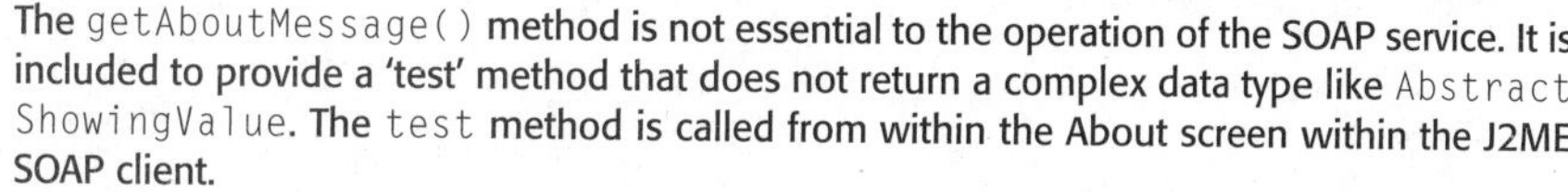

Tip The `getAboutMessage()` method is not essential to the operation of the SOAP service. It is included to provide a 'test' method that does not return a complex data type like `AbstractShowingValue`. The `test` method is called from within the About screen within the J2ME SOAP client.

The `getTodaysShowings()` methods makes a simple call to the underlying `ShowingHandler` to get all the showings for today's date. The behavior is slightly different to that of `getShowingsFutureToday()`, because it was deemed the SOAP service should provide slightly different behavior. Along with the list of showings, `Film` and `TheatreValue` objects are gathered from their respective `Handlers`. `Film`, `Theatre`, and `Showing` values are then aggregated into a single `Value` object by the `aggregateShowings()` helper method. The collection of aggregated results is then transformed into an object array and returned to the caller.

Caution Although a Vector or Collection may be used, object arrays are used as return types for the `getTodaysShowings()` method. Typically, Java style guidelines recommend against the use of arrays, but attempts during development could not get a vector of `AggregateShowingValue` objects to be de-serialized by the kSOAP client. Object arrays, on the other hand, can be de-serialized without error.

Listing 14-9: **WebServicesHandler.java**

```
package bible.tomcat.tccinemas;

import java.util.*;
import java.sql.SQLException;

import bible.tomcat.tccinemas.util.*;

public class WebServiceHandler
    extends Handler
{
    private static final String MSG =
        "Powered by the Tomcat Cinemas SOAP service";

    public WebServiceHandler()
    {
    }

    public static String getAboutMessage()
    {
        return MSG;
    }
```

Continued

Listing 14-9 *(continued)*

```
public static AggregateShowingValue[] getTodaysShowings()
    throws Exception
{
    ShowingHandler sh = new ShowingHandler();
    FilmHandler fh = new FilmHandler();
    TheatreHandler th = new TheatreHandler();

    Collection showings;
    Collection films;
    Collection theatres;

    try
    {
        showings = sh.getShowingsByDate(new Date());
        films = fh.getFilms(false);
        theatres = th.getTheatres(false);

    }
    catch (SQLException e)
    {
        throw new Exception("Error retrieving showing information");
    }

    Collection aggregateShowings = aggregateShowings(showings,
                                                     theatres,
                                                     films);
    AggregateShowingValue[] rv =
        new AggregateShowingValue[aggregateShowings.size()];
    aggregateShowings.toArray(rv);

    return rv;
}

private static Collection aggregateShowings(Collection showings,
                                            Collection theatres,
                                            Collection films)
{
    ArrayList rv = new ArrayList();

    for(Iterator i=showings.iterator(); i.hasNext(); )
    {
        ShowingValue thisShowing = (ShowingValue)i.next();
        TheatreValue thisTheatre = new TheatreValue();
        FilmValue thisFilm = new FilmValue();

        for(Iterator j=theatres.iterator(); j.hasNext(); )
        {
            TheatreValue tmp = (TheatreValue)j.next();
            if(tmp.getId() == thisShowing.getTheatreId())
            {
                thisTheatre = tmp;
```

```
                    break;
                }
            }

            for(Iterator j=films.iterator(); j.hasNext(); )
            {
                FilmValue tmp = (FilmValue)j.next();
                if(tmp.getId() == thisShowing.getFilmId())
                {
                    thisFilm = tmp;
                    break;
                }
            }

            AggregateShowingValue item =
                new AggregateShowingValue(thisShowing,
                                          thisTheatre,
                                          thisFilm);
            rv.add(item);
        }

        return rv;
    }
}
```

Configuration

The deployment descriptor in Listing 14-10 is slightly more complex that the examples in this chapter so far. The first part of the file looks familiar where the following parameters for the Tomcat Cinemas SOAP service are declared:

✦ **Service-URN:** `urn:tomcatcinemas`

✦ **Provider-Type:** Java

✦ **Provider-Scope:** Application

✦ **Provider-Exposed methods:** `getAboutMessage getTodaysShowings`

✦ **Provider-Implementing class:** `bible.tomcat.tccinemas.WebServiceHandler`

✦ **Fault Listener:** `org.apache.soap.server.DOMFaultListener`

As our SOAP service facade returns complex data structures, the deployment descriptor is required to provide additional type mappings.

✦ **Map-Encoding style:** the `encodingStyle` attribute specifies the encoding style to use for the mapping. The standard SOAP encoding style should be used specified by the URL `http://schemas.xmlsoap.org/soap/encoding`.

✦ **Map-Qname Namespace:** the `xmlns` attribute specifies the unique namespace to use for the XML element.

✦ **Map-Qname Element:** the name of the XML element containing the deserialized data structure.

✦ **Map-Java Type:** the fully qualified class name for the object that is being mapped.

- **Map-Serializer:** the class that is used to serialize the Java object to XML.
- **Map-Deserializer:** the class that is used to deserialize the object from XML to a Java representation.

Tip

You may wonder why type mapping was not required for previous examples, even though data was returned from the SOAP service. Fortunately Apache SOAP provides a set of predefined type mappings for primitive Java types, and commonly used classes and collections. For a full list of predefined mappings see `http://xml.apache.org/soap/docs/guide/serializer.html`.

Apache SOAP comes with a number of serializers/deserializers that can be used for mapping your classes to and from XML, avoiding the need for custom serializers/deserializers to be written by the application developer.

You will see that the `ShowingValue` element uses the `BeanSerializer` to serialize and deserialize complex data structures such as the `AggregateShowingValue` class. The `BeanSerializer` can dynamically serialize the contents of any class that conforms to the `JavaBeans` specification using introspection.

Mappings must exist not only for return types, but all fields within complex data structures. Hence the Apache SOAP `DateSerializer` is used for the serialization ad deserialization of `Date` values. This declaration is not strictly necessary as `Dates` should have a predefined mapping.

Listing 14-10: **DeploymentDescriptor.xml**

```
<isd:service xmlns:isd="http://xml.apache.org/xml-soap/deployment"
 id="urn:tomcatcinemas"
 checkMustUnderstands="true">
  <isd:provider type="java"
   scope="Application"
   methods="getAboutMessage getTodaysShowings">
    <isd:java class="bible.tomcat.tccinemas.WebServiceHandler"
     static="false"/>
  </isd:provider>
  <isd:faultListener>
    org.apache.soap.server.DOMFaultListener
  </isd:faultListener>
  <isd:mappings>
    <isd:map encodingStyle="http://schemas.xmlsoap.org/soap/encoding/"
     xmlns:x="tomcatcinemas"
     qname="x:ShowingValue"
     javaType="bible.tomcat.tccinemas.AggregateShowingValue"
     java2XMLClassName="org.apache.soap.encoding.soapenc.BeanSerializer"
     xml2JavaClassName="org.apache.soap.encoding.soapenc.BeanSerializer"/>
    <isd:map encodingStyle="http://schemas.xmlsoap.org/soap/encoding/"
     xmlns:x="tomcatcinemas"
     qname="x:Date"
     xml2JavaClassName="org.apache.soap.encoding.soapenc.DateSerializer"/>
  </isd:mappings>
</isd:service>
```

Like the Context-Based SOAP Service example, Tomcat Cinemas will use an Apache SOAP server embedded within its context. To enable this behavior it is necessary to modify the Tomcat Cinemas `web.xml` file under `web/WEB-INF` to include the Apache-SOAP RPC Router servlet declaration and URL mapping.

Modify `web.xml` in the Tomcat Cinemas work area, and include the snippets contained in Listing 14-11 and 14-12.

Tip The order of elements within `web.xml` is important. Refer to Chapter 8 for more information about the structure of a `web.xml` file.

The `servlet` and `servlet-mapping` elements define the `org.apache.soap.server.http.RPCRouterServlet` class and maps it to the `/servlet/rpcrouter` URL underneath the Web application context. The `RPCRouterServlet` class is included in the Apache SOAP client-side JAR file, and will be made available to the Web application during the deployment process.

Listing 14-11: Apache SOAP Servlet Declaration

```
<servlet>
    <servlet-name>rpcrouter</servlet-name>
    <display-name>Apache-SOAP RPC Router</display-name>
    <description>no description</description>
    <servlet-class>
        org.apache.soap.server.http.RPCRouterServlet
    </servlet-class>
    <init-param>
        <param-name>faultListener</param-name>
        <param-value>
            org.apache.soap.server.DOMFaultListener
        </param-value>
    </init-param>
</servlet>
```

Listing 14-12: Apache SOAP Servlet Mapping

```
<servlet-mapping>
    <servlet-name>rpcrouter</servlet-name>
    <url-pattern>/servlet/rpcrouter</url-pattern>
</servlet-mapping>
```

Building and Deploying

The build file shown in Listing 14-13 combines the SOAP targets used in previous examples into the Tomcat Cinemas build file. Replace the existing `build.xml` in the project work area with the one contained in Listing 14-13.

Listing 14-13: build.xml

```
<project name="Tomcat Cinemas" default="compile" basedir=".">

<!-- ==================== Property Definitions ===================== -->


  <property file="build.properties"/>
  <property file="${user.home}/build.properties"/>


<!-- ==================== File and Directory Names ==================== -->

  <property name="app.name"      value="tomcatcinemas"/>
  <property name="app.path"      value="/${app.name}"/>
  <property name="app.version"   value="0.1-dev"/>
  <property name="build.home"    value="${basedir}/build"/>
  <property name="dist.home"     value="${basedir}/dist"/>
  <property name="docs.home"     value="${basedir}/docs"/>
  <property name="src.home"      value="${basedir}/src"/>
  <property name="web.home"      value="${basedir}/web"/>
  <property name="desc.home"     value="${basedir}/etc"/>


<!-- ================== Custom Ant Task Definitions ================== -->

  <taskdef name="install" classname="org.apache.catalina.ant.InstallTask"/>
  <taskdef name="list"    classname="org.apache.catalina.ant.ListTask"/>
  <taskdef name="reload"  classname="org.apache.catalina.ant.ReloadTask"/>
  <taskdef name="remove"  classname="org.apache.catalina.ant.RemoveTask"/>

  <taskdef name="deploy"    classname="org.apache.catalina.ant.DeployTask"/>
  <taskdef name="undeploy"  classname="org.apache.catalina.ant.UndeployTask"/>

  <target name="deploy" description="Deploy Web application">
      <deploy
          url="${manager.url}"
          username="${manager.username}"
          password="${manager.password}"
          path="${app.path}"
          war="file:///${dist.home}/${app.name}-${app.version}.war"/>
  </target>

  <target name="undeploy" description="Undeploy Web application">
      <undeploy
          url="${manager.url}"
          username="${manager.username}"
          password="${manager.password}"
          path="${app.path}"/>
  </target>
\
<!--  ================== Compilation Control Options =============== -->
```

```
  <property name="compile.debug"       value="true"/>
  <property name="compile.deprecation" value="false"/>
  <property name="compile.optimize"    value="true"/>


<!-- ==================== External Dependencies ======================= -->

<!-- Dummy external dependency -->
  <property name="soap.jar"
      value="D:/soap-2_3_1/lib/soap.jar"/>


<!-- ==================== Compilation Classpath ======================= -->

  <path id="compile.classpath">

    <!-- Include all JAR files that will be included in /WEB-INF/lib -->
    <pathelement location="${soap.jar}"/>

    <!-- Include all elements that Tomcat exposes to applications -->
    <pathelement location="${catalina.home}/common/classes"/>
    <fileset dir="${catalina.home}/common/endorsed">
      <include name="*.jar"/>
    </fileset>
    <fileset dir="${catalina.home}/common/lib">
      <include name="*.jar"/>
    </fileset>
    <pathelement location="${catalina.home}/shared/classes"/>
    <fileset dir="${catalina.home}/shared/lib">
      <include name="*.jar"/>
    </fileset>

  </path>


<!-- ==================== All Target ================================== -->

  <target name="all" depends="clean,compile"
   description="Clean build and dist directories, then compile"/>



<!-- ==================== Clean Target ================================ -->

  <target name="clean"
   description="Delete old build and dist directories">
    <delete dir="${build.home}"/>
    <delete dir="${dist.home}"/>
  </target>
```

Continued

Listing 14-13 *(continued)*

```
<!-- ==================== Compile Target ================================ -->

  <target name="compile" depends="prepare"
   description="Compile Java sources">

    <!-- Compile Java classes as necessary -->
    <mkdir    dir="${build.home}/WEB-INF/classes"/>
    <javac srcdir="${src.home}"
          destdir="${build.home}/WEB-INF/classes"
            debug="${compile.debug}"
      deprecation="${compile.deprecation}"
         optimize="${compile.optimize}">
        <classpath refid="compile.classpath"/>
    </javac>

    <!-- Copy application resources -->
    <copy  todir="${build.home}/WEB-INF/classes">
      <fileset dir="${src.home}" excludes="**/*.java"/>
    </copy>

  </target>


<!-- ==================== Dist Target ==================================== -->

  <target name="dist" depends="compile,javadoc"
   description="Create binary distribution">

    <!-- Copy documentation subdirectories -->
    <mkdir   dir="${dist.home}/docs"/>
    <copy    todir="${dist.home}/docs">
      <fileset dir="${docs.home}"/>
    </copy>

    <!-- Create application JAR file -->
    <jar jarfile="${dist.home}/${app.name}-${app.version}.war"
         basedir="${build.home}"/>

    <!-- Copy additional files to ${dist.home} as necessary -->

  </target>


<!-- ==================== Install Target ================================ -->

  <target name="install" depends="compile"
   description="Install application to servlet container">

    <install url="${manager.url}"
```

```
        username="${manager.username}"
        password="${manager.password}"
            path="${app.path}"
             war="file://${build.home}"/>

  </target>


  <target name="context" depends="compile"
      description="Install to container using context.xml">

      <install url="${manager.url}"
          username="${manager.username}"
          password="${manager.password}"
          path="${app.path}"
          config="file:///${build.home}/WEB-INF/context.xml"/>
  </target>

<!-- ==================== Javadoc Target ============================== -->

  <target name="javadoc" depends="compile"
   description="Create Javadoc API documentation">

    <mkdir          dir="${dist.home}/docs/api"/>
    <javadoc sourcepath="${src.home}"
                destdir="${dist.home}/docs/api"
           packagenames="*">
      <classpath refid="compile.classpath"/>
    </javadoc>

  </target>


<!-- ====================== List Target =============================== -->

  <target name="list"
   description="List installed applications on servlet container">

    <list    url="${manager.url}"
        username="${manager.username}"
        password="${manager.password}"/>

  </target>


<!-- ==================== Prepare Target ============================== -->

  <target name="prepare">

    <!-- Create build directories as needed -->
    <mkdir  dir="${build.home}"/>
    <mkdir  dir="${build.home}/WEB-INF"/>
```

Continued

Listing 14-13 *(continued)*

```
    <mkdir  dir="${build.home}/WEB-INF/classes"/>


    <!-- Copy static content of this Web application -->
    <copy todir="${build.home}">
      <fileset dir="${web.home}"/>
    </copy>

    <!-- Create a context file if required -->
    <filter token="context.docbase" value="${build.home}" />
    <filter token="context.path" value="${app.path}" />
    <filter token="context.appname" value="${app.name}" />
    <copy todir="${build.home}/WEB-INF" filtering="true" >
        <fileset dir="${basedir}">
            <present present="srconly" targetdir="${basedir}">
                <mapper type="glob" from="template.*" to="*" />
            </present>
        </fileset>
        <mapper type="glob" from="template.*" to="*" />
    </copy>

    <!-- Copy external dependencies as required -->
    <mkdir  dir="${build.home}/WEB-INF/lib"/>
    <copy todir="${build.home}/WEB-INF/lib" file="${soap.jar}"/>

    <!-- Copy static files from external dependencies as needed -->
    <!-- *** CUSTOMIZE HERE AS REQUIRED BY YOUR APPLICATION *** -->

  </target>


<!-- ==================== Reload Target =============================== -->

  <target name="reload" depends="compile"
   description="Reload application on servlet container">

    <reload url="${manager.url}"
       username="${manager.username}"
       password="${manager.password}"
           path="${app.path}"/>

  </target>


<!-- ==================== Remove Target =============================== -->

  <target name="remove"
   description="Remove application on servlet container">

    <remove url="${manager.url}"
```

```
       username="${manager.username}"
       password="${manager.password}"
           path="${app.path}"/>

   </target>


<!-- ==================== Soap Deploy Target ========================== -->

  <target name="soapdeploy" depends="compile"
   description="Deploy a SOAP service to the Apache SOAP server">

       <java classname="org.apache.soap.server.ServiceManagerClient"
        classpathref="compile.classpath" fork="yes" >
           <arg value="${soap.url}"/>
           <arg value="deploy"/>
           <arg  path="${desc.home}/DeploymentDescriptor.xml"/>
       </java>

  </target>


<!-- ==================== Soap Undeploy Target ======================== -->

  <target name="soapundeploy"
   description="Undeploy a SOAP service from the Apache SOAP server">

    <java classname="org.apache.soap.server.ServiceManagerClient"
         classpathref="compile.classpath" fork="yes" >
            <arg value="${soap.url}"/>
            <arg value="undeploy"/>
     <arg value="urn:${app.name}"/>
    </java>

  </target>


<!-- ===================== SOAP List Target ========================== -->

  <target name="soaplist"
   description="List installed applications on the Apache SOAP server">

    <java classname="org.apache.soap.server.ServiceManagerClient"
         classpathref="compile.classpath" fork="yes" >
            <arg value="${soap.url}"/>
            <arg value="list"/>
    </java>

  </target>

</project>
```

Upon completion of the previous steps, we are now ready to re-build the new, SOAP service enabled, Tomcat Cinemas application. After deploying the Web application run the following command from the project work area.

```
C:\work\tomcatcinemas\> ant soapdeploy
```

Because there are many different ways of deploying a Web application the `soapdeploy` target is unable to define an appropriate dependency. It is, however, essential that the Web application has been deployed to the Tomcat server before running `soapdeploy`. Otherwise the embedded Apache SOAP server in the `/tomcatcinemas` context will not be operational, and will not accept deploy requests from the service manager client.

Tomcat Cinemas J2ME SOAP Client

Tomcat Cinemas wishes to distinguish itself by providing movie information on the go to its clientele. A J2ME application on a network-connected PDA or a mobile device is the perfect way to deliver information to people out and about.

With the use of the kSOAP library, the J2ME application can take advantage of the newly-created SOAP service. Although not the most efficient means of network communication, SOAP is used in this example to demonstrate the interoperability of SOAP between different vendor clients and servers running on a heterogeneous network.

Because this book is primarily concerned with the development of Web applications with Tomcat, very little attention will be paid to J2ME development and the creation of MIDlets. This section will however familiarize J2SE and J2EE developers with the creation of a J2ME project with the J2ME Wireless Toolkit.

Creating a New Project

The J2ME Wireless Toolkit contains nearly everything required to develop a J2ME application apart from a text editor. It provides a simple IDE (KToolbar) specialized for J2ME applications, a build environment, and a J2ME emulator with skins for default devices. With the use of third part tools, you can also profile, debug, and obfuscate your application.

To create a new project, open the KToolbar and click `New Project...` on the toolbar, or select `File>New Project...` from the menu. A dialog box is displayed.

In the dialog box, enter `tomcatcinemas` in the Project Name field, and for the MIDlet Class Name type `bible.tomcat.tccinemas.TomcatCinemasMidlet`. The `TomcatCinemasMidlet` class is created during the course of this example. The form should look like the one shown in Figure 14-13. Press Create Project when the form is completed.

The next screen will ask the user for the settings for the new project. In this form change the values for MIDlet-Name and MIDlet-Vendor to `Tomcat Cinemas SOAP Client` and `Tomcat Cinemas` respectively. The resulting form should look like that shown in Figure 14-14.

You are not required to fill in the MIDlet-Jar-Size when building and packaging using the J2ME Wireless Toolkit; it is filled in automatically once the package is created.

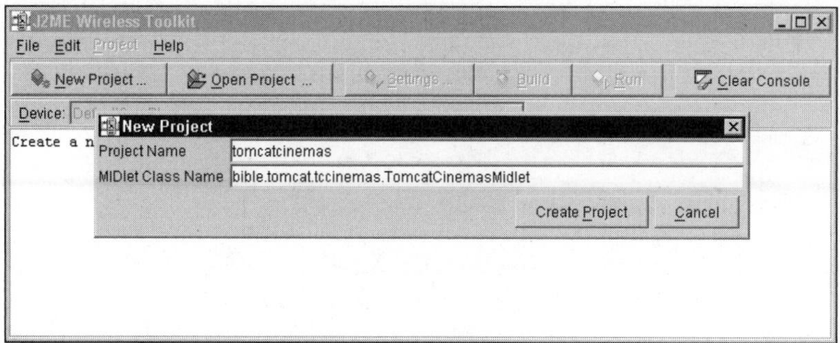

Figure 14-13: New J2ME Project dialog box

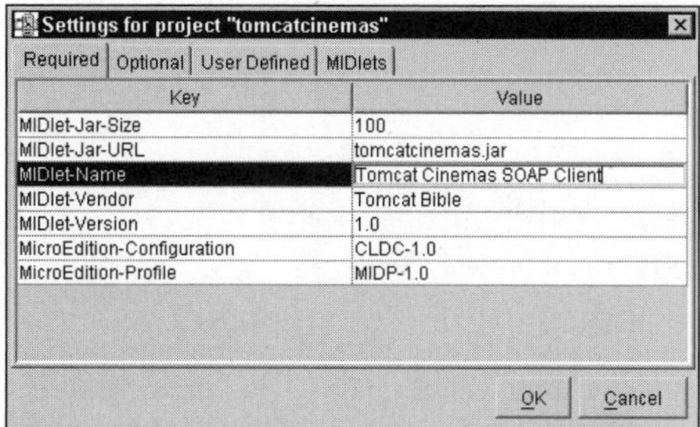

Figure 14-14: Tomcat Cinemas project settings

Click the MIDlets tab, and for the first entry in the list click Edit. This displays the default MIDlet's details. The details displayed in Figure 14-15 determine how the application looks in the application launcher in the mobile device. Change Name to Tomcat Cinemas, and remove the Icon entry. Click OK to close the MIDlet form, and save the details. Click OK on the underlying form to save and close the project settings dialog box.

If you would like an icon to appear alongside the application in the launcher menu, create an icon file in the `res` directory under the project area with the file specified in the Icon field.

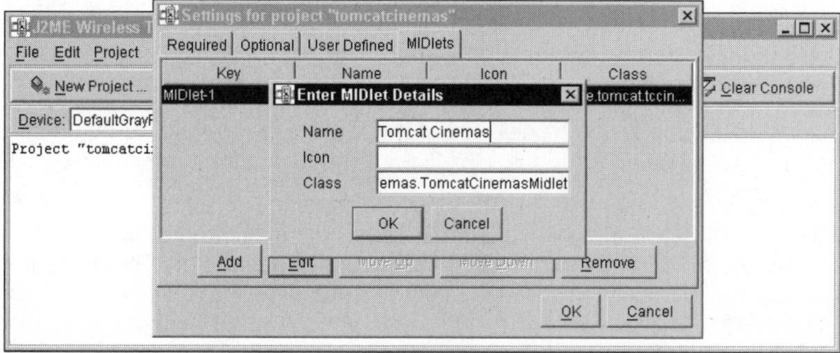

Figure 14-15: MIDlet details

That concludes the creation of the Tomcat Cinemas J2ME project. If you look under the installation folder of the J2ME Wireless Toolkit, C:\WTK104, you will see the project hierarchy resulting from the creation of a new project like that shown in Figure 14-16.

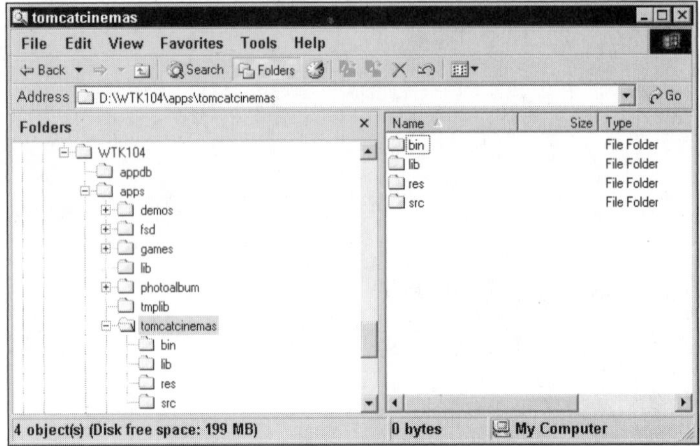

Figure 14-16: Tomcat Cinemas J2ME SOAP client project hierarchy

The rest of the example outlines the steps involved in populating the project with source code and building the project into a packaged J2ME client.

Implementation

The development of a J2ME SOAP client consists of objects extending/implementing the following classes/interfaces:

✦ `org.kobjects.serialization.KvmSerializable`: interface defines methods to get and set properties. The design of the getters and setters is used to make up for the lack of reflection and introspection in J2ME. Classes implementing `KvmSerializable` can be used to realize the `Value` object, or `Model`, pattern.

✦ `javax.microedition.lcdui.Form`: the `Form` is a subclass of `Screen`, which is a container for UI components. A `Form` class will be developed for each screen in the application, acting as `Views`.

✦ `javax.microedition.midlet.MIDlet`: all J2ME applications must extend the `MIDlet` class. The `MIDlet` object can contain all the application logic in a single class, however we chose to logically organize the application `Form` and `KvmSerializable` classes, leaving the MIDlet to behave as a Controller.

As you can see, the J2ME application uses an architecture similar to MVC. Although this may not be the most efficient way to structure a J2ME application, it makes this example easier to understand.

The `KvmShowingValue` object shown in Listing 14-14 is a client-side representation of the `ShowingValue` element returned from the SOAP service. The object provides all the normal `Value` object getters and setters. In addition, it implements `org.kobjects.serialization.KvmSerializable` that provides alternate methods to get and set properties, used instead of reflection on the J2ME platform.

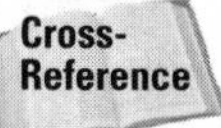

You may recall that the AggregateShowingValue shown in Listing 14-8 is the server-side implementation of the ShowingValue element for the Tomcat Cinemas SOAP service.

Classes implementing org.kobjects.serialization.KvmSerializable can also be mapped to a SOAP data type using the kSOAP API. KvmShowingValue therefore acts as a serializer/deserializer, enabling a direct mapping between Java objects and XML.

The source code in Listing 14-14 should be placed under the project area in the directory C:\WTK104\apps\tomcatcinemas\src\bible\tomcat\tccinemas.

Listing 14-14: **KvmShowingValue.java**

```
package bible.tomcat.tccinemas;

import java.util.*;

import org.kobjects.serialization.*;
import org.kobjects.isodate.*;

public class KvmShowingValue
    implements KvmSerializable
{
    private long _id = 0;
    private String _theatreName = null;
    private String _filmName = null;
    private Date _dateTimeStart = null;
    private int _filmLength = 0;

    public KvmShowingValue()
    {
    }

    public KvmShowingValue(long id,
                           String theatreName,
                           String filmName,
                           Date dateTimeStart,
                           int filmLength)
    {
        setId(id);
        setTheatreName(theatreName);
        setFilmName(filmName);
        setDateTimeStart(dateTimeStart);
        setFilmLength(filmLength);
    }

    //setters

    public void setId(long id)
    {
        _id = id;
```

Continued

Listing 14-14 *(continued)*

```
    }

    public void setTheatreName(String theatreName)
    {
        _theatreName = theatreName;
    }

    public void setFilmName(String filmName)
    {
        _filmName = filmName;
    }

    public void setDateTimeStart(Date dateTimeStart)
    {
        _dateTimeStart = dateTimeStart;
    }

    public void setFilmLength(int filmLength)
    {
        _filmLength = filmLength;
    }

    //getters

    public long getId()
    {
        return _id;
    }

    public String getTheatreName()
    {
        return _theatreName;
    }

    public String getFilmName()
    {
        return _filmName;
    }

    public Date getDateTimeStart()
    {
        return _dateTimeStart;
    }

    public int getFilmLength()
    {
        return _filmLength;
    }

    public Object getProperty(int index)
    {
```

```
    switch (index)
    {
        case 0:
            return new Long(_id);
        case 1:
            return _theatreName;
        case 2:
            return _filmName;
        case 3:
            // date is serialized to a String
            return IsoDate.dateToString(_dateTimeStart,
                                        IsoDate.DATE_TIME);
        case 4:
            return new Integer(_filmLength);
        default:
            throw new IllegalArgumentException("Property [" +
                                               index +
                                               "] is invalid");
    }
}

public int getPropertyCount()
{
    return 5;
}

public void getPropertyInfo(int index, PropertyInfo info)
{
    try
    {
        switch (index)
        {
            case 0:
                info.name = "id";
                info.type = Class.forName("java.lang.Long");
                break;
            case 1:
                info.name="theatreName";
                info.type = Class.forName("java.lang.Long");
                break;
            case 2:
                info.name = "filmName";
                info.type = Class.forName("java.lang.Long");
                break;
            case 3:
                // date is serialized and deserialized as a String
                info.name = "dateTimeStart";
                info.type = Class.forName("java.lang.String");
                break;
            case 4:
                info.name = "filmLength";
                info.type = Class.forName("java.lang.Integer");
```

Continued

Listing 14-14 *(continued)*

```
                    break;
                default:
                    throw new IllegalArgumentException("Property [" +
                                                       index +
                                                       "] is invalid");
            }
        }
        catch (ClassNotFoundException e)
        {
            /*
             * This will only happen during development,
             * throw an exception to make developer aware of the problem
             */
            throw new RuntimeException(
                    "Class declaration in getPropertyInfo() is incorrect: "
                    + e.getMessage());
        }
    }

    public void setProperty(int index, Object value)
    {
        switch (index)
        {
            case 0:
                _id = ((Long)value).longValue();
                break;
            case 1:
                _theatreName = (String)value;
                break;
            case 2:
                _filmName = (String)value;
                break;
            case 3:
                // date is deserialized from a String
                _dateTimeStart = IsoDate.stringToDate(value.toString(),
                                                      IsoDate.DATE_TIME);
                break;
            case 4:
                _filmLength = ((Integer)value).intValue();
                break;
            default:
                throw new IllegalArgumentException("Property [" +
                                                   index +
                                                   "] is invalid");
        }
    }
}
```

The Tomcat Cinemas J2ME SOAP client is made up of many screens; Listing 14-15 and Listing 14-16 show two of the most important screens in the application. Each form is primarily concerned with arranging UI components on the screen to be displayed to the user. As part of this process, the form must prepare data to be shown on the form into a suitable format.

Notice that the forms offer getter methods to access the internal UI components and `Command` objects. These methods called during the event-handling process in the MIDlet. The `TodaysShowingsForm` object also makes public the method `getSelectedShowing()`; this is a helper method to simplify the retrieval of the `ShowingValue` from the `ChoiceGroup` UI component.

Source code for all forms should be placed in the source tree under `C:\WTK104\apps\tomcatcinemas\src\bible\tomcat\tccinemas`.

Listing 14-15: TodaysShowingsForm.java

```
package bible.tomcat.tccinemas;

import java.util.*;

import org.kobjects.serialization.*;

public class KvmShowingValue
    implements KvmSerializable
{
    private long _id = 0;
    private String _theatreName = null;
    private String _filmName = null;
    private Date _dateTimeStart = null;
    private int _filmLength = 0;

    public KvmShowingValue()
    {
    }

    public KvmShowingValue(long id,
                           String theatreName,
                           String filmName,
                           Date dateTimeStart,
                           int filmLength)
    {
        setId(id);
        setTheatreName(theatreName);
        setFilmName(filmName);
        setDateTimeStart(dateTimeStart);
        setFilmLength(filmLength);
    }

    //setters

    public void setId(long id)
    {
```

Continued

Listing 14-15 *(continued)*

```
        _id = id;
    }

    public void setTheatreName(String theatreName)
    {
        _theatreName = theatreName;
    }

    public void setFilmName(String filmName)
    {
        _filmName = filmName;
    }

    public void setDateTimeStart(Date dateTimeStart)
    {
        _dateTimeStart = dateTimeStart;
    }

    public void setFilmLength(int filmLength)
    {
        _filmLength = filmLength;
    }

    //getters

    public long getId()
    {
        return _id;
    }

    public String getTheatreName()
    {
        return _theatreName;
    }

    public String getFilmName()
    {
        return _filmName;
    }

    public Date getDateTimeStart()
    {
        return _dateTimeStart;
    }

    public int getFilmLength()
    {
        return _filmLength;
    }

    public Object getProperty(int index)
```

```
{
    switch (index)
    {
        case 0:
            return new Long(_id);
        case 1:
            return _theatreName;
        case 2:
            return _filmName;
        case 3:
            return _dateTimeStart;
        case 4:
            return new Integer(_filmLength);
        default:
            throw new IllegalArgumentException("Property [" +
                                               index +
                                               "] is invalid");
    }
}

public int getPropertyCount()
{
    return 5;
}

public void getPropertyInfo(int index, PropertyInfo info)
{
    try
    {
        switch (index)
        {
            case 0:
                info.name = "id";
                info.type = Class.forName("java.lang.Long");
                break;
            case 1:
                info.name="theatreName";
                info.type = Class.forName("java.lang.Long");
                break;
            case 2:
                info.name = "filmName";
                info.type = Class.forName("java.lang.Long");
                break;
            case 3:
                // date is serialized and deserialized as a String
                info.name = "dateTimeStart";
                info.type = Class.forName("java.lang.String");
                break;
            case 4:
                info.name = "filmLength";
                info.type = Class.forName("java.lang.Integer");
                break;
```

Continued

Listing 14-15 *(continued)*

```
            default:
                throw new IllegalArgumentException("Property [" +
                                                   index +
                                                   "] is invalid");
        }
    }
    catch (ClassNotFoundException e)
    {
        /*
         * This will only happen during development,
         * throw an exception to make developer aware of the problem
         */
        throw new RuntimeException(
                "Class declaration in getPropertyInfo() is incorrect: "
                + e.getMessage());
    }
}

public void setProperty(int index, Object value)
{
    switch (index)
    {
        case 0:
            _id = ((Long)value).longValue();
            break;
        case 1:
            _theatreName = (String)value;
            break;
        case 2:
            _filmName = (String)value;
            break;
        case 3:
            // date is deserialized from a String
            _dateTimeStart = (Date)value;
            break;
        case 4:
            _filmLength = ((Integer)value).intValue();
            break;
        default:
            throw new IllegalArgumentException("Property [" +
                                               index +
                                               "] is invalid");
    }
}
}
```

Listing 14-16: **ShowingForm.java**

```
package bible.tomcat.tccinemas;

import java.util.*;

import javax.microedition.lcdui.*;
import javax.microedition.midlet.*;

import org.kobjects.isodate.*;

public class ShowingForm extends Form
{
    private StringItem showingItem;
    private StringItem theatreItem;
    private StringItem filmItem;
    private StringItem startTimeItem;
    private StringItem durationItem;
    private Command exitCmd;
    private Command backCmd;

    public ShowingForm(KvmShowingValue sv)
    {
        super("Tomcat Cinemas - Showing");

        exitCmd = new Command("Exit", Command.EXIT, 1);
        backCmd = new Command("Back", Command.BACK, 2);

        if (sv != null)
        {
            showingItem =
                new StringItem("Showing ID: ",
                               new Long(sv.getId()).toString());
            theatreItem =
                new StringItem("Theatre: ",
                               sv.getTheatreName());
            filmItem =
                new StringItem("Film: ",
                               sv.getFilmName());
            startTimeItem =
                new StringItem("Start Time: ",
                               IsoDate.dateToString(sv.getDateTimeStart(),
                                                    IsoDate.TIME));
            durationItem =
                new StringItem("Duration: ",
                               new Integer(sv.getFilmLength()).toString() +
                               " mins");

            append(showingItem);
            append(theatreItem);
            append(filmItem);
```

Continued

Listing 14-16 *(continued)*

```
            append(startTimeItem);
            append(durationItem);
        }
        else
        {
            append("No showing to display");
        }

        addCommand(exitCmd);
        addCommand(backCmd);
    }

    public Command getExitCommand()
    {
        return exitCmd;
    }

    public Command getBackCommand()
    {
        return backCmd;
    }
}
```

Listing 14-17 shows the application controller `TomcatCinemasMidlet`. This object controls all user interaction with the application by implementing the `CommandListener` method `commandAction()`. This method is called every time a user triggers an event; method arguments include the screen on which the event occurred and the command that was invoked. The logic inside the `commandAction()` method uses the arguments to determine what action to take, and if necessary what screen to display as a result of an event.

The logic to display each screen is separated into its own helper method. Inside each display method, data is prepared and passed on to the form used to display the data. Finally, a call is made to have the MIDlet display the form to the user. Data preparation is usually performed by a corresponding helper method.

Special note should be made for the helper method `getTodaysShowings()`. This method retrieves showing information from the SOAP service by building a *Remote Procedure Call* (RPC), and invoking the call using the HTTP transport provided by the kSOAP library.

Cross-Reference

The building and execution of a RPC is similar to that shown for the Apache SOAP client in Listing 14-2. Both pieces of code perform the same task, but each API has slightly different syntax.

After showing information is retrieved from the SOAP service, it is stored as a local property inside `TodaysShowingsForm` in preparation for the next action (envisaged to be a request for detailed information about one of the showings). Upon such an event, the controller retrieves the selected showing by calling `TodaysShowingsForm.getSelectedShowing()`, and passes it to the helper method that displays the showing screen.

Last to be mentioned, but first to be executed, is the MIDlet initialization. The `initTransport()` method prepares a transport mechanism to connect to the SOAP service. In this case HTTP is used as the transport.

During initialization, data type mappings are registered with the transport. Unlike Apache SOAP, the kSOAP library has no default mappings for `Date` types. It is therefore necessary to use the `MarshalDate` class to register date-time type mapping with the transport. `MarshalDate` uses the `IsoDate` utility class to serialize/deserialize to and from date strings.

Complex data types also need a registered type mapping to serialize/deserialize elements appropriately. A direct mapping can be made for the `ShowingValue` complex data type using `KvmShowingValue` class. `KvmShowingValue` is used directly to deserialize to XML to a Java object, and vice versa.

Listing 14-17: **TomcatCinemasMidlet.java**

```
package bible.tomcat.tccinemas;

import java.io.*;
import java.util.*;

import javax.microedition.io.*;
import javax.microedition.midlet.*;
import javax.microedition.lcdui.*;

import org.ksoap.*;
import org.ksoap.transport.*;
import org.ksoap.marshal.*;
import org.kobjects.serialization.*;

public class TomcatCinemasMidlet
    extends MIDlet
    implements  CommandListener
{
    private static final String URL =
        "http://localhost:8080/tomcatcinemas/servlet/rpcrouter";
    private static final String URN = "urn:tomcatcinemas";
    private static final String TODAYS_SHOWS_ACTION = "getTodaysShowings";
    private static final String MSG_ACTION = "getAboutMessage";

    protected HttpTransport http = null;
    private Display display = null;
    private IntroForm intro = null;
    private AboutForm about = null;
    private TodaysShowingsForm todaysShowings = null;
    private ShowingForm showing = null;

    private String version= null;

    public TomcatCinemasMidlet()
    {
```

Continued

Listing 14-17 *(continued)*

```
        display = Display.getDisplay(this);
        try
        {
            version = getAppProperty("MIDlet-Version");
        }
        catch (NullPointerException npe)
        {
            version = "";
        }

        if (version == null)
        {
            version = "";
        }

        initTransport();
        displayIntroScreen();
    }

    protected void initTransport()
    {
        try
        {
            http = new HttpTransport(URL, "");
            http.debug = true;
            ClassMap classMap = new ClassMap(false);

            // add type mapping for Date elements
            MarshalDate md = new MarshalDate();
            md.register(classMap);

            // add type mapping for complex data types
            Class showingValueClass = Class.forName(
                    "bible.tomcat.tccinemas.KvmShowingValue");
            classMap.addMapping("tomcatcinemas",
                                "ShowingValue",
                                showingValueClass);

            // register type mappings
            http.setClassMap(classMap);
        }
        catch (ClassNotFoundException e)
        {
            e.printStackTrace();
        }
    }

    private void displayIntroScreen()
    {
        if (intro == null)
        {
```

```
            intro = new IntroForm();
        }
        intro.setCommandListener(this);
        display.setCurrent(intro);
    }

    private void displayAboutScreen()
    {
        if (about == null)
        {
            String msg = getMessage();
            about = new AboutForm(version, msg);
        }
        about.setCommandListener(this);
        display.setCurrent(about);
    }

    private void displayTodaysShowingsScreen()
    {
        if (todaysShowings == null)
        {
            todaysShowings = new TodaysShowingsForm(getTodaysShowings());
        }
        todaysShowings.setCommandListener(this);
        display.setCurrent(todaysShowings);
    }

    private void displayShowingScreen(KvmShowingValue sv)
    {
        showing = new ShowingForm(sv);
        showing.setCommandListener(this);
        display.setCurrent(showing);
    }

    /**
     * Retrieve showing information from the Tomcat Cinemas SOAP service
     */
    private Vector getTodaysShowings()
    {
        Vector rv = null;

        try
        {
            SoapObject rpc = new SoapObject(URN, TODAYS_SHOWS_ACTION);
            http.setSoapAction(TODAYS_SHOWS_ACTION);

            rv = (Vector)http.call(rpc);
        }
        catch (Exception e)
        {
            System.out.println(http.requestDump);
            System.out.println(http.responseDump);
```

Continued

Listing 14-17 *(continued)*

```
            e.printStackTrace();
            throw new RuntimeException(e.toString());
        }

        return rv;
    }

    private String getMessage()
    {
        String rv = null;

        try
        {
            SoapObject rpc = new SoapObject(URN, MSG_ACTION);
            http.setSoapAction(MSG_ACTION);

            rv = (String)http.call(rpc);
        }
        catch (Exception e)
        {
            System.out.println(http.requestDump);
            System.out.println(http.responseDump);
            e.printStackTrace();
            throw new RuntimeException(e.toString());
        }

        return rv;
    }

    /*
     * Implement CommandListener methods
     */
    public void commandAction(Command c, Displayable d)
    {
        if (d == intro)
        {
            if (c == intro.getOkCommand())
            {
                displayTodaysShowingsScreen();
            }

            if (c == intro.getAboutCommand())
            {
                displayAboutScreen();
            }

            return;
        }

        if (d == about)
        {
```

```
            if (c == about.getBackCommand())
            {
                displayIntroScreen();
            }
            return;
        }

        if (d == todaysShowings)
        {
            if (c == todaysShowings.getOkCommand())
            {
                displayShowingScreen(todaysShowings.getSelectedShowing());
            }

            if (c == todaysShowings.getExitCommand())
            {
                exit();
            }
            return;
        }

        if (d == showing)
        {
            if (c == showing.getBackCommand())
            {
                displayTodaysShowingsScreen();
            }

            if (c == showing.getExitCommand())
            {
                exit();
            }
            return;
        }
    }

    /*
     * Implement Midlet methods
     */
    protected void startApp()
    {
        displayIntroScreen();
    }

    protected void pauseApp()
    {
        // do nothing
    }

    protected void destroyApp( boolean unconditional )
    {
        // do nothing
```

Continued

Listing 14-17 (continued)

```
    }

    public void exit()
    {
        destroyApp( true );
        notifyDestroyed();
    }
}
```

The source code in Listing 14-17 should be placed under the project area in the directory `C:\WTK104\apps\tomcatcinemas\src\bible\tomcat\tccinemas`. Upon completion of this step the development of the Tomcat Cinemas J2ME SOAP client is complete. Proceed to the next step to build and package the application ready for testing.

Configuration

Before the Tomcat Cinemas J2ME project can be built, the external dependencies of the application have to be satisfied. The J2ME SOAP client uses the kSOAP API, therefore all the kSOAP classes need to be available at compile-time, and also included in the packaged application for use at runtime.

The J2ME Wireless Toolkit takes care of external dependences by including any ZIP or JAR files in the project `lib` directory, in the build classpath. During the packaging process, all classes and resources contained in the lib directory are included within the project's JAR file.

To make kSOAP available to the Tomcat Cinemas J2ME SOAP client all the developer has to do is to copy the kSOAP package, `ksoap-midp.zip`, into the project `lib` directory `C:\WTK104\apps\tomcatcinemas\lib`.

Because kSOAP optional classes are only distributed as source code, their installation is not quite as simple. The lack of a binary JAR distribution means the source code must be added into the project source tree. To install the kSOAP optional objects, copy the downloaded `MarshalDate.java` file to `C:\WTK104\apps\tomcatcinemas\src\org\ksoap\marshal`, likewise the `IsoDate.java` file should be copied to `C:\WTK104\apps\tomcatcinemas\src\org\kobjects\isodate`. After building the project, the kSOAP optional classes will be included with the application classes in the `classes` directory.

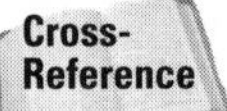

The kSOAP download instructions under the pre-requisites heading explain how to download the kSOAP package and optional classes.

Building and Packaging

Because the KToolbar has a built-in build environment there is no need to create an Ant build file. Simply open the project in KToolbar and press the Build button on the toolbar. Alternatively, select `Project>Build` from the menu. Any compilation errors are displayed in the console window.

After a successful build the following output will appear on the console:

```
Project settings saved
Building "tomcatcinemas"
Build complete
```

At this point the project may be packaged. Select Project>Package>Create Package from the menu, the packaging process will re-build the project and then package the class files and resources. The output of the package process should look like:

```
Project settings saved
Building "tomcatcinemas"
Wrote C:\WTK104\apps\tomcatcinemas\bin\tomcatcinemas.jar
Wrote C:\WTK104\apps\tomcatcinemas\bin\tomcatcinemas.jad
Build complete
```

The Tomcat Cinemas J2ME SOAP client package can now be found in C:\WTK104\apps\tomcatcinemas\bin. The package contains a JAR file containing the class and resource files. The *Java Application Descriptor* (JAD) contains the information to manage and install the MIDlets contained in the JAR file. Looking in the JAD file, you will see properties identical to the project settings created during the creation of a new J2ME project. To change the values contained in the JAD file, select Project>Settings... in KToolbar, or click the Settings button in the toolbar.

The packaged application can now be installed on a mobile device or run in an emulator by double clicking the JAD file.

Applications may be run in an emulator from within KToolbar without the need to package the application. Just press the Run button on the toolbar. Again, the equivalent functionality is also available via the menu by selecting Project>Run.

Consult your mobile phone documentation for information about how to install J2ME applications on the device.

Testing the SOAP Service

Once the Tomcat Cinemas SOAP service has been deployed, user-based testing can be performed using the J2ME SOAP client. This tests the end-to-end operation of the Tomcat Cinemas application, from the database right through to a client-side application running on a mobile device (or an emulator).

Populate the Database

Before we can begin testing, however, the database must be populated with showing data for today's date. New data may be added directly into the database, but a simpler method is to use the Tomcat Cinemas Administration Menu to add Films, Theatres, and Showings.

To operate the Administration Menu, Tomcat must be running. If Tomcat is not running, start it now.

Next, make sure the Tomcat Cinemas Web Application is deployed. The Ant list target can be used for this purpose. Issue the following command in your Tomcat Cinemas work area to list the deployed applications on your Tomcat server.

```
C:\work\tomcatcinemas> ant list
```

A list similar to the following one should be displayed. Make sure the list contains an entry for the /tomcatcinemas context.

```
Buildfile: build.xml

list:
```

```
    [list] OK - Listed applications for virtual host localhost
    [list] /tomcat-docs:running:0:C:\tomcat\webapps\tomcat-docs
    [list] /admin:running:0:../server/webapps/admin
    [list] /soap:running:0:C:/tomcat/webapps/soap
    [list] /webdav:running:0:C:\tomcat\webapps\webdav
    [list] /examples:running:0:examples
    [list] /tomcatcinemas:running:7:D:\work\book\tomcatcinemas/build
    [list] /manager:running:0:../server/webapps/manager
    [list] /:running:0:C:\tomcat\webapps\ROOT

BUILD SUCCESSFUL
Total time: 5 seconds
```

Open the Administration Menu for Tomcat Cinemas by opening `http://localhost:8080/tomcatcinemas/admin` in a browser.

Click the `List Theatres` link and make sure there is at least one `Theatre` available. If no `Theatres` have been created, create a new one now.

Click `List Films` and make sure that there is at least one active `Film` showing. If there are no active `Films`, create a new one.

Click `List Today's Showings` to see if there are any `Films` showings already entered for today. If not, click Add New Showing at the bottom of the table to create a new showing. Figure 14-17 demonstrates the creation of a new showing; make sure the current date is entered, with a time set to a point in the future.

Figure 14-17: Add a new showing for today's date.

Repeat the last step to add another showing for today's date. There should now be two showings listed when you view the All Showings list like that in Figure 14-18.

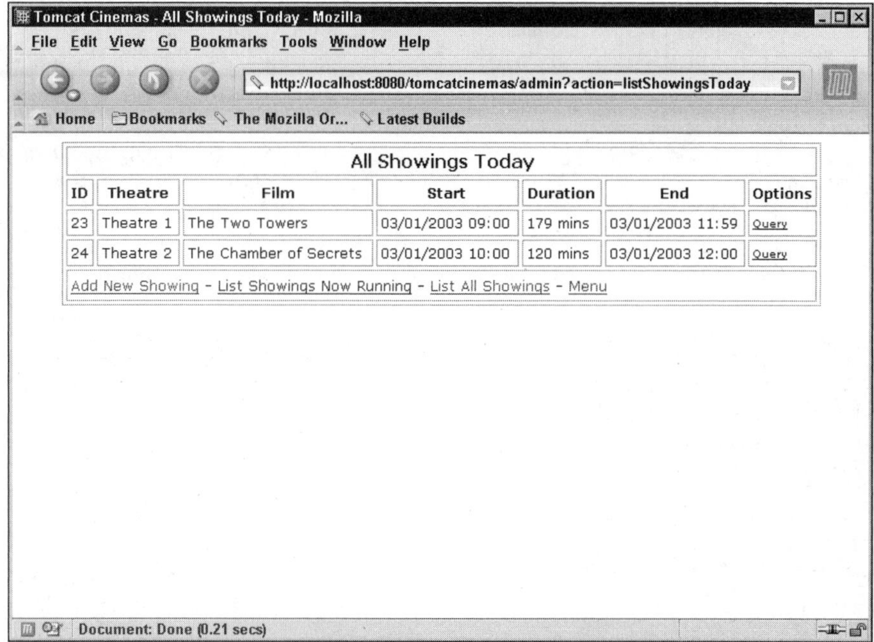

Figure 14-18: All showings for today's date

The Tomcat Cinemas database is now populated. Please proceed and start the SOAP service.

Start the SOAP Service

Again, the Tomcat server must be running for the SOAP service to operate. If Tomcat is not running please start it now.

Make sure the SOAP service has been deployed. From the command line run the command in your Tomcat Cinemas work area:

```
C:\work\tomcatcinemas> ant soaplist
```

The result lists the SOAP services deployed on the Apache SOAP server in the `/tomcatcinemas` context. Make sure the `urn:tomcatcinemas` service is listed.

```
Buildfile: build.xml

soaplist:
     [java] Deployed Services:
     [java]     urn:tomcatcinemas

BUILD SUCCESSFUL
Total time: 9 seconds
```

The SOAP service should now be up and running.

Run the J2ME SOAP Client

Finally, users may test the Apache Cinemas SOAP service using the J2ME SOAP client. For the purposes of this test we will run the J2ME SOAP client in an emulator.

The J2ME Wireless Toolkit is required to run the client MIDlet. Double clicking the `tomcatcinemas.jad` file starts the MIDlet, otherwise the MIDlet may be run from the KToolbar application bundled with the Wireless Toolkit. The instructions focus on the use of KToolbar.

Open KToolbar from the Start menu, and once loaded open the Tomcat Cinemas project. Click `Open Project...`, or select `File>Open Project...` from the menu, and in the dialog box select the `tomatcinemas` project from the list. The workspace now operates on the Tomcat Cinemas J2ME SOAP client.

Click `Run` on the toolbar, or `Project>Run` from the menu to start the Tomcat Cinemas MIDlet class in the emulator. A screen like that shown in Figure 14-19 should be shown.

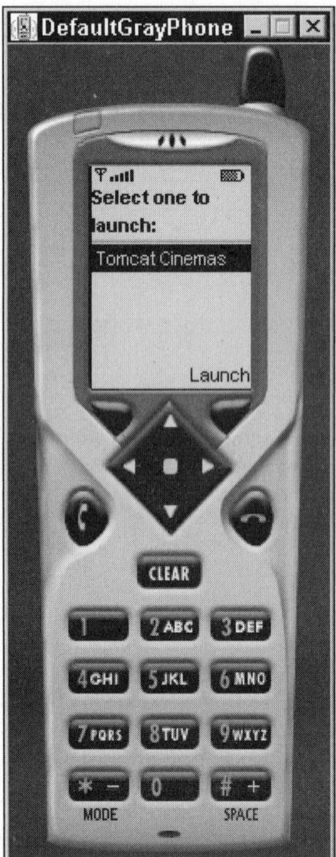

Figure 14-19: Launch the Tomcat Cinemas SOAP client.

Click the Launch soft button. The welcome screen for the Tomcat Cinemas application is displayed. Figure 14-20 shows the Tomcat Cinemas welcome screen.

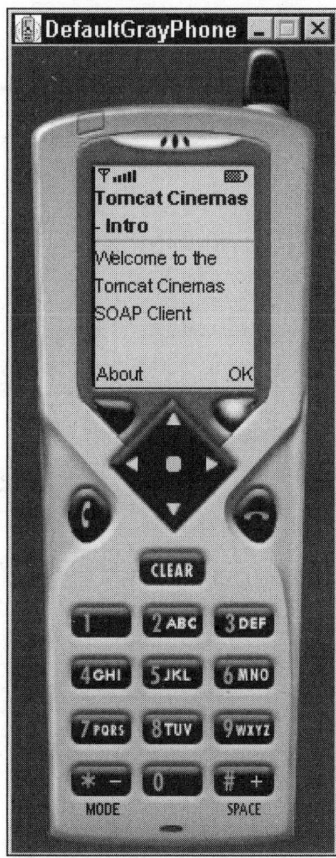

Figure 14-20: Tomcat Cinemas SOAP client welcome screen

Tip

If you have any difficulties running the following test, click the About soft button to run a simple test connecting to the SOAP service. The simple RPC to the SOAP service should return the message string "Powered by the Tomcat Cinemas SOAP service" and display it. If this succeeds you have HTTP connectivity to the SOAP service, and there is obviously a problem with the serialization/de-serialization of the ShowingValue SOAP structure. Try looking at the SOAP deployment descriptor, and make sure all the necessary mappings are correct.

Click the OK soft key to show a list of today's showings. Figure 14-21 shows today's showings (well, only one of them) corresponding to the data supplied in the Configure the Web Application section.

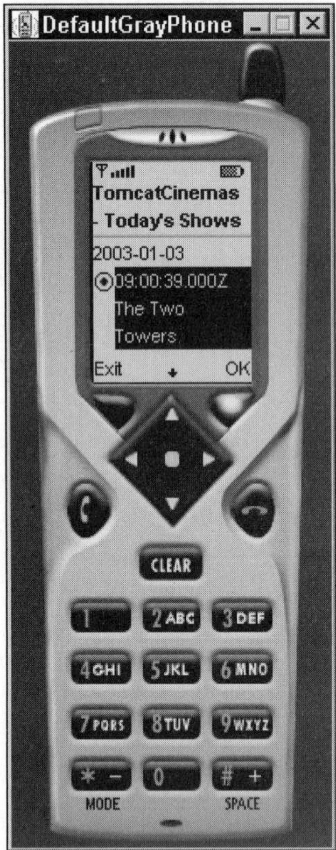

Figure 14-21: Today's showings

A date/time discrepancy of showing times may be observed between Figures 14-18 and 14-21. This behavior is attributed to all date time values being converted into GMT, by the Apache SOAP `DateSerializer`, before the SOAP message is sent to the client, however the J2ME client does not attempt to convert the date time value contained in the SOAP message to the local time zone. Hence the date time discrepancy. J2ME only requires that the "GMT" time zone ID is supported, and unfortunately the J2ME Wireless Toolkit only supports the time zone IDs "GMT" and "UTC". Therefore the J2ME client is unable to convert the date time value back into local time without having to calculate the time zone offset manually. Your mileage may vary attempting to apply a time zone offset on different mobile devices.

To get more information about a showing, scroll through the available showings using the up and down buttons, and make your selection using the center part of the thumb pad. Once a selection has been made, click the OK soft key and a detailed showing form is displayed like that for the film "Two Towers," shown in Figure 14-22.

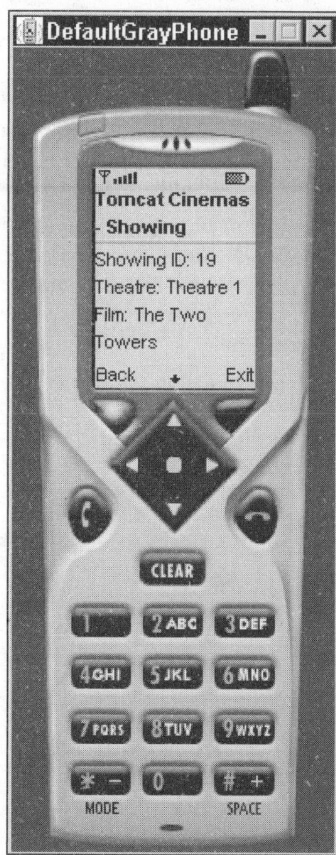

Figure 14-22: Detailed showing view

From here the user can either exit the application after finding the showing they would like to see, or press the back soft button to go back to the list of today's' showings.

Congratulations, Tomcat Cinemas is now wireless! Obviously this example does not make the full functionality of the Tomcat Cinemas Web application available over a mobile device, but it does demonstrate how one might go about making a Web application available to other devices using SOAP.

Although SOAP is used on a mobile device in this instance, one should take caution in using a heavyweight protocol such as SOAP on small devices with limited bandwidth and processing capabilities. Because SOAP is XML-based, the envelope may impede the performance of the application due to communication overhead, and the need to transform data to and from XML on a client with limited processing power. In addition, the size of the SOAP envelope may incur unacceptable user charges over a mobile network.

Summary

In summary, SOAP enables distributed systems to be loosely coupled, allowing open communication between heterogeneous clients and servers. This interchange of data opens up a range of new possibilities of client-server communication over the Web, along with the ability for SOAP services to collaborate easily and flexibly without vendor lock-in.

The examples used throughout this chapter demonstrate the creation of SOAP services. To extend these applications into fully-fledged Web services, the SOAP server must enlist the help of WDSL definitions, and register the service using a UDDI directory. For this purpose it may be worth investigating the Apache Axis project `http://xml.apache.org/axis/`, which provides more functionality and better support for WDSL.

✦ ✦ ✦

Tomcat and Web Servers

In This Chapter

The Role of the Web Server

Popular Web Servers

Connecting Tomcat with a Web Server

Why Use Tomcat with a Web Server?

Tomcat and Microsoft Internet Information Services (IIS)

Tomcat and the Apache HTTP Server

Web servers and servlet engines serve very different purposes in life. One is concentrated on serving files as quickly as possible and the other is dedicated to providing the functionality of a fully-fledged application over the Web. This chapter shows how a Web server can be used in conjunction with Tomcat to leverage the capabilities of both systems.

In the past, Web servers have been extended in an attempt to deliver fully functional, distributed applications. Many technologies, such as PHP, have already provided those sorts of applications. However, increasing demand for highly available, scalable, and robust Web applications has given rise to application servers, such as the Tomcat servlet engine. Application servers are now an integral part of the Internet landscape.

Web servers and application servers do, to a large degree, provide overlapping features. Web servers can be extended to host Web applications, and application servers can serve Web pages. Hence, the distinction between Web servers and application servers can become somewhat blurred.

In previous chapters the reader has been exposed to the myriad of capabilities the Tomcat server has to offer, however Tomcat alone may not be a sufficient platform to host large-scale Web applications. This chapter discusses the strengths and weaknesses of each server in detail to provide the most suitable server architecture for your application.

If the reader finds compelling reasons to connect Tomcat with a Web server, a step-by-step guide is provided to help a developer, or systems administrator, get the two systems up and running and talking to each other.

The Role of the Web Server

In the beginning the World Wide Web was comprised of static Web pages marked up as HyperText Markup Language (HTML) documents. Web servers, also known as *HTTP servers*, were initially designed to host HTML documents and other elements embedded within the HTML document. As seen in Figure 15-1, Web servers serve HTML content to client Web browsers via the *HyperText Transfer Protocol* (HTTP). Incoming HTTP requests for static content are redirected directly to the Web server. Once they arrive the Web server fulfills the request and sends the HTTP response back to the client.

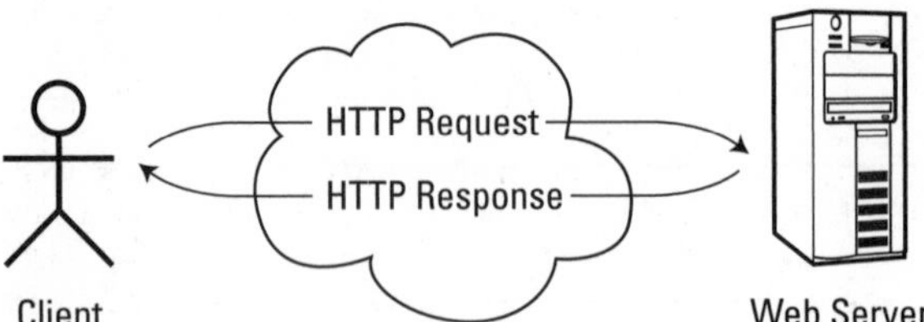

Figure 15-1: Simple HTTP request/response scenario

According to surveying conducted by Netcraft, as of the November 30, 2002 there were 35,686,907[1] Web sites hosted on the Internet. The Apache HTTP Server and Microsoft Internet Information Services (IIS) are the two most predominant Web servers hosting these sites.

Evolution of the Web Server

The rapid evolution of the Web increased the need for richer content and Web-based applications. Therefore, Web servers were required to dynamically generate HTML content. To allow dynamic content generation, Web servers were extended to run server-side programs. Throughout the past many techniques have been used to extend the Web server.

Common Gateway Interface (CGI) was the first technique to be used to facilitate server-side programming on the Web. HTTP requests were forwarded to a program, conforming to the Common Gateway Interface; this program would then interpret the request and generate HTML output. CGI output would then be written in the response to the client browser. CGI brought a level of extensibility to a Web server previously unseen, and allowed Internet developers to create fully-fledged applications over the Web.

Figure 15-2 demonstrates a client interacting with a CGI application. First the client sends a request for the CGI application to the Web server. Here a new instance of the application is forked, and then executed to fulfill the request. Once the request has been fulfilled the application exits and resources are freed.

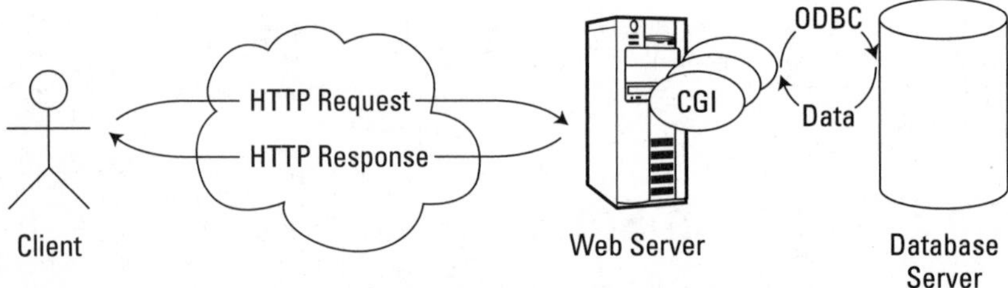

Figure 15-2: Invocation of CGI applications to fulfill HTTP requests

1. www.netcraft.com/survey/

CGI did, however have limitations. A separate process is spawned to fulfill each request. Therefore, under extreme load, the server could rapidly run out of resources and be unable to fulfill incoming requests in a timely fashion. Denial Of Service (DoS) attacks could easily bring down the Web servers running CGI applications. Each CGI program was also extremely vulnerable to security exploits unless the programmer took extreme measures to parse all input taken from the client.

To overcome the limitations of CGI, many Web server vendors provided server extensions as a way of enabling server-side processing. Server extensions allow applications to run in process, giving them direct access to internal components of the Web server. The Web server performs mapping of incoming requests to the appropriate server extension. The request is then processed by the server extension; this may involve executing an application or interpreting a script. Figure 15-3 outlines the request/response workflow using a server extension.

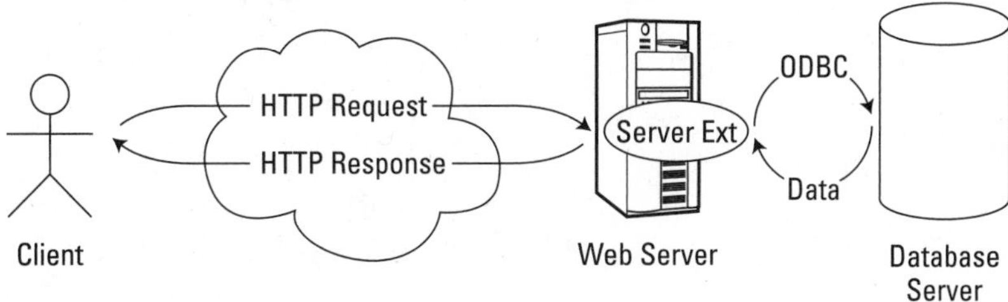

Figure 15-3: Web server using server extension

Microsoft allows the extension of their Internet Information Services via the use of ISAPI; support for Active Server Pages (ASP) within IIS is a good example of a server extension. Apache's HTTP server allows the use of plug-in modules to extend the server's capabilities. A host of plug-in modules are available for Apache, such as `mod_perl` and `mod_php`, just to name a few.

Server extensions run applications in process with the Web server. This allows tighter integration and better management of server resources. However, running server-side programs in the same process space as the Web server can result in application errors causing the entire server to fail.

Many Web servers can be extended using server extensions, two of which are described in the next section.

Popular Web Servers

As mentioned previously, Apache HTTP Server and Microsoft Internet Information Services (IIS) are the most popular Web servers on the Internet. As of November 30, 2002, Apache has the largest install base with approximately 64.69 percent of the[2] market share, IIS with 25.59 percent of the[3] market share. Although it is possible to redirect HTTP requests from the other Web servers to Tomcat, we will focus on the two most common servers used on the Internet today.

2. www.netcraft.com/survey/

3. www.netcraft.com/survey/

Microsoft Internet Information Services (IIS)

"Windows 2000 is a fully Web-aware operating system, with a built-in Web server, Internet Information Services 5.0. It also includes the critical application development services needed to build integrated, component-based applications that take advantage of the Internet."[4]

Caution

Do not confuse IIS with the Personal Web server (PWS) also bundled with Windows 2000 and Windows 9*x*.

Table 15-1 provides a brief summary of IIS features.

Table 15-1: Internet Information Services Features

Current Version:	5.0
Vendor:	Microsoft Corporation
Release Date:	February 2000
Supported Platforms:	Windows 2000 Professional/Advanced Server
Configuration:	Internet Information Services console
Licensing:	Fee-based (Windows 2000)
Tomcat connectivity:	JK2 Jakarta-Tomcat-Connector
Standard Server Extensions:	ASP, SHTML
Third Party Server Extensions:	Perl, jRun, CGI

Apache HTTP Server

"Apache has been the most popular Web server on the Internet since April of 1996. The August 2002 Netcraft Web User Survey found that 63 percent of the Web sites on the Internet are using Apache, thus making it more widely used than all other Web servers combined."[5] Table 15-2 gives a brief overview of the features of the Apache HTTP Server.

4. www.microsoft.com/windows2000/technologies/web/default.asp

5. http://httpd.apache.org/

Table 15-2: Apache HTTP Server Features

Current Version:	2.0.43
Vendor:	Apache Software Foundation
Release Date:	April 1996
Supported Platforms:	Win32, Linux, FreeBSD, Solaris, AIX, HPUX, Irix, OS X , and many others
Configuration:	Text based configuration file (. `/etc/httpd.conf`)
Licensing:	Open source
Tomcat connectivity:	JK2 Jakarta-Tomcat-Connector
Standard Server Extensions:	CGI
Third Party Server Extensions:	`mod_perl`, PHP, and many others

The Role of the Application Server

More recently, specialized application servers have been developed to provide a complete server-side programming environment. These application servers are designed to abstract many common problems faced by Web applications, including distributed component models, session management, database pooling, logging, and fail-over. This frees up the application programmer to concentrate on the task at hand; that is, to implement the required business functionality.

J2EE compliant application servers, such as Tomcat, provide application programmers with a feature-rich environment on which to develop Web applications.

Network Architecture

Today, when a user browses a Web site, the first machine he or she interacts with will most likely be a Web server. The Web server is the gateway into the Web-based application. All user HTTP requests are sent to the Web server; from here requests may be fulfilled immediately, or passed on to an application server for processing. Static content, such as brochureware, is hosted on the Web server, and Web-based applications are hosted on application servers. If necessary, the application server may communicate with a database server, such as MySQL or SQLServer, to retrieve and/or store data used by the application.

Figure 15-4 shows a typical network architecture used in modern Web-based applications.

Note Although each server is shown to reside on individual machines, this is not absolutely necessary. All three servers, Web, application and database, may run on a single machine.

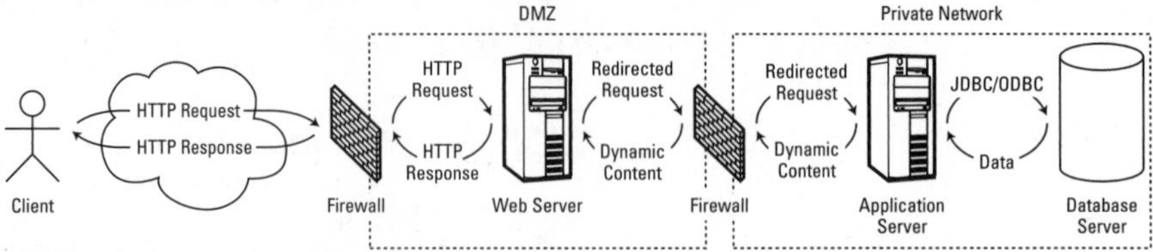

Figure 15-4: Network architecture diagram, demonstrating the use of a Web server situated in front of an application server

Advantages of an Application Server

Advantages of this architecture include the separation of content delivery and content generation. The Web server is simply concerned with accepting HTTP requests and delivering HTML content in a response. If the Web server cannot fulfill the request it redirects it to a server that can, and tunnels the response back to the client. The Web server is dedicated doing what it does best, serving Web content, fast.

The application server, on the other hand, responds to requests for dynamic content. Once processing has been completed the response is sent to the client via the Web server. The application server only runs applications; it is not concerned with serving files.

Caution Serving static content from a Web server means incoming requests are not processed by Tomcat filters or security constraints defined within the Web application's deployment descriptor (`/WEB-INF/web.xml`). Alternate security measures must be adopted to secure sensitive content not hosted on the Tomcat server.

Security is another advantage; the Web server is the only machine that needs to be in the De-Militarized Zone (DMZ). The Web server is put in the front-line, whilst the more vulnerable application and database servers can be placed behind a second firewall, on the internal network. Requests are only routed through the firewall to the application server if they originate from the Web server. Clients are not able to access the application server directly, reducing the likelihood of server specific exploits.

Finally, using a Web server as a gateway allows clustering of a group of Tomcat servers. The group of Tomcat servers may also be load balanced, offering throttling of traffic to each server and fail over capabilities.

Why Use Tomcat with a Web Server?

There are many factors that will influence the decision to use Tomcat in conjunction with a Web server. These may include the need to fit in with an existing network architecture, or the presence of a strict system administration policy.

Alternatively, if working from a clean slate you are free to decide whether to use Tomcat standalone, or in conjunction with a Web server, based solely on the merits of the application. The information outlined in this section describes arguments for and against connecting Tomcat with a Web server based on various requirements and constraints.

If you do decide to use Tomcat with a Web server, a detailed explanation is provided in the next section on how to configure the two servers to cooperate.

Reasons for Using Tomcat with a Web Server

Most large-scale applications require the use of Tomcat with a Web server. The configuration of the Web server and Tomcat does, however, require significant effort. In addition, the development environment and release procedure must support the separation of the Web application into static and dynamic packages, each deployed to a different server.

Application Profile

The profile of your Web-based application is paramount to the decision to separate static and dynamic content generation onto separate servers. If your application incorporates the use of large quantities of static content, such as HTML documents, images, audio, and video, it is sensible to host this content on a Web server and have Tomcat host the portions of the application that generate dynamic content.

Existing Network Infrastructure

If your organization has already invested in dedicated Web servers you may feel the need to use the existing infrastructure for what it was designed; serving Web content. Then again, your company's systems administration policy may dictate that all static content be hosted on such Web servers, in which case you are only limited by the server's ability to connect with Tomcat. Unless there is a good reason not to connect Tomcat with the Web server it may be hard to refuse such policy.

Existing Web Applications

The presence of existing Web-based applications may impact the architecture of your Web application. Redirecting requests to applications through a Web server can be used to invisibly integrate many separate Web applications, giving the perception of synergy between the disparate parts of the site. Connection of Tomcat and the Web server in this fashion also allows distribution of various application components to separate machines.

Server Load

Web servers are efficient at serving static content such as HTML documents and image files. Client requests can be fulfilled with very low response times, using minimal server resources. Servlet engines such as Tomcat are designed to generate dynamic content with the use of JSP and servlet technology. Although Tomcat is able to serve static content it will incur a performance hit and take up valuable resources that could otherwise be used to fulfill requests for dynamic content.

On a site with high performance demands it is preferable to take unnecessary load away from machines with limited concurrent user capabilities, such as Tomcat, and fulfill them on another server. Depending on the profile of the application it may be appropriate to host static content on a dedicated Web server, or load balance over a group of Tomcat servers.

Note It is also possible to start Tomcat in a JVM running in the same process space as the Web server. This allows tighter integration between the two servers, giving Tomcat direct access to the Web server's resources. Also, because Tomcat is started by the Web server, it is not necessary to manage two separate server processes.

Performance Requirements

Non-functional requirements may dictate response times that Tomcat cannot hope to achieve under peak demands. To meet the given response times it may be necessary to distribute content delivery to the Web server, or farm off servlet processing to a group of load-balanced Tomcat servers. In either case it will be necessary to redirect Tomcat requests through a Web server or load balancer.

Load Balancing

Performance and availability requirements may require the use of a cluster of Tomcat servers. Load balancing provides throttling of requests to the least loaded servers in the cluster.

For large-scale applications the investment in dedicated load balancing hardware, such as a CISCO director or Radware traffic management products, is justified, regardless of the hefty price tag. For small to medium scale applications, the cost of dedicated load balancing hardware can be prohibitive. A cheaper alternative may involve the use of a Web server to load balance or cluster a group of Tomcat servers.

Using a single Web server to load balance a group of Tomcat servers may not satisfy all the availability constraints. The system will still have a single point of failure, the Web server. A backup Web server along with fail-over switching technology may still be required to meet the service availability constraints.

Load balancing requires the connection of multiple Tomcat servers with a Web server.

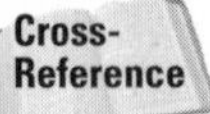

The setup of load balancing and clustering in is discussed in Chapter 16.

Security

Out of the box Tomcat allows HTTP connections on port 8080. Conceivably, Tomcat may be configured to accept all HTTP connections on port 80, the standard HTTP port. Tomcat can therefore pose as a Web server. This may suit a smaller-scale application, but poses many security risks, especially on a Unix platform.

Unix prohibits processes to bind to ports less than 1024, unless they are run as the root user. Therefore server processes must run as root to bind to privileged ports. To overcome this problem the Apache HTTP server listens for connections as root, and once a connection is accepted a child process, running as a less privileged user, is forked to process the request. Because Tomcat runs in a single JVM, it is not feasible to for Tomcat to listen on port 80 as root, and have child threads running as less privileged users.

It is not in any way suggested that Tomcat be run as the root user. Running Tomcat as root opens up the entire server to attacks from badly written or malicious servlets, or server exploits.

It is recommended that HTTP requests arriving on port 80 be redirected to a Tomcat server running on a non-privileged port. This can be achieved by using a connector with the Apache HTTP to redirect the request using the AJP13 protocol on port 8009. This also allows the Tomcat server to be located in a protected network, while the Apache HTTP server runs in the DMZ.

Alternatively, a firewall rule may be used to redirect HTTP traffic on port 80 to Tomcat running on port 8080.

Reasons against Using Tomcat with a Web Server

Tomcat also has a built-in HTTP connector that will be explained in more detail in the next section. A client may make HTTP requests directly to the Tomcat server, making the need to route requests for JSP and servlet resources through the Web server redundant. Although the Tomcat HTTP connector is not as fast as a dedicated Web server, there may be compelling reasons to avoid tunneling requests through a Web server. This largely depends on the non-functional requirements of the Web application.

Application Profile

Applications that consist of little or no static content do not require integration with a Web server. Routing requests through a Web server may offer little benefit and may even degrade the performance of the application, especially if the Web server is under load from other applications.

Smaller and simpler applications may not warrant the overhead of the supporting infrastructure. Quite simply, the time taken to set up the Web server/Tomcat connectivity may outweigh the development time. The size and importance of the application needs to be considered in relation to the effort required to set up Tomcat with a Web server.

Isolated Application

If the Web-based application hosted on the Tomcat server is the first of its kind, or it is to work in isolation from other systems, there may be no need to redirect HTTP requests through a Web server. Also, if all subsequent applications are to be based on the Tomcat server, integration should not be an issue. Applications will interoperate seamlessly.

Closed User Group

A small number of concurrent users will not put a large amount of load on the Tomcat server; therefore, unused resources are available to serve static content via the HTTP connector. It may also be adequate to run the Tomcat server on port 8080, avoiding security concerns raised previously.

If the required response times for static portions of the application can be met using the HTTP connector, it is not necessary to enlist the services of a Web server. Lack of availability requirements may also mean technologies such as fail-over, load balancing, and clustering are not necessary.

Performance Requirements

The non-functional requirements of the application may specify that the response time is not important, or it has been found through benchmarking that Tomcat can fulfill the response times specified without the help from a dedicated Web server.

Prototype

Application developers typically prototype parts of a system during a project's exploration phase to gather requirements and determine scope. During this phase it is essential to focus on the functional requirements such as user interface, data structures, and business rules, rather than non-functional requirements such as response time and availability. Prototypes should have limited reuse and a shorter life-cycle, negating the need for large amounts of supporting infrastructure.

Connecting Tomcat to a Web Server

So you want to use Tomcat with a Web server. For these two servers to collaborate and host a Web application, they must be able to communicate. This implies a network connection, and some sort of protocol between the two servers to transfer incoming requests. What you need is a *connector.*

Connectors are made of two parts: a Web server extension or plug-in module, and a listener on the Tomcat server. The two parts of a connector talk to each other using a variety of transport mechanisms and protocols. The purpose of this communication is to pass off requests from the Web server to Tomcat for processing, and to forward the resulting Tomcat response to the client.

The server extension, or plug-in module, is configured to accept incoming servlet requests, and if the request matches some criteria, it is forwarded to the Tomcat server for fulfillment. The Tomcat connector represents a listener on the Tomcat server that accepts and processes redirected requests. The protocols used to communicate between the connector components depend on the connector used.

This process is outlined in Figure 15-5. Connecting Tomcat with the Web server in this fashion is much cleaner and enables seamless integration with existing Web site and Web-based applications. The Web server provides a single point of entry into the Web application; the client, meanwhile, is oblivious that their request is actually fulfilled by another server.

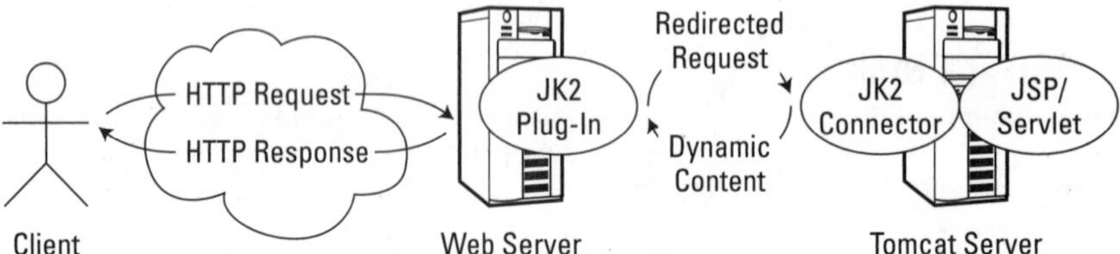

Figure 15-5: Redirecting servlet requests to Tomcat through the Web server

SMNJakarta Tomcat Connectors (JTC)

Connectors enable a client to connect directly to the Tomcat servlet engine. A client may be a browser, a client side application, or a process running on another server.

There are many different connectors available for use with Tomcat; a complete list can be found at `http://jakarta.apache.org/tomcat/tomcat-4.1-doc/config/connectors.html`.

HTTP Connectors

HTTP connectors enable Tomcat to function as a standalone Web server, listening for client requests on the designated port, and sending a response back to the browser.

HTTP/1.1

HTTP/1.1 connector supports the HTTP protocol. The HTTP/1.1 connector allows clients to request static Web content such as HTML, and also executes JSP and servlet based applications.

Caution This connector has been deprecated in favor of the new Coyote HTTP/1.1 connector.

Coyote HTTP/1.1

Essentially the Coyote HTTP/1.1 connector performs the same task as the HTTP/1.1 connector, but uses the Coyote interface. Coyote is a standardized and simplified API used to communicate with the underlying connector; both the HTTP/1.1 and AJP connectors use the Coyote interface. The Coyote HTTP/1.1 connector is enabled by default on port 8080, enabling application developers to start writing JSP and servlet applications without the need to configure Tomcat with a Web server.

Other Connectors

Connectors don't always respond to requests from client browsers. Sometimes it is necessary to allow connections from processes running on other servers. This is certainly the case when connecting Tomcat with a Web server.

AJP Connector

The AJP connector accepts connections from remote clients using the AJP protocol. The protocol enables the contents of a HTTP request to be redirected to the Tomcat server. The protocol has many versions, of which AJP13 is currently recommended for use with `Tomcat 4.1.12`.

Warp Connector

The Warp connector utilizes the Web Application Remote Access Protocol (WARP) 1.0 protocol to communicate with remote clients. WARP is a more effective protocol used to transmit the contents of a pre-processed HTTP request more efficiently than AJP13.

Currently WARP is only supported by the deprecated `mod_webapp` connector, however there is no reason why this more efficient protocol cannot be used by JK2.

Web Server Plug-in Modules

Apache requires server extensions to be written conforming to the module API, Apache modules are distributed as a Dynamically Linked Library (DLL) on the Windows platform or a Shared Object library on Unix-based platforms. IIS server extensions are written according to the ISAPI. The server extension is distributed as a DLL. Binary versions of the server extensions are available separately from `http://jakarta.apache.org/builds/jakarta-tomcat-connectors/`.

JServ

Originally designed to connect a Web server with the JServ servlet engine. The JServ project has been placed in maintenance mode, so it is undergoing no active development. JServ also works with Tomcat 3.x using the AJP 1.2 protocol. JServ only supports the Apache Web server on a Unix OS.

The JServ module is not recommended for use with current Tomcat servers, use JK or JK2 instead.

JK

The JK connector is a replacement for the JServ connector; it simplifies the configuration and makes the connector specific to Tomcat, moving away from the outdated JServ engine. JK also supports many different Web servers on a variety of platforms. JK is available for Tomcat 3.x and 4.x and supports the AJP 1.3 protocol.

JK2

JK2 is the next generation of JK. It has been refactored and incorporates powerful features like load-balancing, and has a simplified configuration. JK will run on Tomcat 3.x and 4.x and supports the same range of OS/Web server configurations as JK. JK2 supports the AJP 1.3 and 1.4 protocols.

JK2 currently is the most widely supported connector, and is used in the installation instructions contained in the following section.

Although configuration between JK and JK2 is very similar, the installation instructions are specific to the JK2 connector.

Webapp

The Webapp connector aims to simplify the Tomcat/Web server setup, including auto-deployment and Web application configuration. Webapp uses the new Web Application Remote Access Protocol (WARP) 1.0 protocol.

The connector requires the use of the Apache Portable Runtime (APR) so Win32 platforms are not supported and is therefore limited to Apache 2.0 on Unix. In the future APR aims increase portability of Apache modules between different platforms.

The Webapp connector has been recently deprecated. As there is no Win32 support for the Webapp connector it is recommended that the JK2 be used instead.

Tomcat and Microsoft Internet Information Services (IIS)

The remainder of this chapter focuses on the configuration of Tomcat with the two leading Web servers available today. First, the Microsoft built-in Web server is covered. Then the Apache HTTP Server.

Existing infrastructure, the deployment platform, and system requirements influence the choice of which Web server to use. Fortunately the same connector may be used for both the Apache HTTP server and IIS, therefore no code changes are necessary and there are only minor configuration differences.

Connectivity between IIS and Tomcat is achieved with the use of the JK2 connector. IIS uses an ISAPI plug-in version of JK2. The connector is distributed as a Dynamically Linked Library (DLL) file. The plug-in is installed as an ISAPI filter, allowing all sites on the Web server to redirect requests to the Tomcat server.

At the conclusion of this section, the reader should have successfully configured IIS to serve a modified version of the JSP and servlet examples. These examples are installed by default with Tomcat. In the modified examples, IIS serves all the static content including HTML and images, and Tomcat makes the JSP and servlet resources available. This testing process is repeated for the Apache HTTP Server.

Internet Information Server (IIS)

IIS is distributed with Windows 2000 Professional and Advanced servers as a built-in Web server, part of the Internet services platform also including FTP and mail delivery services.

Installation

IIS is installed on Windows 2000 by default. If you have uninstalled IIS please consult the Windows 2000 Server Documentation at `www.microsoft.com/windows2000/en/server/iis/default.asp` for instructions on how to remedy the situation.

Testing

Before installation of the JK2 connector can proceed, it must be established that IIS is in fact operational. The following procedure tests the status of the IIS service, and demonstrates that IIS can serve Web content.

Open the Control Panel.

Open the Administrative Tools folder.

Start the Services application.

Double-click IIS Admin Service and select Startup type: Manual, or Automatic. Depending on your preference, IIS will start up with Windows, or you will be required to manually start the server via the services console.

If the service status is Stopped, click Start to start the IIS service.

After you have determined that IIS is running, open a browser and type in the URL, `http://localhost/`. A screen resembling Figure 15-6 should be displayed.

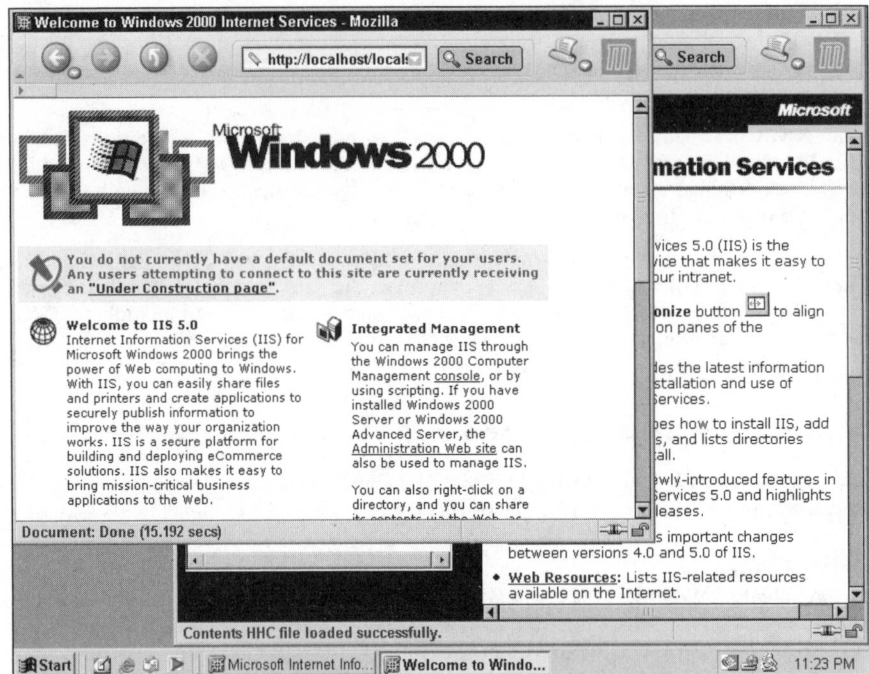

Figure 15-6: Expected result after testing the status of the Windows 2000 IIS service

JK2

Installation of the JK2 connector is not trivial. It is the cause of many difficulties from users attempting to connect Tomcat with IIS. Due to the inherent nature of Windows services, configuration requires the use of an administration console, the Internet Services Manager. As there are many steps in this process involving user input, it is critical that the reader follows the procedure very carefully to avoid configuration issues.

> **Note** It is strictly not correct to suggest that the only way to configure IIS is via the console. Users familiar with Active Scripting will be familiar with methods to configure IIS via the use of scripts. Techniques such as Active Scripting are not covered in this book.

Download

The latest version of the pre-built JK2 adapter can be found at `http://jakarta.apache.org/builds/jakarta-tomcat-connectors/jk2/release/v2.0.1/bin/win32/`.

> **Note** There is no easy way to navigate to this download directory from the Jakarta site!

You will find many files in this directory, one for connecting Tomcat with each Web server. Each has been pre-built for a particular operating system and Web server configuration. The `isapi_redirector2.dll` file is a version of the JK2 server extension specifically built for the IIS 5.0 on the Windows 2000 platform.

The 2.0.2 release of JK2 was built under Windows XP and IIS 5.1 and is therefore only suitable to users running Windows XP.

Select: `isapi_redirector2.dll` and when prompted, save the file to disk.

Installation

Install ISAPI Server Extension

Create a new directory `C:\tomcat\bin\win32\i386`. This directory hosts the JK2 ISAPI server extension. Theoretically the plug-in could live under any directory on the local machine, however, it must be referenced appropriately when creating a virtual directory under IIS.

Copy the downloaded file to `C:\tomcat\bin\win32\i386`.

Update the Windows Registry

The JK2 ISAPI server extension operates based on parameters contained in the Windows registry. Editing of the Windows registry may be performed using the Microsoft Registry Editor; alternatively the user may be more comfortable applying the updates via a `.reg` file containing all the registration entries.

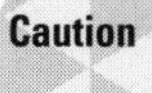

The following steps require changes to your Windows registry; please backup your existing registry before making the changes, because errors when editing the registry may render your system unusable.

1. To open the Registry Editor click Start, then Run.
2. A Run dialog box similar to that shown in Figure 15-7 appears on the screen. Commands can be typed in the Open field, and are run when the user clicks OK. Type **regedit** and then click OK.

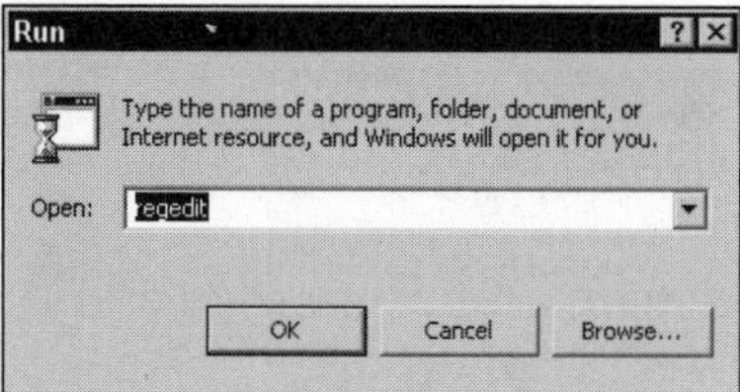

Figure 15-7: The run dialog box used to run the Registry Editor command

The registry editor works in a similar way to Windows Explorer. The registry contains a hierarchical collection of keys. Keys behave similar to directories. Each key is made up of values, and those values can be of type `String`, `Binary`, or `DWORD`. Key values behave in a similar fashion to files. It should be noted that many of the operations available within the Registry Editor are accessible by right-clicking the mouse button.

3. Navigate to the key named `HKEY_LOCAL_MACHINE\SOFTWARE`.
4. Create a new key named `Apache Software Foundation`.

5. In the new key create another key named `Jakarta ISAPI Redirector`.

6. Again, in the new key create a new key named `2.0`.

7. Create a new `String` value and name it `serverRoot`. Assign the value by double-clicking the name. The value should be set to full path to your Tomcat installation `c:\tomcat`.

8. Create a new `String` value with the name `extensionUri` and the value `/jakarta/isapi_redirector2.dll`. This value defines the location of the ISAPI server extension relative to the context root.

A virtual directory will be created later in the installation process. It is important that the registry value `/jakarta/isapi_redirector2.dll` reflects the correct name of the virtual directory created.

9. Add a new `String` value and call it `workersFile`. The value must reflect the location of the workers configuration file `C:\tomcat\conf\workers2.properties`. A detailed description of the format of the workers configuration file is presented in the section titled "Configuration."

10. Finally, a new `logLevel` named value should be created. This defines the level of logging the ISAPI server extension will write, and it can have one of the following values: `DEBUG`, `INFO`,or `ERROR`.

The location of the log file is no longer specified as a registry entry. Unlike the JK connector, JK2 supports the use of a `logger` entry in the workers2.properties file. By default all messages may be viewed via the Windows Event Viewer.

The registry modifications are now complete; your registry should look like the one shown in Figure 15-8. After verifying that all the necessary settings are correct, close the registry editor. Changes to the registry are saved automatically.

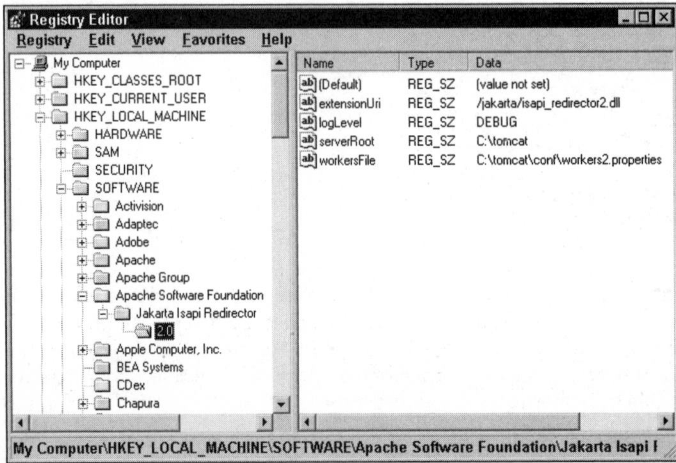

Figure 15-8: Registry editor after successful modifications to Windows registry

Tip

It is not necessary to restart the computer after the registry settings have been added. However, if they are changed IIS does require a restart.

Creating a New Virtual Directory

A new virtual directory must be created under the document root pointing to the JK2 ISAPI server extension. A virtual directory functions like a normal directory under the Web site, but the contents of the directory are located elsewhere on the drive.

Open the Internet Services Manager. The program can be found in the Control Panel, under the Administrative Tools folder.

The Internet Services Manager can be used to modify the properties of all the common Internet services available on the local machine. The management console in Figure 15-9 shows FTP, Web, and SMTP services running on the local machine.

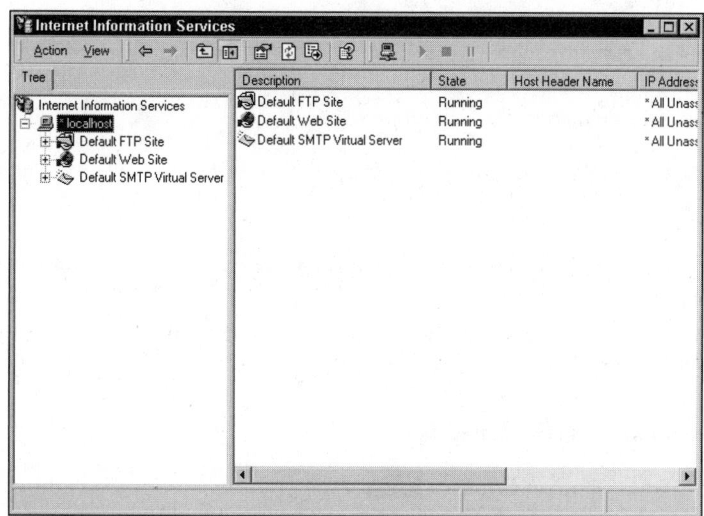

Figure 15-9: Internet services running on the local machine

Open the Default Web Site service. The contents of the Web site's document root are shown.

Tip

The document root for IIS is normally located in `C:\Inetpub\wwwroot`.

To create the new virtual directory right click the Default Web Site and select New then Virtual Directory.

The Virtual Directory Creation Wizard is displayed as shown in Figure 15-10. Click Next to continue.

Figure 15-10: Virtual Directory Creation Wizard

Type `jakarta` in the Alias field and click Next to proceed.

Caution It is essential that the name typed in the Alias field is the same as the `serverRoot` value set in the registry.

Type `C:\tomcat\bin\win32\i386` in the Directory field, or navigate to the appropriate directory where the `isapi_redirector2.dll` can be found. Click Next to continue.

In the Access Permission dialog box, select the Execute (such as ISAPI or CGI applications) check box. The result should look the same as Figure 15-11.

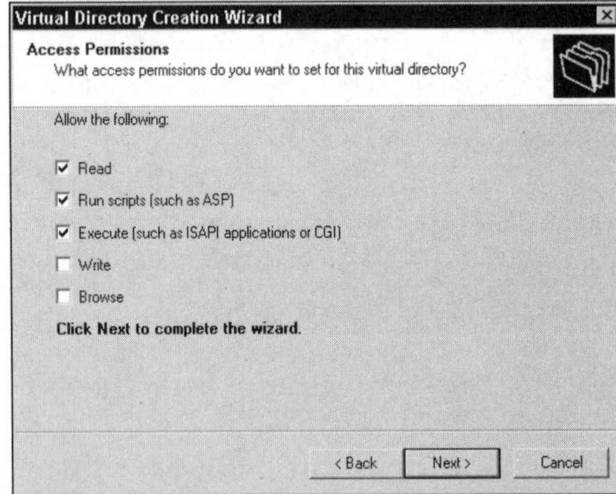

Figure 15-11: Access permission settings for the Jakarta virtual directory

Automatic Registry Update

If you would prefer not to update the registry manually you can quickly add and update entries into the registry using a .reg file. Using this technique saves time in the registry editor and avoids human error creating new registry entries. Note that using the .reg file does not exempt you from backing up your registry

Create a new file named C:\tomcat\bin\isapi_redirector2.reg and copy the contents of the following configuration into the file.

```
REGEDIT4
[HKEY_LOCAL_MACHINE\SOFTWARE\Apache Software Foundation\Jakarta Isapi
Redirector\2.0]
"serverRoot"="C:\\tomcat"
"extensionUri"="/jakarta/isapi_redirector2.dll"
"logLevel"="DEBUG"
"workersFile"="C:\\tomcat\\conf\\workers2.properties"
```

If necessary, make any changes appropriate to your custom installation.

Navigate to C:\tomcat\bin in Windows Explorer and double-click the iis_redirector2.reg file.

A registry editor dialog box is displayed with the following prompt: Are you sure you want to add the information in isapi_redirector2.reg to the registry? Click Yes.

After the registry has been updated a dialog box is displayed: Information in isapi_redirector2.reg has been successfully entered into the registry. Press OK to close the dialog box.

Click Next to complete the Wizard. The virtual directory should now appear under the default Web site.

Add ISAPI Filter to the Master WWW Service

The next step is to add the ISAPI server extension to IIS as a filter. The filter will be applied to all incoming requests; if the request is determined to be for a servlet or JSP, it is redirected to Tomcat.

In the Internet Information Services application, right-click the local computer and select Properties. The local computer should be the first entry under the Internet Information Services tree in the left pane on the screen. The entry reflects the hostname of your computer, Figure 15-12 demonstrates the user right-clicking the local computer named localhost.

A dialog box shows the localhost Properties, as shown in Figure 15-13. In the Master Properties section, in the top half of the pane, select the WWW Service and then click Edit.

Note Applying the JK2 filter to the Master WWW Service allows all Web sites running under that service to redirect requests to Tomcat. However, the JK2 ISAPI plug-in may alternatively be added as a filter to specific Web sites, including the Default Web Site. As a result, only the sites configured with the Jakarta ISAPI filter allow servlet and JSP redirection.

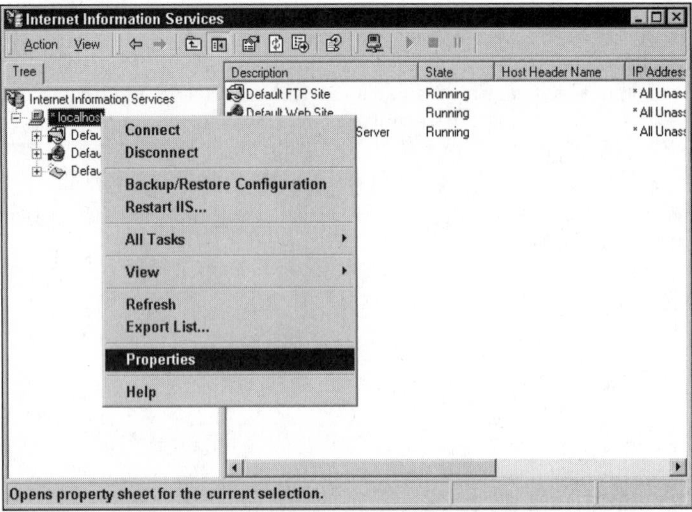

Figure 15-12: Opening the local computer's master properties

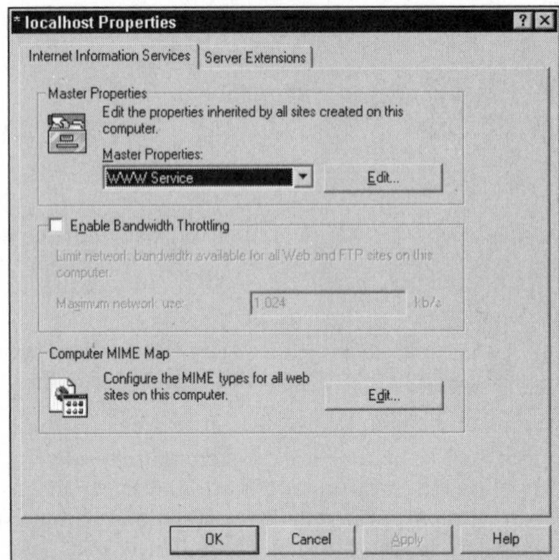

Figure 15-13: Local computer's master properties dialog box

Another dialog box appears, titled WWW Master Properties for localhost. Select the ISAPI Filters tab and then press Add. The screen shown in Figure 15-14 should now be displayed.

In the Filter Properties dialog, type `jakarta` into the Filter Name field. Then enter the location of the executable `C:\tomcat\bin\win32\i386\isapi_redirect2.dll` or browse to the appropriate directory and select the `isapi_redirect2.dll` file. Press OK to add the filter to the list.

The name of the filter is not critical, you may call it whatever you wish. The name `jakarta` is simply used to identify the filter in the list.

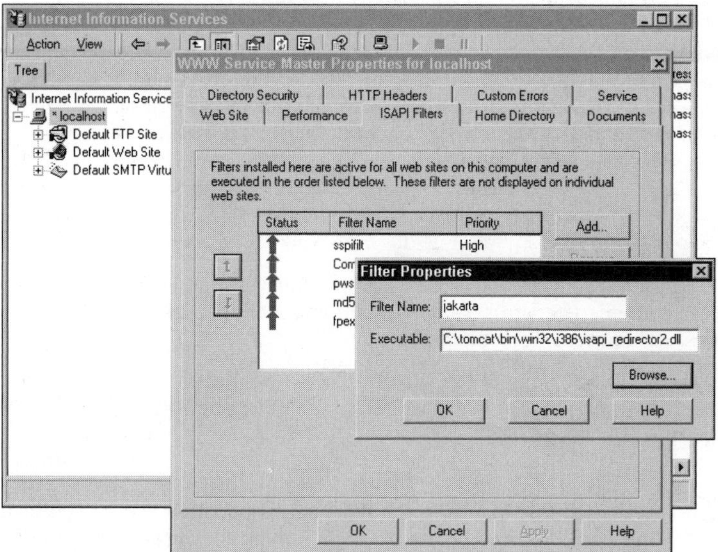

Figure 15-14: Adding filter properties

The filter is now installed and should appear in the filter list. Notice that in Figure 15-15 the status column does not have a green arrow; this means the filter is not yet loaded. Before the filter can be loaded it is necessary to complete the IIS Configuration steps.

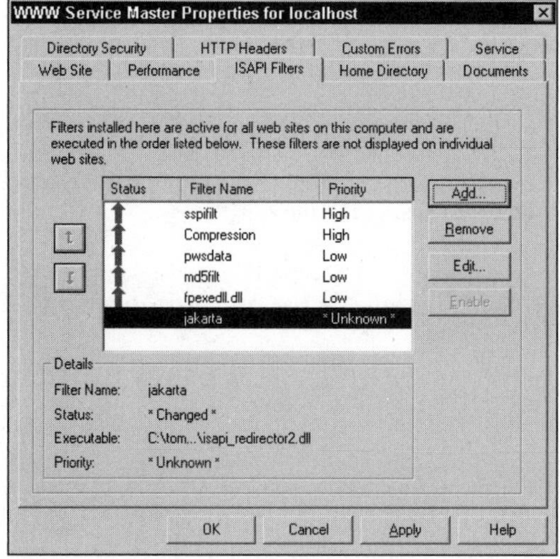

Figure 15-15: Successful addition of the Jakarta filter

Configuration

JK2 redirection behavior is dictated by the `workers2.properties` file. The location of this file is specified in the `workersFile` registration entry. For the purposes of this example assume that the workers file is located in `C:\tomcat\conf\workers2.properties`.

This chapter does not cover the auto-configure feature provided by Tomcat. Auto-configuration is limited to Tomcat and Web servers residing on the same machine, and does not support load balancing and clustering a group of Tomcat servers. Additionally, at the time of writing, the auto-configure feature for JK2 suffered from poor documentation, and was not as widely supported as auto-generated configuration for JK.

A detailed configuration reference for the `workers2.properties` file can be found at `http://jakarta.apache.org/tomcat/tomcat-4.1-doc/jk2/jk2/configwebcom.html`

The following configuration samples describe each individual component of the workers file. All the components combined constitute a bare minimum configuration required to have IIS redirect JSP and servlet requests to Tomcat.

After understanding the components of the workers file, a new JK2 plug-in configuration file needs to be created. In the `C:\tomcat\conf\` directory, create a new `workers2.properties` file containing Listings 15-1 through 15-5.

Logger

By default, the ISAPI redirector plug-in logs to the Windows application event log. However, viewing the output of the Event Log can be frustrating at times. For the purposes of this example, the default logger is overridden in Listing 15-1 to log output to the text file `C:/tomcat/logs/iis_jk2.log`.

Listing 15-1: workers2.properties (Logger Configuration)

```
[logger.file:0]
level=INFO
file=C:/tomcat/logs/iis_jk2.log
```

Shared Memory

A shared memory file is required for reconfiguration and status with multiprocess servers. Listing 15-2 declares the location and suggested size of the file.

Listing 15-2: workers2.properties (Shared Memory Configuration)

```
[shm:]
info=Shared memory file. Required for multiprocess servers
file=c:/tomcat/work/jk2.shm
size=1000000
```

Channel

The channel defines the communication method used to communicate to the Tomcat worker. For the Windows platform, Listing 15-3 shows the use of TCP sockets to connect to each Tomcat process.

Listing 15-3: workers2.properties (channel Configuration)

```
[channel.socket:localhost:8009]
info=Forwarding over socket connection to local tomcat instance.
host=localhost
port=8009
```

Worker

A worker describes the host and port the Tomcat process is listening on. Listing 15-4 uses the AJP 13 protocol over the TCP socket channel to send redirected requests to the Tomcat process.

Listing 15-4: workers2.properties (AJP13 Worker Configuration)

```
[ajp13:localhost:8009]
info=Ajp13 worker, connects to tomcat instance using AJP 1.3 protocol.
channel=channel.socket:localhost:8009
```

URIMapper

The URI entries map incoming requests to workers. The configuration in Listing 15-5 maps all requests for JSP and servlet examples to the Tomcat workers. Wildcards may be used as part of the URI mapping to specify a group of resources to map. Additionally, a port number may be specified at the end of the URI map to redirect requests to virtual hosts running on different ports.

By default, all channels and associated workers run in the `lb:0` group. If left unspecified, URI mappers also default to the `lb:0` group. Therefore, the URI mappers specified for the JSP and servlet examples correspond to the AJP 13 worker running on `localhost:8009`.

Listing 15-5: workers2.properties (URI Mapping Configuration)

```
[uri:/examples/jsp/*.jsp]
info=JSP examples, map requests for all JSP pages to Tomcat.
context=/examples/jsp

[uri:/examples/servlet/*]
info=Servlet examples, map requests for all servlets to Tomcat.
context=/examples/servlet
```

Tomcat

Tomcat must be configured with a connector to listen for redirected requests from IIS. This requires the configuration of the JK2 ISAPI filter, and final, post-configuration steps to ensure the filter is running on IIS.

Configuration

The following configuration is for the Tomcat JK2 Connector, and an example servlet context used for testing.

Coyote JK2 Connector Configuration

The JK2 Connector configuration is located under the Tomcat home at `C:\tomcat\conf\jk2.properties`. The contents of this file are not essential to get the connector up-and-running, because the default values used by the Connector will suit most configurations. The file can, however, be used to override the connector configuration to suit custom installations.

Listing 15-6 shows a JK2 configuration example explicitly defining `channelSocket.port`; the port number the connector shall listen on for socket connections. If it is not declared, the default port 8009 will be assumed.

The `shm.file` declaration defines a shared memory file that is used by multiprocess servers.

Tip Even though this may not be used with single process servers, the following declaration avoids JK2, logging a warning on startup.

Listing 15-6: jk2.properties (Shared Memory Configuration)

```
channelSocket.port=8009
shm.file=c:/tomcat/work/jk2.shm
```

Tomcat Connector Configuration

The Tomcat configuration file, `server.xml`, has been described in detail as part of Chapter 8. The standard Tomcat `4.1.12` installation enables the Coyote JK2 connector by default. This connector accepts incoming requests conforming to the AJP 13 protocol on port 8009. Ensure your Tomcat configuration has the configuration listed in Listing 15-7 enabled to allow the JK2 plug-in channels to connect to the Tomcat workers.

Listing 15-7: Server.xml (Coyote JK2 Connector Configuration)

```
<!-- Define a Coyote/JK2 AJP 1.3 Connector on port 8009 -->
<Connector className="org.apache.coyote.tomcat4.CoyoteConnector"
           port="8009" minProcessors="5" maxProcessors="75"
           enableLookups="true" redirectPort="8443"
           acceptCount="10" debug="0" connectionTimeout="20000"
           useURIValidationHack="false"
           protocolHandlerClassName="org.apache.jk.server.JkCoyoteHandler"
           />
```

Tomcat Examples Context Configuration

For the purposes of this example it is necessary that the Example JSP and servlet contexts are enabled. Listing 15-8 shows the default examples context configured by Tomcat during installation. If the examples context has been removed the contents of the listing are required in `server.xml` to enable the following tests to complete successfully:

Listing 15-8: server.xml (Tomcat Example Context Configuration)

```
<!-- Tomcat Examples Context -->
<Context path="/examples" docBase="examples" debug="0"
         reloadable="true" crossContext="true">
  <Logger className="org.apache.catalina.logger.FileLogger"
             prefix="localhost_examples_log." suffix=".txt"
      timestamp="true"/>
  <Ejb   name="ejb/EmplRecord" type="Entity"
         home="com.wombat.empl.EmployeeRecordHome"
       remote="com.wombat.empl.EmployeeRecord"/>

  <Environment name="maxExemptions" type="java.lang.Integer"
              value="15"/>
  <Parameter name="context.param.name" value="context.param.value"
             override="false"/>
  <Resource name="jdbc/EmployeeAppDb" auth="SERVLET"
           type="javax.sql.DataSource"/>
  <ResourceParams name="jdbc/EmployeeAppDb">
    <parameter><name>user</name><value>sa</value></parameter>
    <parameter><name>password</name><value></value></parameter>
    <parameter><name>driverClassName</name>
      <value>org.hsql.jdbcDriver</value></parameter>
    <parameter><name>driverName</name>
      <value>jdbc:HypersonicSQL:database</value></parameter>
  </ResourceParams>
  <Resource name="mail/Session" auth="Container"
           type="javax.mail.Session"/>
  <ResourceParams name="mail/Session">
    <parameter>
      <name>mail.smtp.host</name>
      <value>localhost</value>
    </parameter>
  </ResourceParams>
  <ResourceLink name="linkToGlobalResource"
           global="simpleValue"
           type="java.lang.Integer"/>
</Context>
```

Post Configuration

After IIS and JK2 have been configured, the Tomcat and IIS servers must be started up.

Start the Tomcat server.

Open the Internet Information Services console and restart the IIS service. To do this, right-click the local computer entry on the left pane and select Restart IIS... as shown in Figure 15-16.

A Start/Stop/Reboot dialog box is displayed. Select Restart Internet Services on localhost; this restarts all the Internet services on the local machine.

In the process of restarting the Internet Services on the localhost, the new `jakarta` ISAPI filter will be loaded.

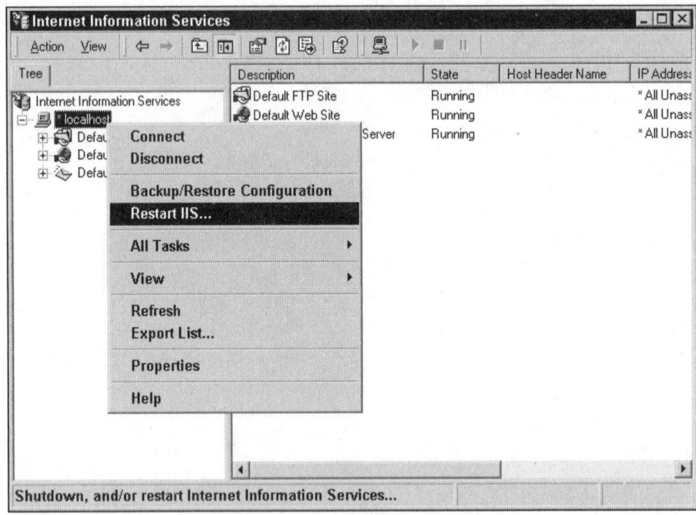

Figure 15-16: Restarting the IIS service

Once IIS has been restarted, check the status of the `jakarta` ISAPI filter.

In the Internet Information Services application, right-click the local computer and select Properties. In the localhost Properties dialog box select the WWW Service and click Edit...

The WWW Master Properties for localhost dialog box should now be displayed. Select the ISAPI Filters tab and check the status of the `jakarta` ISAPI filter. The filter should have a green up arrow in the status column, which indicates that the filter was successfully loaded. See Figure 15-17.

Caution If the `jakarta` ISAPI filter has not loaded, a red down arrow is displayed in the status column. If this happens, first check the JK2 installation steps, including the registry entries. Second, ensure all the necessary configuration files exist, and are free of syntactical errors. Finally, try to restart the IIS services again. If all else fails, attempt to configure the ISAPI filter in the Master WWW Service instead of the Default Web Site. Higher success rates have been shown running the filter in the Master WWW Service.

Finally, to restore the HTTP service on port 80, the Default Web Site should be started. Click the Default Web Site in the left pane and press the Start Item icon on the toolbar. Alternatively, you can right-click the Default Web Site entry and select Start from the pop-up menu.

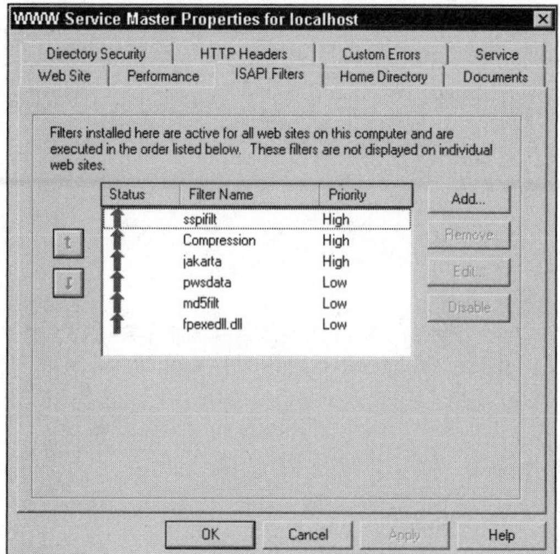

Figure 15-17: Checking the status of the JK2 ISAPI filter

Testing

For the purposes of testing the Tomcat-Apache configuration we are going to split the JSP and servlet examples, which are installed with Tomcat, into dynamic and static content. The dynamic content will be hosted on Tomcat, and the static content will be hosted on the IIS. The following test steps assume that the previous configuration has been applied to both IIS and the Tomcat server.

Caution The following steps assume that your IIS document root is located in `C:\Inetpub\wwwroot\`.

1. Stop the Tomcat server.
2. Stop the IIS Default Web Site from the Internet Information Services console.
3. Copy the existing examples folder `C:\tomcat\webapps\examples` to `C:\tomcat\webapps\examples.old` for safekeeping.
4. Create a new folder, `C:\Inetpub\wwwroot\examples`. This creates an examples context available from IIS.
5. Move the folders `C:\tomcat\webapps\examples\images` and `C:\tomcat\webapps\examples\servlets` to `C:\Inetpub\wwwroot\examples`. Images and servlet resources are only required on the Web server, therefore they are moved from the Tomcat document root.

Note The `servlets` directory does not actually contain any servlets, it only contains static HTML.

6. Copy the folder `C:\tomcat\webapps\examples\jsp` to `C:\Inetpub\wwwroot\examples`. Both the Tomcat and Web server require the contents of the `jsp` directory, hence it is replicated under both document roots. Redundant files are removed from each server in the next step.

7. Remove all static files from the `C:\tomcat\webapps\examples\jsp` folder. This proves without doubt that the static content is served from the Web server.

Do not remove the files `carts.html` and `error.html`, they are included by JSP pages at runtime.

You may want to search for `*.html`, `*.txt` in `C:\tomcat\webapps\examples\jsp` and delete search results.

8. Remove all `.jsp` files from the `C:\Inetpub\wwwroot\examples\jsp` folder. If the redirection to Tomcat is not working, the user will see a HTTP 404 error because the file cannot be found on the Web server.

You may want to search for `*.jsp` in `C:\Inetpub\wwwroot\examples\jsp` and delete search results.

9. Start the Tomcat server.
10. Start the IIS Default Web Site from the Internet Information Services console.
11. Open the URL `http://localhost/examples/jsp/index.html`. You should see the screen shown in Figure 15-18 and the examples should function as normal.
12. Open URL `http://localhost/examples/servlets/index.html`. You should see the screen shown in Figure 15-19, and the examples should function as normal.

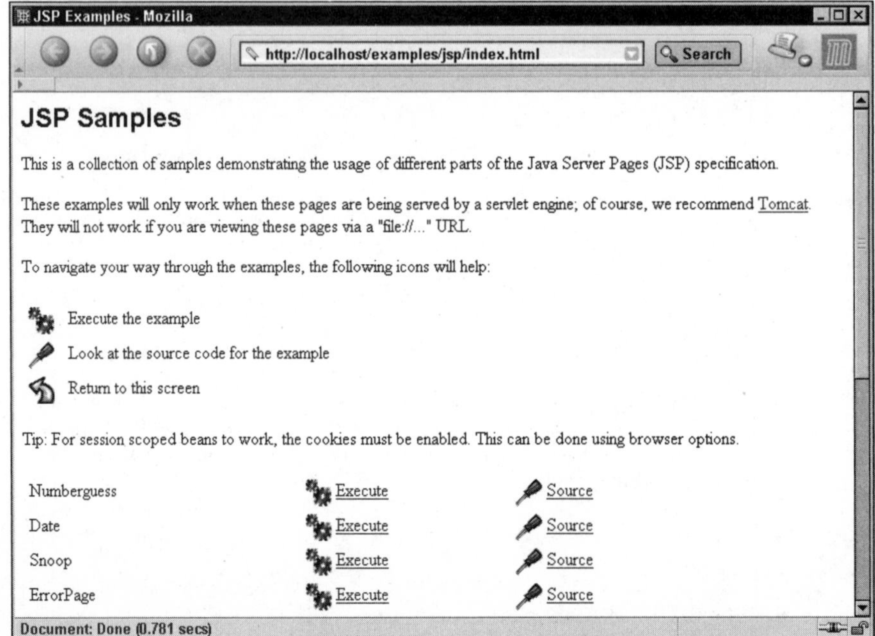

Figure 15-18: JSP test expected results

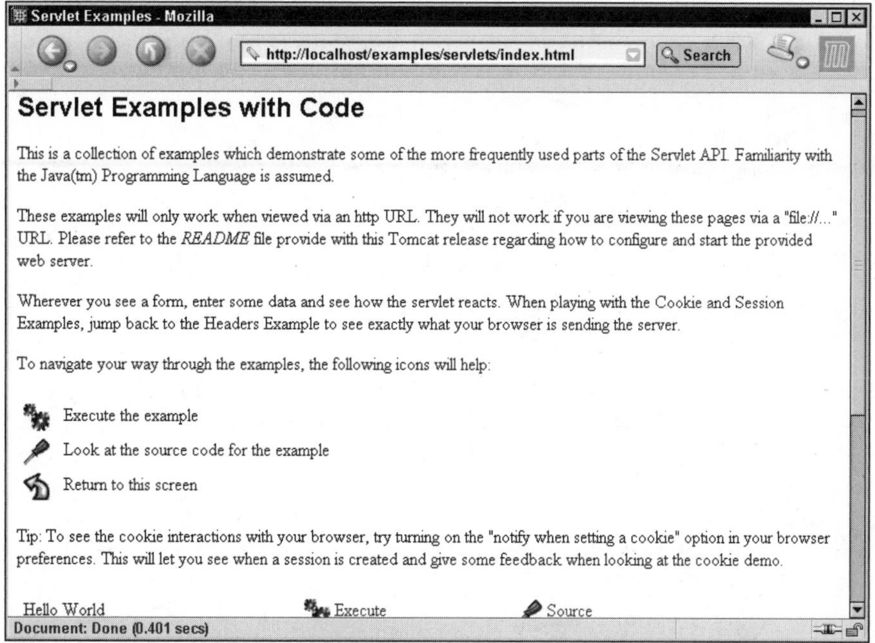

Figure 15-19: Servlet test expected results

13. Open the log file `C:/tomcat/logs/iis_jk2.log` and look for any errors that may have occurred during the test.

Tomcat and the Apache HTTP Server

In this section we configure the Apache HTTP server with the Tomcat servlet engine. You may note that Apache also uses the JK2 connector, and for the purposes of this example many of the configuration files remain the same as those shown in the IIS example. If you aren't already running the most popular Web server on the market, you soon will be after this section!

Apache HTTP Server

Apache HTTP Server, like IIS, uses their own form of server extension to allow Tomcat connectivity. The JK2 connector for the Apache Web server comes pre-built as an Apache module. Platform- and version-specific Apache modules are available from the Jakarta site.

Also check out the multitude of other modules available for you to enhance the functionality of the Apache HTTP server.

Tip Because a large proportion of Apache installations are on Linux, or other Unix variant servers, we also explore Linux-specific Apache HTTP configuration in the section titled "Configuring Apache HTTP Server on Linux."

Tomcat can be configured to run in a JVM internal to the Apache HTTP server. See the section titled "Configuring IIS to Coexist with Apache HTTP Server," after completing the following configuration, for specific steps to enable this feature.

Download

The latest version of the Apache HTTP server is available from `http://httpd.apache.org/`.

To find the download area, select Download! from the left navigation pane. Select a mirror physically close to you then click Change. Apache HTTP server version 2.0.43 is recommended for compatibility with Tomcat 4.1.12 and the JK2 connector.

Select: Win32 Binary (MSI Installer): `apache_2.0.43-win32-x86-no_ssl.msi` and when prompted, save the file to disk.

This particular download (with the .msi extension) requires the Windows Installer 1.1; however there is also a self-extracting version (with an .exe extension) available via the Other Binaries link.

Installation

The executable that has been downloaded is the installer for the Apache HTTP server. To begin the installation, run this program.

Apache HTTP server installer only configures Apache to run on ports 80 or 8080. If you followed the installation instructions in Chapter 2 correctly, Tomcat is already listening on port 8080, and if you happen to have Microsoft IIS installed, it is listening on port 80. Therefore, before you can install the Apache HTTP server, IIS must be disabled, or made to run on a different port. See the section titled "Configuring IIS to Coexist with Apache HTTP Server" later in this chapter.

After a few moments a splash screen is displayed.

Read the instructions on the Welcome Screen and then press Next.

This displays the license screen. Read the license agreement, select "I accept the terms in the license agreement," and press Next.

A screen is displayed titled Read This First. Read the notes before installing Apache and press Next to continue.

The next screen gathers information about your server. Enter the network domain, and the fully qualified server name. Also enter the e-mail address of the server administrator. It is recommended that the Apache HTTP server is run on port 80 so select: "for All Users, on Port 80, as a Service" and press Next.

The next screen describes the setup type for the installation. Select Typical and press Next.

The next step is to configure the destination folder. Press Change to change the current destination folder to `C:\` as shown in Figure 15-20, and press OK, then press Next to proceed. This installs the Apache HTTP server in the folder `C:\Apache2`, which simplifies the path and reduces the likelihood of unusual behavior.

Apache2 is now ready to install. Press Install to proceed.

The installer proceeds to copy all the required files to `c:\Apache2` and subdirectories, as shown in Figure 15-21:

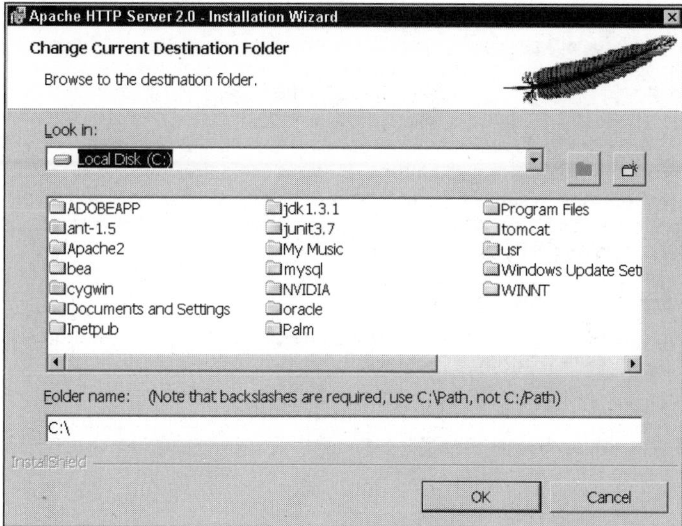

Figure 15-20: Change the destination folder.

During the installation process some console windows are opened by the installer when starting up the Apache service; these should then disappear.

The next screen indicates that the installation has completed. Press Finish to exit.

You now see an Apache Service Monitor in the system tray. The monitor can be used to start and stop the Apache HTTP service.

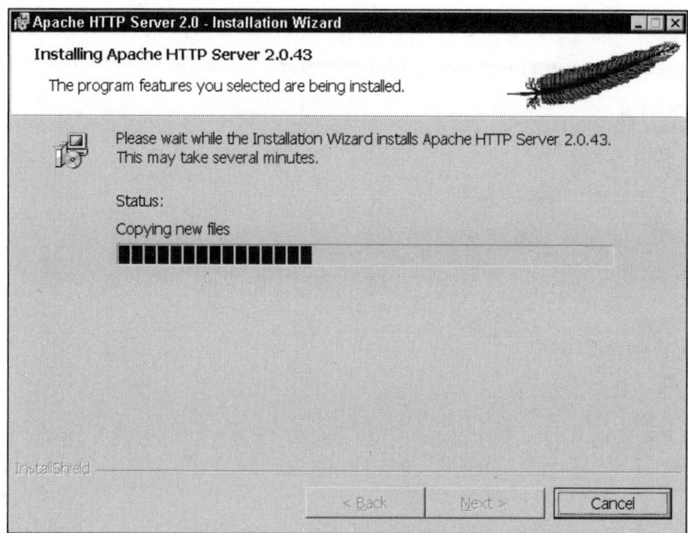

Figure 15-21: Apache HTTP server installation process

Configuring IIS to Coexist with Apache HTTP Server

Internet Information Services (IIS) is Microsoft's built-in Web server. Depending on your Windows installation, IIS may be enabled by default. IIS, if enabled, will be listening for connections on port 80, the well-known HTTP port. You can run into trouble if you prefer to use the Apache HTTP server on this machine because two processes cannot listen on the same port. To workaround this problem there are two options; disable IIS and run Apache on port 80, or alternatively, IIS can be configured to listen on a non-standard port. How you choose to configure IIS depends on your need to run IIS side-by-side with the Apache HTTP server.

Disable Internet Information Services (IIS)

To disable IIS, perform the following steps. After the process has been completed, the IIS service is stopped, and will not be started-up automatically with Windows.

1. Open the Control Panel.
2. Open the Administrative Tools folder.
3. Start the Services application.
4. Double-click the IIS Admin Service and select Startup type: Disabled. This prevents IIS from starting when Windows starts up.
5. If the Service status is Started, click Stop to stop the currently running instance of IIS.

To enable the IIS service at a laterdate, ensure the Apache HTTP server is no longer running and repeat the preceding process with the following exceptions; in Step 4, instead of selecting Disabled, select Manual or Automatic"from the Startup type: drop-down list. In Step 5, click Start to start the IIS service.

Configure IIS to Listen on a Non-Standard Port

Alternatively, if you must run IIS alongside Apache HTTP Server, or another Web server for that matter, you can change the configuration and have IIS listen on a non-standard port. To re-configure IIS to run on a different port, implement the following steps .

1. Open the Control Panel.
2. Open the Administrative Tools folder.
3. Start the Internet Services Manager.
4. Left-click the Default Web Site and select Properties from the pop-up menu.
5. Change the TCP port from 80 to an unused port greater than 1024. Port number 9080 is used for example.
6. Press OK to apply the changes.
7. Close the Internet Services Manager.

You can test that IIS is listening on the designated port by typing the URL, including the port number, into your favorite browser (for example `http://localhost:9080/`).

Testing

Using the Apache Service Monitor, ensure the Apache service status shows a green icon.

If the service status is red, press Start to start the service.

To ensure that the server is correctly working, open a browser and type in the URL, `http://localhost/` and a screen resembling Figure 15-22 should be displayed.

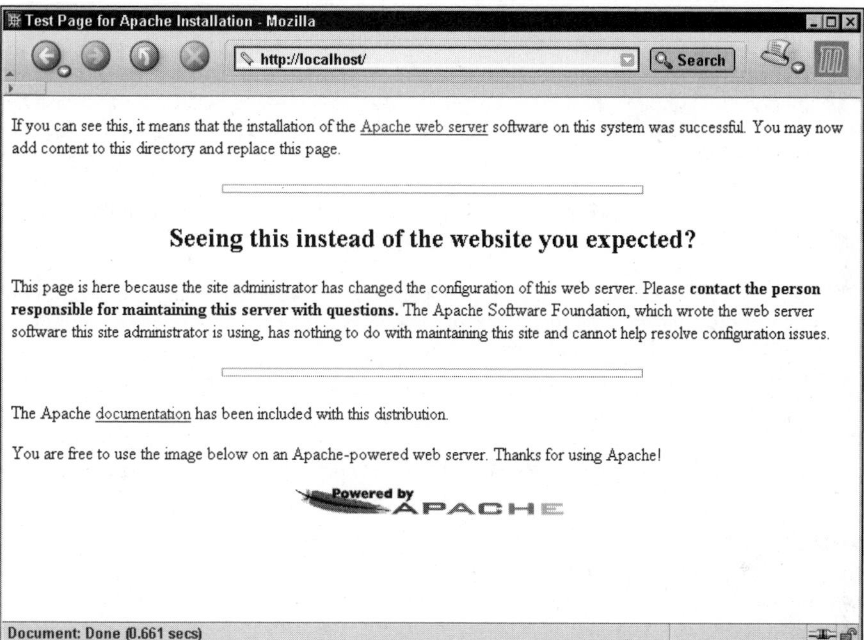

Figure 15-22: Expected result after successful installation of the Apache HTTP Server

Post Install

After the Apache HTTP server has been installed, you can find the configuration file in `C:\Apache2\conf\httpd.conf`. The Configuration section later in the chapter explains exactly how the Apache configuration needs to be modified.

Apache writes all log output to files in the `C:\Apache2\logs` directory. Of note is the `access.log` file and the `error.log` file that records page accesses and server output respectively.

JK2

JK2 is a plug-in module that redirects requests from the Apache HTTP Server to Tomcat.

Download

The latest version of the JK2 DLL can be found at `http://jakarta.apache.org/builds/jakarta-tomcat-connectors/jk2/release/v2.0.1/bin/win32/`.

Select: `mod_jk2-2.0.43.dll` and when prompted, save the file to disk.

There is no easy way to navigate to this download directory from the Jakarta site! You are required to manually enter the URL into the address bar of your favorite browser.

The 2.0.1 release of JK2 was built under Windows 2000 and 2.0.43, it is therefore recommended for Windows 2000 users. The newer 2.0.2 release was built under Windows XP and IIS 5.1 and although it still may work under Windows 2000 it is best suited to users running Windows XP.

There are many files in this directory, one for connecting Tomcat with each Web server. `mod_jk2-2.0.43.dll` is for Apache 2.0.43 (and only 2.0.43).

You can build the source to suit your particular environment using the Jakarta-tomcat-connectors source distribution available from `http://jakarta.apache.org/builds/jakarta-tomcat-connectors/jk2/release/v2.0.1/src/`.

You must download the version of the DLL corresponding to your version of the Apache HTTP server for the module to work. If there is no binary distribution available for your version of Apache, you need to download the source distribution and compile manually.

Installation

The JK2 plug-in module is a lot simpler to install than its IIS counterpart. The process is outlined below.

1. Stop the Apache server.
2. Copy the downloaded file to `C:\Apache2\modules\mod_jk2.dll`.
3. Configure Apache to load the Tomcat-Apache plug-in module, making it available when Apache starts.
4. Add the following statement to the end of the Dynamic Shared Object (DSO) Support section of your `C:\Apache2\conf\httpd.conf` file (approx line 173).

   ```
   LoadModule jk2_module modules/mod_jk2.dll
   ```

5. Start the apache server.

Post Installation

The Apache JK2 module looks for configuration files underneath the Apache home directory `C:\Apache2`. JK2 relies on a `workers2.properties` file that must be created in the `C:\Apache2\conf` directory. The following Configuration section explains the contents of this file.

JK2 configuration is specified using the `workers2.properties` file. However, JK2 can also be configured inside the Apache configuration file `httpd.conf`. The use of the Apache configuration is not covered because of the lack of user documentation, and to keep a level of consistency with the Tomcat-IIS configuration. Some users will, however, prefer to have all their Web server configuration located in the single file. Unfortunately, they will need to reference the JK2 source code for details regarding the accepted configuration parameters.

Configuration

The `workers2.properties` file describes the host(s) and port(s) used by the workers (Tomcat processes), and the patterns that are used to match URI requests to workers.

This chapter does not cover the auto-configure feature provided by Tomcat because auto-configuration is limited to Tomcat and Web servers residing on the same machine, and does not support load balancing and clustering a group of Tomcat servers. Additionally, at the time of writing, the autoconfigure feature for JK2 suffered from poor documentation, and was not as widely supported as auto-generated configuration for JK.

In the `C:\tomcat\conf\` directory, create a new file named `workers2.properties` containing the Listings 15-9 through 15-13.

Detailed configuration information of the workers2.properties configuration may be found at `http://jakarta.apache.org/tomcat/tomcat-4.1-doc/jk2/jk2/configweb.html`.

Logger

By default, the ISAPI redirector plug-in logs to the Windows application event log. However, viewing the output of the Event Log can be frustrating at times. For the purposes of this example, the default logger is overridden in Listing 15-9 to log output to the text file `C:/tomcat/logs/apache_jk2.log`.

Listing 15-9: workers2.properties (Logger Configuration)

```
[logger.file:0]
level=INFO
file=C:/tomcat/logs/apache_jk2.log
```

Shared Memory

A shared memory file is required for reconfiguration and status with multiprocess servers. Listing 15-10 declares the location and suggested size of the file.

Listing 15-10: workers2.properties (Shared Memory Configuration)

```
[shm:]
info=Shared memory file. Required for multiprocess servers
file=c:/tomcat/work/jk2.shm
size=1000000
```

Channel

The channel defines the communication method used to communicate to the Tomcat worker. For the Windows platform Listing 15-11 shows the use of TCP sockets to connect to each Tomcat process.

Listing 15-11: workers2.properties (Channel Configuration)

```
[channel.socket:localhost:8009]
info=Forwarding over socket connection to local tomcat instance.
host=localhost
port=8009
```

Worker

A worker describes the host and port the Tomcat process is listening on. Listing 15-12 uses the AJP 13 protocol over the TCP socket channel to send redirected requests to the Tomcat process.

Listing 15-12: workers2.properties (AJP13 Worker Configuration)

```
[ajp13:localhost:8009]
info=Ajp13 worker, connects to tomcat instance using AJP 1.3 protocol.
channel=channel.socket:localhost:8009
```

URI Mapper

The URI entries map incoming requests to workers. The configuration in Listing 15-13 maps all requests for JSP and servlet examples to the Tomcat workers. Wildcards may be used as part of the URI mapping to specify a group of resources to map. Additionally, a port number may be specified at the end of the URI map to redirect requests to virtual hosts running on different ports.

By default, all channels and associated workers run in the `lb:0` group. If left unspecified, URI mappers also default to the `lb:0` group. Therefore the URI mappers specified for the following JSP and servlet examples correspond to the AJP 13 worker running on `localhost:8009`.

Listing 15-13: workers2.properties (URI Mapping Configuration)

```
[uri:/examples/jsp/*.jsp]
info=JSP examples, map requests for all JSP pages to Tomcat.
context=/examples/jsp

[uri:/examples/servlet/*]
info=Servlet examples, map requests for all servlets to Tomcat.
context=/examples/servlet
```

Tomcat

Tomcat must be configured with a connector to listen for redirected requests from the Apache HTTP server. This requires the configuration of the JK2 plug-in module filter before the separation of static and dynamic content over Apache and Tomcat servers respectively, can be tested.

Configuration

The following configuration is for the Tomcat JK2 Connector, and an example servlet context used for testing.

Coyote JK2 Connector Configuration

The JK2 Connector configuration is located under the Tomcat home at `C:\tomcat\conf\jk2.properties`. The contents of this file are not essential to get the connector up-and-running, because the default values used by the Connector suits most configurations. The file can, however, be used to override the connector configuration to suit custom installations.

Listing 15-14 shows a JK2 configuration example explicitly defining `channelSocket.port`; the port number the connector listens on for socket connections. If it is not declared, the default port 8009 is assumed.

The `shm.file` declaration is also used to defines a shared memory file that is used by multi-process servers.

Tip Even though this may not be used with single process servers, the following declaration avoids JK2, logging a warning on startup.

Listing 15-14: jk2.properties (Shared Memory Configuration)

```
channelSocket.port=8009
shm.file=c:/tomcat/work/jk2.shm
```

Tomcat Connector Configuration

The Tomcat configuration file, `server.xml`, has been described in detail as part of Chapter 8. The standard Tomcat `4.1.12` installation enables the Coyote JK2 connector by default. This connector accepts incoming requests conforming to the AJP 13 protocol on port `8009`. Ensure your Tomcat configuration has the configuration shown in Listing 15-15 enabled to allow the JK2 plug-in channels to connect to the Tomcat workers.

Listing 15-15: Server.xml (Coyote JK2 Connector Configuration)

```
<!-- Define a Coyote/JK2 AJP 1.3 Connector on port 8009 -->
<Connector className="org.apache.coyote.tomcat4.CoyoteConnector"
           port="8009" minProcessors="5" maxProcessors="75"
           enableLookups="true" redirectPort="8443"
           acceptCount="10" debug="0" connectionTimeout="20000"
           useURIValidationHack="false"
           protocolHandlerClassName="org.apache.jk.server.JkCoyoteHandler"
           />
```

Tomcat Examples Context Configuration

For the purposes of this example it is necessary that the example JSP and servlet contexts are enabled. Listing 15-16 shows the default examples context configured by Tomcat during installation. If the examples context has been removed the contents of the listing are required in `server.xml` to enable the following tests to complete successfully:

Listing 15-16: server.xml (Tomcat Example Context Configuration)

```
<!-- Tomcat Examples Context -->
<Context path="/examples" docBase="examples" debug="0"
         reloadable="true" crossContext="true">
  <Logger className="org.apache.catalina.logger.FileLogger"
             prefix="localhost_examples_log." suffix=".txt"
      timestamp="true"/>
  <Ejb   name="ejb/EmplRecord" type="Entity"
         home="com.wombat.empl.EmployeeRecordHome"
       remote="com.wombat.empl.EmployeeRecord"/>

  <Environment name="maxExemptions" type="java.lang.Integer"
              value="15"/>
  <Parameter name="context.param.name" value="context.param.value"
             override="false"/>
  <Resource name="jdbc/EmployeeAppDb" auth="SERVLET"
            type="javax.sql.DataSource"/>
  <ResourceParams name="jdbc/EmployeeAppDb">
    <parameter><name>user</name><value>sa</value></parameter>
    <parameter><name>password</name><value></value></parameter>
    <parameter><name>driverClassName</name>
      <value>org.hsql.jdbcDriver</value></parameter>
    <parameter><name>driverName</name>
```

```
    <value>jdbc:HypersonicSQL:database</value></parameter>
  </ResourceParams>
  <Resource name="mail/Session" auth="Container"
            type="javax.mail.Session"/>
  <ResourceParams name="mail/Session">
    <parameter>
      <name>mail.smtp.host</name>
      <value>localhost</value>
    </parameter>
  </ResourceParams>
  <ResourceLink name="linkToGlobalResource"
            global="simpleValue"
            type="java.lang.Integer"/>
</Context>
```

Testing

For the purposes of testing the Tomcat-Apache configuration we are going to split the JSP and servlet examples, which are installed with Tomcat, into dynamic and static content. The dynamic content will be hosted on Tomcat, and the static content will be hosted on the Apache HTTP server. The following test steps assume that the previous configuration has been applied to both the Apache and Tomcat servers.

1. Stop the Tomcat server.
2. Stop the Apache server.
3. Copy the existing examples folder `C:\tomcat\webapps\examples` to `C:\tomcat\webapps\examples.old` for safekeeping.
4. Create a new folder `C:\Apache2\htdocs\examples`. This creates an examples context available from Apache.
5. Move the folders `C:\tomcat\webapps\examples\images` and `C:\tomcat\webapps\examples\servlets` to `C:\Apache2\htdocs\examples`. Images and servlet resources are only required on the Web server, therefore they are moved from the Tomcat document root.

Note The `servlets` directory does not actually contain any servlets, it only contains static HTML.

6. Copy the folder `C:\tomcat\webapps\examples\jsp` to `C:\Apache2\htdocs\examples`. Both the Tomcat and Web server require the contents of the `jsp` directory, hence it is replicated under both document roots. Redundant files are removed from each server in the next step.
7. Remove all static files from the `C:\tomcat\webapps\examples\jsp` folder. This proves without doubt that the static content is served from the Web server.

Caution Do not remove the files `carts.html` and `error.html`; they are included by JSP pages at runtime.

You may want to search for `*.html` and `*.txt` in `C:\tomcat\webapps\examples\jsp` and delete search results.

8. Remove all `.jsp` files from the `C:\Apache2\htdocs\examples\jsp` folder. If the redirection to Tomcat is not working, the user will see a HTTP 404 error because the file cannot be found on the Web server.

You may want to search for `*.jsp` in `C:\Apache2\htdocs\examples\jsp` and delete search results.

9. Start the Tomcat server.
10. Start the Apache server.
11. Open URL `http://localhost/examples/jsp/`. You should see the screen shown in Figure 15-23, and the examples should function as normal.
12. Open URL `http://localhost/examples/Servlets/`. You should see the screen shown in Figure 15-24, and the examples should function as normal.
13. Open the log file `C:/tomcat/logs/apache_jk2.log`, and look for any errors that may have occurred during the test

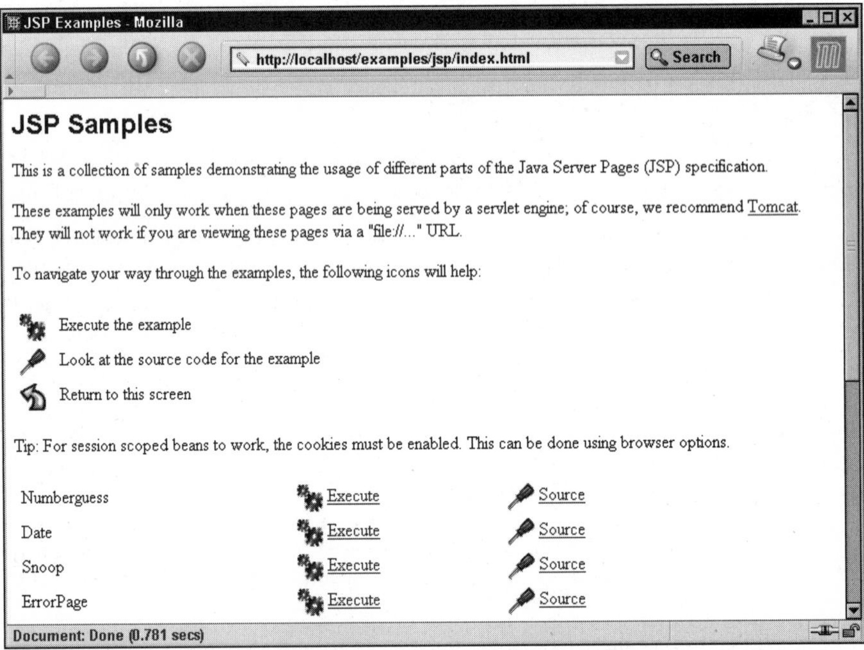

Figure 15-23: JSP test expected results

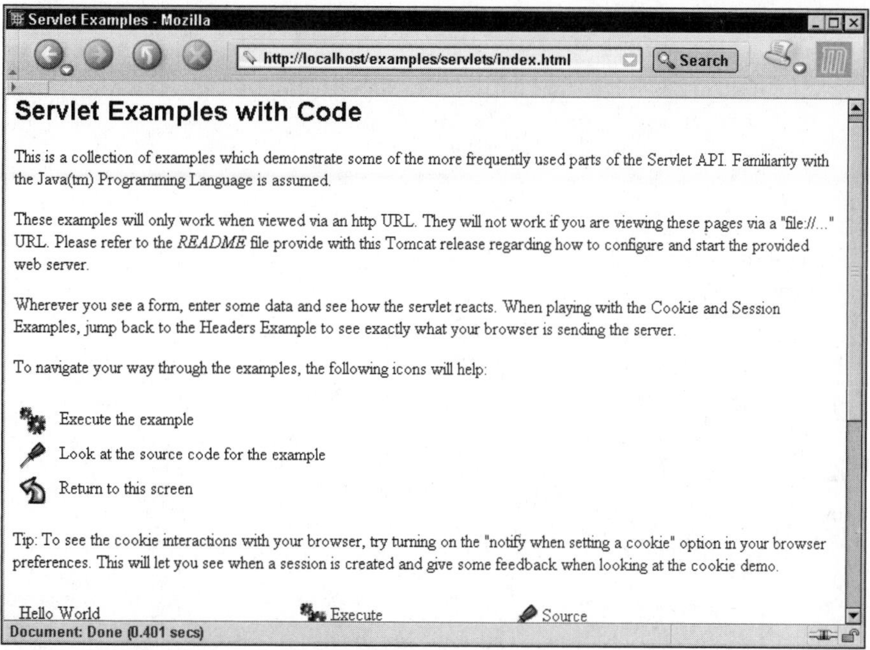

Figure 15-24: Servlet test expected results

Running Tomcat In-process with the Apache HTTP Server

If the Tomcat and Apache HTTP servers are running on the same machine, it is possible to run the Tomcat server in the same process space as the Apache HTTP server. The following configuration explains how this is achieved.

Apache Configuration

To run the Tomcat server in the same process space as Apache, the Tomcat and Apache configuration files must be modified to define a common shared memory file. The following configuration must be added to the `workers2.properties` file:

```
[shm:]
    info=Shared memory file. Required for reconfiguration \
         and status with multi-process servers
    file=c:/tomcat/work/jk2.shm
    size=1000000
```

In addition, for Apache to startup and shutdown the Tomcat server the Apache configuration must define the parameters for the Virtual Machine used to start the in-process container. Also, JNI channels, and associated workers, need to be defined to startup and shutdown the Tomcat container.

```
[vm:]
    info=Parameters used to load a JVM in the server process
    OPT=-Djava.class.path=c:/tomcat/bin/tomcat/jni.jar;\
```

Continued

Continued

```
        c:/tomcat/server/lib/commons-logging.jar
    OPT=-Dtomcat.home=${CATALINA_HOME}
    OPT=-Dcatalina.home=${CATALINA_HOME}
    OPT=-Xmx128M

[channel.jni:jni]
    info=The jni channel, used if tomcat is started inprocess

[worker.jni:onStartup]
    info=Command to be executed by the VM on startup.
    class=org/apache/jk/apr/TomcatStarter
    ARG=start
    stdout=c:/tomcat/logs/jk.log
    stderr=c:/tomcat/logs/jk.log

[worker.jni:onShutdown]
    info=Command to be executed by the VM on shutdown.
    class=org/apache/jk/apr/TomcatStarter
    ARG=stop
```

Tomcat Configuration

For Tomcat to use the same shared memory file defined by the Apache configuration, the following property must be added to the jk2.properties file:

```
shm.file=c:/tomcat/work/jk2.shm
```

Testing

To test the in-process server is operational we will start the Apache server only. If the configuration is correct, both Apache and Tomcat services should be available.

Note: This configuration assumes the previous configuration has been applied to both the Tomcat and Apache servers and that the JSP and servlet example Web application has been split into static and dynamic content (as per the previous section).

Stop Tomcat server (if running).

Stop Apache server.

Start the Apache server; this should start the Tomcat server in-process upon the first request for dynamic content.

Open URL `http://localhost/examples/jsp/`. You should see a screen similar to that seen previously in Figure 15-23. The examples should function as normal.

Open URL `http://localhost/examples/Servlets/`. You should see a screen similar to that seen previously in Figure 15-24. The examples should function as normal.

The Tomcat server is now running in-process with the Apache HTTP server. This configuration simplifies the Windows 2000 startup process as it is only necessary to start Apache as a service, and automatically Tomcat will also be available.

Tomcat and the Apache HTTP Server on Linux

Although this book focuses on installing and configuring Tomcat on a Windows platform, you may be required to connect Tomcat with an Apache HTTP server running on a Unix server. Fortunately, the configuration of the Apache HTTP server does not differ greatly between the Windows and Unix platforms. In the following section the process of connecting an Apache HTTP server running on Linux with a Tomcat server running on Windows 2000 using the JK2 connector is demonstrated.

This section assumes you are familiar with the Linux environment, and are capable of installing RedHat Package Manager (RPM) distributions, or compiling source distributions if necessary. All commands listed assume they are being executed as the root user.

Apache HTTP Server

The following section assumes you have Apache 2.0.43 installed on a Linux server. If you need to upgrade your existing Apache installation search for pre-packaged RPM file from `http://rpmfind.net/linux/RPM/`. Otherwise download and compile the source code from `http://httpd.apache.org/`.

It is also assumed that the Linux Apache host is named `www`. Please replace this hostname with the actual hostname or IP address throughout the following instructions.

JK2 Download

The JK2 module for apache is distributed as a pre-compiled shared object library, or as a source distribution.

The latest version of the JK2 shared object library can be found at `http://jakarta.apache.org/builds/jakarta-tomcat-connectors/jk2/release/v2.0.1/bin/linux/i386/`

There are many files in this directory, one for connecting Tomcat with each Web server. `mod_jk2-2.0.43.so` is for Apache 2.0.43 (and only 2.0.43). Select `mod_jk2-2.0.43.so` and when prompted save the file to disk.

If there is no binary distribution to suit your version of Apache you may be required to download and build the source code from `http://jakarta.apache.org/builds/jakarta-tomcat-connectors/jk2/release/v2.0.1/src/`.

JK2 Installation

Once the JK2 module shared object library has been downloaded, or built manually, copy the file to the Apache modules directory `/etc/httpd2/modules/` using the following command.

```
$ cp mod_jk2-2.0.43.so /etc/httpd2/modules/
```

It pays to make sure the module has the correct permissions by issuing the following command.

```
$ chmod 755 /etc/httpd2/modules/mod_jk2-2.0.43.so
```

Add the following statement to the end of the Dynamic Shared Object (DSO) Support section of your `/etc/httpd2/conf/httpd2.conf` file.

```
$ LoadModule jk2_module modules/mod_jk2-2.0.43.so
```

JK2 is now installed, wait until JK2 has been configured before restarting the Apache HTTP server.

Continued

Continued

JK2 Configuration

Create the JK2 configuration file in `/etc/httpd2/conf/workers2.properties` containing the following listing. Note, the hostname of the remote Tomcat server is assumed to be `tomcat1`. Replace this with the hostname or IP address of your remote Tomcat server.

```
[logger.file:0]
level=INFO
file=/etc/httpd2/logs/apache_jk2.log

[shm:]
info=Shared memory file. Required for reconfiguration and \
     status with multiprocess servers
file=/tmp/jk2.shm
size=1000000

[channel.socket:tomcat1:8009]
info=Forwarding over socket connection to local tomcat instance.
host=tomcat1
port=8009

[ajp13:tomcat1:8009]
info=Ajp13 worker, connects to tomcat instance using AJP 1.3 protocol.
channel=channel.socket:tomcat1:8009

[uri:/examples/jsp/*.jsp]
info=JSP examples, map requests for all JSP pages to Tomcat.
context=/examples/jsp

[uri:/examples/servlet/*]
info=Servlet examples, map requests for all Servlets to Tomcat.
context=/examples/servlet
```

JK2 has now been installed and configured to redirect requests for all dynamic content for the JSP and servlet examples to the Tomcat server. Restart the Apache HTTP server using the System V style startup script for the configuration changes to take effect.

```
$ /etc/rc.d/init.d/httpd2 restart
```

Or, directly using the Apache HTTP server control interface.

```
$ /usr/sbin/apachectl2 restart
```

Tomcat

The Tomcat server is assumed to be set up and running on a Windows 2000 server. Please follow the instructions in Chapter 2 to install the Tomcat server, and configure the Tomcat server according to the section titled "Tomcat and the Apache HTTP Server" in this chapter before proceeding.

Testing

Again to test communication between the Apache and Tomcat servers the JSP and servlet example is used. Copy the contents of the `C:\tomcat\webapps\examples` directory onto the Linux server, the following procedure will outline how to install the static content into the Linux Apache HTTP server document root.

1. Stop the Apache server.

```
$ /etc/rc.d/init.d/httpd2 stop
```

2. Create a new examples directory under the Apache document root.

```
$ mkdir /var/www2/html/examples
```

3. Copy the directories `examples/images` and `examples/servlets` from the copy of the Tomcat examples directory to the Apache document root `/var/www2/html/examples`. Images and servlet resources are only required on the Web server, they should also be removed from the Tomcat document root.

```
$ cp -R examples/images /var/www2/html/examples/
$ cp -R examples/servlets /var/www2/html/examples/
```

4. Copy the folder `examples/jsp` to `/var/www2/html/examples`. Both the Tomcat and Web server require the contents of the `jsp` directory, hence it is replicated under both document roots. Redundant files are removed from each server in the next step.

```
$ cp -R examples/jsp /var/www2/html/examples/
```

5. Remove all `.jsp` files from the `/var/www2/html/examples` directory. If the redirection to Tomcat is not working, the user will see a HTTP 404 error because the file cannot be found on the Web server

```
$ rm -f `find /var/www2/html/examples -name *.jsp`
```

6. Make sure all the static example content has the correct file permissions.

```
$ chmod -R 755 `find /var/www2/html/examples/ -type d`
$ chmod -R 644 `find /var/www2/html/examples/ -type f`
```

7. Start the Tomcat server on the Windows 2000 box.

8. Start the Linux Apache server.

```
$ /etc/rc.d/init.d/httpd2 start
```

9. Open URL `www/examples/jsp/`. You should see roughly the same screen shown previously in Figure 15-23, and the examples should function as normal.

10. Open URL `www/examples/Servlets/`. You should see roughly the same screen shown previously in Figure 15-24, and the examples should function as normal.

11. Open the log file `/etc/httpd2/logs/apache_jk2.log`, and look for any errors that may have occurred during the test

If no errors are displayed in the JK2 log file and the JSP and servlet examples work as advertised, you are finished. Good work, now go have a cup of tea.

Summary

At the conclusion of this chapter you should understand the fundamentals of connecting Tomcat to a Web server using the JK2 Jakarta Tomcat Connector. In addition, given the rationale behind deploying separate parts of your Web application to dedicated servers, you should have a feeling of whether or not your particular application fits the profile warranting the use of Tomcat with a Web server. If your application does fit the profile, redeploying the example JSP and servlet applications across Tomcat and a Web server will give you a good starting point to splitting your application into static and dynamic parts, and deploying each on the appropriate server. If, on the other hand, you decide not to split your application up, you should have enough ammunition to have your manager or systems administrator exempting your Web application from any organizational policies mandating all traffic be redirected through a Web server.

The next chapter explores Tomcat/Web server connectivity by introducing load balancing and clustering with the aid of the Apache HTTP server.

✦ ✦ ✦

CHAPTER 16

Load Balancing and Clustering

In This Chapter

This chapter builds on the knowledge gained in Chapter 15, expanding that to create a group of Tomcat servers managed and directed by a Web server, effectively creating a Tomcat cluster.

During the course of this chapter, the fundamental concepts behind clustering are presented, including different types of fail-over and load balancing. Afterwards a how-to guide explains the process of building your own cluster using multiple Tomcat nodes managed by an Apache HTTP server.

This chapter is intended to be a guide for developers and systems administrators who need to increase the availability, reliability, and scalability of their Tomcat Web applications.

What Is Clustering?

A *cluster* is a group of servers used to provide a unified application or service. Clusters are typically used for large-scale systems requiring high availability, reliability, and scalability.

Availability describes whether or not the application is available, so high availability suggests that the application can still serve clients even under peak server load, and can withstand hardware or software failures.

Reliability is not just a matter of being operational or not, it is a measure of how reliably a server can fulfill requests within a given response interval. If, under peak loads, a server fails to respond in adequate time, it is deemed unreliable. A reliable system can respond to requests under varying loads, always within the given response time limits.

Scalability is the ability to increase or decrease the processing capabilities of the system to meet service demands. Typically systems are scaled up, increasing the number of machines in a cluster to meet the availability and reliability requirements of the service.

Server Farms

A cluster consists of a collection of two or more servers, or nodes, in a loosely coupled group. A group of servers is often called a *farm*, or a *server farm*.

Nodes are connected via a high-speed Local Area Network (LAN) to reduce the overhead of running a distributed application. Obviously a high-speed LAN never has the same level of performance as an application running in a single server, but a single server cannot provide the a level of availability required in large-scale systems.

A cluster normally has a single point of entry into the system. This can be a dedicated load balancer or a Web server, referred to as a *director*. Requests are distributed by the director to individual nodes in the cluster.

Figure 16-1 shows a clustered configuration of six servers with a single director, farming requests to the group.

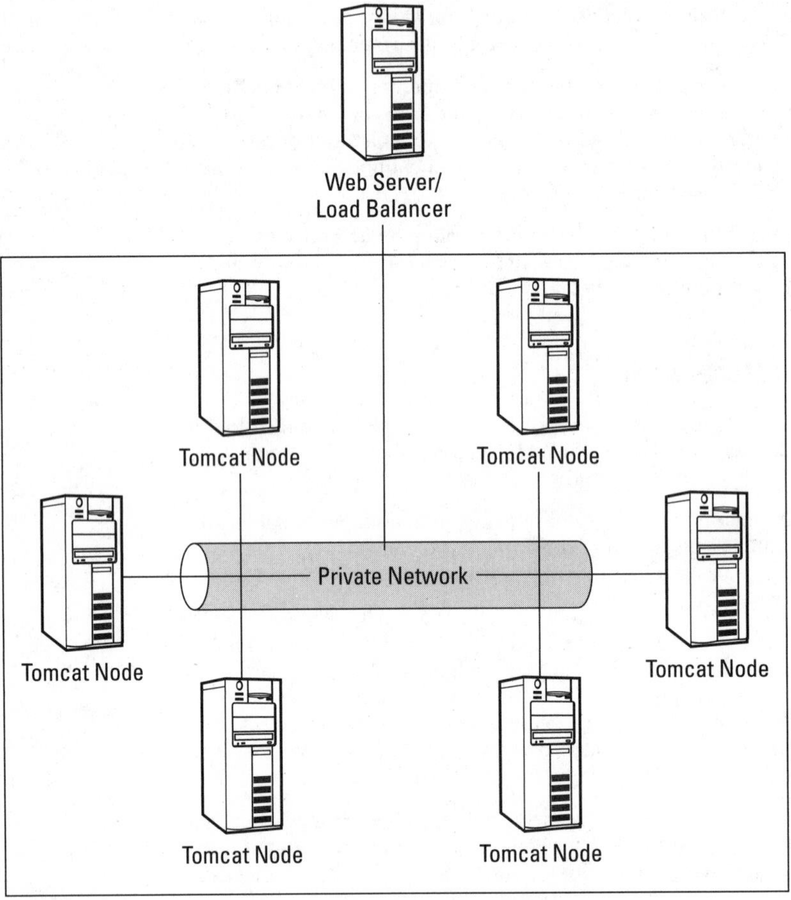

Figure 16-1: Cluster of Tomcat nodes load balanced via a Web server

Fail-Over

Fail-over describes the ability to cope with hardware or software failures by redirecting failed requests to an operational server. The cluster's director is responsible for controlling fail-over to operational servers. This may be achieved by monitoring the reliability of nodes in the cluster, and rerouting incoming requests away from servers that cannot respond within an acceptable time period. At scheduled intervals the director may probe nodes on the cluster to gauge their reliability.

Fail-over can occur on a number of levels, namely request-level and session-level, both of which are explained in the following sections.

Request-Level Fail-Over

Request- level fail-over increases the availability of a system by rerouting incoming requests to an operational server. This enables a level of redundancy provided by other nodes in the cluster; if one node fails another can process its requests.

Additionally, requests that are part of a session may be sent to the node they were serviced by originally, providing sticky sessions. Sticky sessions are typically provided by a load balancer and are explained later. Although, request-level fail-over can almost guarantee the ability to service an individual request, it cannot guarantee the ability to service an entire session made up of multiple requests.

Automatic Session Fail-Over

Automatic session fail-over enables the system to recover from server failure, retaining session information associated with the client request. If a node fails, requests are rerouted to another node in the cluster where the client's session information is replicated. Automatic session fail-over increases the serviceability of session-based transactions.

To support automatic session fail-over, clusters use a technique called *session replication*. By replicating the session information across the cluster each node knows the session information stored on all the other nodes, hence the cluster can be said to have *session affinity*.

Session replication, or session affinity, can be achieved in two ways, broadcasting the session information so all nodes have a copy of the complete set of session data, or, alternatively a single master server stores the complete set of session information and is queried in the event of a failure to provide the rerouted requests with their appropriate session details. Obviously a redundant master server is also required to avoid a single point of failure in the system.

Caution Broadcasting session messages to an entire cluster can have dramatic effects on performance, especially if there are large amounts of information being written to the session, and many nodes in the cluster. It is therefore important to keep the number of nodes in a session-aware cluster to a minimum, and to put data in the session only when absolutely necessary.

The net effect is the ability for session-based requests to be rerouted to another server in the middle of a session, and continue to be serviced without interruption.

Load Balancing

In a single server scenario it is possible that incoming requests cannot be processed quickly enough, resulting in a request backlog and eventually a loss of service to some customers. *Load balancing* attempts to increase the reliability of a system by farming the incoming requests off to nodes within the cluster. In this way, the cluster can share the load on the system as a whole.

Load balancers distribute this load according to an algorithm. This algorithm may be systematic; such as round-robin scheduling, distribution based on server load, distribution based on response time; or even random.

Load balancers can also provide sticky session functionality in which sessions are tagged with a node identifier, and any subsequent requests as part of that session bypass the balancing algorithm and go straight to the node that originally fulfilled the request.

Obviously, the use of sticky sessions reduces the effectiveness of the load balancing algorithm, further exemplifying the importance of keeping session usage at a minimum across the application.

Simple Tomcat Cluster

To begin with, a very simple Tomcat cluster is created. This cluster does not feature any degree of fail-over or load balancing; it simply shows how a group of servers can be used to provide a unified service.

Several examples are used during the course of this chapter to demonstrate the capabilities of a cluster of Tomcat servers. All examples in this chapter are built on a simple network architecture consisting of a Web server and two Tomcat servers, or nodes. The Web server is a single point of access into the cluster.

During the course of this chapter the cluster created in this section is extended to support more sophisticated features such as load balancing, fail-over, and session replication. Therefore, it is essential that the following installation and configuration steps are followed, to create a foundation on which the cluster will be constructed.

A typical scenario for simple clustering involves a Web-based application that is composed of two sub-systems that have vastly different processing profiles. The sub-systems are distributed over two machines. One machine is tuned to provide extremely fast file IO, like that required by a database server. The other server is more suited to intensive processing tasks, for example public/private key generation. If the components were distributed over identical hardware, the application would be unable to meet tight performance and reliability constraints due to a compromise between processing power and file IO. Therefore, specialized hardware is necessary for each sub-system, but it is desirable to have a single point of entry to the entire application.

Simple clustering meets the requirements of the previous scenario by allowing a single access point to the cluster via the Web server. The Web server can then forward requests for each sub-system to a dedicated node on the cluster.

Prerequisites

Clustering relies Tomcat Apache HTTP server configuration described in Chapter 15. Before proceeding you must be able to set up the Apache HTTP server with Tomcat using JK2.

Installation

To demonstrate a simple cluster it is necessary to set up a group of at least two Tomcat servers, and a single Web server. Figure 16-2 shows a Tomcat cluster running on two separate machines, coupled with a Web server on a third machine.

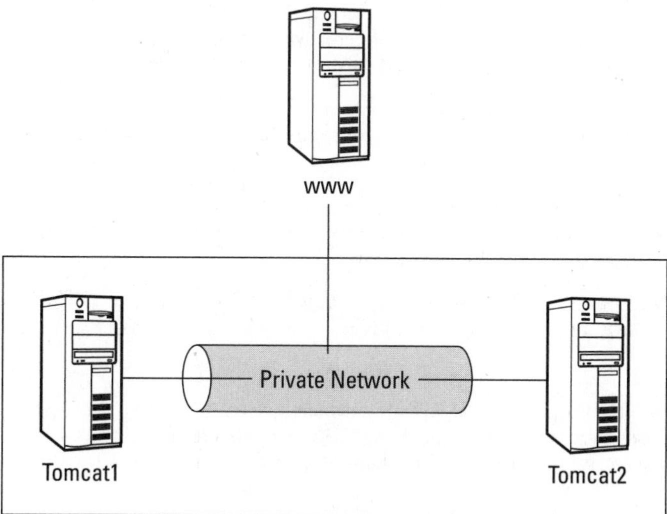

Figure 16-2: Simple Tomcat cluster containing two Tomcat nodes and a Web server

For the purpose of this chapter, it is recommended that the cluster be installed over at least two, preferably three machines. It is possible to install all three servers on a single machine by running multiple instances of Tomcat on the same server, however to adequately test session replication over the cluster using IP muticasting it is preferable to run separate servers over a network.

The following matrix in Table 16-1 outlines the possible server configurations that can be used for the cluster architecture shown in Figure 16-2.

Table 16-1: Server Configuration Matrix

Number of Machines	Web Server (WWW)	Tomcat Server (TOMCAT1)	Tomcat Server (TOMCAT2)
3	Machine 1	Machine 2	Machine 3
2	Machine 1	Machine 1	Machine 2
1	Machine 1	Machine 1	Machine 1

For the remainder of the chapter, the servers are referred to as `WWW`, `TOMCAT1`, and `TOMCAT2`. You now need to install and configure the servers according to the specified network architecture. The number of machines you have available, determines the server configuration you should use.

Install Tomcat 4.1.12 on the first Tomcat server in your cluster. This node is known as `TOMCAT1`. See Chapter 2 for detailed instructions on installing Tomcat.

Install a second Tomcat instance on the second node in the cluster, `TOMCAT2`. If two Tomcat servers are required to co-exist on a single machine see the section in Chapter 8 regarding the configuration of multiple instances of Tomcat.

Install the Apache HTTP server on the host `WWW`. See Tomcat and the Apache HTTP Server in Chapter 15 for an explanation of how to install and configure the Apache HTTP Server with Tomcat.

Caution Clustering does not function on IIS with JK2. Unfortunately, the `isapi_redirector2.dll` plug-in for IIS causes internal server errors when URI requests are mapped to a load balanced group of servers. All examples in this chapter rely on the Apache HTTP server.

Connect all three servers to an internal network.

Configure the Web server `WWW` so incoming requests are redirected to the Tomcat server `TOMCAT1`. Proceed to the simple cluster configuration once connectivity between `WWW` and `TOMCAT1` has been confirmed.

Configuration

The following configuration provides you with a complete configuration to set up a simple tomcat cluster. It does however assume you know to configure the Apache HTTP Server to communicate with Tomcat, and have installed the JK2 module on the Web server.

First it is necessary to declare the JK2 connector configuration. The contents in Listing 16-1 explicitly define the default port the AJP13 Connector listens on. Although the `channelSocket.port` property is optional, it is explicitly defined as 8009; the default value. The `jk2.properties` file must be present in `C:\tomcat\conf` regardless of whether or not any properties are defined.

Listing 16-1: jk2.properties

```
channelSocket.port=8009
```

Listing 16-2 lists the configuration for the first Tomcat node in the cluster. No specific clustering configuration is contained in this file for a simple cluster. We will investigate more complex Tomcat configurations later in the chapter. Special points of interest in the configuration file include the naming of the default virtual host. Hostnames consistent with the cluster Installation section are used throughout this chapter. In this case the first node in the cluster is named `TOMCAT1`.

Also included in the configuration is a simple context `/clustering` that will be used to host JSP files for testing purposes.

Copy the contents of Listing 16-2 into `C:\tomcat\conf\server.xml` on `TOMCAT1`.

Listing 16-2: TOMCAT1 server.xml

```
<Server port="8005" shutdown="SHUTDOWN" debug="0">
    <Service name="Tomcat-Standalone">
        <Connector
            className="org.apache.coyote.tomcat4.CoyoteConnector"
            port="8009" minProcessors="5" maxProcessors="75"
            enableLookups="true" redirectPort="8443"
            acceptCount="10" debug="0" connectionTimeout="20000"
            protocolHandlerClassName="org.apache.jk.server.JkCoyoteHandler"
            useURIValidationHack="false"/>
        <Engine name="Standalone" defaultHost="TOMCAT1"
            debug="0">
            <Host name="TOMCAT1" debug="0" appBase="webapps"
                unpackWARs="true" autoDeploy="true">
                <Context path="/clustering" docBase="clustering"
                    debug="0" reloadable="true" crossContext="true">
                    <Logger
                        className="org.apache.catalina.logger.FileLogger"
                        prefix="TOMCAT1_clustering_log." suffix=".txt"
                        timestamp="true"/>
                </Context>
            </Host>
        </Engine>
    </Service>
</Server>
```

For the second, and subsequent, nodes in the cluster, a `server.xml` file similar to the one displayed in Listing 16-3 must be configured. As you will notice, the only difference between the Tomcat configuration files `TOMCAT1` and `TOMCAT2` are the default virtual host name, and the log file name. Ensure these names reflect the name of your node.

Create a copy of Listing 16-3, with any necessary modifications, in the C:\tomcat\conf directory for each of the remaining nodes in your cluster.

Tip

If you are running multiple instances of Tomcat on the one machine make sure you change the Server: port and Connector: port and redirectPort parameters to avoid a clash with any other Tomcat instances already bound to the given port numbers. For more information regarding the configuration of multiple instance of Tomcat on a single machine see Chapter 8.

Listing 16-3: **TOMCAT2 server.xml**

```
<Server port="8005" shutdown="SHUTDOWN" debug="0">
    <Service name="Tomcat-Standalone">
        <Connector
            className="org.apache.coyote.tomcat4.CoyoteConnector"
            port="8009" minProcessors="5" maxProcessors="75"
            enableLookups="true" redirectPort="8443"
            acceptCount="10" debug="0" connectionTimeout="20000"
            protocolHandlerClassName="org.apache.jk.server.JkCoyoteHandler"
            useURIValidationHack="false"/>
        <Engine name="Standalone" defaultHost="TOMCAT2"
            debug="0">
            <Host name="TOMCAT2" debug="0" appBase="webapps"
                unpackWARs="true" autoDeploy="true">
                <Context path="/clustering" docBase="clustering"
                    debug="0" reloadable="true" crossContext="true">
                    <Logger
                        className="org.apache.catalina.logger.FileLogger"
                        prefix="TOMCAT2_clustering_log." suffix=".txt"
                        timestamp="true"/>
                </Context>
            </Host>
        </Engine>
    </Service>
</Server>
```

If the Apache HTTP server has not been configured to load the JK2 plug-in module, add the following line in Listing 16-4 into the modules section of C:\Apache\conf\httpd.conf.

Listing 16-4: **httpd.conf**

```
...
LoadModule jk2_module modules/mod_jk2.dll
...
```

The workers2.properties file for clustering is very similar to the one use in Chapter 15 for Tomcat and the Apache HTTP Server.

As a cluster contains multiple Tomcat servers, JK2 must be configured to redirect requests to each node in the cluster. A channel must be created for socket-based communication with each node. The channel defines the communication endpoint by means of the remote host and port of the Tomcat engine. Listing 16-5 defines a socket channel for TOMCAT 1 and TOMCAT2.

For redirected requests to be forwarded to Tomcat, at least one worker must be defined for each channel. To communicate between two Windows boxes over a remote connection it is necessary to use a worker using the AJP 13 protocol. The configuration in workers2.properties defines two AJP 13 workers; ajp13:TOMCAT1:8009 and ajp13:TOMCAT2:8009, for each channel; channel.socket:TOMCAT1:8009 and channel.socket:TOMCAT2:8009 respectively.

If WWW and TOMCAT1 reside on the same machine, it is possible increase performance using the JNI channel. Please refer to Chapter 15.

To provide a unified service over a cluster, it is necessary to transparently forward requests to the appropriate node in the cluster. The URI mapping example in Listing 16-5 shows how two URI patterns can be used to redirect requests to different servers. Requests for www/tomcat1/Hostname.jsp are configured to be redirected using the ajp13.TOMCAT1:8009 worker. Likewise, requests for www/tomcat2/Hostname.jsp are redirected using the ajp13.TOMCAT2:8009 worker.

To demonstrate the ability to map a requested URI to a different context on Tomcat server; both requests are redirected to the /clustering context on different servers.

Create a file named workers2.properties containing the contents of Listing 16-5. The new JK2 configuration should be placed in C:\Apache2\, on the Apache HTTP Server (WWW).

Listing 16-5: workers2.properties

```
[shm:]
info=Shared memory file. Required for multiprocess servers.
file=c:/tomcat/work/jk2.shm
size=1000000

[channel.socket:TOMCAT1:8009]
info=Forwarding over socket connection to TOMCAT1 instance.
host=TOMCAT1
port=8009

[ajp13:TOMCAT1:8009]
info=Ajp13 worker, connects to TOMCAT1 instance using AJP 1.3 protocol.
channel=channel.socket:TOMCAT1:8009

[channel.socket:TOMCAT2:8009]
info=Forwarding over socket connection to TOMCAT2 instance.
host=TOMCAT2
port=8009

[ajp13:TOMCAT2:8009]
info=Ajp13 worker, connects to TOMCAT2 instance using AJP 1.3 protocol.
```

Continued

Listing 16-5 *(continued)*

```
channel=channel.socket:TOMCAT2:8009

[uri:/tomcat1/Hostname.jsp]
info=Sample JSP to test tomcat clustering.
context=/tomcat1
group=ajp13:TOMCAT1:8009

[uri:/tomcat2/Hostname.jsp]
info=Sample JSP to test tomcat clustering.
context=/tomcat2
group=ajp13:TOMCAT2:8009
```

Testing

For the purposes of testing a simple cluster a JSP page is included in Listing 16-6 to display the name of the server that is servicing the request.

The test JSP needs to be installed under the `/tomcat1` and `/tomcat2` contexts on the hosts `TOMCAT1` and `TOMCAT2` respectively. On `TOMCAT1` create a new directory titled `C:\tomcat\webapps\tomcat1` and place a file named `Hostname.jsp` from Listing 16-6 in it. Do the same for `TOMCAT2`, placing `Hostname.jsp` in a new directory titled `C:\tomcat\webapps\tomcat2`.

Listing 16-6: `Hostname.jsp`

```
<%@ page import="java.net.*" %>
<% String hostname = InetAddress.getLocalHost().getHostName(); %>
<html>
<body>
    <h1>Hostname</h1>
    <b>Hostname:</b> <%=hostname%>
</body>
</html>
```

Start the `TOMCAT1` and `TOMCAT2` nodes in the cluster, then start the Apache HTTP server.

Open a new browser window and go to the URL `www/tomcat1/Hostname.jsp`. The resulting HTML output in Figure 16-3 shows that the `TOMCAT1` node fulfilled the request.

In the same browser window, open the URL `www/tomcat2/Hostname.jsp`. As expected, the browser displays a page generated from the JSP running on `TOMCAT2`, as shown in Figure 16-4.

After successfully configuring a Tomcat cluster you are now ready to extend the configuration to include load balancing or session replication over the cluster.

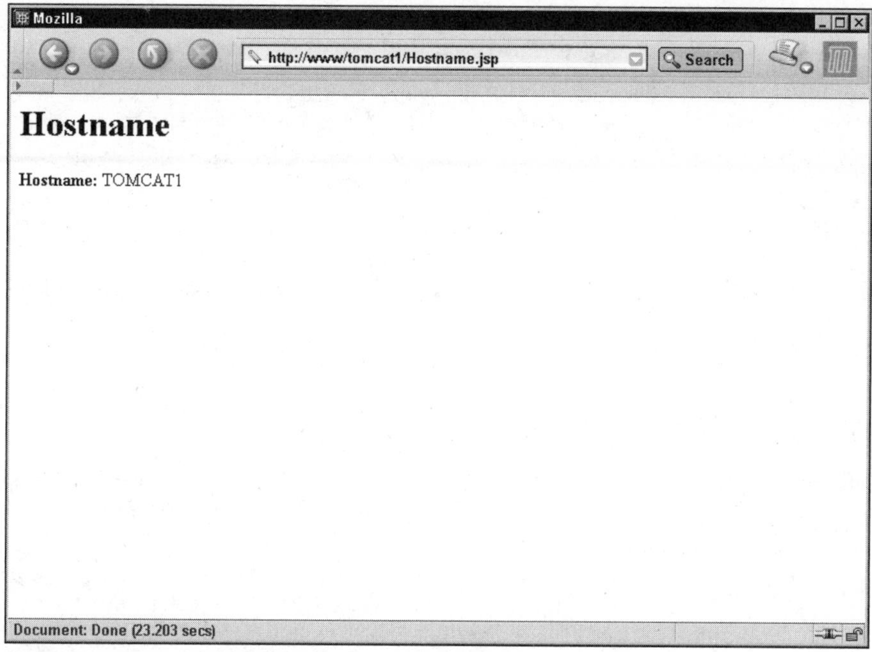

Figure 16-3: Request fulfilled by the `TOMCAT1` node

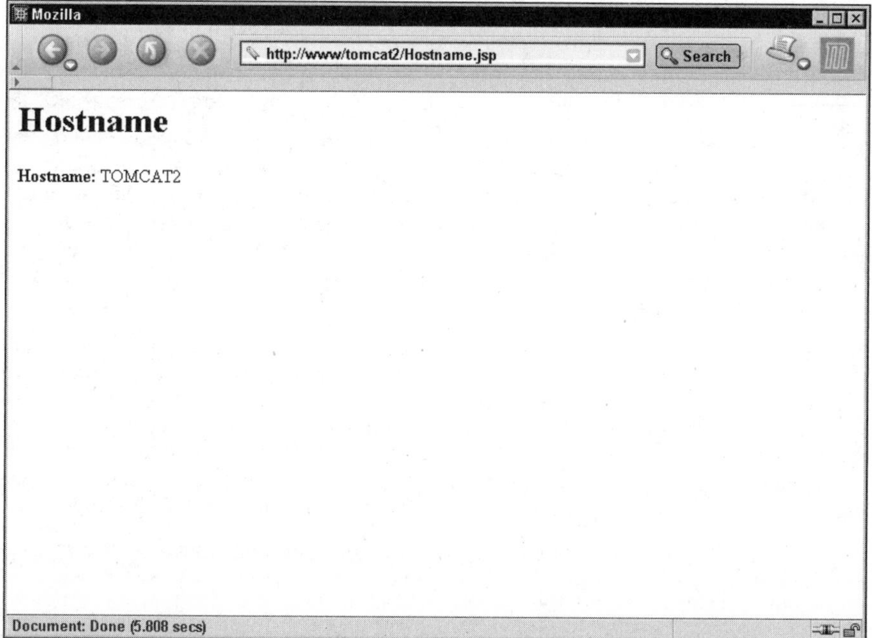

Figure 16-4: Request fulfilled by the `TOMCAT2` node

Hosts File

To assist with the process of testing, the following Hosts file may be useful to reference the Web server and any Tomcat nodes in your cluster. After modifying the IP addresses to suit your network, copy the hosts file in `C:\WINNT\Hosts`.

Hosts

```
127.0.0.1    localhost
192.168.0.1  WWW
192.168.0.2  TOMCAT1
192.168.0.3  TOMCAT2
```

Load Balancing a Tomcat Cluster

Although simple clustering is suitable for improving performance and response times under load, it is unable to deliver a level of availability required by many large-scale Web-based applications.

The need for Web applications to remain available even in the face of hardware and software failure requires fail-over capabilities. In addition, the ability to cope with many simultaneous requests means that load balancing is required to distribute the requests over a group of servers, so no one server becomes overloaded.

However, the need for a system to be available can compete with reliability requirements. If, under a time of high load, one node in the cluster fails, the remaining nodes are under increased load resulting in higher response times and reduced reliability.

The JK2 module not only provides load balancing, it also provides request-level fail-over and sticky sessions as part of the package. When using the load balancing features of JK2, fail-over and sticky sessions almost come for free.

Although sticky sessions are essential for a session-aware Web application to operate on a load balanced cluster, there are several limitations users should be aware of before proceeding. Although request-level fail-over means session-based requests are redirected to a node that can service the request, all session information associated with the request will be lost. Also, session stickiness can reduce the effectiveness of load balancing due to the unpredictable nature of session usage.

Load balancing with request-level fail-over is perfect for Web applications that do not require application state to be stored in session. For example, many Web-based applications avoid the use of session attributes, preferring to pass application state back to the client embedded in the response. All subsequent requests re-send the application state back to the server. In this case, request-level fail-over is sufficient to ensure node failures do not disrupt the client transactions. The storage of application state within the request/response does, however, require additional development effort and can increase the complexity of the application.

Although sticky sessions have limitations, some applications may only rely on session information for authentication purposes. In this case a node failure means the user will be required to re-authenticate, but it does not result in the loss of application state.

The following Configuration section demonstrates how load balancing can be added to the simple cluster example using the JK2 module.

Prerequisites

A Tomcat cluster must be configured according to the previous Simple Tomcat Cluster section.

Configuration

Once a simple cluster is set up, only minor modifications are required to enable load balancing and request-level fail-over. Two changes are necessary; configuration of the cluster to use sticky sessions, and the creation of a load-balanced group of workers.

A Tomcat identifier appended to the session ID enables the JK2 module to recognize sticky sessions, and redirect session-based requests to the appropriate server. When a new session is created the Tomcat ID is appended to the generated session ID. Each server's Tomcat ID must be unique across the cluster, and is specified in the Tomcat configuration file using the `jvmRoute` argument of the Engine Container.

Listing 16-7 demonstrates the specification of a unique Tomcat ID for the first server in the cluster. Along with the configuration to enable sticky sessions, a new context has been defined. This context is used for testing purposes at the end of the section.

Listing 16-7: TOMCAT1 server.xml

```
<Server port="8005" shutdown="SHUTDOWN" debug="0">
    <Service name="Tomcat-Standalone">
        <Connector
            className="org.apache.coyote.tomcat4.CoyoteConnector"
            port="8009" minProcessors="5" maxProcessors="75"
            enableLookups="true" redirectPort="8443"
            acceptCount="10" debug="0" connectionTimeout="20000"
            protocolHandlerClassName="org.apache.jk.server.JkCoyoteHandler"
            useURIValidationHack="false"/>
        <Engine name="Standalone" defaultHost="TOMCAT1"
            jvmRoute="TOMCAT1:8009" debug="0">
            <Host name="TOMCAT1" debug="0" appBase="webapps"
                unpackWARs="true" autoDeploy="true">
                <Context path="/loadbalancing" docBase="loadbalancing"
                    debug="0" reloadable="true" crossContext="true">
                    <Logger
                        className="org.apache.catalina.logger.FileLogger"
                        prefix="TOMCAT1_loadbalancing_log." suffix=".txt"
                        timestamp="true"/>
                </Context>
            </Host>
        </Engine>
    </Service>
</Server>
```

It is essential that every server in the cluster must be configured with a unique `jvmRoute` argument. Otherwise the load balancer will be unable to determine where to forward session-based requests.

The second server in the cluster is configured using a very similar configuration to the first, however, the virtual hostname and the Tomcat ID have been changed to reflect the server hostname in Listing 16-8.

Listing 16-8: TOMCAT2 server.xml

```
<Server port="8005" shutdown="SHUTDOWN" debug="0">
    <Service name="Tomcat-Standalone">
        <Connector
            className="org.apache.coyote.tomcat4.CoyoteConnector"
            port="8009" minProcessors="5" maxProcessors="75"
            enableLookups="true" redirectPort="8443"
            acceptCount="10" debug="0" connectionTimeout="20000"
            protocolHandlerClassName="org.apache.jk.server.JkCoyoteHandler"
            useURIValidationHack="false"/>
        <Engine name="Standalone" defaultHost="TOMCAT2"
            jvmRoute="TOMCAT2:8009" debug="0">
            <Host name="TOMCAT2" debug="0" appBase="webapps"
                unpackWARs="true" autoDeploy="true">
                <Context path="/loadbalancing" docBase="loadbalancing"
                    debug="0" reloadable="true" crossContext="true">
                    <Logger
                        className="org.apache.catalina.logger.FileLogger"
                        prefix="TOMCAT2_loadbalancing_log." suffix=".txt"
                        timestamp="true"/>
                </Context>
            </Host>
        </Engine>
    </Service>
</Server>
```

Each member in a load-balanced cluster must be declared with their own channel, and individual worker process. Each channel, or individual worker, must then belong to a load-balanced group. Finally, a mapped URI defines which load balanced group should be used to fulfill requests.

Firstly the `lb` configuration component in Listing 16-9 defines a new load-balanced group. Group membership is defined by the `channel` or `ajp13` worker configuration component using the `group` parameter. Listing 16-9 shows two channels, one for each server in the cluster, declared to belong to the `lb` load balanced group.

Each `channel` component defines a load balancing factor using the `lbfactor` parameter. The load balancing factor is a ratio relative to the factors defined by other members of the cluster. For example, if two channels are declared both with equal load balanced factors, there will be a 1:1 ratio, and the load balancer will redirect an equal number of requests to each server. If the `TOMCAT1:8009` channel has a load balance factor of 3, and the `TOMCAT2:8009` channel has a load balance factor of 1, `TOMCAT1` will receive three times as many requests as `TOMCAT2`.

Note Load balancing factors and ratios assume that each Tomcat server is available to handle the request.

When a session-based request is received, the load balancer determines where to redirect the request by matching the session ID contained in the request with the `tomcatId` parameter specified in the channel configuration. Alternatively each worker in a channel may specify their own `tomcatId` parameter.

A URI map is also declared in Listing 16-9. The example mapper demonstrates the use of a load balanced group to fulfill all incoming requests for the `/loadbalancing` context.

To configure the JK2 module in your Web server to act as a load balancer, copy the contents of Listing 16-9 into `C:\Apache2\conf\workers.properties`.

Listing 16-9: workers2.properties

```
[shm:]
info=Shared memory file. Required for multiprocess servers.
file=c:/tomcat/work/jk2.shm
size=1000000

[lb:lb]
info=Declaration of a load balanced group.
debug=0

[channel.socket:TOMCAT1:8009]
info=Forwarding over socket connection to TOMCAT1 instance.
host=TOMCAT1
port=8009
lbfactor=1
group=lb
tomcatId=TOMCAT1:8009

[ajp13:TOMCAT1:8009]
info=Ajp13 worker, connects to TOMCAT1 instance using AJP 1.3 protocol.
channel=channel.socket:TOMCAT1:8009

[channel.socket:TOMCAT2:8009]
info=Forwarding over socket connection to TOMCAT2 instance.
host=TOMCAT2
port=8009
lbfactor=1
group=lb
tomcatId=TOMCAT2:8009

[ajp13:TOMCAT2:8009]
info=Ajp13 worker, connects to TOMCAT2 instance using AJP 1.3 protocol.
channel=channel.socket:TOMCAT2:8009

[uri:/loadbalancing/SessionTest.jsp]
info=Sample JSP to test load balancing.
context=/loadbalancing
group=lb
```

After the configuration has been completed, restart each node in the Tomcat cluster, along with the Web server/load balancer, and commence testing of the configuration.

Testing

The following test will demonstrate sticky sessions and request level fail-over on a load balanced Tomcat cluster. The JSP file in Listing 16-10 is used during this test to analyze the creation of new sessions, and observe the host on which the session is being fulfilled.

This example uses sticky sessions to achieve request-level fail-over. However, in the case of node failure session information will be lost. To avoid the loss of session information, automatic session fail-over is required; see the section titled Session Replication Over a Tomcat Cluster.

Create a new JSP file named `SessionTest.jsp` in `C:\tomcat\webapps\loadbalancing`, containing the contents of Listing 16-10. This file should be installed on all nodes in the cluster.

Listing 16-10: SessionTest.jsp

```
<%@ page import="java.util.*, java.net.*" %>
<%
    // the name host attribute stored in the session
    String HOST_ATTR = "host";

    // has a new session been created?
    boolean isNewSession = session.isNew();

    // the session identifier
    String sessionId = session.getId();

    // time the session was created at
    Date creationTime = new Date(session.getCreationTime());

    // time the session was last accessed
    Date lastAccessedTime = new Date(session.getLastAccessedTime());

    // the host the session was created on
    String initHost = (String)session.getAttribute(HOST_ATTR);

    // the current host the session/servlet is running on
    String currentHost = InetAddress.getLocalHost().getHostName();

    // if a session has just been created, store the host on which the
    // session was created
    if (isNewSession)
    {
        initHost = currentHost;
        session.setAttribute("host", initHost);
    }
%>
```

```
<html>
<body>
    <h1>Distributed Session Information</h1>
    <table>
        <tr>
            <td><b>New Session?</b></td>
            <td><%=isNewSession%></td>
        </tr>
        <tr>
            <td><b>Session ID:</b></td>
            <td><%=sessionId%></td>
        </tr>
        <tr>
            <td><b>Session created at:</b></td>
            <td><%=creationTime%></td>
        </tr>
        <tr>
            <td><b>Session last accessed at:</b></td>
            <td><%=lastAccessedTime%></td>
        </tr>
        <tr>
            <td><b>Session created on:</b></td>
            <td><%=initHost%></td>
        </tr>
        <tr>
            <td><b>Session running on:</b></td>
            <td><%=currentHost%></td>
        </tr>
    </table>
</body>
</html>
```

Start the Tomcat server on the host `TOMCAT1`.

Start any other Tomcat servers in your cluster (i.e. `TOMCAT2`).

Start the Apache HTTP Server.

Start a new browser and open the URL `www/loadbalancing/SessionTest.jsp`.

The output of `SessionTest.jsp` displays some of the information contained in the session, along with information regarding when and where the session was created, and the identifier given to the session.

Depending on the load balancing factor you will see output originating from the server on `TOMCAT1` or `TOMCAT2`, assuming your cluster only contains two servers. This example assumes that the request was fulfilled by `TOMCAT1`, as shown in Figure 16-5.

Press `SHIFT-Refresh`. The New Session field is updated to `false`, indicating that this is a repeat visit from a user with an existing session. "The Session last accessed at" should reflect the current time. Because the load balanced cluster uses sticky sessions, the "Session running on" and the "Session created on" fields always reflect the same hostname, meaning a single host fulfills each transaction.

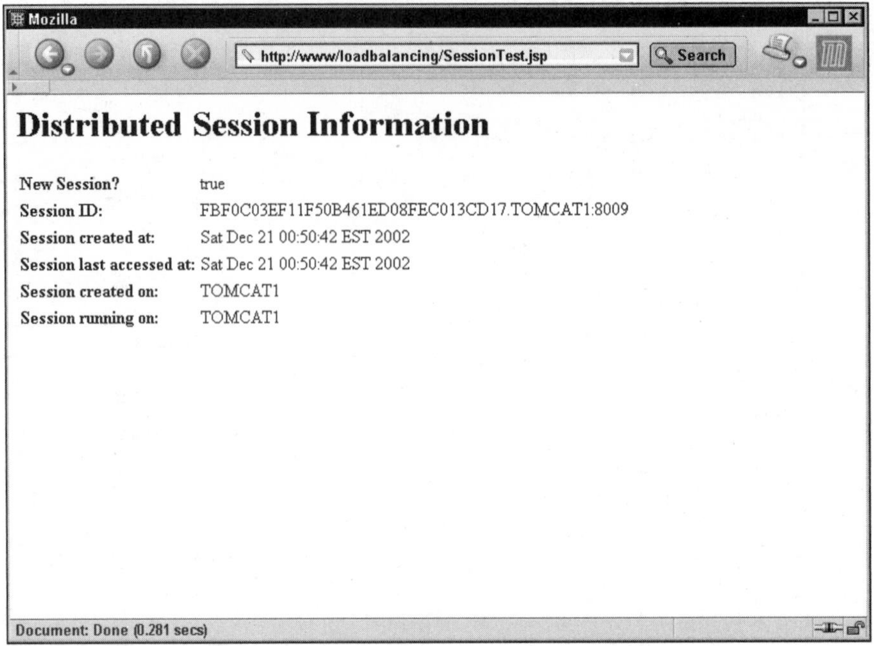

Figure 16-5: Load balanced request fulfilled by TOMCAT1

Holding the SHIFT key while clicking on the Refresh button on your browser performs a hard-refresh, ensuring the browser does not display a cached copy of the page. If the "The Session last accessed at" field does not reflect the last accessed time ensure that a hard-refresh is used.

Create many new sessions in new browser window, observing where the session is created. If there are two Tomcat servers in the cluster and each server has equal load balancing factors, equivalent processing capabilities, and similar load, every new session appears to alternate from one server to the other. Figure 16-6 shows one of the sessions fulfilled by TOMCAT2.

Ensure there is at least one session active on each Tomcat server, then kill the server running on TOMCAT2.

Open a browser window containing a session created on TOMCAT1 and Press SHIFT-Refresh. The session remains running on TOMCAT1 and the "Session last accessed" time should be updated.

However, if you navigate to a browser containing a session created on TOMCAT2, you should notice a short pause whilst JK2 fails-over and sends the request to TOMCAT1. The JSP output now indicates that the previous session has been lost, and a new one created on TOMCAT1, as shown in Figure 16-7. Unfortunately, users mid-way through a transaction lose information, but the application is still available.

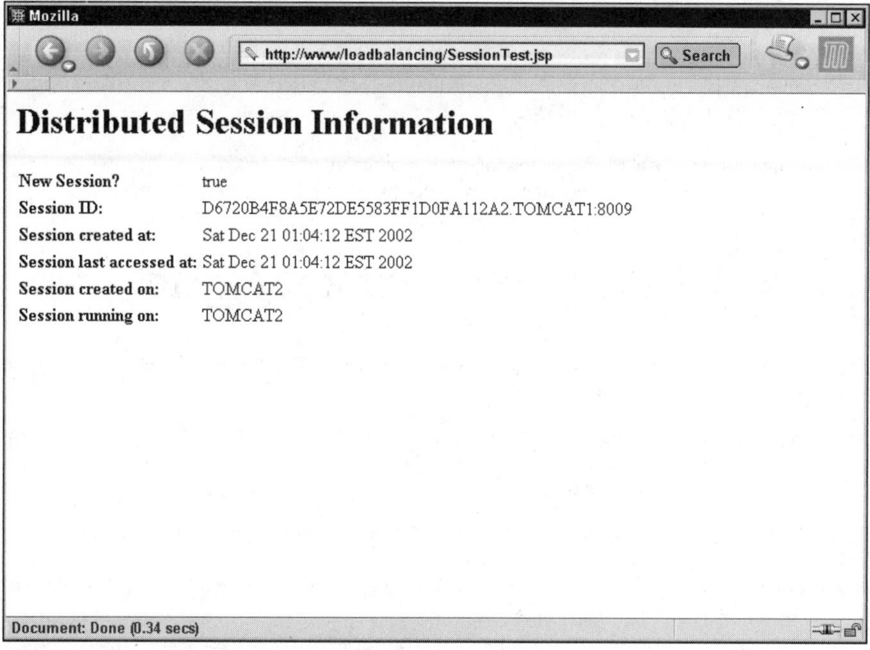

Figure 16-6: Load balanced request fulfilled by `TOMCAT2`

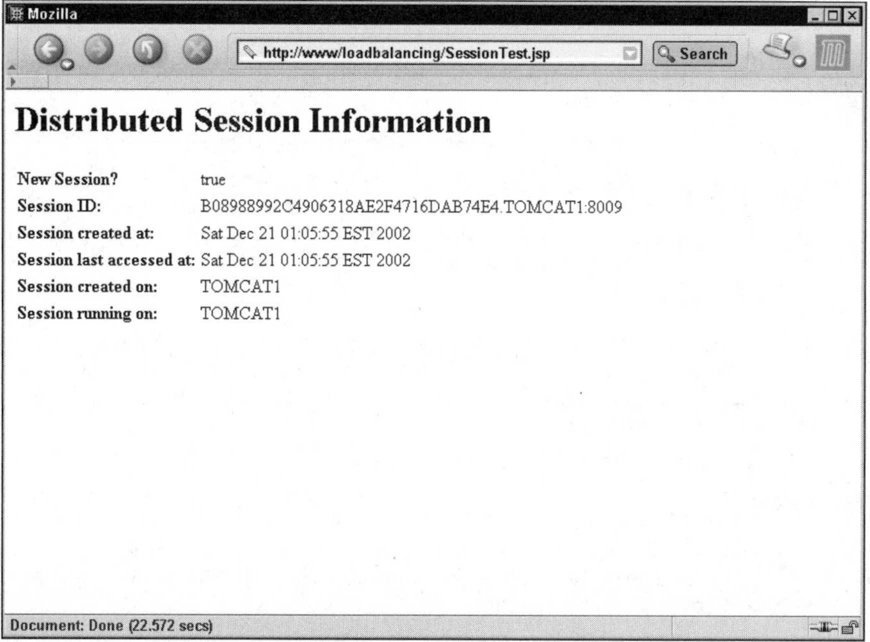

Figure 16-7: Request-level fail-over of session from `TOMCAT2` to `TOMCAT1`

Start the server on TOMCAT2, wait for Tomcat to fully start.

After 60 seconds, incoming requests should be load balanced over all servers in the cluster. All sessions started in the server running on TOMCAT2 are lost, but new sessions should successfully run on both Tomcat servers.

Tip

Change the load balancing factor for each worker in `workers2.properties` and repeat the previous test, observing changes in the number of requests each server fulfills.

Session Replication over a Tomcat Cluster

To overcome some of the limitations of sticky sessions and request-level fail over, it is possible to provide session affinity and automatic session fail-over. Then it is possible to provide a highly available, session-aware application.

In the event of a server failure all requests for the inactive server are redirected to an operational Tomcat server that has a copy of the session state, enabling it to fulfill the request without the loss of session information.

Using session replication with in memory session replication, every node in the cluster has a complete copy of the session state for the cluster. Every time session information is changed on one of the nodes, the changes are broadcast to all other nodes on the cluster, allowing them to update their copy of the session state.

A very good overview of in memory session replication written by Filip Hanik is available from TheServerSide `www2.theserverside.com/resources/article.jsp?l=Tomcat`. The article explains how Tomcat and the JavaGroups library are used together to provide session replication.

Caution

The configuration in TheServerSide article is, however, specific to Tomcat 4.0.x and the Apache mod_proxy module.

In this section the latest version of the Tomcat in memory session replication library will be presented. Notice that the session replication configuration is very similar to that described previously in this chapter, in the section titled "Load Balancing a Tomcat Cluster," the reason being session replication uses the same load balancing configuration, with the addition of the in memory session replication.

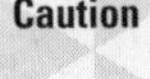

Caution

All installation and configuration steps must be performed on each Tomcat server within the cluster. Care should be taken to ensure identical configurations are applied, as discrepancies may cause session replication to fail. The reader is explicitly notified where customized configuration is required for each server.

Prerequisites

Before session information can be replicated across multiple Tomcat servers, a cluster must first be set up. Please follow the instructions in the section titled "Simple Tomcat Cluster" earlier in this chapter before proceeding.

After you have a working Tomcat cluster, the Tomcat in memory session replication library must be installed on each node in the cluster.

In the new release of Tomcat 5.0, the Tomcat in memory session replication project is integrated into the Tomcat release, enabling session replication out-of-the-box. In the meantime Tomcat 4.1 users may use a BETA version of the Tomcat in memory session replication code available from `http://www.filip.net/tomcat-clustering.html`.

Tomcat in memory session replication uses the java.nio packages; therefore JDK 1.4 must be installed before proceeding. After installing JDK 1.4 you are required to modify the `JAVA_HOME` environment variable, and may also be required to re-install Tomcat.

Download

Go to the Tomcat in memory session replication site at `http://www.filip.net/tomcat-clustering.html`, and select the `tomcat-replication.jar` hyperlink at the bottom of the page.

Installation

Copy or move the downloaded JAR file, `tomcat-replication.jar`, to `c:\tomcat\server\lib` on each Tomcat node in the cluster.

That is it! All we need to do now is configure the session replication for each node.

Configuration

Now that Tomcat in memory session replication library has been installed, you are ready to configure session replication over a Tomcat cluster. The following configuration can be used to enable session replication to an existing Tomcat cluster. To configure a cluster from scratch, please refer to the section titled "Simple Tomcat Cluster" at the beginning of this chapter.

The configuration declares an AJP 13 listener to receive redirected requests from the Apache HTTP Server. Requests are redirected from the Apache HTTP Server to the Tomcat engine. This engine defines the `jvmRoute` attribute that is appended to the session ID, enabling sticky sessions. The host entry identifies a default virtual host for the Tomcat server. For the purposes of the example, the first server in the cluster is identified as `TOMCAT1`.

Although sticky sessions are utilized in this configuration, this is strictly not necessary, as it does not matter which server fulfills an incoming request.

Session replication is configured per context and consists of three sections, a valve, the in memory session replication manager, and a logger. Listing 16-11 defines the `/sessionrpl` context that will be used during testing of this configuration. The context uses a round-robin algorithm specified by setting the `maxKeepAliveRequests` attribute to `1`. The in memory session replication manager responds to changes to session information and broadcasts the changes to the cluster. After each request has been fulfilled the valve calls the manager to replicate the session. If the `Manager` node's `useDirtyFlag` attribute is set to `true`, the session information is only replicated when a session is created or modified, not after every request. Log output for the in memory session replication manager and the context is written to `TOMCAT1_sessionrpl_log.txt`.

Listing 16-11 defines a configuration for the first Tomcat server in out cluster. The `server.xml` file contains the bare-minimum configured to have a load balanced Tomcat server supporting session replication.

Replace the contents of the `C:\tomcat\conf\server.xml` file with Listing 16-11 on the first Tomcat server in the cluster, `TOMCAT1`.

Caution The `tcpListenAddress` attribute in the `Manager` tag must not be set to the loopback address (`127.0.0.1`), or a hostname that will resolve to the loopback address. To check you are not using a loopback address type the following command in a Command Prompt window substituting `tomcat1` with the appropriate hostname:

```
C:\ >ping tomcat1
```

In the result, check that the IP address is not equal to `127.0.0.1`.

```
Pinging TOMCAT1 [192.168.0.2] with 32 bytes of data:
```

Listing 16-11: TOMCAT1 server.xml

```
<Server port="8005" shutdown="SHUTDOWN" debug="0">
    <Service name="Tomcat-Standalone">
        <Connector
            className="org.apache.coyote.tomcat4.CoyoteConnector"
            port="8009" minProcessors="5" maxProcessors="75"
            enableLookups="true" redirectPort="8443"
            acceptCount="10" debug="0" connectionTimeout="20000"
            protocolHandlerClassName="org.apache.jk.server.JkCoyoteHandler"
            useURIValidationHack="false"
            maxKeepAliveRequests="1"/>
        <Engine name="Standalone" defaultHost="TOMCAT1"
            jvmRoute="TOMCAT1:8009" debug="0">
            <Host name="TOMCAT1" debug="0" appBase="webapps"
                unpackWARs="true" autoDeploy="true">
                <Context path="/sessionrpl" docBase="sessionrpl" debug="0"
                    reloadable="true" crossContext="true">

                    <Logger
                        className="org.apache.catalina.logger.FileLogger"
                        prefix="TOMCAT1_sessionrpl_log." suffix=".txt"
                        timestamp="true"/>

                    <Valve className=
                            "org.apache.catalina.session.ReplicationValve"
                        debug="0"/>

                    <Manager className=
                   "org.apache.catalina.session.InMemoryReplicationManager"
                        debug="10"
                        printToScreen="true"
                        saveOnRestart="false"
                        maxActiveSessions="-1"
                        minIdleSwap="-1"
```

```
                    maxIdleSwap="-1"
                    maxIdleBackup="-1"
                    pathname="null"
                    printSessionInfo="true"
                    checkInterval="10"
                    expireSessionsOnShutdown="false"
                    serviceclass=
                       "org.apache.catalina.cluster.mcast.McastService"
                    mcastAddr="228.1.2.3"
                    mcastPort="45566"
                    mcastFrequency="500"
                    mcastDropTime="5000"
                    tcpListenAddress="TOMCAT1"
                    tcpListenPort="4001"
                    tcpThreadCount="1"
                    useDirtyFlag="true">
                    </Manager>
                </Context>
            </Host>
        </Engine>
    </Service>
</Server>
```

For each subsequent Tomcat server in the cluster, an equivalent Tomcat configuration must be applied. Listing 16-13 shows the configuration for the second Tomcat server in the cluster, TOMCAT2. Notice that all host references have been updated to reflect the new server.

Apply the appropriate server.xml configuration for each server in the cluster.

Listing 16-12: **TOMCAT2 server.xml**

```
<Server port="8005" shutdown="SHUTDOWN" debug="0">
    <Service name="Tomcat-Standalone">
        <Connector
            className="org.apache.coyote.tomcat4.CoyoteConnector"
            port="8009" minProcessors="5" maxProcessors="75"
            enableLookups="true" redirectPort="8443"
            acceptCount="10" debug="0" connectionTimeout="20000"
            protocolHandlerClassName="org.apache.jk.server.JkCoyoteHandler"
            useURIValidationHack="false"
            maxKeepAliveRequests="1"/>
        <Engine name="Standalone" defaultHost="TOMCAT2"
            jvmRoute="TOMCAT2:8009" debug="0">
            <Host name="TOMCAT2" debug="0" appBase="webapps"
                unpackWARs="true" autoDeploy="true">
                <Context path="/sessionrpl" docBase="sessionrpl" debug="0"
                    reloadable="true" crossContext="true">
```

Continued

Listing 16-12 *(continued)*

```
                    <Logger
                        className="org.apache.catalina.logger.FileLogger"
                        prefix="TOMCAT2_sessionrpl_log." suffix=".txt"
                        timestamp="true"/>

                    <Valve className=
                            "org.apache.catalina.session.ReplicationValve"
                        debug="0"/>

                    <Manager className=
                   "org.apache.catalina.session.InMemoryReplicationManager"
                        debug="10"
                        printToScreen="true"
                        saveOnRestart="false"
                        maxActiveSessions="-1"
                        minIdleSwap="-1"
                        maxIdleSwap="-1"
                        maxIdleBackup="-1"
                        pathname="null"
                        printSessionInfo="true"
                        checkInterval="10"
                        expireSessionsOnShutdown="false"
                        serviceclass=
                           "org.apache.catalina.cluster.mcast.McastService"
                        mcastAddr="228.1.2.3"
                        mcastPort="45566"
                        mcastFrequency="500"
                        mcastDropTime="5000"
                        tcpListenAddress="TOMCAT2"
                        tcpListenPort="4001"
                        tcpThreadCount="1"
                        useDirtyFlag="true">
                    </Manager>
                </Context>
            </Host>
        </Engine>
    </Service>
</Server>
```

Now that you have at least two session-aware Tomcat servers in a cluster, it is necessary to notify the Apache HTTP Server of any new contexts that contain in-memory session replication. Listing 16-13 shows a `workers2.properties` file containing a URI mapping entry for the new `/sessionrpl` context used for testing.

Copy the contents of `workers2.properties` to the `C:\Apache2\conf` directory, then restart the Apache HTTP Server.

Listing 16-13: workers2.properties

```
[shm:]
info=Shared memory file. Required for multiprocess servers.
file=c:/tomcat/work/jk2.shm
size=1000000

[logger.file:0]
level=INFO
file=c:/tomcat/logs/apache_jk2.log

[lb:lb]
info=Declaration of a load balanced group.
debug=0

[channel.socket:TOMCAT1:8009]
info=Forwarding over socket connection to TOMCAT1 instance.
host=TOMCAT1
port=8009
lbfactor=1
group=lb
tomcatId=TOMCAT1:8009

[ajp13:TOMCAT1:8009]
info=Ajp13 worker, connects to TOMCAT1 instance using AJP 1.3 protocol.
channel=channel.socket:TOMCAT1:8009

[channel.socket:TOMCAT2:8009]
info=Forwarding over socket connection to TOMCAT2 instance.
host=TOMCAT2
port=8009
lbfactor=1
group=lb
tomcatId=TOMCAT2:8009

[ajp13:TOMCAT2:8009]
info=Ajp13 worker, connects to TOMCAT2 instance using AJP 1.3 protocol.
channel=channel.socket:TOMCAT2:8009

[uri:/sessionrpl/SessionTest.jsp]
info=Sample JSP to test session replication
context=/sessionrpl
group=lb
```

After restarting all the clustered Tomcat servers, all session states should be replicated across the entire cluster. Execute the following test to ensure that the configuration has been successful.

Testing

The `SessionTest.jsp` file used for load balancing, described in Listing 16-10, is also used to test session replication. Place this file in a new context on each node that has been set up to broadcast session information over the cluster.

1. Create new context under the `webapps` directory `C:\tomcat\webapps\sessionrpl` for each server. Place `SessionText.jsp` in newly created `/sessionrpl` context.
2. Start the Tomcat server on the host `TOMCAT1`.

Caution

If you get the following error when attempting to start Tomcat please check that you are using JDK 1.4.

```
10 [main] ERROR digester.Digester - Begin event threw error
java.lang.NoClassDefFoundError: java/lang/CharSequence
```

If after installing JDK 1.4 the error still appears make sure the `JAVA_HOME` environment variable has been updated with the location of JDK 1.4. As a last resort re-install Tomcat and see if that solves the problem.

3. Start any other Tomcat servers in your cluster (for example, `TOMCAT2`).
4. Start the Apache HTTP Server.
5. Start a new browser and open the URL `www/sessionrpl/SessionTest.jsp`.
6. The output of `SessionTest.jsp` displays some of the information contained in the session, along with information regarding when and where the session was created, and the identifier given to the session.
7. Depending on the load balancing algorithm you will see output originating from the server on `TOMCAT1` or `TOMCAT2`, assuming your cluster only contains two servers. For the purpose of this example assume that the request was fulfilled by `TOMCAT1`.
8. Press `SHIFT-Refresh`. The New Session field is updated to `false`, indicating that this is a repeat visit from a user with an existing session. "The Session last accessed at" should reflect the current time, and the "Session running on" field indicates where the request was fulfilled.

Tip

Holding the `SHIFT` key while clicking the Refresh button on your browser performs a hard-refresh.

9. Open another new browser window, and open the URL `www/sessionrpl/SessionTest.jsp`. Assuming the Tomcat servers have equal load-balancing factors, and they are equally loaded, the next request should be fulfilled by the server running on `TOMCAT2`. If not, close the browser window and repeat until the "Session running on field" equals the host `TOMCAT2`.
10. Press refresh. "New Session" should now return false and the "Session last accessed" time should be updated.
11. Now kill the Tomcat server running on `TOMCAT2` by pressing `Control-C` in the Tomcat console window.

12. Open the browser window containing the session created on `TOMCAT2` and Press SHIFT-Refresh. The browser may pause briefly while JK2 fails-over and sends the request to `TOMCAT1`. The JSP output in Figure 16-8 now indicates that a session with an identical ID is running on `TOMCAT1`. The "Session last accessed" time is updated to the current time.

If the "New Session" field returns true, session replication has failed. This occurs when the redundant server does not recognize the incoming session ID, and therefore creates a new one, similar to the scenario of load balancing without session replication where session information is lost. Please repeat the previous configuration steps, and ensure IP multicast is operational over your network.

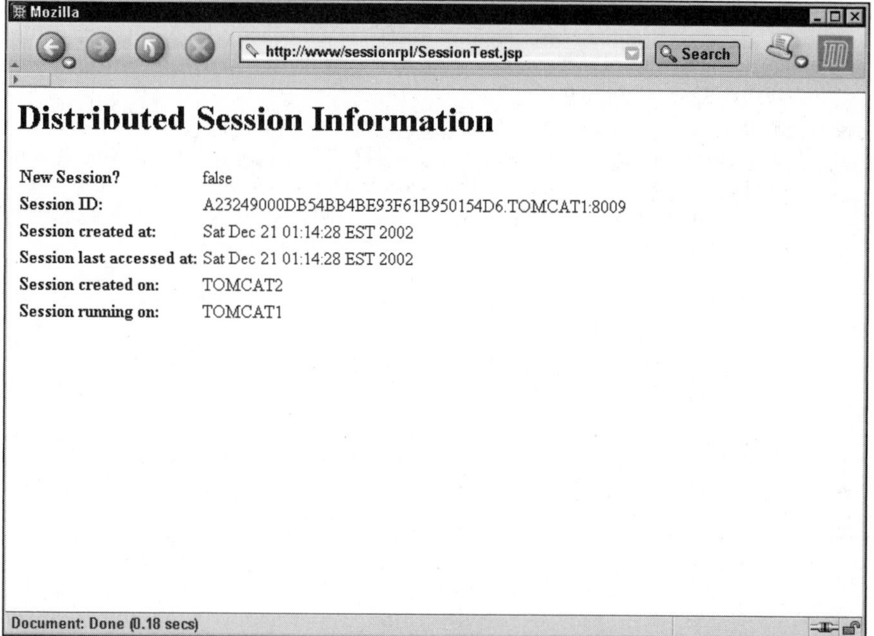

Figure 16-8: Expected response arising from transparent session fail-over from `TOMCAT2` to `TOMCAT1`

13. Start the server on `TOMCAT2`, wait for Tomcat to fully start.

14. Go to the browser containing the session created on `TOMCAT2`. Press SHIFT-Refresh. Confirm the session is running on `TOMCAT2`. If not, wait 5 seconds until the load balancer checks for recovered servers, and try again.

Note

If this behavior is undesirable, you can disable sticky sessions. Without sticky sessions the load balancer redirects the incoming request irrespective of where the session was created. To do this, remove the `jvmRoute` argument in each `server.xml` configuration. Additionally, remove the `tomcatid` fields under each AJP 13 worker in `worksers2.properties`.

15. Both sessions should now behave as normal.

You may wish to investigate other fail-over scenarios to test the behavior of session replication.

Summary

Big congratulations are in order at the completion of this chapter. The topic of clustering is complex, and the configuration of the JK2 module with in memory session replication is not trivial. You should now have a functional cluster of Tomcat nodes distributed across a number of machines, possibly load balanced and with session affinity.

At the conclusion of this chapter, the importance of systems architecture should be stressed. The decision to use clustering is not a light one, and one should go about the selection of hardware and server software carefully. Important evaluations need to be made regarding the suitability of the hardware and software used to construct the cluster to meet the non-functional requirements of your application.

Although the use of a Tomcat in a cluster can increase the availability, reliability, and scalability of a Web application, the use of the Apache HTTP server to manage and direct the cluster may not be suitable for a mission-critical system. Systems with such high importance are justified in the purchase of dedicated load-balancing hardware such as Cisco or Radware products.

✦ ✦ ✦

CHAPTER 17

Tools and Utilities

✦ ✦ ✦ ✦

In This Chapter

JBoss

log4j

Cactus

JMeter

✦ ✦ ✦ ✦

This chapter contains some information about tools, utilities, and even a full J2EE application server. It should not be considered the definitive source of information about these tools, but a useful introduction to their capabilities.

The following products have been chosen either because of their integration with Tomcat or the general applicability of their use with Tomcat.

The first "tool" covered is the JBoss Web application server. Describing all the functionality of JBoss would take a book at least as large as this one, so the information covered is sufficient for investigation, installation, and the initial operation of the server.

The next product covered is the log4j library. log4j is an comprehensive and extensible logging framework, another Apache Jakarta project often used in conjunction with Tomcat to provide more sophisticated logging functionality within Web applications.

Cactus, a testing framework, also is introduced. Cactus is a client/server extension to the JUnit testing toolkit and provides the capability to develop unit tests for Web applications.

The final product discussed in this chapter is the JMeter testing tool. JMeter is a Swing-based GUI application that can perform functional and stress testing of any Web application. JMeter is a very useful tool for developers and deployers to implement high-level test cases for required functionality. Those tests can then be used for stress testing the application.

JBoss

JBoss is an open source J2EE implementation supporting the servlet 2.3, JSP 1.2 and Enterprise JavaBean (EJB) 2.0 specifications. JBoss provides a great entry point into the world of J2EE development and one of its best features is the use of the Tomcat servlet container. This benefit means that many of the things discussed and developed throughout the book are immediately relevant to starting development using a J2EE server.

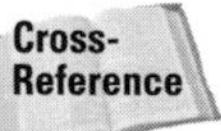

A full list of J2EE components is discussed in Chapter 1.

With any J2EE implementation there are different interpretations of the specification resulting in incompatibilities, but the good news is that the WAR files created in earlier chapters can be deployed and tested on JBoss without any modification. Of course, they don't make use of many of the J2EE features, but they certainly provide a great starting point.

JBoss started in March 1999 as an implementation of an EJB container, and now with the inclusion of a servlet container it provides a full implementation of the J2EE standard.

JBoss has JBoss/Server as the core of the EJB container, including Container Manager Persistence (CMP) and JMX infrastructure, JBossMQ for JMS messaging, JBossMX for handling the JavaMail API.

The default version of JBoss uses the JBossWeb (Jetty) servlet container, however the JBoss developers also support the use and provide a download of JBoss bundled with Tomcat, which greatly eases any configuration issues.

Getting Started with JBoss

So you want to start leveraging the power of EJBs from your Web site? JBoss is definitely a step in the right direction. In this section we will get a JBoss server up and running with an existing JSP and servlet based Web application. The following section on the template J2EE Project will cover the introduction of EJBs to your project.

Download

A binary JBoss package is available from the Downloads area of the JBoss.org Web site. Open `www.jboss.org/` in a browser and click the Downloads link on the left navigation panel.

JBoss 3.0 is the latest release of the JBoss J2EE server. The binary package comes with three different servlet container configurations:

- JBossWeb (Jetty)
- Apache Tomcat 4.1.12
- Apache Tomcat 4.0.6

Because we already have Web applications deployed using the Tomcat 4.1.12 servlet container, the logical choice is to choose the JBoss-3.0.4-Tomcat-4.1.12 package. To download this package select the `JBoss-3.0.4_Tomcat-4.1.12.zip` link. On the next screen choose a mirror site. You are then prompted to save the file to disk.

While you are visiting the `JBoss.org` Web site it is probably a good idea to pick up some documentation. Various JBoss documentation is available via the Documentation link on the left side of the page. The documentation area has some high-quality documentation written by JBoss developers, for a small fee. However, there also some free documentation available. Click the link JBoss 3.0 Getting Started Documentation, which will jump down the page where you can download Draft 3 of the documentation (at the time of writing) and also a copy of the template and example projects.

To download the documentation, select Download Draft 3. Again select a mirror site, and depending on your browser settings you will either be prompted to save the file to disk, or the PDF file automatically opens in the browser. If the PDF automatically opens, but you would like to save the file, go back and right click the `JBoss.3.0QuickStart.Draft3.pdf` link and select `Save File As` from the menu.

To download the template project, select Download Template and Examples `JBoss.3.0TemplateAndExamples.zip` from the documentation area.

We are now ready to move ahead and install the JBoss server.

Installation

The JBoss-3.0.4-Tomcat-4.1.12 package comes bundled with the Tomcat 4.1.12 servlet container and the simple Hypersonic database. These servers, coupled with JBoss, enable a developer to get started developing end-to-end J2EE applications.

Installation of JBoss is as easy as extracting the downloaded package, `jboss-3.0.4_tomcat-4.1.12.zip`. Extract the file to `C:\`. This creates the directory `jboss-3.0.4_tomcat-4.1.12` and the subdirectories shown in Figure 17-1.

After the JBoss server has been installed it is time to install the template and Examples distribution. Theoretically these examples could live anywhere on the file system, but for neatness and consistency they are installed underneath the JBoss distribution. Extract the file `JBoss.3.0TemplateAndExamples.zip` to `C:\jboss-3.0.4_tomcat-4.1.12\examples`. If necessary the tool used to extract the file needs to create the `examples` directory during the extraction process. At the completion of this process you are left with the directories; `template`, `cmp2`, `transaction`, and the subdirectories. The template project is explained in greater detail in the Template J2EE Project later in this section.

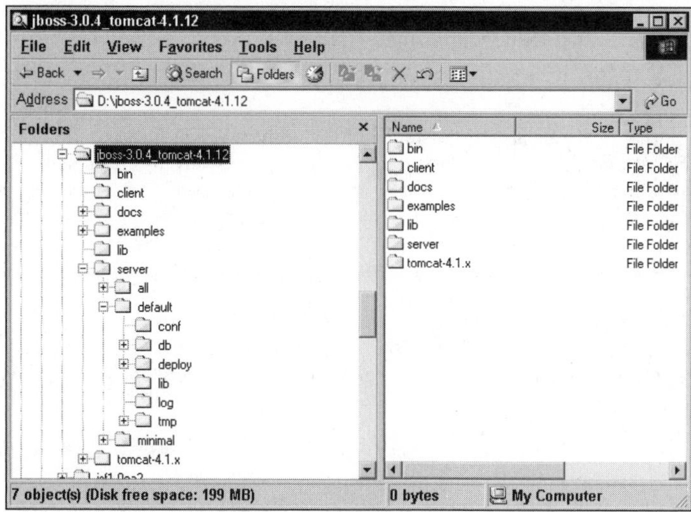

Figure 17-1: JBoss directory hierarchy

The JBoss directories shown in Figure 17-1 have the following purpose:

✦ **bin:** contains the scripts necessary to start and stop the JBoss server. Both Windows and Unix scripts are provided.

✦ **client:** libraries used by EJB clients.

✦ **docs:** don't be fooled, user documentation is not found under the docs folder. The folder does, however, contain the following:

- **dtd:** XML Document Type Definition (DTDs).
- **examples:** Java Connector Architecture (JCA) examples containing configuration files for different JCA configurations.
- **tests:** unit test results in HTML format.

✦ **examples:** JBoss Template and Example projects.

✦ **lib:** common libraries used by both clients and the JBoss server.

✦ **server:** server files organized into three pre-configured server environments. Depending on the arguments passed to the JBoss run script, one of the following environment configurations is used at startup. It is possible for the user to customize and create new server configurations in this directory. If the configuration directory name is passed to the run script, the custom configuration is loaded during JBoss startup.

- **all:** contains all the available services.
- **default:** supports all services except RMI/IIOP and clustering. It is suitable for most applications and is run by default if no arguments are supplied to the startup script.
- **minimal:** the minimal configuration to deploy a Web application. Starts the servlet container, a deployment scanner, and a JNDI server.

✦ **Tomcat-4.1.x:** the bundled Apache Tomcat Servlet container instance.

Unpacking the package creates another instance of the Tomcat server located under tomcat-4.1.x. This instance of Tomcat is preconfigured to operate with the JBoss server. It is feasible that the original instance of Tomcat in c:\tomcat be configured to work with JBoss, but for ease of use, this section concentrates on the bundled version of the Tomcat servlet container.

Configuration

The JBoss default environment is preconfigured out of the box and ready to go. If you wish to change the configuration of JBoss at a later stage, refer to the JBoss Quick Start Guide when modifying the files in C:\jboss-3.0.4_tomcat-4.1.12\server\default\conf (assuming you wish to modify the default environment).

Running

To startup the JBoss server simply execute the Windows batch file C:\jboss-3.0.4_tomcat-4.1.12\server\bin\run.bat. The batch file can be run from the command line, or to run the default environment simply double-click the file in Windows Explorer.

The batch file supports the following arguments, allowing different configuration environments to be loaded at startup:

```
run.bat -c minimal|default|all
```

After running the batch file, a console similar to Figure 17-2 should be displayed with JBoss output written to it. The JBoss server has successfully completed starting up when the following message is displayed.

```
[Server] JBoss (MX MicroKernel) [3.0.4 Date:xxx] Started in 0m:47s:888ms
```

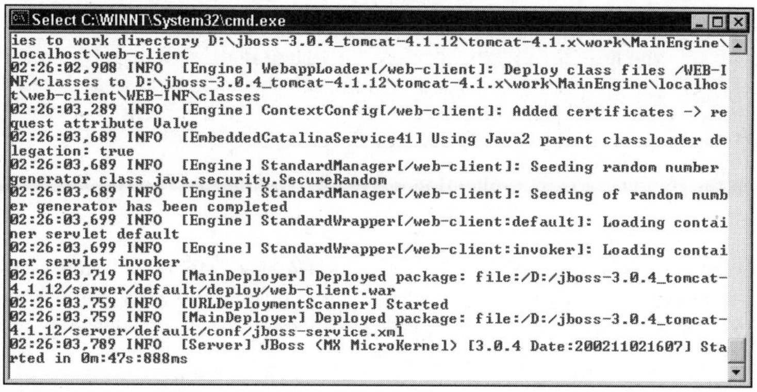

```
Select C:\WINNT\System32\cmd.exe
ies to work directory D:\jboss-3.0.4_tomcat-4.1.12\tomcat-4.1.x\work\MainEngine\
localhost\web-client
02:26:02,908 INFO  [Engine] WebappLoader[/web-client]: Deploy class files /WEB-I
NF/classes to D:\jboss-3.0.4_tomcat-4.1.12\tomcat-4.1.x\work\MainEngine\localhos
t\web-client\WEB-INF\classes
02:26:03,289 INFO  [Engine] ContextConfig[/web-client]: Added certificates -> re
quest attribute Valve
02:26:03,689 INFO  [EmbeddedCatalinaService41] Using Java2 parent classloader de
legation: true
02:26:03,689 INFO  [Engine] StandardManager[/web-client]: Seeding random number
generator class java.security.SecureRandom
02:26:03,689 INFO  [Engine] StandardManager[/web-client]: Seeding of random numb
er generator has been completed
02:26:03,699 INFO  [Engine] StandardWrapper[/web-client:default]: Loading contai
ner servlet default
02:26:03,699 INFO  [Engine] StandardWrapper[/web-client:invoker]: Loading contai
ner servlet invoker
02:26:03,719 INFO  [MainDeployer] Deployed package: file:/D:/jboss-3.0.4_tomcat-
4.1.12/server/default/deploy/web-client.war
02:26:03,759 INFO  [URLDeploymentScanner] Started
02:26:03,759 INFO  [MainDeployer] Deployed package: file:/D:/jboss-3.0.4_tomcat-
4.1.12/server/default/conf/jboss-service.xml
02:26:03,789 INFO  [Server] JBoss (MX MicroKernel) [3.0.4 Date:200211021607] Sta
rted in 0m:47s:888ms
```

Figure 17-2: JBoss console

Note

Looking at the file `C:\jboss-3.0.4_tomcat-4.1.12\server\default\log\boot.log` you may notice several warning messages like the one shown here:

```
WARN  [MainDeployer] The manifest entry in file:/xxx.jar
references URL file:/xxx.jar which could not be opened, entry
ignored
```

Bug 644289 has been submitted to the `sourceforge.net` JBoss.org project bug tracker, attributing the behavior to a classloader problem. The bug details can be viewed by searching the JBoss.org bug tracker at `https://sourceforge.net/tracker/?atid=376685&group_id=22866&func=browse`.

The warning is due to classes that are loaded by more than one classloader causing an IllegalAccessError. A fix has been committed to head of the 3.0 and 3.2 branches of the JBoss source tree, but for the purposes of release 3.0.4 of JBoss the warning can safely be ignored.

Note

The following warning messages may also appear in the log file `C:\jboss-3.0.4_tomcat-4.1.12\server\default\log\boot.log`.

```
WARN  [ServiceController]
jboss.management.single:j2eeType=J2EEDomain,name=Manager does
not implement any Service methods

22:55:07,254 WARN  [ServiceController] jboss:service=XidFactory
does not implement any Service methods
```

These may safely be ignored and should be removed in a future release of JBoss. JBoss output is written to the console in addition to the log output written to the file `C:\jboss-3.0.4_tomcat-4.1.12\server\default\log\server.log`.

Caution

Each server configuration environment contains its own log directory; make sure you look at the correct log files for the running environment.

Testing

What better way to test the new JBoss 3.0.4–Tomcat 4.1.12 installation than to try some of the Web applications developed in previous chapters? Although this will not test all the J2EE capabilities of the server, it will prove the default configuration environment is operational. For a simple J2EE test, refer to the Template J2EE project.

This test deploys the Hello City Web application developed in Chapter 7 to the JBoss–Tomcat server.

Before we proceed it is necessary to build and create a WAR file distribution from the source code presented in Chapter 7. If the HelloWorld example has not been completed, refer back to Chapter 7 or download and install the source code from the books companion Web site.

Assuming the HelloWorld project has been created in `C:\work\hello`, issue the following command from the project root:

```
C:\work\hello> ant dist
```

A new file named `C:\work\hello\dist\hello-0.1-dev.war` should be created.

Deploying the application to JBoss can be done manually by copying the file `hello-0.1-dev.war` to `C:\jboss-3.0.4_tomcat-4.1.12\server\default\deploy`. After the file has been copied the JBoss Deployment Scanner detects the WAR file and deploys the application. The following output is at the tail of the server log or console output:

```
[org.jboss.deployment.MainDeployer] Deployed package: file:/C:/jboss-3.0.4_
tomcat-4.1.12/server/default/deploy/hello-0.1-dev.war
```

Opening the URL `http://localhost:8080/hello-0.1-dev/` in a browser starts up the Hello City Web application on the JBoss server. The result should look like Figure 17-3, and behave like the original application developed in Chapter 7.

Because the JBoss default configuration has the Tomcat manager application disabled, the existing `context`, `deploy`, and `install` Ant targets will not work against the Tomcat instance running with JBoss. Web applications must be deployed using the JBoss Deployment Scanner.

Template J2EE Project

The JBoss 3.0 Quick Start guide refers to a template project that all JBoss examples are based upon. Developers also can use this project as a starting point for J2EE development.

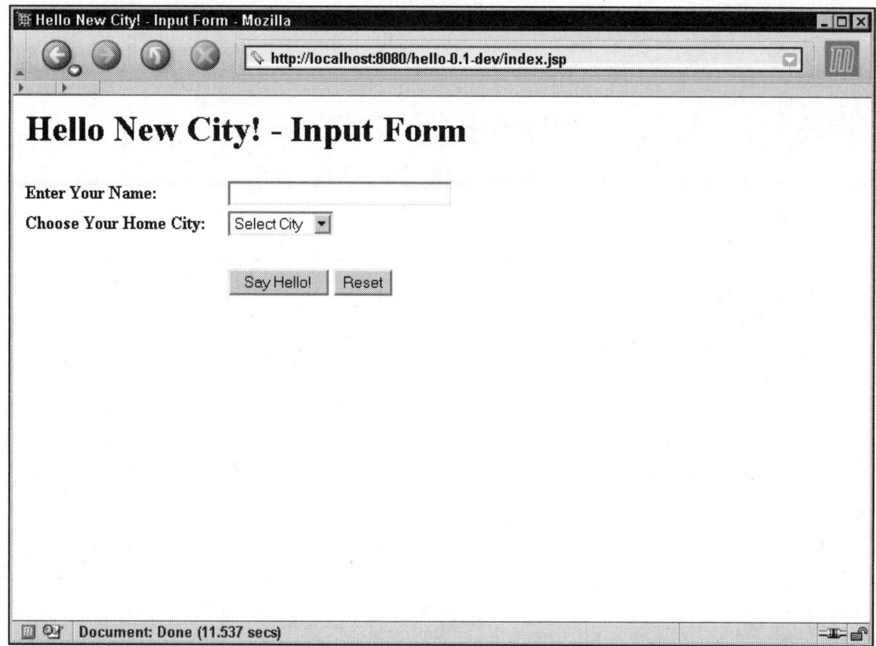

Figure 17-3: Successful test of the Hello City Web application on the JBoss server

The template project provides a simple example of a Web-based application communicating with an Enterprise Java Bean (EJB) containing the application business logic. In this example the business logic is quite simple; a JSP `index.jsp` communicates with the `TestSessionBean` session bean that tests the storage and retrieval of an entity to the internal Hypersonic database. The session bean stores and retrieves data from the database via the `TestEntityBean` entity bean. During insertion the entity bean invokes another session bean, `SequenceGeneratorBean`, that generates a unique ID for the new entity using the database's sequence generator. After a new entity is inserted into the database the unique ID is returned to the JSP and displayed to the user.

Note For more information about session, entity and message driven beans, refer to the JBoss Quick Start Guide or Mastering Enterprise JavaBeans (second edition) by Ed Roman, et al.

This section familiarizes a developer with the template J2EE project by explaining the structure of the project, along with the Ant- and XDoclet-based build system.

Project Structure

The layout of a JBoss J2EE project is not too dissimilar from a Tomcat Web project. The structure of the template project in `C:\jboss-3.0.4_tomcat-4.1.12\examples\template` can be seen in Figure 17-4.

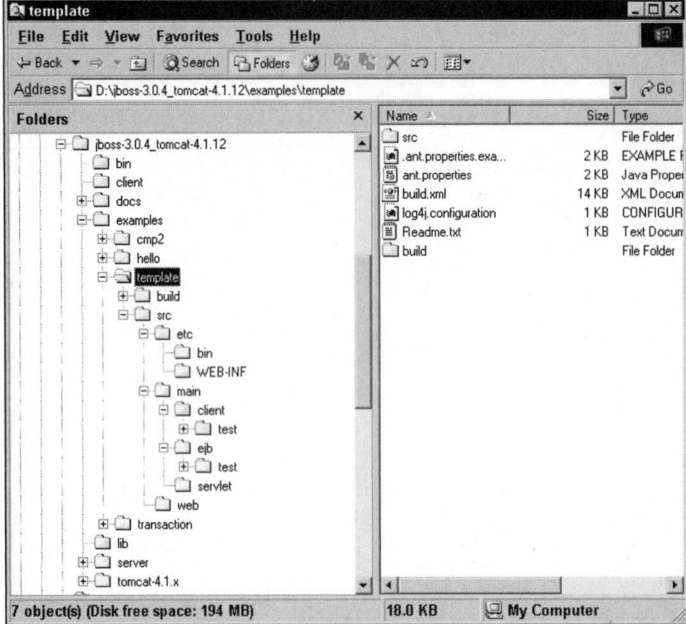

Figure 17-4: JBoss template and example layout

The major difference in the layout is the fact that the source tree contains all the source, configuration, and resource files along with all the Web-based content such as HTML and JSP. Apart from that, the underlying layout of each of these components remains relatively the same. Table 17-1 briefly describes the structure and purpose of each directory within the template layout.

Table 17-1: Template Project Structure

Directory	*Sub Directory*	*Purpose*
build		The build output folder. All compiled objects are placed within this folder along with the complete project structure required to create WAR and EAR distributions.
src		The root of the source tree. Contains all source code, configuration files, Web content, and additional resources required for the project.
src	Etc	Configuration files, including deployment descriptors and properties.
src	Main	Location of all project source code. Source code within this folder is organized into three separate sub folders, `client`, `ejb` and `servlet`. The organizational structure determines how the resulting classes are packaged during the deployment process.
src	Web	Web-based content including HTML and JSP files.

Build System

The JBoss template project uses the Ant build tool as the core of the build system. Sample build scripts are provided with the template project and serve as a solid foundation for any J2EE project. To further ease EJB development the build system utilizes the XDoclet code generation engine, greatly reducing the amount of source files required in a J2EE project.

XDoclet generates all the necessary home and remote interfaces required by Enterprise JavaBeans, along with the creation of container specific configuration. Extra meta-data required to generate these files is included in the EJB source code as JavaDoc tags.

More information about XDoclet can be found from the XDoclet project site at `http://xdoclet.sourceforge.net/`.

Download and Installation

The templates example should have been installed along with the JBoss distribution in the JBoss Installation section. If the `C:\jboss-3.0.4_tomcat-4.1.12\examples` directory does not exist go back and follow the instructions to download and install the JBoss template and examples.

The template build system requires Ant and XDoclet are installed.

Ant

Ant should already be installed as part of Chapter 2, and an example of its usage is given in Chapter 5.

Caution

Ensure the `ANT_HOME` environment variable is set before commencement of using the template project. Type the following command in a Command Prompt window:

```
C:\> echo %ANT_HOME%
```

The result should point to the location of the Ant install directory.

XDoclet

XDoclet can be obtained from `http://xdoclet.sourceforge.net/`. Click the Download/Installation link, and scroll to the Downloading XDoclet area. From here, click the SourceForge download page link.

Version 1.1.2 is the latest stable release; select `xdoclet-1.1.2.zip`, and when prompted save the file to disk.

Installation of XDoclet requires the downloaded file to be unzipped. Extract `xdoclet-1.1.2.zip` to the new folder `C:\xdoclet-1.2.0`. The package creates the sub folders `docs`, `lib`, and `samples`.

The `lib` directory contains all the classes required to run XDoclet, and the `samples` directory contains a useful starting point to integrate XDoclet into your Ant build environment. Refer to the documentation in the `docs` directory for more information.

Configuration

Configuration of the build environment is easy with the use of a separate `ant.properties` file that is used to separate environment specific information out of the build file.

Now you have to copy the `.ant.properties.example` to `ant.properties` and adjust the settings to your needs.

The JBoss template project was obviously designed to work on a Unix system, and suggests that the `ant.properties` file should be named `.ant.properties`. However, as most Windows users will note, the Windows Explorer rename function does not allow you to rename a file in this way. To make things easier for us, modify the build.xml file (at approximately line 9) from

```
<!--
      Give user a chance to override without editing
      this file (and without typing -D each time
      they run it)
   -->
   <property file=".ant.properties" />
   <property file="${user.home}/.ant.properties" />
```

to

```
<!--
      Give user a chance to override without editing
      this file (and without typing -D each time
      they run it)
   -->
   <property file="ant.properties" />
   <property file="${user.home}/ant.properties" />
```

The `.ant.properties.example` file can now be renamed to `ant.properties`.

Listing 17-1 shows the changes necessary to the build environment configuration to suit the recently installed JBoss environment. Please apply the following changes to `C:\jboss-3.0.4_tomcat-4.1.12\examples\template\ant.properties`.

Listing 17-1: ant.properties

```
# Set the path to the runtime JBoss directory containing the JBoss
# application server
# ATTENTION: the one containing directories like "bin", "client", "server"
# etc.
jboss.home=C:/jboss-3.0.4_tomcat-4.1.12
# Set the configuration name that must have a corresponding directory under
# <jboss.home>/server
jboss.configuration=default
# Set the path to the root directory of the XDoclet distribution (see
# http://www.sf.net/projects/xdoclet)
xdoclet.home=C:/xdoclet-1.1.2
# Set this to "true" when you want to force the rebuild of the XDoclet
# generated files (see XDoclet's <ejbdoclet> attribute "force")
xdoclet.force=false
# Set the EJB version you want to use (1.1 or 2.0, see XDoclet's
# <ejbdoclet> attribute "ejbspec")
ejb.version=2.0
# Set the JBoss version you want to use (2.4, 3.0 etc., see XDoclet's
# <jboss> attribute "version")
jboss.version=3.0
# Set the DB type mapping (Hypersonic SQL, PostgreSQL etc., see XDoclet's
# <jboss> attribute "typemapping")
```

```
type.mapping=Hypersonic SQL
# Set the DataSource name your are going to use (java:/DefaultDS etc., see
# XDoclet's <jboss> attribute "datasource")
datasource.name=java:/DefaultDS
# Uncomment this and adjust the path to point directly to JAR file
# containing the servlet classes
# Attention: By uncommenting this line you start the creation of a WAR file
servlet-lib.path=\
C:/jboss-3.0.4_tomcat-4.1.12/tomcat-4.1.x/common/lib/servlet.jar
```

The example J2EE application in the template project is now ready to build.

Building

To build the example J2EE application run the build file from the project work area.

```
C:\> cd C:\jboss-3.0.4_tomcat-4.1.12\examples\template
C:\jboss-3.0.4_tomcat-4.1.12\examples\template> ant
```

XDoclet may display warnings during the code generation process; the warnings indicate the failure to locate class and exception dependencies that XDoclet is yet to generate. All dependencies should be fulfilled by XDoclet before the compilation phase; therefore the warnings may safely be ignored.

The build file compiles and deploys the example J2EE application to JBoss. The following output should be seen at the tail of the console or log file:

```
[MainDeployer] Deployed package: file:/C:/jboss-3.0.4_tomcat-
4.1.12/server/default/deploy/web-client.war
- - - - -
- - - - -
[MainDeployer] Deployed package: file:/C:/jboss-3.0.4_tomcat-
4.1.12/server/default/deploy/ejb-test.jar
```

The EJB component and a Web client to test the application should now be deployed to the JBoss server.

Testing

Along with the JSP interface to the template project, a command line client is also provided. The command line client connects directly to the `TestSession` bean, bypassing the use of the servlet container. The command line client is perfect for testing the EJBs in isolation.

To run the command line client change directories to `build\bin` and execute the batch script.

```
C:\jboss-3.0.4_tomcat-4.1.12\examples\template> cd build\bin
C:\jboss-3.0.4_tomcat-4.1.12\examples\template\build\bin> run-client.bat
```

Output should look like

```
New Entity Id is: 2
```

Note

The ID generated will depend on how many times the client or the Web-client has been run.

Next, the template project may be tested using the Web-based client. Open the URL `http://localhost:8080/web-client/index.jsp`. The output should look like that shown in Figure 17-5.

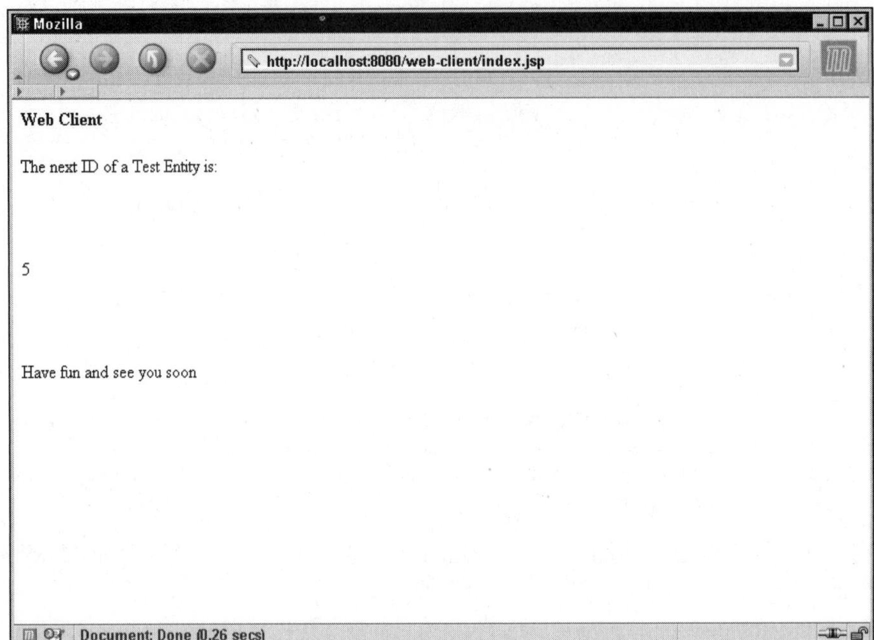

Figure 17-5: Expected results of JBoss template project Web client

The ID generated will depend on how many times the client or the Web-client has been run.

If the tests completed successfully, you can now modify the template project and implement your own fully-fledged J2EE Web applications using EJB technology.

Summary

This concludes a very simple introduction to installing and using Tomcat with JBoss. The brevity of the example really doesn't do justice to the scope of the possibilities to application development with JBoss, but it does confirm how simple the transition from a servlet container (Tomcat) to a J2EE server (JBoss) can be.

In this chapter we have seen a working demonstration of an existing Web-based application running on JBoss with the aid of the Tomcat servlet engine. Furthermore, the overview of the JBoss template project should provide a development team with a springboard for implementing scalable and robust projects using the J2EE suite of APIs.

For more information about the use of EJB refer to the JBoss Quick Start Guide or Mastering Enterprise JavaBeans (second edition) by Ed Roman, et al.

log4j

log4j provides a user customizable logging capability to Java classes. The logging can be enabled or disabled at runtime by the use of configuration files, the changes to which can be automatically detected removing the need to stop and start applications to change logging behavior.

According to the log4j Web site (`http://jakarta.apache.org/log4j`) the overhead of leaving the logging instrumentation in production code is around five nanoseconds per check.

There are three basic components in log4j. These are:

✦ **loggers:** Produce log messages

✦ **appenders:** The output destination of the log messages

✦ **layouts:** The format of the output log message

These can all be created dynamically and configured within the code, but the more common approach is to use a configuration file for the creation of the logging components.

Loggers

Loggers are responsible for the production of log messages and log4j has an extremely interesting method of arranging the relationships of loggers within an application.

Loggers are arranged in a tree-like hierarchy, very similar to a class hierarchy, and this can be utilized in a very convenient manner by having each class that performs logging use the class name as an identifier for the logger. As will become apparent shortly, the logger that is named `tomcat.bible.hello` and the logger `tomcat.bible` have a relationship that can allow for the inheritance of attributes and configuration from the parent to the child. These relationships can also be disconnected, with `tomcat.bible.hello` and `tomcat` having the same relationship provided the intermediate loggers are not specified.

```
Logger myLogger = Logger.getLogger("tomcat.bible");
```

Loggers are identified by a name, and within the application obtaining a logger of the same name obtains an instance of the same logger without creating a new object.

```
Logger another = Logger.getLogger("tomcat.bible");
```

`myLogger` and `another` refer to exactly the same logger instance. This has great benefits because a logger may be created in initialization code, configured appropriately, then utilized throughout the class (or application) without having to pass the logger via parameters. A logger may be obtained at the point when logging is required to be performed, which is extremely beneficial to keeping code maintainable and modular.

There exists a special Logger, the root logger, which always exists and is the root of the tree of all loggers in the application. This logger cannot be obtained by name, but a static method in the `Logger` class can be used to retrieve an instance of this logger.

```
Logger rootLogger = Logger.getRootLogger();
```

For each logger the concept of a logging level exists. This logging level determines if a log message generated passes through the logger into the appenders for output. This mechanism is very similar to the Unix syslog facility and should be familiar to users of those systems. The levels are defined to be:

- DEBUG
- INFO
- WARNING
- ERROR
- FATAL

There are also two special levels, ALL, which has the lowest rank of debugging and turns on all levels, and OFF, which has the highest rank of debugging and turns off all levels.

```
myLogger.setLevel(Level.WARNING);
```

Setting the logging level is not normally performed as part of code, but as part of external configuration files, which is examined in a later section.

As described previously, loggers are arranged in a hierarchy that inherits attributes from parents to children. This also includes the logging level, so a logger that is created from the root logger inherits the logging level of the root logger. The root logger is defined to have a logging level of DEBUG by default, and therefore all loggers by default have a logging level assigned, even if none are ever specifically assigned.

Logging is then a simple matter of invoking one of the methods on the logger that are responsible for generating a message. Each log message must be generated with a level so the priority of the log message can be compared against the log level of the logger to determine if the message should then be displayed. This is achieved by either using the `log(Level lvl, Object obj)` method, or more often one of the convenience methods:

- debug()
- info()
- warn()
- error()
- fatal()

For example, of the following log messages, only the second will be displayed because it has a higher priority than the logging level of the logger.

```
Logger logger = Logger.getLogger("bible.tomcat.hello");
logger.setLevel(Level.WARNING);
logger.debug("about to speak a greeting");
logger.fatal("no speech capabilities found, aborting");
```

The most common approach to obtaining a named logger is not via an explicit string as shown here, but is to use the actual class as follows:

```
Logger logger = Logger.getLogger(HelloWorld.class);
```

Appenders

Appenders are the component that provides a destination for logging messages. Appenders are added to a logger, and there are a number of different types of appenders that are defined in log4j. These are:

- `AsyncAppender`: Performs asynchronous logging. The `AsyncAppender` provides a `addAppender()` method to the appender and other types of appenders (such as `ConsoleAppender`, `JDBCAppender`) and can be added to the `AsyncAppender`. The logger utilizes this appender, which will collect the events and dispatch them to the appenders via a separate thread, preventing the logger from potentially blocking.
- `ConsoleAppender`: a subclass of `WriterAppender` that performs logging to `System.out` or `System.err`.
- `DailyRollingFileAppender`: a subclass of `FileAppender` that performs logging to a file that is rotated on a user specified frequency. The frequency is specified by a `DatePattern` that has the options of rotating the files:
  - At the beginning of each month.
  - On the first day of the week. The first day is defined by the locale.
  - At midnight on each day.
  - At midnight and midday of each day.
  - Every hour.
  - Every minute.
- `ExternallyRolledFileAppender`: A subclass of `RollingFileAppender` that listens on a socket for an external event (a `RollOver` message) that causes the current log file to be rotated.
- `FileAppender`: A subclass of `WriterAppender` that performs logging to a file.
- `JDBCAppender`: Performs logging to a JDBC database.
- `JMSAppender`: Performs logging to a JMS Topic.
- `LF5Appender`: Performs logging to a Swing GUI logging console.
- `NTEventLogAppender`: Performs logging to an NT event system. This appender can only be utilized when installed on a Windows operating system.
- `RollingFileAppender`: A subclass of `FileAppender` that rotates a log file based on the size of the file and keeps a numbered series of backups as part of the rotation.
- `SMTPAppender`: Performs logging via a e-mail message. This appender has a buffer size that collects log messages into a cyclic buffer and a trigger event that causes the e-mail to be sent. The trigger event is set to `ERROR` by default.
- `SocketAppender`: Performs logging to a remote log server, normally a `SocketNode`.
- `SocketHubAppender`: Performs logging to a set of remote log servers.
- `SyslogAppender`: Performs logging to a syslog daemon.
- `TelnetAppender`: Performs logging to a socket that can be viewed in telnet friendly manner.
- `WriterAppender`: Performs logging to a `java.ioWriter` or `java.io.OutputStream` depending on the constructor used.

To add an appender to a logger it is as simple as the following:

```
Appender toFile = new Appender(myLayout, myFile);
logger.addAppender(toFile);
```

However, configuration of this sort is normally done via a configuration file that is described immediately following. In addition, multiple appenders may be added to a single logger to produce output in a variety of forms. Appenders also may be configured to display messages exceeding a particular threshold. This functionality allows for the adding of a ConsoleAppender that has been configured to displays Level.DEBUG and above messages combined with a SyslogAppender that displays Level.ERROR and above messages.

Because appenders are added to loggers and loggers are arranged in a hierarchy that inherits attributes it is reasonable to expect that the appenders are inherited by the children. While this is strictly not how log4j defines the relationship, this is the result that occurs and may produce unexpected results because log messages are sent to all the appenders in the hierarchy.

The result of this arrangement of appenders and loggers in the following example produces three messages to the console, and not possibly the two that were expected.

```
topLogger = Logger.getLogger("bible");
topLogger.addAppender(new ConsoleAppender(myLayout));
helloLogger = Logger.getLogger("bible.tomcat.hello");
helloLogger.addAppender(new ConsoleAppender(myLayout));

topLogger.error("oops"); // 1 message
helloLogger.debug("testing, testing, 1,2,3"); // 2 messages
```

Fortunately log4j provides the capability to inhibit this inheritance of appenders by children. A logger using setAdditivity(false) will inhibit the inheritance; all the children of the logger will not inherit any of the appenders that are higher in the hierarchy. This is best shown using an example. Using the same loggers that have been defined above (topLogger and helloLogger) we shall also add testLogger.

```
testLogger = Logger.getLogger("bible.tomcat.hello.test");
helloLogger.setAdditivity(false);
```

Now testLogger and helloLogger will only output a single message for each log message processed.

Layouts

The final component in the logging trilogy is the layout. Quite simply the layout is the format of the log message. Layouts are used when an appender is created. There are a number of layouts defined by log4j.

- DateLayout: For formatting according to a date specific layout. The options available are any format that can be used by java.text.SimpleDateFormat or any of the predefined options NULL, RELATIVE, ABSOLUTE, DATE, or ISO8601.
- HTMLLayout: Outputs the messages in an HTML table.
- PatternLayout: Outputs the messages according to a user-defined specification similar to printf(). The specification is shown below in Table 17-2.
- SimpleLayout: Outputs the level of the log statement followed by the application-supplied log message.
- TTCCDateLayout: A subclass of DateLayout that implements a specific layout consisting of time, thread, category, and context information.
- XMLLayout: Outputs the log message as an XML element. The XML elements are not sufficient to create a well-formed XML file, and must be used as an external entity within a separate file.

Table 17-2: PatternLayout Specification

Conversion Character	Result
%c	The category of the logging event.
%C	The fully qualified class name of the caller issuing the logging request.
%d	The date of the logging event.
%F	The filename where the logging request was issued.
%l	Location information of the caller generating the logging event.
%L	The line number from where the logging request was issued.
%m	The application supplied message associated with the logging event.
%M	The method name where the logging request was issued.
%n	The platform specific line separator character or characters.
%p	The priority of the logging event.
%r	The number of milliseconds elapsed since the start of the application.
%t	The name of the thread that generated the logging event.
%x	The NDC associated with the thread that generated the logging event.
%X	The MDC associated with the thread that generated the logging event.
%%	The sequence %% outputs a single percent sign (%).

Configuration

Configuration of log4j is performed either via direct manipulation of the logger objects within the code, or more commonly via a configuration file.

The configuration in the code may be done similarly to the examples in the preceding sections, or by the use of the `BasicConfigurator` that will create a logging environment with:

- A `ConsoleAppender` added to the root logger.
- The `ConsoleAppender` uses a `PatternLayout` output to `System.out`.
- The `PatternLayout` using the `TTCC_CONVERSION_PATTERN`.

To use the `BasicConfigurator` is as simple as the following:

```
Logger myLogger = Logger.getLogger(HelloWorld.class);
. . . .
public void init()
{
    BasicConfigurator.configure();
    . . . .
    myLogger.debug("that should just about do it!");
}
```

However, this is still placing the configuration within the application and reduces the ability to change the logging behavior during runtime. The most convenient, and recommended approach to configuring log4j is via a configuration file. There are two types of configuration file readers, the PropertyConfigurator, which will read a file containing Java properties, and a more advanced DOMConfigurator that will read an XML stream. The DOMConfigurator provides a great degree of flexibility for configuration, but for the purposes of this chapter we focus on the PropertyConfigurator because this covers most common uses.

To read from a configuration file it is simply a matter of changing the preceding example to the following:

```
Logger myLogger = Logger.getLogger(HelloWorld.class);
. . . .
public void init()
{
    PropertyConfigurator.configure(configFile);
    . . . .
    myLogger.debug("that should just about do it!");
}
```

By convention the configuration file is called log4j.configuration, and if this is the case, the initialization of the static classes in the Logger automatically loads the file provided the configuration file exists in the CLASSPATH. For a Web application this is simply a matter of placing the file in the WEB-INF/classes.

So, the next step is to download, install, and configure a Web application to make use of log4j.

Download

The Web site for log4j can be found at: http://jakarta.apache.org/log4j/.

1. Select the downloads link from the left navigation pane.
2. This displays the downloads page. Select the latest version from the ZIP link at the top of page and when prompted, save the file to disk.

The direct link to the version used for the examples was

```
http://jakarta.apache.org/log4j/jakarta-log4j-1.2.7.zip
```

Installation

The installation of log4j is very similar to the other Jakarta installations, all of which require unpacking a distribution and making use of a JAR file.

Unpack the distribution to C:\ and this creates a directory hierarchy starting with c:\jakarta-log4j-1.2.7\. This is 7.6MB in size and contains the source, some examples, documentation, and the JAR file that is required to be used in the application.

The log4j JAR file to be used in the applications is located at:

```
c:\jakarta-log4j-1.2.7\dist\lib\log4j-1.2.7.jar
```

Adding Logging to a Web Application

This example updates the Hello City application developed in Chapter 7.

A version of Hello City suitable for modification to follow this example can be downloaded from the book Web site.

Due to the way that the classloaders work in Tomcat, the recommended approach for installing log4j in Tomcat is to include the JAR file as part of the Web application.

There are three steps that need to be performed to add the logging to the Hello City application.

1. Update build.xml to include the log4j.jar and the log4j.properties file.
2. Create a log4j.properties file.
3. Add the logging statements to the application.

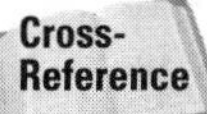

This chapter uses the same files and locations created in Chapter7 for the Hello City Web application. The code modifications will be made to the `CityServlet`.java.

Updating build.xml

There are two parts of `build.xml` that need to be modified. Listing 17-2 shows the sections that require updates highlighted in bold.

Listing 17-2: Updating build.xml

```
<project name="Hello World" default="compile" basedir=".">
. . . .
<!-- ============ External Dependencies ================== -->

<!-- log4j external dependency -->
  <property name="log4j.jar"
          value="c:/jakarta-log4j-1.2.7/dist/lib/log4j-1.2.7.jar" />
. . . .
<!-- =========== Compilation Classpath =================== -->

  <path id="compile.classpath">

    <!-- Include all JAR files that will be included in /WEB-INF/lib -->
    <!-- *** CUSTOMIZE HERE AS REQUIRED BY YOUR APPLICATION *** -->

    <pathelement location="${log4j.jar}"/>

. . . .
<!-- ================ Prepare Target ================= -->
  <target name="prepare">
. . . .

    <!-- Copy external dependencies as required -->
```

Continued

Listing 17-2 *(continued)*

```
    <!-- *** CUSTOMIZE HERE AS REQUIRED BY YOUR APPLICATION *** -->
    <mkdir  dir="${build.home}/WEB-INF/lib"/>

    <copy todir="${build.home}/WEB-INF/lib" file="${log4j.jar}"/>
    <copy todir="${build.home}/WEB-INF/classes"
        file="${basedir}/log4j.properties"/>
  . . . .
  </target>
. . . .
</project>
```

Creating a log4j.properties File

The log4j.properties file controls the logging configuration for the Web application. Create the file in the root directory of the HelloWorld Web application. This is the same directory that contains `build.xml`. Listing 17-3 contains the properties that should be defined for the logging configuration.

log4j uses reflection and the `JavaBean` API to process the properties file. The attributes that are available and the values for the attributes such as `log4j.appender.A1.File` and `log4j.appender.A1.Append` can be deduced by examining the API documentation for the `FileAppender` and looking for the `setXXX()` methods.

Listing 17-3: log4j.properties

```
# set root logger level to ERROR
log4j.rootLogger = ERROR

# set bible.tomcat logger level to DEBUG and appenders called A0 & A1
log4j.logger.bible.tomcat = DEBUG, A0, A1

# A0 is to be a ConsoleAppender
log4j.appender.A0 = org.apache.log4j.ConsoleAppender

# A0 uses SimpleLayout
log4j.appender.A0.layout = org.apache.log4j.SimpleLayout

# A1 is to be a FileAppender
log4j.appender.A1 = org.apache.log4j.FileAppender
log4j.appender.A1.File = c:/tomcat/logs/hello_log4j.txt
log4j.appender.A1.Append = false

# A1 uses a PatternLayout
log4j.appender.A1.layout = org.apache.log4j.PatternLayout
log4j.appender.A1.layout.ConversionPattern = %d{HH:mm:ss} %-5p [%c{1}] %m%n
```

Caution

It may seem like just creating extra work to create a logger `bible.tomcat` rather than just configure the `rootLogger`. The reason that this is done is that there may be other libraries that are also configured to use log4j and to ensure that we only get the messages that we are interested in when running we restrict the logging in this manner.

Those who are curious may wish to change the first line to be:

```
log4j.rootLogger = DEBUG, A0, A1
```

And remove the following line when running the Cactus tests later in the chapter.

```
log4j.logger.bible.tomcat = DEBUG, A0, A1
```

The JUnit/Cactus framework also uses log4j and the amount of debugging information is staggering.

Add Logging Statements to the Web Application

The modifications to the Web application are very simple, and are used to illustrate the creation of loggers in different classes after initialization, which occurs automatically in the log4j package.

The first file to be modified is a servlet in the Web application. In this case it is `CityServlet.java`. Listing 17-4 shows the additional logging in bold. The modifications have been made to show the parameters loaded from the `init-param` elements in the `web.xml`.

Listing 17-4: CityServlet.java

```
package bible.tomcat.hello;

import java.io.*;
import java.lang.*;
import java.util.*;

import javax.servlet.http.*;
import javax.servlet.*;

import org.apache.log4j.*;

public class CityServlet
extends HttpServlet
{
    public final String FORM_PAGE   = "/CityBeanForm.jsp";
    public final String RESULT_PAGE = "/CityResult.jsp";

. . . .

    /*
     * log4j logger
     */
    static Logger logger = Logger.getLogger(CityServlet.class);

    public void init()
```

Continued

Listing 17-4 (continued)

```
    throws ServletException
    {
    . . . .
        while (en.hasMoreElements())
        {
            String p = (String)en.nextElement();

            if (p.startsWith("city.param"))
            {
                String v = ctx.getInitParameter(p);
                if (logger.isDebugEnabled())
                {
                    logger.debug("found parameter ["+p+"] = :"+v);
                }
                greetings.add(createCityBean(v));
            }
        }
        ctx.setAttribute("greetings", greetings);
    }
. . . .
}
```

Note

The use of `logger.isDebugEnabled()` is used with debugging statements so that when the logging level for the logger does not include `DEBUG`, the debug statement is not executed. In many cases this guard is not necessary because the speed of invoking the method is not a great overhead. However, when parameters are constructed as they are in this case, the use of the `isDebugEnabled()` prevents the relatively expensive `String` construction from occurring.

The next file to be modified is `CityBean.java`. Again, the modifications are simple and shown in bold in Listing 17-5.

Listing 17-5: CityBean.java

```
package bible.tomcat.hello;

import org.apache.log4j.*;

public class CityBean
{
    private String  cityName;
    private String  cityAbbrev;
    private String  cityGreeting;

    static Logger logger = Logger.getLogger(CityBean.class);

. . . .
```

```
    public void setCityName(String cn)
    {
        if (logger.isDebugEnabled())
        {
            logger.debug("setCityName: "+cn);
        }
        cityName = cn;
    }

    public void setCityAbbrev(String ca)
    {
        if (logger.isDebugEnabled())
        {
            logger.debug("setCityAbbrev: "+ca);
        }
        cityAbbrev = ca;
    }

    public void setCityGreeting(String cg)
    {
        if (logger.isDebugEnabled())
        {
            logger.debug("setCityGreeting: "+cg);
        }
        cityGreeting = cg;
    }
. . . .
}
```

With the modifications made, compile the Web application and deploy to Tomcat. If any errors in the compilation occur, check the preceding listings and also make sure the `build.xml` is referencing the `log4j.jar` file correctly.

The configuration file that was used creates a file in `c:\tomcat\logs` called `hello_log4j.txt`. The logging occurs when the servlet is initialized and that normally occurs the first time it is accessed unless configured with a `load-on-startup` element in `web.xml`.

Access the servlet with the URL `http://localhost:8080/hello/city` and the browser should display the Hello City! Input Form page. Now, look in the log directory for `hello_log4j.txt`, which should contain lines similar to Listing 17-6.

Listing 17-6: **hello_log4j.txt**

```
01:02:28 DEBUG [CityServlet] [city.param.2] = :MIL:Milan:Ciao
01:02:28 DEBUG [CityBean] setCityAbbrev: MIL
01:02:28 DEBUG [CityBean] setCityName: Milan
01:02:28 DEBUG [CityBean] setCityGreeting: Ciao
01:02:28 DEBUG [CityServlet] [city.param.1] = :MEL:Melbourne:G'day
01:02:28 DEBUG [CityBean] setCityAbbrev: MEL
```

Continued

Listing 17-6 *(continued)*

```
01:02:28 DEBUG [CityBean] setCityName: Melbourne
01:02:28 DEBUG [CityBean] setCityGreeting: G'day
01:02:28 DEBUG [CityServlet] [city.param.3] = :PAR:Paris:Bonjour
01:02:28 DEBUG [CityBean] setCityAbbrev: PAR
01:02:28 DEBUG [CityBean] setCityName: Paris
01:02:28 DEBUG [CityBean] setCityGreeting: Bonjour
```

The first column shows a timestamp, the second column displays the logging level, the third column displays the category of the logging event, and the remainder of the line is the application-supplied message. This matches the format specification in the `log4j.properties` file shown in Listing 17-3.

Summary

This section has provided an introduction to logging using log4j and implementation of that logging in Web applications using Tomcat. log4j is a comprehensive package and the preceding examples provides only a small set of the possible capabilities and configuration options that are available.

Some other areas of particular importance to the Web application area is the ability to track user sessions through the logging and have that information logged as part of the logging, thus allowing for seeing which users and requests generated particular logging messages.

The best source for further information is at the log4j Web site at `http://jakarta.apache.org/log4j`.

Cactus

Cactus is a testing framework for unit testing server-side Java code. It is targeted towards the J2EE framework and has support for testing servlets, EJBs, TagLibs, and filters.

Cactus is an extension of the very popular JUnit testing framework and carries on the philosophy of "test-driven-development" to the server-side development activities that has only been available to component classes via JUnit. JUnit is written by Erich Gamma and Kent Beck, two very strong proponents of agile development methodologies that favor continual testing as part of the development cycle.

More information about JUnit and agile methodologies can be found at `http://www.junit.org`

Cactus provides a client/server layer between the unit testing code and the application that has wrappers for the server interfaces such as `HttpSession`, `HttpServletRequest`, `HttpServletResponse`, that enables the testing to be performed and information to be obtained from the code without any modifications to the code to be tested.

While no code needs to be modified for Cactus to perform much of the testing, it is highly recommended to provide `getXXX()` methods to access attributes that require testing.

As Cactus extends the capabilities of JUnit, many of the JUnit testing frameworks such as the GUI and text-based test running applications also work with Cactus. Cactus also provides a servlet-based test runner that is activated using a browser. The examples in this section cover both types of test activation.

Cactus Test Suite Operation

It is important to understand the operation of Cactus and how to extend the example provided in this section, and to achieve that goal we must first look at how JUnit structures the test components.

JUnit TestCase

There are two basic classes involved in JUnit, the `TestCase` and the `TestSuite`. A `TestSuite` is used to execute one or more `TestCase` implementations.

So, we can look at `TestCase` implementing how the testing will occur. The `TestSuite` determines the testing that will actually take place.

A very simple `TestCase` is shown in Listing 17-7.

Listing 17-7: TestCityBean.java

```
package bible.tomcat.hello.test;

import bible.tomcat.hello.*;

import java.util.*;
import junit.framework.*;

public class TestCityBean extends TestCase
{
    public TestCityBean(String name)
    {
        super(name);
    }

    public void testCreateCityBean()
    {
        CityBean cb = new CityBean();
        assertNotNull(cb);
    }

    public static Test suite()
    {
        return new TestSuite(TestCityBean.class);
    }
}
```

The testCreateCityBean() is an important part of the TestCase because any method that starts with test will be executed when the TestCase is executed by JUnit. The assertXXX() method is the cornerstone of the testing in JUnit. The result of this method call determines the success or failure of a test. The assertXXX() includes the following:

- ✦ assertEquals(Object expected, Object actual). If expected and actual are equal according to the objects equals() method then the test will pass; otherwise the test willfail.
- ✦ assertNull(Object obj). If obj is null, then the test will pass; otherwise the test will fail.
- ✦ assertNotNull(Object obj). If obj is not null, then test will pass, otherwise the test will fail.
- ✦ assertSame(Object expected, Object actual). If expected and actual are the same object then the test will pass, otherwise the test will fail.
- ✦ assertTrue(boolean condition). If condition is true, then the test will pass, otherwise the test will fail.

There also is an assertEquals() for primitive types and for the preceding method signatures there also are methods that provide an additional parameter for a user defined message.

The beantest target described in Listing 17-8 should be added into the Ant build.xml. The recommended location to insert this target is after the all target and before the clean target.

Listing 17-8: **Ant beantest**

```
<target name="beantest" depends="compile" >
  <junit printsummary="yes" haltonfailure="yes" haltonerror="yes"
      fork="no">

      <classpath>
          <path refid="compile.classpath"/>
          <pathelement location="${build.home}/WEB-INF/classes"/>
      </classpath>

      <formatter type="plain" usefile="false"/>
      <test name="bible.tomcat.hello.test.TestCityBean" />
      <classpath>
          <path refid="compile.classpath"/>
          <pathelement location="${build.home}/WEB-INF/classes"/>
      </classpath>
  </junit>
</target>
```

Execute the target with:

```
ant beantest
```

This should display results similar to the following:

```
[junit] Running bible.tomcat.hello.test.TestCityBean
[junit] Tests run: 1, Failures: 0, Errors: 0, Time elapsed: 0.331 sec
[junit] Testsuite: bible.tomcat.hello.test.TestCityBean
[junit] Tests run: 1, Failures: 0, Errors: 0, Time elapsed: 0.331 sec

[junit] Testcase: testCreateCityBean took 0.331 sec
```

Now, that's good, but what if we want to perform lots of tests on the same object? The simple answer is to create lots of `testXXX()` methods in the `TestCase`. This is known as *creating a text fixture*. To support a test fixture there are additional methods that can be added to the `TestCase`.

The `setUp()` method is called prior to each `testXXX()` method and is used to keep all initialization code that may be part of test.

The `tearDown()` method is called after each `testXXX()` method and is generally used to clean up after the test, generally cleaning up whatever actions `setUp()` has performed.

Cactus TestCase

The Cactus `TestCase` has additional complexity due to the server-side nature of the tool. There need to be ways of working with the objects like `HttpServletRequest` to test parameters passing into the servlets, filters, and other server-side objects.

To achieve this there are two additional method signatures:

- `public void beginXXX(WebRequest theRequest)`
- `public void endXXX(WebResponse theReponse)`

The `WebRequest` object is an object provided by Cactus that allows the setting of the HTTP-related parameters that would normally be set by a browser, or relating to the network (such as IP address) that can then be used to test the Web application.

The `WebReponse` can be used to check the results from the operation of the `testXXX()`.

Components Provided by the Test Framework

To allow full access to the server-side environment Cactus provides interfaces into the operation of the Web application and for each type of Web application functionality (servlet, filter, tag library) different components are provided. To work, a Cactus test case must extend not `TestCase` but one of the following:

- **ServletTestCase:** For testing of servlets
- **JspTestCase:** For testing of any Web application functionality that requires access to the `PageContext` or `JspWriter` objects
- **FilterTestCase:** For testing of filters

The following section describes in more detail the objects available within each test case object and their use.

ServletTestCase

The `ServletTestCase` provides access to the following implicit objects:

✦ `request`. This provides access to an object that is like an `HttpServletRequest` and can be used to add headers and cookies in the `beginXXX()` method. The request also provides the ability to set the remote IP address and remote host name of the client to perform testing that could not normally be performed.

✦ `response`. This is an `HttpServletResponse` object and is best used in the `endXXX()` method to check the responses from the test.

✦ `config`. This object is a wrapper around a `ServletConfig` and provides access to the initialization parameters from the `ServletRedirector` element in the `web.xml`.

✦ `session`. This object is an `HttpSession` object and is automatically created by Cactus for every test case. This behavior can be inhibited by using the `WebRequest.setAutomaticSession(false)`. This object is used to examine the session information during the test.

JspTestCase

The `JspTestCase` provides access to the following implicit objects:

✦ `request`, `response`, `config`, `session`. These objects provide the same facilities as the objects of the same name in the `ServletTestCase`.

✦ `out`. This object provides access to the `JspWriter` object.

✦ `pageContext`. This object is used extensively by custom tags to obtain information about the JSP page that contains the tag.

✦ `bodyContent`. The `bodyContent` object is not implicit in the `JspTestCase` and must be obtained by a simple method call, `pageContext.pushBody()`.

Testing custom tags requires some degree of caution because the calls to `pushBody()` must be balanced with `popBody()` or there is a risk the servlet container may not process the tag correctly. The recommended approach is to put the `pushBody()` call in the `setUp()` method and the `popBody()` method in `tearDown()`.

FilterTestCase

The `FilterTestCase` provides access to the following implicit objects:

✦ `request`, `response`. These objects provide the same facilities as the objects ofthe same name in the `ServletTestCase`.

✦ `config`. This object is a wrapper around a `Filter` and provides access to the initialization parameters from the `FilterRedirector` element in the `web.xml`.

✦ `filterChain`. This object is provided to test this filter based on the results of the other filters that form the filter chain.

With the background information out of the way, the next step is to download, install, and implement the Cactus framework.

Download

The first step in using Cactus is to browse to the Cactus home page at `http://jakarta.apache.org/cactus/` to download the software.

1. Select the downloads link from the left navigation pane.
2. This displays the downloads page. Scroll down and under the "Releases" section choose the link "Click here for Cactus Releases."
3. Select the directory `1.4.1`.
4. Select the file `jakarta-cactus-13-1.4.1.zip` and save the file to disk.

The direct link to the version used for the examples was

```
http://jakarta.apache.org/builds/jakarta-cactus/release/v1.4.1/jakarta-cactus-
13-1.4.1.zip
```

Installation

Cactus can be used as a remote testing tool; however this section provides instructions for setting up Cactus with the development and testing done on the same machine.

Note If the testing is performed on a different machine to the Tomcat server, then it is a matter of installing the JAR files listed in the classpath for the JUnit test runner.

As with the log4j section, this installation extends the HelloWorld application developed in Chapter 7. All the paths and environment are consistent with that application.

Cross-Reference Further details about the installation of the tools are provided in Chapter 2.

The following steps describe the process to install the Cactus framework:

1. Extract the downloaded file to `c:\`. This creates a directory hierarchy under `c:\jakarta-cactus-13-1.4.1`. This package consists of the documentation, some examples, and the jar files required to run Cactus.
2. Copy the following jar files from `c:\jakarta-cactus-13-1.4.1\lib` to `c:\tomcat\common\lib`.
   - `cactus-[release].jar`
   - `commons-httpclient-[release].jar`
   - `junit-[release].jar`
   - `aspectjrt-[release].jar`

Note The versions of the releases change depending on the version of Cactus that is installed. There is no need to rename them; just copy them as-is from the Cactus `lib` directory to the Tomcat `lib` directory. Tomcat processes all the JAR files found in that directory on startup to locate classes.

These steps have installed all the components required for the operation of Cactus. The next step is to install the testing configuration for operation with the Web application. The next two sections describe the configuration required for using Cactus with the Web-based test runner and the traditional JUnit text-based test runner.

Even if you do not intend to use the Web test runner, configuration in that section is required to use the JUnit text runner, so read both sections carefully to determine what configuration is required for your application.

Configuring a Web Test Runner

Edit `c:\tomcat\conf\web.xml` and add the elements in Listing 17-9 at the beginning of the file, after the `<webapp>` element:

To keep the example simple, only the `ServletTestRedirector` is configured. If the Web application requires testing of filters, JSP pages, or tag libraries, the `FilterTestRedirector` and the `JspTestRedirector` also may need to be configured.

This will add the configuration for all Web applications on the Tomcat server. This might not be what is desired; however, remember that this is a unit testing tool and should not be installed on a development or deployment system except under very special circumstances. The capabilities provided by Cactus allow for custom creation of requests to the Web applications and having that functionality easily available to an external party may not be appropriate.

Listing 17-9: web.xml

```
<servlet>
    <servlet-name>ServletRedirector</servlet-name>
    <servlet-class>
        org.apache.cactus.server.ServletTestRedirector
    </servlet-class>
</servlet>

<servlet>
    <servlet-name>ServletTestRunner</servlet-name>
    <servlet-class>
        org.apache.cactus.server.runner.ServletTestRunner
    </servlet-class>
</servlet>
```

Then, after the last `servlet` element definition (there are a few provided by Tomcat in addition to the two preceding ones), add the following:

```
<servlet-mapping>
    <servlet-name>ServletRedirector</servlet-name>
    <url-pattern>/ServletRedirector</url-pattern>
</servlet-mapping>

<servlet-mapping>
    <servlet-name>ServletTestRunner</servlet-name>
    <url-pattern>/ServletTestRunner</url-pattern>
</servlet-mapping>
```

The `ServletRedirector` is required by Cactus to perform the unit testing functionality; this servlet must be installed for Cactus to operate.

The `ServletTestRunner` servlet is the optional test running functionality that displays the results in a Web browser.

Configuring Ant with Cactus/JUnit

The easiest approach to the configuration of the JUnit test runner is to use the Ant task to provide the framework to execute the test. Ant is not required to execute the JUnit test runner, further information about creating and executing JUnit test suites can be found in the JUnit documentation on `http://www.junit.org`.

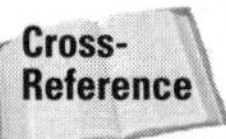

Installation of Ant is covered in Chapter 2. Chapter 5 contains further details on the operation of Ant and the modification of Ant build files.

The `test` target described in Listing 17-10 should be added into the Ant `build.xml`. The recommended location to insert this target is after the `all` target and before the `guitest` target.

Listing 17-10: Cactus Testing Target

```
<target name="test">
  <junit printsummary="yes" haltonfailure="yes" haltonerror="yes"
      fork="yes">

      <classpath>
          <!-- Cactus.properties the classpath -->
          <path location="${basedir}" />
          <path refid="compile.classpath"/>
          <pathelement location="${build.home}/WEB-INF/classes"/>
          <fileset dir="${build.home}/WEB-INF/lib">
              <include name="*.jar"/>
           </fileset>
      </classpath>

      <formatter type="plain" usefile="false"/>
      <test name="bible.tomcat.hello.test.TestHelloWorldServlet"/>

  </junit>
</target>
```

Using the Cactus framework with the JUnit test runner as a client requires the configuration of the location of the Web application context to be tested by the framework. This is achieved by the addition of a configuration file called `cactus.properties`. This file needs to be located in the class path of the JUnit task.

Rather than copy this file into the `build` directory, the simplest approach is to add the `base` directory of the Web application source (represented by the `${basedir}` variable) to the class path for JUnit and create the properties file in `${basedir}`.

Create the file cactus.properties in the same directory as the Ant build.xml for the HelloWorld application with the following contents:

```
cactus.contextURL=http://localhost:8080/hello
```

The configuration file location may also be passed to the JVM by specifying the cactus.config system property using a command line argument such as

```
-Dcactus.config=c:\config\cactus.cfg
```

The final task to be performed when using Ant is to copy the junit-[release].jar file from c:\jakarta-cactus-13.1.4.1\lib to c:\ant\lib. If this step is not performed, Ant cannot find the junit task, and will fail when running.

Integration with a Web Application

The final step is to create the test case for the HelloWorld Web application. These series of tests are aimed at providing an overview of the capabilities of Cactus, but as with other tools covered in this chapter the coverage is deliberately kept at a reasonably simple level.

These unit tests are aimed at testing the CityServlet servlet. It is useful to view the source of CityServlet.java at the same time as working through Listing 17-11 to see the relevance of the tests.

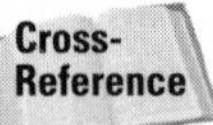

The code for CityServlet.java is in Chapter 7 and also downloadable from the book's Web site.

Listing 17-11 contains the code for the test case; create this file in the directory src\bible\tomcat\hello\test.

Part of the philosophy of the test-driven-development approach is to develop the unit tests in parallel with the development of the functionality.

Readers who are interested in attempting this should read through Listing 17-11 and each unit test section is broken by a small comment within the code. When you get to a comment compile the code and run the test. This gives you a feel for the incremental nature of the development philosophy.

At the end of Listing 17-11 are sections describing how to execute the tests; readers developing the testing servlet incrementally should skip to that section after the first iteration to understand how to perform the test.

Listing 17-11: TestHelloWorldServlet.java

```
package bible.tomcat.hello.test;

import bible.tomcat.hello.*;

import java.io.*;

import javax.servlet.*;
import javax.servlet.http.*;
```

```
import junit.framework.*;
import org.apache.cactus.*;

public class TestHelloWorldServlet extends ServletTestCase
{
    public TestHelloWorldServlet(String theName)
    {
        super(theName);
    }

    public static Test suite()
    {
        return new TestSuite(TestHelloWorldServlet.class);
    }
```

The first test is `testCheckGreetings()` and this uses the implicit `session` object to determine if the servlet is initialized correctly and the `greetings` object was successfully created and placed in the session.

Notice there is no `beginCheckGreetings()` or `endCheckGreetings()` because the test does not need to perform any requests on the servlet.

```
    public void testCheckGreetings() throws ServletException
    {
        CityServlet city = new CityServlet();
        city.init(config);
        assertNotNull("greetings is not null",
            config.getServletContext().getAttribute("greetings"));
    }
```

The next test is `testCheckSelection()`. This test is checking the selection made from a request which is faking the `CityForm.jsp` HTTP POST to the servlet. The URL and parameters are set in the `beginCheckSelection()` method, then the `doPost(request, response)` method in `testCheckSelection()` uses the implicit objects to test the servlet.

The results are checked by examining the values of attributes in the `request` object which are added by the `doPost()` method in `CityServlet.java`.

```
    public void beginCheckSelection(WebRequest req)
    {
        req.setURL("localhost:8080", "/hello", "city", null, null);
        req.addParameter("action", "input");
        req.addParameter("NAME", "jon");
        req.addParameter("CITY", "MEL");
    }

    public void testCheckSelection() throws ServletException, IOException
    {
        CityServlet city = new CityServlet();
        city.init(config);
        city.doPost(request, response);
```

```
        String theGreeting = (String)request.getAttribute("theGreeting");
        assertNotNull("theGreeting is not null", theGreeting);
        assertEquals("theGreeting matches G'day", "G'day", theGreeting);

        String theName = (String)request.getAttribute("theName");
        assertNotNull("theName is not null", theName);
        assertEquals("theName equals jon", "jon", theName);
    }
```

The next test is similar to `testCheckSelection()` except that this test is looking for the results of an error condition, and that the servlet correctly displays an error when a name is not passed as a parameter to the servlet.

Notice how in `beginNoName()` there is no `addParameter("NAME", "x")` unlike in `beginCheckSelection()`.

```
    public void beginNoName(WebRequest req)
    {
        req.setURL("localhost:8080", "/hello", "city", null, null);
        req.addParameter("action", "input");
        req.addParameter("CITY", "MEL");
    }

    public void testNoName() throws ServletException, IOException
    {
        CityServlet city = new CityServlet();
        city.init(config);
        city.doPost(request, response);

        String errorMsg = (String)request.getAttribute("errorMessage");
        assertNotNull("errorMessage is not null", errorMsg);
        assertTrue("errorMessage has 'Please enter a name!",
                   (errorMsg.indexOf("name!") >= 0));

    }
```

`testNoCity()` is similar to `testNoName()` but checks a different parameter, and `testNoInputs()` tests for the correct results when there are no parameters passed to the `CityServlet`.

```
    public void beginNoCity(WebRequest req)
    {
        req.setURL("localhost:8080", "/hello", "city", null, null);
        req.addParameter("action", "input");
        req.addParameter("NAME", "jon");
    }

    public void testNoCity() throws ServletException, IOException
    {
        CityServlet city = new CityServlet();
        city.init(config);
        city.doPost(request, response);
```

```
        String errorMsg = (String)request.getAttribute("errorMessage");
        assertNotNull("errorMessage is not null", errorMsg);
        assertTrue("errorMessage has 'Please choose a city",
                (errorMsg.indexOf("city") >= 0));

    }

    public void beginNoInputs(WebRequest req)
    {
        req.setURL("localhost:8080", "/hello", "city", null, null);
        req.addParameter("action", "input");
    }

    public void testNoInputs() throws ServletException, IOException
    {
        CityServlet city = new CityServlet();
        city.init(config);
        city.doPost(request, response);

        String errorMsg = (String)request.getAttribute("errorMessage");
        assertNotNull("errorMessage is not null", errorMsg);
        assertTrue("errorMessage has both 'name!' and 'city'",
                ((errorMsg.indexOf("city") >= 0) &&
                 (errorMsg.indexOf("name!") >= 0))
                );

    }
```

testCheckOutput() uses the response from the servlet in endCheckOutput() to determine the success of the test. In this case, given the input parameters provided beginCheckOutput(), the servlet should correctly process the results and display the results page produced by CityResult.jsp.

In endCheckOutput() the HTML data is obtained from the response and then a simple match is performed to see if the correct page has been displayed. In many circumstances this may not be a robust and reliable mechanism for determining the success or failure of a test because there may be no simple match that can determine if the page is output correctly.

```
    public void beginCheckOutput(WebRequest req)
    {
        req.setURL("localhost:8080", "/hello", "city", null, null);
        req.addParameter("action", "input");
        req.addParameter("NAME", "jon");
        req.addParameter("CITY", "MEL");
    }

    public void testCheckOutput() throws ServletException, IOException
    {
        CityServlet city = new CityServlet();
        city.init(config);
        city.doPost(request, response);
```

```
    }
    public void endCheckOutput(WebResponse resp) throws IOException
    {
        String expectedResponseContains = "Results Page";

        String html = resp.getText();
        assertTrue("Text matching ["+expectedResponseContains+"] found",
                   html.indexOf(expectedResponseContains) >= 0);
    }
```

testBadOutput() is the companion test to testCheckOutput() in that it tests the results when the input provided is invalid and the servlet displays CityForm.jsp for re-entry of the data.

```
    public void beginBadOutput(WebRequest req)
    {
        req.setURL("localhost:8080", "/hello", "city", null, null);
        req.addParameter("action", "input");
        req.addParameter("NAME", "jon");
        // no city
    }

    public void testBadOutput() throws ServletException, IOException
    {
        CityServlet city = new CityServlet();
        city.init(config);
        city.doPost(request, response);
    }

    public void endBadOutput(WebResponse resp) throws IOException
    {
        String expectedResponseContains = "Input Form";

        String html = resp.getText();
        assertTrue("Text matching ["+expectedResponseContains+"] found",
                   html.indexOf(expectedResponseContains) >= 0);
    }
}
```

After entering either a subset or the entire set of preceding test methods, save the file and compile and then install the Web application in Tomcat. The next two sections describe how to execute the tests using the Web test runner or the JUnit text-based test runner.

Using the Web Test Runner

Open a browser and enter the following URL:

```
http://localhost:8080/hello/ServletTestRunner?suite=bible.tomcat.hello.test.Test
HelloWorldServlet
```

The first part of the URL specifies the ServletTestRunner as the servlet to execute and the second part of the URL (after the ?) specifies the unit test.

Regardless of the number of unit tests that have been entered the results will look something like Figure 17-6.

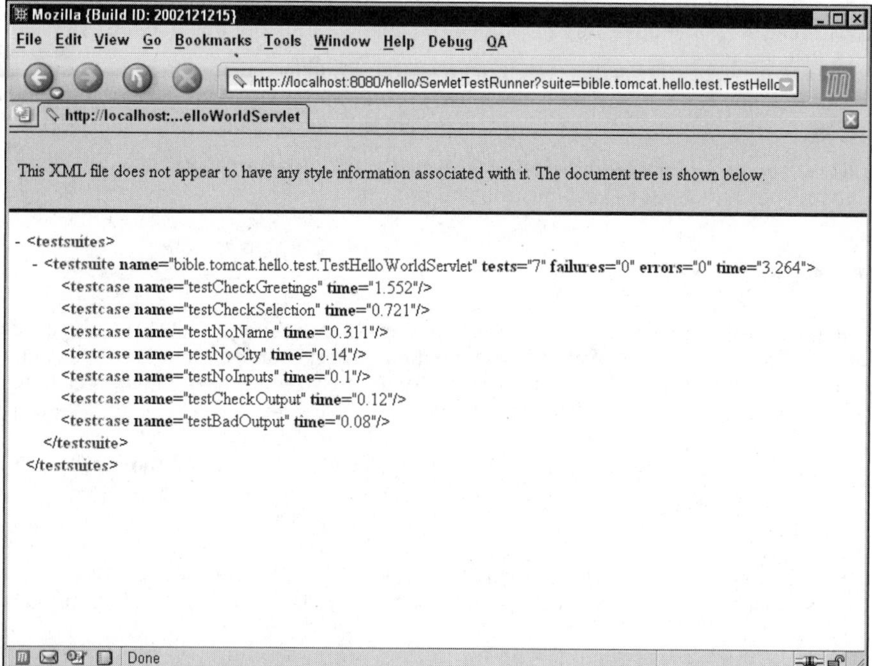

Figure 17-6: Cactus Web Test Runner

Using the JUnit Test Runner

The JUnit Test Runner is even simpler than the Web Test Runner (if that is possible) and is executed by using the following command:

```
ant test
```

This should produce results similar to the following:

```
[junit] Running bible.tomcat.hello.test.TestHelloWorldServlet
[junit] Tests run: 7, Failures: 0, Errors: 0, Time elapsed: 4.717 sec
[junit] Testsuite: bible.tomcat.hello.test.TestHelloWorldServlet
[junit] Tests run: 7, Failures: 0, Errors: 0, Time elapsed: 4.717 sec

[junit] Testcase: testCheckGreetings took 3.565 sec
[junit] Testcase: testCheckSelection took 0.521 sec
[junit] Testcase: testNoName took 0.25 sec
[junit] Testcase: testNoCity took 0.111 sec
[junit] Testcase: testNoInputs took 0.07 sec
[junit] Testcase: testCheckOutput took 0.08 sec
[junit] Testcase: testBadOutput took 0.11 sec
```

Summary

This section has provided an introduction to unit testing using the Cactus framework. As was found with log4j, Cactus is a comprehensive package and the preceding example provides only a small set of the possible capabilities and configuration options that are available.

Obviously, important areas that were not covered include testing for filters and tag libraries. The information and configuration described in this chapter should provide a solid foundation for developers who are looking to utilize Cactus in those areas.

The best source for further information is at the Cactus Web site at `http://jakarta.apache.org/cactus`, and the JUnit Web site as `http://www.junit.org`.

JMeter

JMeter is a testing application from the Apache Group that can be used to test Web sites, databases, and other sorts of applications that might serve information. The focus of the tool is on stress testing rather than unit testing, but it is an extremely useful functionality testing tool for use with Tomcat and Web applications.

Caution JMeter requires a JDK 1.4 or above to run. This should be downloaded and installed prior to downloading JMeter.

Given that JMeter requires JDK 1.4 it may be prudent to run JMeter on a separate computer to test the Web site unless you feel comfortable running JDK 1.4 and JDK 1.3 on the same computer.

Because JMeter is used for stress testing it may provide more realistic results by running the tests remotely as opposed to the same computer. JMeter requires about 30-50MB of memory, which also may impact on any performance information that is collected, depending on the system configuration.

JMeter includes the capabilities for:

- ✦ Testing HTTP, HTTPS, and other servers.
- ✦ Viewing the results in a graphical or tabular form.
- ✦ Functionality testing of Web application components by checking server responses for correctness.
- ✦ Stress testing of Web applications by providing a framework for defining multiple iterations and multiple simultaneous users.
- ✦ Distributed/remote testing.
- ✦ Saving the testing results for later analysis.
- ✦ Stateful/session testing of Web applications by providing functionality to execute a sequence of events that looks to the server as if they came from the same user by providing support for cookies.
- ✦ Testing Web applications using various HTTP authentication schemes including BASIC and FORM.

JMeter is a Java Swing GUI application used to construct a Test Plan that is then executed. The execution can be via the GUI or by a separate non-interactive text-based interface.

This section focuses on using JMeter with the existing applications developed for this book. As with the other sections in this chapter, it only provides initial information about how to download, install, and get started using JMeter. There is significant breadth in JMeter that further exploration is necessary to utilize the product in a production environment.

This section shows how to configure JMeter to:

✦ Create a Test Plan to test the `HelloWorld` Web application by accessing the `HelloWorld` and `HelloCity` servlets.

✦ Create a Test Plan to test the Tomcat Cinemas Web application by creating tests that will:

- Access SSL enabled pages for the Web booking
- Access the Admin pages
- Access the Front Desk pages

At the time of writing JMeter 1.8 was the latest version and still had a number of minor defects. These would generally manifest in the graphical drawing routines for the tree browser, some of the form fields, and some of the graphs drawn.

These defects are generally fairly minor but some are a little frustrating and diminish the user experience.

Download

The first step in using JMeter is to browse to the JMeter home page at `http://jakarta.apache.org/cactus/` to download the software.

1. Select the downloads link from the left navigation pane.
2. Select the directory `release`.
3. Select the directory `v1.8`.
4. Select the file `ApacheJMeter_1.8.zip` and save the file to disk.

The direct link to the version used for the testing is:

```
http://jakarta.apache.org/builds/jakarta-jmeter/release/v1.8/ApacheJMeter_1.8.zip
```

Installation

Remember that JMeter requires a JDK 1.4 or higher to be installed, so if this has not been done, now is a good time to do it. The installation of JDK 1.4 is very similar to the JDK 1.3 installation described in Chapter 2.

The following instructions describe how to install JMeter.

1. Extract the downloaded file to `c:\`. This creates a directory hierarchy under `c:\jakarta-jmeter`. This package consists of the documentation, the source, some examples, and the files required to run JMeter.
2. Edit the `c:\jakarta-jmeter\bin\jmeter.properties` file and uncomment the following line:

   ```
   ssl.provider=com.sun.net.ssl.internal.ssl.Provider
   ```

   This enables JMeter to perform testing of the SSL portions of the Tomcat Cinemas Web site.
3. Edit the `c:\jakarta-jmeter\bin\jmeter.properties` file and comment out the following line:

   ```
   javax.net.debug=ALL
   ```

   When JMeter is performing the SSL testing it produces significant output to the console. If that is not a concern, then this line can be left uncommented.

Note The use of SSL requires the installation of the Sun's JSSE package. Details on using JSSE for application security are provided in Chapter 12.

Provided that `JAVA_HOME` is set correctly to the JDK 1.4 installation, running JMeter is performed by either setting the PATH to the JMeter `bin` directory or running the application directly. This can be performed under Windows by the following command:

```
c:\jakarta-jmeter\bin\jmeter.bat
```

This starts the Java Swing GUI for JMeter.

The HelloWorld Test Plan

The first test plan that will be developed is a simple example to cover most of the basic configuration required for testing Web applications.

The first step is to start JMeter. This should display a window similar to that shown in Figure 17-7.

The left pane is the element tree panel and is used to construct the test plan. The right pane is the control panel for that element and is used to modify attributes related to the currently selected element.

In Figure 17-7, the `Test Plan` element is selected and the attributes for the test plan are shown in the control panel. Change the `name` attribute to `HelloWorld`. There is no save button for the individual panels; the changes are immediately reflected in the memory version of the test configuration. Saving the changes permanently is performed by selecting the File menu and the Save Test Plan option.

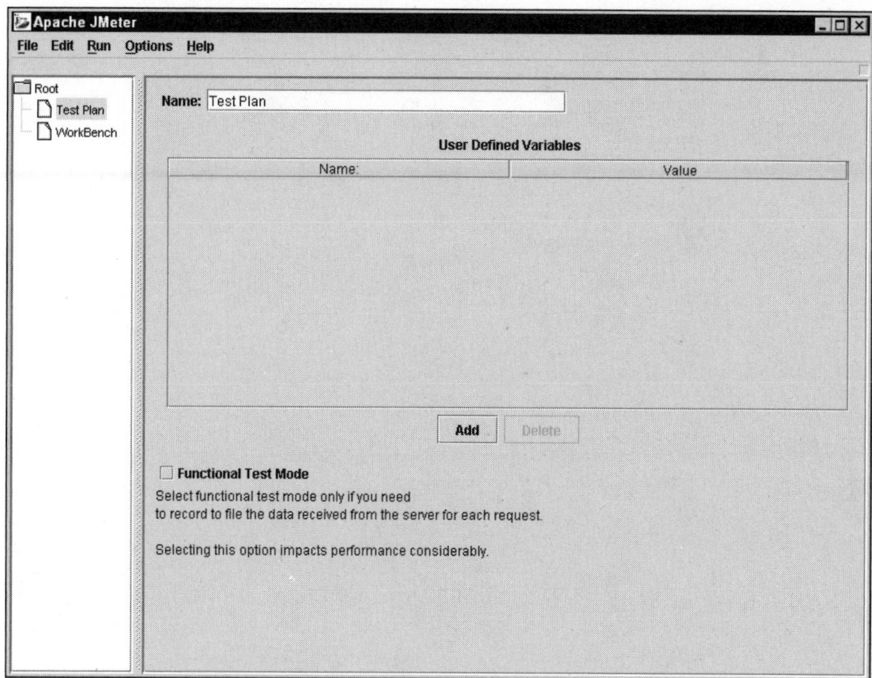

Figure 17-7: JMeter startup screen

The `Test Plan` element is the root element for the test plan. The `Workbench` element is simply an area to store elements when building a test. These elements can then be moved into the `Test Plan` as required.

While the `Test Plan` element may be the root of the test plan, the `Thread Group` element is the driving force behind the testing. The Thread Group provides a container for the requests to be made to the Web application. The Thread Group also can contain most of the other elements available in the element tree.

The `Thread Group` element can be configured to determine the number of threads (concurrent users) that will be accessing the Web application and the number of iterations to be performed.

A new Thread Group may be added as follows:

1. Right-click HelloWorld and select Add->Thread Group.
2. Left-click Thread Group"and change name to **Viewers**.
3. Clear the Forever check box and change Loop Count to **1**.

This should result in a screen that now resembles Figure 17-8.

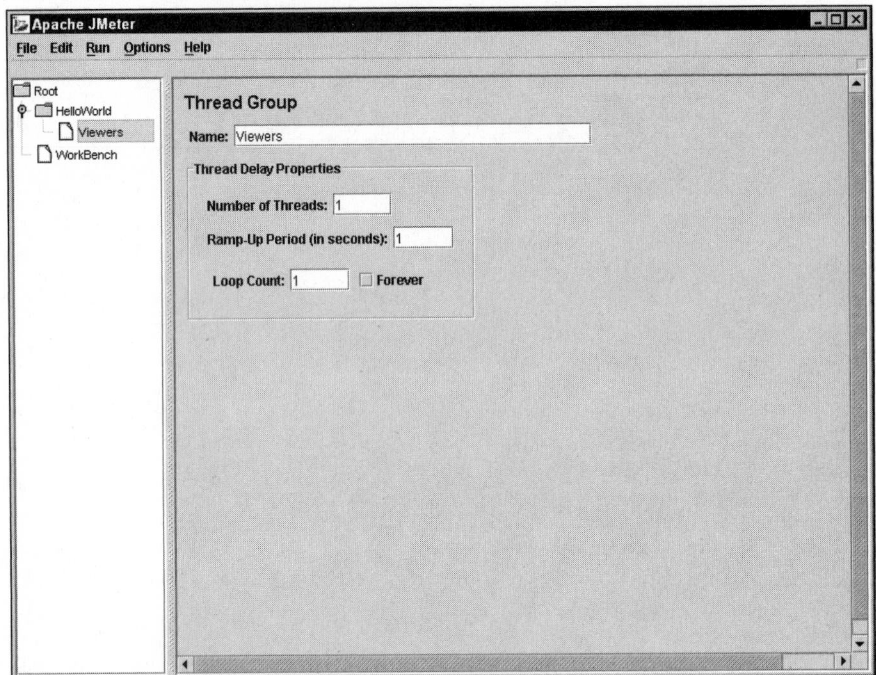

Figure 17-8: Viewers Thread Group

The next step is to get the Thread Group to perform some actions. This is done by configuring an `HTTP Request` element. The `HTTP Request` element can make requests to a Web application.

A new HTTP Request may be added as follows:

1. Right-click Viewers and select Add->Sampler/HTTP Request.
2. Left-click HTTP Request and change the Name to **Servlet Hello World**.
3. Change the Server Name to **localhost**.
4. Change the Port Number" to **8080**.
5. Change the Method to **GET**.
6. Change the Path to `/hello/world`.

This should result in a screen that resembles Figure 17-9.

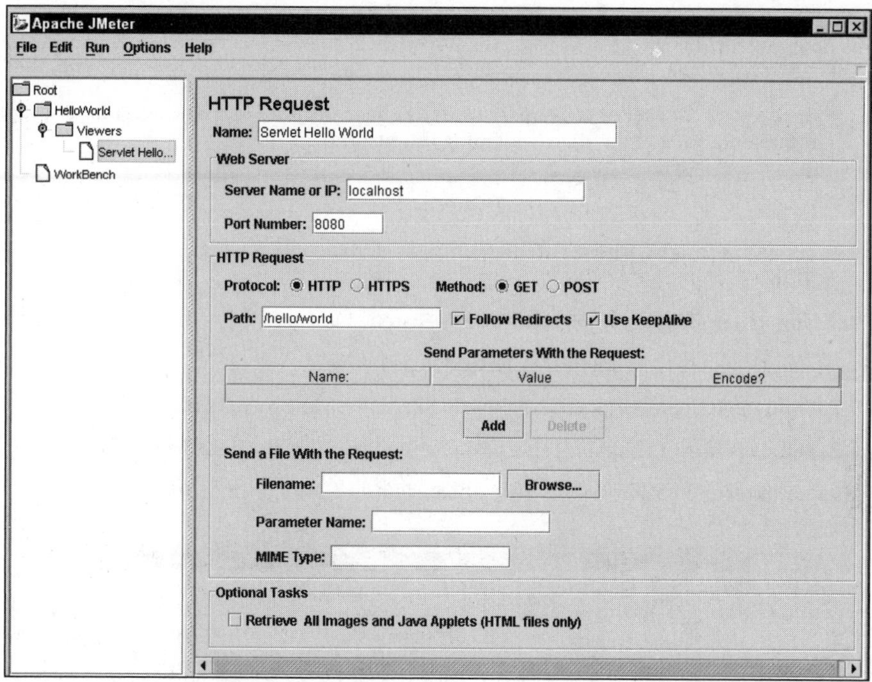

Figure 17-9: Servlet Hello World HTTP request

At this point it looks fairly safe to run the tests. Make sure that Tomcat is started and the HelloWorld Web application developed in Chapter 7 is installed. This can be tested by using a Web browser and opening the URL `http://localhost:8080/hello/world`.

This is a good time to save the test plan configuration. Select the File menu and Save Test Plan as. This displays a standard file dialog box. Choose a sensible location and name for the test plan. We recommend saving it as `HelloWorld.jmx` in the root directory of the Web application development directory.

To run the tests, select the Run menu and then choose the Start option. When tests are running, the GUI displays this by displaying a green square on the top right side of the window, as shown in Figure 17-10. The Start option also is disabled when tests are running. When the tests are completed, the green square returns to a gray color.

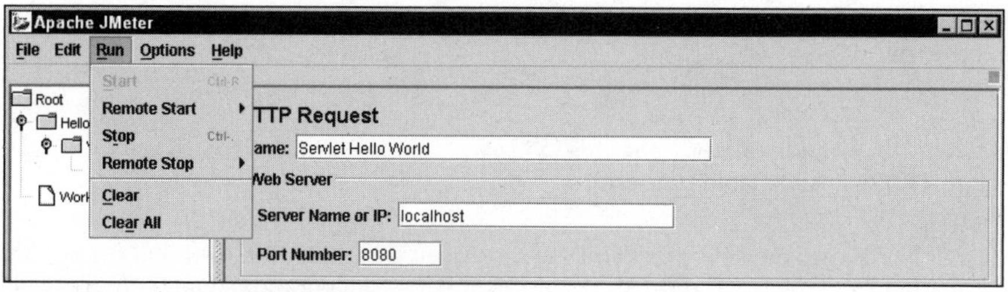

Figure 17-10: Running the HelloWorld test plan

With the test completed, there is one very important configuration that was missed. There was nowhere for the test results to be displayed! Results from testing are collected by an element called a *listener*. There are three basic types of listeners:

- ✦ `Graphical Listeners`. These listeners collect the data and draw graphs or graphical representations of the data to display the results.
- ✦ `Table Listeners`. These listeners collect the data and display the results in a tabular form.
- ✦ `Tree Listeners`. These listeners collect the data and display the results in a tree form.

The first listener to be configured is a `Table` listener.

A new `Results Table` element may be added as follows:

1. Right-click HelloWorld and select Add->Listener/View Results in Table.
2. Left-click View Results in Table and change the Name to **Hello World Table**.

This should result in a screen that resembles Figure 17-11.

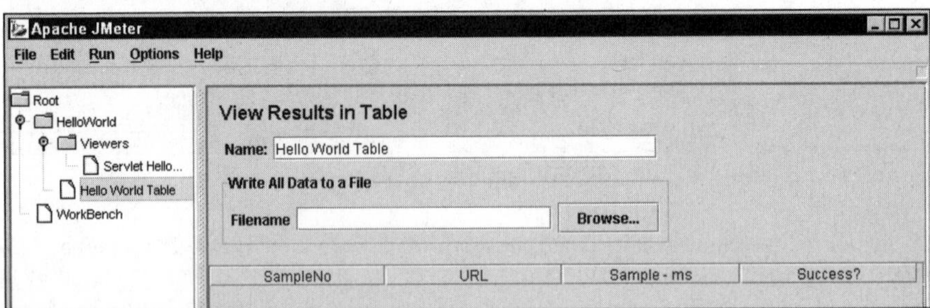

Figure 17-11: Hello World View Results Table

Run the test again, which should result in a screen similar to that shown in Figure 17-12.

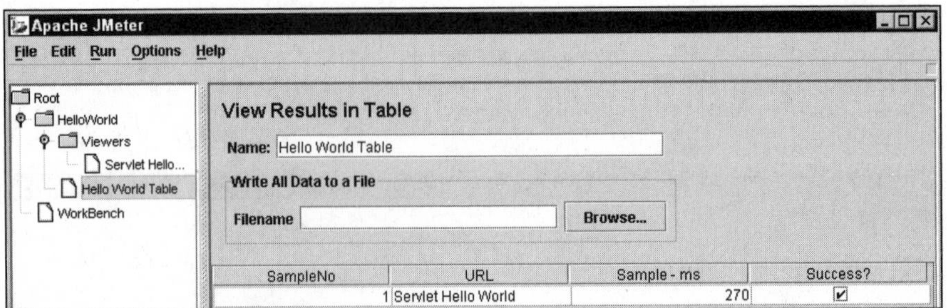

Figure 17-12: Results Table test results

Figure 17-12 shows the single test and the results. At this point, the basics of the configuration are fairly complete. To run a stress test using this configuration, update the Thread Group as follows:

1. Left-click the `Viewers` element.
2. Change Number of Thread" to **10**.
3. Change Loop Count to **5**.

Run the test again. This performs 50 samples, resulting in a screen full of results that can be scrolled through. These samples also can be written to disk by providing a filename.

Tip

The results samples will continue to be added to the results table for every test. To start each test with a blank slate, use the Clear or Clear All options in the Run menu before each test run. The Clear option will only clear the selected listener; Clear All will clear all configured listeners.

If a filename is configured on the results table, the Clear and Clear All options will have no effect until the filename is removed from the configuration.

This isn't particularly interesting viewing, so it's time to configure something with a few graphics.

A new `Results Table` element may be added as follows:

1. Right-click HelloWorld and select Add->Listener/Graph Results.
2. Left-click the `Graph Results` element and change the Name to **Hello World Graph**.

Run the test again. This displays some results on the graph. For a more interesting amount of data change the `Viewers` element Loop Count to **50**. This should result in a display similar to that shown in Figure 17-13.

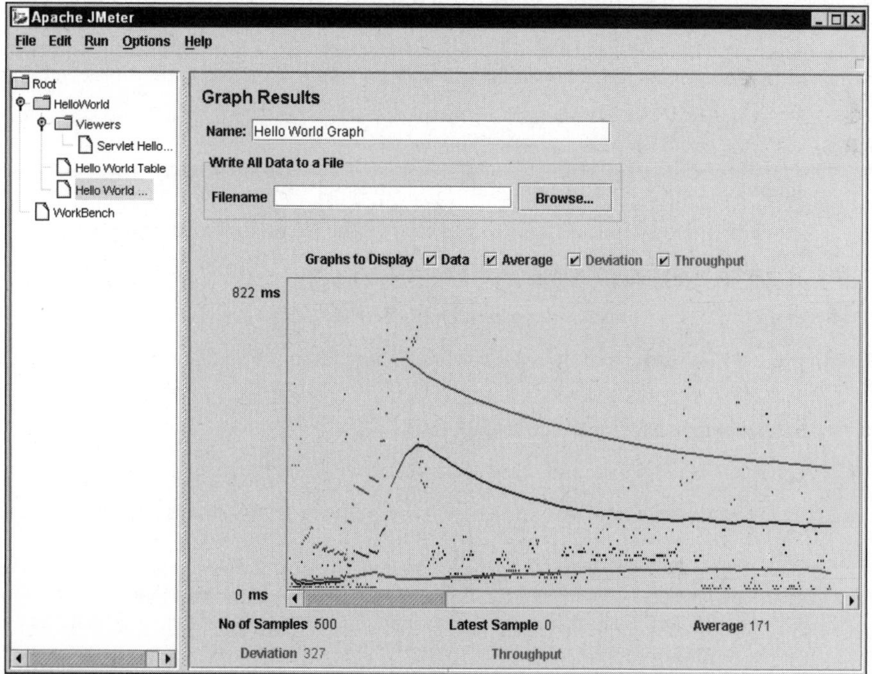

Figure 17-13: Graph results

At this point the Viewers Thread Group isn't really doing much, just sending out a single request on every iteration. It is more common to have a multiple requests within a thread group.

A second HTTP Request may be added as follows:

1. Right-click Viewers and select Add->Sampler/HTTP Request.
2. Left-click HTTP Request"and change the Name to **Hello City**.
3. Change Server Name to **localhost**.
4. Change Port Number to **8080**.
5. Change Method to **GET**.
6. Change Path to **/hello/city**.

Re-run the tests and notice how there are now twice as many samples that are generated. Selecting the `Hello World Table` and `Hello World Graph` elements displays the different views created by the listeners.

Notice how the samples in the Hello World Table are a mixture of the HTTP requests for the Servlet Hello World and the Hello City destinations.

There is one final step in this simple configuration before a more complicated example is attempted. It is worth trying this testing with the Web application not installed or Tomcat not started and examining the results. The Hello World Table will display the results with the Success? column cleared, indicating failure.

However, this doesn't help with testing when the Web application may be installed and responding to requests but returning incorrect information. JMeter provides a very simple string-matching capability that can be configured to determine if the request resulted in the response that was expected. This element is a `Response Assertion` and it is attached to an HTTP Request.

A Response Assertion may be added as follows:

1. Right-click Servlet Hello World and select Add->Assertions/Response Assertion.
2. Left-click the Response Assertion and change the Name to World Assertion.
3. Click Add to add a new Patterns to Test.
4. Select the first line and change it to **Hello World**.

To complete the assertion configuration an assertion listener must be configured to display the results.

An assertion listener may be added as follows:

1. Right-click Hello World and select Add->Listener/Assertion Results.
2. Left-click Assertion Results and change the Name to **Hello World Assertion**.

Tip When adding new elements, or changing the functionality of Assertions, HTTP Request elements, it is very useful to change the Thread Group parameters so that there is only 1 Thread and 1 Loop Count. This minimizes the waiting between tests if there are any mistakes made in the configuration and multiple changes are to be performed.

Run the tests again. This should result in a display similar to that shown in Figure 17-14.

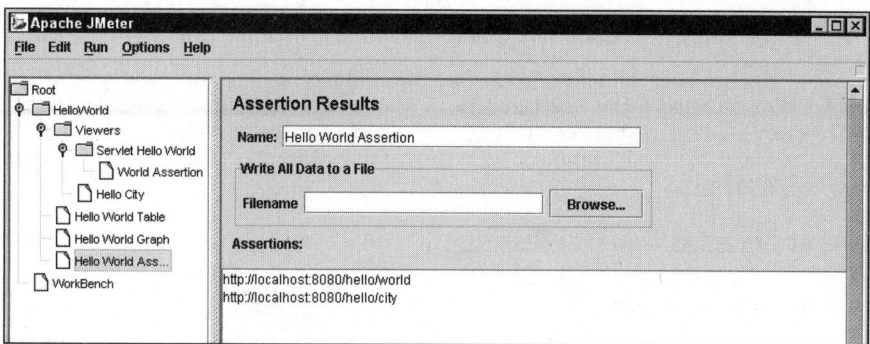

Figure 17-14: Hello World Assertion results

That should have worked, but just to make sure, we will modify World Assertion as follows:

1. Left-click the World Assertion response assertion attached to the Servlet Hello World HTTP request.
2. In the Pattern Matching Rules section of the control panel click Not to reverse the matching criteria. For the response to be successful it must not return content that matches Hello World.

Run the tests again. This should result in a display similar to that shown in Figure 17-15.

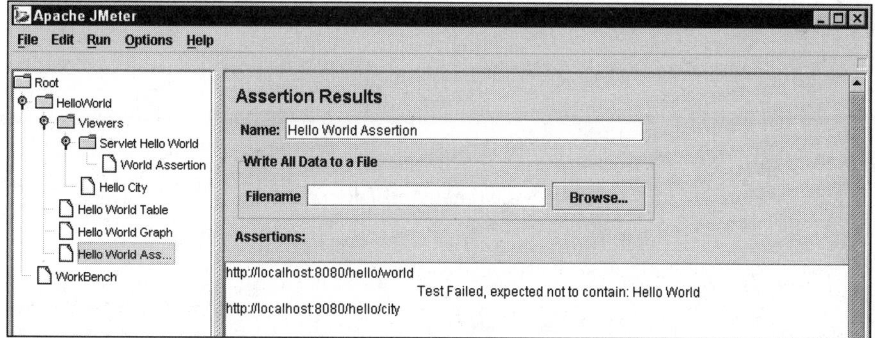

Figure 17-15: A failure in an assertion from World Assertion

That completes the simple test plan. It is a good idea to save the current test plan before moving on to the next section because the next section starts a completely new test plan for the Tomcat Cinemas Web application.

Tip It is recommended that when a test is completed all of the configured listeners are checked to see how the test performed. This becomes more important in the next section where complex tests are added that rely on previous steps. The Assertion Results screen and the results table are often very good places to start when reviewing the test.

The Tomcat Cinemas Test Plan

This section develops a test plan for the Tomcat Cinemas Web application described in Chapter 10 and the additional security implementation in Chapter 12.

The four following subsections include additional techniques and configuration elements compared to the Hello World Test Plan. The elements that have already been discussed in the Hello World Test Plan are not covered in the same detail as the new elements, so if there is any doubt about the configuration or what the control panel should look like then refer to the previous section.

Tomcat Cinemas General Testing

In this test plan there are a number of overall configuration items that exist outside each of the following thread groups.

The first element is the HTTP Request Defaults, which is used to provide the default server name, port, and URL path to be used in following HTTP Request elements. The individual HTTP request elements can override the behavior of the HTTP Request Defaults by providing configuration in the specific element.

Using the HTTP Request Defaults makes the migration of testing from a development test machine to a system test machine and then even the production environment. The `Server Name` attribute only needs to be set in one place in the Test Plan and a single change will update the entire test suite; individual `HTTP Request` elements need not be updated one at a time.

Configure the general elements as follows:

Update the Test Plan as follows:

1. Left-click Test Plan and change the Name to **TC**.

Add an HTTP Request Defaults element:

1. Right-click TC and select Add->Config Element/HTTP Request Defaults.
2. Left-click HTTP Request Defaults and change the Server Name to **localhost**.

Add an Assertion Listener:

1. Right-click TC and select Add->Listener/Assertion Results.
2. Left-click Assertion Results and change the Name to **TC Assertion**.

Add a View Results in Table:

1. Right-click TC and select Add->Listener/View Results in Table.
2. Left-click View Results in Table and change the Name to **TC Results**.

Add a View Results Tree:

1. Right-click TC and select Add->Listener/View Results Tree.

The View Results Tree is an element that contains detailed HTTP request and response information and is extremely valuable when debugging the test configuration and the Web application.

At this stage the configuration should be similar to that shown in Figure 17-16.

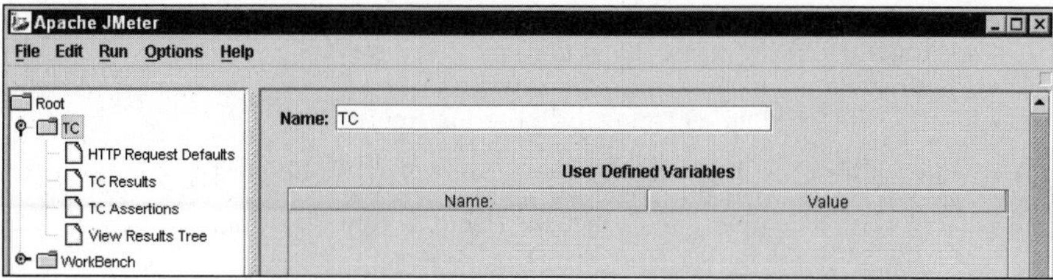

Figure 17-16: General configuration elements for Tomcat Cinemas test plan

That concludes the general configuration for the test plan. There may be a desire to add any of the graphical listeners, such as the Graph Results listener, to the configuration. If that is the case, then do so. The configuration described in this section is a fairly minimal configuration and additional elements of all types should be added as more familiarity is gained with the use of the elements.

Web Booking Testing

The Web booking testing tests the functionality of the Tomcat Cinemas Web application to successfully display a list of the showings remaining today using HTTPS. This is a simple configuration of a Thread Group to simulate the users, an HTTP Request to access the page, and a Response Assertion to check the results.

Because the Web booking is performed over HTTPS and the certificate created for use by Tomcat Cinemas is not trusted, JMeter needs to trust the certificate so the protocol can be performed without any issues.

To select a certificate, use the Options menu and select the SSL Manager option. This opens a standard file dialog box with the default file type set to be PKCS#12. Change the file type to All Files and select the Tomcat installation directory where the `keystore` is available. Select the `keystore` and press Open. Type in the keystore password and press OK.

The keystore password configured in Chapter 12 was "secret".

Caution

You must use the SSL Manager every time JMeter is started to select the keystore. If the keystore is not opened prior to running the tests, a password dialog box is opened for every thread created in the thread group the first time an HTTPS test is run.

The password dialog box can be dismissed by pressing Cancel, however the interruption to the testing appears to cause problems with other concurrently running threads because unusual behavior was exhibited when this occurred.

If the tests are re-run, then the dialog box does not appear and the testing results are consistent.

Add a Thread Group by implementing the following steps:

1. Right-click the TC and select Add->Thread Group.
2. Left-click Thread Group and change name to **Web Booking**.
3. Clear the Forever check box and change Loop Count to **1**.

Note: The Number of Threads and Loop Count are initially set to 1 during configuration. When testing is performed change these values to 5 and 10 respectively.

Add an HTTP request by implementing the following steps:

1. Right-click Web Booking and select Add->Sampler/HTTP Request.
2. Left-click HTTP Request and change the Name to **View Showing**.
3. Change Port Number to **8443**.
4. Change the Protocol to **HTTPS**.
5. Change the Method to **GET**.
6. Change the Path to **/tomcatcinemas/web**.

Add a Response Assertion by implementing the following steps:

1. Right-click View Showing and select Add->Assertions/Response Assertion.
2. Left-click the "Response Assertion" and change the Name to **Valid Response**.
3. Click "Add" to add a new Patterns to Test.
4. Select the first line and change to **Shows Remaining Today**.

The configuration should now look like Figure 17-17.

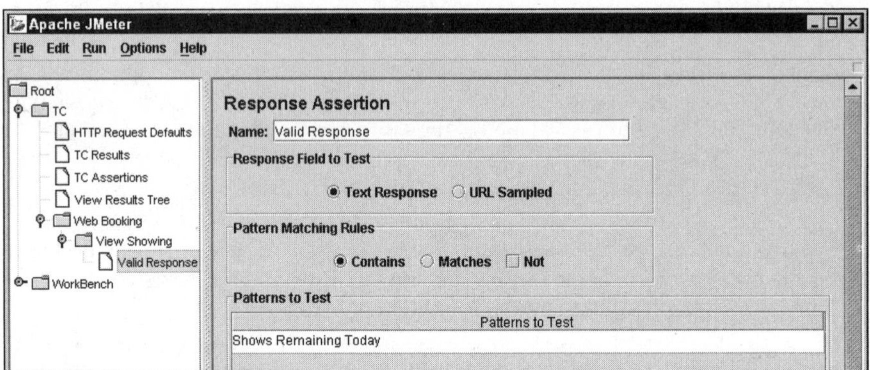

Figure 17-17: Web Booking configuration

Ensure that Tomcat has been started and the Tomcat Cinemas Web application is installed and operational. Run the tests!

Tip: The tests also can be run by using the keyboard shortcut, Control+R.

Select the View Results Tree listener to examine the results. Click the Root folder, which will display a list of the requests performed. Select one of the requests labeled View Showing and the display should look similar to Figure 17-18. The View Results Tree contains the HTTP Request and Response data, including the headers and body.

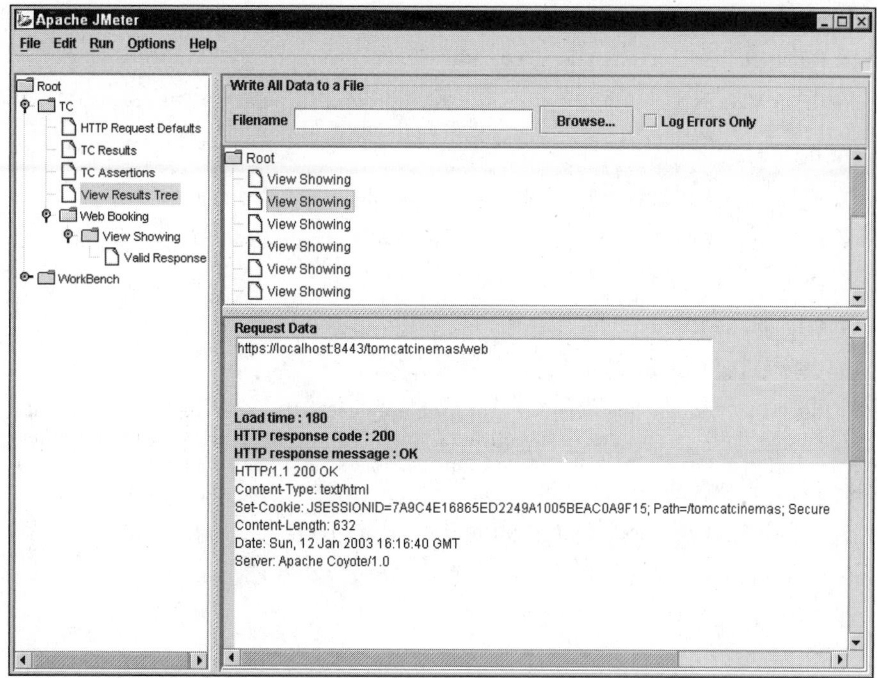

Figure 17-18: View Results Tree

If there are any errors in the View Results Tree from either an HTTP error code or an assertion not successfully met the elements that fail are shown in red text in the view.

The Administration Testing

The Administration testing tests the functionality of the Tomcat Cinemas application to authenticate the Administrator and perform some of the basic tasks available to an authenticated Administration, such as getting a list of the configured theaters and a booking report.

The first step is to identify the authentication mechanism used by the Administration section. Administration uses FORM authentication, and for this to work cookies need to be enabled and form data needs to be sent using POST to a target. Once the Administrator is authenticated, the other tasks can be performed.

Add a Thread Group by implementing the following steps:

1. Right-click TC and select Add->Thread Group.
2. Left-click Thread Group and change name to **Admin User**.
3. Clear the Forever check box and change Loop Count to **1**.

Cookies associated with a thread are handled by an HTTP Cookie Manager. This element also can be used to set custom cookies as part of the testing, but for these purposes we only require the element for the functionality of maintaining the cookies sent from the server to maintain a session.

Add an HTTP Cookie Manager by implementing the following.

1. Right-click Admin User and select Add->Config Element/HTTP Cookie Manager.

To force the Web application to display the login prompt associated with the FORM authentication, a request must be made to a protected resource. This can be done with an HTTP Request.

1. Right-click Admin User and select Add->Sampler/HTTP Request.
2. Left-click HTTP Request and change the Name to **Login Prompt**.
3. Change the Port Number to **8080**.
4. Change the Method to `GET`.
5. Change the Path to `/tomcatcinemas/admin`.

After this HTTP Request has been sent the Web application is expecting the user to fill out the form and send a response. FORM authentication defines the names for the parameters and the action in the FORM. It is simple to provide these and the data for the parameters using another HTTP Request.

1. Right-click Admin User and select Add->Sampler/HTTP Request.
2. Left-click HTTP Request and change the Name to **Login Form**.
3. Change the Port Number to **8080**.
4. Change Method to `POST`.
5. Change the Path to `/tomcatcinemas/j_security_check`.
6. In Send Parameters With the Request add a row with a Name of `j_username` and Value of `boss`.
7. In Send Parameters With the Request add a row with a Name of `j_password` and Value of `boss`.

Tip

During configuration of a test plan it is often desirable to prevent sections of the test plan from executing. In this case there is no need to have the Web Booking thread group running while this configuration is tested.

There are two options available to remove an element from the execute path. The first is to right-click the element and select Disable; the second is to select the element and drag the group to the WorkBench. When the pop-up menu is displayed choose the Add as Child option.

Run the tests again and select the `View Results Tree` element. Click the `Root` element and select the Login Prompt. The results should be similar to Figure 17-19.

Caution

The order of the Login Prompt and Login Form are very important. If these HTTP Request elements are reversed the test will fail. Try it!

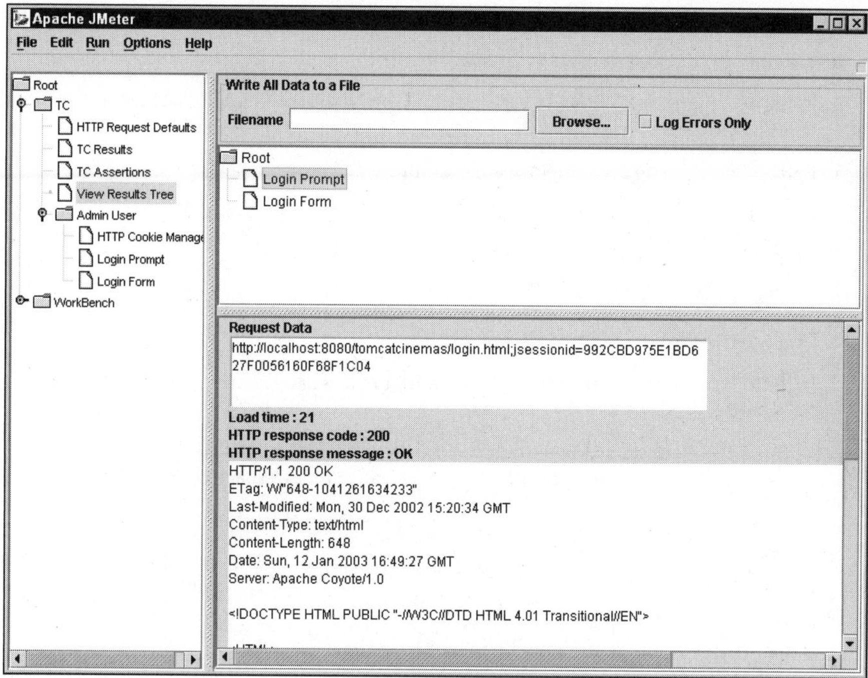

Figure 17-19: Successful administrator authentication

Currently the testing has verified that the Administrator can access the Administration section of Tomcat Cinemas, but now we should add the tasks that the Administrator performs after login.

It would be unusual for an Administrator to login, select a single option then quit, then login again, then select a single option only to quit again immediately. This is what would happen if we were to just add additional HTTP Request elements as part of the Admin User thread group.

Luckily there is a better way, for JMeter has some elements that can be used to control the flow of a thread within a thread group. These elements are all called *Logic Controllers* and the action that needs to be performed in this instance is that after login by the Administrator a series of tasks are performed a number of times. This functionality is provided by using a Loop Controller.

1. Right-click Admin User and select Add->Logic Controller/Loop Controller.
2. Left-click Loop Controller and change the Name to **Finding** and the Loop Count to **5**.

There are two HTTP Requests that are to be performed during the Finding, one for the theater list and another for the booking report.

1. Right-click Finding and select Add->Sampler/HTTP Request.
2. Left-click the HTTP Request and change the Name to **Theatre List**.
3. Change the Port Number to **8080**.

4. Change the Method to `GET`.
5. Change the Path to `/tomcatcinemas/admin`.
6. In Send Parameters With the Request add a row with a Name of **action** and Value of `listTheatres`.
7. Right-click Finding and select Add->Sampler/HTTP Request.
8. Left-click the HTTP Request and change the Name to **Booking Report**.
9. Change the Port Number to **8080**.
10. Change the Method to `GET`.
11. Change the Path to `/tomcatcinemas/admin`.
12. In Send Parameters With the Request add a row with a Name of **action** and Value of `bookingReport`.

Finally, create the Response Assertions for the two HTTP Request to ensure the Administrator remains logged on and that the pages requested are the pages that are served.

1. Right-click Theatre List and select Add->Assertions/Response Assertion.
2. Left-click Response Assertion and change the Name to **Theatre Response**.
3. Click Add to add a new Patterns to Test.
4. Select the first line and change to **List Theatres**.
5. Right-click Booking Report and select Add->Assertions/Response Assertion.
6. Left-click Response Assertion and change the Name to **Booking Response**.
7. Click Add to add a new Patterns to Test.
8. Select the first line and change to **Booking Report**.

Running the test should display a result similar to that shown in Figure 17-20 on the TC Results table.

This thread group contained additional controlling logic to develop more sophisticated test scripts. This is extremely important when attempting to test Web applications that have workflow such as authentication and some tasks. The style of testing would also include a shopping application where items can be added to a shopping basket with a checkout to purchase the added goods.

The Front Desk Testing

The final thread group to be added to the test plan implements the testing of the Front Desk of the Web application. This is very similar to the testing performed on the Administration section with one important difference; the front desk staff must logout after performing their duties because the Web application requires that a single username may only have a single concurrent login.

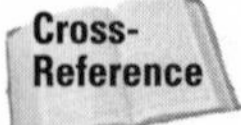

For more information on the Tomcat Cinemas security implementation see Chapter 12.

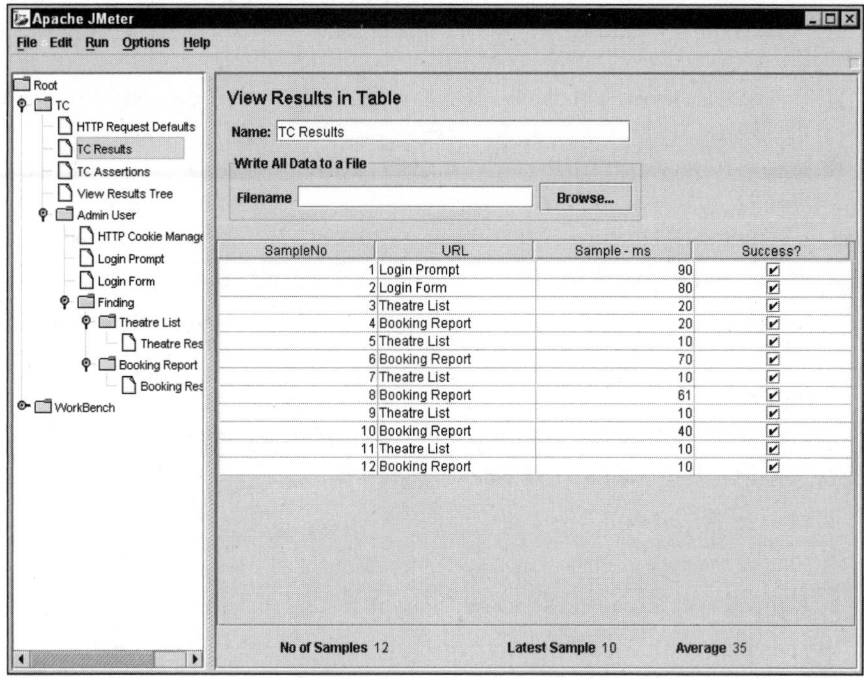

Figure 17-20: Admin User test results

The Front Desk authentication is the same as the Administration so we can use the same process in both cases, but with a different user. The front desk staff also performs a number of tasks after authentication so a Loop Controller will be implemented. The additional step of logging out after the tasks have been completed is implemented by using an HTTP Request.

To add an HTTP Cookie Manager, implement the following steps:

1. Right-click Front Desk and select Add->Config Element/HTTP Cookie Manager.

Add the login prompt and login form for authentication:

1. Right-click Front Desk and select Add->Sampler/HTTP Request.
2. Left-click the HTTP Request and change the Name to **Login Prompt Staff**.
3. Change the Port Number to **8080**.
4. Change the Method to `GET`.
5. Change the Path to `/tomcatcinemas/frontdesk`.
6. Right-click Front Desk and select Add->Sampler/HTTP Request.
7. Left-click HTTP Request and change the Name to **Login Form Staff**.
8. Change the Port Number to **8080**.

9. Change the Method to `GET`.
10. Change the Path to `/tomcatcinemas/j_security_check`.
11. In Send Parameters With the Request add a row with a Name of `j_username` and Value of `staff1`.
12. In Send Parameters With the Request add a row with a Name of `j_password` and Value of `staff1`.

Add the tasks to be performed by the authenticated staff by using a Loop Controller:

1. Right-click Front Desk and select Add->Logic Controller/Loop Controller.
2. Left-click Loop Controller and change the Name to **List Showings** and the Loop Count to **10**.
3. Right-click the List Showings and select Add->Sampler/HTTP Request.
4. Left-click HTTP Request and change the Name to **FD Screen**.
5. Change the Port Number to **8080**.
6. Change Method to `GET`.
7. Change the Path to `/tomcatcinemas/frontdesk`.
8. Right-click FD Screen and select Add->Assertions/Response Assertion.
9. Left-click the Response Assertion and change the Name to **FD Response**.
10. Click Add to add a new Patterns to Test.
11. Select the first line and change to **Current User: staff1**.

Finally, add in the HTTP Request that will log out the front desk staff.

1. Right-click Front Desk and select Add->Sampler/HTTP Request.
2. Left-click HTTP Request and change the Name to **Staff Logout**.
3. Change the Port Number to **8080**.
4. Change the Method to `GET`.
5. Change the Path to `/tomcatcinemas/frontdesk`.
6. In Send Parameters With the Request add a row with a Name of **action** and Value of `logout`.

Change Front Desk to have a Loop Count of **5**. Running the test should display a result similar to that shown on Figure 17-21 on the TC Results table.

The next step in the testing now is to combine all of the tests and have them execute simultaneously. This simulates a real world environment where the Web application needs to service requests for Web bookings, administration, and front desk functionality simultaneously.

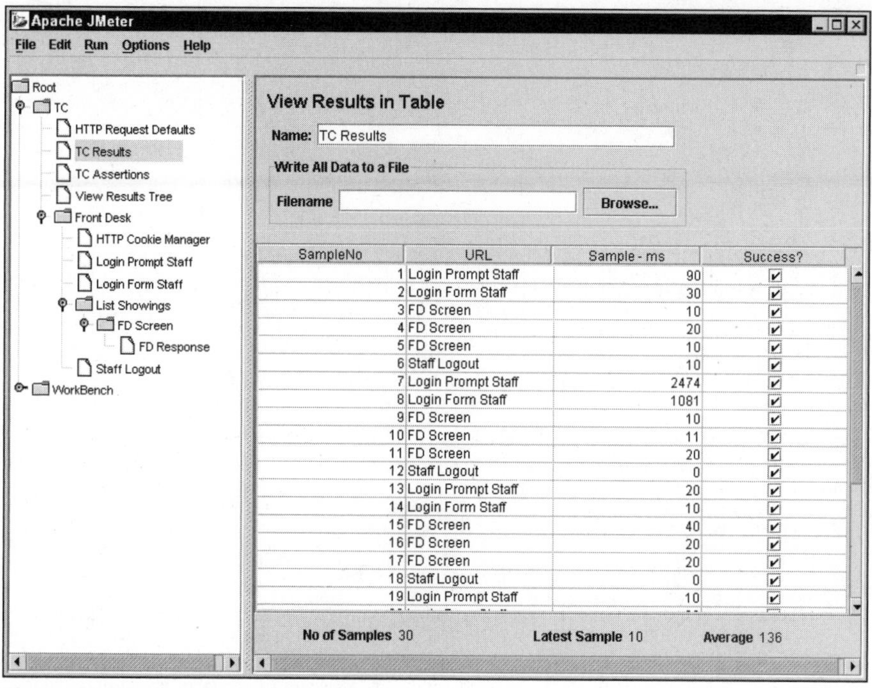

Figure 17-21: Front Desk test results

Summary

JMeter provides an application for performing different types of testing of Web applications. These tests can be used for functionality testing to validate the correctness of Web applications during development or user acceptance testing. Other testing supported by JMeter is performance testing and reporting that can be used to identify bottlenecks in either application design of even hardware resources.

JMeter is a tool that can be integrated into a development and deployment testing strategy to increase the reliability and performance of Web applications, hopefully prior to deployment of the Web application.

The best source for further information is at the JMeter Web site at `http://jakarta.apache.org/jmeter`.

✦ ✦ ✦

CHAPTER 18

Customizing Tomcat

✦ ✦ ✦ ✦

In This Chapter

Why Customize Tomcat?

Setting up a Development Environment

Developing and Deployment of Custom Code

✦ ✦ ✦ ✦

The first 17 chapters of the book describe how to work with the functionality of the Tomcat releases provided by the Apache Tomcat developers. The previous coverage of the components that are part of the Tomcat installation is important to effectively using the Tomcat server in the default configuration.

This chapter changes all of that and provides an understanding of how to extend the functionality of Tomcat to enable it to be customized to suit the particular operating environment specific to you.

This chapter is not about making changes to configuration files and adding Web applications as defined by the Servlet Specification; it is about changing and enhancing the base functionality the Tomcat server provides using the interfaces and framework the Tomcat developers have provided.

This chapter discusses the options for customization and helps you decide if you really want to change Tomcat or if there are other alternatives to performing modifications.

After deciding that there is no choice but to get down and write some code. This chapter shows how to work out where to get information and plan the work to be developed.

Next it covers how to set up a development environment and what additional activities need to be performed to make changes to the Tomcat server.

Finally, the chapter presents three different examples, each highlighting different sorts of customization that can be applied to Tomcat.

Choices for Customization

You first need to decide whether you need to change Tomcat to get the functionality you require, or solve your problem another way. The decision should not be made in a hurry; long-term consequences need to be factored into the decision making process. Customizing Tomcat may provide a short-term benefit, but that may be outweighed by the cost of development, maintenance and integration with future releases of Tomcat.

To asses what course of action to take, it is important to understand what customizing Tomcat entails. The Tomcat developers have provided a framework for providing alternative implementation of the elements used by the Tomcat server.

The server.xml has many elements that have a className as an attribute. To provide an alternative implementation for these elements, the developers have defined Java interfaces and implemented a standard version of the implementation for use by Tomcat.

The choices available are quite extensive because elements from Server and Service down to Valves and Loggers all are capable of replacement by alternative implementations. In reality many of the outer elements (like Server and Service) are unlikely candidates for modification and it is the Realms, Valves, Loggers, and Listeners that are more likely to require custom development to provide installation specific functionality.

After examining the desired functionality to be implemented, it is first worth assessing if there are alternative solutions. For example, the Valve implemented in Tomcat has very similar functionality to the Filter defined in the Servlet Specification. Implementing the functionality as a Valve inhibits the successful migration of the Web application from Tomcat to an alternative servlet container, which may not be a suitable outcome.

To assess the options, it is prudent to examine alternative servlet containers to see if they have the functionality that is required for the Web application. After all, Tomcat is one option provided for Web application developers and the portability of Web applications is an enormous benefit, so why not make use of it under these circumstances.

Another option is to implement the functionality in the Web application if possible. This is the Valve/Filter situation described previously and maintains portability of the Web application.

A further option is to look at third-party tools or libraries that provide the missing functionality. This might require the examination of libraries such as Log4J to be used for Web application logging as an alternative to the Tomcat logging functionality.

After assessing the options and still coming up with the answer "enhance Tomcat" you can determine what form those modifications will take. Obviously, what is modified depends heavily upon what functionality is required. Table 18-1 provides a list of the elements and the general areas of responsibility.

Table 18-1: Tomcat Elements

Element	*Functionality*
Server	Represents the entire server. Handles startup, shutdown, and communication with contained elements
Service	Represents a group of one or more Connectors that use the same Engine to process the incoming requests
Engine	Represents the capabilities of an entire servlet processing engine.
Connector	Represents the component that handles the receipt of requests from clients and returning responses to clients.
Host	Represents a virtual host that is serviced by an Engine.
Context	Represents a Web application
Valve	Represents a request processing component that can perform specific tasks on the input to an Engine, Host or Context

Element	Functionality
`Logger`	Represents a message and exception processing component that is attached to an `Engine`, `Host`, or `Context`
`Realm`	Represents a component that provides a standard interface to an authentication scheme
`LifecycleListener`	Represents a component that processes Lifecycle events (for example start, stop)

The examples in this chapter examine the following:

- A custom error report, implemented as a Valve and used in conjunction with the Host attribute `errorReportValveClass`. The first example provides the functionality to change the look of the default Tomcat error page using a Cascading Style Sheet.
- A custom access log, implemented as a `Valve`. The second example creates an access log valve that rolls over to new log files every month rather than every day.
- A custom logger, implemented as a `Logger`. The third and final example is a `Logger` that generates output that can be directed to a Unix syslogd.

It is important to at least read all the examples even if you only want to implement the `Logger`. The later examples use knowledge built from the previous examples.

Where Can I Find Out More?

The first step in implementing a `Valve` or `Logger` is to examine both the available documentation and the source code. The Tomcat source is available for download, so it makes good sense to make use of the best documentation available, the source itself.

The API documentation is available as part of the Tomcat installation and the Javadoc for the internal implementation is available at :

```
c:\tomcat\webapps\tomcat-docs\index.html
```

The source for Tomcat is available for download separately and can be found at:

```
http://jakarta.apache.org/tomcat
```

Select Source Code from the left navigation pane, under Download, and follow the instructions to download the source. This chapter refers to the source code download root directory as `c:\tomcat-src`.

As the examples are developed, reference is made to the available source code, so having it easily available assists in following and understanding.

Development Environment

Developing the custom elements for Tomcat is not the same as developing a Web application. There are not the same considerations for packaging files into WARs or having `web.xml` descriptor files. The custom element development is more like a standard Java application development using the Tomcat libraries as part of the environment.

Note: The examples in this chapter expect the environment installed in Chapter 2 and then configured in Chapter 5.

Setting up a Development Directory Structure

As we did with the Web application development in Chapter 7, we will create a development environment using Ant build files, as well as an appropriate source directory structure.

Create the base development directories:

```
mkdir c:\devel
cd c:\devel
mkdir extend
cd extend
```

Create the source directories:

```
mkdir src\bible\tomcat\extend
```

Creating the build File

The simplest way to use the Tomcat libraries as part of the build process is to take the standard Tomcat Ant `build` file that was created in Chapter 5 and remove most of the Web application specific parts. This leaves a `build.xml` as shown in Listing 18-1.

Listing 18-1: build.xml

```
<project name="extend" default="compile" basedir=".">

    <property name="app.name"      value="extend"/>
    <property name="build.home"    value="${basedir}/build"/>
    <property name="catalina.home" value="c:\tomcat"/>
    <property name="dist.home"     value="${basedir}/dist"/>
    <property name="docs.home"     value="${basedir}/docs"/>
    <property name="src.home"      value="${basedir}/src"/>

<!--  Control Options  -->

    <property name="compile.debug"       value="true"/>
    <property name="compile.deprecation" value="false"/>
    <property name="compile.optimize"    value="true"/>

<!-- Classpath -->
```

```
    <path id="compile.classpath">

<!-- Include all elements that Tomcat uses internally -->
        <pathelement
            location="${catalina.home}/common/classes"/>
        <fileset dir="${catalina.home}/common/endorsed">
            <include name="*.jar"/>
        </fileset>
        <fileset dir="${catalina.home}/common/lib">
            <include name="*.jar"/>
        </fileset>
        <pathelement
            location="${catalina.home}/shared/classes"/>
        <fileset dir="${catalina.home}/shared/lib">
            <include name="*.jar"/>
        </fileset>
        <pathelement
            location="${catalina.home}/server/classes"/>
        <fileset dir="${catalina.home}/server/lib">
            <include name="*.jar"/>
        </fileset>

    </path>

<!-- All Target -->
    <target name="all" depends="clean,compile"
        description="Clean build and dist, then compile"/>

<!-- Clean Target -->
    <target name="clean"
        description="Delete old build and dist directories">
        <delete dir="${build.home}"/>
        <delete dir="${dist.home}"/>
    </target>

<!-- Compile Target -->
    <target name="compile"
        description="Compile Java sources">

<!-- Compile Java classes as necessary -->
        <mkdir    dir="${build.home}/classes"/>
        <javac srcdir="${src.home}"
            destdir="${build.home}/classes"
            debug="${compile.debug}"
            deprecation="${compile.deprecation}"
            optimize="${compile.optimize}">
            <classpath refid="compile.classpath"/>
        </javac>
    </target>

<!-- create distribution package -->
    <target name="dist" depends="compile"
```

Continued

Listing 18-1 *(continued)*

```
        description="Create binary distribution">
        <mkdir    dir="${dist.home}"/>

<!-- copy mbeans descriptor file -->
        <copy failonerror="false"
            todir="${build.home}/classes/bible/tomcat/extend"
            file="mbeans-descriptors.xml" />

<!-- Create application JAR file -->
        <jar jarfile="${dist.home}/${app.name}.jar"
            basedir="${build.home}/classes"/>
    </target>

<!-- Copy JAR file -->
    <target name="install" depends="dist">
        <copy file="${dist.home}/${app.name}.jar"
            todir="${catalina.home}/server/lib" />
    </target>


<!-- Javadoc Target -->
    <target name="javadoc" depends="compile"
        description="Create Javadoc API documentation">

        <mkdir dir="${dist.home}/docs/api"/>
        <javadoc sourcepath="${src.home}"
            destdir="${dist.home}/docs/api"
            packagenames="*">
            <classpath refid="compile.classpath"/>
        </javadoc>
    </target>
</project>
```

Some minor changes in the file are not readily noticeable at first glance:

✦ Removal of the `<property file=".."/>` lines

✦ Addition of the `<property name="catalina.home" value="c:\tomcat"/>` line

✦ Removal of the Javadoc dependency in the dist target

✦ Adding in the `<mkdir    dir="${dist.home}"/>` line to the dist target

Note This file and all the source files for the project are available from the Web site for the book.

With the development environment set up it is time to move on to the first example.

Custom Error Reporting (CSSErrorReportValve)

The default Tomcat Error Reporting implemented for a Host is `org.apache.catalina.valves.ErrorReportValve`. When this class is used any errors produced by Tomcat result in a display similar to that shown in Figure 18-1.

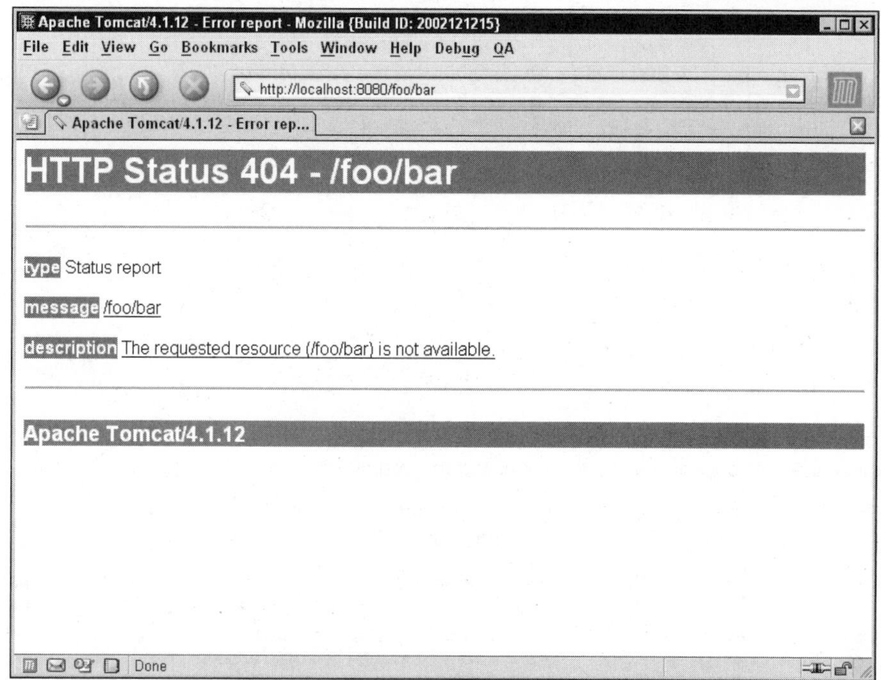

Figure 18-1: Default Tomcat error report output

While this is suitable for many environments there may be installations where even critical errors should have an appropriately styled error page that is consistent with the branding of the rest of the site.

Tip Web applications can provide individual error pages that relate to specific Web applications using the `<error-page>` element in the `web.xml` descriptor. This option provides a default implementation for those requests that are not directed at a specific Web application or where the developers have not implemented the `<error-page>` element in the Web application descriptor.

To provide an implementation that is not only suitably styled for all Web applications on the host, but an implementation where the style can be modified without resorting to calling on a software developer, the first example provides an error report class that outputs an HTML page that uses a Cascading Style Sheet (CSS).

Fortunately the standard ErrorReportValve provides much of the required functionality for processing the error and support for the Lifecycle events in implementing a Valve. Because this is substantially similar we shall merely extend the ErrorReportValve rather than re-implementing it all again.

Much of the functionality that is extended from the ErrorReportValve is discussed in the next example. This allows the first example to concentrate on the key code required to implement a Valve rather than all the supporting code.

With this in mind, the first thing is to do is look at the structure of a Valve. The Valve interface is defined in org.apache.catalina.Valve and can be found in the Tomcat source at tomcat-src\catalina\src\share\org\apache\catalina\Valve.java.

The interface for a Valve is as follows:

```
package org.apache.catalina;

public interface Valve
{
    public String getInfo();
    public void invoke(Request request, Response response,
                       ValveContext context)
}
```

The getInfo() method is a standard Tomcat method found in many of the classes. It returns a formatted string consisting of the class name and a version number.

The invoke() method is used to perform the actions required of the Valve. This is the method that is of most interest in customizing the Valve.

There are a number of Valves in Tomcat and all require similar processing to install into a Container. To provide a modular and maintainable structure the Tomcat developers have created an abstract base class for the Valve implementations, called ValveBase. This class is defined in tomcat-src\src\catalina\src\share\org\apache\catalina\valves\ValveBase.java.

Containers are a particular type of element in the server.xml. The Host and Context are examples of a Container. More information about Containers and the elements in server.xml can be found in Chapter 8.

From ValveBase the ErrorReportValve provides a concrete class that generates the standard error report, as shown in Figure 18-1. The ErrorReportValve class is defined in tomcat-src\src\catalina\src\share\org\apache\catalina\valves\ErrorReportValve.java and provides an implementation for the invoke() method, as shown in Listing 18-2.

Listing 18-2: ErrorReportValve invoke() Method

```
public void invoke(Request request, Response response,
                   ValveContext context)
throws IOException, ServletException {

    // Perform the request
    context.invokeNext(request, response);
    ServletRequest sreq = (ServletRequest) request;
```

```
        Throwable throwable =
            (Throwable)sreq.getAttribute(Globals.EXCEPTION_ATTR);

        . . . .
        . . . .

        try {
            report(request, response, throwable);
        } catch (Throwable tt) {
            tt.printStackTrace();
        }
    }
```

The processing for the error can only occur if the request fails. Like a Filter, the `Valve` invokes the next `Valve` in the chain, if there is one, by calling `invokeNext()`.

The `report()` method encapsulates all the report generating functionality, and is how we can successfully implement the custom error reporting `Valve` as shown in Listing 18-3.

Create a file `c:\devel\extend\src\bible\tomcat\extend\CSSErrorReport.java` with the contents of Listing 18-3.

Listing 18-3: CSSErrorReportValve.java

```
package bible.tomcat.extend;

import java.io.*;
import java.util.*;
import java.net.*;
import javax.servlet.*;
import javax.servlet.http.*;

import org.apache.catalina.*;
import org.apache.catalina.connector.*;
import org.apache.catalina.util.*;
import org.apache.catalina.valves.*;

public class CSSErrorReportValve
extends ErrorReportValve
{

    /**
     * Default style if no style sheet has been provided
     */
    private static final String H1_STYLE =
        "H1{font-family : sans-serif,Arial,Tahoma; "+
        "color : yellow;background-color : #0086b2;} ";

    private static final String H3_STYLE =
        "H3{font-family : sans-serif,Arial,Tahoma; "+
```

Continued

Listing 18-3 *(continued)*

```
    "color : yellow;background-color : #0086b2;} ";

private static final String BODY_STYLE =
    "BODY{font-family : sans-serif,Arial,Tahoma; "+
    "color : black;background-color : white;} ";

private static final String B_STYLE =
    "B{color : yellow;background-color : #0086b2;} ";

private static final String HR_STYLE = "HR{color : #0086b2;} ";

/**
 * The descriptive information related to this implementation.
 */
private static final String info =
    "bible.tomcat.extend.CSSErrorReportValve/1.0";


private String   _css = "/errorstyles.css";
private boolean  _hasStyleSheet = true;

private int debug = 0;

public String getStyleSheet()
{
    return _css;
}

protected void report(Request request, Response response,
                      Throwable throwable)
throws IOException
{
    if (!(response instanceof HttpServletResponse))
    {
        return;
    }
    HttpServletResponse hsr = (HttpServletResponse)response;
    int sc = ((HttpResponse)response).getStatus();
    String msg = RequestUtil.filter
             (((HttpResponse)response).getMessage());

    if (msg == null)
    {
        msg = ""; // for convenience
    }

    // Do nothing on a 1xx and 2xx status
    if ((sc < 300) || (sc == HttpServletResponse.SC_NOT_MODIFIED))
    {
        return;
```

```
}

// Do nothing if there is no report for the specified status code
String report = null;
try
{
    report = sm.getString("http." + sc, msg);
}
catch (Throwable t)
{
    System.out.println(
        "CSSErrorReportValve failed to find status "+sc);
}

if (report == null)
{
    return;
}

Throwable rootCause = null;
if (throwable != null)
{
    if (throwable instanceof ServletException)
    {
        rootCause = ((ServletException) throwable).getRootCause();
    }
}

StringBuffer sb = new StringBuffer();

// render the standard head and title elements
sb.append("<html><head><title>");
sb.append(ServerInfo.getServerInfo()).append(" - ");
sb.append(sm.getString("errorReportValve.errorReport"));
sb.append("</title>");

// if we have a style sheet, then output the sheet
if (hasStyleSheet(request.getContext().getServletContext()))
{
    sb.append("<LINK REL=StyleSheet HREF=\"");
    sb.append(getStyleSheet());
    sb.append("\" TYPE=\"text/css\">");
}
else
{
    sb.append("<STYLE>");
    sb.append(H1_STYLE);
    sb.append(H3_STYLE);
    sb.append(BODY_STYLE);
    sb.append(B_STYLE);
    sb.append(HR_STYLE);
    sb.append("</STYLE> ");
```

Continued

Listing 18-3 *(continued)*

```
}

// ** start of HTML body output **
sb.append("</head><body><h1>");
sb.append(sm.getString("errorReportValve.statusHeader",
                       "" + sc, msg)).append("</h1>");
sb.append("<h3>[CSSErrorReportValve] error report page</h3>");
sb.append("<HR size=\"1\" noshade>");
sb.append("<p><b>type</b> ");

if (throwable != null)
{
    sb.append(sm.getString("errorReportValve.exceptionReport"));
}
else
{
    sb.append(sm.getString("errorReportValve.statusReport"));
}

sb.append("</p><p><b>");
sb.append(sm.getString("errorReportValve.message"));
sb.append("</b> <u>").append(msg).append("</u></p>");
sb.append("<p><b>");
sb.append(sm.getString("errorReportValve.description"));
sb.append("</b> <u>");
sb.append(report);
sb.append("</u></p>");

if (throwable != null)
{
    StringWriter stackTrace = new StringWriter();
    throwable.printStackTrace(new PrintWriter(stackTrace));
    sb.append("<p><b>");
    sb.append(sm.getString("errorReportValve.exception"));
    sb.append("</b> <pre>");
    sb.append(stackTrace.toString());
    sb.append("</pre></p>");
    if (rootCause != null)
    {
        stackTrace = new StringWriter();
        rootCause.printStackTrace(new PrintWriter(stackTrace));
        sb.append("<p><b>");
        sb.append(sm.getString("errorReportValve.rootCause"));
        sb.append("</b> <pre>");
        sb.append(stackTrace.toString());
        sb.append("</pre></p>");
    }
}

sb.append("<HR size=\"1\" noshade>");
sb.append("<h3>");
```

```
        sb.append(ServerInfo.getServerInfo()).append("</h3>");
        sb.append("</body></html>");
        // ** end of HTML body output **

        try
        {
            Writer writer = response.getReporter();
            if (writer != null)
            {
                Locale locale = Locale.getDefault();

                try
                {
                    hsr.setContentType("text/html");
                    hsr.setLocale(locale);
                }
                catch (Throwable t)
                {
                    System.out.println(
                        "CSSErrorReportValve failed to set headers  :"+
                         t.getMessage());
                }

                writer.write(sb.toString());
                writer.flush();
            }

        }
        catch (Exception e)
        {
            System.out.println("CSSErrorReportValve failed to output  :"+
                               e.getMessage());
        }
    }

    private boolean hasStyleSheet(ServletContext ctx)
    {
        java.net.URL css = null;
        try
        {
            css = ctx.getResource(_css);
        }
        catch (MalformedURLException e)
        {
            css = null;
        }
        return (css != null);
    }
}
```

There isn't very much processing code in `CSSErrorReportValve`. Most of the `report()` method is concerned with building up a large `StringBuffer` that contains the HTML to be displayed.

The important code has been bolded and these sections are how the CSS is found in the Web application. These sections enable allow the general output of the error page to be set on a host-by-host basis but each individual Web application can provide custom styles to suit the Web application. The `getResource()` method in `hasStyleSheet()` is used to find the file `errorstyles.css` from the root of the Web application. If the file exists, then the HTML output includes an HTML `<LINK>` tag otherwise the HTML output inserts the default styles using a `<STYLE>` tag.

Now it is time to compile and test the code.

```
ant install
```

Compile the code, create a jar called `extend.jar`, and place that into `c:\tomcat\server\lib` (or to wherever `CATALINA_HOME\server\lib` is pointing). If there are any errors during the compilation, make sure the environment is set correctly and the code is the same as Listing 18-3.

Caution A Warning occurs during the `'dist'` target relating to copying an `mbeans-descriptors.xml` file. This can be safely ignored at this stage and will be addressed a little later in this section.

The first test is to see how to configure and troubleshoot the installation. Before starting Tomcat, edit a `Host` element in `server.xml` so that it looks like the following:

```
<Host name="localhost" appBase="webapps"
        errorReportValveClass="bible.tomcat.extend.CSSErrorReportValve" >
```

The `errorReportValveClass` is the important attribute. Tomcat will load all the JAR files in the `server\lib` directory so the classes in `extend.jar` will be available for Tomcat to use.

Start Tomcat and enter the same URL as before, `http://localhost:8080/foo/bar`.This should produce output similar to that shown in Figure 18-2.

The output from `CSSErrorReportValve` has new colors and has some additional output showing the creator of the page. If the output doesn't look like this, or Tomcat fails to start, check that the medications have been made correctly and check the logfile for errors.

Tip Make sure Tomcat is not running while these classes are copied because Tomcat will not monitor the `server\lib` directory for changes.

If you have had to look in the Tomcat logs to assist in the debugging you may see the following exception:

```
ServerLifecycleListener: Exception processing event
  ContainerEvent['StandardEngine[Standalone].StandardHost[localhost]',
  'addValve','ErrorReportValve[localhost]' ]

javax.management.MBeanException:
     nested exception is java.lang.Exception: ManagedBean is not found with
     CSSErrorReportValve
java.lang.Exception: ManagedBean is not found with CSSErrorReportValve
at org.apache.catalina.mbeans.MBeanUtils.createMBean(MBeanUtils.java:783)
. . . .
. . . .
```

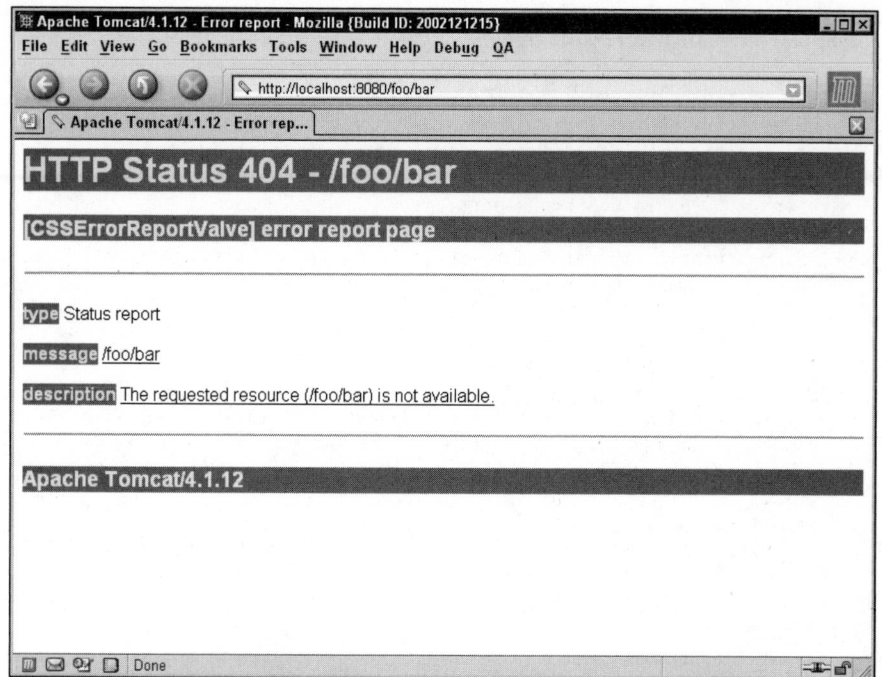

Figure 18-2: Default output from `CSSErrorReportValve`

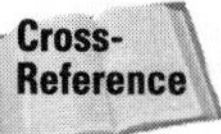

See Chapter 8 and Chapter 11 for more information about configuring Tomcat for logging and debugging.

This is not a critical error, and the Valve will continue to operate correctly. The exception is due to the `Listener` elements installed for using the Administration Tool. The `ManagedBean` interface that it uses has found a `Valve` that it doesn't understand anything about. There are three options available at this stage:

1. Ignore it.
2. Remove the `ServerLifecycleListener` element from `server.xml`, or
3. Install a custom `ManagedBean` descriptor file to inform the `ServerLifecycleListener` about the new `Valve`.

Option 2 is not a good choice if you want to use the Administration Tool. Removing this element stops the Web application from working properly.

Looking at option three seems to be the best course of action, because even though the error isn't critical it will be potentially confusing for other administrators of the system and it looks pretty ugly!

Create a file containing the XML shown in Listing 18-4 in the root directory of the development.

Listing 18-4: mbeans-descriptors.xml

```
<!DOCTYPE mbeans-descriptors PUBLIC
 "-//Apache Software Foundation//DTD Model MBeans Configuration File"
 "http://jakarta.apache.org/commons/dtds/mbeans-descriptors.dtd" >
<mbeans-descriptors>
    <mbean       name="CSSErrorReportValve"
            className="org.apache.catalina.mbeans.ClassNameMBean"
          description="Error reporting valve using errorstyles.css"
               domain="Catalina"
                group="Valve"
                 type="bible.tomcat.extends.CSSErrorReportValve" >

    <attribute   name="className"
          description="Fully qualified class name of the managed object"
                 type="java.lang.String"
            writeable="false"/>

    <attribute   name="debug"
          description="The debugging detail level for this component"
                 type="int"/>

    </mbean>
</mbeans-descriptors>
```

Now rebuild and re-install the `extend.jar`. The error that was occurring earlier when copying files should now disappear. The JAR file contains the `ManagedBean` descriptor, however Tomcat needs to be configured to find that file. Modify `server.xml` so the `Listener` element for the `ServerLifecycleListener` looks like the following.

```
<Listener className="org.apache.catalina.mbeans.ServerLifecycleListener"
    descriptors="/bible/tomcat/extend/mbeans-descriptors.xml"
    />
```

The `descriptors` attribute contains a path to locate a `ManagedBean` descriptor file. If there are more descriptor files, this can be extended to include more paths that are comma separated.

Restart Tomcat and look in the log files. If everything has proceeded as planned, the exceptions will be missing. If they still exist, make sure they are the `ManagedBean` exceptions and not something else, and also make sure the new JAR file has been installed.

In this diversion to clean up the logging, we've moved away from the original goal to provide a CSS file that can be managed without changing code. Create a CSS file called `errorstyles.css` containing the code in Listing 18-5.

Listing 18-5: errorstyles.css

```
H1
{
    font-family : serif ; color : black; background-color : yellow;
}

H3
{
    font-family : serif ; color : black ; background-color : yellow;
}

BODY
{
    font-family : sans-serif ; color : black; background-color : white;
}

B
{
    color : white; background-color : black;
}

HR
{
    color : black;
}
```

This file can be copied to any of the Web application directories that we want to test. Because we are using a Web application that doesn't exist, this request will be sent to the default Web application, or the Web application with the path as a blank string. The Tomcat configuration that is used has defined that to be in the directory:

```
c:\tomcat\webapps\ROOT
```

So, copy `errorstyles.css` to `c:\tomcat\webapps\ROOT` and enter the URL `http://localhost:8080/foo/bar`. This should result in a screen similar to that shown in Figure 18-3.

If the screen doesn't look like Figure 18-3 the check the following things:

- ✦ Is `extend.jar` in `CATALINA_HOME\common\lib`?
- ✦ Is `errorstyles.css` in `CATALINA_HOME\webapps\ROOT`?
- ✦ Are there any errors or exceptions in the log files?
- ✦ Was the `server.xml` file updated correctly?

These are the most likely sources of error when working with customizing Tomcat and the preceding instructions provide a guide to the parts of the system that required modification. These instructions vary slightly depending on the installation environment, but provided the installation proceeded as described in Chapter 2 everything should match very closely.

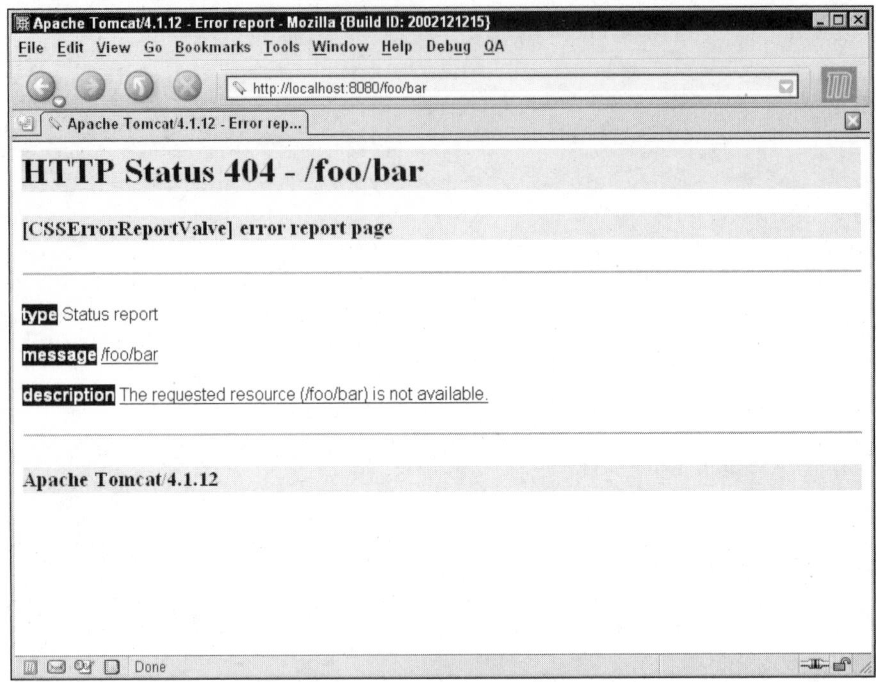

Figure 18-3: Styled output from `CSSErrorReportValve`

Custom Access Log (MonthlyAccessLog)

The standard Tomcat access log implementation generates a new access log for each day and the access log contains a timestamp for the creation day within the log. This generates many, many individual log files within the `logs` directory of a Tomcat installation and provides complications for access log processing software such as Webalizer (`http://www.mrunix.net/webalizer/`).

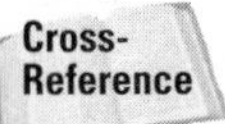

Details about configuring the access log `Valve` can be found in Chapter 8.

To reduce the number of files related to the access logs, this example creates an access log `Valve` that works on a monthly rather than daily basis. The logfile has a timestamp, but this only includes the year and month.

This example provides a framework for creation of a new access log `Valve`. Feel free to make changes to the example to suit your specific needs. Remove the `datestamp`, or change the file archiving strategy to something more complicated.

The `CSSErrorReportValve` covered most of the ground on configuring and installing the development environment; this example builds on that pre-existing framework.

As with the `CSSErrorReportValve`, the `MonthlyAccessValve` implements the `org.apache.catalina.Valve` interface. The default access log `Valve` is represented by the class

AccessLogValve; however, this class has been declared final so it cannot be extended like the CSSErrorReportValve. There is no option but to develop the entire Valve from the beginning.

Because the source from Tomcat is available it would have been possible to change AccessLogValve so that it was no longer final and then extend it to create MonthlyAccessLogValve. This is an option, but not one chosen for this example.

Create a file c:\devel\extend\src\bible\tomcat\extend\MonthlyAccessLogValve.java with the contents of Listing 18-6.

MonthlyAccessLogValve is a reasonably large class, but much of its code is very simple. Take care when entering the source code; due to its length there are more opportunities for errors to creep into the typing.

Listing 18-6: MonthlyAccessLogValve.java

```
package bible.tomcat.extend;

import java.io.*;
import java.text.*;
import java.util.*;
import javax.servlet.*;
import javax.servlet.http.*;
import org.apache.catalina.*;
import org.apache.catalina.util.*;
import org.apache.catalina.valves.*;

public class MonthlyAccessLogValve
    extends ValveBase
    implements Lifecycle
{
```

The attributes of the Valve; are all capable of being set by attributes in server.xml.

```
    private String _directory = "logs";
    private String _prefix = "monthly_log.";
    private String _suffix = "";
    private boolean _resolveHosts = false;
    private static final String _info =
        "bible.tomcat.extend.MonthlyAccessLogValve/1.0";
```

Variables used as part of the logic of the code.

```
    private String _dateStamp = null;
    private boolean _combined = false;
    private StringManager _sm =
        StringManager.getManager(Constants.Package);
    private boolean _started = false;
    private PrintWriter _writer = null;
```

Continued

Listing 18-6 *(continued)*

Variables used in creating the timestamps for the access log, and for the filename.

```
private static final String _months[] =
{ "Jan", "Feb", "Mar", "Apr", "May", "Jun",
  "Jul", "Aug", "Sep", "Oct", "Nov", "Dec" };
private SimpleDateFormat _fileNameFormatter = null;
private SimpleDateFormat _clfDateFormatter = null;
private String _timeZone = null;
private Date _currentDate = null;
private long _dateCreated = 0L;
private long _newFileCheck = 0L;

// For the listeners
private LifecycleSupport _lifecycle = new LifecycleSupport(this);

public MonthlyAccessLogValve()
{
    super();
}
```

This next block of code is the implementation that is used for getting and setting of the attributes.

```
public void setDirectory(String directory)
{
    _directory = directory;
}

public String getDirectory()
{
    return (_directory);
}

public void setPrefix(String prefix)
{
    _prefix = prefix;
}

public String getPrefix()
{
    return (_prefix);
}

public void setSuffix(String suffix)
{
    _suffix = suffix;
}

public String getSuffix()
{
    return (_suffix);
```

```
    }

    public void setResolveHosts(boolean resolveHosts)
    {
        _resolveHosts = resolveHosts;
    }

    public boolean isResolveHosts()
    {
        return _resolveHosts;
    }
```

The example code has a simplified set of rules for what the pattern can contain. The pattern can only be the Common Log Format, entered as `common`; or the Combined Log Format, entered as `combined`.

```
    public void setPattern(String pattern)
    {
        _combined = false;
        if (pattern.equals(Constants.AccessLog.COMBINED_ALIAS))
        {
            _combined = true;
        }
    }

    public String getInfo()
    {
        return (_info);
    }
```

Log a message depending on the setting of the pattern attribute. Some of the pattern attributes assume the request/response is HTTP, and as a result only give an option of `-` if it is invalid in an HTTP context. If the Request/Response is not HTTP then those HTTP-specific attributes are displayed as `*`.

The `invoke()` method is the externally serviced method for a `Valve`; it operates in a similar manner to the `service()` method of a `Servlet`.

```
    public void invoke(Request request,
                       Response response,
                       ValveContext ctx)
    throws IOException, ServletException
    {
        // Pass this request on to the next valve in our pipeline
        ctx.invokeNext(request, response);
```

Each user request, such as `http://localhost/index.html` means there are potentially many requests for resources. This generates things like:

- `GET /index.html`
- `GET /image1.gif`
- `GET /image2.gif`

Continued

Listing 18-6 *(continued)*

For each GET, invoke() is called, so only create a new date every second. This section of code provides a guard against not creating a new Date object for each call of invoke(). Because the log file timestamp accuracy is only one second, there is no point in getting a new Date more than once every second.

```
long now = System.currentTimeMillis();
if ((now - _dateCreated) > 1000)
{
    _currentDate = new Date(now);
    _dateCreated = now;
}
Date logDate = _currentDate;
```

The following section of code creates a StringBuffer to hold the output of the access log message. This message is in a defined format, either Common Log Format or Combined Log Format. Combined Log Format is just Common Log Format with some additional fields at the end of the log message. This makes the logic for processing each incoming request and generating the required log message very simple and straightforward.

```
StringBuffer rv = new StringBuffer();
String tmp = null;
ServletRequest req = request.getRequest();

HttpServletRequest hreq = null;
if (req instanceof HttpServletRequest)
{
    hreq = (HttpServletRequest) req;
}

// %h - hostname or IP address
if (isResolveHosts())
{
    rv.append(req.getRemoteHost());
}
else
{
    rv.append(req.getRemoteAddr());
}

// %l - defined to be '-' by the CLF
rv.append(" - ");

// %u - username or '-'
if (hreq != null)
{
    tmp = hreq.getRemoteUser();
    if (tmp == null)
    {
        rv.append("- ");
    }
    else
    {
```

```
            rv.append(tmp).append(" ");
        }
    }
    else
    {
        rv.append("* ");
    }

    // %t - Date and Time in CLF [ dd/Mmm/YYYY:HH:MM:SS TZ ]
    rv.append("[");
    rv.append(_clfDateFormatter.format(logDate)).append(" "); // CLF
    rv.append(_timeZone).append("] ");                        // Time Zone

    // "%r" - the first line of the request
    rv.append("\"");    // "
    if (hreq != null)
    {
        rv.append(hreq.getMethod()).append(" ");
        rv.append(hreq.getRequestURI());
        if (hreq.getQueryString() != null)
        {
            rv.append('?');
            rv.append(hreq.getQueryString());
        }
        rv.append(" ");
        rv.append(hreq.getProtocol());
    }
    else
    {
        rv.append("UNKN * *");
    }
    rv.append("\" ");

    // %s - status code
    if (req instanceof HttpServletRequest)
    {
        rv.append(((HttpResponse)response).getStatus()).append(" ");
    }
    else
    {
        rv.append("000 ");// nothing else I can do here !
    }

    // %b - bytes sent or '-'
    int length = response.getContentCount();
    if (length <= 0)
    {
        tmp = "-";
    }
    else
    {
        tmp = "" + length; // gak!
```

Continued

Listing 18-6 *(continued)*

```
        }
        rv.append(tmp);

        // now if we are combined, add the extra stuff in !
        if (_combined)
        {
            // "${Referer}"
            rv.append(" \"");
            if (hreq != null)
            {
                tmp = hreq.getHeader("referer");
                if (tmp == null)
                {
                    tmp = "-";
                }
                rv.append(tmp).append("\" \"");

                // "${User-Agent}"
                tmp = hreq.getHeader("user-agent");
                if (tmp == null)
                {
                    tmp = "-";
                }
                rv.append(tmp);
            }
            else
            {
                rv.append("*\" \"*");
            }
            rv.append("\"");
        }
        log(rv.toString(), logDate);
    }
```

The next section of the class contains the methods to work with the log files, including opening, closing, and actually writing the message to the log file.

```
    public void log(String message, Date logDate)
    {
        long now = logDate.getTime();
        if ((now - _newFileCheck) > 1000)
        {
            _newFileCheck = now;
```

The following code checks to see if the date component of the log file name (the year and month) is the same as a string created using the current date. If the two strings are different, then it must be a new month or the first time a log message has been received for the current month. The currently open log file will be closed, and a log file matching the current date will be opened.

```
            String newDate = _fileNameFormatter.format(_currentDate);
            if (!newDate.equals(_dateStamp))
            {
                synchronized (this)
                {
                    if (!newDate.equals(_dateStamp))
                    {
                        close();
                        _dateStamp = newDate;
                        open();
                    }
                }
            }
        }

        if (_writer != null)
        {
            _writer.println(message);
        }
    }
```

The open() method opens a new log file, creating directories if required. The close() method closes the current log file, setting the datestamp field to null.

```
    private synchronized void open()
    {
        File dir = new File(_directory);
        if (!dir.isAbsolute())
        {
            dir = new File(System.getProperty("catalina.base"),
                           _directory);
        }
        dir.mkdirs();

        try
        {
            String pathname = dir.getAbsolutePath() + File.separator +
                _prefix + _dateStamp + _suffix;
            _writer = new PrintWriter(new FileWriter(pathname, true),
                                      true);
        }
        catch (IOException e)
        {
            _writer = null;
        }
    }

    private synchronized void close()
    {
        if (_writer == null)
```

Continued

Listing 18-6 *(continued)*

```
        {
            return;
        }
        _writer.flush();
        _writer.close();
        _writer = null;
        _dateStamp = "";
    }
```

As part of the `Common` and `Combined` log formats the time zone is displayed in the format `+|-HHMM` and there is no convenient methods for doing that within Java. To keep the `log()` method tidy, this functionality has been put into the following method.

The `getRawOffset()` method returns a value in microseconds which is then converted to minutes. This is important because there are time zones which are not on the hour boundaries and the software may need to work in places like Adelaide (GMT+0930) and Newfoundland (GMT-0330).

```
    private String createTimeZoneFormat(TimeZone tz, Date now)
    {
        int raw = (tz.getRawOffset() / 60000);
        if (tz.inDaylightTime(now))
        {
            raw += 60;
        }
        int hours = raw / 60;
        int mins = raw - (hours*60);

        StringBuffer sb = new StringBuffer();

        if (hours >=0)
        {
            sb.append('+');
        }
        else
        {
            sb.append('-');
            hours *= (-1);
            mins *= (-1);
        }

        if (hours < 10)
        {
            sb.append('0');
        }
        sb.append(hours);

        if (mins < 10)
        {
            sb.append('0');
        }
```

```
        sb.append(mins);

        return sb.toString();
    }
```

The next group of methods is required as part of the Lifecycle interface and controls the addition and removal of listeners for this component. The Lifecycle interface has the benefit of providing access to the `start()` and `stop()` methods, which provide convenient opportunities to initialize the `Valve`, and to shut it down cleanly.

```
    public void addLifecycleListener(LifecycleListener listener)
    {
        _lifecycle.addLifecycleListener(listener);
    }

    public LifecycleListener[] findLifecycleListeners()
    {
        return _lifecycle.findLifecycleListeners();
    }

    public void removeLifecycleListener(LifecycleListener listener)
    {
        _lifecycle.removeLifecycleListener(listener);
    }
```

The `start()` method is used to create all the various date formatters. These formatters provide a convenient means of creating the various date and time stamps for both the log messages and for the name of the file.

```
    public void start()
    throws LifecycleException
    {
        if (_started)
        {
            throw new LifecycleException
                (sm.getString("accessLogValve.alreadyStarted"));
        }
        _started = true;

        _currentDate = new Date();
        TimeZone tz = TimeZone.getDefault();
        _timeZone = createTimeZoneFormat(tz, _currentDate);
```

The standard formatters provided cannot generate a three-letter month in the format required for the output. The strings that are needed to be output are passed to the constructor for the `SimpleDateFormat` and they are used as an alternative. The strings that are used are only in English, so a potential enhancement at a later stage may be to have a multi-lingual implementation of this class.

```
        DateFormatSymbols shortMonths = new DateFormatSymbols();
        shortMonths.setShortMonths(_months);

        _fileNameFormatter = new SimpleDateFormat("yyyy-MMM", shortMonths);
        _fileNameFormatter.setTimeZone(tz);
```

Continued

Listing 18-6 *(continued)*

```
        _clfDateFormatter = new SimpleDateFormat("dd/MMM/yyyy:HH:mm:ss",
                                                  shortMonths);
        _clfDateFormatter.setTimeZone(tz);
        _dateStamp = _fileNameFormatter.format(_currentDate);

        open();

    }

    public void stop()
    throws LifecycleException
    {
        if (!_started)
        {
            throw new LifecycleException
                (sm.getString("accessLogValve.notStarted"));
        }
        _started = false;

        close();

    }
}
```

As with the first attempt at installing `CSSErrorReportValve`, if the `MonthlyAccessLogValve` is compiled and installed Tomcat generates the `ManagedBean` exception messages in the log file, so update `mbeans-descriptors.xml` to include the contents of Listing 18-7. The new XML is shown in bold.

Listing 18-7: Updated mbeans-descriptors.xml

```
<!DOCTYPE mbeans-descriptors PUBLIC
 "-//Apache Software Foundation//DTD Model MBeans Configuration File"
 "http://jakarta.apache.org/commons/dtds/mbeans-descriptors.dtd" >
<mbeans-descriptors>
    <mbean       name="MonthlyAccessLogValve"
            className="org.apache.catalina.mbeans.ClassNameMBean"
          description="Valve that generates a web server access log"
               domain="Catalina"
                group="Valve"
                 type="bible.tomcat.extends.MonthlyAccessLogValve" >

    <attribute   name="className"
          description="Fully qualified class name of the managed object"
                 type="java.lang.String"
```

```
            writeable="false"/>

    <attribute   name="debug"
          description="The debugging detail level for this component"
                 type="int"/>

    <attribute   name="directory"
          description="The directory in which log files are created"
                 type="java.lang.String"/>

    <attribute   name="pattern"
          description="The pattern used to format our access log lines"
                 type="java.lang.String"/>

    <attribute   name="prefix"
          description="The prefix that is added to log file filenames"
                 type="java.lang.String"/>

    <attribute   name="resolveHosts"
          description="Resolve hosts"
                   is="true"
                 type="boolean"/>

    <attribute   name="suffix"
          description="The suffix that is added to log file filenames"
                 type="java.lang.String"/>
    </mbean>
    <mbean       name="CSSErrorReportValve"
            className="org.apache.catalina.mbeans.ClassNameMBean"
            . . . .
    </mbean>
</mbeans-descriptors>
```

Next, update server.xml to include a MonthlyAccessLogValve as shown in Listing 18-8. The Valve can be configured in any of the Engine, Host, or Context elements. For the purposes of the example it will be configured in the Engine, but configuration in a production environment like a Host or Context is more likely.

Listing 18-8: server.xml Configuration

```
<Valve className="bible.tomcat.extend.MonthlyAccessLogValve"
    prefix="ENGINE_monthly." suffix=".log"
    pattern="common"/>
```

Now it is time to compile and test the code. Stop Tomcat first, then type the following:

```
ant install
```

If there are any errors during the compilation make sure the environment is set correctly and that the code is the same as shown in Listing 18-4. If there are any problems it might be worth removing all the old class files and existing JAR files by using `ant clean`.

Start Tomcat and check the logs for errors. If any errors have occurred check the following list for likely causes.

- ✦ Was the `server.xml` file updated correctly with the `Valve`?
- ✦ Was the `mbeans-descriptors.xml` file updated correctly with the new `mbean` element?
- ✦ Was a new `extend.jar` file created with the Managed Bean descriptor file and then installed?

If there are no errors, open a browser and enter the following URL

```
http://localhost:8080/
```

This should create a file in the `logs` directory with the following format:

```
ENGINE_monthly.YYYY-Mmm.log
```

Where `YYYY` is the current year and `Mmm` is the three letter abbreviation for the current month. Open the logfile and there should be entries similar to the following.

```
127.0.0.1 - - [22/Dec/2002:01:48:14 +1100] "GET /index.jsp HTTP/1.1" 200 -
127.0.0.1 - - [22/Dec/2002:01:48:14 +1100] "GET /tomcat.gif HTTP/1.1" 200 1934
127.0.0.1 - - [22/Dec/2002:01:48:14 +1100] "GET /jakarta-banner.gif HTTP/1.1"
200 8006
127.0.0.1 - - [22/Dec/2002:01:48:14 +1100] "GET /tomcat-power.gif HTTP/1.1" 200
2324
```

The values for the date, time, and time zone should have appropriate values for the current locale and time. If the file is not created, check that the `Valve` was correctly configured and if the entries in the log file are not very close to the preceding log entries check that the code for the `Valve` was entered correctly.

Custom Logger (SyslogLogger)

The default Tomcat logger provides a mechanism for logging messages to a file resident on the disk of the local machine. In a distributed or decentralized management environment it is desirable to have errors, especially critical errors, reported to a central location.

For many years on Unix operating systems this logging and notification system has been handled by the `syslog` daemon (`syslogd`). This daemon is installed by default on many if not all variants of Unix, including Linux, and has a configuration file stored in `/etc/syslog.conf`.

Caution Due to the recent focus on securing systems, `syslogd` no longer listens for messages over a network connection. This option needs to be enabled if the Tomcat server is not on the same system as the syslogd processing the messages.

The default Tomcat `Logger` implemented is `org.apache.catalina.logger.FileLogger`. The `Logger` outputs messages created by elements to a file specified in the attributes of the `Logger`. The `FileLogger` and the other loggers that are in `src\catalina\share\org\apache\catalina\logger` all extend from `LoggerBase`. `LoggerBase` is an abstract base class that provides the implementation of the `org.apache.catalina.Logger` interface.

This example uses the `Logger` infrastructure to implement a `SyslogLogger` that accepts messages from elements and uses the syslog protocol to transmit the messages to a `syslogd`.

The protocol for the syslog protocol is defined in RFC 3164 and can be found at `www.faqs.org/rfcs/rfc3164.html`. As an alternative to developing the implementation there are many syslog clients (emitters of messages) that have been implemented in Java. For this example we download and use one of those rather than re-inventing the wheel.

Because many developers may be using Windows rather than a Unix operating system we use a Java implementation of the `syslogd` that can be run on Windows for the purposes of testing.

The syslog client chosen for this example is a very simple class available in source form from ICE Engineering (`www.trustice.com/java/syslog/`). This package was chosen because it is

✦ Simple

✦ Self-contained

✦ Doesn't contain any other functionality (like log4j does)

✦ Has a Java-based syslogd available for download

✦ Available under the GNU Public License (GPL)

The next sections describe the process for installing the required components and configuring the syslogd. When that is complete, coding can commence!

Installation of Syslog Client

The syslog client package is available from `ftp://ftp.gjt.org/pub/users/time/java/syslog/syslog.zip`. Download this file and unzip to create a directory structure. This creates a directory, `syslog-1.2`, and a source hierarchy, `com\ice\syslog`. There is a test client in the package but that is not needed for this example.

Because this package contains the source, all that is needed is to copy the required source files into the development source and include the compiled classes in the `extend.jar`.

Create the directory structure `c:\devel\extend\src\com\ice\syslog` and copy the following files into that directory

✦ `Syslog.java`

✦ `SyslogDefs.java`

✦ `SyslogException.java`

That's it! When the `SyslogLogger` is compiled and packaged these classes are included in the JAR and are available to be used.

Installation of syslogd on Windows

The syslogd can be downloaded from `ftp://ftp.gjt.org/pub/users/time/java/syslog/syslogd.zip`. Download this file and unzip it to create a directory structure. This creates directory `syslogd-2.2`.

The important directory for this package is the subdirectory `application`. This example uses the configuration file provided with the package, so there is no need to make any modifications. To run the syslogd, create a batch file, or a shortcut that contains the following:

```
cd c:\syslogd-2.2\application
C:\jdk1.3.1\bin\java.exe -classpath "./syslogd.jar" com.ice.syslogd.SyslogD
```

Use the appropriate directories for where the application was unpacked, and where `java.exe` is located. When creating a shortcut, ensure that the `Start In` field contains the path to the `application` directory.

Using the shortcut or the batch file runs a graphical application that shows the log messages in a window. An example is shown in Figure 18-4.

Configuration of syslog under Unix

The configuration mechanisms for each version of Unix vary slightly but the general principles are the same for each.

To enable the logging that is generated by the `SyslogLogger` a new configuration stanza needs to be added to the syslog configuration file `/etc/syslog.conf`. Add in the following:

```
# save local0 messages to their own log
local0.*                        /var/log/local0.log
```

That is all that is required to for a Tomcat to access the syslogd on a local system. If Tomcat is installed on a remote system from the syslogd, then `syslogd` needs to be configured to accept messages from the network.

Under RedHat Linux the options are stored in a file called `/etc/sysconfig/syslog` which is sourced when `syslogd` is started and stopped via the `/etc/rc.d/init.d/syslog` script. The options line in this file should be modified to include the `-r` option as shown:

```
SYSLOGD_OPTIONS="-r -m 0"
```

Restart `syslogd` to include the configuration and option changes using

```
/etc/rc.d/init.d/syslog restart
```

That's all the configuration required for the syslog daemon, and with the syslog client class as part of the development source tree it's now time to develop the logger.

Create a file `c:\devel\extend\src\bible\tomcat\extend\SyslogLogger.java` with the contents of Listing 18-9.

Listing 18-9: SyslogLogger.java

```
package bible.tomcat.extend;

import org.apache.catalina.*;
import org.apache.catalina.logger.*;
import org.apache.catalina.util.*;
import org.apache.catalina.valves.*;
```

Import the Syslog classes that were included into the development.

```
import com.ice.syslog.*;

public class SyslogLogger
    extends LoggerBase
```

```
    implements Lifecycle
{
    protected static final String _info =
        "bible.tomcat.extend.SyslogLogger/1.0";
    private String _host = "localhost";
    private Syslog _syslog = null;

    public String getInfo()
    {
        return _info;
    }

    public void setHost(String host)
    {
        if (host != null)
        {
            _host = host;
            _syslog = null;
            createSyslog();
        }
    }

    public String getHost()
    {
        return _host;
    }
```

The `log()` method is the only method required to be implemented after extending `LoggerBase`. The facility for the logger is `LOG_LOCAL0` and the severity is `LOG_DEBUG`. Both should be modified to suit the purposes of the installation, but work effectively for this example.

```
    public void log(String msg)
    {
        if (_syslog != null)
        {
            try
            {
                _syslog.syslog(
                               SyslogDefs.LOG_LOCAL0,
                               SyslogDefs.LOG_DEBUG,
                               msg
                               );
            }
            catch (SyslogException e)
            {
                System.err.println("Exception during logging :: "+
                                   e.getMessage());
            }
        }
        else
        {
```

Continued

Listing 18-9 *(continued)*

```
            System.err.println("Syslog object is null.  Logging disabled");
        }
    }

    private void createSyslog()
    {
        if (_syslog == null)
        {
            try
            {
                _syslog = new Syslog(_host,
                                     SyslogDefs.DEFAULT_PORT,
                                     "Tomcat Syslog",
                                     SyslogDefs.LOG_PERROR);
            }
            catch (SyslogException e)
            {
                System.err.println("Exception creating a Syslog :: "+
                                   e.getMessage());
            }
        }
    }
```

As with the `MonthlyAccessLogValve`, the `Lifecycle` methods are used to initialize the state of the `Logger` and create the `Syslog` object used for the client side of the protocol.

```
    /*
     * Lifecycle methods for starting and stopping the Logger
     */
    public void start()
    throws LifecycleException
    {
        if (_started)
        {
            throw new LifecycleException("SylogLogger already started");
        }
        createSyslog();
        _started = true;
    }

    public void stop()
    throws LifecycleException
    {
        if (!_started)
        {
            throw new LifecycleException("SylogLogger not started");
        }
        _started = false;
    }
```

```
    /*
     * Lifecycle methods required by contract.
     */
    private LifecycleSupport _lifecycle = new LifecycleSupport(this);
    private boolean _started = false;

    public void addLifecycleListener(LifecycleListener listener)
    {
        _lifecycle.addLifecycleListener(listener);
    }

    public LifecycleListener[] findLifecycleListeners()
    {
        return _lifecycle.findLifecycleListeners();
    }

    public void removeLifecycleListener(LifecycleListener listener)
    {
        _lifecycle.removeLifecycleListener(listener);
    }


}
```

Next, add in the `ManagedBean` configuration as shown in Listing 18-10. The XML in bold identifies the new section.

Listing 18-10: **Updated mbeans-descriptors.xml**

```
<!DOCTYPE mbeans-descriptors PUBLIC
 "-//Apache Software Foundation//DTD Model MBeans Configuration File"
 "http://jakarta.apache.org/commons/dtds/mbeans-descriptors.dtd" >
<mbeans-descriptors>
    <mbean       name="SyslogLogger"
            className="org.apache.catalina.mbeans.ClassNameMBean"
          description="Logger that sends output to syslog"
               domain="Catalina"
                group="Logger"
                 type="bible.tomcat.extends.SyslogLogger" >

    <attribute   name="className"
          description="Fully qualified class name of the managed object"
                 type="java.lang.String"
            writeable="false"/>

    <attribute   name="debug"
          description="The debugging detail level for this component"
                 type="int"/>
```

Continued

Listing 18-10 *(continued)*

```
    <attribute   name="host"
          description="Hostname of target syslogd"
                 type="java.lang.String"
            writeable="false"/>

    </mbean>
    <mbean       name="MonthlyAccessLogValve"
            className="org.apache.catalina.mbeans.ClassNameMBean"
          description="Valve that generates a web server access log"
    . . . .
    </mbean>
    . . . .
    . . . .
</mbeans-descriptors>
```

Next, update server.xml to include a SyslogLogger as shown in Listing 18-11. The Valve can be configured in any of the Engine, Host, or Context elements for the purposes of the example it is configured in the Host. Change the host attribute to match the host running the syslog daemon, or leave it as it is.

Listing 18-11: server.xml Configuration

```
<Logger className="bible.tomcat.extend.SyslogLogger"
             host="localhost" />
```

Now it is time to compile and test the code. Stop Tomcat first, then type the following:

```
ant install
```

If there are any errors during the compilation make sure the environment is set correctly and that the code is the same as shown in Listing 18-10. If there are any problems it might be worth removing all the old class files and existing JAR files by using ant clean.

Now it is time for the moment of truth. If you are using the Java syslogd, start it now. Then start Tomcat. This should result in many messages being generated by Tomcat and displayed in the Main Window, as shown in Figure 18-4, or the logfile if using the Unix syslogd, as shown in Listing 18-12.

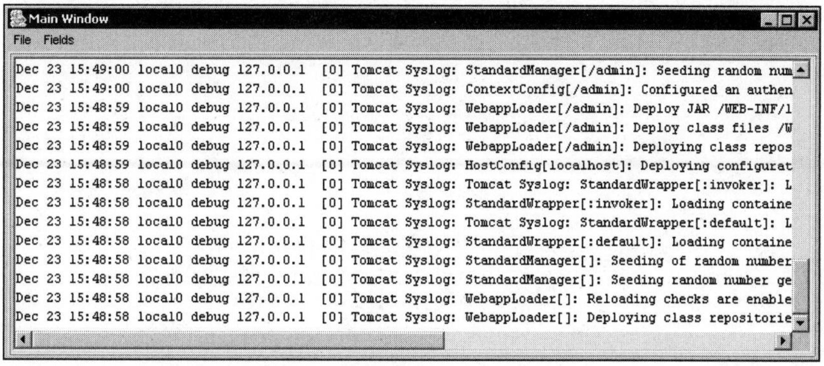

Figure 18-4: Syslog messages displayed in Java `syslogd`

Listing 18-12: Syslog Messages in /var/log/local/local0.log

```
Dec 23 15:55:52 192.168.1.220 Tomcat Syslog: StandardWrapper[/tomcat-
docs:invoker]: Loading container servlet invoker
Dec 23 15:55:52 192.168.1.220 Tomcat Syslog: Tomcat Syslog:
StandardWrapper[/tomcat-docs:invoker]: Loading container servlet invoker
Dec 23 15:55:52 192.168.1.220 Tomcat Syslog: HostConfig[localhost]: Deploying
web application directory webdav
Dec 23 15:55:52 192.168.1.220 Tomcat Syslog: StandardHost[localhost]: Installing
webapplication at context path /webdav from URL file:C:\tomcat\webapps\webdav
Dec 23 15:55:52 192.168.1.220 Tomcat Syslog: WebappLoader[/webdav]: Deploying
class repositories to work directory C:\tomcat\work\Standalone\localhost\webdav
Dec 23 15:55:52 192.168.1.220 Tomcat Syslog: StandardManager[/webdav]: Seeding
random number generator class java.security.SecureRandom
Dec 23 15:55:52 192.168.1.220 Tomcat Syslog: StandardManager[/webdav]: Seeding
of random number generator has been completed
```

Summary

This chapter provides an introduction to the functionality that can be customized in Tomcat. The examples in this chapter were chosen to show how relatively simple it is to add new functionality to the Tomcat server.

There are many other areas that can be explored, with the next most likely customization requirement being a custom implementation of a `Realm` to integrate with enterprise authentication systems.

✦ ✦ ✦

Index

Continued

D

Continued

G

H

J

Continued

Continued

Continued

Continued

S

Continued

Continued

Continued

Continued

X